MICRONESIA
HANDBOOK

DIANA LASICH HARPER

MICRONESIA HANDBOOK

FIFTH EDITION

NEIL M. LEVY

MOON
TRAVEL
HANDBOOKS

MICRONESIA HANDBOOK
FIFTH EDITION

Published by
Avalon Travel Publishing
5855 Beaudry St.
Emeryville, CA 94608, USA

Printed by
Colorcraft Ltd.

Please send all comments,
corrections, additions,
amendments, and critiques to:

MICRONESIA HANDBOOK
MOON TRAVEL HANDBOOKS
5855 BEAUDRY ST.
EMERYVILLE, CA 94608, USA
e-mail: travel@moon.com
www.moon.com

Printing History
1st edition—1985
5th edition—January 2000

5 4 3 2 1 0

ISBN: 1-56691-162-1
ISSN: 1088-095X

Editors: Gina Wilson Birtcil, Marion Harmon, Jeannie Trizzino
Production & Design: Carey Wilson
Cartography: Brian Bardwell, Mike Morgenfeld
Index: Sondra Nation

Front cover photo: Rock Islands, Palau © David W. Hamilton/The Image Bank 1999

All photos by Neil M. Levy unless otherwise noted.
All illustrations by Bob Race unless otherwise noted.

Distributed in the United States and Canada by Publishers Group West

Printed in China

CONTENTS

MAPS

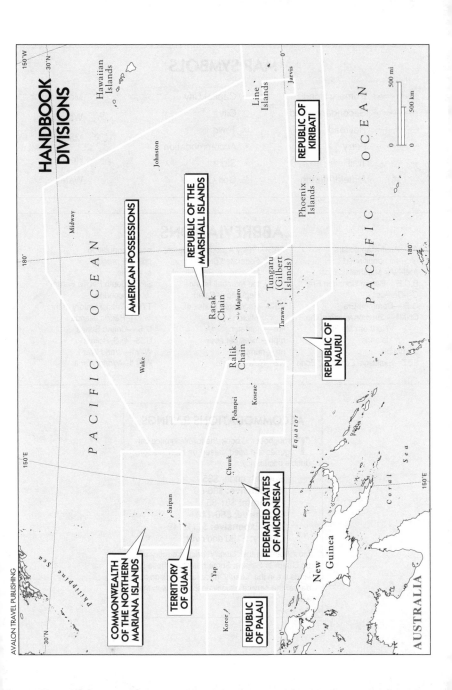

AVALON TRAVEL PUBLISHING

HANDBOOK DIVISIONS

Hawaiian Islands

Midway

Johnston

PACIFIC OCEAN

Line Islands

Jarvis

REPUBLIC OF KIRIBATI

0   500 mi

0   500 km

AMERICAN POSSESSIONS

REPUBLIC OF THE MARSHALL ISLANDS

Ratak Chain

Majuro

Phoenix Islands

PACIFIC OCEAN

Wake

Ralik Chain

Tungaru (Gilbert Islands)

Tarawa

REPUBLIC OF NAURU

Saipan

Chuuk

Pohnpei

Kosrae

Equator

COMMONWEALTH OF THE NORTHERN MARIANA ISLANDS

TERRITORY OF GUAM

FEDERATED STATES OF MICRONESIA

Yap

Koror

REPUBLIC OF PALAU

New Guinea

Coral Sea

AUSTRALIA

Philippine Sea

MAP SYMBOLS

═══	Primary Road	⊛	Capital City	▲	Mountain
═══	Secondary Road	○	City		Waterfall
├──┼──┤	Railroad	○	Town		Mangrove
··········	Ferry	•	Accommodation		Reef
- - - - -	Trail	▪	Sight		Water
✗	Airfield/Airstrip	⚑	Golf Course		

ABBREVIATIONS

A$—Australian dollars
a/c—air conditioned
AMI—Air Marshall Islands
B.C.E.—Before Common Era
C—Celsius
C.E.—Common Era
CNMI—Commonwealth of the
    Northern Mariana
    Islands
d—double
EEZ—Exclusive Economic Zone

FAS—Freely Associated States:
    Federated States of
    Micronesia, Republic of
    the Marshall Islands,
    Republic of Palau
FSM—Federated States of
    Micronesia
km—kilometer
mph—miles per hour
no.—number
NZ—New Zealand

pop.—population
pp—per person
s—single
SPF—South Pacific Forum
tel.—telephone
TTPI—Trust Territory of the
    Pacific Islands
U.S.—United States
US$—U.S. dollars
WW I—World War I
WW II—World War II

ACCOMMODATIONS RATINGS

Throughout this book, the following price categories are used, based on high season, double occupancy:

Budget: under $35
Inexpensive: $36-60
Moderate: $61-85
Expensive: $86-110
Very Expensive: $111-149
Luxury: $150 and over

Most hotels in the "Luxury" price category are on Guam or Saipan. Some hotels on those islands are in the "Luxury" price range, but do not deliver the service usually associated with that word.

ACKNOWLEDGMENTS

First I wish to give thanks to and express admiration for the work of David Stanley, author of the first three editions of *Micronesia Handbook,* the first guidebook to the region. I have relied on his work, his files, and his advice.

I am grateful to the staff of Moon Publications for their assistance. I particularly wish to thank Jeannie Trizzino for her editorial encouragement and judgment. Thanks also to Dave Hurst and cartographer Mike Morgenfeld. And thanks to Bill Newlin, Moon's publisher and my friend, who took the chance that a law professor could write plain English.

A number of scholars and writers shared their expertise with me. Father Frances X. Hezel of the Micronesian Seminar deepened my understanding of Micronesian history. John M. van Dyke, Professor of Law, University of Hawaii, helped me understand the legal problems facing Micronesia, as did my former student Chuck Greenfield and Nina Eejima. Pia Anderson, University of California at Berkeley, was a great resource on the archaeology and anthropology of Micronesia.

My appreciation also goes to Giff Johnson of the *Marshall Islands Journal* and to Gene Ashby, author of *Pohnpei: An Island Argosy,* who both provided valuable input. Tim Rock shared his knowledge of diving and of Guam. Jack D. Haden of Australia shared extensive information on Nauru and Kiribati.

Many people within the travel industry supplied me with ideas and facts. Mike Musto of Trip-N-Tour Micronesia was a very useful source of information about travel, as was Layne Ballard of Central Pacific Dive Expedition. My sincerest thanks to Remy Meraz and Christina Martinez of Continental Airlines, who got me to Micronesia and back, and helped ensure that I could provide accurate airline information.

Many people living in Micronesia added to the enjoyment of my travels and helped me get to know the region. On Guam, thanks to Anthony Corn of the Guam Art Council and to artist Anita D. Bento. On Rota, thanks to Justin Manglona. On Kosrae, thanks to Madison T. Nena, Nora Conroy, and Matthew Blumkin. On Pohnpei, thanks to Wendolin Lainos from Ict Ieh Tours, and Andrea and Charles Hillyer. And thanks to Steve Vosseller, who surfs on Yap. On Saipan, I wish to thank Bill Stewart, Micronesia's preeminent cartographer, and Nancy Weil and Kurt D. Burkhart. I was aided on Palau by Dorji Roberts, Scott Benbow, and the Palau Visitors Authority's Clint Parry. A special thank you to my guide in Kiribati, Anita Awira, and to Peace Corps volunteers Kevin Campopiano on Abemama and Arlene Morton on Tarawa.

My most special thanks go to Jane Levy, my wife, who not only accompanied me to parts of Micronesia, but also used her knowledge as a librarian, museum curator, and basket weaver to contribute to the arts and crafts sections of this handbook, as well as the Booklist.

Special Credit

Many of the antique engravings included in this book were taken from *Oceanie, ou Cinquième Partie du Monde* by M.G.L. Domeny de Rienzi. Domeny, a colorful French adventurer, self-proclaimed soldier of fortune, and professor of geography, published several books. *Oceanie* was first published by the prominent 19th-century French publishers, Firmin Didot Frères, as part of a multivolume work on the history of the peoples of the world.

PREFACE

THE TRAVEL WRITER

Preparation

To expand the universe of the possible,
> the travel writer records events that have not occurred
> and even events that could not occur.

Words define the travel writer's journey,
> but the journey composes his words.
> Intuition cannot replace investigation.

Heisenberg's Uncertainty Principle
> complicates the travel writer's task,
> as he tries to capture a languid, tropical vacation
> while meticulously gathering reliable information.

Commitment

The travel writer heads West,
> towards the sunset,
> towards island countries whose names he cannot pronounce
> towards islands he thought existed only in World War II movies
> —hoping to find Amelia Earhart,
> —hoping to find J.C. Penney.

The travel writer appears
> to move about with a sense of purpose,
> but is as purposeless as life's other travelers.
> Having no sense of direction, however,
> he never knows he's lost.

The travel writer sees all,
> questions all,
> assumes nothing,
> fears he would become confused
> in a universe he understood.

"Who am I to judge?" he asks.
> "Must I find out who I'm not
> before I find who I am?"

Undertaking

The travel writer permits himself
     the silly questions
     he always has been too repressed to ask.

The travel writer leaves phrases,
     not footprints,
     on the pathways.
     He wonders whether to use the word "landmark"
     to describe what he sees underwater.

Frightened in a five-seat Cessna,
     the travel writer knows that
     if he does not look out the window,
     he is not up in the air.

The travel writer is used, confused,
     but seldom knowingly abused.
     He has perfected the art
     of plagiarizing unwritten sources.

When hotel owners learn he is the travel writer,
     they tell him their dreams,
     believing that in doing so,
     their dreams become reality.

The travel writer believes those dreams,
     but to preserve the mystery of travel,
     he omits writing them.

The travel writer says,
     "Conception is easy.
     Details are killing me."
     His pregnant wife agrees.

Like Gregor Samsa,
     the travel writer is a commercial traveler,
     the travel writer shares rooms with gigantic insects.
     Perhaps will awaken, one day, to find himself metamorphosed.

HOW WAS YOUR TRIP TO MICRONESIA?

Micronesia is constantly changing. Have you made new and interesting discoveries you wish to share with readers of future editions? I'd love to hear from you. Of course, everything will be field-checked, but you might help me discover fascinating aspects of Micronesia that I might otherwise miss. Moon Publications strives to make each edition better than the last, and you can be part of the process.

Keep in mind that between the time this book went to press and the time it reached the shelves, hotels have opened and closed, restaurants have changed hands, and roads have been repaired or fallen into disrepair. Also, prices may have increased; therefore, all prices should be regarded as approximations and are not guaranteed by the publisher or author.

Note: Authors, editors, and publishers wishing to see their publications listed in our Booklist can send review copies to the address listed below. Hotel owners, tour operators, and divemasters: the best way to keep your listing in *Micronesia Handbook* up-to-date is to submit current information about your business. There is never any charge or obligation for a mention.

Address all correspondence to:

Micronesia Handbook
Avalon Travel Publishing
5855 Beaudry St.
Emeryville, CA 94608, U.S.A.
e-mail: travel@moon.com

. . . each day is a journey
and the journey itself is home
~Basho

INTRODUCTION

Halfway between the real and the make-believe lies the magical.

Micronesia's land area covers about 1,245 square miles, and the ocean area 4,500,000 square miles. There are plenty of things to enjoy in Micronesia, but if you don't love the ocean, this is probably the wrong destination for you.

Micronesia is *the* diver's paradise, and much more. The land, though small in area, is tremendously varied. There are high volcanic islands and flat sandy atolls. These far-flung islands host a great diversity of cultures as well: cultures alive today and cultures that left mysterious archaeological remains.

Today, Micronesia's people, definitely citizens of the global village, combine traditional values with Western culture. Micronesia is exotic, but not altogether foreign. As one hotel owner asked, "Where else can you find a place this exotic, where people speak English and use American currency?"

Although many people have never heard of Micronesia (you may be the first on your block to

visit it), this vast region includes thousands of lush tropical islands scattered between Hawaii and the Philippines. The name means "Little Islands." The total landmass of Micronesia is about that of Rhode Island or the Los Angeles basin. About 500,000 people live there.

While Tahiti and Fiji are household words, most Americans are unaware of this enormous area, which the United States administered after World War II. Today Guam remains a United States territory; the Northern Marianas are part of the American Commonwealth; and the Federated States of Micronesia, the Republic of the Marshall Islands, and the Republic of Palau, though independent—by "Compacts of Free Association"—have a special relationship to the United States in which the U.S. continues to provide certain services and controls security in these "Freely Associated States" (FAS).

Five prior colonial powers, in turn, controlled parts of Micronesia through the centuries. Spain, Germany, and Japan were forced out in wars, while Britain and Australia left voluntarily.

You have in your hands the new edition of the original travel guidebook to Micronesia. It

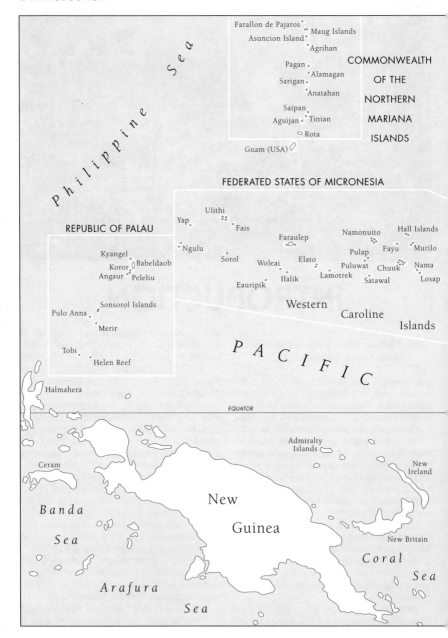

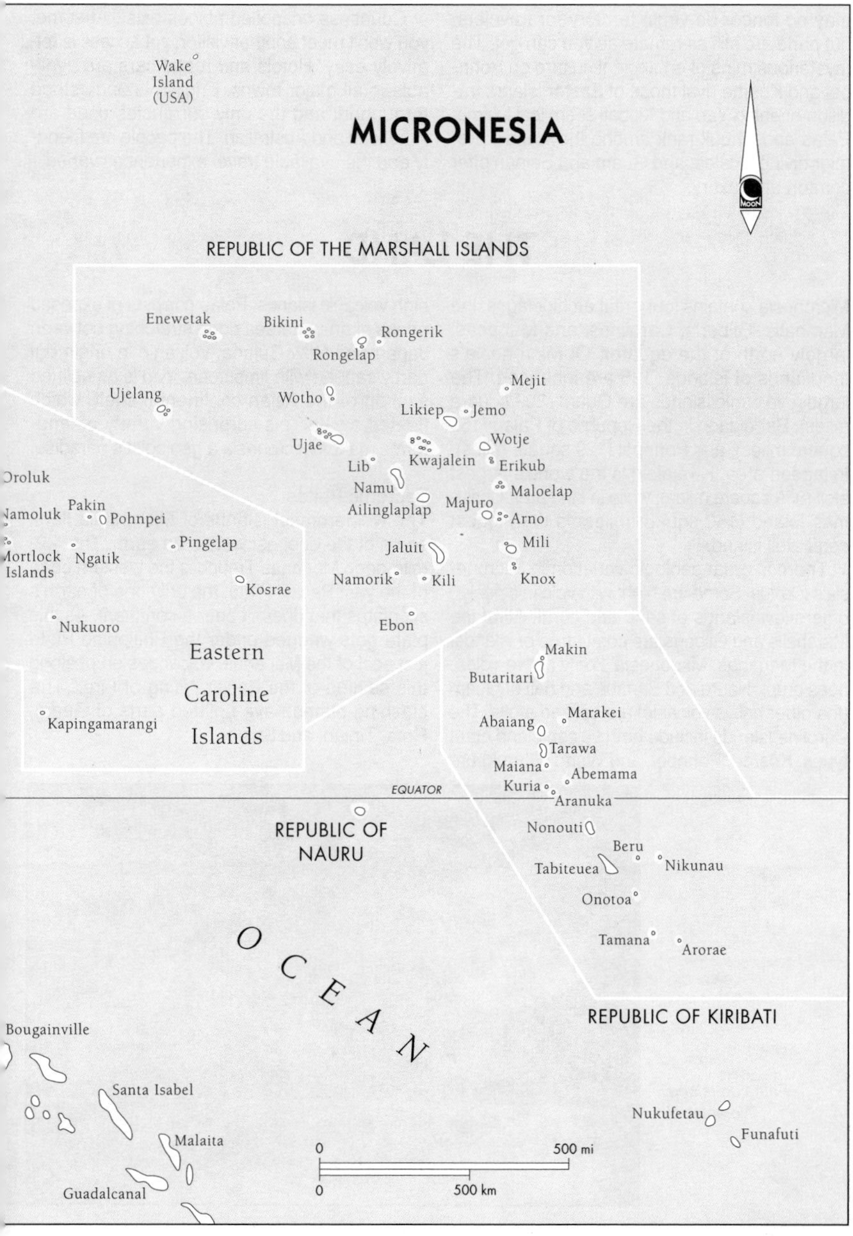

MICRONESIA

REPUBLIC OF THE MARSHALL ISLANDS

Wake Island (USA)

Enewetak

Bikini

Rongerik

Rongelap

Ujelang

Wotho

Mejit

Likiep · Jemo

Ujae

Wotje

Oroluk

Lib

Kwajalein

Erikub

Namoluk

Pakin

Namu

Maloelap

Pohnpei

Ailinglaplap

Majuro

Arno

Mortlock
Islands

Ngatik

Pingelap

Jaluit

Mili

Nukuoro

Kosrae

Namorik

Kili

Knox

Ebon

Eastern

Makin

Caroline

Butaritari

Islands

Abaiang

Marakei

Kapingamarangi

Tarawa

Maiana

Abemama

Kuria

Aranuka

EQUATOR

REPUBLIC OF
NAURU

Nonouti

Beru

Tabiteuea

Nikunau

Onotoa

Tamana

Arorae

O C E A N

REPUBLIC OF KIRIBATI

Bougainville

Santa Isabel

Malaita

Nukufetau

Funafuti

Guadalcanal

0   500 mi

0   500 km

may no longer be virgin territory for travelers, but parts are still as remote as you can get. The mysterious ruins of an ancient culture on Pohnpei and Kosrae rival those of Easter Island; tradition-oriented Yap and Kiribati seem lost in time; Palau and Chuuk rank among the world's premier diving locales; and Guam and Saipan offer comfort and luxury.

Countless unspoiled places exist. At some, you won't meet another visitor, yet access is relatively easy. Hotels and rental cars are available in all major towns. English is understood throughout and the only currencies used are American and Australian. The people are friendly and the available travel experiences varied.

THE LAND

Micronesia contains four great archipelagos: the Marshalls, Gilberts, Carolines, and Marianas, largely north of the equator. Of Micronesia's thousands of islands, 125 are inhabited. The largest volcanic islands are Guam (209 square miles), Babeldaob in the Republic of Palau (153 square miles), and Pohnpei (129 square miles). In lagoon area, Kwajalein is the world's largest atoll (839 square miles), while in land area Christmas Island (150 square miles) is the biggest coral atoll island.

There is great geologic variation in Micronesia's islands. Some are high, with volcanic peaks, others low islands of sand and coral. All of the Marshalls and Gilberts are coral atolls or islands. In the Marianas, Micronesia's only active volcanoes erupt. Nauru and Banaba and half of Guam (the other half is volcanic) are uplifted atolls. The Caroline Islands include both volcanic and coral types. Kosrae, Pohnpei, and Weno (Chuuk) are

high volcanic islands. Palau consists of exposed peaks of an undersea ridge stretching between Japan and New Guinea, volcanic in origin but partly capped with limestone. Yap is an uplifted section of the Asian continental shelf, which floated away. This surprising variety of landforms makes Micronesia a geologist's paradise.

Tectonic Plates

The westernmost islands of Micronesia flank some of the deepest waters on earth. The 4.2-mile-deep Marianas Trench is the western edge of the vast Pacific Plate, the only one of earth's six plates that doesn't bear a continent. As this plate gets wedged under the Philippine Plate just east of the Marianas, volcanoes erupt along this section of the Pacific "Ring of Fire." The clashing plates have uplifted parts of Guam, Rota, Tinian, and Saipan.

Falealop Island, Woleai Atoll

PAUL BOHLER

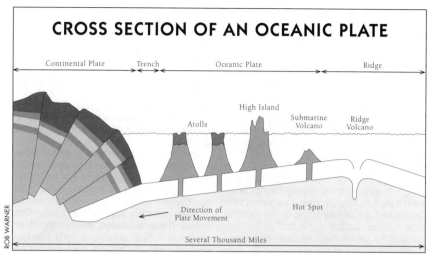

CROSS SECTION OF AN OCEANIC PLATE

Continental Plate   Trench   Oceanic Plate   Ridge

High Island
Atolls   Submarine Volcano   Ridge Volcano

Direction of Plate Movement   Hot Spot

Several Thousand Miles

ROB WARNER

Atoll Formation

In 1952 scientists at Enewetak in the Marshalls managed to drill through to volcanic rock, 4,244 feet deep, for the first time on any Pacific atoll, confirming Charles Darwin's Theory of Atoll Formation. The famous formulator of the theory of evolution surmised that atolls form as high volcanic islands that then subside into lagoons. The original island's fringing reef grows into a barrier reef as the volcanic portion sinks. When the last volcanic material finally disappears below sea level, the coral rim of the reef, now an atoll, remains to indicate how big the island once was.

Of course, all this takes place over millions of years, but deep down below any atoll is the old volcanic core, as the researchers at Enewetak found. Darwin's theory is well illustrated at Chuuk, where a group of high volcanic islands remains inside the rim of Chuuk's barrier reef; these islands are still sinking. Return to Chuuk in 25 million years and all you'll find will be a coral atoll like Majuro or Kwajalein.

Hot Spots

High or low, all the islands have a volcanic origin best explained by the Conveyor Belt Theory. A crack or "hot spot" opens in the sea floor and volcanic material escapes upward. A submarine volcano builds up slowly until the lava finally breaks the surface, forming a volcanic island.

The Pacific Plate moves northwest approximately four inches a year; thus, over geologic eons a volcano disconnects from the hot spot or crack from which it emerged. As the old volcanoes move on, new ones appear to the southeast, and the older islands are carried away from the cleft in the earth's crust from which they were born.

The island then begins to sink under its own weight, perhaps only half an inch a century, and erosion cuts into the volcano—by this time extinct. In the warm, clear waters a living coral reef begins to grow along the shore. As the island subsides, the reef continues to grow upward. In this way a lagoon forms between the reef and the shoreline of the slowly sinking island. This barrier reef marks the old margin of the original island.

The process is helped along by rising and falling ocean levels during ice ages. Rainwater causes a chemical reaction, which converts the porous limestone into compacted dolomite, giving the reef a more dense base. Eventually, as the volcanic portion of the island sinks completely into the lagoon, the atoll reef is the volcanic island's only remnant.

As the hot spot moves southeast, in an opposite direction to the sliding Pacific Plate (and shifting magnetic pole of the earth), the process is repeated, time and again, until whole chains of islands ride the blue Pacific. In the Marshall,

Gilbert, and Line Islands this northwest-southeast orientation is clearly visible. Although the Carolines are more scattered, the tendency, from Namonuito to Kapingamarangi or Kosrae, is still discernible. In every case, the islands at the southeast end of the chains are the youngest. This rule also applies in the South Pacific.

Life of an Atoll

A circular or horseshoe-shaped coral reef bearing a necklace of sandy, slender islets of debris thrown up by storms, surf, and wind is known as an atoll. The central lagoon of huge Kwajalein atoll is more than 80 miles wide. But the width of dry land on an atoll is usually less than a mile from inner to outer beach. Entirely landlocked lagoons are rare; passages through the barrier reef are usually found on the leeward side. Atolls are seldom higher than 15 feet. Because of this low elevation, the best way to grasp its concept is from an airplane.

A raised or elevated atoll is one that has been pushed up by some trauma of nature to become a coral platform rising as much as 200 feet above sea level. Steep, cave-pocked oceanside cliffs frequently surround raised atolls. A good example of this type is eight-square-mile Nauru.

Where volcanic island remains, there is often a deep passage between the barrier reef and shore; the reef forms a natural breakwater that shelters good anchorages. Soil derived from coral is poor in nutrients, while volcanic soil is fertile. Dark-colored beaches come from volcanic material; the white beaches of travel brochures are coral based.

Modern society is threatening the world's atolls. The dangers of the greenhouse effect and global warming are more severe in atoll countries than anywhere else. Water levels could rise by three feet in 50 years, 10 feet by the year 2100. On atolls this will mean the intrusion of more salt water into the groundwater supply, especially if accompanied by droughts. If the sea level rises more quickly than the coral reef can grow upward, lagoons could lose their vitality and islands would become more exposed to storms. In time, entire populations could be forced to evacuate, and whole countries like the Marshall Islands and Kiribati could be flooded. It's the ultimate irony that isolated specks such as islands in the Marshalls or Kiribati may be the first to feel catastrophic effects from the smog of Beijing or Detroit.

On a local level, two current practices are also harming atolls and their lagoons. First, there is increasing evidence that atoll islands form and then others re-form as the ocean takes sand from one place to another. Traditional societies could move with the islands' shifts. Of course, with modern notions of property, islanders are more likely to build sea walls and the like to stop these processes. But these processes might be necessary for the health of the atoll.

Additionally, particularly on populous atolls, outlying islanders often wish to be connected to the most populous island, which may have electricity and jobs. Since the atoll countries are not wealthy, such islands usually are connected by causeways, rather than by high suspension bridges. These causeways, usually built with an insufficient number of costly culverts, interfere with ocean tides that had previously flushed the lagoon to keep it clean.

CORAL REEFS

Just below the surface of the water lies a different, surprising, and magical world: the coral reef. To understand how a basalt volcano becomes a limestone atoll, it is necessary to know a little about the growth of coral. A reef is created by the accumulation of millions of tiny calcareous skeletons left by generations of microscopic animals called polyps. Though the skeleton is usually white, the living polyps are of many different colors. Coral literally build their community on the skeletons of their ancestors. They thrive in clear, salty water where the temperature never drops below 70° F (21° C). Conversely, they are very susceptible to environmental damage. For example, on Saipan's west coast, the coral is stressed due to runoff from agricultural and residential development.

Coral needs a base less than 150 feet below the water's surface on which to form. Colonies grow slowly upward until they reach the low tide level, after which development extends outward on the edges of the reef. Virtually every living creature on a coral reef serves a function to others. The ability to create symbiotic relationships is a skill necessary for survival. Sunlight is critical for coral growth. Colonies grow more quickly on the ocean side of an atoll, as opposed to the lagoon side, due to clearer water and a greater abundance of food. A strong, healthy reef can grow up to two inches a year.

Fresh or cloudy water inhibits coral growth, which is why villages and ports all across the Pacific are located at the reef-free mouths of rivers. These are also the best spots to surf.

A piece of coral is a colony composed of large numbers of polyps, individual organisms. Polyps extract calcium carbonate from the water and deposit it in their skeletons. Most reef-building corals also contain encrustations of microscopic algae within their cells. The algae, like all green plants, obtain their energy from the sun, and contribute this energy to the growth of the reef's skeleton. As a result, corals behave (and look) more like plants than animals, competing for sunlight just as terrestrial plants do. Many polyps are also carnivorous, supplementing their energy by capturing organic particles and, by using minute stinging tentacles, tiny planktonic animals.

The crown-of-thorns starfish (Acanthaster planci) *feeds on living coral.*

Coral Types

Corals belong to a broad group of sea creatures that includes polyps, soft corals, stony corals, sea anemones, sea fans, and jellyfish. Stony corals such as brain, table, staghorn, and mushroom corals have external skeletons and are important reef builders. Soft corals, black corals, and sea fans have internal skeletons. Fire corals have a smooth, velvety surface and yellowish brown color. The many varieties of soft, colorful coral and anemones might seem inviting to touch, but beware, many can inflict painful stings. Besides, all coral is fragile and can be destroyed by even casual, inadvertent touching. Keep your hands and feet off to contribute to the continuing health of the reef.

Coral, like most life forms in the Pacific, colonized the ocean from the fertile seas of Southeast Asia. Thus the number of species declines

as you move east: the Western Caroline islands have three times as many varieties of coral as Hawaii. More than 600 species of coral make their home in the Pacific, compared with only 48 in the Caribbean. The diversity of coral colors and forms is an endless delight.

Exploring a Reef

Exploring a healthy, thriving coral reef is one of life's great joys. Reefs are the most densely populated and ecologically complex living space on earth, a world of indescribable beauty. Enjoy it, treasure it, protect it. It is fragile. Use all precautions to avoid contact that will harm.

Snorkeling over a reef is usually best at high tides. It is safest to snorkel inside the reef. However, snorkeling the outer "drop-off" is thrilling for its variety of fish and corals. Only strong swimmers with good ocean experience should do so, however. If you are swimming out, rather than being taken by a boat, come out only on a calm day to avoid being knocked back onto the

---

RULES OF THE REEF

Sam's Dive Shop on Palau recommends the following environmental protection rules for all divers and snorkelers:

- Avoid wearing gloves so that you will avoid the temptation to touch.
- Do not collect live or even dead coral or shells.
- Establish neutral buoyancy and keep fins off the bottom.
- Avoid damage to reef life through carelessly moving equipment.
- Never chase, ride, or harass aquatic life.
- Do not spear or collect fish while using scuba.
- Do not throw anything out of the boat, not cigarette butts nor pull tabs.

acropora

staghorn fire coral
(Millepora accicornis)

CORALS OF THE PACIFIC

table coral

mushroom coral
(Fungia fungites)

elkhorn fire coral
(Millepora platyphylla)

brain coral
(Meandrina)

honeycomb coral (Favia matthaii)

DIANA LASICH HARPER

reef by waves. Before going in, make yourself aware of any currents from channels that drain tidal flows. Observe the direction the water is flowing. If the flow is mild, swim into it so that your return, when you may be more tired, is easier. If the flow is strong, don't go in. If you misjudge, and get caught in a strong flow, swim across the current rather than against it. If you can't resist the pull at all, it is best to conserve your energy, let yourself be carried out, and when the current diminishes, swim along the outer reef face until you find somewhere to come back in.

Coral reefs are fragile and complex ecosystems, providing food and shelter for countless species of fish, crustacea (shrimps, crabs, and lobsters), mollusks (clams and mussels), and other living creatures. Hard coral grow less than two inches a year and it can take 10,000 years for a coral reef to form. Though coral look solid, they're fragile and easily broken. By standing on them, breaking off pieces, or carelessly dropping anchor you can destroy in a few minutes what took so long to form. Once a piece of coral breaks off it dies, and it may be years before living coral reestablishes itself at that place.

We recommend you do not remove coral, seashells, plant life, or marine animals from the sea. In a small way, you are upsetting the delicate balance of nature. This is a particular problem along shorelines frequented by large numbers of tourists, who can strip a reef in very little time. If you'd like a souvenir, content yourself with what you find on the beach. Also think twice about purchasing jewelry or souvenirs made from coral or seashells. Limited-production traditional handicrafts that incorporate shells are one thing, but by purchasing unmounted seashells or mass-produced coral curios, you are contributing to the destruction of the marine environment.

CLIMATE

Temperatures are uniformly high, year-round, and rainfall usually is well distributed. The Gilbert and Line Islands in the Southern Hemisphere get less rainfall from July to November, while the Marshalls, Carolines, and Marianas are somewhat drier and less humid from December through April. The Marianas enjoy Micronesia's most pleasant climate, with lower temperatures and moderate rainfall. Kosrae and Pohnpei are among the rainiest places on earth. The Gilberts are drier than the Marshalls.

Much of Micronesia is subject to periodic droughts. During the 1997-1998 El Niño, the current that usually brings rain to Micronesia moved, leaving the Marshalls, Carolines, and Marianas with extreme water shortages.

Travel during the rainy season is almost as easy as during the dry, since the rains are usually brief and heavy, instantly cooling the air and nurturing the thick vegetation. Also, much of the rain falls at night. For divers, though, the rainy season is slightly less favorable as rivers flush more sediment into the lagoons; however, the waters tend to be still at this time, allowing diving at places inaccessible during the windier dry season. The reduced number of visitors during the wet season also compensates for the higher precipitation.

The northeast tradewinds blow steadily west across much of Micronesia from December through March, changing to calms, easterlies, or southeast trades in summer. Throughout Micronesia, winds out of the west bring rain. The tradewinds are caused by hot air rising near the equator and then flowing toward the poles at high altitude. Cooler air drawn toward the vacuum is deflected to the west by the rotation of the earth. Micronesia's proximity to the equator explains the seasonal shift in the winds, as the intertropical convergence zone between the northeast and southeast trades (or doldrum zone— where the most heated air is rising) moves north of the islands in summer.

A tropical cyclone or typhoon (hurricane) forms when thunderstorms release heat and the hot air rises. Cooler air rushes in toward the low pressure area created, spinning around the eye counterclockwise in the Northern Hemisphere, clockwise in the Southern Hemisphere. The main typhoon season in Micronesia is the rainy season, May through December, although typhoons can occur in any month. These storms are usually generated in the east and move west. Thus typhoons are far less common in the Marshalls than farther west.

Micronesia enjoys the cleanest air on earth— air that hasn't blown over a continent for weeks. To view the night stars in the warm, windless sky is like witnessing creation anew.

FLORA AND FAUNA

The variety of animal species encountered on Pacific islands declines as you move away from the Asian mainland. Island birdlife is more abundant than land-based fauna, but still reflects the decline in variety from west to east. The flora too reflect this phenomenon. Although some plant species spread by means of floating seeds or fruit, more commonly, wind and birds effect the movement. The microscopic spores of ferns, for example, can be carried vast distances by the wind.

Flying foxes and insect-eating bats were the only mammals to reach Micronesia without the aid of man. Ancient navigators introduced wild pigs, dogs, and chickens; they also brought along rats and mice. Jesuit missionaries introduced the water buffalo or carabao to Guam in the 17th century.

Birdwatching is not only interesting, it also can open unexpected doors. Good field guides are few (ask at local bookstores, museums, and cultural centers), but a determined interest will bring you in contact with fascinating people and lead to great adventures. The best time to observe forest birds is in the very early morning—they move around a lot less in the heat of the day.

Toward the end of World War II, the Solomon Islands brown tree snake began to establish itself in Guam, probably having hitchhiked on a military supply plane. It proceeded to wipe out virtually all land based birds on Guam. Today, all Pacific tropical islands attempt to avoid the introduction of this voracious snake. Guam has experimented with eradicating this pest, at least from small areas. It is too early to be optimistic.

Micronesia's high islands support a great variety of plantlife, while the low islands are restricted to a few hardy species such as breadfruit, cassava (tapioca), pandanus, and coconuts. On atolls, taro must be cultivated in deep organic pits.

Mangrove forests are common along high island coastal lagoons. The cable roots of the saltwater-tolerant mangroves anchor in the shallow upper layer of oxygenated mud, avoiding the layers of hydrogen sulfide below. The tree provides shade for tiny organisms dwelling in the tidal mudflats—a place for birds to nest and for fish or shellfish to feed and spawn. The mangroves filter and purify water flowing from land to sea and perform the same task as land-building coral colonies along the reefs: as sediment is trapped between roots, the trees extend farther into the lagoon, creating a unique natural environment. In this fashion, over the centuries, mangroves add to the size of their islands.

The past decades have seen widespread destruction of mangroves, which is tragic, considering that the ecological benefits of this fragile environment are not fully known. On many of the islands of Micronesia, canals have been maintained for centuries through mangrove forests. Canoe trips are a marvelous way to explore these wonderful ecosystems.

MARINELIFE

It's believed that most Pacific marine organisms evolved in the triangular area bounded by New Guinea, the Philippines, and the Malay Peninsula. This "Cradle of Indo-Pacific Marinelife" includes a wide variety of habitats and has remained stable through several geological ages. From this cradle the rest of the Pacific was colonized. In a very real sense, unless the Pacific Ocean remains biologically viable, world civilization, and perhaps human life itself, will simply vanish. This ocean supplies the bulk of protein for the Pacific Rim. The oxygen provided to the atmosphere by Pacific Ocean algae dwarfs that supplied by the Amazon rainforest.

Exploring the Ocean

Think of the ocean as a friend or a lover, but one known to have a bit of a temper on occasion. The happiest moments of my life have been spent in the ocean. Following some basic rules can make your time in the ocean relatively safe.

- Remember: we are land mammals, and the ocean is not our natural habitat.
- Know your limits—don't exceed them.
- Seek out advice from locals.

- Realize that some ocean creatures don't like you in their territory.
- In times of difficulty, use your brain before your muscles.
- Never, ever think you have the ocean figured out.

Fish

Micronesia's richest store of life is found in the underwater world of the lagoon and the surrounding ocean. While diving

> *Seven days a week*
> *fish dart among the coral.*
> *Very clear water.*

or snorkeling, you are likely to come across angelfish, bonito, butterfly fish, eels, grouper, harp fish, jacks, mahi, mullet, parrot fish, stingrays, surgeonfish, swordfish, trumpet fish, tuna, and countless more.

A wonderful book that will help you to realize the complexity of fish and better understand their social lives is *Watching Fishes—Understanding Coral Reef Fish Behavior,* Roberta Williams and James Q. Wilson (Pisces Books, 1992).

Dolphins

While most people use the terms dolphin and porpoise interchangeably, true porpoises lack the dolphin's beak (although many dolphins are also beakless). There are 62 species of dolphins and only six species of porpoises, all highly intelligent mammals. Dolphins leap from the water and many legends tell of them saving humans, particularly children, from drowning (perhaps the most famous concerns Telemachus, son of Odysseus). Dolphins often follow schools of tuna. Net fishing of tuna, still practiced by some commercial fishing companies, drowns many dolphins.

A Word of Caution

Sharks are present in most of the Pacific. Their danger has been greatly exaggerated. Your chance of being injured driving to the beach is many times greater than your chance of injury by a shark. Of some 300 different species, only 28 attack humans. Most dangerous are the white, tiger, hammerhead, and blue sharks.

Sharks are least dangerous in waters such as those of Micronesia where food is abundant. If you see a shark, don't panic

and thrash about—this could attract an attack. Get away as calmly and quickly as possible, unless you're with someone knowledgeable, such as a local divemaster, who says it's okay to stay. Avoid swimming in places where sewage or edible wastes enter the water or where fish have just been cleaned.

Among the troublesome sea creatures you may encounter, jellyfish are the most common. Their sting is painful, but rarely serious. Carry a bottle of meat tenderizer with you to the beach, and if stung, apply it to the affected area as quickly as possible.

Although stonefish, crown-of-thorns starfish, cone shells, and eels are hazardous, injuries resulting from any of these are rare. Stonefish rest on the bottom and are hard to see due to camouflaging that makes them look like a sandy ocean bottom; their dorsal fins inject a painful, sometimes lethal poison, which burns like fire in the blood if you happen to step on one. Treat the wound by submerging it, along with an opposite foot or hand, in water as hot as you can stand for 30 minutes (the opposite extremity prevents scalding due to numbness). If a hospital or clinic is nearby, go there immediately. Fortunately stonefish are not common, and if you keep your feet off the bottom, you further reduce any risks.

Never pick up a live cone shell; some varieties have deadly stingers that can dart out from the pointed end and reach any part of the shell's outer surface. Eels hide in reef crevices by day; most are dangerous only if you poke your hand or foot in at them. Don't tempt fate by approaching them in a manner they might interpret as threatening. Sea urchins ("living pincushions") are common in tropical waters, most usually on rocky shores or reefs. The pins on

The relatively harmless blacktip reef shark (Carcharhinus melanopterus) may be seen in shallow lagoon water.

DIANA LASICH HARPER

some can even go through a fin. Quill punctures are painful and can become infected if not treated. The quills on many species have small barbs, like fish hooks, which make their removal difficult. The folk remedy for removal is to soak the area in vinegar or urine for 15 minutes. But if the quill is still in two weeks later, consult a doctor.

REPTILES

Saltwater crocodiles live in the mangrove forests of the Western Carolines. They are so endangered it is almost impossible to find one, let alone be attacked by one. Six of the seven species of sea turtles are facing extinction due to overhunting and overharvesting of eggs. For this reason, importing any turtle product is prohibited in most Western countries.

Although the yard-long monitor lizard may look fearsome, it's no threat to humans and is beautiful to watch if you are lucky enough to see one. The adaptable monitor can climb trees, dig holes, run quickly on land, and catch fish swimming in the lagoon. It'll eat almost anything it can catch, from insects to snails, smaller lizards, rats, crabs, birds, and bird eggs.

The Pacific ridley turtle (Lepidochelys olivacea) *is one of the rarest of the seven species of sea turtles. Pacific ridleys eat crustaceans, fish eggs, and some vegetation.*

Geckos and skinks are small lizards often seen on the islands. The skink hunts insects by day; its tail breaks off if you catch it, but a new one quickly grows. The gecko is nocturnal and has no eyelids. Adhesive toe pads enable it to pass along vertical surfaces, and it changes color to avoid detection. Unlike the skink, which avoids humans, geckos often live in people's homes where they eat insects attracted by electric lights. Its ticking call may be a territorial warning to other geckos.

COCONUT CRABS

The coconut crab *(Birgus latro)* is a nocturnal creature that lives under logs, in holes, or at the base of pandanus or coconut trees. The females lay their eggs in the sea and the tiny crabs float around a few months, then crawl into a seashell and climb up the beach. When a crab is big enough, it abandons the shell and relies on its own hard shell for protection. Its food is ripe pandanus or coconut. The crab will appear dark blue if it eats coconuts, rich orange if it feeds on pandanus. First it will husk a coconut using its two front claws, then break the nut open on a rock. It might take a crab two nights to get at the meat. Coconut crabs can grow up to three feet across. Although undoubtedly tasty, they are endangered in much of Micronesia and should not be eaten.

LOUISE FOOTE

HISTORY

History creates a community's past. To be comprehensible, it must employ a construct to simplify otherwise unmanageable amounts of data. By making sense, history differs from reality.

Micronesians

The earliest arrivals to Micronesia left relatively few artifacts that withstood centuries of tropical weather. Thus, there is much guesswork in piecing together Micronesia's earliest human history. What follows is a summary of the best guesses by archaeologists, historians, and anthropologists, subject, of course, to continual revision.

Austronesian-speaking Micronesian peoples entered the Pacific from Southeast Asia more than 3,000 years ago. The first islands they located were probably the Marianas, followed by the Western Carolines. From this base they settled the Eastern Caroline, Tungaru, and Marshall Islands. Beads uncovered at Yap prove that some contact was maintained with Southeast Asia, where the beads were manufactured. In the westernmost atolls of Micronesia, an Indonesian-style loom is still used to make hibiscus-fiber skirts.

The first Micronesians lived from fishing, gathering, and agriculture. Many islanders used pottery, and all made tools from stone, shells and bone. They cultivated breadfruit, taro, pandanus, coconuts, cassava, and (on the volcanic islands) yams. Pigs, chickens, and dogs were kept for food, but the surrounding sea yielded the most important source of protein. Most Micronesian societies were matrilineal; the husband and children became members of the wife's landholding matrilineage. Patrilineal Yap was an exception. From chiefly clans came the ruling male chiefs. The paramount chiefs of Palau, the Marshalls, Pohnpei, and Yap are still influential figures.

Micronesians were the greatest sea voyagers in the world and sailed huge outrigger canoes between the Carolines and the Marianas. To navigate they read signs from the sun, stars, currents, swells, winds, clouds, and birds. Yap was an important trading center, in regular contact with Palau and the islands to the east. Annual expeditions brought tribute to the powerful islands of Ulithi and Yap.

Old stories in the Carolines tell of a great empire, of which we unfortunately know little. The magnificent ruins of Kosrae and Pohnpei, the stone money of Yap, the *latte* stones of Guam, Rota, and Tinian, and the basalt monoliths and terraces of Babeldaob add to the mystery, but testify to complex, wealthy cultures. It is hard to believe that the extraordinary navigators who lived on atolls did not keep some continual contact with the Philippines, Indonesia, and perhaps mainland Asia.

Magellan

Magellan was the first European to sail on the Pacific. He proved that one could sail around the world. In the late 15th century the Portuguese exercised control of the trade route around the tip of Africa to the spice islands of Indonesia and the riches of China, forcing the Spaniards to find another route for the trade they desired. The king of Spain outfitted Magellan with five ships for one of the greatest journeys in history.

In September 1519, Magellan's fleet of five ships sailed southwest across the Atlantic toward South America. On 21 October, Magellan sighted a cape, and then a bay-like opening. Two ships investigating the channel discovered that the flood tide was stronger than the ebb, indicating a passage. Magellan crossed what became known as the Strait of Magellan in a hideous, but remarkable, 38-day voyage, losing two ships in the process to the tempestuous weather and currents.

On 28 November 1520, the three surviving ships entered the Pacific. The ships sailed northwest for months across this unimaginably vast sea. Worms reduced their biscuits to powder, and the crew had to hold their noses as they drank the water. Rats were a delicacy.

The ships finally sighted land on 24 January 1521, and 11 days later came upon people in swift outrigger canoes near Guam. The islanders (Chamorros) took Magellan's skiff. In vengeance, he took 40 armed men ashore, burned 50 houses and boats, killed seven men, and recovered his skiff. By 9 March his fleet had arrived northeast of the Moluccas (Maluku, Indonesia) at Samar in the present-day Philippines. Magellan converted the rajah of Cebu and 3,000 of his subjects to Christianity. Magellan was killed while leading a similar expedition to convert and subdue the neighboring island of Mactan. One of the ships, however, sailed on alone across the Indian Ocean, around the Cape of Good Hope, and north through the Atlantic, reaching Seville, Spain, in September 1522. These survivors were the first men known to have circumnavigated the globe. One hundred seventy men died on the voyage.

The circumnavigation was perhaps not as important an event as is sometimes implied in history books. No one else bothered to do it until Sir Francis Drake in 1578. The Strait of Magellan remained a dangerous, difficult crossing. For centuries, the major direct route to Asia from Europe was around Africa. The predominant route for the Spanish was indirect: to Mexico and Central America by boat, across land to the Pacific, and then travel by its Pacific fleet.

European and American Colonialism

Micronesia was not soon colonized. It was not an important objective of the Spanish, Portuguese, or the later Pacific colonial power, the Dutch. No permanent base was set up on Guam until 1668. Even then, Spain's interest in Guam was to use it as a support base for their galleons trading the silver of Mexico for the tea, silk, and spices of the Philippines. Little attention was paid to the Carolines or Marshalls until 1864 when the first resident German trader set up shop in the Marshalls, followed in 1869 by a post on Yap. The Germans established a protectorate over the Marshalls in 1878 and attempted to extend this to all of the Caroline Islands in 1885. The Spanish protested that they had already claimed the area. In 1874 the Pope mediated the Spanish-German dispute and ruled in favor of the Spanish on most issues, although he gave the Germans trading rights and permitted them to annex the Marshalls.

In the 1830s British whalers and traders from Australia became active in the Carolines and Marshalls. Americans arrived in the 1850s. These newcomers brought catastrophic epidemics and foreign control over the surviving native people and their traditional way of life. Protestant missionaries established themselves on Pohnpei and Kosrae by 1852. The British established a protectorate over the Gilberts in 1892.

In 1898 the Spanish-American War shattered Spain's colonial empire, and the United States took advantage of the occasion to annex Guam and the Philippines. The Spanish had little choice other than to sell the Carolines and Northern Marianas to the Germans in 1899 for 25 million pesetas.

The Germans set about organizing the lucrative copra trade. To force the islanders to make copra for sale, they established a poll tax in 1910; those who couldn't pay were required to

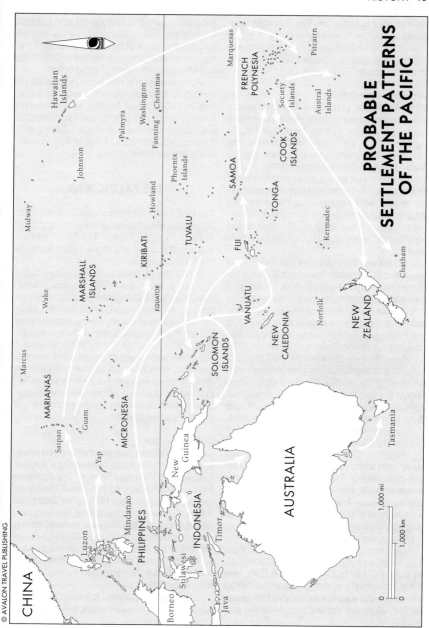

PROBABLE SETTLEMENT PATTERNS OF THE PACIFIC

work on road construction. The Pohnpeians revolted against this slave labor and killed the German governor. A German warship soon arrived, and the rebel leaders were executed and buried in a mass grave.

Japanese Imperialism

When World War I broke out, Germany essentially abandoned its Pacific possessions, bringing its Pacific fleet back to the European war. By agreement with the British, the Japanese took the Northern Marianas, the Carolines, and the Marshalls from the Germans without a fight, about the only part the Japanese played in World War I. Japanese traders had long been calling at the islands, so the change had little immediate impact on the Micronesians. Nauru and the German colonies in the South Pacific (Samoa and New Guinea) were seized by Australia and New Zealand.

After the war the Japanese government was appointed to administer the former German territories north of the equator under a League of Nations mandate binding them to an agreement not to build "fortifications or military and naval bases." In 1922 the neutralization of this part of the Pacific was further guaranteed by a treaty between the United States and Japan. In 1935, however, Japan withdrew from the League of Nations and began building large military bases on some of the islands. Finally, they annexed Nanyo Gunto (their name for Micronesia) outright. The headquarters of the Japanese South Seas Government or Nanyochokan was at Koror.

Big Japanese business interests in 1921 founded the Nanyo Kohatsu Kaisha (South Seas Development Co., Ltd.). The Japanese built sugar mills in the Marianas and mined bauxite and phosphate in Palau. They also developed commercial fishing, trochus shell production, and agriculture. After 1931 Japanese citizens were allowed to purchase or lease Micronesian land and large tracts passed into their hands by dubious means.

Japan encouraged emigration to Micronesia. The number of Japanese colonists skyrocketed from 3,671 in 1920 to 84,476 in 1940, two-thirds of the total population. Japan had turned Micronesia into a part of Japan, with little regard for the indigenous people. Japan was the only imperialist power that had attempted to supplant the local population. The society they developed had three classes of people: Japanese at the top, Korean and Okinawan workers in the middle, and Micronesians *(toming)* at the bottom.

Micronesians continued to live by subsistence agriculture and making copra, spectators on the sidelines of Japanese development. Interisland travel by canoe was banned and the authority of the traditional chiefs undermined. Before WW II, immigrants controlled almost all economic activities in the cash economy.

THE PACIFIC WAR

The First World War eliminated Germany from Micronesia, New Guinea, and Samoa, and gave Japan the central Pacific. The Second World War expelled Japan and left the United States as the dominant power.

In 1942 the Japanese used their military bases in Palau to attack the Philippines and Indonesia; Chuuk was a springboard for their assault on the Solomons and New Guinea. With the Japanese conquest of Guam, Nauru, and Tungaru the whole of Micronesia was under one rule for the first time in history. For the Micronesians the war years were ones of forced labor, famine, and fear. They watched as their islands were ravaged by foreign armies. Five thousand Micronesians died in a war in which no foreign power seemed concerned with the interests or the liberty of the islanders.

The Rising Sun

Japan had hoped to become the dominant power in Asia and the Pacific by establishing a "Greater East Asia Co-prosperity Sphere." The Japanese high command decided to achieve their ends through force. In July 1941, after Japanese troops occupied French Indochina, the American, British, and Dutch governments declared an iron and oil embargo against Japan. When it became evident to the Japanese that they would have to fight to protect their oil supply from Dutch-held Indonesia, they prepared for war against the United States.

The Japanese planned to shatter the American fleet in one massive attack, creating a large

Admiral Isoroku Yamamotu planned the attacks on Pearl Harbor and Midway. He remained commander in chief of the Japanese combined fleet until a Betty bomber in which he was a passenger was shot down over Bougainville in the North Solomon Islands by American P-38s on 18 April 1943.

ter of Pacific Ocean control. This overextended their supply lines. They occupied Tulagi in the Solomon Islands in May and started building an air base on Guadalcanal. Landings took place throughout New Guinea, and a Japanese fleet advanced toward Port Moresby. En route it was intercepted by Allied naval units. Although the ensuing Battle of the Coral Sea—an air battle between navies that never sighted each other—is now judged a draw, the Japanese invasion fleet turned back. Less than a month later, on 4 June, another Japanese invasion fleet became locked in the Battle of Midway: American aircraft sank four Japanese carriers, with their planes and elite crews. Japan had lost its naval superiority in the Pacific. Its strategy of landing a knockout punch to the United States had failed.

The Setting Sun

From July to November 1942, Australian and Japanese armies fought back and forth across New Guinea's Kokoda Trail near Port Moresby. Simultaneously, Japanese soldiers struggled in the Solomons to recapture Guadalcanal from the Americans. By the end of 1942 the Japanese had lost both campaigns. A number of indecisive naval engagements accompanied the jungle war in the Solomons, but the end result was a further weakening of Japanese aerial strength. The spring and early summer of 1943 saw a stalemate between Australia and Japan, while the United States rebuilt its strength.

In the wide Pacific, the advantage lies with the side on the offensive, as the Japanese learned when they tried to defend a vastly scattered front against overpowering mobile naval units. The Allied strategy was to approach the Philippines from two directions, with the United States and Australian armies fighting their way up through New Guinea, and the U.S. Navy thrusting across the central Pacific. By mid-1943 troops under Gen. Douglas A. MacArthur and Admiral Halsey began the long campaign in the Solomons (New Georgia, Bougainville) and New Guinea (Salamaua, Lae, Finschhafen, Madang). Large Japanese armies were bogged down in China and elsewhere, enabling the Allies to concentrate their forces at the weak points, neutralizing and bypassing entrenched strongholds (for example Chuuk) where the price of conquest would have been too great.

defensive perimeter and thereby cutting off aid to its opponents in China. The Pearl Harbor attack on 7 December 1941, for all its seeming brilliance, did not meet the Japanese strategic goal, since the main United States aircraft carriers were out of the harbor and survived the attack. The attack did not take the United States out of the war, as the Japanese high command had hoped. But it did delay the ability of the United States Navy to interfere with Japan's occupation of Southeast Asia. Hong Kong, Shanghai, Malaya, Singapore, the Dutch East Indies, Burma, and the Philippines all fell to the Japanese by April 1942. And China was temporarily cut off from much-needed assistance from the United States.

Then came the Doolittle bombing raid on Tokyo on 18 April 1942. This raid was more than a piece of bravado by the Americans. The Japanese decided that to protect their homeland from further bombing, they had to widen their perime-

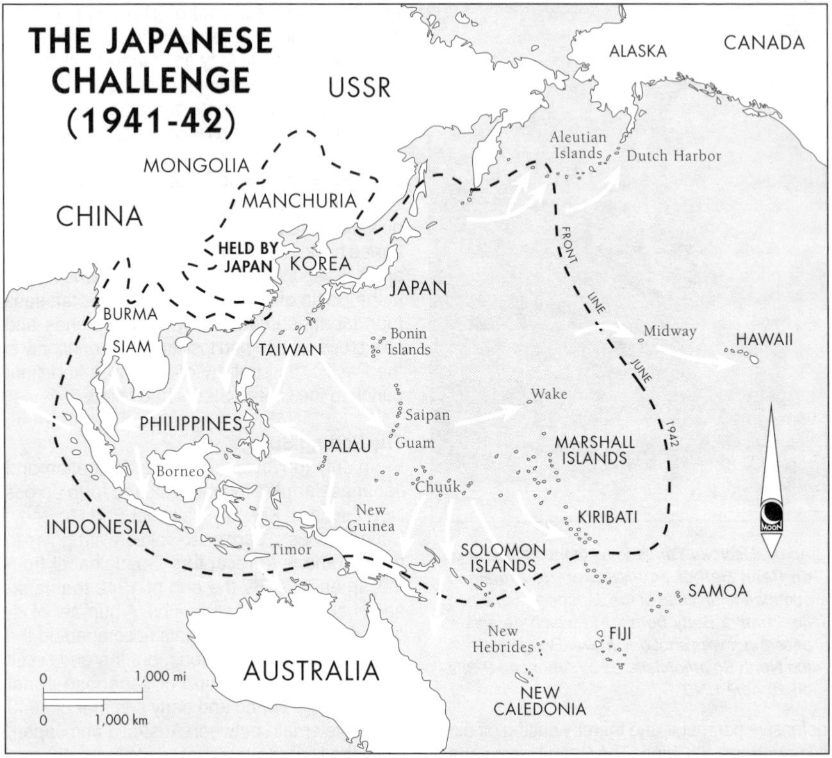

THE JAPANESE CHALLENGE (1941-42)

USSR

ALASKA   CANADA

MONGOLIA

CHINA   MANCHURIA

HELD BY JAPAN KOREA

JAPAN

BURMA
SIAM   TAIWAN

Bonin Islands

Midway   HAWAII

PHILIPPINES

Saipan   Wake

PALAU   Guam   MARSHALL ISLANDS

Borneo

Chuuk

INDONESIA

New Guinea

Timor

KIRIBATI

SOLOMON ISLANDS

SAMOA

New Hebrides   FIJI

AUSTRALIA   NEW CALEDONIA

Aleutian Islands   Dutch Harbor

FRONT LINE   JUNE   1942

0   1,000 mi
0   1,000 km

© AVALON TRAVEL PUBLISHING

The central Pacific naval offensive under Adm. Chester W. Nimitz began in November 1943, with landings at Tarawa and Butaritari in Tungaru. Casualties were high at these battles, but they enabled the Allies to perfect amphibious landing techniques. In February 1944, the Americans captured Kwajalein and Enewetak in the Marshalls. They destroyed the Japanese fleet in Chuuk lagoon. By this time, United States carrier forces were strong enough to overcome Japanese opposition, but at a heavy price if the plans entailed an amphibious landing, rather than mere aerial and naval bombardment.

The Philippines and Beyond

In June 1944 the United States landed on Saipan to secure advanced bases for bombing Japanese home islands. The Japanese Navy engaged the Allies in the Battle of the Philippine Sea, losing three carriers and 480 planes, and leaving the Philippines open to attack. Tinian and Guam were then taken by the Americans.

By July 1944, Japanese weakness was clearly evident, and United States submarines began to take a crippling toll on their merchant shipping. In September, the New Guinea and central Pacific offensives converged when Morotai (near Ternate) and Peleliu (Palau) were captured, providing dual springboards for the Philippines campaign.

The American landings at Leyte in the Philippines in October led to the largest naval battle of all time, the Battle of the Leyte Gulf. The Japanese lost 24 major warships, including all their remaining carriers, compared to a U.S. loss of only six smaller ships. For the first time, the Japanese made large scale use of kamikaze-piloted planes. In January 1945, the Americans landed at Lingayen on Luzon, and by early March the remaining Japanese had been driven into the mountains, where they would hold out until the end of the war, but not before Manila was destroyed in battle.

The next stage in the war was to be the invasion of Japan itself. The first of a damaging series of incendiary bombings of Japanese cities by Tinian-based B-29s occurred on 24 November 1944. In March 1945 more than 80,000 civilians died in the incendiary bombing of Tokyo.

To gain advanced air bases able to provide fighter cover for the bombers, U.S. Marines landed at Iwo Jima on 19 February 1945. Although it took five bitter weeks, they finally cleared the island of defenders. In early 1945, the British reconquered Burma, reopening the road to China. In April, United States forces invaded Okinawa to secure an advanced naval base, but Japanese defensive positions and kamikaze attacks exacted serious casualties.

Finally, on 6 August 1945 the United States ushered in the atomic era, dropping an atom bomb on Hiroshima. Days later it dropped a second on Nagasaki. The planes had taken off from Tinian in the Northern Marianas. The Japanese, at the emperor's insistence, surrendered the day after the Nagasaki bomb. The United States justified its use of atomic weapons on civilians with claims that had it invaded Japan instead, there would have been an even greater loss of life to American soldiers, as well as to Japanese military personnel and civilians.

Half a million Japanese soldiers and civilians died in this senseless war, far from their shores. Of the 50,000 Micronesians, 10% were killed as

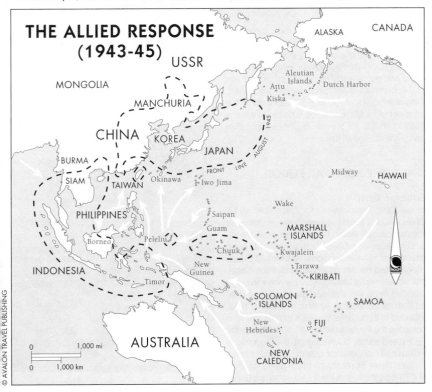

THE ALLIED RESPONSE (1943–45)

Task Force 38.3 enters the Ulithi lagoon, returning from strikes in the Philippines, 11 December 1944.

NAVAL HISTORICAL CENTER, WASHINGTON, D.C.

foreign armies fought back and forth across the islands in a brutal struggle the islanders could only lose. All Japanese military and civilians died in battle, committed suicide, or were repatriated at the end of the war. The prewar infrastructures and economies of Micronesia were obliterated. Bitter memories of the war are still vivid in the minds of older Micronesians, who associate the destruction with the prewar Japanese occupation and militarization of the area.

THE POSTWAR PERIOD

Strategic Trust

In the Cairo Declaration of 1 December 1943, Churchill and Roosevelt announced that after the war, Japan would be stripped of all the island possessions it had obtained in 1914. Soon after the Japanese surrender, the United States Navy called for the annexation of Micronesia, but the Truman administration, sensitive to being branded neocolonialist, opted instead for a United Nations trusteeship, which it received in 1947. Included in the trusteeship were islands that now compose the Republic of the Marshall Islands, the Federated States of Micronesia, the Republic of Palau, and the Commonwealth of the Marianas.

The Trust Territory of the Pacific Islands (TTPI) was the last of the 11 trusteeships under the United Nations to attain self-government. It

had been the only one designated a "strategic" trust, meaning that the United States could establish military bases and conduct nuclear tests. Originally administered by the U.S. Navy in 1951, control over the trusteeship passed to the Department of the Interior, although the Northern Marianas remained under naval rule until 1962. At first Micronesia was administered from Honolulu, but in 1954 the Office of the High

aviator's grave, Japanese Cemetery, Peleliu

Commissioner shifted to Guam, and in 1962 the Trust Territory headquarters moved to Saipan. There were six districts: Marshall Islands, Ponape (Pohnpei), Truk (Chuuk), Yap, Palau, and the Northern Marianas.

Military Use

Immediately after World War II, General MacArthur proposed an "offshore island perimeter" to defend American interests in the Far East. After the withdrawal from Vietnam in 1973, United States strategists resurrected plans for a chain of island-based military installations facing the Pacific Rim from Japan to the Indian Ocean. Micronesia offered a wide perimeter on islands that were immune from massive local opposition. The Pentagon obtained leases over much of the Northern Marianas in 1976. In a 1983 vote, the Marshallese approved a Compact that delivered the Kwajalein missile range to the United States for 30 years. For decades, only the Palauans resisted United States pressure for bases.

Currently, with the cold war over and conventional military deployments winding down worldwide, the United States has shifted to a strategy of a small number of high-tech bases, such as that at Kwajalein. Islanders often see themselves in a no-win situation. On the one hand, there are some continued antimilitary feelings. On the other hand, there is also fear of the economic hardship the islands would face if there were a precipitous, uncompensated withdrawal by the United States.

The American Role in Micronesia

It is clear that the United States objective in World War II was not to bring liberation to Micronesia. The goal was purely strategic—to rid the islands of Japanese bases. Nonetheless, the situation of Micronesians improved with the defeat of Japan. Japan, unlike previous colonial rulers, encouraged large scale emigration of its people to Micronesia. At the start of WW II, the population of Micronesia was two-thirds Japanese. Micronesians had been reduced to a politically impotent minority within their own homeland. With all the drawbacks of American rule, Micronesia today, with the exception of Guam, is again overwhelmingly populated by its native population. Micronesians have the potential to fashion their own future.

This did not take place from American design, however. The United States, during its trusteeship, paid only lip service to the goal of preparing Micronesia for self-rule. From the start, United States policy was to preserve Micronesia for strategic use, while denying military access to foreign powers. The welfare of inhabitants was considered only in relation to this primary purpose, despite article six of the U.N. Trusteeship Agreement. That provision, at least in theory, bound the United States to "promote the economic advancement and self-sufficiency of the inhabitants."

Instead, two decades of neglect followed by two decades of often ill-conceived federal programs eroded the self-sufficiency of Micronesia's economies. In the early 1960s independence fever swept the third world, and it appeared the United States might lose control of its strategically located Trust Territory. In 1961 a visiting United Nations mission leveled heavy criticism at Washington for its neglect. In response, President Kennedy appointed a commission headed by economist Anthony M. Solomon to explore a future for Micronesia. The Solomon Report recommended agricultural development, capital improvements, and new health and welfare programs.

In 1963 President Kennedy issued National Security Action Memorandum 145, setting forth as policy "the movement of Micronesia into a permanent relationship with the United States within our political framework." United States assistance to the TTPI jumped from $6.1 million in 1962 to $17 million in 1963, $67.3 million in 1971, and $138.7 million in 1979. Despite the flood of money, essential services (water, electricity, communications, sanitation) remained as bad as ever. Most of the money went into government salaries rather than into creating an economic infrastructure.

After 1966 large numbers of Peace Corps volunteers arrived in Micronesia; at the high point, 900 volunteers were at work on less than 100 inhabited islands. Many volunteers openly sided with the Micronesians, providing legal advice on how to defend their rights.

Political Development

The United States exported its political structures to Micronesia, undercutting the power of traditional chiefs. When the first Congress of Micronesia met on Saipan in 1965, American officials were taken aback by the political sophistication and solidarity displayed by the Micronesian legislators. In 1966 this Congress asked President Johnson to appoint a status commission to expedite the transfer of political control from American officials to elected Micronesian leaders. Negotiations toward a new status began in 1969. In 1971 the Micronesians rejected an offer of commonwealth status.

Frustrated United States officials fell back on a "divide and conquer" strategy, helping to fragment Micronesia into four separate entities. The CIA was brought in to spy on the Micronesian leaders (see front page, *Washington Post,* 2 December 1976). In 1975 the United States sliced off the Northern Marianas to form the Commonwealth of the Northern Marianas, with large tracts of land leased by the military.

Free Association

Despite the withdrawal of the Marianas delegates, a draft constitution for a "Federated States of Micronesia" was prepared. On 12 July 1978 a plebiscite was held throughout the Trust Territory. Voters in the Marshalls and Palau (the most strategically significant areas) rejected the constitution and elected to separate from the other districts, forming political entities of their own. This reflected, in part, an awareness of their stronger bargaining position and an unwillingness to share future benefits. A few months later the Congress of Micronesia was dissolved, and the four central districts (Kosrae, Pohnpei, Chuuk, and Yap) banded together, proclaiming the constitution of the Federated States of Micronesia on 10 May 1979. The Marshall Islands also attained self-government in 1979, and in 1980 Palau gained significant self-rule.

In 1983, voters in the Marshall Islands and the FSM approved Compacts of Free Association with the United States. This phrase came from the fact that under the United Nations trusteeship, any continuing relationship with the United States had to be given with the "free" consent of the governed. The Compacts were formally adopted by the United States in 1986.

The 15-year Compacts granted two independent entities—the Republic of the Marshall Islands and the Federated States of Micronesia— full control over their internal and foreign affairs. In exchange for billions in financial support, the United States retained the right to use the islands for military purposes for 15 years. The U.S. has veto power over any Micronesian action in conflict with this right. Only the people of the Northern Marianas are U.S. citizens, although the others have the right of free entry to the States.

In 1986 the U.N. Trusteeship Council approved the termination of the trusteeship in the Marshall Islands, the Federated States of Micronesia, and the Northern Marianas, and— though the status of Palau remained unresolved—the U.S. declared the trusteeship terminated in the three in October 1986. Late in 1990 the Soviet Union withdrew its previous objections to these moves, and in December 1990 the U.N. Security Council voted 14 to 1 (with Cuba dissenting) to dissolve the Trust Territory in the Marshalls, FSM, and the Northern Marianas. In 1991 the TTPI headquarters was moved from Saipan to Koror (Palau). On 17 September 1991 the Federated States of Micronesia and the Marshall Islands were admitted to the United Nations. Palau finally ratified a Compact in 1994.

The Future

For the past several centuries, Micronesia's destiny was determined, in large part, by colonial powers that fought to control its strategic locations. Today, with the exception of Guam and the Commonwealth of the Northern Marianas, the islands of Micronesia are independent, though the nations of the former Trust Territory certainly can be said to remain within an American sphere of influence.

How will history judge the American administration of Micronesia? The Spanish came to use the islands of Micronesia as way stations for their far flung empire. They successfully spread their religion, often by murderous means. The Germans had little regard for preserving Micronesian culture and tried to force the Micronesians into plantation economies. The Japanese developed the islands by opening the floodgates to uncontrolled Asian immigration and militarization. Had they not started a disastrous war, Micronesia today would undoubtedly be as Japanese as Okinawa or Hokkaido, retaining an unassimilated Micronesian minority.

The American approach to Micronesia instilled economic and political dependency, which served military ends. The United States, however, unlike the Japanese, protected Micronesian land rights. During the Japanese period much land was alienated to Japanese settlers. Under the TTPI most of this land went back to its original owners. And today, with the exception of Guam, Micronesians retain their land rights.

Today the United States seems ambivalent about spending millions of dollars a year to support the Freely Associated States. Its obligations to make Compact payments to the Marshall Islands and the Federated States of Micronesia expire in 2001. With the end of the cold war, it is not clear to what extent the United States still considers these nations crucial to its own defense. A precipitous, unplanned withdrawal of support or even a great lessening of support, after years of economic dependence, would be disastrous for the islanders.

Meanwhile, the Japanese are an increasing economic force in Micronesia. Even the Philippines, the People's Republic of China, and Taiwan are all anxious to exploit the region's resources.

International Relations

The Republic of the Marshall Islands, the Federated States of Micronesia, the Republic of Palau, the Republic of Nauru and the Republic of Kiribati all belong to the United Nations.

All are also members of the **South Pacific Forum** (G.P.O. Box 856, Suva, Fiji Islands), a regional grouping concerned with economic development, trade, communications, fisheries, and environmental protection. At their annual meetings, the heads of government of the SPF countries express their joint political views. Meetings held in Micronesia have included the 1976 and 1993 meetings on Nauru, the 1980 and 1989 meetings on Tarawa, the 1991 and 1998 meetings on Pohnpei, and the 1996 meeting on Majuro. At the 1985 Forum meeting the South Pacific Nuclear Free Zone treaty was signed. The 1989 meeting condemned driftnet fishing and set up a mechanism to monitor the greenhouse effect.

The **South Pacific Forum Fisheries Agency** (P.O. Box 629, Honiara, Solomon Islands), formed in 1979, coordinates the fisheries policies of the member states and negotiates licensing agreements with foreign countries. In 1988 the Federated States of Micronesia and Marshall Islands became parties to the **South Pacific Regional Trade and Economic Cooperation Agreement** (SPARTECA), which allows certain island products duty free entry to Australia and New Zealand; Kiribati and Nauru also belong.

All of the countries included in this book belong to the **South Pacific Commission** (P.O. Box D5, Nouméa Cedex, New Caledonia). The SPC was established in 1947 by the postwar colonial powers; Australia, France, the Netherlands, New Zealand, the United Kingdom, and the United States. The Netherlands withdrew in 1962. As the insular territories attained self-government they were admitted to membership. In October each year, delegates from the member governments meet at a **South Pacific Conference** to discuss the Commission's program and budget. The SPC promotes regional economic and social development through annual conferences, research, and technical assistance, and is strictly nonpolitical. Fields of activity include food, marine resources, environmental management, rural development, community health, education, and statistical studies.

LOUISE FOOTE

ECONOMY

In 1994, the United Nations held a conference on Barbados to deal with the plight of the world's small island nations. Its final report, titled "Report of the Global Conference on the Sustainable Development of Small Island Developing States" dealt with problems the Micronesian nations share in common with similar ocean countries. The report focused on the importance of these countries, stating:

Small island developing States have sovereign rights over their own natural resources. Their biodiversity is among the most threatened in the world and their ecosystems provide ecological corridors linking major areas of biodiversity around the world. They bear responsibility for a significant portion of the world's oceans and seas and their resources. The efforts of small island developing States to conserve, protect and restore their ecosystems deserve international cooperation and partnership.

The report also focused on the competitive disadvantages these nations have:

Those disadvantages include a narrow range of resources, which forces undue specialization; excessive dependence on international trade and hence vulnerability to global developments; high population density, which increases the pressure on already limited resources; overuse of resources and premature depletion; relatively small watersheds and threatened supplies of fresh water; costly public administration and infrastructure, including transportation and communication and limited institutional capacities and domestic markets, which are too small to provide significant scale economies, while their limited export volumes, sometimes from remote locations, lead to high freight costs and reduced competitiveness. Small

islands tend to have high degrees of endemism and levels of biodiversity, but the relatively small numbers of the various species impose high risks of extinction and create a need for protection.

Because of the small landmass of small island countries, such as those of Micronesia, as well as their fragile ecologies, they face a problem today with which the world has been unwilling to come to terms: economic growth must be sustainable. Civilization cannot exist for long by destroying resources through onetime use.

Regional differences within Micronesia are great, with the Marshall Islands and the FSM having a per capita gross domestic product of less than $2,000 a year, Palau about $4,000 a year, and Guam and the Northern Marianas both more than $15,000 a year. In Kiribati the GDP is less than $1,000 per capita. About two-thirds of the population of the Marshall Islands and Palau lives in urban areas, while only about a third of the people of the FSM and Kiribati are in urban areas. By the same standards Guam and the Northern Marianas are almost totally urbanized.

Self-Sufficiency?

In 1961 imports to Micronesia led exports by two to one; by 1975 this had increased to 15 to one. In 1984 the U.S. provided $124 million in aid to the Trust Territory of the Pacific Islands, more than it spent in Guam and American Samoa combined. Most American aid went to consumption rather than public investment. Large numbers of Micronesians continue to flock to urban areas to lead a lifestyle supported by United States payments. The average government worker earns much more than a villager.

Most of Micronesia is no longer self-sufficient. It has entered into consumer economies. Micronesians today eat imported food—in many places the taro patches are abandoned, breadfruit is unharvested. Rice, the current staple, is imported. It is unclear whether the islands can support today's dense populations in a consumer lifestyle on a sustainable basis. Individual Micronesians may continue to solve their economic problems by migrating to countries with better economic prospects. This would, however, continue to be socially disruptive to island life.

Under the Compacts, the FAS is required to spend 40% of its U.S.-provided Compact payments on capital improvements such as roads, airports, harbors, sewers, and water supply systems. This of course does not insure that the money is effectively used to create a modern infrastructure. Japanese aid is tied to specific projects, with Japanese companies doing all of the work. Much Japanese aid to Micronesia is linked to fishing rights negotiations.

PANDANUS

Apart from the coconut tree, the pandanus shrub is one of the most widespread and useful plants in the Pacific. Among other things, the islanders use the thorny leaves of the pandanus, or screw pine, for weaving mats, baskets, and fans. The seeds are strung into necklaces. The fibrous fruit makes brushes for decorating tapa cloth and can be eaten. The aerial roots can be made into fish traps.

Health and Welfare

Despite some impressive medical facilities, the quality of treatment is low. Proper sewers and water systems are not in place. Large numbers of people fall victim to diseases that have been eradicated in Western countries. Health care is geared more toward curing disease than preventing it. Nutritional education is abysmal, though Pohnpei's drive to promote a return to breast feeding, rather than the continued use of formula, is a notable exception, as is Kiribati' campaign to encourage its people to return to eating fresh vegetables. Imported foods of poor nutritional value have created new health problems. Cigarette smoking is almost universal.

Education

New schools have been built. Palau Community College at Koror offers vocational training. The College of Micronesia—FSM at Pohnpei handles teacher training. A school of nursing operates at Majuro. Practical technical and agricultural education has largely been left to Jesuit institutions, such as the Pohnpei Agricultural and Trade School (PATS). Micronesians also attend United States colleges. Many remain in the States, or return to the islands with few opportunities to use their education because of chronic underemployment.

Law of the Sea

As plentiful as the oceans are, we humans have proven ourselves clever enough to rob them clean of fish. The great cod banks of the North Atlantic have been destroyed. With the technological advances of the last several decades, we can, with very little difficulty, wipe the Pacific clean of its tuna in a very short number of years.

The industrialized nations want tuna. Tokyo wants its sashimi. San Francisco wants its blackened ahi. Lower grade tuna still finds its way into cat food. As long as the industrialized nations put their short-term interests ahead of the long-term notion of sustainable yield, the destruction will continue.

Even when treaties are passed to protect ocean environments, without a great deal of foreign assistance the small nations of Micronesia cannot adequately police their own waters.

States have traditionally exercised sovereignty over a three-mile belt of territorial sea along their shores. The high seas beyond these limits could be freely used by anyone. But on 28 September 1945, President Harry Truman declared United States sovereignty over the natural resources of the adjacent continental shelf. United States fishing boats soon became involved in an acrimonious dispute with several South American countries over their rich anchovy fishing grounds, and in 1952 Chile, Ecuador, and Peru declared a 200-nautical-mile Exclusive Economic Zone (EEZ) along their shores. In 1958 the United Nations convened a Conference on the Law of the Sea at Geneva, which accepted national control over continental shelves up to 650 feet deep. Agreement could not be reached on extended territorial sea limits.

National claims multiplied so much that in 1974 another U.N. conference was convened, leading to the signing of the Law of the Sea Convention at Jamaica in 1982 by 159 states and other entities. This complex agreement of 200 pages, nine annexes, and 320 articles extended national control over 40% of the world's oceans. The territorial sea claims were increased to 12 nautical miles and the continental shelf defined as extending 200 nautical miles offshore. States were given full control over all resources, living or nonliving, within this belt.

Largely due to provisions for the regulation of undersea mining, most industrialized countries, including the United States, still have not ratified the treaty. But a sufficient number of other countries ratified for it to be binding on the ratifying countries.

Many aspects of the Law of the Sea have become accepted in practice. The EEZs mainly affect fisheries and seabed mineral exploitation; freedom of navigation within the zones is guaranteed. The Law of the Sea increased immensely the territory of oceanic states, giving them real political weight for the first time. The land area of the seven political entities covered in this book comes to only 1,245 square miles, while their EEZs total 4,500,000 square miles!

Fisheries

Tuna is the second most important fishing industry in the world (after shrimp and prawns), and 66% of the world's catch is taken in the Pacific. The western Pacific, where most of the is-

EXCLUSIVE ECONOMIC ZONES (EEZ)

© AVALON TRAVEL PUBLISHING

lands of Micronesia are located, is twice as productive as the eastern, with fish worth more than a billion dollars extracted annually. Although tuna is one of the few renewable resources the Micronesian islanders have, for many years the U.S. government (at the behest of the tuna industry) attempted to deny them any benefit from it by claiming that since the fish were "migratory," they were not subject to protection by the EEZ nation. Thus American purse seiners claimed they were not subject to licensing fees for fishing within the 200-nautical-mile EEZs.

In 1985, when Kiribati signed a fishing agreement with the Soviet Union, the United States finally got the message. In 1987 the U.S. government agreed to a $60 million aid package, which included licensing fees for American tuna boats to work the EEZs of the 16 member states of the South Pacific Forum Fisheries Agency (including Palau, the Federated States of Micronesia, Kiribati, the Marshall Islands, and Nauru) for five years. The settlement, small potatoes for the U.S. but big money to the islanders, was seen as an inexpensive way of forestalling "Soviet advances" in the central Pacific. In 1990 the question of whether island governments would be allowed to control their valuable tuna resources seemed settled when the U.S. Congress voted overwhelmingly to impose management on tuna stocks in the U.S. EEZ. The "migratory" fish finally had owners.

The Forum Fisheries Agency, which negotiated the Tuna Treaty, now handles all fishing agreements between FFA member states and the United States, Korea, Japan, and Taiwan. Japan has resisted signing multilateral fisheries agreements, preferring to deal with the Pacific countries individually. As a means of buying influence, fisheries development in Micronesia has been sponsored mainly by Japan rather than the United States, with Japanese-built freezer plants established throughout the region. The Tuna Treaty now provides U.S. assistance to FFA countries in creating fishing industries of their own. The bitter irony of local fish being sent to Japan to be canned, then sold back to islanders at high prices, is all too real.

Until recently, purse seiner operations led to the drowning of tens of thousands of dolphins a year in tuna nets. Herds of dolphins often swim above schools of yellowfin tuna in the eastern Pacific; thus unscrupulous purse seine operators would deliberately set their nets around the marine mammals, crushing or suffocating them. In 1990, after a tuna boycott spearheaded by the Earth Island Institute, H.J. Heinz (StarKist) and other American tuna packers announced that they would can only tuna caught using dolphin-safe fishing methods. Neither longline nor pole-and-line tuna fishing involves killing dolphins. Dolphins do not associate with tuna in the western Pacific. Because Micronesia has always been a dolphin-safe tuna fishing area, the number of U.S. boats operating here increased when the canneries stopped buying tuna caught off Central and South America.

Another devastating fishing practice, the use of driftnets up to 40 miles long and 50 feet deep, only began in the early 1980s. By the end of the decade 1,500 Japanese, Taiwanese, and Korean fishing boats were setting 18,600 miles of these nets across the Pacific each night. These plastic "walls of death" indiscriminately capture and kill everything that bumps into them, from whole schools of tuna or salmon, to dolphins, seals, whales, blue sharks, sea turtles, and many other endangered species. Thousands of seabirds are entangled as they dive for fish in the nets. Driftnets are extremely wasteful, as up to 40% of the catch is lost as the nets are hauled in, and an equally large proportion has to be discarded because the fish are too scarred by the net to be marketable. Lost or abandoned "ghost nets" continue their gruesome harvest until they sink from the weight of corpses caught in them. This practice, which makes fisheries management impossible, was strongly condemned by the South Pacific Forum at its 1989 meeting on Tarawa, and driftnet fishing boats were banned from the 11.4 million square miles of ocean included in the EEZs of the 16 member states. This act was mostly symbolic, as driftnetters often operate in international waters and don't pay licensing fees to anyone. In December 1989 the United Nations General Assembly passed a resolution calling for a moratorium on driftnetting in international waters after 30 June 1992. In 1990 the U.S. Congress passed a bill prohibiting the import of any fish caught with driftnets. Under mounting international pressure, Japan agreed in 1991 to end its driftnet fishing.

Tourism

Virtually every major island in Micronesia encourages tourism. Guam is the second leading tourist destination in the Pacific (behind Hawaii), and Saipan is third. Because most travellers to Guam and Saipan are from Asia, both islands suffered downturns from their peaks in the early 1990s(Guam more than 800,000, Saipan more than 500,000) due to the downturn in the Asian economies in the late 1990s. The FAS altogether receives about 80,000 tourists a year, with Palau alone accounting for about half of these arrivals. While less than 10% of tourists visiting Guam are Americans, the majority of visitors to the Federated States of Micronesia are from the U.S.

THE PEOPLE

Contemporary Life

The landmass of Micronesia is small, making it one of the most densely populated areas on earth. The population growth rate is over three percent. More than half the inhabitants are under age 15. The demographic curve will make these islands even more crowded in the future, even with continued emigration.

Many Micronesians reside in Guam, Hawaii, and California, where employment opportunities are better. This is a pattern occurring over much of the Pacific. For example, considerably more Cook Islanders live in Auckland, New Zealand, today than live in the Cooks. Such migration may solve problems of individual families, but may also have disastrous cultural effects. Often it is young parents who move to earn a living and to remit earnings back to the islands where grandparents raise the young.

Language

Micronesians speak Austronesian languages different from those of Polynesia. Eleven major languages are spoken: Chamorro and Palauan are classified as Indonesian, while Yapese, Ulithian, Chuukese, Pohnpeian, Kosraean, Nauruan, Gilbertese, and Marshallese are Micronesian, and Kapingamarangi is Polynesian. Contemporary Chamorro is a mixture of the original tongue and Spanish. Frequently, one Micronesian language is unintelligible to people from another island. Thus, communication between people from different islands is most often in English.

Religion

Micronesia today is overwhelmingly Christian. Missionaries of many Christian denominations are active in Micronesia. Some, such as clean-cut young Mormons wearing white shirts and ties, are highly visible. Assemblies of God, Baptists, Catholics, Evangelicals, Jehovah's Witnesses, Lutherans, Methodists, Pentecostals, Presbyterians, Seventh-Day Adventists and Baha'is are also present. Only Palau maintains an indigenous religious movement, the United Sect (Ngara Modekngei).

M.G.L. DOMENY DE RIENZI

ARTS AND CRAFTS

Dance and song are the most important art forms of Micronesia, conveying the legends and history of the people. Dancing marks celebratory occasions. Single front line dances are common. Because of the generally differentiated roles of men and women in traditional Micronesian cultures, few dances involve men and women dancing together. Micronesian dance resembles Polynesian dance in many ways, including an emphasis on movements of arms, hands, and fingers, the prominence of group dances, and the use of sitting dances.

Simplicity of form is the cornerstone of Micronesian handicrafts. Although the region is culturally diverse, there is a common thread of design concepts emphasizing angular, geometric shapes. Patterns used in woven textiles on one island, for example, may show up in tattooing and woodcarving on another. Traditional art in the Micronesia region has similarities to Melanesian and Indonesian art, demonstrating Micronesian contacts with those areas. The primary media for traditional arts are woven fabrics (both loom and braided items) woodcarving, and architecture.

Except in the Marianas, handicrafts sold in Micronesia are authentic handmade products; they're easily distinguished from mass-produced Filipino knockoffs. Considering the time that goes into Micronesian handicrafts, prices are low (don't bargain). Many of the handicraft outlets are soft sell, low profit or cooperative ventures.

When making purchases, avoid objects made from turtle shell. Such items frequently are manufactured from endangered species and are prohibited entry into the United States and many other countries.

In Micronesia today, particularly on Guam, a new school of painting is developing. Artists trained in Western art, often in the United States, are creating paintings using Western techniques but retaining an island influence.

Weaving

Textiles traditionally played an important public role. They marked rank and social status. Special textiles were worn for ritual occasions and life cycle events. Fabrics even served as currency. In parts of the Caroline Islands, banana and hibiscus-fiber fabrics were woven on a loom. Today, colorful cotton mill thread is frequently used. Both types of textiles may be purchased by visitors.

In the rest of Micronesia, as in most of the Pacific, braided or plait work predominates. Plaiting fashions a wide variety of utilitarian items, including sleeping mats, wall coverings, canoe sails, baskets, and clothing. Dried coconut fibers and pandanus leaves are the most common materials. Marshall Island plait work is elaborately and richly patterned. Traditionally, the fineness of the design indicated the origin of the mat makers and the family status. Some designs could only be used by royalty.

A Yap woman weaves with a simple back-strap loom, which in the Pacific is found only in the Caroline Islands. Only narrow material can be woven on this type of loom.

Woodcarving

Breadfruit is the wood most often carved (especially for model and actual canoes), although coconut, ironwood, and hibiscus are also used. In Palau, a great revival of hardwood carving took place this century. The finely carved war clubs of the South Pacific are not common in Micronesia, where men most often fought with sling and spear. But warriors in the Gilberts carried shark-tooth-edged swords and wore woven body armor. The only masks known in Micronesia were those of the Mortlocks.

Architecture

Architecture in Micronesia is an important art form. Not to be missed are the beautiful historic sites of Nan Madol on Pohnpei and Lelu on Kosrae. The *latte* stones of the Marianas are remnants of an architecture found nowhere else in Oceania. These physically impressive stones consist of columns larger at the base than the top, crowned by a capstone, usually of coral. Arranged in rows, the purpose of these monumental works is not known for certain, though many archaeologists believe they were used as foundations of aristocratic or communal dwellings.

Other prehistoric sites include the sculpted hills of Babeldaob in Palau, vast prehistoric terraces carved from natural formations. Also in Palau are the stone-sculptured faces of Melekeok and Badrulchau. Yap's ancient stone walkways should be thought of as horizontal, but functional ruins, still serving their ancient purpose today.

Traditional buildings, particularly for community purposes, are still in use in Yap and Kiribati. These beautiful structures are typically rectangular in shape, built on elevated platforms. Their steeply sloping roofs are made from coconut or pandanus leaves. The sides are built from local, natural materials and have shutters rather than glass. Thus, depending on weather conditions they can be open and breezy, or protected from the elements.

Shipbuilding

Micronesian large-scale voyaging canoes are probably the finest outriggers ever built and perhaps the world's fastest sailing crafts. They are superbly designed and crafted with superior sails, riggings, and steering apparatus. Common characteristics of Micronesian voyaging canoes include asymmetrical sides and double-ended hulls, with high ends and sharp bottoms. Forms and details of construction vary from island group to island group. Some canoes, particularly ceremonial ones, have beautiful prow ornaments. Many islands had a tradition of racing small model canoes, and these small models are now available for purchase in some localities.

COCONUTS PAVE THE WAY

Could the islands of the Pacific have been settled if the coconut had not arrived there first?

Micronesians came to the islands with fruit to be planted and animals to be bred. But what could they do while these matured and bred?

If there were drought, they could drink coconut milk. They could eat coconut meat until the breadfruit trees they planted grew. Or they could fry the fish they caught in coconut oil.

The palm trunk became lumber, and coconut fronds became a roof. Coconut palm leaves became hats and mats. In the hands of skilled craftspeople, the coconut husk became twine. Coconut shells made containers for water, fish, and bait. The roots yielded medicine, and the outer husk became charcoal. The palm tree could be tapped for its sweet liquid, which could be turned into molasses. And if the settlers had a rough week? Nothing eased the pain quicker than some fermented coconut toddy.

In the words of an old Pohnpei saying: *"Sohte wasa ehu ni turke nih me sohte ah doadoahk"*— "There is no part of the coconut tree to throw away."

AISLINN RACE

M.G.L. DOMENY DE RIENZI

ON THE ROAD

Tourist activity for most of Micronesia dates back only to 1962. Beginning in the 1930s the Japanese cut non-Japanese visitors down to a trickle. The United States did the same from World War II until 1962. It was not until 1968 that Continental Airlines got together with local business interests to create a new joint venture, then known as Continental Air Micronesia, or "Air Mike," which began service from Honolulu to Saipan in 1968.

Airstrips were gradually upgraded in all the district centers of the old Trust Territory of the Pacific Islands, and by 1970 Air Mike's Island Hopper, from Honolulu to Guam, was calling at Majuro, Kwajalein, Pohnpei, and Chuuk. Feeder services flew to Saipan, Yap, and Koror. Isolated Kosrae became part of Continental's world in 1986.

ACCOMMODATIONS AND FOOD

Rooms

Moderately priced hotels can be found in most of the towns in Micronesia. Guam and Saipan also have large, high-rise tourist hotels. Prices range from $40 to $375. Many hotels in Micronesia, particularly the more expensive ones, will offer corporate and "local" discounts. Nobody is ever very clear about the exact requirements to qualify for each, but they are determined in part by how many vacant rooms the hotel has at the time. Be sure to inquire, particularly if you are calling from Micronesia to make the reservation. During certain months, such as December, there can be accommoda-

tion shortages. It is best to make arrangements in advance.

There aren't many hotels on the outer islands, but in the Marshalls and Federated States, island mayors or chiefs will help visitors find a place to stay. Most atolls in Kiribati have inexpensive Island Council rest houses. Radio ahead to let them know you're coming. Elementary school teachers in remote areas are often very hospitable and may offer to put you up. Always try to find some tangible way to show your appreciation, such as paying for groceries or giving a gift. Don't be afraid to offer cash if a stranger puts himself or herself out financially for you.

ACCOMMODATIONS RATINGS

Throughout this book, the following price categories are used, based on high season, double occupancy:

Budget: under $35
Inexpensive: $36-60
Moderate: $61-85
Expensive: $86-110
Very Expensive: $111-149
Luxury: $150 and over

Most hotels in the "Luxury" price category are on Guam or Saipan. Some hotels on those islands are in the "Luxury" price range, but do not deliver the service usually associated with that word.

Camping
Camping is not common in Micronesia. A tent, however, can save the budget traveler a lot of money and provide convenient shelter. It's rarely too difficult to find people willing to let you camp on their land. Since most land in Micronesia is privately owned it's important to ask permission first. Often the village mayor or chief can help make arrangements.

On the main islands, if you find a place to camp, it is usually not safe to leave your tent unattended. Dismantle it daily and ask your host to store it for you. As yet, the only regular campgrounds are on Guam. On the outer islands, however, there should be no problem: in fact, when you ask for a camping spot, you'll often be invited to stay in the family's house—an offer that can be difficult to refuse.

Food
All the towns have reasonable restaurants serving Island, American, Chinese, and Japanese food from $4 to $8. Almost everywhere in Micronesia you can eat very fresh fish. Tuna sashimi is cheap and available all over Micronesia. The Japanese left Micronesians with an enduring taste for white rice, to which the Americans added sugar, bread, and beer. On the outer islands you'll find a fare of rice, breadfruit, taro, and reef fish, plus the more prosaic canned mackerel and Spam. Guam and Saipan have a large number of excellent, expensive restaurants.

Breadfruit grows on trees. (Remember Captain Bligh? He was carrying breadfruit on his ill-fated voyage.) Taro is an elephant-eared plant cultivated in freshwater bogs. Its roots are a starchy staple. Although yams are considered a

BREADFRUIT

Breadfruit *(Artocarpus altilus)* grows on tall trees with large green leaves. From Indonesia, ancient voyagers carried it to all of Micronesia. "Breadfruit Bligh" was returning from Tahiti with a thousand potted trees to provide food for slaves in Jamaica when the famous mutiny occurred. Propagated from root suckers, this seedless plant provides shade as well as food. A well-watered tree can produce as many as 1,000 breadfruits a year. Joseph Banks, the botanist on Captain Cook's first voyage, wrote: "If a man should in the course of his lifetime plant 10 trees, which if well done might take the labour of an hour or thereabouts, he would completely fulfill his duty to his own as well as future generations."

DIANA LASICH HARPER

prestige food, they're not as nutritious as breadfruit and taro. Yams can grow up to 10 feet long and weigh hundreds of pounds. Papaya (pawpaw) is widely available. Atoll dwellers especially rely on the coconut for food. The tree reaches maturity in eight years and then produces about 50 nuts a year for 60 years.

If you are going to an outer island, it is best to bring your own drinking water or carry purification material, as potable water may not be available.

Also take as many edibles with you as possible. Imported foods are always more expensive there than in the main towns, and often staples such as bread are not available.

Keep in mind that virtually every food plant you see growing on the islands is owned by someone. Fishing floats or seashells washed up on a beach, or fish in the lagoon near someone's home, may also be private property under local laws and customs.

HEALTH

Micronesia is a healthy place, but it is in the tropics. Taking a few basic precautions minimizes risks.

Don't go from winter weather into the hot tropics without a rest. Don't expect to be able to keep up the same pace here as you do at home. Airplane cabins have low humidity, so drink lots of water or juice on the flight coming over. It's also best to forgo coffee and alcohol, which will further dehydrate you. Divers must understand and follow the prescribed waiting period after diving before taking airplane flights.

Tap water is unsafe to drink in most of Micronesia other than Guam (check locally). Bottled water is available on all major islands. Avoid brushing your teeth with water unfit to drink. Avoid raw vegetables. Peel fruit or wash it in bottled or treated water. Cooked food is less subject to contamination than raw. If you wish to avoid the cost of bottled drinks, take along water purification tablets or units, available at many sporting goods and travel stores. There are now tablets available that will take the bad taste out of water you have purified using iodine.

Medicine is often unavailable. If there are medicines you must take regularly, carry twice as much as you need. Split that supply in half and on travel days keep half on your person and half in your baggage to avoid the danger of losing your supply. Before the trip, speak to your doctor about carrying antibiotics and antidiarrheal medicine with you. Note: Even such basics as aspirin are often unavailable on outer islands, so be prepared.

You can see a doctor at government hospitals in the major towns, but although the cost of medical attention is low, on too many islands so is the quality. If you fall seriously ill get a flight

home or to a country with higher medical standards as soon as possible. On the outer islands, clinics deal only in basics.

Sunburn

You may think you don't burn, but everyone burns in tropical sun. Begin with short exposures, perhaps half an hour to an hour the first day, a bit more if it is overcast. Remember you can burn even on cloudy days. If you are a snorkeler, you can protect your back and shoulders with a T-shirt while in the ocean. Use a sunblock with a high sunscreen factor, remembering your nose, lips, forehead, neck, hands, and feet. If you go swimming, reapply periodically. Calamine ointment soothes burned skin, as does coconut oil.

Ailments

Cuts and scratches take a long time to heal in the tropics. An antibiotic cream speeds healing and helps prevent infection. To prevent infection from coral cuts wash the area with soap and fresh water, then rub vinegar or alcohol into the wounds—painful, but effective.

> *Mosquito*
> *Do I offend you*
> *As much as you offend me?*

Many places in Micronesia, though not all, have mosquitos. If you (like most people) are susceptible to them, keep yourself covered when hiking. Be particularly careful around sunrise and sunset when they are at their hungriest. Bring mosquito repellent with you. (I owe unswerving devotion to Cutter's.) At night in your hotel room, keep all unscreened doors and windows closed. Most will be screened. And consider using the nearly universally available Chinese mosquito coils.

Food spoils quickly in the tropics. You may experience diarrhea at some point during the trip. If so, be certain to keep up your intake of water. Particularly if you are sweating, be sure to replenish your salts. Most cases of diarrhea are self-limiting and require only simple replacement of fluids and salts. If the diarrhea is persistent or you experience fever, drowsiness, or blood in the stool, take these developments seriously. If you are at an island such as Palau where decent medical care is available, consult a doctor. If you are on an island without adequate modern medical care, consider flying elsewhere.

There are incidents of *ciguatera* (seafood poisoning) in Micronesia. It doesn't matter whether the fish is cooked or raw. Local residents will have experience knowing which species to avoid, and thus there is virtually no worry about *ciguatera* while eating in restaurants. There's no treatment except to relieve the symptoms (tingling, prickling, itching, nausea, vomiting, erratic heartbeat, joint and muscle pains), which usually subside in a few days. If you suspect ciguatera, seek immediate medical care.

Vaccinations and Diseases

Malaria is nonexistent, and there have been no cholera outbreaks in almost two decades. Many immunization centers refuse to administer the cholera vaccination because it's only 50% effective for six months and bad reactions are common.

Tetanus, diphtheria, typhoid fever and polio shots are not required, but they're a good idea if you're going to remote islands. Tetanus and diphtheria vaccinations are given together and a booster is required every 10 years. Typhoid fever boosters are required every three years, polio every five years. There is now a shot available to prevent certain forms of hepatitis. A yellow fever vaccination is required only if you've recently been in an infected area such as parts of South America or central Africa.

Dengue fever is a mosquito-transmitted disease. Signs are headaches, sore throat, pain in the joints, fever, rash, and nausea. It can last anywhere from five to 15 days, and although you can relieve the symptoms somewhat, the only real cure is to wait it out. It is painful, but dengue fever is rarely fatal to an adult. Of course, seek medical attention if you suspect this disease.

Leprosy and elephantiasis are hard to catch and are now found only on a few remote islands. Sexually transmitted diseases are rampant in much of Micronesia. AIDS has not reached epidemic proportions, though cases have been reported. Local public health authorities fear for the future unless there are radical changes in current island sexual practices.

> *Wishing to catch fish*
> *a fisherman follows the birds.*
> *Birds follow the boat.*

INFORMATION AND SERVICES

Regional tourist information offices and diplomatic posts are listed in an appendix at the end of this book, most with phone numbers as well as websites, if applicable. William H. Stewart, Economic Service Counsel, has designed an intriguing series of tourist maps, packed with interesting anecdotes on Palau, Guam, Kosrae, Pohnpei, Saipan, and Chuuk. These and a standard selection of tourist brochures are available from tourist offices. Also see our Booklist at the end of this book.

TOURIST

i

INFORMATION

Peace Corps volunteers are always good sources of information, and you'll find them in the most unlikely corners of the Republic of Kiribati and the Federated States of Micronesia.

Visas

Entry to Micronesia is easy. No visa is required to visit the Marshalls, Federated States, Palau, or Northern Marianas for a stay of up to 30 days. If you're leaving on the next connecting flight, you won't need a visa for Nauru either. Entry requirements to Kiribati are more complicated (turn to the Kiribati chapter for details). Citizens of most countries other than America and Canada need a United States visa to enter Guam. Inquire from the American embassy or consulate in your home country.

Technically, United States citizens, with proper identification, can enter the Marshalls, Federated States, Palau, Guam, and Northern Marianas without a passport. But since individual customs officials have varying ideas as to what is proper, we advise everyone, Americans included, to carry a passport when traveling in Micronesia. Passports are required for Americans to stay in Nauru or Kiribati.

All Micronesian countries require proof of onward passage upon arrival. If you arrive without it, you may be required to purchase a ticket on the spot or be refused entry. You may also be required to prove that you have sufficient funds. United States citizens don't require an onward ticket to enter Guam or the Northern Marianas.

Money, Measurements, and Mail

American currency (US$) is used throughout Micronesia, except in Kiribati and Nauru, where Australian dollars (A$) circulate. In this book, prices are quoted in US$ in US$ areas and A$ in the A$ areas (Kiribati and Nauru), unless otherwise noted. At last report, US$1=A$1.53.

Credit cards are accepted at the large hotels and by car rental agencies in most US$ areas, but cash is easier at restaurants and shops. To avoid wasting time hassling at banks for cash, it's best to bring enough traveler's checks to cover your out-of-pocket expenses. On Yap, even some car rentals will not take credit cards. On the outer islands, credit cards are useless. Dollars in the country's currency should be in small denominations. Post offices in the US$ areas cash U.S.

MICRONESIAN TIME

	STANDARD TIME	
	HOURS FROM GMT	**TIME 1200 GMT***
California	– 8	4 a.m.
Hawaii	–10	2 a.m.
International Date Line		**Sunday**
		Monday
Majuro, Kosrae	+12	midnight
Tarawa, Nauru	+12	midnight
Pohnpei	+11	11 p.m.
Chuuk, Yap	+10	10 p.m.
Guam, Saipan	+10	10 p.m.
Palau, Japan	+ 9	9 p.m.
Philippines	+ 8	8 p.m.
Hong Kong	+ 8	8 p.m.

*GMT is Greenwich mean time, the time at London, England. California adopts daylight saving time from April to October.

MICRONESIA POSTAL CODES

Note: When mailing a letter from outside the U.S. to the Marshall Islands, the Federated States of Micronesia, Palau, Guam, and the Marianas, include "via U.S.A." in the address.

COUNTRY		POSTAL CODE
Republic of the Marshall Islands	Majuro	MH 96960
	Ebeye	MH 96970
Federated States of Micronesia	Kosrae	FM 96944
	Pohnpei	FM 96941
	Chuuk	FM 96942
	Yap	FM 96943
Republic of Palau	Koror	PW 96940
Guam	Agana	GU 96910
	Tamuning	GU 96911
	Dededo	GU 96912
	Barrigada	GU 96913
	Yona	GU 96914
	Santa Rita	GU 96915
	Merizo	GU 96916
	Inarajan	GU 96917
	Umatac	GU 96918
	Agana Heights	GU 96919
	Guam Main Facility (GMF)	GU 96921
	Asan	GU 96922
	Mangilao	GU 96923
	Chalan Pago	GU 96924
	Piti	GU 96925
	Sinajana	GU 96926
	Maite	GU 96927
	Agat	GU 96928
	Yigo	GU 96929
	Talofolo	GU 96930
	P.O. Boxes, Tamuning	GU 96931
Commonwealth of the Northern Marianas	Saipan	MP 96950
	Rota	MP 96951
	Tinian	MP 96952
Republic of Nauru		Rep. of Nauru, Central Pacific
Republic of Kiribati		Rep. of Kiribati, Central Pacific

postal money orders, a good way to have money sent from the States.

A small stack of U.S. one- and five-dollar bills for minor expenses is always handy when traveling.

Make sure your traveler's checks are expressed in US$; other currencies may be difficult to exchange or subject to special service charges. To report stolen American Express traveler's checks call the Hong Kong office, tel. (852) 2801-7300 collect, or on Guam, tel. (671) 472-8884. If you'll be visiting Kiribati or Nauru, have your bank order a few Australian dollar traveler's checks.

Tipping has become widespread, though as yet it's a way of life only on Guam and Saipan. The serving staff in restaurants that cater mostly to foreign businesspeople or tourists expect to be tipped, but those in places patronized mostly by Micronesians do not. When in doubt, tip.

The electric current throughout the American portion of Micronesia is 110 volts, 60 cycles, with standard American outlets. In Kiribati it's 240 volts, 50 cycles, with Australian outlets.

Regular U.S. postal rates apply throughout Micronesia (except in Kiribati and Nauru). Always specify airmail when posting a letter. Mail leaves Micronesia faster than it arrives. All the countries included in this book issue their own postage stamps (except Guam and the Northern Marianas, which use U.S. stamps). These stamps, available at local post offices, make excellent souvenirs. Many stamps will also be available on colorfully printed first day cover envelopes.

All mail is delivered to post office boxes. In this book you'll find the box numbers of most businesses we discuss. Postal codes appear in the "Micronesia Postal Codes" appendix and in each chapter. Micronesian post offices will hold general delivery mail. If you're mailing a letter

---

MICRONESIA COUNTRY CODES

To call the following countries in Micronesia from the United States, dial the international access code 011, followed by the country code, then the phone number.

COUNTRY	COUNTRY CODE
Republic of the Marshall Islands	692
Federated States of Micronesia (all)	691
Republic of Palau	680
Republic of Nauru	674
Republic of Kiribati	686

The following are now on the United States telephone grid. From the United States merely dial 1 (*not* 011), followed by the area code, then the phone number. Calls cost a small fraction of the rate of calls to the above numbers.

AREA CODE	
Guam	671
Commonwealth of the Northern Marianas	670

---

to Micronesia from outside the United States, include "via U.S.A." in the address and be sure to use the correct five digit zip code.

Telephone

Except for Guam and the Northern Marianas, to call direct to a phone number in Micronesia from the United States, dial the international access code 011, then the country code, then the number. The country code for each island state is listed in the back of this book, as well as in each chapter.

Guam and the Northern Marianas are now on the United States telephone "grid." You merely dial a "1" before the country code (not 011). Calls to Guam and the Marianas now cost merely a fraction of the cost of calls to the rest of Micronesia, which are always very expensive. You can access toll-free numbers (800, 888, etc.) from Guam and the Northern Marianas.

WHAT TO TAKE

Packing

Decision number one is whether you wish to travel only with carry-on baggage. If you wish to do so, the trade-off will be worldly possessions for not having to stand in numerous lines. Assemble everything you simply must take and cannot live without—then cut the pile in half. Keep on cutting until it fits. Today, luggage is available that can be turned from a hand-carried piece into a backpack. If you decide to travel with more baggage, take along a day pack. Either way, when checking in for flights carry anything that can't be replaced with you.

If you are planning to dive almost anywhere in Micronesia other than Guam, Palau, and Yap, you will want to take along all your gear other than weights and tanks. This will make it impossible to travel light.

Camping Equipment

A small nylon tent guarantees you a place to sleep every night. It must be mosquito- and waterproof. Get one with a tent fly. It's usually too hot to get into a sleeping bag in the tropics, so you could leave that item at home. A sheet is ideal. You don't really need to carry a bulky foam pad as the ground is seldom cold. A mosquito net can come in handy if you're visiting remote areas.

Clothing

For clothes take loose-fitting cotton washables, light in color and weight. Synthetic fabrics are hot and sticky, and most of the things you wear at home will be too heavy for the tropics. Coin-operated laundromats are found across Micronesia, so you don't need to take a lot of clothes. Be prepared for the humidity. Take along one lightweight long-sleeved shirt and long pants. They provide mosquito protection in the evenings and warmth in the occasionally over air conditioned restaurant.

Micronesians dress informally for both business and social occasions, but it's important to know that the dress code in the islands is strict. For women, in much of Micronesia wearing short skirts, halter tops, bathing suits, and other brief attire in public places is considered offensive. Women should wear clothing that covers the knees. On outer islands especially, women should wear a knee-length dress or wrap a yard-long piece of cloth around their thighs. Shorts usually are okay for men, as long as they are not too short. Men will want a clean shirt for evenings, but only Mormon missionaries wear ties.

Take comfortable, broken-in shoes. Divers' rubber booties are lightweight and perfect for both crossing rivers and reef walking, though an old pair of sneakers may be just as good.

Accessories

Micronesia provides wonderful scenery for photographers, both above water and below. It is best to bring along your own equipment and film. Consider taking an underwater camera with you. Several are now available for about $200. Not only will you be able to shoot underwater, these cameras are easier to care for above water since you do not need to take care against rain and humidity. Serious underwater photography for divers requires much more elaborate cameras and lights.

A mask, snorkel, and fins are essential equipment. Divers should bring their own regulator, buoyancy compensator, and tank pressure gauge (tanks, backpacks, and weight belts can usually be rented locally).

Much of travel entails cutting or tying. Bring along a Swiss army knife and a cord. A pocket flashlight, matches, and a water bottle are often handy. Sunglasses are a must. If you wear prescription glasses, bring along an extra pair since Micronesia does not have one-day eyeglass service.

Remember your driver's license and, if you dive, your scuba certification card.

GETTING THERE

Some principles for every Micronesia traveler:

- Unless you have unlimited time, flying is the only way to travel; boats take too long.

- Distances are great. Even air travel takes time. Airfare is expensive.

- You cannot always get there from here. You cannot always pick a destination and choose a flight to get you there. It may not be possible to fly from one island to another without serious backtracking or waiting a week. The available flights and how they connect determines where you visit, unless you have unlimited time and money.

- Many travel agents are not knowledgeable about Micronesia flights. Try to find a specialist. Some are listed below under "Travel Agents." As with travel anywhere, flights, routes, and prices change.

- The **International Date Line** is a mystical concept. Cross the line heading west, and it's suddenly tomorrow; cross it heading east, and it's suddenly yesterday. Always think about the Date Line when planning. Airlines will use the date and the day of the week at the flight's place of *origin*. The Date Line even moves around. The United States base at Kwajalein is now on the same date as the rest of the Republic of the Marshall Islands, one day later than the United States. All of Kiribati is now west of the Line.

- Understand the difference between inconvenience and tragedy.

- Travel inevitably entails time in transit: this time can be minimized, endured, slept through, or if all else fails—enjoyed.

- Never trust anyone who gives you directions and ends by saying, "You can't miss it."

Continental Airlines

The main regional air carrier is **Continental Airlines.** (Until 1998, Continental Airlines' Micronesia flights were run under the name Continental Air Micronesia, or Air Mike). Since Continental reabsorbed Air Mike, there have been ongoing changes in schedule. Your best chance for up-to-date information is to call Continental Airlines International at (800) 231-0856; visit its website at: www.continental.com; or call one of the travel agents listed below. The merger has improved connections between flights within Micronesia and other Continental flights that connect with the U.S. mainland or Asia. Continental and Northwest Airlines (tel. 800-447-4747) have an alliance that also can be used to connect with Continental's Micronesia routes. Continental's Guam office can be reached at tel. (671) 647-6453, fax (671) 646-9219.

Although Continental offers nonstop flights from Honolulu to Guam, a popular routing among travelers is the Island Hopper service aboard a Boeing 727. This routing starts in Honolulu and stops in Majuro, Kwajalein, Kosrae, Pohnpei, Chuuk, and Guam. (The Island Hopper makes the same stops in the opposite direction from Guam.) In Guam you can change to other Continental flights continuing to Yap, Koror, or Saipan. If you know you're going to do this, buy a through ticket to your turnaround point—this is usually cheaper than buying a separate ticket in Guam.

In your planning, always remember the International Date Line. For example, an Island Hopper that leaves Honolulu on Monday arrives in the Marshall Islands, the other side of the Date Line, on Tuesday. Thus if you wish to stay in Majuro for a week, you would take a flight out on Tuesday (Marshall Island time) the following week.

Continental offers a number of different fares. Of course, the most expensive is flying without advance ticket purchase. If you purchase your ticket 21 days in advance, it will be significantly less expensive. To take advantage of this plan, however, you must stay in Micronesia for a minimum of seven days and a maximum of three months. Continental also offers its Circle Micronesia fare. This plan too must be purchased in advance. It allows two free stops within Micronesia, and additional stops at $50 each. You can use the Island Hopper only in one direction, without any backtracking. This fare usually works best for any extensive tour of Micronesia, but cannot be used to fly from Guam to Saipan.

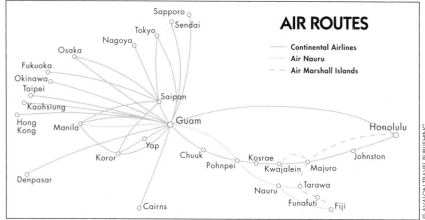

AIR ROUTES

Continental Airlines
Air Nauru
Air Marshall Islands

Sapporo
Sendai
Tokyo
Nagoya
Osaka
Fukuoka
Okinawa
Taipei
Kaohsiung
Hong Kong
Manila
Koror
Denpasar
Saipan
Guam
Yap
Chuuk
Pohnpei
Kosrae
Kwajalein
Nauru
Tarawa
Funafuti
Fiji
Majuro
Johnston
Honolulu
Cairns

© AVALON TRAVEL PUBLISHING

Continental also offers its Visit Micronesia discount to those who live in Micronesia.

Remember to inquire about penalties if you purchase a discounted fare and are unable to make the trip. There probably will be no cash refund, and there may also be a penalty for changing flights.

Flying times are six hours from Honolulu to Majuro or California, seven and a half hours from Honolulu to Guam nonstop, and about two hours on most flights within Micronesia itself. The Island Hopper takes almost 16 hours from Honolulu to Guam.

Continental is highly reliable, with excellent on-time records and few baggage problems. The service on Continental's Micronesia flights is friendly and personal. You begin to enjoy the charms of Micronesia from the time of takeoff.

Aloha Airlines

Aloha Airlines has a once-a-week flight from Honolulu to the Marshall Islands, stopping at Majuro and Kwajalein. The plane leaves Honolulu on Thursday and returns the following day (Saturday because of the International Date Line) to Honolulu. Aloha's toll-free phone number is (888) 477-7010; its Honolulu phone number is (808) 485-2220. Aloha's website is www.alohaair.com.

Air Nauru

Air Nauru, flag carrier of the tiny Republic of Nauru, provides service between Micronesia and

the South Pacific, flying on Wednesday from Nauru to Pohnpei to Guam to Manila, returning the opposite route. This mostly aids travelers who are arriving from or traveling to Australia, New Zealand, or other South Pacific points via Nauru. Most Air Nauru fares are calculated point to point via Nauru. To work out a route, combine any two of these one-way economy fares out of Nauru itself: Brisbane ($328); Melbourne ($369); Sidney ($369); Guam ($257); Manila, Philippines ($414); Nadi and Suva, Fiji ($214); Pohnpei, FSM ($219); and Tarawa, Kiribati ($109). These prices are one way, quoted in U.S. dollars. You can get updated routes and costs on-line at its website: www.airnauru.com.au.

To contact Air Nauru by phone from the United States, the best procedure is simply to call Air Nauru's Guam office, Pacific Star Hotel, Tamuning, GU 96931, tel. (671) 649-7106, fax (671) 649-4856. You can also try their general sales agent at 5757 West Century Blvd., Suite 660, Los Angeles, CA, 90045, tel. (310) 670-7302, fax (310) 338-0708.

Air Nauru's head office is in the Republic of Nauru, tel. (674) 444-3141, fax (674) 444-3705. Other offices are located at: Level 49, Nauru House, 80 Collins St., Melbourne, VIC 3000, Australia, tel. (613) 9653-5602, toll-free in Australia (800) 060-609, fax (03) 9654-4925; Ratu Sakuna House, Victoria Parade, Suva, Fiji Islands, tel. (679) 312-417, fax (679) 302-861; Ground Floor, Pacific Star Building, Makati Ave.,

Makati City, Philippines, tel. (632) 818-3580, fax (632) 817-7386.

Air Marshall Islands
Air Marshall Islands (P.O. Box 1319, Majuro, MH 96960, tel. 692-625-3733) flies to Tarawa, Funafuti, and Fiji. This allows a side trip to the Republic of Kiribati or a connection to the South Pacific. Check for any reduced roundtrip excursion fares. You can look at AMI's entire schedule on-line at its website: www.rmiembassyus.org/amisked.html.

From Europe
No direct flights connect Europe to Micronesia. The easiest access is usually a flight from Europe to California, Honolulu, or Manila, where you join one of Continental Airlines' routes described above. With Continental Micronesia absorbed into Continental Airlines and considering Continental's relationship with Northwest Airlines, those two airlines frequently have the best connections with Continental's flights within Micronesia. In any event, for the Continental portion of your ticket, go to a large professional travel agency and inquire whether it has Micronesia experience, or call Continental Airlines yourself.

European travel agencies specializing in round the world travel via Micronesia include **Reisbureau Amber,** Da Costastraat 77, 1053 ZG Amsterdam, Holland (tel. 20-685-1155); **Malibu Travel,** Damrak 30, 1012 LJ Amsterdam; **Trailfinders,** 42-50 Earls Court Rd., Kensington, London W8 6EJ, England (tel. 071-938-3366); and **Globetrotter Travel Service,** Rennweg 35, 8001 Zurich, Switzerland (tel. 01-211-7780).

Ticket Tips
Airline tickets are sometimes refundable only in the place of purchase, so ask about this before you invest in a ticket you may not use. Nearly every Pacific island requires that you have an onward ticket as a condition for entry, thus careful planning is necessary. A travel agent may be able to help you, provided the agent knows where Micronesia is!

Always reconfirm your onward reservations after arriving on an island, to minimize the possibility of being bumped from your continuing flight. If you are using a small interisland airline, always allow a 26-hour stopover between connecting flights; there are very few extra planes sitting around in Micronesia.

If your flight is delayed more than four hours ask the airline for a meal voucher. If the flight is canceled due to mechanical problems with the aircraft, the airline will likely cover hotel and meals. If they reschedule the flight on short notice for reasons of their own, or you're bumped off an overbooked flight, they will likely also pay.

To compensate for no-shows, airlines often overbook. To avoid being bumped, check in early and go to the departure area well before flight time. In some airports, flights are not called over the public address system, so keep your eyes open. Overbooked airlines often offer meals, rooms, and cash to volunteers willing to relinquish their seats.

Baggage
Continental Airlines allows two pieces of checked baggage plus a carry-on on their big DC-10s and 727s, but the smaller commuter airlines may limit you to as little as 30 pounds. If you'll be changing aircraft at a busy gateway city, think twice before checking your baggage straight through to your final destination. Though a nuisance, it's safer to collect it at the transfer point and check it in again.

TRAVEL AGENTS

Many travel agents have little or no experience dealing with Micronesia. Below we list agents with experience who we believe keep current on Micronesian travel. Many of these agents specialize in diving or fishing trips, but almost all will also arrange flights and hotels.

Many experienced divers consider Micronesia the world's ultimate diving destination. Chuuk, Guam, Palau, and Yap each offer totally different diving experiences. You can often save money by booking dives directly with the dive shops listed in the individual chapters of this book. You can write or call ahead, or just wait to talk once you get there.

But unless you've got lots of time and are philosophical about disappointments, you may wish to go on an organized diving tour. When pricing diving tour packages, inquire whether airfares are included. Even when they are included, it is usually only from, and then back to, Hawaii. Ascertain what equipment you should bring with you. Unless you are taking part in a dive certification program, you must have proof of certification. Prices of dive tours aren't cheap, but the convenience of having all your arrangements made for you by a company able to pull weight with island suppliers is often worth it.

(For information about dive live-aboards, look at the individual chapter about the island of your interest).

Continental Airlines runs its own tour service. It can be reached by calling tel. (800) 634-5555 or (760) 724-5307.

Mike Musto's **Trip-N-Tour** (2182 Foothill Dr., Vista, CA 92084, tel. 800-348-0842 or 760-724-0788, fax 760-724-9897, e-mail: info@trip-n-tour .com, website: www.trip-n-tour.com) is the largest and most experienced Micronesian specialist. Mike offers dive packages to the Marshalls, Chuuk, Pohnpei, Yap, Palau, Guam, Saipan, Tinian, and Rota. Usually the farther away your diving destination, the more expensive. Mike can also handle your flight and hotel reservations if that is all you desire.

Poseidon Ventures (359 San Miguel Dr., Newport Beach, CA 92660, tel. 800-854-9334 or 949-644-5344; or 505 N. Belt, Suite 675, Houston, TX 77060, tel. 713-820-3483) offers diving tours to Chuuk, Palau, Yap, and Pohnpei. It will also book flights and hotels for nondivers.

New to Micronesia, but not new to dive tours, is **Dive Tours** (18219 Strack Dr., Spring, Texas 77379, tel. 800-433-0885, fax 281-257-1783, e-mail: info@divetours.org). The folks there can arrange diving in Yap, Palau, Chuuk, and Guam. They also can take care of all bookings with the Outrigger chain's Micronesian hotels.

Tropical Adventures (111 2nd Ave. N, Seattle, WA 98109, tel. 800-247-3483 or 206-441-3483, fax 206-441-5431), now affiliated with Dive Tours, has been sending divers to Micronesia since 1973. Check its website at www .divetropical.com.

Layne Ballard of **Central Pacific Dive Expedition** (150 Yorba Street, Tustin CA 92780, tel. 800-846-3483 or 714-426-0265, fax 714-426-0267) can arrange independent travel or tours. He specializes in dive tours to the Marshalls and other islands reached by Continental Airlines.

In conjunction with Marshall Dive Adventures, he can arrange diving in exotic locales such as Bikini atoll.

Another outfit specializing in diving is **Dive Discovery,** 1005 A Street, Suite 202, San Rafael, CA 94901, tel. (800) 886-7321, fax (415) 258-9115, e-mail:info@divediscovery.com.

Interested in fishing? **International Anglers,** (P.O. Box 2232, Napa, CA 94558, tel. 800-477-2076 or 707-226-2076, fax 707-226-2850) can arrange trips to Palau or to Majuro and Bikini in the Marshalls.

Ocean Voyages Inc. (1709 Bridgeway, Sausalito, CA 94965, tel. 800-299-4444 or 415-332-4681, fax 415-332-7460) arranges "share-boat" yacht tours throughout Micronesia, and diving is often possible. This is worth checking out if you enjoy sailing as much as diving and want to get away from the usual diving sites.

Oceanic Society is a nonprofit, ecological organization founded in 1972. Through **Oceanic Society Expeditions** (Fort Mason Center, Building E, San Francisco, CA 94123, tel. 800-326-7491 or 415-441-1106, fax 415-474-3395), it runs educational tours and work projects on both Palau and Midway Island. Expeditions are led by expert naturalists and are ideal for individuals wishing to get close to nature without sacrificing too many creature comforts.

Valor Tours, Ltd. (10 Liberty Ship Way, Sausalito, CA 94965, tel. 800-842-4504 or 415-332-7850) runs a tour to Pacific battle sites in November each year for U.S. veterans. In 1998, the 11-day escorted package tour went to Majuro, Wotje, and Mili in the Marshalls; Tarawa in Kiribati; Peleliu in the Republic of Palau; Guam; Saipan; and Tinian. The tour, including roundtrip airfare to Hawaii, cost $2,450. Valor President Robert Reynolds also designs tours for veterans to the Solomon Islands.

Swingaway Holidays (22 York St., Sydney, NSW 2000, Australia, tel. 29-9237-0300) has beach holiday packages to Guam, Saipan, Pohnpei, Chuuk, Palau, and Yap from Australia. They use the best hotels available and prices include airfare but not meals. Participants travel individually on any flight departing Sydney or Brisbane for Guam. This may be cheaper than buying a regular ticket and paying for your accommodation directly.

GETTING AROUND

By Air

Local **commuter airlines** such as Air Marshall Islands, Air Kiribati, and Pacific Missionary Aviation Air operate domestic services within the individual island groups. Most flights to outer islands are on propeller planes, sometimes on 19-passenger planes, often on four- or six-seaters. In 1998 there was an air crash of a small Paradise Air plane coming from Anguar to Palau. All aboard died.

By Ship

If you have a great deal of time, you can really get the feel of Micronesia by taking a field trip ship. These depart fairly frequently from Majuro, Pohnpei, Chuuk, Yap, and Tarawa; you should be able to get on if you're flexible. You'll also need a sense of humor because no one seems to know anything until just a few days prior to departure. It's useless to write ahead requesting reservations. If you happen to be there as the ship's about to leave, you're in luck.

The purpose of the field trips is to transport local passengers and freight. Field trips are for the adventurous; there are few comforts. Deck space is about seven cents a mile. The cabins are usually reserved by government officials, but if you manage to get one it's 10 cents a mile, plus another $10 a day for meals. The cheapest way to go is to stretch your own mat on deck and eat your own food. When buying your ticket, don't ask for a complete roundtrip as they'll compute it by adding up all the interisland fares. Pick one of the farthest islands and buy a ticket to there. Buy another one-way ticket at the turnaround point, or fly back. The ships visit many islands twice, on the outward and inward journeys, so you could stop off and pick it up on the return.

A ship might stop at each island for anywhere from a few hours to four days. You can sleep on board or go ashore and camp. Ask the island mayor or chief for permission—usually no problem. As sailing time approaches, keep a close eye on the ship. Rely only on the captain or Field Trip Officer (FTO) for departure information. Even so, cases have been reported where a ship got an emergency call from another island, gave one blast of its horn, took up the tender, and sailed away. Travelers off walking at the far end of the island have been left to catch a flight back. The ships are usually crowded at the beginning and end of the journey, but comparatively empty at the turnaround point.

The islanders and crew on board may give you food, so have something to give back. If you give the cook some rice, he may be kind enough to cook it for you. A jar of instant coffee will come in handy as there's always plenty of hot water. The hot water is also good to heat up bags of Japanese ramen, but you'll need a bowl. You'll often be invited to feast ashore.

By Canoe

Never attempt to take a dugout canoe through even light surf: you can be swamped. Don't try to

ancient stone walkway on Yap

pull or lift a canoe by its outrigger: it will break. Drag the canoe by holding the solid main body. A bailer is essential equipment. If you get off the beaten track on an island, it's likely that a local friend will offer to take you out in his canoe.

By Ocean Kayak

Ocean kayaking is the fastest growing sport in Micronesia. In some colder water locations, kayaking is mainly for the young and hardy. But in Micronesia's warm water, particularly within enclosed lagoons, anyone can join in. You can rent kayaks, with or without guides, on almost any of the major islands. They provide a wonderful way to get to locations without using an internal combustion engine, which is likely to frighten off wildlife.

By Road

In Micronesia, on all islands other than Guam and Saipan, roads are for walking and automobiles are merely tolerated. Wherever you are driving, watch out for young children on the road. On many islands, the speed limit may be 15 miles per hour. This is for pedestrian safety as well as to avoid damage to your car, since the roads are often potholed and made of gravel.

Also be aware that your automobile insurance from home may not provide coverage in Micronesia. Discuss this with your insurance agent before you leave. Not all car rental companies in Micronesia offer insurance.

Car rentals are available at all the airports served by Continental Airlines. At Guam and Saipan several well-known rental companies compete for your trade, while operators on some of the other islands are of the rent-a-wreck variety. Generally, only the agencies on Guam and Saipan accept reservations. The price is usually calculated on a 24-hour basis (around $40), so you can use the car the next morning. Mileage is included in the price.

Shared taxis prowl the roads of Tarawa, Majuro, Ebeye, and Chuuk, offering lifts along their routes at low rates. You don't really need to rent a car on those islands. Taxi vans and minibuses on Pohnpei also charge per head. See the individual airport and hotel listings for information on airport transfers. Hitchhiking is fairly easy throughout Micronesia, except on Guam.

By Bicycle

Cycling in Micronesia? Sure, why not? You'll be able to go where and when you please, stop easily and often to meet people and take photos—really *see* the islands. It's great fun, but it's best to have bicycle touring experience. Most roads are flat along the coast but be careful on coral roads, especially inclines: if you slip and fall you could hurt yourself badly. Rainy islands like Pohnpei can start to seem inhospitable.

A sturdy mountain bike with wide wheels, safety chain, and good brakes might be best. Thick tires and a plastic liner between tube and tire will reduce punctures. Know how to fix your own bike. Take along a good repair kit (pump, puncture kit, freewheel tool, spare spokes, chain links, etc.) and a repair manual; bicycle shops are few to nonexistent in the islands. Don't try riding with a backpack; sturdy, waterproof bike bags are required. You'll also want a good lock.

Continental Airlines will carry a bicycle free as one of your two pieces of checked luggage within Micronesia. On domestic U.S. flights such as Los Angeles to Hawaii, however, Continental charges $30. You can avoid this charge by checking your bike straight through to your first stop in Micronesia. Interisland commuter airlines usually won't accept bikes on their small planes. Boats sometimes charge a token amount to carry a bike.

M. G. L. DOMENY DE RIENZI

REPUBLIC OF
THE MARSHALL ISLANDS
INTRODUCTION

Ask almost any Marshallese what is the country's main tourist attraction and you will be told with pride, "the warmth of her people."

The Marshall Islands are as remote a chain of islands as exists on the planet. This remoteness allowed the Marshalls to avoid significant Western interest and control until the middle of the 19th century. But the isolation melted away in the face of modern transportation when the 20th century landed on the Marshallese, who have retained an ambivalent attitude toward Western technology.

The Republic is composed of narrow coral islands without much land. Few have extra space for garbage disposal. Throwing garbage onto infertile atoll land was functional when garbage was biodegradable, but this habit became quite

dysfunctional with the emergence of non-biodegradable garbage. Cans, building materials, and plastic now lie everywhere on the narrow circle of sand that makes up Majuro atoll, the capital and commercial center of the Marshalls.

Twentieth-century waste litters the Marshalls. At the end of the runway of Majuro's International Airport, lying on the ground for several decades, sat the remains of a Western Pacific airplane. Through the years, the plane had been picked apart for spare parts or just for the sheer fun of it. A wing sat unattached to the fuselage. The remaining parts were removed only recently. The fuselage now sits on a barge in the lagoon, and the wing forms the bottom of a landfill project.

However, the Marshallese would like to turn their most spectacular garbage into treasure. As the United States pushed westward across the Pacific during World War II, it destroyed an

THE MARSHALLS AT A GLANCE

	POP. (1999 EST)	LAND AREA (SQ. MI.)	LAGOON AREA (SQ. MI.)
RATAK CHAIN			
Ailuk	488	2.08	68.46
Arno	1,656	5.02	130.77
Aur	438	2.16	92.59
Bikar	0	0.19	14.44
Erikub	0	0.58	88.92
Jemo	0	0.08	none
Likiep	482	3.98	163.71
Majuro	31.261	3.56	113.94
Maloelap	796	3.78	375.56
Mili/Knox	854	6.14	294.71
Nejit	445	0.73	none
Taka	0	0.23	35.95
Tsongi	0	1.24	30.12
Utirik	409	0.93	22.12
Wotje	646	3.17	241.04
RALIK CHAIN			
Ailinginae	0	1.08	40.93
Ailinglaplap	1,715	5.68	289.69
Bikini	10	2.32	229.42
Ebon	741	2.20	40.08
Enewetak	715	2.28	387.99
Jabat	112	0.23	none
Jaluit	1,709	4.36	266.29
Kili	602	0.35	none
Kwajalein	13,677	6.33	839.30
Lae	319	0.58	6.83
Lib	115	0.35	none
Namorik	814	1.08	3.24
Namu	801	2.43	153.51
Rongelap	0	3.09	387.76
Rongerik	0	0.66	55.37
Ujae	448	0.73	71.78
Ujelang	0	0.66	25.48
Wotho	90	1.66	36.64
TOTAL	**59,343**	**69.94**	**4,506.64**

enormous number of Japanese ships, planes, guns, and bunkers, which now litter sea and land. Many nations faced with such a situation would consider it a problem to be solved, but the Marshallese look at it as an opportunity. Like their Micronesian cousins on the island of Chuuk in the Federated States of Micronesia, the Marshallese are attempting to build a tourist industry around wreck diving, confident that divers will come to view the refuse.

During the 1940s and 50s, the United States carried out a series of nuclear tests on the Marshalls, dropping atomic and hydrogen bombs on Bikini and Enewetak atolls. Today, most Marshallese think the United States should be forced to complete a cleanup. Others believe the radioactivity of these atolls must be accepted. They reason that since things could not be much worse, industrialized countries should be invited, for a price, to dump additional atomic and toxic wastes here.

The Land

Majuro, the capital and commercial center of the Marshalls, will not please those seeking an unspoiled island paradise. It contains small areas of tropical beauty, but most of the atoll is a vibrant,

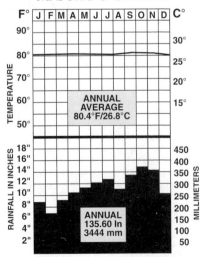

MAJURO'S CLIMATE

ANNUAL AVERAGE 80.4°F/26.8°C

ANNUAL 135.60 In 3444 mm

gutsy, overcrowded slum. Ebeye, an island on Kwajalein atoll, and the Marshall's second population center, has even greater overcrowding. Take the time to get away to outer atolls, however, and you'll discover islands of beautiful beaches, breadfruit, coconut palms, and pandanus. Services may be few, but the people are friendly and there is a sense of adventure in the air.

The 1,225 Marshall Islands are grouped together in 29 atolls (20 inhabited), five low islands (Jabat, Jemo, Kili, Lib, and Mejit), and 870 reefs. The atolls are narrow coral rings, usually with white sandy beaches enclosing turquoise lagoons. The southern atolls' vegetation is thicker due to heavier rainfall. Although the land mass of the Marshall Islands comprises only 70 square miles, the islands are scattered over 775,000 square miles of the central Pacific Ocean. Its position as the first island group west of Hawaii led to bitter battles during World War II. Its geo-

graphical isolation from industrialized countries and their media made them seem perfect to the United States as a place to test nuclear bombs too large or dirty for Nevada.

The Marshalls boast the largest atolls in the world, arrayed in two chains 150 miles apart and 800 miles long. The northeastern or Ratak ("Sunrise") Chain includes the large atolls of Mili, Majuro, Maloelap, Wotje, and Likiep; the southwestern or Ralik ("Sunset") Chain includes Jaluit, Ailinglaplap, Kwajalein (the world's largest atoll), Rongelap, Bikini, Enewetak, and others. The Marshall Islands' government also claims the United States-held island of Wake (Enen Kio) to the north, but is not expected to invade.

Climate

The Marshall Islands' climate is tropical oceanic, cooled by the northeast trades. From January to March the climate is drier. The summer months

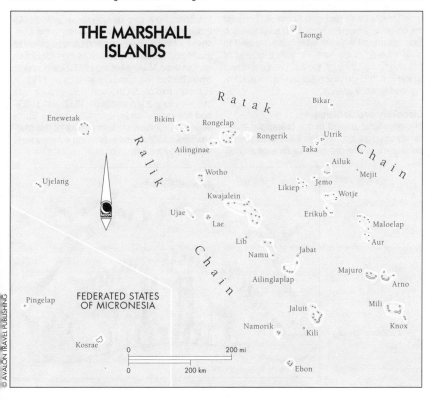

are most likely to have the still air and water that divers prefer. The northern islands of the Marshalls are cooler than the southern atolls, and receive less rainfall. Typhoons are rare, although March, April, October, and November can be stormy. During the 1997-1998 El Niño, the islands experienced severe drought as the rain-bearing current moved away. From January-June 1998, residents of Majuro received water only one day a week. Extra water for emergencies was limited to one gallon per person, and the wait for such emergency rations could be two hours long. Hotels had to limit water use by guests to several hours a day.

HISTORY

Origin of the Marshall Islands

The first humans, Uelip and his wife, lived on the island of Ep. One day a tree began to grow from Uelip's head and split his skull. Through the crack were born his sons, Etau and Djemelut. Etau quarreled with his father and decided to build a home of his own. He took a basket of soil and flew off through the air. The basket had a hole in it through which soil drained out, forming the Marshall Islands.

Discovery and Settlement

Micronesians arrived in the Marshalls thousands of years ago, though there is academic debate as to a more precise time of arrival.

They were extraordinarily skilled navigators. Keen observers of the ocean, they discovered that the location of distant islands affected wave patterns. Thus, by studying those patterns, a Marshallese navigator could locate islands that were too low to be seen over the horizon. They created "stick charts" made of sticks and cowrie shells to help memorize the patterns. With this navigation system, far superior to anything Europeans possessed at the time, the Marshallese were able to sail their large outrigger canoes between distant atolls.

There is no record of any single chief controlling the entire group, although the Ralik Chain was occasionally united. Because land is so scarce in the Marshalls, it is highly valued. Traditionally, tribute in the form of the produce of the land was rendered to the chiefs.

European Contact

The first recorded European on the scene was the Spaniard Alvaro de Saavedra, in 1528. Although Spain made a vague claim to the Marshalls in 1686, it never attempted to colonize the region. The islands were named for British captain John Marshall of the HMS *Scarborough,* who charted the group of islands in 1788. A Russian explorer, Otto von Kotzebue, made two trips to the Marshalls (in 1817 and 1825), and his careful observations provided Europeans with their first clear picture of the Marshallese and their atolls. Ensuing whalers were repelled by the islanders.

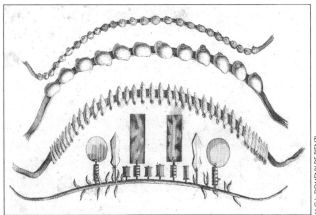

traditional jewelry

FIELD MUSEUM OF NATURAL HISTORY, CHICAGO

MARSHALLESE STICK CHARTS

To travel to islands over the horizon, the people of the Marshalls learned to read the wave patterns of the sea. When uniform ocean currents and wind drifts are interrupted and reflected by numerous atolls and reefs, they form certain kinds of swells that show the direction of land. This phenomenon can be clearly seen today in aerial photographs and pictures taken from weather satellites. The patterns could be felt by an experienced navigator as waves slapped against the side of the canoe. These stick charts were used as memory aids to help navigators memorize the patterns.

The first German trader established himself on Ebon in 1861; in 1878 Chief Kabua of Ebson and Jaluit, ancestor of the first president of the Republic of the Marshall Islands, signed a treaty with the Germans giving them use of Jaluit and protection for their traders. In exchange, the Germans supported his supremacy among the islanders. The German government declared a protectorate over the Marshalls in 1885 and two years later set up headquarters on Jaluit. The Germans ruled indirectly through the Marshallese chiefs and did not attempt mass colonization. A small European business staff was in charge of copra production.

In 1888 the traders merged into the Jaluit Gesellschaft, which agreed to cover Germany's costs of administration in exchange for a monopoly. By 1899 the Jaluit company had 10 stations in the Marshalls and ships that purchased coconut meat throughout the Carolines. In 1905, a devastating hurricane swept across the Marshalls, destroying buildings and plantations. Unable to recover, the company returned control of the area to the German government in 1906, which joined it to other Micronesian islands it had purchased from Spain in 1899.

Japanese Contact

The Japanese, who had traded in the Marshalls since 1890, took the islands from the Germans in 1914, after the start of World War I. No fighting occurred because the Germans withdrew to strengthen their European war effort. The Japanese set up a naval administration. In 1920, Japan received a mandate from the League of Nations to administer Micronesia, including the Marshalls. The copra trade was turned over to a company called Nanyo Boeki Kaisha. Direct Japanese rule replaced the authority of the traditional chiefs and the number of Japanese officials steadily increased.

The Japanese, in violation of the terms of their mandate, began building military bases on some of the atolls in 1935. The Marshalls were a staging area for the 1941 Japanese invasion of what is now Kiribati, the Gilbert Islands. The United States captured Kwajalein and Enewetak from the Japanese in February 1944, after bloody battles. Japanese bases on Jaluit, Maloelap, Mili, and Wotje were neutralized by aerial bombardment, and the survivors, both Japanese and Marshallese, were left to sit out the war. From Kwajalein and Majuro, the United States Navy struck west into the Japanese-held Carolines and Marianas.

In 1947 the Marshall Islands became part of the Trust Territory of the Pacific Islands, administered by the United States. Although under United Nations auspices, the Trust Territory was made a "strategic" trust, meaning that the United

States was allowed to create military bases. From 1946 to 1958 the United States violated the most basic responsibilities of trusteeship by carrying out a massive nuclear testing program on the northern atolls of Bikini and Enewetak. In 1961, Kwajalein became the army's Pacific Missile Range, a target for Intercontinental Ballistic Missiles (ICBMs) test fired from California.

Independence

In a vote of the people on 12 July 1978, Marshallese voters chose to separate from the other districts of the Trust Territory of the Pacific Islands. They approved a constitution of their own the following year, and on 1 May 1979 formed a Marshall Islands government. In September 1983, the Marshallese electorate voted for a Compact of Free Association with the United States. The Compact was approved by the United States in 1986, and payments to the Marshalls under the agreement began in 1987, bringing the Marshalls about $1 billion over the next 15 years.

In December 1990, the United Nations Security Council formally terminated the trusteeship arrangement in these islands and the following September accepted the Republic of the Marshall Islands as a member.

GOVERNMENT

The legislature is modeled on the British parliamentary system. But the government, like all politics in the Marshalls, remains strongly influenced by the ancient, traditional hierarchy. The constitution provides for a 33-senator Nitijela (Parliament) elected every four years. Majuro has five seats; Kwajalein three; Ailinglaplap, Arno, and Jaluit two each; and 19 other districts one each. The voting age is 18.

The Nitijela elects the president from its ranks, and the president chooses his cabinet from the elected members of the Nitijela. If the house passes two votes of no confidence, the president must step down, dissolve the Nitijela, and call new elections. Legislative powers are centralized in the Nitijela, there being no states or provinces.

The two political groupings are the ruling RMI party and a loosely formed opposition group. Many of the elected members of the Nitijela are

also customary chiefs *(iroij)*. The traditional high chief Amata Kabua, first president of the Marshall Islands, exercised firm personal leadership since self-government began in 1979 until his death in 1996. After a short tenure by interim president Kunio Lemari, Amata's first cousin, Imata Kabua, *iroij* of Kwajalein, took over the presidency.

The Council of Iroij (consisting of 12 hereditary traditional leaders) deliberates on matters relating to land, custom, and tradition. A Traditional Rights Court rules on land rights.

The capital of the Marshall Islands is D-U-D (Darrit-Uliga-Delap) on Majuro; Ebeye (on the Kwajalein atoll), Jaluit, and Wotje are administrative subcenters. Each of the 24 inhabited islands and atolls has a mayor and an island council, organized according to municipal constitutions, which govern the consumption of alcoholic beverages, among other things.

ECONOMY

The Republic of the Marshall Islands, like most small Pacific island nations, will have a great deal of difficulty regaining economic self-sufficiency. After political independence, the Republic remained economically dependent on payments under the Compact of Free Association from the United States—these payments accounted for more than half of the government's budget. Excluding Compact payments, in 1993 the Marshalls imported $62 million of goods and services, and exported $9 million.

The local economy, though not its social structure, is aided by Marshallese who work abroad, usually in the United States, and remit money back to family members still living in the Marshalls. Under the Compact, Marshallese are eligible to join the U.S. armed forces. The economy is hampered by one of the highest birthrates in the world. This has swelled population and created a great number of children who need to be supported. Much economic development money has not been effectively utilized. As stated in 1995 by Rube R. Zackhras, Minister of Finance:

The problem facing RMI is colossal. There is no doubt that dependence of the economy on massive foreign aid, imported food, raw material and capital goods and on expatriate human resources has to be reduced if we are to reduce the negative impact of the eventual termination of Compact funding. We have to create alternative sources of employment, income and government revenue that would take the place of Compact funding. In addition, we have to meet the needs of a fast growing population more than half of which consists of young dependents who do not contribute to incomes of family.

There is still a degree of subsistence agriculture (coconuts, breadfruit, pandanus, bananas, taro, sweet potatoes, yams, pigs, chickens, reef fish), particularly on the outer islands. But most Marshallese are in a cash/consumer economy.

Payments from the United States, under the Compact of Free Association, fueled the Marshalls' economy. Although the Compact payments were intended to build an economic infrastructure, they were spent in large measure to build an oversized government bureaucracy. Government workers outnumbered those in the private sector. Payments under the Compact were in essence mortgaged when the Marshalls issued bonds backed by future payments. In 1998, the debt service on the bonds equalled almost $20 million, roughly one-third the amount of Compact dollars and services for the year. When the RMI government began to downsize in the late 1990s, the loss of governmental salaries depressed the entire retail economy as well. This led to disinvestment by foreign business interests that previously had provided goods and services. It seems clear that unless the United States enters into a second Compact, with significant payments, further economic collapse will occur. Negotiations are scheduled to begin in 1999.

The Marshalls have attempted to expand the role of private businesses. Copra and coconut oil are the most significant agricultural exports. Almost all trade is with the United States and Japan. Income enterprises are underway, farming giant clams *(Tridacna gigas)* and exporting live tropical fish to aquarium stores.

The Marshalls, like other Micronesian nations, allow foreign fishing fleets, using foreign labor, to harvest enormous amounts of tuna from its waters. Thus the Marshalls receive relatively little income from the taking of perhaps its greatest natural resource. One possible bright spot for the Marshalls is that the PM&O shipping company and Starkist have entered into a letter of understanding to build a tuna loining plant. At this plant, the tuna would be filleted and cooked before being shipped off to be canned. The government granted a minimum wage waiver, but believes that the plant will lead to 300 jobs for Marshallese at $1.50/hour.

The Kwajalein Missile Range brings in more than $25 million a year in salaries paid to Marshallese workers at the base, $11 million annual rent paid by the military, and taxes on the salaries of American expatriates. But with the Cold War over, the United States is cutting back on the size and scope of this base.

The Republic of the Marshalls has built up business as a "flag of convenience" for the registration of foreign-owned ships. Its ship registry is now the 10th largest tonnage in the world.

THE PEOPLE

Of the 29 atolls and five individual low islands, 24 are inhabited. Almost half the population of the Marshalls lives on Majuro and close to a quarter on Ebeye, making these islands among the most densely populated in the Pacific. From 1980-88, the Marshalls' birthrate was more than 4.24%, close to the theoretical limits of population growth. Since then, aggressive family planning promotions have decreased the rate, which nonetheless remains high. More than half the population is under age 15.

Westernization and the breakdown of the traditional family have led to many of the problems associated with urban poverty: alcoholism, high rates of teenage suicide, and out-of-wedlock teenage pregnancy. What is perhaps more remarkable is the degree to which some traditional values have survived the effects of colonialism, the destruction of World War II, and the Cold War era nuclear testing program.

For most people on Majuro, rice has replaced more nutritious traditional starches, such as breadfruit, taro, and other root plants. Some families eat few fresh vegetables or even fresh fish, living instead on a diet of canned and processed foods. Such eating habits have led to obesity and even cases of blindness in children from lack of vitamin A.

Outer islanders, particularly the young, continue to migrate to Majuro and Ebeye, though often they are unable to find suitable employment once they arrive. Another important social development in the Marshalls is that many young adults will spend at least part of their life working in Hawaii, Guam, or the United States mainland. If they return to the Marshalls, their cultural values obviously have become changed by their off-island experiences.

Most Marshallese are Protestant. Missionaries of many creeds are active on Majuro. Many social activities focus on the churches. Eight grades of education are compulsory. High schools teach in English. For postsecondary education, students can go on to the College of the Marshall Islands (CMI), a teacher training facility on Majuro, which in 1991 became affiliated with the University of the South Pacific in Fiji. CMI offers a nursing program that serves all of Micronesia.

Marshallese society is traditionally matrilineal: chiefly titles descend through the mother. Under these traditional rules, each Marshallese person belongs to the *bwij* (clan) of his or her mother and has the right to use the land and other common property of that *bwij.* Alongside this is "blood" lineage *(bodokodok),* which is inherited from the father. The *dri jerbal* till the land. The head of the *bwij* is the *alab,* a spokesman between commoners *(kajur)* and the chiefly families *(iroij).* The paramount chiefs *(iroijlaplap)* are the Marshallese equivalent of royalty. As the money culture expands, Marshallese women are losing control of the land as family property is often sold to local men. Only Marshallese can own land in the Marshall Islands, although outsiders may lease it.

Language

Marshallese, the official language, belongs to the Austronesian family of languages (formerly known as Malayo-Polynesian) and is related to Gilbertese and some languages of the Carolines. People of the Ratak and Ralik Chains speak mutually comprehensible dialects. *Yokwe* (YAG-way) is the Marshallese greeting; "thank you" is *kommol.* Kids often shout *belle* or *dribelle* (foreign people) at visitors; answer them with *yokwe.* If they are small enough you might try an-

swering back *driMazjal* (Marshallese people)—it usually gets a laugh.

ARTS AND ENTERTAINMENT

Arts and Crafts

The Marshalls produce a good supply of traditional handicrafts that are readily available for purchase by tourists. Plentiful supplies of pandanus and coconut fiber, plus the relaxed pace of atoll life, led to a variety of handicrafts. The best baskets in Micronesia are made in the Marshalls, especially those made by the Bikini refugees now living on Kili Island. You can also find woven coasters, wall hangings, pandanus hats, grass skirts, belts, purses, headbands, necklaces, fans, and mats, all made by Marshallese women.

The men do woodcarvings of sharks, eels, and canoes. Marshallese stick charts *(wapeepe),* which record the way ocean swells reflect and bend as they near land, make unique souvenirs.

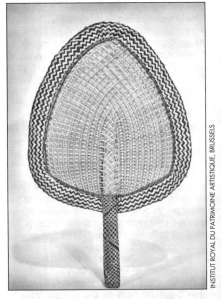

a Jaluit fan made of coconut, pandanus, and hibiscus fibers

INSTITUT ROYAL DU PATRIMOINE ARTISTIQUE, BRUSSELS

Holidays and Events

Public holidays include New Year's Day (1 January), Memorial Day and Nuclear Victim's Remembrance Day (1 March), Good Friday, Constitution Day (1 May), Fisherman's Day (first Friday in July), Labor Day (first Monday in September), Manit Day (last Friday in September), Independence Day (21 October), President's Day (17 November), Thanksgiving (first Friday in December), and Christmas Day (25 December).

Constitution Day, commemorating the Marshallese constitution, which took effect 1 May 1979, is a good time to see Marshallese singing and dancing, and other traditional activities. On the first Saturday of the month (or the next), the **Outrigger Marshall Islands Cup,** sponsored by the Outrigger Hotel, is held. Boat races, featuring the best from all the atolls, compete in a men's division and a women's division.

Aging Week (last week in May) features exhibitions of handicrafts, traditional Marshallese medicines, and cooking. Fisherman's Day marks the beginning of a famous game fishing tournament organized by the Marshalls Billfish Club in Majuro. Alele Week (last week in August) also hosts dancing, singing, handicrafts, and other cultural activities. At Christmas, singing and dancing unfold in the churches all day.

PRACTICALITIES

Accommodations and Food

The only full-service hotels and restaurants are on Majuro, Ebeye, and the American base on

---

> **MARSHALL ISLANDS**
> **COUNTRY CODE: 692**

Kwajalein. Taxes on rented rooms are three percent of the bill plus $2 a day. On outer islands, camping is generally acceptable, provided you first obtain permission of the landowner (usually no problem).

Hotel Robert Reimers (RRE) runs small outposts on Arno, Wau, Mili Atoll, and Bikini. MEC (Marshalls Electric Company) has a small guest house on Jaluit. (For details, see discussion of each atoll.) Additional accommodations for visitors are available on Mili and a few other outer atolls, but reliable information is hard to obtain. One way to arrange a stay on an outer island is to go to the Nitijela and ask for the senator from the atoll of your interest. The senator will be able to outline the accommodations situation and perhaps suggest local contacts. Although you can simply show up on the outer islands, to be assured of a good reception it's much better to make prior arrangements with the Island Council. The Ministry of Internal Affairs (P.O. Box 18, Majuro, MH 96960, tel. 692-625-3240) has a radio link with most of the atolls and is experienced in arranging stays. Give them plenty of time to contact the island's mayor and make the arrangements. You can also seek assistance from the Marshall Islands Visitors Authority (MIVA), P.O. Box 5, Majuro, MH 96960, tel. (692) 625-6482, fax (692) 625-6771, e-mail: tourism@ntamar.com.

guest cottages on Mili-Mili

If you arrange to stay with someone as a guest, ask whoever made the arrangements what to take along as a gift (a large jar of instant coffee, T-shirts, music cassettes, or flashlight and batteries, for example—but not alcohol, which is prohibited on some outer islands). Although Marshallese hospitality is genuine, adequate reciprocation (monetary or otherwise) is customary. Airline baggage limits permitting, take your own food and bottled water or water purification system with you to the outer islands, as local stores carry only basics like sugar, rice, and flour.

Visas

Although United States citizens do not legally need a passport to enter the Marshalls, to avoid hassles it's best to carry one. No visa is required of United States citizens for stays up to 30 days, but anyone intending to stay more than 30 days should obtain a Marshalls entry permit in advance through their local sponsor. Visa extensions beyond the initial 30 days are hard to come by without an adequate reason. Everyone other than United States and Canadian citizens must already have a United States visa if they are going east to Hawaii or west to Guam. All visitors must have an onward or return air ticket and are forbidden from engaging in political activity.

After clearing customs at Majuro, visiting yachts must obtain a permit from the Ministry of Interior and Outer Islands Affairs to cruise to the other atolls.

Money, Mail, and Measurements

American currency is used. Food and other essentials can cost almost twice as much on the outer islands as they do in Majuro, if they can be found at all. Bargaining is not customary in the Marshalls and tipping is expected only in tourist-oriented establishments.

The Marshall Islands issues its own colorful postage stamps. Domestic United States postal rates apply. Packages mailed to the United States are frequently opened for postal inspection. The electric voltage is 110 volts/60 cycles, and American appliance plugs are used.

The Marshall Islands are west of the International Date Line. If you are coming from Hawaii, you lose a day. Government offices are most reliably open weekday mornings.

Health

A vaccination certificate against cholera or yellow fever is required if arriving from an infected area. Typhoid and polio immunizations are not required, but recommended. There's a hospital on Majuro and one on Ebeye. Try to avoid either. If something is seriously wrong and time permits, fly out to Honolulu or Guam. Only dispensaries are available on the outer islands. Be aware: sexually transmitted disease and tuberculosis rates on Majuro and Ebeye are high.

The Marshall Islands experiences cases of *ciguatera* (seafood poisoning) more than other parts of Micronesia. There is little if any danger, however, in restaurants. And on outer islands, where it is most prevalent, older residents can offer guidance on which species of fish to avoid.

Don't drink the tap water in the Marshalls. At best the water is brackish, and it may well be contaminated. Buy bottled water, available in Majuro and Ebeye. Most years, from January through April water is rationed on Majuro. Be thoughtful and minimize your use.

Information

Upon request, the Marshall Islands Visitors Authority (MIVA), P.O. Box 5, Majuro, MH 96960, tel. (692) 625-6482, fax (692) 625-6771, e-mail: tourism@ntamar.com, will send you material. Request its very useful *Marshall Islands Visitor's Guide.*

You may also wish to order the *Marshall Islands Guidebook* for $10 by writing to its publisher, the *Marshall Islands Journal,* P.O. Box 14, Majuro, MH 96960. This booklet includes a Marshallese dictionary, maps of all the atolls, much background information on the country, and fairly comprehensive phone listings.

The Alele Museum (P.O. Box 629, Majuro, MH 96960, tel./fax 692-625-3226) sells hard-to-find books such as *Collision Course at Kwajalein* (1984, $8), by Giff Johnson, and *Man This Reef* (1982, $11), by Gerald Knight. These books can be shipped by airmail. You can write for a complete list. The museum also sells the *Marshall Islands Guidebook.*

The weekly, privately owned *Marshall Islands Journal* (P.O. Box 14, Majuro, MH 96960) comes out on Friday (50 cents) in English and Marshallese. Annual subscription rates to the *Journal* are $87 to the United States, $233 elsewhere (airmail). The *Journal* includes a wealth of interesting local news from an independent perspective, so be sure to pick up a copy first chance you get. It advertises itself as "The World's Worst Newspaper" (which it's not).

The Guam-based *Pacific Daily News* is usually available in D-U-D. Cable TV is available, including CNN and ESPN. Also available are TV programs that were broadcast in San Francisco on other networks a week earlier.

What to Take
You're allowed to bring in one bottle of liquor and two cartons of cigarettes—a good idea if you need them, as they're heavily taxed. Cosmetics are also expensive locally. Color print film can be purchased in D-U-D. Women visitors should be aware that local women dress conservatively, the custom is against wearing shorts above the knees.

Getting There
Majuro Airport (MAJ) is eight miles west of town and has no bank or tourist information. Handicrafts are sold at two shops that sometimes open for international flights. A shared taxi to D-U-D costs $2 pp, although most hotels offer free shuttles. The airport departure tax is $20 on international flights. The HNR Restaurant at the airport does not inflate prices. Since service is often slow, do not assume you can fit in a quick bite right before a flight. Flights are announced in a gentle, unamplified voice so pay attention to the time, particularly if you are in the restaurant.

Continental Airlines (tel. 800-231-0856 or 692-625-3209, fax 692-247-7646) flies from Honolulu to Majuro and back two or three times a week, depending on demand, on its Island Hopper service between Honolulu and Guam. It can cost almost as much to fly Honolulu to Majuro as to Honolulu to Guam, with stops in Majuro, Kosrae, Pohnpei, and Chuuk. Reconfirm your onward flight when you arrive in Majuro.

Aloha Airlines has a once a week flight from Honolulu to the Marshall Islands, stopping at Majuro and Kwajalein. The plane leaves Honolulu on Thursday and returns the following day (Saturday because of the International Date Line) to Honolulu. Its toll-free phone number is (888) 477-7010. Aloha's Honolulu phone number

is (808) 485-2220. Aloha's Website is www.alohaair.com.

Air Marshall Islands (tel. 692-625-3733) flies to Tarawa and Funafuti. Check for any reduced roundtrip excursion fares. You can look at AMI's entire schedule on-line at www.rmiembassyus.org/amisked.html.

Layne Ballard of **Central Pacific Dive Expedition** (150 Yorba St., Tustin, CA 92780, tel. 714-426-0265 or 800-846-3483, fax 714-426-0267) can arrange independent travel or tours. He specializes in dive tours to the Marshalls and other islands reached by Continental Airlines. In conjunction with Marshall Dive Adventures, he can also arrange diving in exotic locales such as Bikini atoll.

Other travel agencies that can also arrange fishing trips to the Marshalls are **International Anglers,** P.O. Box 2232, Napa, CA 94558, tel. (800) 477-2076 or (707) 226-2076, fax (707) 226-2850; and **Kaufmann's Fly Fishing Expeditions,** 8861 SW Commercial St., Tigard, OR 97223, tel. (800) 442-4359, fax (503) 684-7025. From England, you might try **Harris Holidays,** tel. (440) 1375-396-688, e-mail: diving@harris-travel.com.

Getting Around
By Air: Government-owned **Air Marshall Islands** (P.O. Box 1319, Majuro, MH 96960, tel. 692-625-3733, fax 692-625-3730) uses safe, reliable 19-seat Dornier propeller aircraft to provide service to all 26 airstrips in the Marshalls weekly or twice a month. AMI flies from Majuro to Airok ($89) and Jeh ($82) on Ailinglaplap, also weekly to Likiep ($120), Maloelap ($69), Wotje ($93), and Tinak on Arno ($41), twice weekly to Mili ($56), Jaluit ($85), and Kili ($93), and six times a week to Kwajalein ($125). All fares are one way. Checked baggage limits are 30 pounds on domestic flights, 44 pounds international. Often the flights are full.

Special services sometimes allow weekend trips to Arno and Jaluit. Occasionally AMI offers Sunday day trips to outer islands such as Maloelap or Mili for about $75 including a lunch of local foods—a great opportunity if your travel plans coincide. A flight arrival on an outer island is the main social event of the week for the residents.

By Boat: Time permitting, a leisurely way to experience the Marshall Islands is on a field trip

a supply ship
at Majuro

DAVID STANLEY

ship. These 600-ton ships make five different field trips from Majuro: west (1,510 miles), north (695 miles), south (680 miles), central (530 miles), and east (175 miles). Theoretically the ships visit all the atolls every month or two. Fares run about 25 cents a mile with cabin, 15 cents a mile on deck. The cabins are usually full. Meals are $10 a day extra, but the food served is poor. It's best to take along your own.

To find out what's available, inquire at the **Government Transportation Office** (tel. 692-625-3469) beside the dock, as soon as you arrive on Majuro. If something's leaving that same day, jump on it—otherwise, you might have to wait a couple of weeks. Another possibility is to fly to an island that the field-trip ship will be visiting shortly and ride back to Majuro. Note that alcoholic beverages are prohibited on many outer islands.

THE RATAK CHAIN

MAJURO

Majuro atoll, 2,273 miles southwest of Honolulu, is a series of islands circling the Majuro lagoon. Originally, 64 islands surrounded the oval lagoon; causeways now enable you to drive the 35 miles from Rita to Laura. Some say Rita and Laura—World War II code names—are named for Hollywood stars Rita Hayworth and Lauren Bacall.

Before the war Majuro was just another outer atoll, Jaluit being first the German and then the Japanese administrative center. But on 1 February 1944 the Americans landed unopposed on Majuro and built a fighter strip near where Gibson's Department Store now stands, while naval units anchored in the lagoon. Take the time to explore and you'll find Majuro an interesting place to spend a few days.

D-U-D

The present capital of the Marshall Islands bears the title D-U-D Municipality—the initials stand for Darrit-Uliga-Delap, originally three islands but now joined by a road into one strip. D-U-D is three miles long and at most places a couple of hundred yards wide. It's a conglomeration of administrative buildings, businesses, department stores, supermarkets, small groceries, beer outlets, and densely packed houses of plywood and corrugated iron or tin roofs. Don't expect a pristine paradise: it is heavily littered and cars outnumber coconuts palms. Almost 30,000 Marshallese from every atoll in the country and a couple of hundred Americans now live here.

Rita, the residential community at the northeast end of D-U-D, is quite lush with many mature breadfruit, papaya, and plumeria trees. You can easily walk the several miles to Rita from Uliga, the commercial center of the island, or you can take a cab out for 50 cents and walk back. It is probably the best place to get a feel for daily life in Majuro. The lushness of the area causes a mosquito problem, however, so bring along the bug juice.

Uliga features the **Reimers Store** and hotel, the post office, the library and courthouse, as well as many restaurants and bars.

The small **Alele Museum** (open Monday 10 a.m.-noon, Tuesday and Wednesday 9 a.m.-noon and 1-4 p.m., Thursday closed, Friday 9 a.m.-noon, Saturday 10 a.m.-1 p.m., Sunday closed) has a collection of models of traditional sailing ships and stick charts, as well as a display of traditional weaving and ropes. It also has an extensive collection of seashells from the Marshalls.

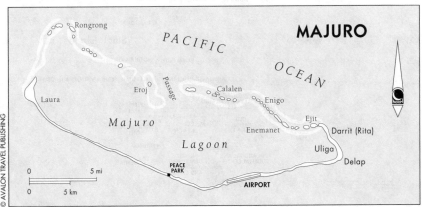

© AVALON TRAVEL PUBLISHING

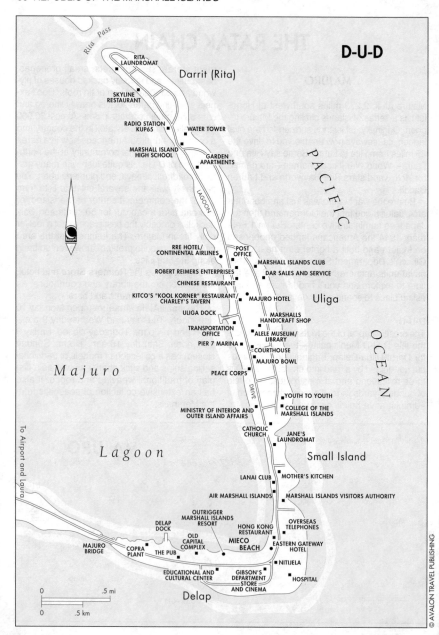

D-U-D

Rita Pass

RITA
LAUNDROMAT

Darrit (Rita)

SKYLINE
RESTAURANT

RADIO STATION
KUP65

WATER TOWER

MARSHALL ISLAND
HIGH SCHOOL

GARDEN
APARTMENTS

PACIFIC

LAGOON

RRE HOTEL/
CONTINENTAL AIRLINES

POST
OFFICE

MARSHALL ISLANDS CLUB

ROBERT REIMERS ENTERPRISES

DAR SALES AND SERVICE

CHINESE RESTAURANT

KITCO'S "KOOL KORNER" RESTAURANT/
CHARLEY'S TAVERN

MAJURO HOTEL

Uliga

ULIGA DOCK

MARSHALLS
HANDICRAFT SHOP

TRANSPORTATION
OFFICE

ALELE MUSEUM/
LIBRARY

PIER 7 MARINA

COURTHOUSE

MAJURO BOWL

PEACE CORPS

Majuro

YOUTH TO YOUTH

MINISTRY OF INTERIOR AND
OUTER ISLAND AFFAIRS

COLLEGE OF THE
MARSHALL ISLANDS

CATHOLIC
CHURCH

JANE'S
LAUNDROMAT

Lagoon

Small Island

LANAI CLUB

MOTHER'S KITCHEN

AIR MARSHALL ISLANDS

MARSHALL ISLANDS VISITORS AUTHORITY

To Airport and Laura

OUTRIGGER
MARSHALL ISLANDS
RESORT

DELAP
DOCK

HONG KONG
RESTAURANT

OVERSEAS
TELEPHONES

OLD
CAPITAL
COMPLEX

MIECO
BEACH

EASTERN GATEWAY
HOTEL

MAJURO
BRIDGE

COPRA
PLANT

THE PUB

NITIJELA

EDUCATIONAL AND
CULTURAL CENTER

GIBSON'S
DEPARTMENT
STORE
AND CINEMA

HOSPITAL

Delap

DRIVE

OCEAN

MOON

0   .5 mi

0   .5 km

© AVALON TRAVEL PUBLISHING

The museum sells a few books on the Marshalls, first day postal covers, and T-shirts depicting local legends. The T-shirts make excellent souvenirs; children's sizes sell for $5 and adult sizes $12. They come with a printed card explaining the legend depicted.

Adjoining the museum is the **library** (Mon.-Thurs. 10 a.m.-6 p.m., Friday 10 a.m.-5 p.m., Saturday 9 a.m.-1 p.m.), which has moderately recent American news magazines and a good reference section on Micronesia.

Behind the Alele Museum is one of the island's great institutions—the **Marshalls Handicraft Shop** (P.O. Box 44, Majuro, MH 96960, tel. 692-625-3566). This enormous crafts store is now more than 25 years old and was largely responsible for the revival in Marshallese handicrafts. It is cooperatively owned and run by women. Of the purchase price for crafts, 80 cents of each dollar goes directly to the artist. Mary Lanwi, one of the guiding spirits of the Handicraft Shop, is keenly aware of the degree this institution has empowered women of the Marshalls who otherwise had few economic options. The enormous inventory allows you to see the diversity of handicrafts being produced throughout the Republic. Baskets sell for $15-20, stick charts are in the same price range, and items such as woven coasters are as little as $1.35. Craftswomen are frequently at work at the store, and with an advance request, the store can often arrange particular demonstrations. They will mail purchases home and will also accept mail orders.

Next to **Robert Reimers Enterprises** is a covered table area that pretty much serves as the town square. Old men play checkers (coral vs. pop-tops). It's the easiest place in town to sit down and get to know locals—everyone is quite friendly.

The most interesting architecture on the island is the *Nitijela* (Parliament) complex in Delap. This thoroughly modern building is monumental in feeling; its steel-green windows set into the sand-colored structure echo the dominant colors of the atoll and its lagoon.

Opposite the new *Nitijela* is **Gibson's Department Store,** which, like Reimers, is a general store, selling clothing as well as food. Gibson's recently built a three-screen movie theater at this location. In the early evening, or on weekends, at **Mieco Beach Park** across from the Gibson complex, one can often find a soccer or softball game. Several hundred yards farther down is the Educational Cultural Center, which accommodates sports events and public meetings.

To Laura

A mile and a half past Mieco Beach is the **Majuro Bridge,** built with Japanese aid money in 1983. It's the highest point on the atoll, roughly 12 feet above sea level at high tide. A channel was cut through the lee side to allow better access to the sea for small boats, which could then avoid the long detour around Calalen Island. On the ocean side, on both sides of the channel are often pretty clean waves. When the waves reach four feet, a nice left forms off the red buoy to the left of the channel (looking out from the bridge). Some caution though; aside from the channel, the bottom is a very hard reef that should not be surfed, and there are frequently dangerous currents in the channel as the tide goes out. This is not a place for anyone but experts. As always, if possible, check conditions with a local.

As you continue around the island toward Laura, you won't find many public beaches. Do not go to a beach in front of someone's home without asking permission, since the beach is considered the homeowner's property. If you find an owner, however, permission to use the beach will usually given. A thank you will go a long way, and perhaps a drink or candy for any kids, but no money should be offered.

Opposite the airport, on a clear day, you can look across the lagoon and see small islands dotted along the circumference of the lagoon. Right past the runway is a place to park, a nice spot to picnic or to snorkel. The **Japanese Peace Park,** created a couple of miles past the airport in 1984, is another nice spot to picnic or snorkel.

You are now in the area the people of crowded D-U-D call the "countryside," an area of coconut and pandanus plantations, a tremendous change from the bustle and dense population of nearby D-U-D. The island here widens to a quarter of a mile across, then broadens still further at the end, Laura town.

Laura had been the big town on the atoll until the United States arrived during the war and chose to concentrate development on the D-U-D side. Now it is a very laid-back community. You'll often see people hanging out, enjoying midday barbecues. It is very lush with many banana, taro, and pumpkin patches. There are a number of stands for snacks and drinks. Once the road gets to Laura, it is unpaved for the last mile or so, but it is still easily passable by any car or bike. The road splits to a lagoonside road and one on the oceanside. The lagoonside road comes back to meet the oceanside road, so either road leads to the beach at the end of the island.

Just beyond the end of the paved road is the 10-foot-high Japanese **typhoon monument,** which memorializes Emperor Hirohito's assistance to Majuro after a typhoon in 1918.

At the end of the island, you'll come to a beautiful beach and **snorkeling** locale. Admission is $1 for adults, 25 cents per child. It's clean, has both a shower and an outhouse, and is one of the few useable white sand beaches on the island. It is a fairly easy place to snorkel but watch out for tidal movements, particularly as you get closer to the channel. At high tide, the reef begins about 300 feet from shore and can be easily spotted from shore by its darker color amid the turquoise.

Accommodations

Although Majuro is nothing but island, it has no beach resorts in the usual sense of those words, in part because there are so few white sand beaches. Even hotels on the lagoon are usually built behind a seawall, which protects the hotel but makes access to the water difficult. Oceanside hotels also have poor access to the water.

Unless indicated otherwise, rooms have private baths, are air conditioned, will probably have a small refrigerator, and may even have a TV.

Budget hotels in Majuro are not particularly cheap. This does not mean that owners are making a fortune; it is costly to build and maintain even a rudimentary hotel here. You could try the **Ajidrik Hotel** (inexpensive) (P.O. Box E, Majuro, MH 96960, tel. 692-625-3171, fax 692-625-3712), centrally located in Uliga. Its 15 rooms go for $50 s, $56 d. Sitting in the shade of its uncompleted (and probably never to be completed) three-story monolith are some older units of the **Eastern Gateway Hotel** (moderate) (P.O. Box 106, Majuro, MH 96960, tel. 692-625-3337). These units have the forlorn look of being in a permanent construction zone. They are located on a nice lagoonfront beach in Delap, a couple of miles south of the business center, but opposite the *Nitijela*. The rooms are $55 s, $67 d. Use these two hotels only if necessary.

Only slightly more expensive is the **Hotel Marshall Islands** (moderate) (P.O. Box 14, Majuro, M.H. 96960, tel. 692-625-3000, fax 692-625-3136), opened in 1995. The hotel is adjacent to the venerable Marshall Islands Club, one of the best bars on the island. The hotel bills itself as "Oceanside Splendor, Booze in the Blender." Rooms are $65 s, $80 d. Particularly on weekends, noise can float up from the adjacent bar, so request a room toward the back of the hotel. The hotel also has a small outer-lagoon islet facility on Kidanen Island, complete with kayaks.

The newest hotel in Majuro, and the one with the most amenities, is the upscale **Outrigger Marshall Islands Resort** (expensive) (P.O. Box 3279, Majuro, MH 96960, tel. 692-625-2525, fax 692-625-2500). From within the United States, reservations can also be made by calling (800) 688-7444. This 150-room hotel is located on the lagoon, not far from the government buildings. The hotel was built by the government to accommodate visitors to the 1996 South Pacific Forum. Now run by the Outrigger chain, it is too large for Majuro's present needs—the two most distant wings are usually left vacant. It is the only hotel on Majuro with a swimming pool (saltwater) and exercise room. Rooms start at $125, with commercial travelers being offered rates as low as $75. Its restaurant, **Enra** (meaning breadbasket), is the most elegant on the island, sensibly stressing local food.

Older, but more interesting, is the recently refurbished **Hotel Robert Reimers** (P.O. Box 1, Majuro, MH 96960, tel. 692-625-5131, fax 692-625-3783) known to everyone on Majuro as the RRE Hotel. The main part of the hotel is on the second floor, above the Ace hardware store, in the center of Uliga. It has 12 units with lanais overlooking the lagoon (our favorite units) at $95. It also has 10 downstairs rooms and five windowless upstairs rooms for $75. The hotel has three new lagoonfront suites, with bedroom and living room for $225, as well as new single-room beach units that cost $125. These oceanfront units are built with traditional high thatched roofs but are air conditioned. RRE is conveniently located for business in Majuro. Its restaurant, the Tide Table, serves breakfast, lunch, and dinner. Go up to the bar at happy hour, 5 p.m. It is easy to meet local government officials, expats, or visiting businesspeople. Any visiting tuna boat captain or outer island teacher volunteer will probably pass through; it's a great place to meet the quirky adventurers who have chosen such lives. RRE is also the best place in town from which to arrange fishing or diving trips.

Less lively, but an acceptable choice, is **Royal Garden Hotel** (moderate) (P.O. Box 735, Majuro, MH 96960, tel. 692-247-3701, fax 692-247-3705), on the ocean, a couple of miles west of the Majuro Bridge. The 24 rooms rent for $75 s, $85 d. It's located on a stretch of ocean that offers good reef walking at low tide, but not really any swimming. It's in clean, pleasant surroundings and has a restaurant with a beautiful ocean view. You'll probably want a car if you stay here.

For a longer stay on Majuro, call Brian and Nancy Vander Velde of the **Garden Apartments** (P.O. Box 1603, Majuro, MH 96960, tel./fax 692-625-3811). They rent apartments in Rita, prices starting at $350/month or $150/week.

Food

Majuro has a good choice of restaurants, at varying price ranges. **Kitco's "Kool Korner" Restaurant,** near the Ajidrik Hotel, serves dishes like hotcakes and eggs ($2) and fried chicken with chips ($3). **The Deli,** between Robert Reimers Enterprises and the post office, sells takeaway breakfast foods, sandwiches, and Chinese dishes that can be eaten at their sidewalk picnic table area. Thursday and Friday at noon the Deli sets up a barbecue that serves up some of the best food in town: a chicken or beef teriyaki plate with a soda is about $5.

The **Tide Table Restaurant** at the RRE Hotel, is a good choice for a nice dinner out. Dinner with a couple of beers will cost less than $20. Try the seared blackened ahi, very rare inside, in spicy mustard sauce.

A bit more expensive for dinner is the **Enra,** at the Outrigger Marshall Islands Resort. The spacious dining room has a view over the lagoon. The Enra has begun to stress the use of local produce when possible. Lunches are less expensive (about $7 for the entree) and feature sashimi and marinated fish dishes.

The **Skyline Restaurant** in Rita and the **FAB** in Delap, both owned by Prianga Fernando, an immigrant electrical engineer from Sri Lanka, offer the same menu, featuring local, Chinese, and American dishes as well as curries from his homeland. Huge portions are reasonably priced, most $4-5. Beer is served.

The **Royal Garden Hotel** serves meat and seafood. The food is not exceptional and the dinner bill will run $8 to $10. Lunch is cheaper with burgers at about $3.

Savannah's near Gibson's (in the old Quik Stop Coffee Shop building) is the restaurant of Al Wong, former manager of the Tide Table. The fish dishes are best, and main courses will run about $10. There is a bar in the back room that usually has music Friday and Saturday nights at 8 p.m.

Japanese Flavor Garden Restaurant, open for lunch and dinner, is located near the Royal Garden Hotel one mile west of the Majuro Bridge. It serves reasonably priced meals (primarily Japanese, but also hamburgers), which you may carry back into their lagoonside garden and eat at the covered picnic tables. It's a good place to stop if you're driving. The restaurant is called the "Stone House" by locals because of all the coral used in construction.

Blue Lagoon, offers local takeaway foods, ready-made for picnics. It is located about one mile from the airport, heading toward D-U-D.

Located in the building next to the Air Marshall Islands office, **Lanai Bar and Oriental Restaurant** (Lanai Club) offers mediocre but filling Chinese rice plate lunches for $5. It has views out to the lagoon. Food is cooked outside and can be eaten there or inside the air-conditioned restaurant.

Recently opened in Majuro are three additional Chinese restaurants. Just south of the Eastern Gateway Hotel is **Hong Kong Restaurant.** The **Canton Restaurant** and **Yue Yuan** are both near RRE, but on the ocean side of the road. The prices (dishes start at about $6) and quality of the three seem similar. They all will sell take-away and are open for American-style breakfasts as well.

Food is served at the expanded **Majuro Bowl.** In Uliga, **Yoon's** restaurant and bakery specializes in Korean food. One can also order pizza and other food as well as eat on the oceanside terrace of the small **Chit Chat Cafe** located next to the Marshall Islands Club. It is the only restaurant in Majuro that stays open till 2 a.m.

Tipping is expected at American-style restaurants, such as the Tide Table and Enra, but not in the Marshallese restaurants.

Entertainment

Majuro has two great bars, the Tide Table at the RRE Hotel, which is *the* place to meet other travelers, and the Marshall Islands Club. The **Tide Table** has a great view out over the lagoon and serves a fine local beer on tap. There is frequently a live band on Tuesday and Saturday nights.

Nearby, but on the ocean side of the island, is the **Marshall Islands Club,** also with its own local tap beer. Cool breezes blow in from the ocean when, as usual, the storm shutters are up. It is a big barn of a place, with pool tables, shuffleboard, a classic bar, and music blaring from large speakers. It is the perfect vision of a tropical bar. It is a proven fact that if you sit at a table alone, with a pen and paper, you will instantly become a writer. It is that type of place.

The white sand beach curved into the distance, a cruel reminder that I am no more a coconut than a leaf of spinach is a can of sardines.

The Marshall Islands Club often serves free *pupus* (snacks) during happy hour. Order a pizza or try their $2 snacks anytime: sashimi, fried fish pieces, chicken wings, nachos, or giant-clam meat. A live band plays after 10 p.m. certain nights ($3 cover), as advertised on signs at the door.

Other drinking spots include **Charley's Tavern,** next to Kitco's Restaurant, a cocktail lounge that is retro without trying (live music Mon.-Sat.), with free *pupus* 5-7 p.m.; the **Lanai Club,** on Delap's Small Island (karaoke at 7:30 Wednesday nights); **The Pub,** near the new dock in Delap; and the lounge above the **Majuro Bowl.** All are bars that have music late on weekend nights. The Pub is a favorite late-night dancing spot for the younger crowd.

Most bars on Majuro have a happy hour, with reduced prices weekdays from 5 to 6:30 p.m. On weekend nights, the streets are active and the discos start hopping around 11 p.m. Most bars are closed on Sunday.

There is a three-screen movie house in the Gibson's complex, and the **Majuro Bowl** in Uliga.

Sports and Recreation

Majuro is a good place to go diving: the underwater attractions beat the above-water sights fins down. The lagoon offers coral pinnacles, abundant sea life including sea turtles and reef sharks, and there are fine walls, channels, and wrecks to visit. There is even good shore diving. Laura is an exceptionally good place for shore diving or snorkeling. Take special care with ocean currents if you are on the ocean side of the atoll or near a pass.

The United States dumped a large number of jeeps and trucks off Rita as it was leaving the island. Known as the "parking lot," divers can swim to it from land. Because of difficult currents at times in the channel, it is best to visit it only with a local dive professional. There are also oceanside walls to dive at the 25-mile marker and at the 28-mile marker.

The most reliable dive outfit, operating out of the RRE Hotel, is the **Marshall Dive Adventures** (P.O. Box 1, Majuro, MH 96960, tel. 692-625-3250, fax 692-625-3505). MDA charges $90 for a two-tank dive, $110 to dive neighboring Arno atoll. They will take snorkelers for considerably less. MDA also dives Mili Atoll, with divers able to stay at RRE's small eco-facility on Wau island. MDA also is the sole diving company to dive Bikini atoll. Diving, room, and board (but not airfare) runs $2,750, plus $1,000 more to fish each day.

There are also small, independent dive operators on Majuro. Before using one it's a good idea to verify its reliability with local sources. You might check with the Visitors Authority.

The Marshalls are a great place to fish. There are few, if any, places on earth with a greater variety of game fish: blue marlin, mahimahi, sailfish, tuna, and wahoo. Charter boats for deepsea fishing can be arranged directly, for example, through the RRE Hotel ($400 half day, $600 full day). However, the **Marshall Charter Boat Association** (P.O. Box 244, Majuro, MH 96960, tel. 692-625-3478, fax 692-625-3017, e-mail: piimaj@ntamar.com) can get you in touch with any of its members, who collectively have 10 charter boats of varying size. One of the biggest events on Majuro is the annual **Billfish Tournament** during the first weekend in July.

Shopping

The largest department stores and supermarkets are **Robert Reimers Enterprises (RRE)** in Uliga, the **Long Island Grocery Store,** and **Gibson's Department Store** in Delap. A four percent government sales tax is added to all sticker prices.

The best spot for purchasing traditional handicrafts is the **Marshalls Handicraft Shop** (open weekdays; P.O. Box 44, Majuro, MH 96960, tel. 692-625-3566), just behind the Alele Museum. It has a great selection of baskets, fans, coasters, mats, Kili bags, wall hangings, stick charts, and model canoes at reasonable prices. It will mail purchases for you. Another nonprofit crafts outfit, run by Youth to Youth in Health, is **Jenok to Jenkwad** (P.O. Box 3149, Majuro, MH 96960, tel. 692-625-8326, fax 692-625-5449), located on the main road just north of the College of the Marshall Islands. It specializes in customizing crafts, such as for corporate promotions.

Crafts are also sold at the **Busy Hands Club,** next to the Catholic church, and at the RRE Hotel.

Services

The **Bank of Guam** (tel. 692-625-3322) and the **Bank of Marshall Islands** (tel. 692-625-3636) have branches opposite one another near Robert Reimers Enterprises in Uliga. The **Bank of Hawaii** (tel. 692-625-3741) is at the Gibson's complex in Delap. The banks are open weekdays 10 am.-3 p.m., Friday till 6 p.m.

The downtown post office next to the RRE complex in Uliga has Marshallese stamps and first day covers (open weekdays 8 a.m.-noon and 1-4 p.m., Saturday 8-11 a.m.). There's a branch post office at Gibson's in Delap.

Calls to the U.S. are $2 a minute, station to station, to Guam $3 a minute, to Europe $5 a minute. There's a three-minute minimum to Europe.

To place radio telephone calls to the outer islands, go to radio station KUP65 near Marshall Islands High School in Rita. They're open 24 hours a day and the charge is 50 cents a minute.

Health

The **Majuro Hospital** (tel. 692-625-3399) in Delap provides X-ray, laboratory, emergency, outpatient, and inpatient services. Avoid going there if at all possible. There's a pharmacy at the hospital.

D-U-D tap water is unsafe to drink unless boiled or treated. You can, however, buy bottled water at any market.

Getting Around

Swarms of shared taxis prowl up and down Lagoon Drive in D-U-D, 50 cents to $1 pp a ride within town, depending on the distance. Flag one down anywhere, though the taxis are often full. They run until midnight, sometimes later on the weekend. Cruising buses charge 25 cents a ride within D-U-D. The price of a taxi to Laura must be negotiated in advance, but should be about $15 each way.

Blue and white minibuses run four times a day between D-U-D and Laura ($1.50 pp one-way), but there is no service on Sunday. Look for them in the parking lot in front of the RRE Hotel in Uliga; the stop is marked with a sign reading Bus Parking Only.

Small cars rent for $45-50 a day (extra for insurance) at **DAR Sales and Service** (P.O. Box 153, Majuro, MH 96960, tel. 692-625-3174) behind Robert Reimers Enterprises and at the airport. **RRE Hotel** (tel. 692-625-5131, fax 692-625-3783) in Uliga also rents cars, as well as **Deluxe Rent-a-Car** (tel. 692-625-3665) opposite the Pub in Delap.

Foreign driver's licenses are accepted for one month. At most agencies you must be at least 25 years old to rent a car. The excellent taxi service and limited roads make renting a car optional. One possibility is to rent a car just for one day, to drive to Laura.

OFFICIAL FIRST DAY COVER

Undersea Glory

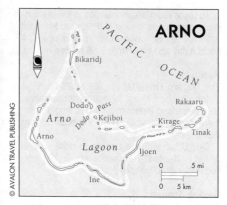

ARNO

PACIFIC OCEAN

Bikaridj

Dodo Pass
Arno
Dodo
Kejiboi
Arno

Rakaaru
Kirage
Tinak

Lagoon
Ijoen

Ine

0   5 mi
0   5 km

© AVALON TRAVEL PUBLISHING

ARNO

You can see Arno, one of the five most populous atolls in the Marshalls, as a thin line along the horizon east of D-U-D; small outboard motorboats often journey between the old dock on Majuro and Arno ($10). If you have to arrange to go with a sportfishing, diving or snorkeling boat, the trip will be much more expensive. In either case, keep the tides in mind because Arno is not accessible by boat at low tide. Both Ine and Tinak Islands have airstrips, with flights from nearby Majuro about once a week—the easiest way to escape city life. RRE has several rooms for rent on Arno for $50 per night. To make arrangements, call RRE in Majuro at (692) 625-5131.

More than a hundred islets sit on Arno's peculiarly shaped barrier reef, which twists around three lagoons! The beautiful beaches and quiet communities make a visit worthwhile. Arno lobsters are famous. With persistence, you can visit the oyster and clam farm on Enerik Island. Black pearls are harvested here. A Japanese fishing project functions on Arno, with local fishermen using small boats to supply a cold storage facility.

MILI

On Mili-Mili, the major island on Mili Atoll, you will soon discover that the tourist is the main attraction. You will probably be the only one on the island and you will be fussed over, particularly by the school-age children who will want to practice their (limited) English with you. Mili-Mili is the picture-perfect atoll, from coconut palms to white sand beaches.

After Kwajalein, Mili, 93 miles south of Majuro, is the largest atoll in land area in the Marshalls. During the war, Mili was the only place in which there was a revolt by concerted action of Micronesians and Korean and Okinawan forced labor crews. The revolt was brutally suppressed. Recent burial finds make clear that the Japanese retaliated with mass executions, including of children and noncombative women.

There are Air Marshall Islands (AMI) flights from Majuro ($56 one way) twice a week. A speedboat also arrives every two weeks ($5). Camping is no problem, but food supplies on Mili are very limited so it's best to bring your own. Take care with the drinking water.

The plane to Mili, a 19-seater Dornier 228, lands in a narrow slot through a thicket of breadfruit, coconut palms, and pandanus. Prevailing winds are off the lagoon. Since the plane lands into the wind, it usually lands facing the lagoon and close to it. It will seem that half the island greets your plane. There are only a few vehicles on the whole island, but they will be out to meet the plane to see if you need help with your luggage. Toward your right are four thatched huts on the beach, run by Neija Daniel, who also has a small store next door. The huts rent for $28 a night. This is a great opportunity to see, from the inside, the ingenious design of traditional Marshallese house construction. Cooling breezes come in when you lift the thatched window coverings. Running water is outside and toilet facilities are in an outhouse. Marshall Dive Adventures on Majuro, tel. (692) 625-3250, may be able to line up a stay in advance.

When the lagoon is still, often the case during summer, there is wonderful snorkeling off to the right of the cottages as you face the beach. When the wind has been blowing, you can actually get a small, sloppy, but makeable wave in the lagoon.

Mili has many Japanese war relics, including submerged wrecks for diving enthusiasts. On land, wrecked Zeros, bunkers, and large guns—are scattered in the bush and difficult to find. It is best to use a guide. You might try Emos Kimej, who lives in a two-story structure just on the other side of the airplane slot from the cottages. He is

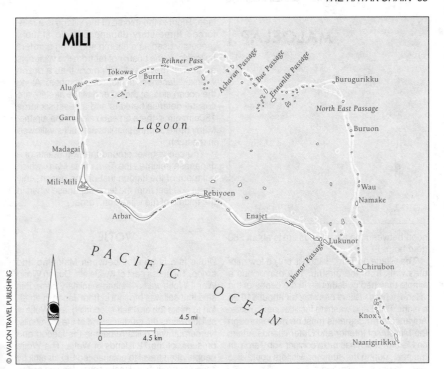

old enough to tell you about life under Japanese rule and the coming of the American forces.

Take a walk down Main Street parallel to the lagoon. Most life on Mili-Mili is on the lagoon, not the ocean. Main Street is a wide dirt lane with virtually no traffic. Past the schoolhouse, you'll see an old Japanese bunker. The remains of Japanese roads and runways are visible everywhere. Today grass grows up through them: the island itself is defeating the material remains of Japanese Imperial rule.

RRE Hotel (tel. 692-625-5131) runs an interesting, small eco-resort on privately owned **Wau Island,** on the opposite side of the lagoon from Mili-Mili. Most visitors are divers and six at a time can be accommodated. You will fly into Mili-Mili, where you will be met by the dive boat and taken on a wreck dive. Depending on the weather, the boat will then take you to Wau across the lagoon or outside, on the ocean. There are three cabins for guests on Wau; all

are simple, basic, and clean, with indoor toilets and running water most of the time. If you come in a group for diving, meals will be prepared for you. If you are traveling alone, bring your own food. The charge is $50 per night.

At Wau you will be taken on drift dives to see turtles, stingrays and other large fish. RRE also runs a giant clam farm on Wau. You can reach the giant clams by snorkeling from shore. They are incredibly beautiful creatures, with enormous variations in the color and patterns of their mantels. Many have a brilliant luminescence.

MALOELAP

Maloelap atoll, 106 miles north of Majuro, has the largest lagoon in the Ratak Chain, with 71 islands on the reef. AMI flies from Majuro to Taroa twice a week, to Kaven every other week. Chartering a speedboat for the ride across the la-

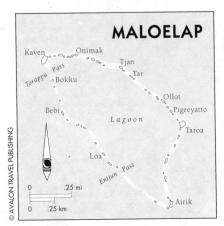

MALOELAP

Kaven, Onimak
Torappu Pass, Bokku
Tjan
Tar
Ollot
Bebi, *Lagoon*
Pigeeyatto
Taroa
Loa
Enijun Pass
Airik

0 .25 mi
0 .25 km

© AVALON TRAVEL PUBLISHING

lage. Right in the middle of the village is a reinforced three-story Japanese radio station, presently used as a church and living quarters by locals. In the bush, not far from the village, is an aircraft graveyard, with more than a dozen wrecked Japanese fighters and bombers. Along the ocean side, at the far end of the airstrip, are coastal defense bunkers and at least six large 150mm guns, three on each side of the airstrip. Many more Japanese ruins are half swallowed in the bush.

You can snorkel around the twin masts of a Japanese freighter, the *Toroshima Maru,* which poke out of the lagoon just off the beach, only about 300 feet from the large Japanese wharf in the middle of the village on Taroa.

goon between the two islands costs about $60 (four hours).

The village on Taroa Island is only a few minutes walk from the airstrip. The mayor has a simple thatched guesthouse in the center of the village, where visitors can stay for about $10 pp a night. Toilet and washing facilities are outside. Advance arrangements must be made through the Ministry of Interior and Outer Islands Affairs on Majuro, which has radio contact with Taroa. In the past, during the summer, visitors could also sleep in empty classrooms.

In 1941, Maloelap became the easternmost Japanese bastion in the Pacific, but on 29 January 1944 a United States air strike from the carrier *Enterprise* against the X-shaped runways on Taroa terminated Maloelap's role as a fortified base. The United States forces never bothered to land on neutralized Maloelap. About two-thirds of the 3,000 Japanese stationed on Maloelap died in the original and subsequent air strikes or from starvation, as they were marooned on an island that could not support them.

Today numerous Japanese guns, bunkers, bombs, and large concrete buildings are hidden in the thick undergrowth of Taroa. Two Zero aircraft lie beside the airstrip. A large concrete Japanese power plant, its rusted generators still inside, sits between the airstrip and the vil-

WOTJE

Wotje is a large atoll between Maloelap and Likiep, 150 miles east of Kwajalein. During World War II Wotje was a Japanese military base. It is said that soil was brought in from Japan in an effort to make the atoll self-supporting, and Wotje is still known as the garden island of the Marshalls. Numerous war relics remain in the lagoon and on some of the 72 islands of Wotje. The Wotje people often travel to uninhabited Erikub atoll by speedboat to fish and make copra. Plan on camping or staying with locals if you visit.

LIKIEP

Likiep is another sizable atoll, with 65 islands arranged around its shallow lagoon. About a century ago, a German named Adolph Capelle and a Portuguese named Anton deBrum bought Likiep from the chief; their descendants still jointly own the atoll. The deBrum mansion, former headquarters of Likiep's coconut plantation, has been restored with support from the Endowment for Historic Preservation of the Micronesia Institute, Washington, D.C. Thousands of glass plate photos taken by Joachim deBrum are kept at the Alele Museum on Majuro.

THE RALIK CHAIN

KWAJALEIN ATOLL

Kwajalein atoll, 274 miles from Majuro, is the world's largest atoll. Its 176-mile-long coral reef encloses a boomerang-shaped lagoon of 840 square miles. This atoll is a tale of two islands. Kwajalein Island, known as Kwaj, is home to the United States Army's Missile Range. Ebeye, a mere three miles away, is home to more than 12,000 Marshallese, more than 1,000 of whom work on the base. Until 1958 the U.S. Navy used Kwajalein as the main support facility for its nuclear testing program on Enewetok and Bikini.

When the 1963 Limited Test Ban Treaty drove nuclear testing underground, the base on Kwajalein Island was converted to testing the accuracy of missile systems. In 1964 control of the atoll passed from the navy to the army, which set up the Kwajalein Missile Range now officially called USAKA (United States Army Kwajalein Atoll). For many years, the central two-thirds of

the lagoon was closed to small crafts since it was used as a target for intercontinental ballistic missiles fired from California. Missiles aimed at Kwajalein were often themselves used as targets for antiballistic missiles. Since such tests are now quite infrequent, the entire lagoon is usually open for diving or fishing boats. Kwajalein is still an essential element in the Pacific Barrier radar system, which detects and tracks orbiting satellites, but in the late 1990s, like other U.S. military establishments, it was somewhat scaled back.

The compensation of landowners for the base has been a bone of contention. A 1969 "sail-in" reoccupation of the test zone by 200 islanders won enhanced recognition of their rights. During a second sail-in in 1979, landowners occupied missile range facilities on Kwajalein and Roi-Namur, a smaller base on the north end of the atoll. As a result, the United States dramatically increased lease payments. Nonetheless, in 1982 more than 1,000 Marshallese launched Operation Home-

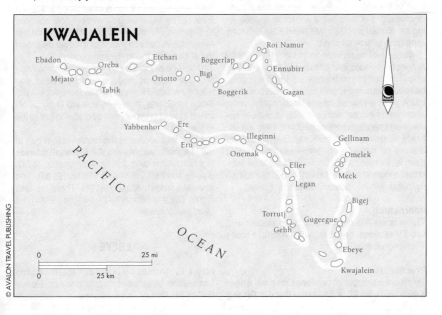

KWAJALEIN

Ebadon
Oreba
Etchari
Boggerlap
Roi Namur
Mejato
Oriotto
Bigi
Ennubirr
Tabik
Boggerik
Gagan

Yabbenhor
Ere
Eru
Illeginni
Gellinam
Onemak
Omelek
Eller
Meck
Legan

Bigej
Torrutj
Gugeegue
Gehh
Ebeye
Kwajalein

PACIFIC

OCEAN

0   25 mi
0   25 km

coming, reoccupying 11 islands inside the security zone, where they camped for four months.

Under the 1986 Compact of Free Association, $11 million a year "rent" was to be paid for the military use of Kwajalein atoll for 30 years. However, it was unclear to whom the payments should be made. Monies had at first been distributed on a per capita basis. Today $7 million is distributed to senior landowners in proportion to their rank under the traditional system. These senior landowners theoretically held land for the benefit of all Marshallese, but since no mechanisms are in place to require fair distribution, often hundreds of thousands of dollars a year are used for nothing other than personal gain. The other $4 million a year goes to the Kwajalein Atoll Development Authority (KADA).

About 3,000 Americans live on **Kwajalein Island,** primarily employees of private American corporations doing research for the Defense Department. It is difficult to get advance permission to stay on the base unless you have business there or are visiting someone. If you ask the stateside Army for permission, it will be denied with bureaucratic excuses. But if you are staying on nearby Ebeye, it is relatively easy to take a boat to Kwajalein and walk around the nonrestricted areas of the base. If you know anyone living on Kwajalein, they will have little difficulty arranging overnight stays.

Kwaj has the reputation of being a wealthy American suburb lost in the middle of the Pacific Ocean. It is true there are swimming pools, baseball diamonds, and other amenities. The military did an excellent job landscaping; most apartments are set within stands of mature coconut and pandanus trees. Best yet, there are virtually no private cars on Kwaj. Everyone gets around on funky, rusty one-speed bikes. But Kwaj is not particularly opulent. Its upscale suburban reputation comes mainly from its proximity to the grinding poverty of nearby Ebeye.

Information
There is an AM and an FM radio station and two TV stations, one run by the Armed Forces Television Network.

Practicalities
There are a number of cafeterias on Kwaj where a meal will cost $3 or $4. At the **Pacific Dining Room** a cafeteria-style lunch buffet costs $5; the salads are safe to eat.

Kwaj Lodge is the only hotel on the island. Rooms for government travelers are $35 or less and for others $49 or less. There are 12 private rooms, 24 semi-private. Reservations *must* be made by your "personal point of contact" on the island. The Lodge can also arrange rooms in bachelor quarters for as little as $5 per night.

Getting There
Continental Airlines flights between Majuro and Kosrae touch down on Kwajalein. Ebeye does not have its own airport, and people going to Ebeye must also deplane here. If you are deplaning, your luggage is lined up by American authorities and sniffed by drug detecting dogs. The search holds up passengers for almost an hour, quite an inconvenience. Afterward, passengers proceeding to Ebeye are referred to Marshall Islands Immigration. After clearance, they're bused to a lagoonside wharf and sent on by free ferry.

In the past, to visit Ebeye one had to obtain an "Entry into Ebeye" permit from the Immigration office in the *Nitijela* building in Delap on Majuro. The permit was issued automatically if you had hotel reservations or some other place to stay on Ebeye. The Marshall government now appears to dispense with this requirement for American or Marshallese passengers, but it would be safest to confirm with the Immigration office.

If you have neither an American nor a Marshallese passport, and are going to Ebeye, you will be escorted from airport to ferry dock. With those passports, however, you will likely be allowed to walk on your own, and able to get to the restaurants.

Kwajalein serves as the northwestern hub of the Marshalls, with weekly **Air Marshall Islands** flights to Airok and Jeh on Ailinglaplap ($74), weekly to Ujai ($183) and Wotho ($190), and several a week to Majuro ($125). There are also flights twice a month to Enewetok ($154); all fares are one way.

EBEYE

About 10 minutes by boat from the Kwajalein base is the Marshallese community on Ebeye (EE-bye). Though on a tropical atoll island, it

children on Ebeye

people, one-fifth of the population of the Marshall Islands, live there now. After a disastrous storm in 1988, and with United States aid, the "reconstruction" of Ebeye began. Water and electricity were connected to most dwellings. The main streets were paved, and a combination power/desalination plant was built. But today the power plant is no longer reliable and the desal unit is barely functioning. During the El Niño drought of 1997-98, the U.S. Army brought water in on barges.

A small number of new residences have been built, but most homes remain plywood shacks piled on each other. When a visitor remarks on the conditions of poverty, he or she is immediately told how much better things are since the reconstruction.

More than 1,000 Ebeye workers commute by boat to work on Kwaj. Due to the lack of other sources of employment in the Marshalls, and despite living conditions on Ebeye, its population continues to grow as Marshallese from other atolls arrive looking for jobs on the base or support from relatives already established here.

Ferries run by the United States Army leave Ebeye to Kwaj about every half hour 5:30-8:30 a.m. and return on a similarly timed schedule in the afternoon.

has the harsh, parched look of a Sonoran desert barrio that was picked up and dropped here so that Kwaj could have a supply of cheap labor. The best reason to visit Ebeye is if one is a truly avid diver.

As you walk the streets of Ebeye, the Marshalls' second-largest town, at dusk, you will be overwhelmed by the number of young children, almost as if a universe had been created containing only nine-year-olds. They sit, they run, they pick nits out of each other's hair. They play ball, often substituting sticks for bats or beach balls for the basketballs they cannot afford. They are poor, charming, and beautiful; they smile easily. I dread the thought of returning in four years to a universe populated solely by adolescents, made sullen by despair.

In 1951 construction of the naval station on Kwajalein Island forced the evacuation of the 450 Marshallese inhabitants to Ebeye, one-tenth the size of Kwajalein. By 1967, 4,500 people were jammed onto Ebeye's 80 acres amid appalling sanitary conditions. More than 12,000

Sights

Visitors can walk around Ebeye in an hour or two. There is little to see other than the people. The nicest time for a walk is dusk. As the sun sinks and the temperature cools, the children come out to play. On the south end of the island is a **beach park** with good snorkeling if you can bear the noise from the island's nearby electrical generator (when it is functioning). The **post office** is about 50 feet south of the Anrohasa Hotel and the **new hospital** is about a quarter mile north of it. In the late afternoon and evening, people fish from the pier serving the boats from Kwaj.

A poorly maintained causeway links Ebeye to a series of smaller islands. The first island, with a bandstand and cabanas, is the private reserve of major landholders; the second island with hydroponically grown vegetables under glass is also privately owned.

Along the second causeway, the lagoon has a spectacular 200-foot wall to dive. It is pretty easy to spot from the causeway. All kinds of great snorkeling spots present themselves. To get here, it is probably best to arrange for a taxi to drop you off and to pick you up. Although taxi rides on Ebeye itself are only 25 cents, you will have to negotiate a price for a ride out to the causeways. There are no services, so bring your own food and water.

The next island has some nice FEMA-built housing. On the lagoon side of the island, near the housing, is a well-preserved Japanese war relic, an armored personnel carrier. The causeway ends five miles from Ebeye.

Ebeye presents other opportunities for diving and snorkeling. There are some beautiful coral pinnacles, which can be seen while snorkeling. Divers can visit the 600-foot wreck of the *Prinz Eugen,* a pocket battleship that had been a companion ship to the infamous *Bismarck.* Its bow lies at 200 feet and its stern protrudes above the water. Arrangements for diving should be made with the Kwajalein Atoll Dive Resort, P.O. Box 5159, Ebeye, Kwajalein, MH 96970, tel. (692) 329-3100, fax (692) 329-3297.

Accommodations

Be certain to make advance hotel reservations on Ebeye, as there are only two hotels. There is usually a vacancy, but there are *no* alternatives, not even a bus station or an airport in which to spend the night. The island is too crowded to find a place to pitch a tent. The **Anrohasa Hotel** (expensive) (P.O. Box 5039, Ebeye, Kwajalein, MH 96970, tel. 692-329-3161, fax 692-329-3248) should probably be your first choice. Located by the lagoon, just south of the ferry landing, it has 24 rooms, 18 in a new wing. All rooms are air conditioned, with private baths. Rates for rooms begin at $87, the cheapest rooms being in the old wing. The hotel has two rooms with cooking facilities and two suites for $150 each. There's a bar, restaurant, and laundromat on the premises.

The hotel discounts commercial travelers 10% but charges four to six percent for use of a credit card to pay the bill. Have traveler's checks ready.

At the south end of Ebeye is the **DSC Hotel** (inexpensive) (P.O. Box 5097, Ebeye, Kwajalein, MH 96970, tel. 692-329-3194, fax 692-329-3310), run by Immigration officer Rudy Paul. The seven air-conditioned rooms with private facilities are $57, $47 per night for stays of four

nights or more. The rooms are on the third floor (no elevator) above the DSC grocery store.

Food

There are really only two acceptable restaurants on Ebeye. **Bob's Island Restaurant,** overlooking the ferry pier, is a local favorite. It serves breakfast ($3-4), lunch, and dinner (main course $7-10). Barbecue is their specialty and it's very good. The pleasant dining room overlooks the lagoon as does an outside patio. Bob's has a full bar; the clientele includes both locals and visitors from Kwaj.

Anrohasa Restaurant is also worth a visit but beware of the TV—always on and blaring. Try the sweet bread from their bakery for breakfast. The menu is mainly Chinese and mediocre, but a number of local dishes such as *"U"*—a coconut porridge—are served. No booze is served in the restaurant, though the hotel has a separate bar.

Entertainment

Mon La Mike is a nightclub that opens on the weekend at about 11 p.m. Admission for women is free; men pay $10. It can get rowdy as patrons get increasingly drunk, so it is probably best to leave by 1 a.m.

Services

To make overseas calls on Ebeye, go to the NTA office on the south end of the island. It is open 24 hours a day and can accept a modem. Both the Bank of Guam and the Bank of Marshall Islands operate branches on Ebeye.

JALUIT ATOLL

The Germans set up a trading post on Jaluit in 1878, and when the Marshalls became a colony in 1885, the Germans headquartered here. In 1914 Jaluit became the Japanese administrative center. Later, the Japanese built an airstrip on nearby Emiej Island and shipped tons of soil from Kosrae and Pohnpei to create vegetable gardens on the island. By 1941 the population of Jabwor village was 3,000. The United States bombed and bypassed the Japanese base on Jaluit during World War II; some war wreckage remains.

JALUIT

Boggenadick
Urbett
Ngain
Lijeron
Rua
Medyado
Northeast Pass
Imrodj
Anbor
Jaluit
Lagoon
Emiej
Pinglap
Southeast Pass
Jabwor
Ali Pass
Elizabeth
Southwest Pass
Jaluit
South Point

0   10 mi
0   10 km

Today bananas and breadfruit are grown; copra, seashells, and handicrafts are exported. There's a public high school in Jabwor at the north end of Jaluit, one of 91 reef islands composing the atoll. Swept channels lead from three passes to lagoon anchorages off Emiej and Jaluit Islands. The dock and petroleum storage facility at Jaluit sports a big Mobil Pegasus sign. Jaluit is accessible twice weekly by air from Majuro ($85 one way), 56 miles northeast.

M.E.C. (Marshalls Energy Company) rents basic rooms for $50. To make arrangements, call their main Majuro office at (692) 625-3507.

AILINGLAPLAP ATOLL

Ailinglaplap, 150 miles west of Majuro, is a large, copra-growing atoll. Several passages provide entry into the lagoon. Phosphate deposits have been located on some of the 56 islands. Traditionally, the high chiefs of the Ralik Chain resided on Ailinglaplap, which is located halfway between Majuro and Kwajalein.

BIKINI ATOLL

From 1946 to 1958, 23 atmospheric nuclear blasts shook Bikini atoll. They left behind a legacy of contamination, cancer, leukemia, thyroid problems, miscarriages, and irreversible genetic damage for those downwind from the blasts. The full effects are not yet known.

For the initial series of tests, a captured Japanese war fleet and several U.S. naval vessels, including the aircraft carrier USS *Saratoga,* were positioned in Bikini lagoon to test the use of atomic weapons against naval forces. On 1 July 1948 "Able" was dropped on 90 ships by a B-29 from Kwajalein. On 25 July an underwater explosion code named "Baker" contaminated the atoll. "Charlie," the third test, was canceled when it became apparent that radiation would endanger U.S. personnel.

In February 1946 American officials had informed the inhabitants of Bikini that their islands were needed temporarily "for the good of mankind and to end all world wars." The 166 Bikinians were taken to uninhabited Rongerik atoll, but in just two years it became apparent that Rongerik lacked the resources to support them, and they had to be evacuated again.

After a few months on Kwajalein, Bikinians were resettled on Kili Island, an isolated dot in the ocean just southwest of Jaluit. Most Bikinians remain there today, even though Kili is quite a step down. Bikini's 36 islands are six times larger than Kili in land area. Kili does not even have a protected lagoon, and fishing is often impossible due to weather conditions. Other Bikinians live on Ejit Island at Majuro.

In the 1960s and 1970s the United States undertook a cleanup of Bikini so that its people could return home. It's now clear that the cleanup was done in a haphazard manner, and the Atomic Energy Commission failed to take sufficient tests before they declared, in 1969, that Bikini was once again safe for habitation. Islanders working in the cleanup process itself suffered significant radiation injuries.

After lawsuits and pleas to American benevolence, a $6 million trust fund was set up by the U.S. government in 1978, and a further $20.6 million placed in a resettlement fund. In 1984 the United States promised to spend $42 million on another cleanup, and in 1988, $90 million was allocated by Congress for a final cleanup. In 1996 scientists convened by the International Atomic Energy Association were saying again that the remaining rehabilitation of the atoll islands would be easy and inexpensive. Decontamination alternatives include flushing sea water through the soil to leach out the contaminants, scraping off the top half yard and replacing it with uncontaminated soil, and applying potassium-rich fertilizer to block the uptake of cesium-137 by plants.

As of the end of 1997, the **Nuclear Claims Tribunal,** funded by the United States, had made total payments of $63 million to 1,549 claimants, victims of atomic radiation.

The Bikini Lagoon did come back to health more quickly than projected. Marshall Dive Adventures currently dives Bikini atoll. In addition to more usual dives, divers may visit the wrecks created by the nuclear tests. Divers can visit the Japanese battleship *Nagato,* the U.S. aircraft carrier *Saratoga* (the world's only divable aircraft carrier), the destroyer *Anderson,* and the submarine *Apogon.*

You can contact MDA or make arrangements through Central Pacific Dive Expeditions. Trips to Bikini last one week. RRE runs a small hotel there. The price for a week's stay, including meals, is $2,750 if you are diving, $3,750 if you wish to try your luck at the atoll's superb fishing. If you do not wish to do either of these activities, a lower charge can be negotiated.

Bikini's local government council has a marvelous website on the nuclear history as well as the current situation on Bikini at: www.bikiniatoll.com.

ENEWETAK ATOLL

Enewetak (Eniwetok) is an almost perfectly circular atoll 20 miles in diameter. In December 1947, officials in Washington announced that it was to be used for nuclear tests, and the 145 inhabitants were immediately moved to Ujelang atoll, with one-quarter the land area and a fifteenth the lagoon area of Enewetak. From 1948 to 1958, 43 nuclear tests rocked Enewetak. On 1 November 1952 the world's first hydrogen ex-

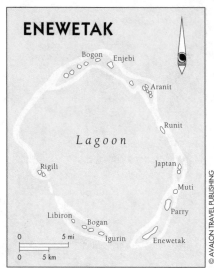

plosion was detonated here, unleashing more explosive force than all the wars of history combined, and completely vaporizing one of the islands of Enewetak; in 1958 another hydrogen device destroyed a second.

In 1976, the United States Congress appropriated funds for a $110 million cleanup operation on Enewetak by the Defense Nuclear Agency. The contaminated waste was scraped off the surface of the atoll and buried in a bomb crater on Runit Island under a gigantic cement dome 18 inches thick. The material will remain a hazard to human life for thousands of years, and there have already been reports that the dome is cracking.

The Department of Energy reports that the southern islands of the atoll are now safe for habitation, but the northern islands will be unsafe for the next 300 years. In 1980, 542 people returned from Ujelang to Japtan Island on Enewetak. Like the people of Bikini, the Enewetakese remain a disrupted community whose future is clouded by uncertainty.

RONGELAP ATOLL

On 1 March 1954, 15 megaton "Bravo," the largest and dirtiest of the hydrogen bombs, was tested on Bikini. This colossal explosion had a force equal to 1,200 Hiroshima bombs, more than twice what its designers expected. The blast sent up a 22-mile-high cloud, which dropped 1.5 inches of fine white dust on Rongelap atoll four to six hours later, turning the water yellow, contaminating the food, and burning the unprepared people standing in the open. Children played in the radioactive material as if it were snow. The United States Navy destroyer *Gypsy,* which had been stationed a mere 19 miles from Rongelap lagoon on the day of the test, quickly sailed off. The population of Rongelap was not evacuated for 48 hours. The evacuees experienced all the symptoms of radiation exposure. At the time United States officials blamed the contamination on an unexpected wind shift, but 27 years later four retired U.S. airmen who had operated the weather station on nearby Rongerik shed new light on the matter. They reported that the test was allowed with full knowledge that for weeks previous, the prevailing wind had been blowing directly at these islands. United States government documents declassified in the mid-1980s confirmed that U.S. officials knew that the wind was blowing toward Rongelap before the Bravo test.

Under an agreement signed in 1996, the United States created a $5 million trust fund to begin work to prepare Rongelap Atoll for resettlement by the Rongelap community, which numbers more than 2,500 people and is now living on Mejatto Island in Kwajelein atoll and elsewhere. The Rongelap victims and their descendants receive about $320 per year and some medical services.

> *I have gone to the ends of the earth,*
> *where innocence is nourished by nuclear waste,*
> *where names are clear, but not their purpose.*
> *How can I explain the smiles of the children,*
> *smiles that go dim when eyes go blind,*
> *smiles that go sullen from blameless poverty.*
> *I have gone to the ends of the earth,*
> *but I can return untouched*
> *if only I can harden my heart.*

GORDON OHLIGER

FEDERATED STATES OF MICRONESIA

INTRODUCTION

The Federated States of Micronesia (FSM) is the largest and most populous (about 105,000 people) political entity to emerge from the Trust Territory of the Pacific Islands. It includes all of the Caroline Islands except for what is now in the Republic of Palau. International flights go to the state capitals: Pohnpei, Kosrae, Chuuk, and Yap. Pohnpei (formerly Ponape) is a lush, volcanic island, with much to entice the hiker and historian. Kosrae, another high island, has better beaches and friendly, easygoing people. Chuuk (formerly Truk) is best known for its spectacular underwater wreck sites. Yap remains a stronghold of traditional Micronesian culture.

Each of these four islands offers some of the conveniences, and some of the drawbacks, of modern Western life. Even on these four main islands, you'll usually encounter a natural, relaxed affability. The outer islands of the country offer the adventuresome a glimpse of a more tradi-

tional way of life, often idyllic and always slow. Most outer islands lack hotels, cars, and electricity. But don't expect to find "happy natives" without knowledge of the world around them— today it's difficult to find anyplace where the young, at least, are totally unfamiliar with Western music or movies.

The Land

The Eastern Caroline Islands include Kosrae, Pohnpei, and Chuuk states, while Yap and the Republic of Palau form the Western Caroline Islands. More than 1,550 miles lie between Kosrae and Yap, yet the FSM totals only 270 square miles in land area, with Pohnpei alone accounting for almost half that land.

This huge island group, named for King Charles II of Spain, includes almost every type of oceanic topography: outer island atolls; high volcanic islands such as Pohnpei and Kosrae; Yap, now a large island of sedimentary rock, but geologically a piece of Asia that drifted away; Fais, a raised atoll; and Chuuk, an atoll to be, with remnants of its volcanic core still poking out of the lagoon. Nearly a thousand smaller coral islands and reefs complete the scene.

The vegetation is also varied. Coconut palms, pandanus, and breadfruit flourish on the low islands. On the high islands, mangrove forests along the coasts are home to salt-resistant plants; inland you'll find coconut groves on the flats, rainforest up the slopes, and ferns or grasslands near the summits. Other than fruit bats, many species of which are endangered, most of the terrestrial fauna was introduced by man. There is a relative lack of land birds, though there are a number of unique species found nowhere else. Numerous shorebirds and seabirds make up for the relatively small number of land birds. Marinelife in the lagoons, on the reefs, and in the open ocean is truly what Micronesia is about.

Climate

Heavy rainfall usually drenches the Carolines, although the quantity decreases as you move west from Pohnpei to Yap. Pohnpei gets measurable rainfall 300 days a year—it's wet January-February and even wetter March-December. At Chuuk the rain falls mostly at night, hardest just before sunrise. The rain often comes in short, heavy downpours, presenting only a temporary inconvenience to travelers, while providing the residents with water for crops, washing, and cooking. Humidity is high year-round.

The northeast trades blow across the Eastern Carolines December-April; southeast winds prevail July-September. Yap gets northeast winds November-May, changing to southwest July-October.

The Western Caroline Islands spawn more tropical typhoons than any other area on earth, an average of 19 a year! September-November is peak typhoon season, and most of the storms move northwest toward Asia. Typhoons rarely occur in the Eastern Caroline Islands. On Pohnpei, near the equator, the sun rises near 6 a.m. and sets just after 6 p.m. every day of the year.

The El Niño worldwide weather pattern in 1997-1998 brought severe drought to the FSM. The prevailing current shifted, dropping Micro-

FSM AT A GLANCE

	POP. (1989)	LAND AREA (SQ. MI.)
State of Kosrae	7,317	42.31
State of Pohnpei	33,700	133.34
Ant	nil	0.73
Kapingamarangi	473	0.50
Mwoakilloa	209	0.46
Ngatik	603	0.66
Nukuoro	349	0.66
Oroluk	nil	0.19
Pakin	nil	0.42
Pingelap	518	0.69
Pohnpei	31,548	129.03
State of Chuuk	53,319	49.18
Chuuk Lagoon	43,712	38.57
East Fayu	nil	0.15
Etal	420	0.73
Houk	346	1.08
Kuop	nil	0.19
Losap	795	0.39
Lukunor	1,279	1.08
Murilo	694	0.50
Nama	897	0.27
Namoluk	310	0.31
Namonuito	994	1.70
Nomwin	624	0.73
Pulap	541	0.39
Pulawat	477	1.31
Satawan	2,230	1.78
State of Yap	11,178	45.72
Eauripik	118	0.08
Elato	121	0.19
Fais	301	1.08
Faraulep	223	0.15
Gaferut	nil	0.04
Ifalik	653	0.39
Lamotrek	385	0.39
Ngulu	38	0.15
Olimarao	nil	0.08
Pikelot	nil	0.04
Satawal	560	0.50
Sorol	nil	0.35
Ulithi	1,016	1.81
West Fayu	nil	0.04
Woleai	844	1.74
Yap	6,919	38.69
TOTAL	**105,514**	**270.55**

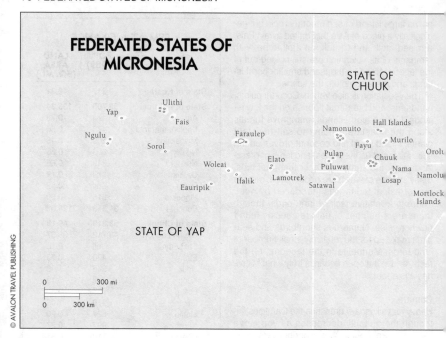

FEDERATED STATES OF MICRONESIA

STATE OF CHUUK

STATE OF YAP

© AVALON TRAVEL PUBLISHING

nesia's usual rain onto California. Particularly hard-hit were the outer atolls, which have no mountains to trap moisture and only the most limited water storage facilities. Many outer islanders moved to their state capital during the drought and needed assistance from the United States Federal Emergency Management Agency (FEMA) to be able to return to their home islands to begin rebuilding agricultural production.

Toward Self-Government
Until 1978 the FSM, along with most of Micronesia, was administered as part of the Trust Territory of the Pacific Islands, a United Nations trusteeship area administered by the United States. Thus the history of the region up to that point must be treated as a whole. In July 1978 a draft FSM constitution was approved by voters in Kosrae, Pohnpei, Chuuk, and Yap. The constitution was defeated in votes in Palau and the Marshalls, which then became separate political entities.

On 1 October 1982, American and FSM negotiators at Honolulu signed the Compact of Free Association, which was approved by the United

States Congress in 1985. Under the terms of this 15-year agreement, the FSM received a total of about $1.3 billion. In exchange, the Compact gave the United States military access to the FSM, while denying such access to other powers.

The Compact payments expire in 2001. Negotiations will begin in 1999 for a new Compact. But with the Cold War over, it is unclear whether the United States will wish to continue payments at or near the original level.

Government
The FSM constitution went into effect on 10 May 1979—now celebrated as Constitution Day. Under it, each of the four states has a locally elected governor and legislature, while the central government meets at Palikir on Pohnpei. The 14-member National Congress of FSM includes one member-at-large elected from each state for a four-year term. The president and vice president are chosen by the Congress from among these at-large members. Thus, they cannot be from the same state. The other 10 members serve two-year terms, apportioned accord-

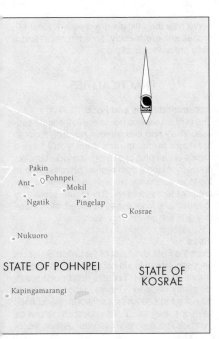

Pakin

Ant○ ○Pohnpei
           ○Mokil
   Ngatik   Pingelap
                    ○Kosrae

○Nukuoro

STATE OF POHNPEI

STATE OF KOSRAE

○Kapingamarangi

ing to population: Chuuk, five members; Pohnpei, three; Kosrae, one; and Yap, one. There are no political parties. The national government has primacy over state governments. In Chuuk, Pohnpei, and Yap states, the role of traditional chiefs is recognized by the state constitutions.

Economy
Payments under the Compact have supported the FSM's standard of living and maintained its balance of trade, since imports dwarf exports. The payments are made to the government, which consequently is bloated, employing two-thirds of the workforce. Employment is often based more on politics than on governmental need. Compact payments far surpass local taxes, though revenue also comes in through fishing licenses and tourism. FSM's main exports are tuna and copra, but most tuna fishing in the FSM's 200-nautical-mile Exclusive Economic Zone is carried on by foreign boats using foreign crews.

There are few private businesses other than retail outlets, which sell consumer goods, and a few service industries, such as tourism. Under the Compact, textiles manufactured in the FSM may be imported into the United States free of quotas. One Taiwanese company set up a factory on Yap in to take advantage of this. The company's entire workforce, however, remains foreign. Recently, a garment plant was built on Pohnpei.

Most food and almost all elements of modern life are imported. Outside the towns, reef fishing and subsistence agriculture do continue. Tourism is being encouraged—wisely, slowly. There's no rush to jump on the Guam/Saipan bandwagon. Instead smaller, locally controlled developments are going ahead. Land can only be leased (not purchased) by outsiders, and new businesses must have 51% local ownership. In 1990 Pohnpei received 9,534 visitors, Chuuk 7,654, and Yap 3,984, nearly half of them from the United States and another quarter from Japan.

In the late 1990s, the downturn in the Asian economies cut deeply into the tourism of all Pacific Island nations. At the same time, with the Cold War over, Western countries felt less political motivation to help sustain the economies of the isolated Pacific Island nations. The leaders of Micronesia, as well as those of the United States, speak of the necessity of the Freely Associated States (FSM, Palau and the Marshall Islands) developing "sustainable" economies. But the small populations and geographic isolation of these nations may make it impossible for them to compete effectively in the world market. Thus, if the United States thinks it is in its interest not to allow a power vacuum to occur in the mid-Pacific, it may find itself needing to reach a new Compact with the Federated States that includes significant new payments. A precipitous drop in payments would devastate the economy of the FSM and probably cause further out-migration. Currently about 15% of FSM's citizens live off-island, with large communities in Honolulu, Guam, and California.

The People
Ethnically, the Federated States' population is overwhelmingly Micronesian, with several thousand Polynesians on two outlying atolls in Pohnpei State and in Kolonia. There are small but significant American and Asian expat communities on the major islands. About a third of the population lives in urban or semi-urban areas. Eight different languages are spoken in the FSM: Chuukese,

Kosraean, Kapingamarangi, Nukuoran, Pohnpeian, Ulithian, Woleaian, and Yapese. Many are totally dissimilar, making English the common language for interisland communications. Traditionally, most of the societies have been matrilineal, although the influence of missionaries has created a patrilineal system on Kosrae. The Polynesian islands of Kapingamarangi and Nukuoro have always been patrilineal.

Most Yapese are Catholic, most Kosraeans Protestant. Pohnpei and Chuuk are split between Catholics and Protestants, with Chuuk leaning toward Catholicism. Nearly half the population is under 15. Birthrate continues to be astoundingly high and is offset by continued out-migration. The life expectancy is 58-59 for men, 62-64 for women. The suicide rate among young Micronesian males ages 15-24 is high. FSM citizens have unrestricted entry rights to the United States, though Guam is attempting to limit access.

Holidays and Events
Holidays include: New Year's Day (1 January), President's Day (third Monday in February), Traditional Culture Day (31 March), FSM Constitution Day (10 May), Micronesian Day (12 July), United Nations Day (24 October), FSM Independence Day (first Friday in November), and Christmas Day (25 December).

There are also state holidays such as Kosrae Constitution Day (11 January), Sokehs Rebellion Day (24 February, Pohnpei), Yap Day (1 March), Kolonia Independence Day (17 May), Kosrae Liberation Day (8 September), Pohnpei Liberation Day (11 September), Chuuk Charter Day (26 September), Kosrae Self-Government Day (3 November), Pohnpei Constitution Day (8 November), and Yap Constitution Day (24 December). Try to be in Colonia on Yap on 1 March or in Kolonia on Pohnpei on 11 September to see canoe races, customary dancing, and other traditional events. There are the various municipal Constitution Days on Pohnpei. On Kapingamarangi, Taro Patch Day is celebrated on 15 March.

Conduct
Micronesians expect Western women to dress modestly. Male visitors calling on government offices should avoid dressing too casually. Observe how the officials are dressed. Most Micronesians are friendly, so a big smile and a hello are never out of place.

PRACTICALITIES

Accommodations and Food
The only full-service hotels are in the state capitals. You'll find inexpensive restaurants in all the major towns. In rural areas you'll have a choice of camping or staying with local families; on many islands, both require permission from the local landowner, householder, chief, or government representative. Try to find some way to repay any kindnesses received. Nonmonetary gifts are always very welcome.

Visas
Since the FSM is not part of the United States, its entry requirements are not the same as those of Guam and Hawaii. Tourists don't need a visa for a stay of up to 30 days, although officials may want to see an onward ticket. If you don't have one, they may insist you purchase one on the spot. This applies to everyone, Americans included.

Citizens of countries other than the United States must carry a passport. United States citizens are not technically required to have a passport, only proof of citizenship such as a birth certificate or naturalization papers. But we urge all Americans also to carry valid passports to ease entrance and save time. Nationalities other than Americans and Canadians going on to Hawaii must have a valid United States visa in their passport. Some nationalities also need a visa to stay in Guam. Check with a United States consulate.

You get a new entry permit every time you cross a state boundary; $10 exit fees are the norm. Each time through immigration control earns you another 30 days without leaving the Federated States. Permit extensions are a nuisance, so when you arrive ask for all the time you may need. The maximum stay without an extension is 30 days.

Anyone considering arriving by yacht should apply for an FSM vessel permit in advance from: Chief Immigration Officer, FSM National Government, Palikir, Pohnpei, FM 96941 (tel. 691-

320-5844, fax 691-320-2234). Ports of entry are Lelu and Okat on Kosrae, Kolonia on Pohnpei, Weno on Chuuk, Ulithi, and Colonia in Yap State. Upon sailing from one state to another, yachts must clear customs.

Money, Measurements, and Phone

U.S. currency is used. Credit cards are now fairly well accepted at hotels and car rentals, except on Yap. It is most convenient to carry U.S. cash or U.S.-denominated traveler's checks in small denominations.

To call direct from the U.S. to a telephone number in the FSM, dial 011-691 and the seven-digit number. To call from one FSM state to another, dial a "1" before the seven-digit number. Off-island calls within the FSM are $1 a minute, cheaper at night. Calls out of the country are quite expensive. It is sometimes less expensive for a person in the United States to initiate the call. Most public telephones in the FSM accept FSMTC telephone cards, which can be purchased at phone company offices. The same card can be used in Kosrae, Pohnpei, Chuuk, and Yap.

Standard American 110-volt, 60-cycle appliances are used. The FSM issues its own postage stamps, but U.S. domestic postal rates apply. There's a one-hour time change between Pohnpei and Chuuk.

Getting There

One must change planes at Honolulu if coming from the United States mainland. Most visitors come to the Federated States on **Continental Airlines** (formerly Continental Air Micronesia or "Air Mike") Island Hopper service between Hawaii and Guam. Depending on the season, the flight is available two or three times a week in each direction. From the east it runs Honolulu to Majuro to Kwajalein to Kosrae to Pohnpei to Chuuk to Guam. In scheduling stopovers, remember that the flight crosses the International Date Line between Hawaii and Majuro in the Marshall Islands.

Continental also has a daily nonstop flight in each direction between Honolulu and Guam. At times, there are additional flights between Guam, Chuuk, and Pohnpei. Yap is on the Guam to Palau route. A change of planes at Guam is necessary if you are coming from any other FSM destination.

In 1998, Continental Airlines absorbed Continental Air Micronesia. For years, though a wholly owned subsidiary, it had been run independently. Since the merger, there have been ongoing schedule changes. Your best chance for up-to-date information is to call Continental Airlines International at (800) 231-0856; visit its website at: www.continental.com; or call one of the travel agents listed in the "On the Road" chapter. The merger has improved connections between flights within Micronesia and other Continental flights that connect with the U.S. mainland or Asia. Continental and Northwest Airlines (tel. 800-447-4747) have an alliance that also can be used to connect with Continental's Micronesia routes.

Air Nauru flies to Pohnpei. The Wednesday flight runs Nauru to Pohnpei to Guam to Manila. This can be helpful if you are traveling to or from Australia, New Zealand, or other South Pacific points via Nauru.

Dark with twisted paths,
canals of the mangrove swamp.
—An egret soaring.

STATE OF KOSRAE

Because of its profile, Kosrae is called the "Island of the Sleeping Lady." Legend tells that Kosrae was shaped by the gods from the transformed figure of a sleeping woman. Her good looks might make you wish to linger, to know her better. And she won't disappoint.

Particularly if you are coming from the crowded, flat islands of the Marshalls, you can't help becoming excited by this island's central mountains enshrouded in dense, green rainforest, among the most pristine rainforests existing in Micronesia. In some places, the mountains run directly to the ocean; more frequently they run to low-lying plains created over eons by mangroves reaching into the ocean, trapping runoff soil, and creating their own landfill.

Views are reminiscent of Rarotonga in the Cook Islands, or Oahu's windward side 30 years ago. Breadfruit, papaya, mango, taro, coconut palms, bananas, Kosrae's famed green, seedless tangerines, jacaranda, and colorful flowers grow everywhere.

Formerly Kusaie, Kosrae (ko-SHRY) is a single 42-square-mile island, the easternmost of the Carolines and, after Pohnpei, the second-largest island in the Federated States. It fulfills the tropical island fantasy: lush green interior circled by alternating coral beaches and mysterious mangrove forests. The rugged interior, inaccessible except with a guide, is crowned by Mt. Finkol (2,069 feet). A broad valley between Mt. Finkol and Mt. Mutunte divides the island in two, with a deep harbor at each side.

Orientation

Five traditional villages lie along the coast. Heading clockwise around the island from the airport, they are: Tafunsak, Lelu, Malem, Utwa, and

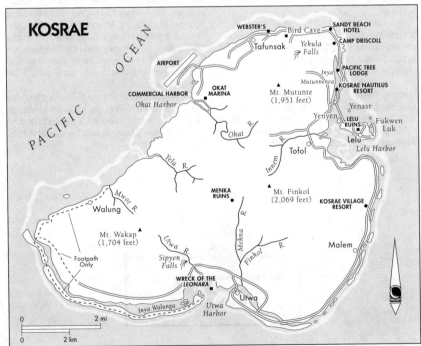

KOSRAE

© AVALON TRAVEL PUBLISHING

KOSRAE'S CLIMATE

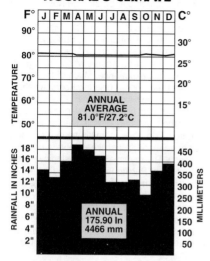

ANNUAL AVERAGE
81.0°F/27.2°C

ANNUAL
175.90 In
4466 mm

Walung (which is part of Tafunsak municipality). A coastal road circles about two-thirds of the island but does not reach Walung.

The road to Walung is a political hot potato, many villagers preferring privacy to the "progress" a road would bring. A compromise plan has been proposed under which the road would circle the island while going near, though not through, Walung. Under this plan, however, the road would go through pristine forest.

Lelu, the largest village, sits on Lelu Island, connected to Kosrae by a causeway. The view from Lelu of forested volcanic peaks in profile on the western horizon is majestic. The skyline from here resembles the sleeping lady of the legend.

Most government offices, the hospital, tourist office, immigration office, post office, communications center, police station, banks, Continental Airlines, high school, and library are located at Tofol, Kosrae's administrative center, about 2.5 miles from Lelu by road. Tofol is not so much a town as it is a stretch of road where buildings are strung somewhat close together.

History

Hundreds of years ago a feudal aristocracy ruled Kosrae from Lelu Island. The rulers built themselves a great stone city called Insaru, the ruins

and canals of which you see today. These ruins give a feel for the aristocracy's material wealth—such prosperity allowed the legendary Isokelekel and his 333 warriors to conquer Nan Madol, Pohnpei's capital.

Whalers brought diseases that reduced the number of Kosraeans from 10,000 or more to a mere 300 in just a few decades. The whalers were followed in 1852 by Congregational missionaries from Hawaii who came to convert the survivors. Those few survivors, having lost faith in the power of their own gods, were receptive to the new religion. Today, Kosraeans are much more likely to think of this conversion as the beginning of their redemption, rather than the death of their old culture. The survival of the Kosraean people and their language, in the face of the devastation brought by the West, is a tribute to the vitality of their traditional culture.

Unscrupulous traders came as well, including the notorious pirate, Bully Hayes, whose ship *Leonora* sank at Utwa Harbor in 1874. Hayes is thought to have buried his treasure in the vicinity, but nothing has been found—yet.

Thousands of Japanese immigrants came to Kosrae in the period between the two world wars, outnumbering Kosraeans and forcing them to abandon their villages and to move to the interior. During WW II this Japanese community was reinforced by Japanese military troops. Although the United States bypassed strategically isolated Kosrae, it did bomb the island, killing three Kosraeans in an attack on Japanese forces, including the mother of a future governor of Kosrae, Thurston Siba. Before the bombing, and particularly afterward, the Japanese subjected Kosraeans to forced labor and made it a criminal act for a native Kosraean to pick fruit from trees.

Kosraeans are linguistically separate from the people of Pohnpei, an island almost 300 miles away. Nonetheless, Kosrae was part of the district of Pohnpei until January 1977. At that time, Kosrae demanded and was granted status as a separate state within the Federated States.

The People

Kosraeans are warm and friendly, usually quite eager to meet visitors. Most Kosraeans speak some English. Much of the island is underemployed. Many women do some subsistence farming while many men still fish. Life is slow and entertainment is often a meal with family or friends. There are no movie houses, nightclubs, or bowling alleys.

Church services are an integral part of Kosraean culture and social circles. The population is overwhelmingly Congregationalist, though there are also three Mormon churches, an Assembly of God congregation, a Baptist church, a Catholic church, and a Seventh-Day Adventist school. As the *Kosrae Visitor's Guide* points out, there are rules of expected behavior, even for tourists, on Sundays:

- *Do* wear long pants and a shirt (men).

- *Do* wear a dress (women).

- *Do* feel free to attend church (the Kosraeans are noted for their choral singing), visit friends, read, and relax.

- *Do not* collect seashells, snorkel, water-ski, or scuba dive.

- *Do not* drink alcoholic beverages.

It is illegal to drink or fish on Sunday and almost all stores and offices are shut. Commercial dive shops and fishing boats do not operate. So sit back and relax—this might be the day you discover the joys of a peaceful Sabbath. If you are not up to the rigors of such leisure, visiting the Lelu ruins is acceptable, but no guide will be available.

Each of the villages has a blue and white Congregational church. They are surprisingly large for the size of the population and they are invariably packed on Sunday. Services begin at 10 a.m. (this appears to be the one Kosrae event that begins punctually). Men and women sit on opposite sides of the center aisle. Most churches have an additional 4 p.m. Sunday service and also welcome visitors to choir practice.

One cannot know Kosrae without taking part in the church experience. Much of the hour is filled with sensational, uniquely Kosraean choral singing. One solo woman singer will set the tone, using a series of high-pitched wailing notes. The rest of the choir then joins in. Men and women sing separate parts, sometimes in a call-and-response mode, other times in very complex harmony. The rhythms and phrasing owe more to traditional Pacific Island music than to the New England hymns from which the songs were derived. The Kosraeans took what they were taught and adapted it to their own needs. Regardless of your own religious beliefs (or lack of them) you will be moved by the spiritual feel around you. It is an experience not to be missed.

SIGHTS

Kosrae has a road that circles about two-thirds of the island. Most of it is flat and can easily be walked. Cars are tolerated by the people and animals using it. The greatest difficulty in walking the road is that cars will often stop to inquire if you would like a lift.

Prismatic basalt "logs" stacked atop giant volcanic blocks demonstrate the architectural evolution of Kosrae's Lelu ruins.

On the other hand, off-road hikes through the mountains or the mangroves should usually be undertaken only with a guide. Trails are not well kept, and a guide will sometimes need a machete to clear new growth. Further, because of the dense canopy on many parts of the island, it is very easy to become disoriented on a cloudy day.

Your hotel can probably arrange a guide for you. If not, feel free to call another hotel, particularly the Kosrae Village Resort or the Kosrae Nautilus Resort. The Kosrae Tourist Office, P.O. Box 600, Kosrae, FM 96944, tel. (691) 370-2228, fax (691) 370-2187, e-mail: kosrae@mail.fm, can also make arrangements.

You can also try to contact guides directly. For most hikes, try Emilson Phillip, tel. (691) 370-4405, or Tadao Waguk, tel. (691) 370-5080. For climbing Mount Finkol, speak to Hanson Nena, tel. (691) 370-3344. For touring the mangroves on the northeast coast, call Emilson.

Guides for half days usually charge about $25, for a full day, $50.

Around the Island

As you drive round the island from the airport in a clockwise direction, you will come upon a road to the left in about a mile. This road leads to the village of **Tafunsak**. It has a great feel—not much going on. It's a funky, old, quiet town with a beautiful large church.

If you turn left when you get to the coast, the road is quite scenic, going through mangroves and densely verdant small hills. The road eventually runs out—turn back along the coast. If you continue straight, less than a mile past Tafunsak this road rejoins the round-the-island road.

Several miles farther, inland of the road, is the Army Corps of Engineers' Camp Driscoll. The Civic Action Team (referred to as CAT), tel. (691) 370-2324, is a United States military unit dedicated to providing infrastructure support to the island. It also provides emergency and minor medical care to travelers, free of charge.

Next to CAT is the **Tropical Breeze** store. It has excellent baked goods, including donuts and turnovers as well as other snack food. It is the only store on Kosrae open on Sunday.

Lelu

Lelu town occupies an island across the harbor from Tofol, connected to the main island by a causeway. On the left side of the causeway you'll find a pier with a ladder that leads down to a swimming hole used by local kids. This is the best spot on Kosrae to swim laps, if that is your inclination. On the right is the Aquaculture Center, which grows giant clams. A local produce market takes place on the causeway most weekday mornings.

Lelu is a relaxed town. The tall concrete building on the main street near Thurston's Enterprises dates from 1915. It served as the storehouse of an American trader who dumped stones from the nearby ruins into Lelu Harbor to extend his dock.

Lelu Ruins

When they built their fortress at Lelu, Kosrae's rulers thought they were building a stronghold, a sanctuary, a gated community for the ruling class. They never dreamt they were constructing an archaeological site.

Kosrae's leading land attraction are the Lelu Ruins, located in Lelu town. Lelu flourished as the feudal capital of Kosrae from 1400 to 1800; the king and high chiefs had their residences here. The city once covered the entire flat portion of Lelu Island and included 100 large, walled compounds, perhaps larger than Nan Madol on Pohnpei. Its power was such that warriors from Lelu were able to invade Pohnpei, overthrow the Saudeleurs, and conquer Nan Madol in the 17th century.

One of the most impressive archaeological sites in the Pacific, the ruins are similar in style to, and predate, Nan Madol off Pohnpei. Yet the Lelu Ruins are more accessible since they sit right in the center of town. The heart of the site is just a few minutes' walk down a footpath that begins beside the security fence on the west side of Thurston's Enterprises on the main street. Parts of the ruins are quite muddy after rain, so wear good walking shoes. As soon as you get deep enough into the site to be unable to hear the refrigerator at the Thurston store, the centuries roll back. You see the enormity of the material culture, the wealth and organization that allowed such massive construction.

You will enter the ruins at *Kinyeir Fulat,* a living area including a feast house. It is surround-

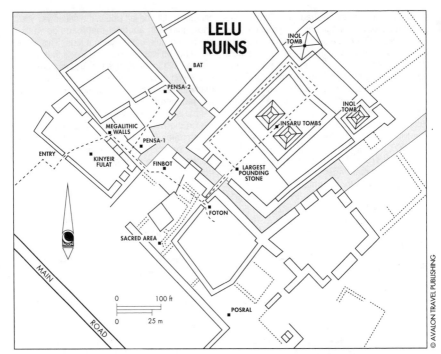

ed by some of the highest walls in the ruins, up to 20 feet. It is thought to have been the westernmost part of the city in 1400, when it fronted on the lagoon.

There are other important sites from this early period. *Finbot* is probably from the same period. *Foton* is a well-preserved dwelling compound, with excellently constructed basalt prism walls. *Posral* was the king's residential quarters, surrounded by sacred compounds.

Ancient coral and rock walkways run through the ruins, permitting striking glimpses of the ancient city. Archaeologists believe that the crisscrossed, five-sided basalt logs that were the basic building material were floated on rafts all the way from Utwa. Many Kosraeans, assuming their ancestors were too intelligent to do this much work to construct a monument, maintain that the city was built in a night by two magicians.

The prismatic, stacked basalt architecture often rests on walls of massive basalt boulders. These walls reach as high as 20 feet and, like

Incan architecture, the stones were carefully fitted so that mortar was unnecessary. The height of the base of each residence corresponded to social rank. You can still see the network of canals that brought ocean-going canoe traffic through the city.

Note the flat grooved *seka*-pounding stones at Pensa-1 and at the entrance to *Insaru. Insaru* holds the truncated pyramid tombs of the kings whose bodies were placed in crypts. When a corpse completely decayed, the bones were taken to a reef off Lelu and dropped into a deep hole. These ocean-going people had intuited that life came from the sea. Their burial process reflected this belief by returning the remains to their origin.

Other points of particular interest include *Pensa*-1, *Pensa*-2, and *Bat* residential areas, all believed to have been constructed only several hundred years ago. The *Inol* tombs are also believed to be from this later period.

Many parts of the Lelu Ruins are overgrown. Although the government recently posted explanatory notes in parts of the ruins, you will get the most from your visit if you hire a guide. The going price seems to be $25. There is also a $3 admission charge for those on arranged tours. You can make arrangements through the Kosrae Museum, tel. (691) 370-3078, your hotel, or the Tourist Office in Tofol, tel. (691) 370-2228. You can also contact directly two experienced guides: Albert Welly, tel. (691) 370-3022, or Jorim Mike, tel. (691) 370-3815.

Lelu Hill

A trail behind a small cemetery not far from the old wharf leads to the summit of Lelu Hill (355 feet) which the Japanese fortified during WW II. You pass a couple of their air raid shelters near the trailhead, then proceed straight ahead on the main trail until reaching a switchback as you approach the summit. A short distance along this trail, a **tunnel** hewn from solid rock winds 100 feet back into the hill. Continue along the same overgrown track toward the south side where another tunnel cuts through the hill. Japanese trenches, foxholes, and caves still girdle Lelu Hill in rings, but all known wartime guns have been removed. As with most trips off the roads of Kosrae, hire a guide.

Tofol

For an easy glimpse of the interior, take a ride or a stroll up the dirt road that leads off to the right, 1.1 miles past the junction of the round-the-island road and the causeway. If you reach the ****

Star construction company, you've come about 100 yards too far. The way leads past lush tropical gardens onto the plateau between Mt. Finkol and Mt. Mutunte. It is best not to leave the road unless you are with a guide. Paths are not regularly maintained, and all land bordering the road is privately owned.

About two miles past the turnoff to Lelu is Tofol, the site of all governmental and most private business on the island. There is a new public library within the high school complex. It's open Mon.-Thurs. 8 a.m.-4 p.m. In addition to its regular collection, it has an excellent Micronesia reference section including many government documents.

To save money (a false economy) the **Kosrae Museum** (tel. 691-370-3078, fax 691-370-3767) was moved from its prior location adjacent to the Lelu Ruins to Tofol. Since the museum focuses on the ruins and their excavation, it's a good idea to visit it before visiting the ruins themselves. Unfortunately, its current quarters are too small for it to exhibit the entire collection. It is said that this museum location is only "temporary," but in Micronesia the difference between "temporary" and "permanent" may be in the distant future.

The museum is open Mon.-Thurs. 9 a.m.-3 p.m. Call ahead to verify that it actually will be open when you plan to visit. At other times, the museum may be opened in response to your call. Mr. Berlin Sigrah is the museum's director.

As you continue around the island, the road gets progressively worse. In places, the road is

early 19th-century houses at Kosrae

not paved, or is potholed. Still, even in an ordinary car, one can drive to Utwa. Drive *slowly*. Never think you should drive faster than a local in a pickup truck. The drive is beautiful and your patience will be well rewarded. Toward the water you'll see beautiful vistas of mangroves growing on reefs, literally forming the island. Inland you'll find great views up deep canyons toward the mountains. Most beaches are privately owned, and you should ask permission at a nearby house before using one. Permission will most usually be granted.

Allow at least two hours for the roundtrip from the Kosrae Village Resort to Utwa and back, even with only minimal time sightseeing.

Malem

Malem itself is not a particularly picturesque town.

In Malem is the **PMS store,** its name set in concrete, the initials of the store owner, I am told. I tried to verify the story, but the store clerk yelled at me.

During the first month in June, the residents of Malem celebrate the return to their village after the surrender of Japanese forces at the end of World War II.

Right past Malem lie reefs extending out a great distance. At low tide they make for interesting tidepool viewing. Wear good sturdy footwear.

Utwa

Utwa is the village at the mouth of the Finkol, Kosrae's largest river. It serves as the base for exploring the island's south side. From here you can take off by outrigger or canoe to explore the mangrove forest of the recently founded **Utwa Walung Conservation Area.**

The backwater canoe journey can be arranged through your hotel or the **Utwa-Walung Marine Park,** (P.O. Box 539, Kosrae, FM 96944, tel. 691-370-3483, ask for Madison Nena, fax 691-370-2321). You might also try calling guide Tadao Waguk at (691) 370-5080. Rates vary between $25 and $35 pp, depending upon the length of the trip.

The time of day for the trip will be determined by the tides because the channel is not passable at low tide. You begin by traversing a wide lagoon with a magnificent view of the forested

mountains. Then you enter the shallow, 20-foot-wide **Utwa-Walung Mangrove Channel** *(Inya Walunga)* for a close look at the magnificent mangrove forest, a unique ecological environment. You will see fantastically twisted shapes that are these trees' root structures. Ferns and palms overgrow the channel to form an overhead tunnel. With luck, you may get to see a giant monitor lizard, some of which are six feet long. It is said the Japanese brought them in to control the island's rat population. It turned out that, like us, the lizards much prefer to eat birds' eggs or fresh mangrove crabs.

To Menka Ruins
Slippery, difficult trail
Ate a sweet mango

From Utwa, you can also hike to the **Menka Ruins** or to the top of **Mt. Finkol.**

Mt. Finkol (2,069 feet) is Kosrae's highest peak. This grueling hike should only be undertaken by accomplished hikers accompanied by a local guide. You wade up the Finkol River quite a distance, then scramble through the slippery rainforest to the top. Wear rubber booties or some old tennis shoes. There are sweeping views of the entire island from the grassy summit.

A wonderful hike out of Utwa is up to the **Menka Ruins.** The hike through the forest and up to the ruins will take about an hour and should be done only with a guide. In Kosraean lore Menka, even older than Lelu, is the home of Sinlaku, goddess of breadfruit.

Hiking to the Menka Ruins will leave you wet, muddy, exhilarated, and if you are old enough to have grown children, exhausted as well. You hike to the site up a river valley, the trail crossing the river back and forth. The hike is through one of the best preserved rainforests in Micronesia. You will see giant *ka* trees whose size and majesty compare to California's redwoods. For generations, the people of Kosrae have cultivated small plots amid the large trees, without destroying the forest. Along with mango, banana, and papaya trees, you will see taro, cabbages, cucumbers, watermelons, and even tomatoes growing. The land is so fertile and well-watered by rain that crops grow with a minimum of work. But remember, in Kosrae, every piece of land, every tree, has an owner.

Along the trail grow pepper plants, from which the ancient Kosraeans made *seka*. This narcotic drink is known on Pohnpei as *sakau*. The drink is seldom still used on Kosrae, but it does remain very central to Pohnpeian life. It is said (by Kosraens) that even today the best *sakau* comes from plants grown on Kosrae.

The Menka Ruins have not been reconstructed or even fully surveyed. There are perhaps a hundred stone foundations of residential areas. Some have been cleared, but most haven't. The scope of the ruins offers proof that once a large population lived here.

One area was surely a *seka* bar. Still in place are the large pounding stones with carved indentations. Smaller rocks were used to pound

---

GREETINGS FROM THE UTWA WALUNG CONSERVATION AREA

The Conservation Area includes much biodiversity, from rare fish to rare trees, as well as historical ruins and unspoiled beauty. We are pleased for you, our guests, to enjoy these things.

But these are things we in Kosrae also value. In the Conservation Area are things we want to keep. Our land and our seas are our home, our "supermarket," our culture, and our history. The Utwa Walung Conservation Area is our own attempt to keep our island the way we want it to be, for our children and for the generations to follow them. We are proud of it.

It is not a national park in the Western sense. It is not government land. The government does not make the rules. This conservation area is based in our communities. Individual landowners who want to keep their environment in its current healthy state have placed their land within the Conservation Area. We can still come and collect resources—crabs for food, mangrove trees for building—but we are doing it sustainably.

This is a new concept in conservation, and we are doing it in the Kosraean way, with some help from the South Pacific Regional Environment Program. Its boundaries are still growing as more lands are placed under its care. It is growing organically, just as the trees and plants around you.

---

the pepper root in these indentations to extract its psychoactive liquid.

Take a few dollar bills with you. At one stop on the way down, there may be children who will offer you fresh fruit and perform a few traditional dances.

Walung

Walung is not yet connected to the rest of the island by road. This makes it difficult to reach but keeps it an "unspoiled" spot: a long palm-fringed beach, no electricity, no stores, no roads, no cappuccino, and the *New York Times* is delivered only twice a decade. It is possible to walk into Walung either from Utwa or from Okat Harbor, near the airport. From either direction, the hike is beautiful but arduous and should not be attempted without a guide.

Easier is a boat from the **Okat Marina** (tel. 691-370-2629), just past the bridge from the airport. A roundtrip costs about $35, depending on how long you want the boat to wait for you in Walung. The trip takes about an hour each way. If you coordinate the trip with a tide table, you will be able to go through the mangroves at high tide and outside the reef at low tide. You can also negotiate for the boat to stop en route for handline fishing or snorkeling. This trip can also be arranged through your hotel.

Okat Marina also offers a once-in-a-lifetime experience: for $50 you can fish all night. It is for the hardy only: no cabin, probably no sleep, and certainly no sympathy if you become seasick. But when else might you have the chance to fish by handline for large bottom fish with people who do this for a living, not for the experience?

ACCOMMODATIONS

Although Kosrae has only six hotels, containing in total about 60 rooms, the traveler has a fair amount of choice because each hotel appeals to a slightly different market.

The first hotel you reach heading clockwise toward Tofol from the airport is the **Sandy Beach Hotel** (moderate) (Donald Jonah, P.O. Box 6, Kosrae, FM 96944, tel. 691-370-3239, fax 691-370-2109). It's about halfway between the airport and Tofol. All of its 16 beachfront rooms have two double beds, are air conditioned, have refrigerators, and overlook the ocean. The hotel has two stories so specify if you prefer downstairs (immediacy to the beach) or upstairs (better views). The rooms are $55 s, $72 d. The hotel still maintains an old one-room thatch cottage that rents for $42 s, 55 d.

Rooms are clean and spacious, but plain with little decoration. The charms of the hotel outweigh this small drawback. Kosraeans Donald Jonah, his son Ronald, and daughter-in-law Ruth are fantastic hosts. At the beach you can view tidepools during low tide or go snorkeling during high tide to enjoy the interesting ecology of sea grasses directly in front of the hotel. The tide usually pulls to the left as you face the water. Head out into the current so that you have an easy return, going with the flow when you return. If you are skilled in ocean swimming, you may be able to traverse the reef if the breakers

KOSRAE COUNTRY CODE: 691

are *small* by walking at low tide and swimming at high. The reward lies in deep-water snorkeling over coral.

About one-half mile before the turnoff to Lelu is the **Pacific Tree Lodge** (moderate) (P.O. Box 51, Lelu, Kosrae, FM 96944, tel. 691-370-2102, fax 691-370-3060). This hotel, built in 1992, is uniquely designed. Six cottages, each with two units, surround a squared-off section of mangrove forest, a joy to see with its active birdlife. Each unit backs onto more mangroves that have grown right up to the glass doors. The rooms are quite comfortable and are a good value at $55 s, $75 d. There is a restaurant on the premis-

LEGEND OF THE MUTUNNENEA CHANNEL

One day the King of Kosrae went to visit his relatives on the opposite side of the island. As he came to the Harbor of Okat, he saw a very beautiful girl swimming nearby. He ordered his servants to capture the girl and take her with them. So his servants captured the girl and took her to the King's palace in Lelu. The girl happened to be the daughter of a snake.

After a while the snake mother became worried about her daughter because she had been gone for almost two days. The mother left her home to look for her daughter and slid to the South, but she was not there. Then she went West, but she was not there either. Nor was she to the North or East. Everywhere the snake went she gouged out a big channel in her tracks that we see as a channel around Kosrae today.

The snake finally came to Lelu Harbor. There she crawled beside a rock under a boathouse to rest. The next morning one of the king's servants went to throw garbage out and saw a big snake resting her head on a rock. He hurried back to the palace and the first person he met was the snake's daughter. He told her about the snake, and she knew at once that it was her mother. So she begged the servant to keep silent about what he had seen, and he agreed not to tell anyone. That night the girl went to her mother and told her to crawl to the king's palace and hide herself in the rafters of the ceiling of

one of the big houses there. By morning, after working all night to hide herself, the snake mother was well concealed.

One day a servant was out walking beside the king's court when he heard a strange noise. He looked around but could not find where it came from. He began to walk away when he again heard the unfamiliar noise at the top of the house. When he spotted the snake, he could hardly believe his eyes. He then quickly ran off to report to the king what he had seen. The king suspected that it was the girl's mother and she had come to take the girl away. So he made a plan to kill the snake mother. He ordered all the women to go to the Innem River to wash clothes. While the women were gone he then ordered the men to set fire to the house where the snake was hiding.

They set fire to the house and as it burned, ashes from the fire carried by the wind floated down onto the lap of the girl. She knew what was happening and hurried back to the king's palace. By the time she arrived at the palace, her mother had been burned to death. She cried as she jumped into the fire to die with her mother, and she was burned to death. The only thing left as a reminder of this sad story is the irregular channel made by the mother snake while searching for her beautiful daughter long ago.

—Emilson Phillip

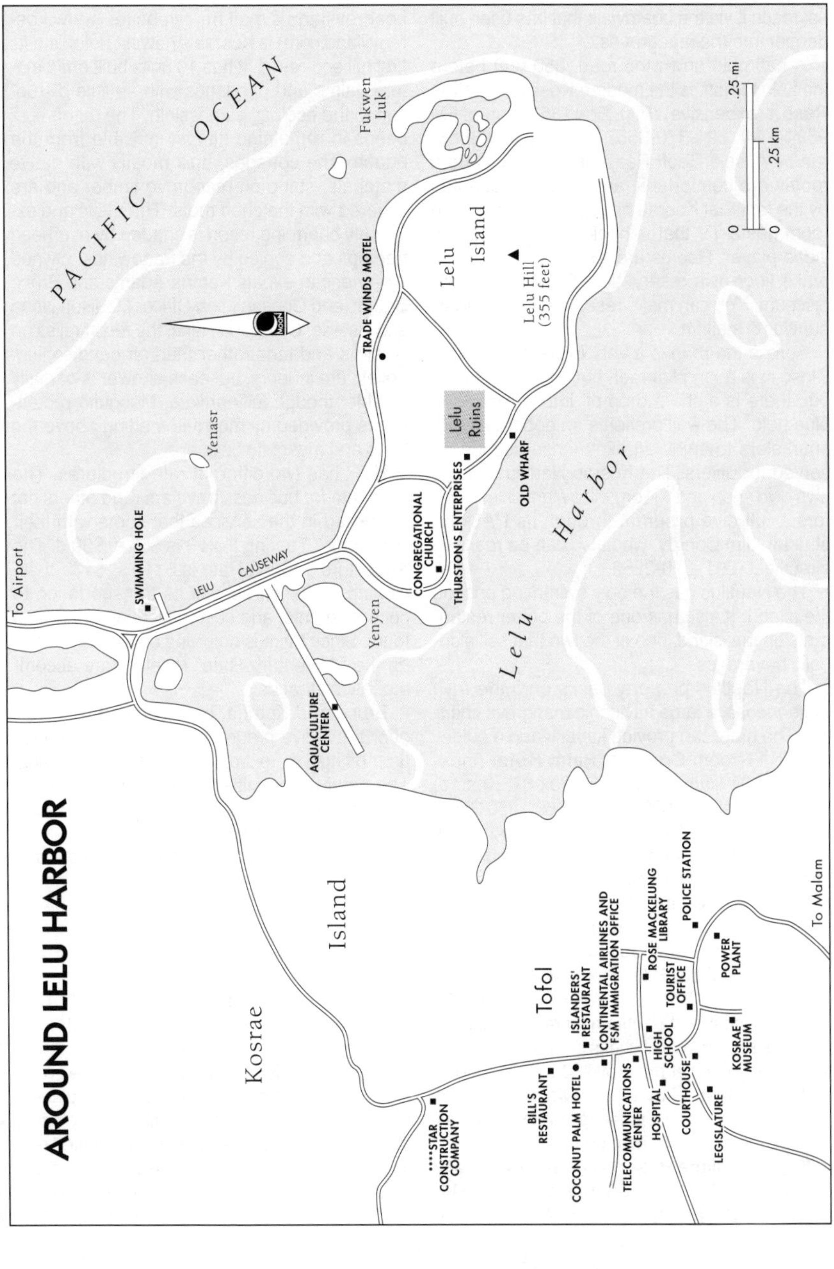

AROUND LELU HARBOR

© AVALON TRAVEL PUBLISHING

PACIFIC OCEAN

Fukwen Luk

Lelu Island

Lelu Hill
(355 feet)

TRADE WINDS MOTEL

Yenasr

Lelu Ruins

SWIMMING HOLE

LELU CAUSEWAY

CONGREGATIONAL CHURCH

THURSTON'S ENTERPRISES

OLD WHARF

Lelu Harbor

Yenyen

AQUACULTURE CENTER

Kosrae Island

Tofol

STAR CONSTRUCTION COMPANY

BILL'S RESTAURANT

COCONUT PALM HOTEL

ISLANDERS' RESTAURANT

CONTINENTAL AIRLINES AND FSM IMMIGRATION OFFICE

TELECOMMUNICATIONS CENTER

HOSPITAL

HIGH SCHOOL

COURTHOUSE

LEGISLATURE

KOSRAE MUSEUM

ROSE MACKELUNG LIBRARY

TOURIST OFFICE

POLICE STATION

POWER PLANT

To Malam

To Airport

0   .25 km

0   .25 mi

es; reach it via the boardwalk that has been built deeper into the mangroves.

A half mile down the road, 350 feet before the Lelu turnoff, is the modern **Kosrae Nautilus Resort** (expensive) (P.O. Box 135, Kosrae, FM 96944, tel. 691-370-3567, fax 691-370-3568) run by Aussie Geoff Raaschou. All 16 modern rooms are comfortable and clean. Undaunted by the fact that Kosrae has no TV station, each room has a TV that is hooked up to a central video player. Rooms are $83 s, $104 d. If you make your own reservation, they offer a 15% discount. You can make reservations by e-mail: nautilus@mail.fm.

Across the road is a very interesting beach. Close in is a long flat reef, but about 150 yards out, there is a sharp drop-off into a very deep blue hole. The wall presents an opportunity for snorkelers to enjoy an experience usually reserved for divers. The Kosrae Nautilus has its own dive shop and will organize night dives. It offers a full dive program through its PADI instructor, Jim Conroy, who also can be reached directly at (691) 370-2252.

The Nautilus has the only swimming pool on the island. It also has one of the better restaurants on the island, one of the two that sell alcoholic beverages.

The Nautilus property backs onto the *Inya Mutunnenea,* a large navigable mangrove channel. The hotel can provide kayaks and a guide.

The 11-room **Coconut Palm Hotel** (inexpensive) (William Tosie, P.O. Box 87, Kosrae, FM 96944, tel. 691-370-3181, fax 691-370-3084) in Tofol charges $40 s, $45 d. Located in the heart of town and not very scenic, it primarily attracts commercial visitors. Parts of it are a bit rundown, so ask for a renovated room.

Close to the Lelu Ruins but off the island's main road is **Trade Winds Motel** (inexpensive) (Thurston K. Siba, P.O. Box 248, Kosrae, FM 96944, tel. 691-370-3991, fax 691-370-3047). Although most of the units now rent on a long-term basis, units with kitchens are often available for the economical price of $30 s, $40 d. This motel is managed by Island Office Supply in Tofol, so if you show up unexpectedly, you may find no one around to help you.

Kosrae Village Resort (expensive), usually called "KVR" (P.O. Box 399, Kosrae, FM 96944, tel. 691-370-3483, fax 691-370-5839, e-mail: kosraevillage@mail.fm, website: www.kosraevillage.com) is Kosrae's newest hotel and its first full eco-resort. It has 10 units built amid mature palms and pandanus with as little disruption to the ecology as possible. The resort succeeds in remaining almost invisible from the beach. The cottages, built mostly with native materials, stand on mangrove timber and are covered with thatched roofs. The rustic and extremely charming resort is shaded by overhead treetops and cooled by the tradewinds. Owned by American expats Katrina Adams and Bruce Brandt, and Conservation Officer Madison Nena and his wife, Christiana Nena, the resort relies on screens and fans rather than air conditioning. Toilets are indoors, but each shower is partially outside, though fully private. Mosquito protection is provided by mosquito netting above the beds and mosquito coils.

KVR has two different rate structures. The daily rate for business travelers (and others not interested in the services that come with their "Adventure Touring Rate") is $65 s, $99 d. The Adventure Touring Rate is $115 s, $170 d, including breakfast as well as transportation to cultural events, and customized land and boat tours. Since there is no diving on Sunday, those on the "Adventure Rate" receive free accommodations that day.

Bruce and Katrina, both certified by PADI, offer a full dive program. There is even a nice drop-off right in front of the hotel for shore diving. The hotel is committed to the physically challenged. All parts of the resort are fully wheelchair accessible. Bruce and Katrina are licensed to instruct and dive with challenged divers and they can devise a program to meet any needs.

FOOD

Kosrae's restaurants, never the island's high point, have been improving. Restaurants now offer more local dishes and produce. A fair amount of food is grown or caught on the island and its surrounding lagoon. At local get-togethers there are mounds of ahi sashimi, boiled lobsters and mangrove crabs, and plates of smoked reef fish. The local sukiyaki contains papaya as well as meat. Also popular are nutritious starch dishes including rice mixed with coconut meat; breadfruit cooked in taro leaves; sliced taro; and a gelatin tapioca made by chopping tapioca and mixing it with poi and copra, then covering it with sweetened coconut milk. On special occasions, *fafa* might be served. This fantastic dish of chopped taro balls served in a sweet coconut sauce by tradition may be prepared only by certain families.

Inum, the restaurant at the Kosrae Village Resort, is the island's best. The traditional Kosrae-style architecture and atmosphere of the dining room are splendid, and the food is very good. Local ahi is served both as a pepper steak or tempura style for $7; tasty mangrove crab is $10-20 depending on size. A sirloin Pohnpein pepper beefsteak is $8.50. The restaurant rotates local dishes such as *um mas* (baked breadfruit) and *kutak* (steamed taro). The resort has a full-service bar, with a wide selection of beers. For the lowest prices, join the happy hour, Mon.-Sat. 4-6 p.m. At about 7:30 Thursday evenings, there is a performance by a children's traditional dance troupe.

The second-best restaurant on the island, also with a bar, can be found at the **Kosrae Nautilus Resort** restaurant. First, cross the lobby of the hotel and buy your very own mandatory drinking permit for $3, good for one month. For dinner, try a huge sashimi appetizer ($3.50) followed by a grilled tuna steak ($10.50). An excellent local side dish is *Ainpat* ($1.50), which consists of banana and soft taro or breadfruit cooked with coconut milk. If you have a sweet tooth, leave room for the crepes à la mode.

The Nautilus has happy hour Monday, Wednesday, and Friday, 3:30-6 p.m., with 30% off drink prices. Friday is a particularly good day to meet expats and other travelers.

Bill's Restaurant opposite the Coconut Palm Hotel in Tofol, serves breakfast, lunch, and dinner. It's clean and has a luncheonette look to it. Most full breakfasts run $5. A ramen lunch will set you back three and a half bucks. No lunch or dinner entree costs more than $6. A treat at Bill's any time of day is frigid coconut milk served in the shell for $1.

Islanders' Restaurant is almost across the street from the Coconut Palm. During the week, at breakfast or lunch, it's a good place to get a feel for the local working community, native and expat. The cook does very well with local fish.

Very few lunches or dinners cost more than $6.

You get to the **Treelodge Restaurant** by walking over a boardwalk that begins at the back of the Pacific Tree Lodge. The restaurant is beautifully set in the mangroves, on the *Inya Mutunnenea,* and the view is a pleasure during the day. Don't go there if you are in a rush as service can be quite slow. Portions are big and you can fill up on fried chicken for $5. The restaurant is open-air and not air conditioned.

Primarily used by its guests, but open to the public, is the restaurant at the **Sandy Beach Hotel.** Call ahead to make sure it's open. It's in a small, simple room with a wonderful view out to the beach. Breakfasts are good and reasonably priced. Try the pancakes. Dinners are also reasonably priced. Mangrove crab and lobster are occasional treats. If you want one, order in advance so that the restaurant can be sure to accommodate your wish.

If you have access to cooking facilities or are staying with a local family, buy fish, crab, and lobster at the **Okat Marina** across the bridge from the airport. "Mom and Pop" stores sometimes will have signs advertising they are selling tuna that day.

RECREATION

Diving

Whatever Kosrae may lack in nightlife, it makes up for in outdoor, daytime recreational activities. In addition to hiking, as discussed above, there are incredibly varied water activities including diving, surfing, fishing, kayaking, canoeing through mangrove forests, snorkeling, and reef walking.

The Kosraean dive community, in a project begun by Geoff Raaschou, placed 56 mooring buoys around the island. Thus, boats no longer have to drop anchor. This is a wonderful accomplishment because every dropped anchor can damage the reef. Kosrae thus is protecting its superb drift diving. There are walls to dive as well as several wrecks. Visibility is often 100 feet, and more during summer. There are four dive shops on Kosrae. Prices are comparable, usually about $80 for a two-tank dive; price may vary depending on how many other divers go out that day. All dive shops will also take snorkelers at a much lower rate, usually about $20 pp, but again price depends on how many other people are going out.

Kosrae Nautilus Resort (P.O. Box 135, Kosrae, FM 96944, tel. 691-370-3567, fax 691-370-3568, e-mail: nautilus@mail.fm) is a good spot for anyone. Kosrae Village Resort's **Sleepy Lady Divers,** (P.O. Box 399, Kosrae, FM 96944, tel. 691-370-3483, fax 691-370-5839, e-mail: kosraevillage@mail.fm, website: www.kosraevillage.com) is Kosrae's first PADI five-star diving center and is also a good diving establishment for anyone. It is also *the* place for divers with disabilities. **Phoenix Sports Club** (P.O. Box PHM, Kosrae, FM 96944, tel. 691-390-3100, fax 691-370-3509) is Japanese owned, a branch of the company on Pohnpei. There are a good number of Japanese-speaking guides and instructors, as well as those with some knowledge of English. Ask Max to show you how he can attract fish using air bubbles. On the Sandy Beach Hotel premises, Ronald Jonah runs a small dive operation called the **Dive Caroline** (P.O. Box 6, Kosrae, FM 96944, tel. 691-370-3239, fax 691-370-2109).

Surfing

Kosrae may not make the cover of *Surfer* magazine, but it has some great waves. First, a word of caution: breaks here are over coral, with coral heads often protruding from the reefs. Generally, surf only near high tide. Second, you might even wish to wear a surfing helmet. Bodysurfers and spongers, please take particular care. As usual, try to talk to locals before surfing. The waves here are never crowded and there is no localism. If you are walking along carrying your board, someone in a pickup will invariably offer you a ride.

Surfing is usually best July to October, or November if you are lucky. The trades lighten during those months and the swells generally come from the east, northeast through southeast. Malem channel, opposite the municipal building, has a wave that breaks left as well as right. There are two breaks off Lelu channel: Lelu South and Lelu North. Each breaks on a northerly swell. Lelu North as well as Mother Lode, an outside break beyond the Blue Hole in front of the Nautilus, is makeable at double overhead, breaking in 15 feet of water. Teachers is off a channel

east of Tafunsak. East of the airport is a break called "Airport." Another break is off Shark Island, but with that name you're on your own.

Only recently have Kosraeans begun to surf. The local Malem surf club has about 10 members, all locals, who surf on donated boards, arrangements made by legendary philanthropic surfer, Ed Puikunas, who we hear is now surfing Mount Shasta in California.

OTHER PRACTICALITIES

Shopping

Kosrae has a continuing handicraft tradition. Work includes woven bags, hats, fans, headbands, trays, food utensils, taro pounders, purses, model canoes, carved sharks, coconut- or pandanus-fiber carrying cases, and decorative wall hangings. Gathered skirts with colorful tropical flower appliqué sell for $25-30.

The **Kosrae Community Action Program** has a wide selection of handicrafts and can put you in touch with local artisans. Call (691) 370-3217 or drop into their office, Mon.-Thur. 8 a.m.-4 p.m. in the green building next to Bill's Restaurant. If you are interested in seeing a carver at work, ask your hotel to arrange for you to visit Peter Lick in his workshop.

You can also buy handicrafts, T-shirts, postcards, and the like from the visitor's booth at the airport. The shop opens only when commercial flights are scheduled.

There are ongoing vegetable markets: next to the courthouse in Tofol, on the Lelu causeway, between Lelu and Tofol, and on the beach side of the road, going north to Tafunsak, just past Sandy Beach Hotel. All keep idiosyncratic hours. Excellent fresh, local produce include tangerines, papaya, watermelons, bananas, oranges, limes, cucumbers, cabbages, eggplants, string beans, sweet potatoes, breadfruit and taro.

Services

A Bank of Hawaii branch (tel. 691-370-3230) is next to the Islanders' Restaurant at Tofol. Below the nearby Coconut Palm Hotel are the Bank of the FSM (tel. 691-370-3225) and the post office. In the new office building about 100 yards away are Continental Airlines (tel. 691-370-3224) and the FSM Immigration office (tel. 691-370-3051).

Able to grow in salt water, mangroves trap runoff from the interior and thus, over centuries, expand the size of the island.

Overseas calls can be placed at the Telecommunications Center (open 24 hours) in Tofol. The office also has a computer available to the public for Internet access.

Address mail to Kosrae, FM 96944.

There's a coin laundry at Thurston's Enterprises in Lelu.

Most Kosrae state government employees are on a four-day work week, Mon.-Thurs. 8 a.m.-4 p.m. National government offices, such as Immigration and the Post Office, are open on Friday. All in all, *don't* count on getting much business done on Kosrae on Friday, Saturday or Sunday.

Information
You can pick up brochures on Kosrae or locate a guide at the Division of Tourism (P.O. Box. 600, Kosrae, FM 96944, tel. 691-370-2228, fax 691-370-2187, e-mail: kosrae@mail.fm), in a traditional-style thatched building at Tofol. The tourist

office also sells the book *Kosrae, The Sleeping Lady Awakens* by Harvey Gordon Segal ($14), and William H. Stewart's *Tourist Map of Kosrae* ($2.50). You're most likely to find someone there Mon.-Thurs. early in the morning. Justus Alokoa in this office is a good source of information and can help with practical arrangements.

Peace Corps volunteers are another excellent source of information.

TRANSPORTATION

Getting There
Flights land at the **airport** (KSA) at Okat, eight miles from Tofol. Visitors with hotel reservations are usually picked up at the airport; those without reservations will have no trouble hitching a lift. There's a $10 departure tax.

Continental Airlines Island Hopper heads west from Hawaii two or three days a week, depending on the season. It also stops at Kosrae when heading east from Guam. You can reconfirm your onward flight at the Tofol office, tel. (691) 370-3224. Remember that because of the International Date Line, you lose a day traveling from Honolulu to Kosrae. The Line is located between Honolulu and the Marshall Islands.

Private yachts can dock at either Lelu or Okat Harbor, without charge.

Getting Around
Kosrae's public transportation is virtually nonexistent, unless you include hitching in your definition of public transportation. There is a bus, but its main function is to take government workers to and from work. There is one taxi cab company, AA Taxis, tel. (691) 370-2639, with several sedans and one van. From Tafunsak village to Tofol the charge is $1 pp, with a minimum charge of $2 per cab. If you flag down a cab with room, it will pick you up for $1. The price of longer trips, past Tofol, should be negotiated with the owner, Alik Albert.

Hitchhiking is an option on Kosrae—it is that sort of place. If you are walking, people will often offer a ride, even if you haven't asked. Additionally, hotel owners will often take you for short rides if they are not too busy. Most hotel owners, for a fee, will also arrange longer trips and tours.

Nonetheless, if you plan on extensive sightseeing, you will want to rent a car. The going price seems to be about $50 per day. Many rental cars have manual shifts, while some imports from Japan have right-hand drive; specify what you want. Your hotel management can arrange a rental for you at a fair price. If you wish to arrange a car yourself, try calling **Thurston's Enterpris-** **es** (tel. 691-370-3245, fax 691-370-3047), **Webster's** (tel. 691-370-3116, fax 691-370-2116), **Bill and Sue's Auto Rental** (tel. 691-370-3181, fax 691-370-3084), or **Island-U-Drive**(tel. 691]-370-4582). There are gas stations in all villages on the main road.

STATE OF POHNPEI

INTRODUCTION

Pohnpei is mysterious—tropical mountain rainforests, mist-shrouded waterfalls, coastal mangrove forests—particularly after 5 p.m., when it is most usually seen through one's drug of choice: paralyzingly potent *sakau* made from the roots of a pepper plant, alcohol, betel nut, or locally grown (illegal) marijuana.

The island of Pohnpei (spelled Ponape until 1984), eight outlying atolls, and Minto Reef make up the State of Pohnpei, about halfway between Honolulu and Manila. Pohnpei Island, 12 by 14 miles, is the largest in the FSM. Local author Gene Ashby calls Pohnpei "the outer edge of Paradise."

The rugged, rainforested slopes of the interior rise to 2,540 feet at Nahnalaud ("Big Mountain") and Ngihneni ("Giant's Tooth"), shrouded in lush tropical vegetation nurtured by endless precipitation. Pohnpei's peaks generate the island's heavy rains by catching passing clouds and wringing the moisture from them. The torrential rains swell the 42 streams and rivers, which thunder down from the uplands in high cascades. Pools at the feet of the falls, and the rivers themselves, allow excellent freshwater swimming.

> *When Pohnpei's bright orange hibiscus flower falls prey to the tropical sunlight, it turns saffron yellow, tinged by burgundy, more elegant in death than in life.*

Nearly all the shore is skirted by intact mangrove forests. At Kitti, for example, the forest is almost a mile wide. Canoes must wind through twisting channels to reach the lagoon. Because of the mangrove forests, there are no beaches on Pohnpei itself. However, there are great beaches from which to snorkel and dive on nearby reef islets. There are three types of islands in Pohnpei's lagoons: coral, volcanic, and artificial. Creating artificial islands through landfill is not just a modern activity. The ancient residents of Pohnpei did so also.

Aside from the main town, Kolonia, the most heavily populated areas on Pohnpei are Sokehs Island and Madolenihmw (mad-o-LEN-ee-um). Pohnpei is one of the few islands in the Pacific with monumental ruins from every period of its

Pohnpei's Kepirohi waterfall is a great place to swim.

MICRONESIA REGIONAL TOURISM COUNCIL

POHNPEI'S CLIMATE

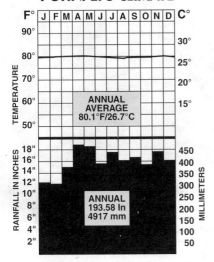

history: Micronesian, Spanish, German, Japanese, and American.

Kaselehlia, like *aloha,* translates into hello or goodbye, but to visitors it means "Welcome to Pohnpei."

Climate

An island does not contain a lush, tropical forest without a lot of rain. Kolonia gets roughly 16 *feet* of annual rainfall, but twice that amount falls on the mountains of the interior. Much, though by no means all, of the rain falls at night.

Even lush Pohnpei suffered severe drought during the 1997-1998 El Niño worldwide climate pattern. Residents received water only every other day. The conditions on some of Pohnpei State's outer atolls, such as Pingelap, were so disastrous that many residents moved to Pohnpei for the drought's duration.

The Founding of Pohnpei

According to one Pohnpei legend, long, long ago people sailed from a distant island in search of new land. On their way they met an octopus who told them of a shallow place in the sea stretching from north to south. They reached the place, but found only a tiny coral islet that fit between canoe and outrigger. So they used magic to call coral

and rocks to help build the island. Since waves broke the stones, they planted mangroves to protect their work and put a reef around the island to keep the sea away. As they brought more soil, the island grew. They built an altar and piled rocks on top of it. Thus Pohnpei got its name from *pohn* (on) *pei* (the altar).

All the people returned to their home island, except for one couple who remained and had many children. A second group arrived and helped enlarge Pohnpei, but all still lived in caves. Finally, a third group landed on the island bringing vegetables. They taught the others how to build houses of grass and small trees. Later, other groups came, each contributing to the Pohnpei of today.

History

Pohnpei was divided into three kingdoms by a line of native kings, the Saudeleurs, who ruled from Nan Madol, beginning in the 13th century. The Saudeleur dynasty was overthrown by the legendary warrior Isokelekel, who arrived with 333 comrades from Kosrae. Isokelekel established the first line of Nahnmwarkis, who are the current traditional chiefs. In the legends of Pohnpei (though not Kosrae) Isokelekel actually was a descendant of Pohnpei's earlier rulers who had been banished to Kosrae by usurpers.

Pohnpei was sighted by Alvaro de Saavedra in 1529. Pedro Fernando de Quirós, leader of a Spanish expedition, passed Pohnpei on 24 December 1595 but didn't land. The islanders were left in peace until the second quarter of the 19th century, when whalers arrived. In 1854 the American whaler *Delta* brought a smallpox epidemic to Pohnpei, wiping out half the population and leading to the abandonment of Nan Madol. A few years later the American ship *Pearl* brought measles, which killed many more. Whaling declined after 1865 when the Confederate raider *Shenandoah* sank 40 Yankee whaling ships in the North Pacific, four of them at Pohnpei.

One chance arrival, James F. O'Connell, shipwrecked here off the *John Bull* in 1827, entered local lore as the "Tattooed Irishman." O'Connell danced an Irish jig to ingratiate himself with the local chiefs. His book, *A Residence of Eleven Years in New Holland and the Caroline Islands,* is a colorful mix of sailor's tales and interesting facts about old Pohnpei.

a Japanese AA gun in a bamboo thicket on Sokehs Mountain (Pohndolap)

DAVID STANLEY

The Spanish laid vague claim to these islands in the 16th century but only arrived to occupy Pohnpei after the Germans claimed the Carolines in 1885. The Spanish built a town wall and fort at Kolonia, the remains of which you can visit today. The Germans bought the islands from Spain in 1899, took over the outpost at Kolonia, and developed the copra trade. Pohnpei became the capital of German Micronesia.

German rule was often harsh. In 1910 members of the Kawath clan of Sokehs killed four German officials in a rebellion brought on by forced labor for road building. The Germans brought soldiers from New Guinea to capture those responsible for the rebellion. Seventeen Pohnpeians were executed and 426 exiled to Angaur Island, Palau, to work in phosphate mines. Land owned by the rebel clans at Sokehs and Palikir was confiscated and given to outer islanders.

The Germans were forced off Pohnpei at the start of World War I in 1914 and the Japanese occupied the island. In a short period, they completed a road fit for vehicles around part of the island.

Thousands of Japanese colonists arrived and by 1941 they outnumbered the Pohnpeians three to one. Pohnpei was not a strategic base for the Japanese during World War II. The United States chose to bypass it, but launched more than 200 bombing attacks against the island. During much of the Trust Territory period Pohnpei was a quiet backwater.

After the war, as in the rest of Micronesia, the Japanese were repatriated. Pohnpei had more intermarriage than most other islands. Since the Japanese spouse was not allowed to stay in Micronesia, mixed families had to choose between moving to Japan or being split up. Not until the 1970s were the small number of Japanese in mixed marriages allowed to return.

Pohnpei is now the capital of the FSM. Considering its relative isolation it is surprisingly cosmopolitan. Micronesians from other states come to attend to the business of government. Kolonia has a fairly large expat community, primarily Americans and Filipinos, with a smaller number of Chinese.

Economy

Since Pohnpei is the capital of the Federated States of Micronesia, government plays the dominant role in the local economy. Education is important because Pohnpei is home to the main campus of the College of Micronesia—FSM. It recently moved from Kolonia to a new complex out at Palikir. The Pohnpei Agricultural and Trade School (PATS) is the only one of its kind in the region.

In 1995, at the inauguration for his second term, Pres. Bailey Olter called for an economy based upon the notion of "sustainable living." This concept is critical for all nations on this consumer-oriented planet. But the problem created by consuming more than nature can replenish hits the limited ecologies of small island nations particularly painfully. Olter maintained that for Pohnpei, sustainable living must revolve around agriculture, tourism, and the fisheries.

Over the past decades, agriculture has not fared well. There has been a clear decline in subsistence farms. However, Pohnpei is famous for its yams *(kehp),* which grow up to 10 feet long—a cluster can weigh a thousand pounds. Other traditional crops are taro, breadfruit, cassava, and sweet potatoes. Pohnpei's black pepper is thought by many to be the tastiest in the world.

Pohnpei was hard-hit in the general economic slowdown of FSM in the late 1990s.

Kaselel shampoo and Oil of Pohnpei soap are made from coconut oil by Pohnpei Coconut Products Inc. (P.O. Box 1120, Pohnpei, FM 96941), near PATS in Madolenihmw. This company also produces Marekeiso oil for use on body and hair and "Oil of Pohnpei" suntan oil. These excellent products are sold at handicraft outlets around Kolonia and can be ordered by mail.

Genuine Pohnpei pepper can be ordered through the mail from Pohnpei Agricultural Development, Inc., P.O. Box 1479, Pohnpei, FM 96941. Both white and black pepper, ground or whole, is available.

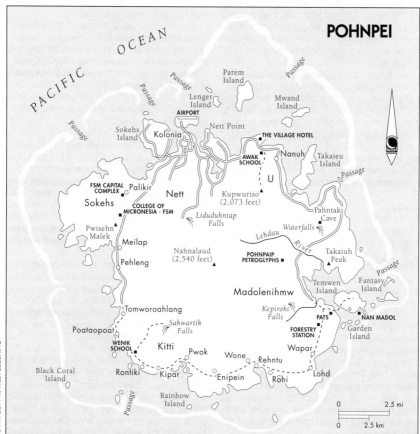

The People

The state's population is approximately 34,000, about a fifth of which lives in Kolonia. Pohnpeians outside Kolonia don't live in compact villages, but in groups of individual houses with land around each. People generally are easygoing and friendly.

Influential lines of chiefs and nobility control the five municipalities other than Kolonia: Sokehs, Nett, U, Madolenihmw, and Kitti. Each has a Nahnmwarki, or High Chief, and a Nahnken, or Talking Chief. Below the hereditary nobility are other social classes of landowners and commoners, a complex social hierarchy. Descent is matrilineal, with children becoming members of the mother's clan and inheriting their prestige and property from it. It's hard to discern differences in caste from appearances; whenever in doubt, visitors should address or greet older people first.

Immigrants from outer islands such as Pingelap, Mwoakilloa (formerly Mokil), and the Mortlocks make up about a quarter of the population of Pohnpei Island. Some formed separate communities, each with its own language, on Sokehs Island, where they were resettled in 1912 on lands seized by the Germans during the 1910 rebellion. At Porakiet, on the west side of downtown Kolonia, live about 1,000 Polynesians from Kapingamarangi atoll.

Crafts

Pohnpei has an outstanding tradition of loom woven sashes of intricate patterns. Certain patterns and colors belonged to specific families and copying was not permitted. In fact, some sashes belonged to the nobility, and a commoner could be put to death for wearing such a belt. Sashes were sometimes heavily decorated with glass beads and tiny shells.

Still available for purchase is the dance paddle. Dance paddles in Pohnpei come in various sizes, typically with a white line design of an intricate geometric pattern on the flat of the blade. The edges of the blade are decorated with pandanus fiber. Other local crafts include carefully scaled model canoes, wooden sea animals and fish, and woven items such as wall hangings, trays, handbags, baskets, fans, and mats. Pohnpei is also noted for its unique stools, a seat with a built-in coconut grater.

SIGHTS

Kolonia

Kolonia is more a town than a colony or city. You can look for downtown Kolonia, only to realize you are in it. One is never more than a couple of dozen feet from the nearest chicken or pig. A road that is a continuation of the causeway road from the airport lies at sea level parallel to Kolonia Harbor. On this road are many of the island's small businesses, the public market, and such retail outlets as hardware stores. Most of central Kolonia is about 100 feet higher, with some residential areas higher still. The town thus has an interesting topography.

Because Pohnpei is the capital of the Federated States, everyone in town seems to speak English; in this way someone from Kosrae can communicate with someone from Yap or Chuuk.

Before World War II, Kolonia had a population of 10,000 Japanese nationals (in all there were 13,000 Japanese on Pohnpei and only 5,900 Micronesians). Kolonia and its environs are again approaching that size in population, and it's mostly Micronesians this time.

The **Pohnpei Lidorkini Museum** (open Mon.-Fri. 10 a.m.-5 p.m.) is a good place to start a visit to Kolonia. The small museum has excellent model canoes, some six to eight feet long. Also inside is a small Pohnpeian assembly house (Nahs) with tools of sakau-making. The museum's strongest feature is its focus on uses of native materials such as sakau and the coconut palm. Because of its artifacts from Nan Madol, it's great to visit the museum before going to that site.

For further information on the museum, contact Museum Director Henter P. Lawrence (P.O. Box 250, Education Department, Kolonia, Pohnpei, FM 96941, tel. 691-320-5299, fax 691-320-5155). Next door to the Lidorkini Museum is the **Nahnsehling Maritime Center,** with exhibits relating to the use of the ocean.

In the park on the north side of Kolonia is the **old Spanish wall,** which now doubles as the left field fence for a baseball field. Built in 1887 (earlier than the "Green Monster" at Fenway), it marked the western boundary of Fort Alfonso XIII, which extended north and east to the lagoon. Just across the park is the **Catholic mission.** Only the apse and belfry remain from the

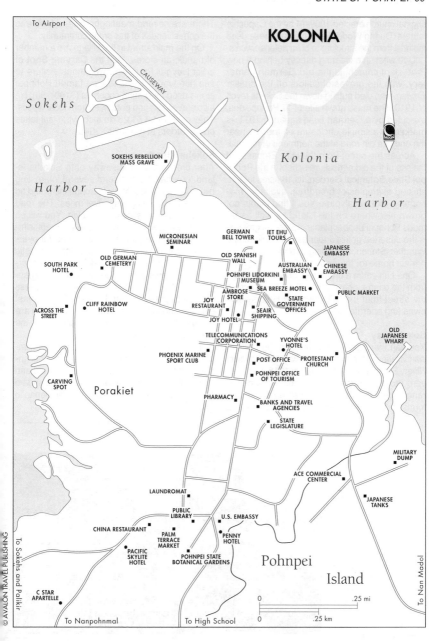

KOLONIA

To Airport

CAUSEWAY

Sokehs

Harbor

Kolonia

Harbor

SOKEHS REBELLION
MASS GRAVE

MICRONESIAN
SEMINAR

GERMAN
BELL TOWER

IET EHU
TOURS

JAPANESE
EMBASSY

OLD GERMAN
CEMETERY

OLD SPANISH
WALL

AUSTRALIAN
EMBASSY

CHINESE
EMBASSY

SOUTH PARK
HOTEL

POHNPEI LIDORKINI
MUSEUM

AMBROSE
STORE

SEA BREEZE MOTEL

PUBLIC MARKET

CLIFF RAINBOW
HOTEL

JOY
RESTAURANT

STATE
GOVERNMENT
OFFICES

ACROSS THE
STREET

JOY HOTEL

SEAIR
SHIPPING

OLD
JAPANESE
WHARF

TELECOMMUNICATIONS
CORPORATION

YVONNE'S
HOTEL

CARVING
SPOT

Porakiet

PHOENIX MARINE
SPORT CLUB

POST OFFICE

PROTESTANT
CHURCH

POHNPEI OFFICE
OF TOURISM

PHARMACY

BANKS AND TRAVEL
AGENCIES

STATE
LEGISLATURE

MILITARY
DUMP

ACE COMMERCIAL
CENTER

LAUNDROMAT

JAPANESE
TANKS

PUBLIC
LIBRARY

U.S. EMBASSY

CHINA RESTAURANT

PALM
TERRACE
MARKET

PENNY
HOTEL

Pohnpei

PACIFIC
SKYLITE
HOTEL

POHNPEI STATE
BOTANICAL GARDENS

Island

C STAR
APARTELLE

To Nanpohnmal

To High School

To Sokehs and Palikir

To Nan Madol

0   .25 mi

0   .25 km

© AVALON TRAVEL PUBLISHING

original church erected 1909-14 by the Capuchin fathers. During World War II the Japanese used material from the structure to build defense works.

Due west, in a clearing directly behind a new Protestant church, is the **old German cemetery,** with the graves of sailors off the cruiser *Emden,* who died putting down the Sokehs revolt of 1910. The mass grave site of 17 Pohnpeians, executed by a German firing squad in 1911, is marked by a simple enclosure on the left, near the end of a dirt road at the north end of Kolonia.

Across the street from the U.S. Embassy at the site of the old agriculture school is the **Pohnpei State Botanical Garden.** Its 18 acres feature striking examples of breadfruit, avocado, mahogany, and eucalyptus. You'll find plants not grown elsewhere on the island as well as famous Pohnpei pepper plants. Inside the grounds is the deserted gothic Japanese Agriculture and Weather Station, a building that would make a perfect home for the Addams Family.

One can then catch a great view of Sokehs Island from the open-air bar **Across the Street,** across the street from the Cliff Rainbow Hotel, which owns and operates it.

Sokehs Bay

You can then take a stroll through the Polynesian village of **Porakiet** on your way back to town. Ninety Polynesians settled here in 1918 after a severe drought on their native atoll, Kapingamarangi. Open thatched houses sit on stone platforms and the residents have an outdoor lifestyle.

There are several meetinghouses, a tribute to the cohesiveness of this small community.

On the main street in the village are a number of handicraft stores. Visit the **Carving Spot** of artist Heyger Paul, who welcomes visitors to see him work. He makes the famed Pohnpei stools used for grating coconuts ($100-150). He also carves fish and porpoises from local woods. They cost about $1.25 an inch. Mr. Paul takes phone orders at (691) 320-3648.

Sokehs Island

After crossing the causeway onto Sokehs Island, one has the choice of several interesting hikes. The easiest is to walk around the island on the road, about six fairly level miles. The road presents a great slice of island life. You will be joined by happy children and see well-kept, simple homes. The island has a wonderful overgrown feel; looking inland, one sees fantastic volcanic outcroppings, toward the right are ever-changing views of the water seen through mangroves. The west side of Sokehs Island is less heavily populated than the east. On the east side are shops for drinks and the like. If you are going to circle the island, bring water because the west side has few services.

The road around the island has been improved. Although there are still about 2.5 unpaved miles, the roadbed has been graded and it's not difficult to drive around, even in a standard car. Thus the road, whose construction began in 1890, is now near completion.

Massive volcanic plugs poke skyward just below the summit of Sokehs Rock (Paipalap).

DAVID STANLEY

VICINITY OF KOLONIA

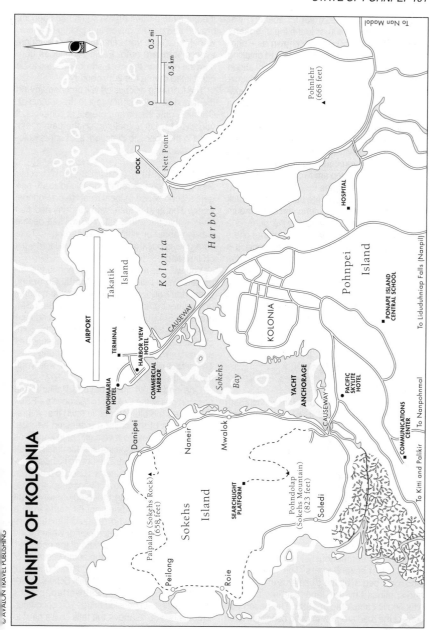

© AVALON TRAVEL PUBLISHING

To Nan Madol

0.5 mi
0.5 km

N

Pohnlehr
(668 feet)

DOCK

Nett Point

HOSPITAL

Kolonia

Harbor

Takatik
Island

AIRPORT

TERMINAL

HARBOR VIEW
HOTEL

PWOHMARIA
HOTEL

COMMERCIAL
HARBOR

CAUSEWAY

KOLONIA

Pohnpei
Island

PONAPE ISLAND
CENTRAL SCHOOL

To Liduduhniap Falls (Nanpil)

Sokehs
Bay

YACHT
ANCHORAGE

CAUSEWAY

PACIFIC
SKYLITE
HOTEL

COMMUNICATIONS
CENTER

To Nanpohnmal

To Kitti and Palikir

Danipei

Naneir

Mwalok

Sokehs
Island

SEARCHLIGHT
PLATFORM

Pohndolap
(Sokehs Mountain)
(823 feet)

Soledi

Paipalap (Sokehs Rock)
(658 feet)

Peilong

Roie

A more difficult hike, great for scenery, war relics, and birdwatching, is to the top of **Sokehs Mountain** (823 feet), locally known as Pohndolap. Just after the causeway, instead of taking the road to the right, take the road straight ahead that winds up the hill. When the paved road turns left, go straight on the overgrown former Japanese military road. Follow this path for about a 25-minute walk, until it switchbacks steeply to the mountaintop.

You'll know you're getting there when you start seeing good views of Kolonia. Take care to note which way you came so you can find your way back down. On top are two large double-barreled Japanese AA guns to the right and a six-inch naval gun in a concrete bunker at the back of the hill to the left. At the north end of the mountain, some distance beyond the AA guns, is a metal Japanese searchlight platform that offers stunning views of Sokehs Rock and Kolonia. It is best to take this hike with someone who has done it before. The Office of Tourism & Parks, tel. (691) 320-2421, can provide you with the name of a guide.

The climb to the top of **Sokehs Rock** (658 feet), or Paipalap (Peipapap), though spectacular, should only be taken by excellent hikers with some climbing ability, accompanied by someone familiar with the path. There have been serious accidents on the Rock.

South of Kolonia

A road, partially paved, runs four miles south from Kolonia past the rock crusher along the dirt road to **Liduduhniap Falls** at Nanpil (admission of several dollars may be charged). The road follows the Kahmar River (good swimming) then climbs, affording a good view of the island's lush interior. The area around the falls has been cleared; the road runs right up to it. After rains, the way can be muddy and cars can bog down. You pass a hydroelectric project on the way to the falls.

Around the Island

Pohnpei has tremendously improved its roads over the last several years. The round-the-island road, begun by the Spaniards in the 1890s and continued by the Japanese in the 1930s, was finally completed in 1985. The paved portions of the road are now in good condition. Even the unpaved portion on the south has been improved and can be driven in a pickup or a four-wheel drive, or if you can drive slowly enough, even a standard auto. Paving continues from both the east and the west, and is expected to be completed during the 20th century.

The following discussion will proceed around the island from the southwest to the southeast. Certainly until the paving project is complete, if you wish to visit something on the east coast, head in the opposite direction, east out of Kolonia instead.

West and South

Going west on the round-the-island road, one gets a good sense of local rural life on Pohnpei today. The land is lush, with gardens and fruit trees within the rainforest. You will see people walking about or sitting on their porches. Take care driving because many young children walk on the road.

You will see a well-marked turnoff to the impressive nine-building **FSM Capital Complex,** opened at Palikir in 1989. It houses the national government offices, the Congress of the FSM, and the FSM Supreme Court. The buildings are completely modern, but the roof lines, the color of material, and the basalt log-shaped supports are reminiscent of traditional meetinghouses. The area is open and quite attractive, well worth the detour.

One and a half miles beyond Palikir is the new campus of the College of Micronesia—FSM. It replaced the old campus in town that will remain a part of the college extension service. The school is next to a volcanic plug known as **Pwisehn Malek** ("Chickenshit Mountain") that towers above the road. The prismatic basalt formations indicate the materials used to build Nan Madol. When a lava flow is very deep, the material cools slowly into these columnar basalt crystals. *Pwisehn Malek* got its name from a legendary rooster who relieved himself here (thereby creating the outcropping) while racing around the island on an errand of the gods.

Two waterfalls flow off the southwest side of Pohnpei in Kitty municipality, a difficult one-hour hike up a muddy track from Wenik School. Water that feeds the first falls, **Sahwarlap,** passes under the first suspension bridge you encounter. Trouble is, you're above the falls so it's hard to get a clear view. Just beyond the bridge, work your way over to the edge of the cliff for a view of **Sahwartik,** the higher of the two falls. Be aware that this path can be quite slippery. Do not attempt to climb the falls.

South and East
The **Pohnpei Agricultural and Trade School** (PATS) at Madolenihmw is a Jesuit-run secondary school, offering 160 Micronesians four-year courses in construction, mechanics, horticulture, and animal husbandry. Tours of PATS are offered 1-4 p.m. A small **coconut products plant** run by **Kaselel Company** near the Temwen Causeway produces excellent coconut oil soap, shampoo,

and skin cream. Sold in tiny pandanus baskets, they make wonderful souvenirs.

Nan Madol
If you ever visit Pohnpei, if you are ever even close to Pohnpei, you *must* see Nan Madol. Period.

This celebrated archaeological site is located on artificial islands in the lagoon by Temwen Island, off the east coast of Pohnpei. These islands are home to impressive stone compounds and varied basalt buildings. Legend tells how Nan Madol was formed by the *hunani,* Olsihpa, and Olsohpa, causing the stones to fly into place. Usually "hunani" is translated "magicians," but in

NAN MADOL RUINS

Temwen Island

KONDEREK

NAN DOWAS

NAN MWOLUHSEI

PEHI EN KITEL

PEHIKAPW SAPWAWAS

KARIAHN

PEINERING

PAHN KADIRA

IDEHD

DARONG

Passage

KELEPWEL

Moon

Lagoon

PAHNWI

0 .1 mi

0 .1 km

© AVALON TRAVEL PUBLISHING

LOUISE FOOTE

the mysterious ruins of Nan Madol

the Pohnpeian tradition, "hunani" implies people of occult skills, with an unusual degree of enlightenment.

The most usual means of visiting Nan Madol today, as it was in traditional times, is from the sea. One enters a break in the seawall and comes to the monumental plaza on Nan Dowas surrounded by basalt logs, forming walls 25 feet high. As you approach the island, you will be overwhelmed by the grandeur of the construction. You can only imagine the feeling it inspired in visitors from other islands when they arrived for commerce or to pay tribute to Nan Madol's rulers. Like Piazza San Marcos in Venice, the grandeur of the city made a foreign policy statement. All visitors who wished to enter the royal quarters had to crawl in through a low opening, thus increasing the disparity between them and the king.

A mighty seawall flanks the site on three sides, with open channels between the 80 artificial islands. One is awed by the society that was able to construct Nan Madol; all of the huge basalt logs that went into the project had to be brought by bamboo rafts! New archeological finds indicate that the earliest levels may have been built as early as the 7th century and that building continued until the 16th century. When Europeans began to colonize Pohnpei, Nan Madol had only recently been abandoned.

The main islets to visit are Pahnwi, with a seawall of monoliths; Kariahn, the burial place of priests; Pahn Kadira, the administrative center; Kelepwel, housing servants for Pahn Kadira; Idehd, the religious center; Pehi en Kitel, the burial place of chiefs; Darong, center for ceremonial clamming; Peinering, coconut-oil-producing center; Pehikapw Sapwawas, the communication or drumming center; Nan Mwoluhsei, a huge boulder from which warriors jumped to prove their bravery; Konderek (place of funeral rites), and the greatest ruin of all, Nan Dowas, the war temple or fortress.

Nan Dowas is the most spectacular island, the only one surrounded by monumental walls. Some of its walls have partially collapsed, most likely from the long, steady pressure of breadfruit tree roots. Many of the other islands of Nan Madol have not been excavated, or even properly surveyed. One would need a lifetime to explore the entire compound, particularly since some of the islands are completely overgrown today. Currently, an attempt is being made to remove some of the trees obstructing views or destroying key portions of the site.

Many hotels can arrange a trip for you, most charging about $50. Closest to the site, the Village Hotel has its own touring service. Most tours also take you snorkeling in the lagoon and conclude with a swim in the Kepirohi waterfall. If you prefer to spend additional time at the site, discuss this with your guide and boatmates before taking off.

Tides affect what you will be able to see and do at Nan Madol. If you will be on Pohnpei for a period of time, arrange the trip at high tide. At that time a small motorboat can go through many of the canals, allowing you to visit many of the basalt sea walls protecting some of the lesser artificial islands. Walking across the canals at low tide is a more difficult alternative. You must choose between walking in mud or using tricky underwater coral stepping stones.

It's more fun to be guided through the canals by kayak. Most tour operators can arrange this. And during much of the tide, a kayak can go though canals that contain insufficient water for a motorboat.

A much less desirable alternative is to wade or snorkel to the ruins from Joy Island or to cross the footbridge from Temwen Island. This is much more difficult and should only be done at low tide. Enterpoint Minimarket, about a quarter of a mile past PATS if you veer to your right, advertises ferry service to Nan Madol, tel. (691) 320-3026. It is pretty much hit or miss whether the service will be available when you wish.

The high chief of Madolenihmw, Ilten Selten, 23rd Nahnmwarki since the fall of the Saudeleur dynasty, lives on Temwen and charges a $3 pp entrance fee to visit the ruins. A representative of the chief may approach you on the site to collect it.

East and North

Just past the turnoff to PATS, **Kepirohi Falls** (admission $3 adult, $1.50 child) pours over basalt cliffs into an idyllic swimming pool. Take the path near the bridge where the boats dock. Pyramid-like **Takaiuh Peak** rises across Madolenihmw Harbor. The secure yacht anchorage just west of the point of land opposite Temwen's north end makes this a good port of call for yachties.

Several miles farther down the road are the **Pohnpaip Petroglyphs.** Shortly after you make the turnoff, someone will come out to charge you $3 pp and, in return, guide you. It is a very short, easy walk to the rocks. On the right of the path are a number of standing rocks, some with petroglyphs. On the left is one huge stone, perhaps 100 feet square. Parts of the huge rock are hollow, which you can tell by tapping it with a stone. There is a petroglyph of a woman with a baby inside—the birthing stone. Even without the petroglyphs, this would be a wonderful spot for a picnic. It is set on a beautiful plateau at the base of the mountains.

Farther north, a sign on the right will direct you to the **Pahntakai Cave and Waterfall.** Drive to the end of the road, and someone will ask you for $3 and point you in the direction of the cave, about a mile away. Camping is permitted at this beautiful and remote site.

ACCOMMODATIONS

Pohnpei has a six percent room tax. Most hotels offer free transfer service from the airport, so ask. There's no suitable place to camp in Kolonia itself—you have to go a bit outside. Whenever

---

POHNPEI COUNTRY CODE: 691

camping on Pohnpei, get permission from the landowner, especially if houses are near your campsite.

Hotels

On the hill behind town is the large **Cliff Rainbow Hotel** (moderate) (P.O. Box 96, Kolonia, Pohnpei, FM 96941, tel. 691-320-2415, fax 691-320-2417), expanded to accommodate the 1998 meeting of the South Pacific Forum. Rooms are comfortable, though not exciting. It works fairly well for both English and Japanese speakers. Rooms start at $40 s, $48 d in the old wing and go as high as $85 s, $95 d in the new wing. It is probably the best choice on the island if you are on business and need a telephone in your room. The least expensive rooms are the best value. It is a 10-minute walk or a $1 cab fare to almost anyplace in town. A small restaurant on the premises is open for breakfast, lunch, and dinner. This full-service hotel also can make arrangements for your touring or diving needs.

Close to the U.S. Embassy is the **Penny Hotel** (moderate) (P.O. Box 934, Kolonia, Pohnpei, FM 96941, tel. 691-320-5770, fax 691-320-2040, e-mail: penny@mail.fm). The hotel is well situated, overlooking the **Pohnpei State Botanical Garden** and an upscale residential neighborhood. This 15-room hotel charges $65 s, $75 d. Although there is no restaurant on the premises, there are a good number nearby.

The friendly, modern **Joy Hotel**(moderate) (P.O. Box 484, Kolonia, Pohnpei, FM 96941, tel. 691-320-2447, fax 691-320-2478, e-mail: ponape@mail.fm) could be said to be in the heart of town if Kolonia were the type of town that could be said to have a center. The 10 a/c rooms with fridge and TV are $65 s, $85 d. Most of the clientele is Japanese, but the hotel also does a good job with English-speaking guests. Excellent Japanese meals are served in the dining room.

The **South Park Hotel** (moderate) (P.O. Box 829, Kolonia, Pohnpei, FM 96941, tel. 691-320-2255, fax 691-320-2600) also caters to Japanese travelers, but unfortunately does not work well for English speakers. It has six rooms in the old wing at $40 s, $45 d, none too pleasant, and 12 nice rooms in the new wing at $75 s, $85 d. All rooms are a/c, but the new rooms have better beds, cable TV, refrigerators, and in-room phones. Most of the new rooms have unsurpassed views of Sokeh Rock and Island.

Sea Breeze Hotel (inexpensive) (P.O. Box 692, Kolonia, Pohnpei, FM 96941, tel. 691-320-2065, fax 691-320-2067), next to the Australian Embassy, is a clean but rather spartan place. Rooms that overlook the water are $55 s, $60 d, five bucks less for rear rooms.

Serious drawbacks plague both the **Harbor View Hotel** (inexpensive) (P.O. Box 1328, Kolonia, Pohnpei, FM 96941, tel. 691-320-5244, fax 691-320-5246), with rooms for $35 s, $50 d, and **Pwohmaria Beach Resort** (moderate) (P.O. Box 1416, Kolonia, Pohnpei, FM 96941, tel. 691-320-5942, fax 691-320-5941), with rooms for $50-72 s, $60-78 d. Both isolated hotels are near the airport but removed from town life. The Pwohmaria bungalows are nice, but most rooms are not air conditioned. Despite the name and the impression from its brochure, it is near the commercial harbor and is not a beach resort. The Harbor View is on the docks, noisy, and suited only for those who are truly harbor freaks. The Harbor View can smell quite ripe when the wind blows from the tuna wharf.

In the last edition of this book, we described the **Pacific Skylite Hotel** (moderate) (P.O. Box 1687, Kolonia, Pohnpei, FM 96941, tel. 691-320-3672, fax 691-320-3708) as overpriced. It has since reduced its rates to $66 s, 75 d, a reasonable level. The hotel's bar has become a hangout for the expat crowd.

The **Village Hotel** (expensive) (P.O. Box 339, Pohnpei, FM 96941, tel. 691-320-2797, fax 691-320-3797, e-mail: thevillage@mail.fm), six miles east of Kolonia at U, is undoubtedly the best vacation hotel on Pohnpei—nothing is a close second. It's probably the most romantic hotel in all of Micronesia: great lodging, great food, everything seems to get done for each guest. Its 20 Pohnpei-style thatched bungalows with bamboo walls, oversized waterbeds, ceiling fans, and private bath run $80-95 s, $90-105 d (depending on the view from the room). Air conditioning is unnecessary here as the tradewinds blow through the screening surrounding the rooms. Patti and Bob Arthur wisely opted for ceiling fans instead. They also wisely opted to leave telephones out of the rooms.

It is hard to believe this hotel is more than 20 years old. The Village, awarded for its accomplishment as an ecotourism hotel, was ahead of its time when founded and has been able to maintain its edge.

Apartments

Pohnpei has several apartment hotels that take day guests. Their prices are quite economical, particularly if you are traveling with a family. If you cook at home, your savings will increase.

In the heart of town is **Yvonne's Hotel** (inexpensive) (P.O. Box 688, Kolonia, Pohnpei, 96941, tel. 691-320-4953), with many units having kitchens. Rentals start at $45 s, $55 d.

Farther from town on the road to the communications center is the 12-unit **C Star Apartelle** (moderate) (P.O. Box 279, Kolonia, Pohnpei, FM 94961, tel. 691-320-3460, fax 691-320-3399). Prices start at $60 s, $75 d, with a three-bedroom unit going for $125. Discounts are offered for commercial travelers there for a longer stay. There is a Chinese restaurant on the premises.

Resort Islands

There are islands in the Pohnpei lagoon with guest facilities. These "resorts" provide simple cottages, usually without indoor plumbing or electricity. They are inexpensive and provide a chance to slow down, if you don't mind roughing it. Unless you make other arrangements, be sure to bring water, food, and mosquito netting.

The nicest is **Black Coral Island** (P.O. Box 1519, Kolonia, Pohnpei, FM 96941, tel. 691-320-4869) off the southwest side of Pohnpei. To stay a night costs only $5 pp, but to get there, a boat will cost $35 roundtrip per boatload. The rooms are simple boxes, but there are toilet facilities and plenty of water. To be safe bring your own drinking water or purification system. There are great views back to Pohnpei. You can swim across to a neighbor island or snorkel in the channel between the two. Be conscious of the extent and direction of the tide.

Lenger Island Resort (P.O. Box 667, Kolonia, Pohnpei, FM 96941, tel. 691-320-2769) has seven units, renting at $7 pp. The island is a five-minute boat ride past the airport.

Both of these resort islands also take day guests.

HEG's Garden Island Resort, formerly Joy Island, (P.O. Box 175, Kolonia, Pohnpei, FM

96941, tel. 691-320-3586) is set on a sandy reef islet near Nan Madol on the southeast side of Pohnpei. It is not clear whether it is still in operation. If you can make arrangements, bring all your supplies with you.

FOOD

Pohnpei has interesting, reasonably priced Japanese restaurants.

The **Joy Restaurant** (lunch Mon.-Sat., dinner Sunday only) is the most interesting spot in town for lunch. Terrific Japanese bento box lunches are $5-8. It is a popular restaurant with expats, local business people, and government workers. On crowded days someone may be seated with you at your table, which is a great way to meet people.

The nearby **Joy Hotel Restaurant** serves a similar though less extensive menu at prices comparable to the Joy Restaurant. The food is as good (or better) than at the Joy Restaurant, though the atmosphere is missing the energy.

The **PCR Restaurant,** recently moved to a new location on the outskirts of Kolonia on the road to Nan Madol, in the old Nantehlik Hotel building. It overlooks an expansive inlet of salt and fresh water as well as Nett Point. Though it specializes in Japanese cuisine, it also serves pasta dishes. Prices vary widely, but some excellent chicken dishes cost about $9. It has a festive feel to it.

The **South Park Hotel Restaurant** serves Japanese food not quite as good as at the above three restaurants, but at a higher price. Dinner with a beer will cost about $20. From the lanai is a great view of Sokeh Rock. But a better way to enjoy the view is to skip the meal here and get a happy hour beer ($1.50) next door at the Cliff Rainbow's Across the Street Bar.

Sei's Restaurant is about 50 feet before the turnoff to the U.S. Embassy. It's housed in a wonderful room, quite spacious, with a high beamed ceiling and planked floor. The tables are large and well spaced. Sei's is now a Japanese food buffet: lunch $6.50, dinner $8.50. Mounds of tuna sashimi, vegetable and fish tempora, rice noodle dishes, etc. Very tasty.

The **China Restaurant** (closed Sunday) offers fairly good, though expensive, Chinese food. Its special group menus for four or more are the best buys.

SAKAU

Listen for the rhythmic pounding leading to a *sakau* house. *Sakau,* made from a pepper shrub root, is pounded on a flat stone and squeezed through hibiscus fibers to produce a mildly narcotic, powerfully anesthetizing drink similar to Fijian *kava,* but stronger. The *sakau* is generously served in a half-coconut shell. The taste is a combination of woodiness and chalk. Getting *puputa* (high) on *sakau* is a strange experience: even if your head stays reasonably coherent, when you try to get up, your knees may have disappeared.

The *sakau* bars of Kolonia are usually simple huts with signs in front. You can also find *sakau* for sale in the villages on Pohnpei. A *nahs* is an assembly house for drinking it.

One health concern is that *sakau* may be made with untreated water. Unless you have a cast-iron stomach, you may wish to make inquiries before drinking.

The **Cafe Ole** is a small, inexpensive luncheonette next to the Ambros Store. It serves both made-to-order and steam table lunches, as well as breakfast.

The Cliff Rainbow Hotel also has a restaurant serving breakfast, lunch, and dinner. The food is okay. Most dinners run about $12.

My favorite restaurant on Pohnpei is the elegant **Tattooed Irishman** at the Village Hotel. It is covered but open-air, perched above the mangrove forest with a view to the ocean below. In the distance, even Sokehs Rock can be seen. The food is excellent and plentiful, the service the best in Micronesia. Dinner with a beer or two will cost you about $20. The restaurant also serves breakfast and lunch, as well as a great Sunday brunch that allows for leisurely dining.

OTHER PRACTICALITIES

Entertainment

Pohnpei is blessed (or from another perspective—cursed) with some of the great bars of the Pacific.

Across the Street, across the street from the Cliff Rainbow Hotel, which operates it, overlooks the water and beautiful Sokehs Rock. This comfortable, covered, open-air room serves beer for $1.50 during happy hour.

The **Tattooed Irishman** at the Village Hotel also has an open-air bar with an unsurpassed ocean view. Its island ambience makes it a fantastic place to watch the sunset.

Since the demise of the venerable **Palm Terrace Bar,** three bars have taken up the slack as the best places to meet the expat community after 5 p.m. The bar in the **Pacific Skylite Hotel** is often the most crowded, but the other two are much more scenic. **Rumors** is in the mangroves, down by the small boat marina. To get to Rumors, at the junction in front of the Skylite, take the road toward Sokehs and look for Rumors' large sign, on the right within several hundred yards. Happy hour is 4-6 p.m. Saturday and Sunday it opens at noon. Snacks are available, but there is no meal service. **Club Cupid** is located 0.7 miles farther toward Sokehs from Rumors. It too has a sign on the right to lead the way. Up a hill, it has panoramic views and most evenings, yes, karaoke.

Pohnpei's main dance club is **Club Flamingo.** It gets going at about 11 p.m., and keeps going and going.

A multiscreen theater in Kolonia, behind the Ace Commercial Center, opened in late 1998.

Sports and Recreation

Divers should bring their own regulator, buoyancy compensator, and gauges with them. A certification card is required for all equipment rentals and scuba trips. Too much sediment from heavy rainfall runoff precludes diving from the main island. But numerous small white sand islands on the surrounding barrier reef allow for excellent channel diving. From December through February, waters are more likely to be rough.

The biggest dive shop on Pohnpei, with the nicest boats, is the **Phoenix Marine Sport Club** (PMSC) (P.O. Box 387, Pohnpei, FM 96941, tel. 691-320-2362, fax 691-320-2364). It focuses on Japanese-speaking business. While it accommodates English-speaking divers, there may be language difficulties with some employees. Make sure you are comfortable communicating with your divemaster. Diving on the dropoffs just outside the reef passes costs $65 for two tanks, including lunch and drinks (four-person minimum). This includes tanks, but you will have to pay

extra for any other equipment you rent. Diving at Ant and Pakin atolls costs $75 for two tanks.

Phoenix will also take nondivers for a day of picnicking and snorkeling, usually at Black Coral Island or Ant for $55 pp, lunch $5 extra (five-person minimum). Trolling in a 30-foot boat costs $400 per boat, reef fishing costs $300 per boat.

If you don't have a large group to split the costs, much less expensive for fishing is **Micro Tours** (P.O. Box 459, Pohnpei, FM 96941, tel. 691-320-2888, fax 691-320-5528). Trolling costs $100 pp and reef fishing is $75 pp. They will also take you to Ant for snorkeling for $50 pp.

Iet Ehu Tours (P.O. Box 559, Kolonia, Pohnpei, FM 96941, tel. 691-320-2959, fax 691-320-2958), a very good outfit, offers a full range of diving, $65 pp to the Pohnpei reef, $80 pp to Ant or Pakin atoll, including lunch. Fishing costs $125 for trolling, $50 for bottom fishing, with lunch included (prices per person will be reduced if more than one person is fishing). Iet Ehu also arrange ocean and land tours and overnights. They can arrange seeing Nan Madol by kayak. They also can arrange a trip to the **Mwakot Cultural Center,** which includes seeing a traditional dance, having lunch, and taking part in the *sakau* ceremony. The charge is $30 pp. If you like, this visit can be part of a full-day trip around the entire island at $50 pp. At times Iet Ehu can be difficult to reach, so call in advance to make arrangements.

There are a fair number of small tour and diving operators that open and close with some regularity. The Pohnpei Office of Tourism keeps a fairly up-to-date list (P.O. Box 66, Kolonia, Pohnpei, FM 96941, tel. 691-320-2421, fax 691-320-6019).

Shopping

Excellent Polynesian handicrafts such as woodcarvings of dolphins and sharks, shellwork, woven wall hangings, coconut graters, model outrigger canoes, canoe bailers, mobiles, food and oil bowls, tackle boxes, and fish or eel traps are available at Porakiet. On the main street through Porakiet, try **Kapinga Store** or, right next to the Cliff Rainbow Hotel, **Actouka Boutique,** which also sells used English-language pocketbooks. Joy Restaurant also sells crafts.

Pohnpei now has supermarkets that can meet most of your needs. Probably the best is the expanded **Palm Terrace Store.** It offers a 10%

An imposing tino *figure from Nukuoro, 400 km (249 miles) southwest of Pohnpei. Abstract female images of this kind were draped with flowers and mats during island ceremonies.*

RAUTENSTRAUCH-JOEST MUSEUM, COLOGNE, GERMANY

discount on Thursday, Friday and Saturday. The Chuuk Trading Company has opened the **Sokehs Shopping Center,** with a grocery and a small department store. It is located on the round-the-island road, about two miles south of the turnoff to Sokehs Island. **Ambros Stores** has a grocery, small department store, and hardware store in downtown Kolonia. There is a **Best Buy** bulk discount store near the Pacific Skylight Hotel.

Services
The Bank of Hawaii (tel. 691-320-2543) and Bank of Guam (tel. 691-320-2550), both open Mon.-Thurs. 9:30 a.m.-2:30 p.m. (till 4 p.m. on Friday), have adjacent branches in the com-

mercial block just below the Pohnpei Legislature. A couple of good travel agencies are in offices above them. The Bank of FSM (tel. 691-320-2724) is in lower Kolonia.

You can place long distance telephone calls from the Telecommunications Corporation on the main street near the post office. You can also hook up to the Internet from their computers for $4 per hour. Address mail to Pohnpei, FM 96941.

The FSM Immigration office (tel. 691-320-2606), across from the baseball field and next to the old Spanish wall, will give visa extensions 30 days at a time, up to 90 days maximum.

Several countries have diplomatic missions in Kolonia. The Chinese Embassy, tel. (691) 320-5575, is near the Public Market. Above the Bank of FSM, across the street is the Australian Embassy (P.O. Box S, Kolonia, Pohnpei, FM 96941, tel. 691-320-5448). The Japanese Embassy is also across the street from the Australian Embassy. The United States Embassy (P.O. Box 1286, Kolonia, Pohnpei, FM 96941, tel. 691-320-2187) is near the Pohnpei State Botanical Gardens on the south side of town.

Information
The Pohnpei Office of Tourism (open weekdays, P.O. Box 66, Kolonia, Pohnpei, FM 96941, tel. 691-320-2421, fax 691-320-6019), beside the small Japanese tank on Main St., can provide current information on local resorts on reef islands and cultural events. There is a separate Pohnpei Visitors Bureau (P.O. Box 1949, Kolonia, Pohnpei, FM 96941, tel. 691-320-4851, e-mail: pvb@mail.fm).

One of the best travel books you will ever read is *Pohnpei, An Island Argosy* by Gene Ashby (Rainy Day Press, P.O. Box 574, Kolonia, Pohnpei, FM 96941). Gene explores every aspect of Pohnpei, and copies are usually available at souvenir shops and restaurants in Kolonia. Gene also edited two volumes of legends written by his students at the College of Micronesia: *Micronesian Customs and Beliefs* and *Never and Always.*

In 1996, the **Nature Conservancy** (P.O. Box 216, Kolonia, Pohnpei, FM 96941, tel. 691-320-4267) put together a wonderful pamphlet, *Pohnpei: An Ecotourist's Delight,* that sells for $2. The pamphlet describes 20 interesting sites on Pohnpei. It explains how difficult it is to hike to

Pohnpei. It explains how difficult it is to hike to each and also provides phone numbers for individual guides.

For scholars and serious students, the **Micronesian Seminar,** P.O. Box 160, Pohnpei, FM 96941, tel. (691) 320-4067, under the auspices of the Catholic Church, contains a great reference library on all aspects of Micronesia. The seminar director is Father Frances X. Hezel, SJ, Micronesia's preeminent scholar.

GETTING THERE

Pohnpei Airport (PNI) is on Takatik Island, connected by causeway to Kolonia. Most hotels offer shuttles to meet the flights. Car rental booths and a snack bar open for arrivals and departures. They are located about 100 yards toward the left as you leave the terminal building. Airport departure tax is $10. Signs warn against the spitting of betel nut juice. Take heed!

Continental Airlines Island Hopper heads west from Hawaii toward Guam (and back) two or three times a week, depending on the season. Remember that because of the International Date Line, you lose a day travelling from Honolulu to Pohnpei. Reconfirm your onward reservations at the airport upon arrival or by phone at (691) 320-2424.

Air Nauru has one flight a week from Nauru to Pohnpei, Guam, and Manila. From Nauru you also can make connections to or from Kiribati or the South Pacific.

Pacific Missionary Aviation no longer offers regular service from Pohnpei Island to other islands in the state. Presently, Pingelap and Mwoakilloa are only accessible by sea or by expensive chartered plane.

GETTING AROUND

Field Trips
The **Island Affairs Office** (tel. 691-320-2710), near the governor's office behind the Pohnpei legislature, offers two monthly field trips on the MV *Micro Glory*. The four-day eastern trip visits Mwoakilloa and Pingelap ($31 cabin roundtrip), while the nine-day southern trip calls at Ngatik, Nukuoro, and Kapingamarangi ($89 cabin

roundtrip). Cabin passengers must pay $2 pp daily extra for berthing. The ship has seven double cabins, usually booked well in advance; deck fares are about one-third these amounts.

Check with **SeAir Transportation Agency** (tel. 691-320-2866) downtown for boat tickets to Mwoakilloa ($6.24), Pingelap ($9.78), and Kosrae ($18.30). All fares are deck class (no cabins available) and meals are extra.

Boats to the outer islands routinely leave anywhere from 48 hours to a week late. Complaining will not be productive.

By Road
Taxis are the mainstay of Pohnpei's public transport. Flag down any cab you see or have your hotel call one of the more than 15 companies now operating. Any trip within Kolonia or out to the airport is $1 pp. For longer trips the fare will be higher but negotiable. To anywhere other than the farthest locations, however, the price should not be more than $2 pp.

Hitching on the roads to and from Kolonia isn't too difficult; there's not much traffic, but drivers will take you if they have room. Assume, however, that any pickup truck that stops to give you a ride outside Kolonia will expect you to pitch in a couple of bucks toward expenses.

Car Rentals
About a dozen agencies, large and small, rent cars for $40 and up a day with unlimited mileage. Check the rental time and fuel level marked on your contract before you drive off—and make sure there's a spare tire. Insurance is not always available. Be particularly careful driving off paved roads since it is easy to ding the car. Most car rentals will deliver and pick up at your hotel. It is easiest to have your hotel make the arrangements for you. If you wish to do so yourself, at the airport are: **Budget,** tel. (691) 320-8075, fax (691) 320-8909; and **Penny Rent A Car,** tel. (691) 320-5579, fax (691) 320-2040.

THE OUTER ISLANDS

Pakin and Ant
These two small atolls off the west coast of Pohnpei have wonderful beaches and excellent snorkeling and diving. Each is a day trip

from Pohnpei. Ant is easier to get to because it is closer (about one and a half hours by motorboat) and entry is not as dependent on high tide as is Pakin. Numerous seabirds nest on **Ant,** and diving or snorkeling in the S-shaped pass is superb during slack tide. Beware of strong currents when the tide is running. Ask about trips to Ant at Iet Ehu, Micro Tours, or Phoenix. Tour operators can arrange an overnight on one of Ant's beautiful palm-filled islands, dropping you off one day and picking you up the next. The island has no services, so bring everything you need. Yachties should obtain permission from the Nanpei family in Kolonia before visiting.

On the way to Ant atoll, I saw a family of dolphins. Their ancestors came from the sea, developed on land, returned to the sea. On a good day surfing—I get it.

Ngatik (Sapwuahfik)
Southwest of Pohnpei, Ngatik was resettled by Pohnpeians after the crew of a British whaler massacred all the male inhabitants in 1837. About 600 people live there now.

Mwoakilloa (Mokil)
This clean, jewel-like atoll 97 miles east of Pohnpei consists of three islands: Coconut, Taro, and Home. The atoll's 200 residents all live on Home. Lined with coral stones, Main Street runs right down the middle of Home, from the elementary school to the airstrip at the far end. Canoe houses and kitchens line the lagoon side of the road, while sleeping houses are on the ocean side. There's only one store in the village, often completely sold out.

The eastern field-trip ship from Pohnpei often calls at Mwoakilloa, both on the outward and inbound journeys, allowing a stop in between of a couple of days. Camp at the airstrip or ask about accommodations at the Municipal Building. Mwoakilloa is mostly for avid snorkelers, as you can soon exhaust the above-water attractions. Red coral washes onto the ocean beaches.

Pingelap
Pingelap, between Pohnpei and Kosrae, is a three-island atoll (pop. 518) with a big sunken taro patch *(inipwel)* behind the village. The snorkeling is good off the east end of the airstrip. The wide main island takes several hours to walk around at low tide. At night, Jan.-April, islanders using hand-held nets catch flying fish they attract with burning torches.

The chief magistrate can arrange accommodations at the Municipal Building, or ask for storekeeper Larry Lundstrum, who sometimes takes in guests. There are several small stores on Pingelap.

Oliver Sacks, in his fascinating *The Island of the Colorblind* (Alfred A. Knopf, New York, Toronto, 1997), investigated the lives of those on Pingelap with achromatopsia, or total color blindness. While this condition is extremely rare in

Sunday school
at Pingelap

DAVID STANLEY

most of the world, on Pingelap about 10% of the population has it. Because of this high incidence, Sacks can study not only the condition itself, but also how a society reacts if the condition is not rare.

Polynesian Islands

The people of Nukuoro and Kapingamarangi atolls are Polynesians. There are 42 tiny islands on the **Nukuoro** reef but most of the 350 people live on the largest.

Although 33 islets compose **Kapingamarangi** atoll, 366 miles southwest of Pohnpei, most of the population of 500 lives on the adjacent islets of Touhou and Ueru, which are linked by a concrete bridge. Tiny Touhou, which you can walk around in 10 minutes, houses the majority. The homes are arranged in clusters, each of which belongs to a different family. Yachts require a pilot to enter the lagoon, where an American plane and a Japanese ship lie submerged. Overwater toilets are a quaint part of Kapinga.

> *Often doctoral students and other researchers into Pohnpeian culture are stymied by incomplete answers from Pohnpeian informants. Traditionally, to tell all that one knows about a subject or a story is thought to cause the informant to lose part of himself. Legends, like knowledge of traditional medical cures told by elders, might only be passed on in their complete forms to selected family members, oftentimes the youngest male member. Since it is unlikely that the youngest will inherit land, the secret knowledge could be his legacy from the family.*
>
> —Gene Ashby, *An Island Argosy*

STATE OF CHUUK

INTRODUCTION

Driving on Weno's lush north shore, the road though paved is deeply potholed. I slowed down as I saw two children and their young mother sitting in the roadway, cutting coconuts with machetes. Behind them stood a corrugated metal shed on which had been spray-painted 90210.

Near the lagoonside market sat a brown-skinned woman, gold encircling her two front teeth. She wore a flower garland, a lava lava, and a Snapple T-shirt.

Chuuk is caught between two worlds, and most visitors to Chuuk, other than those who come for its unique wreck dive sites, don't like it at all. All international flights land on Weno. Though nestled in one of the most beautiful settings on earth, Weno is a dirty island. Trash and wrecked cars lie scattered along potholed roads. Sea walls wreck the visual unity of the lagoon shore.

Weno deteriorated between 1995 and 1998. People became visibly poorer. Fewer foreign businesses continued to provide goods and services. The island's infrastructure declined. The main road through the commercial section became so poorly maintained that in many spots it became inadvisable to drive at more than five miles per hour. Electricity was not always available. For a time, when landing lights for approaching airplanes had to be turned on, electricity to the hospital first had to be turned off. Chuuk's only museum had no lights for months on end.

The State of Chuuk (known to generations of sailors and other foreigners as Truk) consists of 11 high, mangrove-fringed volcanic islands in Chuuk Lagoon and a series of 14 outlying atolls and low islands. The lagoon, 40 miles across at its widest point, is circled by one of the world's longest barrier reefs. Submerged in the lagoon is a Japanese fleet, destroyed by United States air power in 1944.

The reef-locked islands in the lagoon, the heart of the state and home to more than 75% of its people, like Pohnpei and Kosrae, have lush central peaks. Even Weno has a spectacular setting. The state's outer island groups, the Halls, Westerns, and Mortlocks, resemble the palm and sand atolls of the Marshalls. Visitors can explore three aspects of Chuuk: Weno (formerly Moen), the state's administrative center; the other islands in Chuuk Lagoon, all rural; and the outlying atolls—in all, 290 islands from which to choose.

Wartime Chuuk

In Chuuk, World War II is simply called *the* World War, or even *the* War. What the rest of the world calls World War II hit Chuuk with particular brutality. Chuuk was the main Japanese naval base in the central Pacific, the "Gibraltar of the Pacific," protected by the encircling reef and giant guns in caves and tunnels guarding the passes. Most of the entrenched firepower was taken off obsolete cruisers and battleships and positioned on the hillsides. The Japanese had four airstrips in Chuuk lagoon, two on Weno and one each on Etten and Parem.

On 17 February 1944, the United States unleashed Operation Hailstone, one of the most devastating aerial attacks in history. For two days and one night, aircraft from nine carriers hammered the islands in 30 waves. Submarines posted outside the passes caught fleeing vessels. Japan lost 250 planes, nearly 60 vessels, and thousands of men, compared to United States' loss of only 26 aircraft. The 180,000 tons of shipping sunk set a two-day World War II record.

This defeat would have been even more devastating except for an American reconnaissance flight over the lagoon on 4 February that tipped the Japanese off to the impending attack. On 10 February all the Japanese warships present (including a battleship, two aircraft carriers, five heavy and four light cruisers, and 20 destroyers) withdrew to Palau. Most of the ships wrecked in the lagoon were merchant ships converted to war use. It is difficult to under-

Under Chuuk lagoon lies a Japanese navy. Sailors presumed dead

stand, however, how the same Japanese Navy that three years earlier had realized the vulnerability of American ships in Pearl Harbor could think that Chuck Lagoon could be protected from a massive air assault.

The 45,000 Japanese survivors on Chuuk were bypassed as the United States forces moved on to capture Saipan. Both Japanese and Chuukese suffered famine due to the ensuing American blockade. In 1946 the United States Navy established the present administrative center on Weno, replacing the earlier center on Tonoas Island (Dublon).

Economy

Chuuk's economy clearly declined during the late 1990s. Certainly one factor was the drop in Compact payments. But blame must also be placed on the government, which some have called inept and even corrupt. During the heyday of Compact payments, Chuuk still managed to be on the verge of bankruptcy. More than other parts of Micronesia, a government bureaucracy that did little for the good of the people kept expanding. In 1998 a new faction took over the state government, which gave some people hope for better government management.

Today Chuuk faces difficult problems. It is unlikely that Compact payments will return to their 1980s level. The downturn in the Asian economy hurt tourism by limiting Asian wreck divers. For Chuuk to attract other tourists, it must improve its infrastructure and overcome its reputation. This is crucial for all of Micronesia. The Federated States of Micronesia is the largest country in the region, the State of Chuuk contains more than half the population of the Federated States, and Weno is the capital of Chuuk. The future of the whole region depends, at least in part, on the rejuvenation of Weno.

On Weno, businesses are scattered but are primarily located on or near the road between the airport and the boat dock. Small, scarcely stocked stores can be found in the other villages of Weno, with even fewer stores on the other islands in the lagoon. Weno is home to a tuna fleet, but sees little benefit from it.

There are no credible statistics concerning the economy of the other islands within the lagoon. Some people commute to Weno either for government jobs or to sell farm products. On some of the islands, such as Fefan, people have substantial gardens. But the line between someone considered "unemployed" and someone who is a "subsistence" fisherman or farmer is a fine one. Western economic concepts are difficult to apply to this third world economy.

Many Chuukese lack sufficient education and management skills needed by the cash economy. A small number of Americans supply some needed skills. Filipinos are often in middle management. This threatens to become a vicious cycle, with many Chuukese feeling further alienated from the cash economic sector.

The 1997-1998 El Niño drought hit Chuuk's outer islands particularly hard. Even after the drought ended in May 1998, it took months for crops to be replanted and become mature.

The People
More than half of the 105,000 citizens of the FSM live in the State of Chuuk. Weno accounts for about 17,000. The Hall and Mortlock Islands to the north and south of Chuuk Lagoon are closely related in language and customs, but the people of the Western Islands are culturally more closely related to islanders farther west in the Carolines.

Chuuk is the only place in Micronesia where tourists regularly get into beefs with locals. For several years, the United States Peace Corps thought it unsafe to station women here. During the day, as well as at night, one sees obviously intoxicated teenagers. Stores post guards. A significant number of Chuukese men and teenagers become drunk on the weekend, especially on government paydays, the second and fourth Friday of each month. Violence is often sparked between locals, but visitors can

also become victims. It is best neither to wander around Weno those evenings nor to go to local bars. Weno is not an island to explore at night unless you know your way around.

If you are silly enough to provoke a direct, clear disagreement with a Chuukese, at some point you will be told, "This is Chuuk." This simple statement is shorthand for "You are asking for something that is not done here. Stop being rude, the topic is closed." At that point back off and try a new approach to what you wish to accomplish. Sometimes, when you make a statement or ask a question of a Chuukese, you may be met with a long silence. The silence may be embarrassingly long—for you. Do not take this pause as a sign of mental weakness or anger. It is merely the Chuukese way. The Chuukese are experts at waiting. To try to rush the conversation would be counterproductive: this is Chuuk.

Crafts
Outer islanders make fine handicrafts, such as the *tapwanu* masks of the Mortlocks, the only masks made in Micronesia. Representing a benevolent spirit, these masks were worn at dances to ward off typhoons, or used to ornament the gable of the men's house. Originally carved from the wood of the breadfruit tree,

CHUUK'S CLIMATE

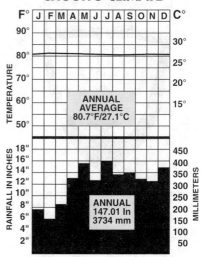

they're now made from lighter hibiscus wood and have been renamed "devil masks."

Chuuk love sticks and war clubs also are unique. At one time every Chuukese male had an individually designed love stick. Love sticks were up to 13 feet long, so the young man could thrust the object through the wall of a hut and reach the girl of his affections, who might be sleeping on the other side of the room. He would then entangle her hair in the long stick and tug to wake her. She would know by the feel of the stick whose it was; if she pulled it inside the hut he could enter; if she shook it she was coming outside; and if she pushed it out, he was rejected. Dr. Freud would have had a field day analyzing this custom.

The frightening wooden war bludgeons and shark-tooth-studded knuckle-dusters of Chuuk were designed for less romantic encounters. Handbags, baskets, trays, stools, wall hangings, *lava lava,* and grass skirts complete the crafts scene. Note that many objects, nontraditional for Chuuk, such as carved faces and story

The tapwanu *mask of the Mortlock Islands is the only type of mask known in Micronesia, and may once have ornamented the gable of a men's house. Carved from the wood of the breadfruit tree, it was thought to protect the fruit of that tree during storms.*

boards, are also sold. Some are quite decorative and interesting.

Many women in Chuuk wear truly beautiful tortoiseshell combs in their hair. They are occasionally seen for sale and in all honesty are more beautiful than imitation plastic ones. However, the real material often comes from severely endangered species and should not be bought for that reason. Further, it is illegal to import this material into the United States and most European countries.

Health

Take extra care with the water on Weno. Don't drink tap water without first boiling or chemically purifying it. Be careful with raw fruit or vegetables you suspect were washed in local, untreated water. Avoid the hospital on Weno if at all possible. If serious medical attention is needed, take the first plane out to Hawaii or Guam.

WENO

Try to get your head past the dirt of Weno; it is nestled in one of the most beautiful settings on earth. The view from Weno across newly forming mangrove forests as the sun sets behind the Tol group can be sublimely beautiful. The commercial center, an industrial zone amid housing, stretches along the west shore of Weno from the airport to beyond the port. Nantaku, the governmental center of Chuuk State, is on the saddle road heading east. Dense forests and grasslands fill the interior of this, the second-largest island in the lagoon.

Western Weno

If this island has a downtown, it is the small-boat harbor and the market in front of it. Lagoon island women come by boat to sell avocados, pineapples, and beautiful leis made of plumeria and soft green leaves. Rice, clothing, and other goods are sold out of panel trucks. The area is jumpy, dirty, quirky, and filled with tropical energy. Men sit in the boats they used to transport people from the lagoon islands, waiting to return them at the end of the day. The Seaside Restaurant overlooks it all.

Nearby is the **Chuuk Ethnographic Exhibition Center,** accessible from the Chuuk Visitors Bureau (open weekdays 8 a.m.-5 p.m., admission $1.50). Here there are *tapwanu* devil masks, *fenai* love sticks of mangrove wood, *tor lava lava* skirts of hibiscus fiber, model canoes, war clubs, fish traps, war relics, and other crafts. You will see World War II artifacts that take up half of the museum. Note: you'll see them better if the museum ever fixes the electrical problems that left it in semidarkness for months on end during 1998. Check first, and bring a flashlight if the lights are not back on.

For groceries, head to the corrugated metal **Truk Trading Company** (TTC) or nearby **Shigeto's.** TTC is the best place in town to get hardware, clothing, or photographic supplies. Both stores are on the inland side of the road, about 150 feet past the commercial pier when coming from the airport.

A big **Japanese gun** is in a tunnel dubbed "Nefo Cave," a short walk up from the governor's residence at Nantaku. Follow the road due south from the courthouse as far as a large,

green water tank. The tunnel is 150 feet to the right. There's an excellent view of Weno center and the lagoon from here.

The Japanese had an airstrip at **South Field,** the level area just east of the Truk Blue Lagoon Resort (formerly Truk Continental Hotel). As you approach this part of the island, the land gets more lush and you will see occasional taro patches as well as bananas and breadfruit trees. A **coconut processing plant** now sits on the vast concrete platform that once sloped into the lagoon to permit seaplane traffic. Inside the factory you can see soap, body oil, and shampoo being made from copra. Drop into the Hotel and its beachside bar to enjoy the superb lagoon view.

Roads run along the north and west sides of Weno. It's a three-hour walk on a level footpath along the southeast coast between the ends of these roads. Eastbound you get a good view of grassy Mt. Witipon. There's a beach at **Nukanap** where you can stop for a swim.

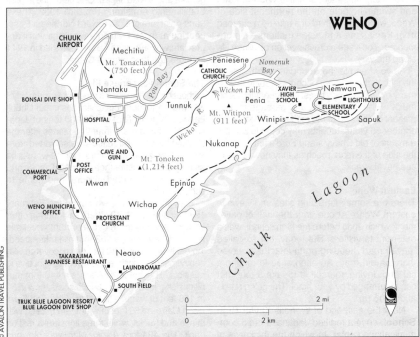

Northern Weno

To climb to the grassy summit of **Mt. Tonachau** (750 feet), take the road beside the rock crusher past the airport up as far as the U.S. Air Force Civic Action Team (CAT) headquarters. The overgrown trail follows the power lines that run up the ridge just before it. It's a stiff climb that can be slippery near the top. High, sharp grass on the slopes forces you to stay on the trail. Bring your camera. One legend explains that Tonachau is a great octopus whose arms once stretched across the lagoon; another claims the hero Soukatau brought the great basalt knob atop Tonachau with him from Kosrae. Soukatau's son, Souwoniras, built his *wuut* (meetinghouse) on the mountain.

Tunnuk holds a Catholic enclave, home of the Cathedral Parish and the Chuuk Vicariate. At **Fairo** village on the lagoon near Tunnuk is a traditional *wuut* built by Puluwat islanders in 1990, with support from the Micronesian Institute, as a community center. A canoe house stands alongside.

To reach the small, attractive **Wichon Falls** and swimming hole on the northeast side of Weno, walk about a third of a mile up a dirt road from Peniesene and ask directions—it's unmarked. You'll see a cross-section of village life along the way.

As you head farther round the north side of the island, the scenery becomes very lush with many old, wild mango trees. Unfortunately, as on much of the island, junk and garbage is ever present by the side of the road and the ocean. In another 50 years, tourists may come to see the remains of old Chevy's and Ford's left to rot by the side of the road, much as they now come to see naval wrecks.

Eastern Weno

There are some interesting sites and views in eastern Weno. At one time the lack of pavement, which ends before the high school, was a deterrent to visitors. But today, the so-called "paved road" heading north is actually worse than the dirt road. An alternative to renting a car and driving yourself is to take a tour that can be arranged by your hotel. The going rate is about $15 pp.

Near the east end of Weno is **Xavier High School,** once a fortified Japanese radio communications center, to which the thickness of the cement walls and the steel hatches on the windows attest. After the war, Jesuits purchased the building for $1,000 and turned it into the best four-year high school in Micronesia, with about 150 students coming from throughout the region. The view of the lagoon from the roof is excellent.

An abandoned **Japanese lighthouse** *(totai)* in reasonably good condition stands on the highest point of the Sapuk Peninsula. Get there by following a footpath from the elementary school near Xavier High School, or from Or village to the east. Someone claiming to be the lighthouse owner may ask $1-2 pp at Or, which is fair enough, but pay only after you're shown the way. Ownership of the lighthouse is in dispute and you may be asked for money more than once. There is a fine view from the lighthouse.

Just below, at the bottom of the slope to the northeast, are several huge **eight-inch naval guns** in big metal housings. The guns are off an Italian armored cruiser purchased by Argentina and sold to Japan. One bears the imprint Stabilimento Armstrong Pozzuoli 1902. These guns point straight out toward Northeast Pass. Looking at these fearsome weapons you'll appreciate why the United States decided in 1944 to bomb and then bypass Chuuk.

The Sunken Japanese Fleet

Without doubt, the world's greatest assortment of war wreckage for divers to visit lies under Chuuk Lagoon. A ghost fleet of 180,000 tons of Japanese ships and more than 270 planes litter the shallow lagoon bed. Little was salvaged from the wartime air strikes; almost all the wrecks lie as they sank, most of them around Tonoas and Fefan, now shrouded in coral and home to schools of fish.

Sixty ships went down during the February 1944 air strike, and 40 others sank during other attacks. Among the most important wrecks is the *Shinkoku Maru,* a 503-foot oil tanker standing eerily upright just 40 feet down, covered with heavy marine growth, a site where a night dive is possible. The *Yamagiri Maru* is a 440-foot munitions ship loaded with 18-inch shells, now in 50 to 120 feet of water. The holds of the *San Francisco Maru,* in 150 feet of water, are packed with mines and trucks, while three light tanks rest on deck. The 494-foot *Aikoku Maru* was blown in

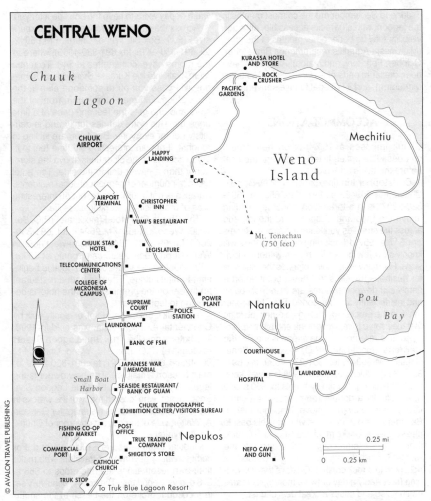

CENTRAL WENO

Chuuk Lagoon

CHUUK AIRPORT

KURASSA HOTEL AND STORE

ROCK CRUSHER

PACIFIC GARDENS

Mechitiu

Weno Island

HAPPY LANDING

CAT

AIRPORT TERMINAL

CHRISTOPHER INN

YUMI'S RESTAURANT

Mt. Tonachau (750 feet)

CHUUK STAR HOTEL

LEGISLATURE

TELECOMMUNICATIONS CENTER

COLLEGE OF MICRONESIA CAMPUS

SUPREME COURT

POWER PLANT

Nantaku

Pou Bay

POLICE STATION

LAUNDROMAT

BANK OF FSM

COURTHOUSE

JAPANESE WAR MEMORIAL

Small Boat Harbor

SEASIDE RESTAURANT/ BANK OF GUAM

HOSPITAL

LAUNDROMAT

CHUUK ETHNOGRAPHIC EXHIBITION CENTER/VISITORS BUREAU

FISHING CO-OP AND MARKET

POST OFFICE

Nepukos

TRUK TRADING COMPANY

COMMERCIAL PORT

SHIGETO'S STORE

NEFO CAVE AND GUN

CATHOLIC CHURCH

TRUK STOP

To Truk Blue Lagoon Resort

0   0.25 mi

0   0.25 km

© AVALON TRAVEL PUBLISHING

half by an American dive bomber, itself destroyed in the explosion. The largest wreck in the lagoon, the *Heian Maru,* a 526-foot submarine tender, lies 50 feet down.

Near Etten, and accessible to snorkelers, is the *Fujikawa Maru,* a 437-foot armed aircraft ferry still containing Zero planes. Its stern is perhaps 20 feet below the surface at low tide. The front gun is clearly visible from the surface, as is the hoist for loading the ship, now dubbed the "Devil's Altar."

The *Dai Na Hino Maru,* between Fefan and Uman Islands, is also accessible to snorkelers.

A 372-foot munitions ship, the *Sankisan Maru,* full of 50mm ammunition, is covered with soft coral formations 50 feet down. Submarine I-169 *Shinohara* was lost because someone forgot to close the storm ventilation valve in the bridge when the 330-foot sub dove to avoid an air raid in April 1944. You can also visit a number of submerged Japanese planes off Etten.

June to September are the calmest months in the lagoon, with all wrecks accessible, although visibility may be better other months of the year. (Micronesia Aquatics recommends September, October, February, and March). All wrecks have been declared parts of an Underwater Historical Monument, and it is illegal to take souvenirs.

ACCOMMODATIONS

Chuuk imposes a 10% tax on hotel room charges. The prices listed below are the cost before the tax is added on.

Christopher Inn (inexpensive) (P.O. Box 37, Chuuk, FM 96942, tel. 691-330-2652, fax 691-330-2207) is in a three-story concrete building above the Stop and Shop, toward the left and across the street as you leave the airport. Rooms are $47 s, $57 d (including tax), and they will knock off a few bucks for rooms without televisions. For many years, this hotel was the mainstay for business travelers to Chuuk, but it unfortunately slid downhill. Rooms are extremely basic and insufficiently air conditioned. But Christopher Inn is in the process of putting up a new building that may serve to rejuvenate the entire enterprise.

About a mile north of the airport is the **Pacific Gardens** (moderate) (P.O. Box 494, Weno, Chuuk, FM 96942, tel. 691-330-4639, fax 691-330-2334), which opened in 1993 in a well-kept, modern building. A room that rents for $50 s, $60 d, is actually a double room; there is a small kitchen but no oven or stove. Manager Levy I. Banadera is a gracious host who tries his best to please guests. Unlike most hotel rooms in Chuuk, there is even some color used to decorate the rooms. A word of caution: the Pacific Gardens is right next to a rock crusher. On days that it is running (reportedly a day or two a month), it creates much noise and raises a great deal of dust.

The Quiet Corner restaurant is in the building, as is a bar that serves as a disco on the weekend. Things can get quite noisy on those nights for those wishing to sleep. There's an on-site laundromat where you can do your own

wash or pay extra to have the hotel do it for you.

Across the street is **Kurassa Hotel** (inexpensive) (P.O. Box 64, Weno, Chuuk, FM 96942, tel. 691-330-4415, fax 691-330-4355), where all the rooms have kitchenettes at $48. To rent a room, walk into the Kurassa Store, where someone will pass you off to someone else in the back office. Old men hang out in front of the store and one gets the feel and pace of a time gone by. This hotel defines funky and is definitely not for everyone. But if you are willing to rough it, it has an interesting old-time feel to it. Try to get one of the older units above the store, rather than a newer unit to the side. The hotel has a fair number of permanent, local residents. Kurassa is not a rural village, but an interesting slice of urban island, working class life.

The **Chuuk Star Hotel** (moderate) (P.O. Box 1230, Weno, Chuuk, FM 96942, tel. 691-330-2040, fax 691-330-2045) is the newest hotel in Weno. It provides clean, safe rooms at $60 s, $70 d. Only three years old, the hotel is beginning to hit its stride. There is both a restaurant and a bar on the premises, and the hotel is beginning to feel lived in.

The Truk Continental Hotel, originally built by Continental Air Micronesia, was sold in 1998. The hotel is now the **Truk Blue Lagoon Resort** (expensive) (P.O. Box 340, Weno, Chuuk, FM 96942, tel. 691-330-2727, fax 691-330-2439, e-mail: blresort@mail.fm). The new owner is the legendary Kiniuo Aisek, the Blue Lagoon Dive Shop owner, who located many of the wrecks in the lagoon. Joining him is his daughter Gardinia A. Walter, wife of the current governor of Chuuk, Ansito Walter.

Regular room rates are $100 s, $120 d. For commercial or government travelers who make their own reservations the rate drops to $68 s, $78 d, a very good buy. The hotel is beautifully set in a coconut grove on the beach near the southwest corner of the island. There is great snorkeling right in front of the hotel's beach. On a map, it may look like the hotel is isolated, but is only a 15-minute taxi ride to the airport for a 50-cent fare. The hotel has the best restaurant on the island and a separate bar with a deck onto the beach.

This hotel is favored by divers who do not wish to deal with the rest of Weno. It has somewhat the feel of a giant, stationary "live-aboard." The resort offers economical combination rates

---

CHUUK COUNTRY CODE: 691

for stays and dives; the longer the stay, the deeper the discount.

The hotel was allowed to run down during the last years of ownership by Continental. A significant renovation is now planned. The hotel has its own desalination plant and is not connected to Weno's water system. During 1998, the system was not working properly, and even after the end of the El Niño drought, water was rationed to certain morning and evening hours. Check the status of the water system when calling for reservations.

The Truk Blue Lagoon Resort owns a small island in the lagoon, between Uman and Tonoas islands, about 15 minutes by motorboat from the resort. There is a small hut with a shower and a kitchen. Tents are provided for sleeping. The outing costs $65 pp, per night.

The **Truk Stop** (expensive) (P.O. Box 546, Weno, Chuuk, FM 96942, tel. 691-330-4232, fax 691-330-2286), located about one mile south of the airport, has 23 rooms. The hotel is well run and clean, with a restaurant on the premises. For better or worse, it is located in the heart of Weno's commercial district. Its clientele is mainly business and government travelers, with rooms that start at $90 and go to $104 for lagoonfront rooms. This is more than room rates offered business travelers at the Truk Blue Lagoon, which in our opinion is a superior hotel.

Falos Beach Resort (inexpensive) is run through the **Pacific Gardens** (P.O. Box 494, Weno, Chuuk, FM 96942, tel. 691-330-4639 or 691-330-2606, fax 691-330-2334). It's located on a lagoon island surrounded by a white sand beach, a 30-minute ride from Weno. A night's stay is $45 s, $50 d. It is only for the hardy and the not easily bored. Cottages are concrete and square; rooms do have screens and occasional electricity. There are two outhouses, and the "shower" consists of a bucket and some fresh water.

The island can be a lovely spot for a day trip. The price is $35 pp, with a two-person minimum. This includes lunch and transportation to and from the island. The snorkeling is great.

FOOD

Rainbow Restaurant is on the first floor under the Christopher Inn. Lunch and dinner average

$7, but a good bowl of ramen is $3.50. The menu includes fish, Filipino, Japanese, and Chinese dishes. The restaurant is quite clean, but not sufficiently air conditioned. **Yumi's Restaurant,** opposite the airport, also has Filipino dishes.

The **Seaside Restaurant** overlooking the small boat harbor is a nice place to stop for coffee and to get a feel for Weno. It is not particularly clean so take care ordering food.

Breakfast or lunch at the **Quiet Corner Restaurant** in the Pacific Gardens hotel runs about $6. It has a good selection of Filipino, American, and Chinese dishes. For dinner, $13 will get you anything on the lunch menu along with soup, salad, and dessert. Comparable is the restaurant at the **Chuuk Star Hotel.**

The **T & S Cafeteria,** located on the road between the FSM Supreme Court and the power plant, offers breakfasts and lunches at reasonable prices.

The expensive **Takarajima Japanese Restaurant** is on the west side road, near the Truk Blue Lagoon Resort. Dinner with a couple of beers will cost $25 or more. It has a nice Japanese decor, including some great saltwater aquariums, but the food is not special.

The restaurant at the **Truk Stop** overlooks the lagoon and has outdoor tables. Its prices have risen over the last several years. Try the "local plate," a sampling of chicken, fish, tapioca, and cooked bananas in a coconut sauce ($7.50). In the evening, dinners average about $15, a little less for seafood.

The best and most festive restaurant on the island is at the **Truk Blue Lagoon Resort.** It is located by the lagoon with lovely views out. Service has improved since the change in ownership. Alcoholic drinks are available in the restaurant or the adjacent bar.

OTHER PRACTICALITIES

Entertainment

Local bars open and close with some regularity. It is probably safest for travelers to avoid these spots, particularly on payday Fridays—the second and fourth Friday of each month. Hotel restaurants and bars are more likely to be safe. If you must disco, try Yumi's or the bar beneath the Pacific Gardens, and keep alert as the evening progresses. Fights sometimes usually break out.

Sports and Recreation

Chuuk offers the best **wreck diving** in the world. Very few tourists visit Chuuk for any other reason. There is no place else to see this many wrecks in such a small area—and all in a warm ocean. Wreck diving poses technical challenges, beyond those usually encountered during other types of dives. Know your limits. Do not explore inner passages that make you uncomfortable. There is less supervision of divers in Chuuk than at most other dive locations. Thus, even more than usual, it must be you who sets the limits. As in most of Micronesia, bring all your own equipment, other than tanks and weights.

Micronesia Aquatics (Clark Graham, P.O. Box 57, Chuuk, FM 96942, tel. 691-330-4096, e-mail: cgraham@mail.fm, website: www.padi.com/dive/micrones122a/home.htm) has offered reliable scuba services since 1974. Diving is $65 pp (two tanks), $80 if you are a single diver. Snorkeling from the boat costs $35 pp.

Blue Lagoon Dive Shop (Gradvin K. Aisek, P.O. Box 429, Chuuk, FM 96942, tel. 691-330-2796, fax 691-330-2439) offers diving at a similar price. Gradvin's father, Kimiuo Aisek, was an Operation Hailstorm eyewitness. He is a local legend for locating most of the lagoon's wrecks. He founded this company in 1973. A two-tank dive costs $75, snorkeling $35 pp. The shop will also arrange fishing or tours of nearby Tonoas Island. Discount prices are available to those who also stay at the Truk Blue Lagoon Resort.

Sundance Tours and Dive Shop (P.O. Box 85, Chuuk, FM 96942, tel. 691-330-4234, fax 691-330-4451), located next to the Truk Stop, opened in 1990 and also offers an array of diving packages. A two-tank dive is $70 pp, and a day snorkeling and sightseeing is $50 pp. Sundance caters primarily to Japanese clientele. English-speaking divers should verify that there are no communication problems with their dive master.

If you wish to snorkel, it will be cheaper to go to the small-boat harbor and bargain for someone to take you to one of the many nearby wrecks. Make sure they know of a wreck in shallow water; this way four people can go for about $30.

Two live-aboard dive boats, the SS *Thorfinn* and the *Truk Aggressor,* serve visiting scuba divers. The SS *Thorfinn* charges $2,000 for a one-week, Sunday-to-Sunday package (accommodation, meals, and diving included). The *Truk Aggressor* also offers a week package for $2,295. At those prices, the live-aboard boats are more expensive than staying at a hotel and diving with the companies mentioned above, but you get almost unlimited diving and save time not having to shuttle back and forth from the dive sites each day. These boats particularly appeal to divers who are not interested in exploring Chuuk or putting up with its difficulties.

Passage on these boats must be booked ahead, either through one of the dive wholesalers listed under "Travel Agents" in the "Getting There" section of the On the Road chapter, or by contacting **Seaward Holidays Micronesia Inc.** (P.O. Box DX, Weno, Chuuk, FM 96942, tel. 691-330-4302, fax 691-330-4253) for the SS *Thorfinn;* Aggressor Fleet (Drawer 1470, Morgan City, LA 70381, tel. 504-385-2416, or from the United States, toll-free at 800-348-2628, fax 504-384-0817, website: www.aggressor.com) for the *Truk Aggressor* only; or **Live/Dive Pacific** (74-5588 Pawai Place, Building F, Kailua-Kona, HI 96740, tel. (800) 344-5662, fax (808) 329-2628, website: www.pac-aggressor.com) also for the *Truk Aggressor* only.

Many hikes around Weno involve crossing private property, and property owners may be upset if you undertake such a walk without permission. Ask directions of any adults you meet, then ask if it's okay to continue.

Shopping

Sundance Tours beside the Truk Stop sells baskets, fans, wall hangings, coasters, shell necklaces, T-shirts, love sticks, and woodcarvings. Beware of black coral and turtle shell products which are prohibited entry to the United States and many other nations for environmental reasons. Handicrafts can also be purchased at Yumi's opposite the airport and the **Small Industries Center** near the Truk Trading Company. **Big Mama's Nupoko Barker Co.** sounds more like a biker's bar than a handicrafts store. Unfortunately, store hours are sporadic at best. Try calling (691) 330-2169.

The **Chuuk Coconut Authority** (P.O. Box 1009, Chuuk, FM 96942, tel. 691-330-2628, fax 691-330-2777) on Weno produces Misimisi body oil, Tirow suntan oil, Saram shampoo, and Afata bath soap from local copra. These quality products are exported worldwide. You can visit the factory adjacent to the Truk Blue Lagoon Resort.

Three percent sales tax is added to all sticker prices in Chuuk.

Address mail to Chuuk, FM 96942.

Services
The Bank of Guam (tel. 691-330-2331, open Mon.-Fri. 10 a.m.-3 p.m.) and the Bank of FSM (tel. 691-330-2353, open Mon.-Thurs. 8:30 a.m.-2:30 p.m., Friday 8:30-4 p.m.) have branches on Weno. Only the Bank of Guam will change foreign currencies.

You can place long distance phone calls at the Telecommunications Center (open 24 hours) near the airport. Long distance calls can be placed from many hotel rooms, but you must go through an operator and must charge the call to your hotel, rather than to a calling card.

Avoid the Chuuk Hospital if at all possible.

Information
The Chuuk Visitors Bureau (P.O. Box 1142, Chuuk, FM 96942, tel. 691-330-4133, fax 691-330-4194) is open weekdays 8 a.m.-5 p.m.

CHUUK LAGOON AT A GLANCE

	POP. (1999)	AREA (ACRES)	HIGHEST POINT (FEET)
Eot	361	119	201
Fanapanges	606	388	392
Fefan	4,042	3,265	1,030
Fono	482	81	201
Parem/Totiw	375	484	237
Patta	1,825	832	648
Polle	1,320	2,240	681
Romanum	711	185	168
Tol/Wonei	6,250	5,375	1,487
Tonoas/Etten	3,949	2,300	1,171
Tsis	476	151	250
Udot	1,598	1,218	799
Uman	3,056	1,161	951
Weno	16,121	4,668	1,237
other lagoon islands	nil	200	13
reef islands	nil	1,015	13
TOTAL	**41,172**	**23,682**	**1,487**

GETTING THERE

Chuuk International Airport (TKK) is within a mile of the business center on Weno. Avoid using its bathrooms. A small counter serves cold drinks and coffee at flight times. To get a taxi from the airport, turn left as you leave the terminal and walk out to the main street where cabs pass frequently during daylight hours. Reconfirm your onward flight at the Continental Airlines office (tel. 691-330-2424, fax 691-330-2944) at the airport, open daily 8 a.m.-5 p.m. There's a $10 departure tax.

Continental Airlines Island Hopper heads west from Hawaii to Chuuk two or three days a week, depending on the season. It also stops at Chuuk when heading east from Guam. Remember that because of the International Date Line, you lose a day between Honolulu and Chuuk.

Currently, there are no scheduled flights to the outer islands.

GETTING AROUND

Outside of Weno, most of what is above sea level in Chuuk State sees very few travelers. There are opportunities to escape to the outliers. Boats constantly leave for lagoon islands, and there are regular departures to the even more remote outer islands. These locations, however, have no facilities, such as hotels and restaurants, for travelers. Further, residents of islands in the lagoon sometimes exhibit hostility toward outsiders. Therefore, if you plan to stay on one of these islands, make arrangements with a local family before departing Weno. The Chuuk Visitors Bureau can help you make a contact.

Field Trips
The field trip ships *Micro Trader* and *Micro Dawn* depart Weno approximately every two weeks on a week-long journey along one of four different routes: Upper Mortlocks, Lower Mortlocks,

Hall Islands, and Western Islands. The trip to the Westerns is the best, but it only goes once a month at most. There are basically three types of trips: medical evacuations, trips to pick up or drop off high school students, and regular field trips, when the boat becomes a sailing supermarket, bringing supplies to the residents of the islands it visits.

Schedules don't matter much on these trips as the ship can be diverted at any time for emergencies. During the 1997-98 El Niño and the months following, the ships had to be pressed into service, delivering food and water to the drought-stricken outer islands. The ships usually leave in the late afternoon, but they're often delayed until the next day at the last minute, even after the ship is fully loaded and all passengers are aboard. If this is the case, everyone has to get off and find somewhere else to spend the night.

Passage costs three cents a mile deck, 10 cents a mile cabin (plus $2 a night for berthing). The *Micro Trader* has eight two-berth cabins, but government officials have priority on these. Even though you may have been promised a cabin you can't really be sure you actually have one until just before the ship leaves. And once you're underway you may be asked to give up your cabin in case of medical need. You can always travel deck.

Three meals are provided at $13 a day. Passengers who take meals with the ship's officers pick up morsels of useful information along with what they get on their plates. There's no obligation to take every meal (you only pay for those you consume). Take along a good supply of food and bottled water, and get a cabin if at all possible as the local color of deck passage will wear off after a couple of nights.

The ship usually stops at each island on its route for a couple of hours, and you're free to go in on the ship's boat for a look around. In rough weather, landing on some islands gets dicey through the crashing surf. Take along small gifts to give to people who show you around their island.

For field trip information check with the **Department of Transportation**, P.O. Box 189, Chuuk, FM 96942, tel. (691) 330-2592, located in the warehouse beside the commercial port—they have the most reliable information on cabin availability.

Other Boats

Smaller municipal boats make more frequent trips from Weno to the outer islands, for example the *Ik No. 3* to Kuttu in the Lower Mortlocks, the *Ik No. 1* to Puluwat, the *Toku* to Tamatam, and the *Fuun Matau* to Pulap. The large motor vessel *Miss Nama* sails to Nama twice a week, leaving Weno Tuesday and Friday afternoons (four hours, $8 pp, $1 for each

CHUUK LAGOON

Pis

North Pass

Falos

Fono

Northeast Pass

Weno

Romanum

Patta   Tol   Eot

Piaanu Pass

Polle   Fana-panges   Udot   Parem   Totiw   Fefan   Tonoas   Etten

Tsis   Uman

Salat Pass

PACIFIC

South Pass   Otta Pass

OCEAN

Kuop

0   10 mi

0   10 km

© AVALON TRAVEL PUBLISHING

piece of luggage, one way), and there are similar services to Losap and Pis.

Some of the above are actually fishing boats owned by outer islanders and offer no comforts or safety standards.

It is best not to show up on an outer island without first having made arrangements for your stay.

By Road

Weno's road system has fallen apart. The road on the most heavily travelled west side is so full of potholes that traffic moves at less than 10 miles per hour.

By day, taxis are Weno's public transportation system. Cars and pickups with taxi signs in the front windows continually cruise the roads, so getting around is cheap. These shared taxis charge 50 cents pp. At night, however, they stop running. Do not be caught far from your hotel at night unless you have arranged for your return. One taxi service is now operating 24 hours a day. Call (691) 330-3733.

Rental cars from **VJ Car Rental** (tel. 691-330-2652) at Christopher Inn are $45 a day. **Truk Stop Car Rentals** (tel. 691-330-4232, fax 691-330-2286) has older cars at $35 a day, newer cars at $50 a day, plus 13% tax. **Kurassa Hotel** (tel. 691-330-4415) rents a few cars for $45 including tax. Other hotels can also make arrangements for you. Considering the excellent daytime taxi service, it's not always necessary to rent a car on Weno.

ISLANDS IN THE CHUUK LAGOON

Chuuk Lagoon's islands form the largest island group in the Carolines. Ninety-eight islands and islets are in the group, 41 of them on the barrier reef encircling the lagoon. Five major passes allow ships to enter. All the other large volcanic islands within the lagoon offer a simpler, more traditional lifestyle than Weno; each is beautiful in itself and for its views of the others. Although mangroves predominate along the shores, there are also beaches.

During the Japanese period, the lagoon islands were divided into two groups: the Shiki Islands (including Weno, Tonoas, Etten, Fefan, Parem, and Uman) and the Shichiyo Islands (Udot, Fanapanges, Tol, and the others). The present administration divides these islands into Northern Namoneas (Weno and Fono), Southern Namoneas (Fefan, Parem, Tonoas, Totiw, Tsis, and Uman), and Faichuk (Eot, Fanapanges, Polle, Patta, Romanum, Tol, Udot, and Wonei).

Transportation

Go to the small-boat harbor to catch a ride to other lagoon islands. Serving commuters who work, shop, or sell their produce on Weno, the boats leave the Chuuk lagoon islands in the early morning and depart for the return trip in the afternoon. All of the small *yamma* boats based in remote villages operate this way. One can usually find a boat to Fefan, Uman, Parem, Udot, or Tol for about $3 one way. But you must spend at least one night on each island. Tol is the farthest away, so boats going there leave earlier. Different boats serve the east and west sides of Fefan, and there are several routes to Tol. Be sure to clarify exactly where the boat is going.

However, there is a more convenient, but slightly more expensive, way to visit these islands. Go down to the small-boat harbor around 9 a.m. During the day, the boatmen who brought people into Weno usually just sit in their boats waiting to return. Some will be quite happy to take you to another island, wait for you to explore, and then return (before their afternoon customers finish work). You can also negotiate snorkeling side trips or trips to the barrier reef and its islets.

A word of caution: Some of the boatmen view tourists as easy pickings. Be certain that you and the boatman agree on an itinerary and a price before you leave. Specify clearly whether the price is per person or for the whole boat and write it down. Don't let the boatman try to change it at the end of the day because of a "misunderstanding." If during the trip you wish to change the itinerary, agree to a new price in advance of the change. A four- or five-hour trip to one of the closer islands should not cost more than $25 per boat, $35 to Tol or the outer reef. You should be willing to pay some in advance for the boatman to buy gasoline, but have him quote one all-inclusive price. Some boatmen will want to charge you an additional amount for fuel, but you really have no idea how much gas is needed.

TONOAS

Chuuk Lagoon

Tonof — Wonpiepi — SITE OF JAPANESE NAVAL HOSPITAL — Sapou

Mt. Tonofefin (813 feet)

Kuchua

Bay

TOYO'S COFFEE SHOP

Roro — Nemwanon

GENERAL'S CAVE

Nechap — Muanon — SITE OF JAPANESE GOVERNOR'S RESIDENCE — TUNNEL WITH ELECTRIC GENERATOR — SCHOOL — Enin — TWO JAPANESE AA GUNS

JAPANESE NAVAL CEMETERY — FORMER SPORTS FIELD — RUINS OF JAPANESE CIVIL HOSPITAL

MUNICIPAL BUILDING — CATHOLIC MISSION — SITE OF SHINTO SHRINE — Nukanap

DONUT SHOP — TAMASHIRO MEMORIAL

GUN IN CAVE

Mt. Tonomwan (1,132 feet)

Saponong — MELTED JAPANESE OIL TANKS

Pwene — Takeshima Channel

Nukuno — BUNKER — Sapun — Ichimantong

JUNIOR HIGH SCHOOL (FORMER JAPANESE SEAPLANE BASE)

RUINS OF JAPANESE NANYO FISHING PLANT

0   0.5 mi
0   0.5 km

© AVALON TRAVEL PUBLISHING

Tonoas

From the look of it today, it's hard to believe that Tonoas, the Japanese Natsu Shima or Summer Island, once housed the largest Japanese naval installation outside the home islands. As you walk around the island, however, evidence surfaces: wrecked buildings, melted oil tanks, an abandoned Japanese hospital, piers, and torn-up railway tracks.

In 1814 a Spaniard, Manuel Dublon, arrived to collect bêche-de-mer, and from that time until the official change back to the original Tonoas in 1990, the island was called Dublon, a name still in common use.

In 1899 the Germans made Tonoas a base for the copra trade. The Japanese also built their Chuukese capital, Tokyo, here, centering on the area between the present Municipal Building and Catholic mission. Until late 1946 thousands of Japanese prisoners were held on Tonoas awaiting repatriation. The overcrowding forced the U.S. Navy to build their base on Weno, which has

been Chuuk's administration center ever since.

Don't miss the old **Japanese seaplane base,** now the junior high school, with its vast fields of concrete sloping into the lagoon, bomb shelters, and view of the old airstrip.

A $2.2-million wharf called **Ichimantong** juts into the lagoon on the south side of Tonoas, within sight of the crumbling remains of a Japanese dock built 40 years earlier.

Two **Japanese AA guns** sit at the top of the peninsula beyond the hospital ruins, but you'll need a guide to find them.

The most unusual sight on Tonoas is a little out of the way and generally overlooked. It's the **General's Cave**—actually a network of tunnels beginning beside the road at Roro. Still used as a typhoon shelter, the cave can easily accommodate the entire population of Tonoas. Bring a flashlight and go under the hill and out the other side. Then climb to the top and find your way down to the nearby Protestant Church.

Across the road from the church are two meeting halls. The one nearest the water is the **Hall of the Magic Chickens.** A legend tells that an ancient sorcerer called all the chickens of Tonoas together and had them level the top of the hill behind the church in a single night. Even today it is said that anyone who eats chicken in this hall will assume fowl (foul?) characteristics and suffer other terrifying consequences. Because of this legend, people on Tonoas would rather starve than eat a local chicken. Imported chickens are apparently okay.

Fefan

Fefan is a center for market gardening and handicrafts. Most of the boats from Weno stop at Mesa on the east side.

For strong hikers, from Sako Store at Fason, just south of Mesa wharf, hike up to the center of the island along an old Japanese road that leads to Unufouchy, where five large **Japanese naval guns** congregate and afford fine views. After visiting the guns continue down the other side to Saporanong on the west coast. Many other Japanese guns still sit in caves on the sides of Fefan's mountains, such as those above **Inaka.** You can see these if you're very keen. There are also three small field guns near the road just north of Mesa wharf.

An easier hike is along the flat, round-the-island road. You could walk around the entire island in about five hours. To take a shorter hike, have your boatman drop you at one pier and pick you up at another. This walk is a delightful series of smiles, greetings, and sights. Simple, nice homes sit along the way, placed within gardens, taro patches, papaya trees, and pineapple terraces. Cascading down hillsides, or in stone walls, you will see some of same type basalt rock used to build Lelu and Nan Madol.

The stores on Fefan are few and poorly stocked. Bring in your own food and drink.

Tol

Only 18 miles southwest of Weno, Tol is the outback of the lagoon, with numerous villages and few visitors. A throng of curious children will surround you as you disembark and follow wherever you go. Just as many Micronesians consider Chuukese to be contentious, many Chuukese consider the people on Tol to be extremely contentious. Considering the lack of services on Tol, it is best not to travel there unless you have a local contact. If you go, no matter what happens, don't get angry or show irritation.

Tol (13 square miles, pop. approx. 8,000), Polle, and Patta—known collectively as the Faichuk Islands—are separated from each other by narrow channels and mangrove forests. The Japanese forced Chuukese to dig canals between the islands to allow their patrol boats free

NATIONAL ARCHIVES, WASHINGTON, D.C.

Dive-bombers fly over Fefan, 29 April 1944.

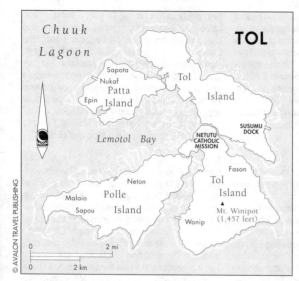

Chuuk Lagoon

TOL

Sapota
Nukaf
Epin — Patta
Island

Tol
Island

SUSUMU
DOCK

Lemotol Bay

NETUTU
CATHOLIC
MISSION

Fason

Neton
Malaio
Sapou
Polle
Island

Tol
Island

Mt. Winipot
(1,457 feet)

Wonip

0 — 2 mi
0 — 2 km

© AVALON TRAVEL PUBLISHING

OUTSIDE THE CHUUK LAGOON

The Outer Islands

Sizable populations inhabit the 11 atolls and three single islands of the Mortlocks, Halls, and Westerns. No cars clog these very traditional islands, so no highways are needed. People here are usually extremely hospitable. Keep in mind, however, that some islands have a limited food supply and are unable to accommodate visitors.

To stay on an outer island, make advance arrangements by radioing ahead to an island mayor. If it's known you're coming there will be time to spread the burden among several households. It is diplomatic to work through the Chuuk Visitors Bureau on Weno (P.O. Box 1142, Chuuk, FM 96942, tel. 691-330-4133, fax 691-330-4194, open weekdays 8 a.m.-5 p.m.).

Each outer island has both an elected mayor and a hereditary chief. Either can give permission for visitors to stay on the island. If you arrive unannounced on an island it may be better to ask to see the chief, but if arrangements are made prior to your arrival you'll probably work through the mayor, who will be in closer contact with Weno. The mayor will often speak better English than the chief. Pay a courtesy call on both the chief and the mayor if you're planning to stay awhile. Mostly they want to know who you are, why you've come, and how long you'll be staying.

The Mortlocks

The Mortlock or Nomoi Islands (pop. approx. 6,500) southeast of Chuuk Lagoon include the Upper Mortlocks (Nama and Losap), the Mid-Mortlocks (Namoluk, Etal, and the northernmost islands of Satowan atoll), and the Lower Mortlocks (Lukunor and southeastern Satowan). **Nama** (pop. approx. 900) is a single island without a lagoon. Many in the Mortlocks feel alienated from and dominated by the rest of the State of Chuuk and periodically argue for their own state within FSM.

circulation. The highest peak in the state (1,457 feet) is on Tol. The Chuuk greater white-eye, one of the rarest birds of Micronesia, is found in the rainforests of Tol.

Tol's inhabitants attempted to secede from Chuuk State a few years ago to form a state within the FSM because they felt they were not getting a fair share of the state budget. Although the move passed the FSM Congress, the president vetoed it.

The Tol administrative center is Fason; the Susumu boat drops you there. You can also take a boat over to Polle, leaving Weno almost daily at 1:30 p.m. The best beaches on Tol are at Sapou and Malaio villages, at the west end of Polle. Giant **Japanese cannons** meant to defend Piaanu Pass still lie in huge caverns chiseled from solid rock, two above Sapou, two more above Malaio. All four can be seen in a morning.

The boat from Malaio to Weno stops at Epin on Patta along the way. If you decide to stop, visit the **cave** dug by the legendary turtles, Nukaf and Sapota, a short walk from Epin.

A relatively easy three-hour walk along an old Japanese road from Malaio brings you to the Netutu Catholic mission, set on both sides of a canal. Netutu is less than an hour's walk from Fason. Hiking north toward Patta is much more difficult.

Satowan atoll's land area totals only a couple of square miles, but its lagoon is the second largest in Chuuk State. The old Japanese airstrip was on Satowan Island (pop. approx. 850) but it's now completely planted with coconut and breadfruit trees and the new airstrip is on Ta (pop. approx. 300). At low tide, you can walk on the Satowan reef from Ta Island to Satowan Island in two hours. **Japanese guns** still lurk beneath Satowan's lush vegetation. You can continue northwest on the barrier reef along the east side of the atoll from Satowan to Moch (pop. approx. 850) in the five hours surrounding low tide, passing many small islands along the way. Unless you've arranged transport, you will have to wait for a low tide to return.

The Japanese government has built a modern plant to freeze fish on Oneop Island (pop. approx. 550) on Lukunor atoll.

The Hall Islands
Sixty miles north of Chuuk Lagoon, the Hall Islands (Pafeng) consist of the twin atolls of Nomwin and Murilo, each with less than a thousand residents, and the uninhabited single island, East Fayu. The Hall Islanders are closely related to the people of Chuuk Lagoon and speak the same dialect. The houses in the group have tin or concrete roofs, and boats are made of fiberglass with outboard motors.

THE WESTERN ISLANDS

Some of the last vestiges of old Pacific culture persist on the western Chuuk and eastern Yap Islands. The inhabitants of the central Carolines have much more in common with each other than they do with the high islanders on Yap proper or those of Chuuk Lagoon. Here amid the sapphire blue waters and smell of plumeria, nearly every house is built of native materials, most of the men wear loincloths, and women walk about bare breasted.

You can still see outriggers carved from breadfruit logs, though the use of fiberglass boats with outboard motors has increased. Large thatched canoe houses serve as men's social clubs, workshops, and schools. You'll still find old navigators here, men who can travel hundreds of miles to islands they've never seen, without a compass

or charts, just from watching the sun, stars, wind, waves, birds, and fish. They travel in sailing canoes between the states of Chuuk and Yap and can predict a typhoon when all seems calm. Yet the young, like young everywhere, appear eager to adopt at least the outward trappings of "world village" culture.

The Westerns include Namonuito, Pulap, and Puluwat atolls, plus Houk (Pulusuk) Island. Chuuk's most skilled navigators reside on Tamatam, Houk, and Puluwat.

Puluwat
Puluwat atoll (pop. approx. 500) is a cluster of five islands, the largest of which are Puluwat and Alet. The one passage into Puluwat's small lagoon leads to an excellent protected anchorage between these two, where cruising yachts sometimes can drop anchor.

All people live on Puluwat Island. These days the large thatched canoe houses lining the lagoon are more likely to shelter one of the island's dozen fiberglass outboards than traditional canoes. The atoll's vegetation is dense and there's usually an ample supply of fish and vegetables, though it suffered during the El Niño drought.

A tall concrete **Japanese lighthouse,** pocked with bullet holes from wartime strafing, still stands at the west tip of uninhabited Alet, just above the beach. You can climb the spiral stairway almost to the top. It's a 90-minute walk along the reef from the village to the lighthouse; many harmless small blacktip reef sharks patrol the

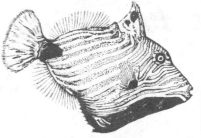

The undulate triggerfish (Balistapus undulatus) *gets its name from a triggerlike mechanism controlling the dorsal fin, which the fish uses to wedge itself into coral crevices when threatened.*

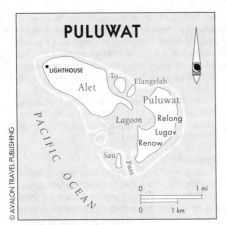

PULUWAT

LIGHTHOUSE

Alet

To Elangelab

Puluwat

Lagoon Relong

Lugav

Renow

Sau

Pass

PACIFIC OCEAN

© AVALON TRAVEL PUBLISHING

0   1 mi

0   1 km

shore on the ocean side. A junior high school has been built beside the lighthouse.

Houk

Houk (Pulusuk) is a relatively large, heavily vegetated island with only a fringing reef (no lagoon) and about 500 residents. Ships sailing between Chuuk and Houk usually call at Pulap or Puluwat first, as a straight line from Weno to Houk is obstructed by dangerous reefs.

Houk is one of the most traditional and isolated islands of Micronesia. Magnificent outrigger canoes are kept in large thatched boathouses along the beach. The breadfruit trees of Houk are incredibly tall and the food supply is adequate. A brackish lake, home to small fish, is used for bathing and washing clothes.

Pulap Atoll

Pulap and Tamatam are small islands on the Pulap reef, each with a single village and a total population of about 1,000. The islands lie on opposite sides of the atoll, with about five miles of lagoon between them. Both are so small you can look right across them. When typhoons strip

the coconuts and breadfruit from the trees and the residents are forced to depend on taro, they can suffer serious famines.

Tamatam is a very traditional island, clean and breezy with houses along the ocean side and a friendly, welcoming people. The two verdant ends of Tamatam are separated by a narrow sandy strip. The island's many huge outrigger canoes can carry as many as 10 men or more to the outer islands of Yap.

Namonuito Atoll

Namonuito's huge triangular lagoon is the largest in the Caroline Islands. The atoll's five inhabited islands are Onoun (Ulul), Magur, Ono, Onari, and Pisaris. Namonuito is somewhat less traditional than the other Western Islands to the south.

Onoun Island (pop. approx. 500) is a long, broad coral strip at the west end of the lagoon. Coconut-covered Onoun is the largest of the Namonuito islands and the best able to receive visitors. Taro is planted in swampy pits in the center of the island and the food supply is adequate. It's a "developed" island with roads (no cars), stores (closed), an airstrip (no scheduled service), and a large, modern junior high school (many students). The concrete-surfaced airstrip, a 15-minute walk north of the main village, was completed by a United States Air Force Civic Action Team in 1991. There's good snorkeling on the lagoon side, cool breezes and fiery sunsets on the ocean side.

The other four Namonuito islands have small populations and limited food supplies. Magur is the northernmost island of Chuuk State. Landing on Ono is dangerous during rough weather. At tiny Pisaris, in the southeast corner of the Namonuito lagoon, visiting ships must anchor far from the island due to treacherous coral shoals in this corner of the lagoon. The shallow waters on the lagoon side protect Pisaris from heavy seas, so landing itself is easy at high tide. Magur and Onari are also reasonably approachable.

STATE OF YAP

INTRODUCTION

Yap is the most traditional state within the Federated States of Micronesia. Things operate at a slow pace here. The state constitution gives the island chiefs veto power over state legislation relating to culture or matters of tradition. Yapese tourism officials say they want "controlled tourism," rather than the uncontrolled growth that occurred on Guam and Saipan. If this is inconvenient at times, remember that it's *they* who are in charge, not tourists. A public outcry stopped a major Japanese resort development. If you think everything isn't arranged just to please you, you're right.

Most tourists come to Yap for diving, particularly to view manta rays. But Yap offers much on land as well. One of the most exciting aspects of Yap is its system of ancient stone pathways. Villages and taro patches are often linked by ancient stone paths, many of which are raised. The builders took dirt from adjoining land to raise the road bed. The remaining depressed pits became easier to irrigate for taro. The paths are so well engineered, with stones holding up the edges and a system of culverts allowing drainage, that they have withstood centuries with only minimal upkeep. As you walk these paths, usually well shaded, you feel the presence of an early, great civilization that was able to produce the abundance needed to sustain these massive public works.

Life on Yap continues to revolve around its villages—most still have meetinghouses—even when the lifestyle in other respects does not remain traditional. The main roads bypass the villages, but you can reach them by driving or hiking on lanes that connect with the roads or by using the ancient stone walkway system.

The State of Yap consists of three islands interconnected by bridges (Yap, Gagil-Tomil, and Maap), nearby Rumung (closed to tourists), and 15 inhabited outer islands. Together the outer islands stretch 625 miles east but total only seven square miles. All the outer islands are low-lying atolls, except Fais, a raised atoll. The northeast tradewinds make sandy beaches more common on the western and southern shores, but none are near Colonia, the main town.

A barrier reef surrounds the main island cluster. Yap is not volcanic, and the land and hills are more gentle than, for example, Palau. Geologically, it was a part of the Asian mainland that drifted away. The landscape varies from coastal villages flanked by majestic coconut palms to the open pandanus and scrub meadows of the upland interior. There are a few sandy beaches, but most of the coast is fringed by mangrove forests.

History

The Yapese were, and the outer islanders still are, the greatest voyagers of the Western Pacific, able to travel incredible distances in outrigger sailing canoes, using only stars and waves as their guides. The Yapese name for Yap Proper is Wa'ab, while the outer islands are Remetau. Traditionally, all of the outer islands that now belong to Yap State, plus the Westerns and Halls in Chuuk State, and the Marianas, were under the rule of the high chief of Yap.

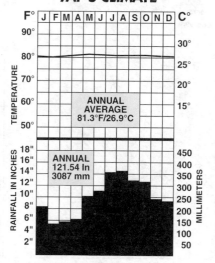

YAP'S CLIMATE

ANNUAL
AVERAGE
81.3°F/26.9°C

ANNUAL
121.54 In
3087 mm

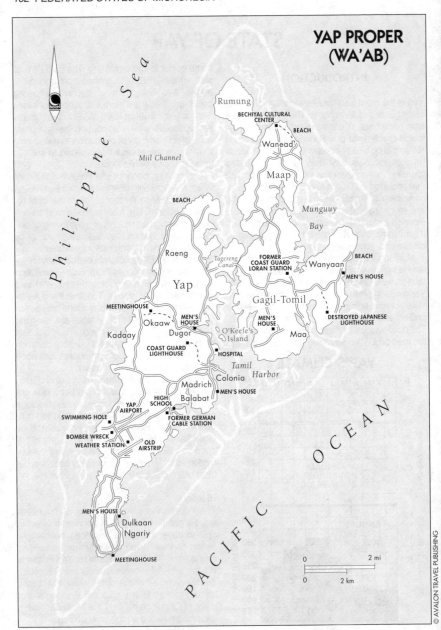

YAP PROPER (WA'AB)

Philippine Sea

Mil Channel

Rumung

BECHIYAL CULTURAL CENTER

BEACH

Wanead

Maap

Munguuy Bay

BEACH

Raeng

Tagereng Canal

FORMER COAST GUARD LORAN STATION

Wanyaan

BEACH

MEN'S HOUSE

Yap

Gagil-Tomil

MEETINGHOUSE

Okaaw

MEN'S HOUSE

O'Keefe's Island

MEN'S HOUSE

DESTROYED JAPANESE LIGHTHOUSE

Kadaay

Dugor

Maa

COAST GUARD LIGHTHOUSE

HOSPITAL

Tamil Harbor

Colonia

Madrich

Balabat

MEN'S HOUSE

YAP AIRPORT

HIGH SCHOOL

SWIMMING HOLE

FORMER GERMAN CABLE STATION

BOMBER WRECK

WEATHER STATION

OLD AIRSTRIP

OCEAN

PACIFIC

MEN'S HOUSE

Dulkaan

Ngariy

MEETINGHOUSE

PACIFIC

0   2 mi

0   2 km

© AVALON TRAVEL PUBLISHING

DAVID STANLEY

Stone money and betel palms flank the traditional meetinghouse at Okaaw on the path across Yap.

In 1869 the Germans set up a trading post. Their claims to the island prompted Spanish from the Philippines to occupy Colonia in 1885. Spain sold its claim to Yap back to the Germans 14 years later.

One of the most unusual characters of the European period was Capt. David O'Keefe, an Irish-American who was shipwrecked on Yap in 1871. Nursed back to health by a Yapese medicine man, he caught a steamer to Hong Kong when he was able. He returned a year later with a Chinese junk, which he used to launch a successful 30-year trading career. The highly developed Yapese culture of the time had an elaborate scale of financial valuations based on stone money. The type of stone used for this money didn't exist on Yap. Traditionally, the stones were brought hundreds of miles from Palau by raft, a perilous undertaking which, of course, gave the stone money its value. O'Keefe used his ship to bring the stones from Palau and traded it for copra and sea cucumbers, becoming very influential in the process. "His Majesty" imported bricks from Hong Kong to build a residence on Taraang, the small island in the middle of Tamil Harbor. Many years later, Burt Lancaster played O'Keefe in the movie, *His Majesty O'Keefe*.

The Japanese occupied Yap in 1914. In the years immediately following the war, it became an international cause célèbre. Yap housed a key installation in the international cable system through which the United States could communicate with its colony, the Philippines. Presumably because of this installation, President Woodrow Wilson wanted Yap excluded from the Japanese mandate from the League of Nations for Micronesia. The Japanese wanted it included. A compromise was finally reached in 1922, the island staying within the mandate, but Japan making concessions as to foreign access.

As on other islands of Micronesia, the Japanese soon outnumbered the local population. World War II was a difficult time for the Yapese as the Japanese forced them to work on defense installations, breaking their stone money unless they cooperated. The United States bombed Yap, but bypassed it without an invasion. The remaining Japanese, now cut off from receiving supplies from Japan, expropriated Yapese food, making life even more difficult for the local population.

Government

Under the Yap State Constitution, if the elected governor of Yap State is from Yap Proper, then the elected lieutenant governor will be from an outer island, and vice versa. The Office of Outer Islands Affairs assists the governor in coordinating outer island development.

There are two councils of chiefs: the Council of Pilung from Yap Proper and the Council of Tamol from the outer islands. The chiefs carry considerable influence in state and national elections. The councils have veto power over legislation affecting traditional customs.

There are 10 municipalities on Yap Proper: two are separate islands (Rumung and Maap), Tomil and Gagil share an island, and Yap Island has six municipalities.

Within the Federated States, Yap has a reputation for good government. It lives within its budget. Unlike any other states, it keeps well-

Yap Supreme Court Judge Constantine Yinuz in his home village of Kadaay

maintained, low-cost dirt roads. Villages, working communally, keep the island free from excessive litter.

Economy

Yap continues more traditional economic activities, such as fishing and taro production, than any other major island in Micronesia. As in much of Micronesia, the government is the largest industry and survives because of Compact payments from the United States. There is very little industry on the island, and even that tends to be foreign-owned enterprises using foreign labor, such as the textile plant not far from the airport. Goods thus produced may be sold in the U.S. under a quota-free, tax-free status granted by the Compact. Several hundred foreign workers live in dormitories. The Yap government gets little more than tax revenue, while absorbing extra strain on the local infrastructure.

The People

Of the more than 11,000 residents of the state, about a third live on the outer islands, the rest on Yap. The population is 95% Catholic. At the peak of its empire, Yap may have held as many as 45,000 people. European- and Japanese-imported diseases probably reduced the population to about 10,000 in 1869 and to less than half that in 1950. Since then the population has rebounded.

The number of jobs available to high school graduates is limited, particularly outside the government. The best students go abroad for schooling and often fail to return. For the outer islanders especially, finding a way forward without economic dependence or the need to emigrate is not easy.

A rigid caste system governed Yap in the old days. The village of origin accounted for the Yapese caste; those from strong, powerful villages were of the highest caste. The people take their surnames from their land parcels rather than from their parents, an example of how sacred land is to them. Each village has a chief, the highest chiefs coming from the highest caste villages.

The overlapping concepts of caste, village of origin, and property rights continue to exert an influence, sometimes pernicious, today. A child born on Yap to outer-island parents remains an outer islander. About 1,000 outer islanders (so defined) now live on Yap. Until the mid-1980s outer islanders, considered of lower caste than those from Yap itself, who moved to Yap were restricted to living in the crowded town of Madrich. Although things have loosened up somewhat today, hardly any outer islanders actually own land on Yap Proper. It is difficult for "lower" caste islanders, particularly women, to be considered for higher paying, higher prestige jobs.

Traditional society drew sharp distinctions between the roles of men and women. Women farmed, men fished. Even today, in some traditional families, a girl, or even a mature woman, cannot begin to eat dinner until her brothers are finished. She also may not contradict statements made by those brothers.

Traditionally, a village would have a *pebai* (meetinghouse) and a *faluw*. The *faluw* would be built beside the seashore on a large stone platform with a high thatched roof. It would serve as a school, meeting place, dormitory for young men, and a storage area for fishing gear. Many *pebai* and *faluw* were destroyed during World War II, and others were allowed to deteriorate afterward. But there still are large numbers of *pebai* and a smaller number of *faluw* that can be visited today. Women's houses *(dapal)* are found only on the outer islands. Always ask permission before entering a *faluw*.

Note too the *wunbey* (stone platforms) and *malal* (dancing grounds). Yapese dances include the bamboo, marching, sitting, and standing dances. The dancing could mark the inauguration of a new building, a high school graduation, or the commemoration of the death of an important person.

Today, only a small minority of women on Yap, mainly outer islanders, still walk in town bare breasted, wearing *lava lava* made of hibiscus and banana fiber, or cotton cloth. You'll see these women shopping or chatting with friends. Why is it so surprising to see a bare-breasted woman hop into a Nissan Bluebird and ride off? *Lava lava* often have woven designs which tell a woman's history, such as her island of origin. Yapese culture is sufficiently flexible that appealing patterns from North American Indians recently have been incorporated into the design repertoire.

More men and many young boys and teenagers wear the *thu* (loincloth). The color of the *thu* tells of the origins, and thus the caste, of the wearer. A pure outer islander's *thu* will be white or blue. If a man is from Yap, the *thu* will probably be multicolored. If he is mixed, he will wear red.

Four languages are spoken in Yap State: Yapese, Ulithian, Satawalese, and Woleaian. In Yapese *mogethin* means "hello," *kefel* "goodbye," *sirow* "excuse me," and *kammagar* is "thank you."

THE BETEL NUT HABIT

Betel nut chewing on Yap is universal, even among children, and for many, continual. All men and most women carry baskets made of coconut leaves in which they keep the necessary nuts, lime, and leaves. A green nut is split open, sprinkled with dry lime made from coral, and wrapped in a piece of a pepper leaf. The bundle is inserted into the mouth and chewed whole for 20 minutes or so.

If you are interested in trying betel nut, almost anybody on Yap will be happy to help you. First-time users should not do so on an empty stomach. The first experience will produce a sense of well being, accompanied by a lightheadedness that lasts for about 15 minutes. As with tobacco, after habitual use, the pleasure is less, but the absence of the drug may lead to feelings of deprivation and in some cases depression. Betel nut chewing turns saliva and teeth bright red. The casual, though not the habitual, user can brush the color away. The red saliva should be spit out, not swallowed. All pavements on Yap have red stains from the continual spitting this activity entails. The YCA building, knowing the futility of "No Spitting" signs, merely used betel nut red-colored pavement. Top quality betel nuts are grown on Yap and are exported. Importing betel nut to some American states and other Western nations is not legal.

JANE M. LEVY

Stone Money

Stone money *(rai)* was as much a pillar of Yapese society as gold is of ours. Although cash is used today for most commercial transactions, the big circular stone "coins" (and smaller stone and shell money for certain specific purposes) are still of considerable value to the Yapese. A Japanese count in 1929 revealed 13,281 pieces of stone money. About half that number survive today, and the money may be seen in every village. The money resembles a flat gristmill with a hole in the middle, so two or more men could carry it on a pole.

The largest piece (on Rumung) is 13 feet across and would take a dozen men to move. Although important, size is not the only factor in determining the value of a coin. A smaller piece may be worth more due to its age and history. Thus the exact value of a stone, like paper money in the United States during much of the nineteenth century, is open to negotiation.

Stones are seldom moved since who owns what is common knowledge. A particular piece of money might be owned by someone in another village. None of this should sound very odd to any modern Westerner, since it is much the method used by governments today. If, for example, the U.S. must make a gold payment to France, the gold is not shipped from the New York Federal Reserve Bank across the Atlantic Ocean to France. The gold may not even be moved at all. It is much easier merely to change the ownership sign on top of a stack of gold, or on a hard disk.

Sitting or standing on stone money is forbidden. Stone money cannot be taken out of Yap.

Crafts

Yap is an excellent place to purchase quality handicrafts. *Lava lava* are woven from hibiscus and banana fibers or from cotton, and usually have interesting lined patterns. There is a variety of basketry woven from pandanus and coconut, including women's soft handbags. Woven baskets for betel nuts make good souvenirs, as do the distinctive combs with long teeth made of bamboo. The *yar,* a traditional form of currency, is a large, polished mother-of-pearl shell tied to a handle woven of coconut fiber. Other craft items include hair ornaments, carved spoons, shell belts, colorful hibiscus fiber necklaces, fans, model canoes, and woodcarvings.

Three main gift shops are located within walking distance of each other in Colonia. The **Women's Cooperative** has very reasonable prices. The **I.L.P.** store, next to O'Keefe's Kanteen, dedicates half its shop to handicrafts. The **Tropical Touch,** in the YCA, is run by Mary Figir. It is exclusively a handicraft gift shop and has a wide selection of quality items at reasonable prices. Particularly outstanding is the collection of *lava lava,* made from traditional hibiscus and banana fibers or modern cotton thread.

Many small stores carry selections as well. The Manta Ray Bay Hotel, the Pathways Hotel and the E.S.A Hotel all have gift shops.

The **Ethnic Art Institute of Micronesia,** located near Aces Market, runs a program in which

stone money coin, rai, resting in front of a meetinghouse

PAUL BÖHLER

Yap Day festival, Gagil

elders teach craft skills to younger artists. Visitors are welcome to watch the artisans work on Tuesdays and Thursdays. Tours should be arranged in advance. Call (691) 350-6000 or fax (691) 350-4279. Inquiries can also be made to the institute's sponsor, the Robert Gumbiner Foundation for the Arts (5456 The Todeo, Long Beach, CA 90803, U.S.A., tel. 562-433-5459, fax 562-439-2473). The institute also sells its quality reproductions of museum pieces from throughout Micronesia at the airport outlet Trader's Landing, open for outgoing international flights.

Yap resident expat artist Ruth Glenn Little recently opened the exciting **Yap Art Studio and Gallery,** (P.O. Box 949, Colonia, Yap, FM 96943, tel. 691-350-4180, e-mail: rglenn@mail.fm). It is located on the road to Gagil-Tamil, just before the hospital turnoff, about a half mile north of central Colonia. Ruth trains local artists in a four-year apprenticeship program. You can see them at work in the gallery, which also sells story boards and features natural fiber *lava lava* as well as those made of thread. The shop carries scenes of Yap, both in watercolors and prints, by Ruth and by her students. The gallery is open Mon.-Fri. 8:30 a.m.-4:30 p.m., or call (691) 350-4180 for an appointment. The gallery will give you a lift from your hotel if you need one.

Events

A *mitmit* is a traditional festival where one village hosts another in an exchange of gifts and obligations. The completion of a major village project and high school graduations can also occasion traditional singing, dancing, and feasting. Yap Day (1 March) is a celebration with sporting events, traditional dancing, contests, and feasts. If you are in Micronesia at that time, try to get to Yap for this colorful event.

Conduct

Roads and walkways (except short paths leading directly to someone's home) are publicly owned. But most other land outside Colonia is privately owned. Since land along the pathways is private, do not pick flowers or fruit. You need permission to use a beach, approach a *faluw,* collect shells, camp, or walk around a village, but it may be difficult to determine who has authority to give it. Do the best you can. If no one is there, use your judgment to decide what to do. Off the main roads, if you smile and greet everyone you meet, you'll rarely be refused permission to proceed. At times, however, people with or without authority to do so may ask for several dollars in exchange for permission.

Don't infringe on fishing grounds or disturb fish traps. Many people, particularly older people, object to having their pictures taken. Don't take pictures of anyone without permission. Don't point at people or pat children on the head. The local custom is that women do not expose their legs above the knees. It's considered ill-mannered to step over another person's outstretched leg or basket or to walk in front of someone who is speaking. A group should walk single file rather than abreast. Yapese walking through a strange village will tell people they meet the purpose of their visit. They sometimes carry a piece of green vegetation in one hand to show peaceful intentions as they pass through a village; carrying a small basket called a *way* (pronounced "Y") serves a similar purpose.

SIGHTS

Colonia and Environs
The Yapese name for Colonia is Donguch, meaning "Small Islands." The point where the government offices and legislature sit, once a tiny island, is now connected to the rest of Colonia by fill. The offices were built on the foundations of a **Spanish fort.** The state legislature nearby occupies the site of what once was a **Japanese shrine.**

Urban life in Colonia revolves around the two-story, modern **YCA** (Yap Cooperative Association) building. It contains the island's largest grocery store, a video store, the Bank of Hawaii, the Bank of FSM, and the Continental Airlines office. It also seems to be the place for Yapese to hang out in town in the morning, meeting friends and neighbors.

In the Yap Small Business Center, behind the Coop building, opposite the Marina, there is a **flea market** on the first Friday of each month, beginning at 10:30 a.m. It is an interesting event. Homemade foods are usually also sold, and it is a chance to see much of the outer islander community

For a superb view of Yap, follow the jeep track from the Catholic mission above Colonia up Medeqdeq Hill to the **Coast Guard Lighthouse.**

You can take a beautiful walk on a traditional stone path right in town. It begins in the narrow space between a church and the Ocean View Hotel. At first, the path is a gentle uphill climb till it levels off above the mangroves. There are some houses along the path, but it gives a wonderful away-from-it-all feeling, remarkable considering you are still in town. In about a half mile, you will come to a fork in the road. To the right, the stone path falls into disrepair in another several hundred feet. It is a lovely walk though I have no idea what, if anything, lies beyond it. The left fork leads to a paved road. Heading left

on that road will take you downhill and back to town; toward the right, the road leads up to Medeqdeq summit.

Directly south of Colonia is the outer islanders' colony of **Madrich.** A Spanish trading post was once here and the place is named after Madrid. Until the 1980s it was the only place on the island where outer islanders were allowed to live. It is crowded, vibrant, and a bit squalid. Less than a mile farther along, **stone money** lines each side of the road in front of the Ruul Municipal Office at Balabat. The paved road dead ends into a dirt road. Make a right turn and a few hundred feet beyond, the second small road to the left leads to another **stone money bank** and a *faluw*.

Continue to the south end of the road where a **dancing ground** rests between two stone platforms *(wunbey).* A stone path leads off to the right. All this can be seen on foot from Colonia in a couple of hours, or in less than an hour by car.

South of Colonia
The unused **old airstrip,** parallel to, and south of, the present strip, was built by the Japanese. More than a dozen Japanese planes are in fragments near it, most of them destroyed on the ground by Allied aircraft. Notice the gun half hidden in the vegetation between the weather station and the old airport terminal.

Beside the highway, just a few hundred feet south of the crossroads and to the west of the road, is a wrecked **Japanese bomber** with German engines. Notice the small insect-eating plants in this area.

Driving farther south on the well-maintained main dirt road, opposite St. Ignatius of Loyola Church, is a dirt path to the left. This path hits a wider dirt road where, if you make a right, the road goes through mangroves to the ocean. It is not a place to swim, but a pleasant spot for a picnic. There is even a barbecue pit set up.

Less than a mile farther down the road is another left-hand turnoff that leads to the village of Dulkaan. The path down is lovely, lined with hibiscus. It is probably best to do this one-quarter mile on foot, as the residents do not seem to appreciate tourists driving through their village.

Better still is a visit to Ngariy, which one reaches by a path off to the left of the main road, about a mile farther south. The village has a new meeting hall and an old platform. The Ngariy road

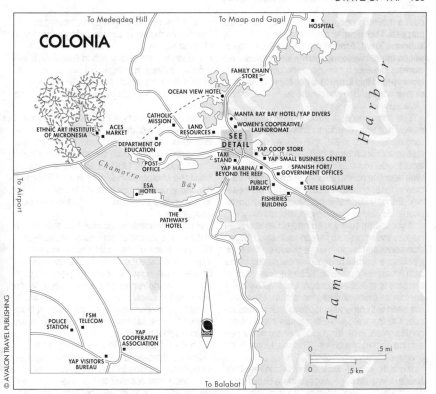

dead ends into the unpaved coastal road. A few feet to the right lie the remains of a stone path lined with stone money. The path leads down to the water through the mangroves; the walk down from the main road is less than a quarter mile. Bug repellent is a must, but this trip is well worth it. It's extremely picturesque and gives a feel for how wealthy Yap once was.

North of Colonia

Two wonderful villages quite near each other are **Okaaw** and **Kadaay.** From the YCA building in Colonia, take the road toward the airport for approximately 1.4 miles. You will see a broad dirt road leading to the right. Take it and go right again at the next fork. About two miles farther, you'll see an unmarked road to the left that leads to the village of Kadaay. Unless you want to miss one of the most beautiful spots on the island, do

not take the road. Instead park the car and get out. About 20 feet down the road to Kadaay, off to the left, lies a fantastic, restored stone walkway. It wanders through a vision of what tropical life was like when homes, rainforest, and agriculture blended with each other and the earth.

The path is raised above fields of taro, banana plants, and betel nut trees. You pass magnificent banyan trees. There is one fork in the path; both branches lead to Kadaay, so whichever you take down, take the other back up.

Once in the village, check out the well-maintained meetinghouse, set near a dancing area, and the stone money bank and sitting areas, complete with stone backrests. The village is one of the most peaceful spots I have ever visited.

In front of the meetinghouse, note the stone backrest with a carved lizard. To the people of Yap, the lizard is the dumbest of animals because it climbs coconut trees for no apparent purpose. Therefore, to call someone a lizard is a supreme insult. Around the turn of the century, village morale was low, and the villagers ceased working together for the common good. One villager carved this lizard to show the rest the error of their ways and to encourage them toward better behavior.

The charge to walk through the village is $2, money that goes directly to the village. For prices ranging from $20 to $40, the village offers package tours. Such tours can include a dinner of local foods and traditional dancing by children. With advance notice, the village will arrange for a master to teach you the rudiments of local weaving. Either your hotel or the Visitors Bureau should be able to make arrangements for you.

If you return to the road and go another half mile, to the right you'll see an unmarked, broad stone path that begins near a house on the right, just before a small bridge. The beginning of the path measures a majestic 12 feet across. Most of the path is shaded by coconut palms. As is the custom in much of Yap, the sides of the path are lined with ornamental plants, such as hibiscus. On the trail, several stones have petroglyphs. Also, look for a piece of stone money serving as part of a bridge. This must have been a village of very high rollers.

It is a 10-minute walk to the village meetinghouse. It is quite large, but in a state of disrepair. The house is surrounded by stone money, one piece being at least eight feet in diameter. From here you can continue to hike across the island. Follow the stream that winds through a bamboo forest punctuated with immense banyan trees and taro patches until you meet up with the road; take it down to Dugor on the east coast. This trip can be done in less than three hours on foot—if you don't get lost. But the trail is difficult to follow in spots and you may wish to hire one of the village children as a guide.

Gagil-Tomil

If you take the main road north from Colonia, in just over six miles there is a turnoff on the right marked Tamiling School that turns into a broad, good-quality dirt road. In about 1.5 miles, you reach the pretty hilltop village of Bogol. Make a right-hand turn in front of bright blue St. Peter Chanel church. About 50 feet farther, on your right, you will come to a beautiful meetinghouse. The meetinghouse is surrounded by a great deal of stone money.

If instead you take a left in Bogol, you will wind up in Maa, a village that organizes ceremonial dancing which hotels can arrange for their guests. The going price is $30 pp for the show.

The main road, if heading north, turns to dirt at the **Maritime Academy,** which is about a half mile past where a paved road comes in from the left. Originally built by the United States Coast Guard as a LORAN station, in January 1990 the Micronesian Maritime and Fisheries Academy, operated by Pacific Missionary Aviation, opened. It closed in 1997, but there is talk of it reopening.

Past the Maritime Academy, take the left fork and the road will end at the beach in the village of Wanyaan, one of the most charming spots in Yap. You will see the beautiful Wanyaan men's house on the right. Respect the people's wish that you do not enter or photograph it. Much stone money lies along the pathway. Many homes, even some modern ones, rest on high, stacked stone foundations. There are many thatched-roof homes.

The road then leads to a beach with four thatch-covered cabanas. Behind the beach is an enclosed cabana for changing and a shower. The beach provides excellent snorkeling, though at high tide it is a *long* swim out to the deep waterholes. The area is now privately operated as **Sea Breeze Park,** with a bar that is open Wednesday through Sunday. On Thursday, Friday and Saturday evenings, you get free sashimi with your beer. If you arrive when the bar isn't open, be sure to stop at the small store on your right as you enter Wanyaan to pay the $1 pp admission fee.

Maap

Near the northern tip of Maap is the **Bechiyal Cultural Center.** Unfortunately, much of the Center was destroyed by Typhoon Fern in December 1996. However, the men's house still stands. A new community house, perhaps the finest on Yap, was completed in 1999, constructed under the supervision of Joe Tamag, who still hand weaves coconut fiber rope, which was used in construction. The white sandy beach

The Bechiyal men's house overlooks a sandy beach.

at Bechiyal slopes far out into the lagoon, which makes it fairly safe for children, but snorkelers have to swim quite a distance to reach the reef. Collecting live seashells is not allowed. There are several good short hikes in the vicinity, including walks along the beach. A $2.50 pp sightseeing fee is charged. It may be possible to stay for the night in the men's house. Contact Marietta T. Fathal at the Yap Visitors Bureau.

You can now drive to Bechiyal, but consider taking the beautiful 30-minute hike to get there. If you are driving, go straight when you come to a fork in the paved road—do not take the road to the left. The road then becomes a dirt road that ends at a wooden footbridge. To get to the Cultural Center, you walk through two of the most traditional villages on the island, Wanead and Tooruw. On the walk stay on the main track until it hits a T and only a small path lies ahead. Take that small path, which gets muddy when wet and leads to the Center. Wear good walking shoes.

Bechiyal faces the forbidden island of **Rumung,** whose people have decided they're not yet ready for tourism.

ACCOMMODATIONS

Colonia is home to most of the state's hotels and restaurants. (There is one other hotel on Yap Island, and one hotel is under construction on Ulithi atoll.) The tap water is not suitable for drinking, and during the dry season, usually January through April, only two hotels, **The Pathways** and the **Manta Ray Bay Hotel,** have enough water to assure it being available all day long. Add 10% room tax to the hotel rates. Many places on Yap still do not take credit cards. Be certain to have sufficient United States dollars or traveler's checks with you.

The most charming stay in Colonia is at **The Pathways** (very expensive) (P.O. Box 718, Colonia, Yap, FM 96943, tel. 691-350-3310, fax 691-350-2066, e-mail: pathways@mail.fm). Overlooking Chamorro Bay, its eight attractive thatched cottages are set on a hillside and rent for $115 s, $125 d, with a filling continental breakfast thrown in. Each rustic, screened unit has a private balcony overlooking the bay, a private bath, ceiling fans and air conditioning, and no telephones or TVs. The cottages are separated by lush vegetation, including such exotica as torch ginger and betel nut trees, and are connected by picturesque wooden walkways, all set into the hillside. There is a bar and the breakfast restaurant attached.

Beside the harbor in the center of town is the **Manta Ray Bay Hotel** (very expensive) (P.O. Box MR, Yap, FM 96943, tel. 691-350-2300, fax 691-350-4567, e-mail: yapdivers@mantaray.com, website: www.mantaray.com), a modern three-story building opened in 1990. The 22 a/c rooms begin at $115 s, $140 d. Rooms have phones, TVs and VCRs. Rooms with water views cost more, and prices may also be higher during peak seasons. The hotel admirably serves the divers'

YAP COUNTRY CODE: 691

needs, as it also runs the leading dive shop on the island, Yap Divers, located next door. Boats leave from a dock behind the hotel reception area. If you plan to dive every day, this is a particularly good choice, as the hotel offers reduced combination package rates to those staying a minimum of three nights.

The **ESA Bay View Hotel** (expensive) (Erenna and Silbester Alfonso, P.O. Box 141, Colonia, Yap, FM 96943, tel. 691-350-2139, fax 691-350-2310, e-mail: esayap@mail.fm) on Chamorro Bay has a new 22-room, three-story building, constructed in 1997. Its rates are $85 s and $95 d. The air-conditioned rooms have telephones and TVs. Surprisingly, the hotel did not secure a water supply and had to ration water during the 1998 drought. The hotel still rents rooms in its older building next door (inexpensive) at $45 s, $55 d. The rooms are dreary and aged, but are probably the best budget choice in Colonia today.

The **Ocean View Hotel** (inexpensive) (P.O. Box 130 Colonia, Yap, FM 96943, tel. 691-350-2279, fax 691-350-2339) is near the ocean, but few rooms have interesting ocean views. Run by the likeable Joe Tamag, the hotel has a familial feel, but also has a crowded, close feel to it. Rooms are $40. It too can have water problems, and should be used as a last resort.

The **Destiny** (luxury) (P.O. Box 428, Colonia, Yap, FM 96943, tel. 691-350-4188, fax 691-350-4187) is located in the village of Anooth, on the southern tip of Yap. These two beautifully constructed cottages each have a small kitchenette. They are isolated, with few surrounding services, and are quite overpriced at $150 per night.

The **Village View Resort** (inexpensive) (Alphonso Ganang, P.O. Box 758, Colonia, Yap, FM 96943, tel. 691-350-3956, fax 691-350-4640, e-mail: villageview@mail.fm) is located on a lovely white sand beach in north Maap, about 10 miles from Colonia. Because much of the road to the resort is unpaved, it takes about 30 minutes to reach from town. It has five buildings on the beach, each with two units. Each unit has a bedroom facing the beach, a kitchenette,

and a nice patio. These air-conditioned houses rent for $55 s, 65 d. Bring your own food, though the local store has some canned goods and plenty of beer and sodas. O.R.C. Diving, affiliated with a Japanese dive company, is located on the premises.

Scheduled to open with 26 rooms in mid-1999 is the upscale **Trader's Ridge Resort,** with a restaurant and Yap's first swimming pool. For more information call (691) 350-6000, fax (691) 350-4279, or write to Trader's Ridge Resort, P.O. Box B, Colonia, Yap, FM 96943.

In addition to the places listed above, the **Visitors Bureau** (P.O. Box 988 Colonia, Yap, FM 96943, tel. 691-350-2298, fax 691-350-7015, e-mail: yvb@mail.fm, website: www.visityap.com) can arrange stays in Yapese homes, costing about $25 pp a day. Of particular interest would be a stay at the cottage rented by Cyprion Muguncey in Wanyaan village. The simple yet charming cottage is raised six feet above the beach. There are two beds and electricity, with toilet facilities in Cyprion's home next door. You can also speak to him about prepared meals. Kayaks are available for rent. You can reach him directly at P.O. Box 400, Colonia, Yap, FM 96943, tel. (691) 350-3344.

FOOD

The best restaurant on Yap, by a long shot, is at the **Manta Ray Bay Hotel.** Located on the third floor, it overlooks Tamil Harbor. The restaurant's large room is not air conditioned, but it does catch the trade winds. (There is also a smaller air-conditioned room if that is your preference). The chef is Jamaican Bill A.D. Munn, who joined the Manta Ray Bay Hotel after a stint at Pacific Palau Resort. His wife, Caroline, bakes wonderful breads and cakes. Fish served at the Manta Ray is always fresh, usually caught that day. You can also chose from a chicken or a beef dish, as well as tasty pizza. Dinners cost $12-19. There is no printed menu; as you enter the restaurant notice the chalkboard listing the day's offerings. Your order will be taken as you enter.

The **Yap Marina,** located past the YCA, has a breezy terrace overlooking the bay where sandwiches, full meals, (breakfasts about $5, dinners about $7), and cheap treats (cold coconuts $1, ice cream $1.25) are served. Alcohol is also served after 1 p.m. and at happy hour the price of a Foster's drops to $1.50.

On the main street, right past the YCA building, is **O'Keefe's Kanteen,** with a nice bar and outdoor patios. A sign outside the bar proclaims:

O'Keefe's Kanteen
Established 1874—Historic Pub

When I asked owner Don Evans how the bar could be that old since it wasn't there in 1995, he looked sheepish and told me that a bar owned by O'Keefe was located here in 1874. He proudly pointed to some bricks in a walkway and said, "They were made in Hong Kong and might have been from the original tavern."

Be that as it may, O'Keefe's is a fine place to have a brew. It is a room where locals, expats and travelers meet. After 5 p.m. on Friday, much of the expat community gathers here. A half barbecued chicken costs $4.50. Other dinners are served Monday through Friday, but the food comes from the **I.L.P. Sakurakai Restaurant** next door. Those meals are primarily Filipino cooking, with dinners running about $8. If you wish to eat in an air-conditioned room, move over to the Sakurakai. O'Keefe's is closed Saturday and Sunday, but Sakurakai stays open.

The ESA Hotel's **Wum ra Restaurant** has moved to the hotel's new building. The air-conditioned restaurant's service has greatly improved. It offers a mixed menu, with many Japanese-style dishes. Fish is your best bet. Dinners cost about $8.

In 1997, the **Yap Small Business Center** was built at a cost of more than $1 million. Some say that it was a waste of money because more than a year later only one room was rented. I disagree. A million dollars is not too much to pay for one first-rate doughnut shop, particularly if it is the only one in the State. **Cecil's Doughnuts** sells doughnuts for 45 cents, coffee for 50 cents, and cold coconuts for 35 cents.

One other choice is the open-air **Ocean View Restaurant** in front of the Ocean View Hotel.

Drinkers staying on Yap for more than 30 days must obtain a drinking permit ($5) from the police.

OTHER PRACTICALITIES

Sports and Recreation

If you are going to Palau, rightly famous for its diving, do yourself a favor and arrange a couple of days to dive in Yap as well. Yap's diving is sufficiently varied that it can also make a wonderful destination by itself. Depending on the time of year, diving takes place at sites all around the island. One of the favorites is Gilman Wall off the southwest tip of the lagoon. From a depth of 35-40 feet a vertical wall plunges 650 feet. Large fish abound, including barracuda, tuna, and jacks, plus eagle rays, turtles, moray eels, and harmless sharks. The water is clear, prime diving spots are only a short boat ride away, and the hard corals are spectacular.

Yap is perhaps the best spot on earth to see manta rays. These beautiful and peaceful cousins to the shark return day after day to be cleaned of parasites by cleaner wrasses who make their living this way. By showing up at the cleaning stations, you can stay beneath them and see these graceful, ethereal creatures, some with 12-foot wingspreads, swim above you. It is not unusual for three or more mantas to circle a cleaning station, each taking its turn. Every manta has unique markings, and folks from Yap Divers have identified and named more than 60 of them.

Yap Divers (Bill Acker, P.O. Box MR, Colonia, Yap, FM 96943, tel. 691-350-2300, fax 691-350-4567, e-mail: yapdivers@mantaray.com) is the oldest, largest, and most established dive shop on Yap. It's by the Manta Ray Bay Hotel in Colonia and runs under joint management. The charge for a two-tank dive including a sandwich and beverages is $95. A one-tank night dive is $45. Certification cards are carefully scrutinized. Snorkelers may go along with the divers for $45 pp.

Beyond the Reef is managed by David Vecella and Jesse Faimaw. Located on the marina, advance arrangement can be made through P.O. Box 609, Yap, FM 96943, tel. (691) 350-3483, fax (691) 350-3733, e-mail: beyondthereef@mail.fm. Its prices are usually a few bucks less than Yap Divers'.

O.R.C. Diving at the Village View Hotel is primarily for Japanese divers. We cannot recommend an additional dive shop, **Nature's Way.**

We are troubled that it rents too much of its equipment from others to be able to ensure proper maintenance.

Beyond the Reef and **Yap Angler,** another enterprise of Bill Acker's, also run fishing trips. Full-day charters at Yap Angler are $125 pp, a half day for $75, with a two-person minimum. Beyond the Reef charges $130 pp for a full day and $95 for a half day. It has no minimum number of those fishing.

On Yap, you can troll for tuna, wahoo, or mahi. Another experience is to go "whipping" for giant trevally. The boat will go out to the reef, where you will cast and pull the lure back very quickly. Hooking into a 20-50 pounder will be an experience you won't soon forget. Yap's fishing companies encourage those fishing to "catch and release" unless the fish has been injured in the fight. They also do not use stainless steel hooks. That way, the hook will not permanently remain in a fish that gets away.

Surfer (and legal counsel to the Yap State Legislature) Steve Vosseller tells us that the reefs near Goofnuw, Miil, and Quatlirow channels are Yap's most consistent surf breaks. Although most spots are surfable even at low tide, high tide is usually better and safer. Boogie boarding should only be done at high tide. It is customary to ask permission from the nearest village before surfing.

As in much of Micronesia, kayaking is beginning to take off on Yap. Divers often go kayaking the day before they fly off, when they cannot dive. It is possible to kayak in the lagoon or through the mangroves. Palau's Planet Blue Kayaks has opened a branch, **Yap's Planet Blue Tours** run by Patricia Acker (P.O. Box MR, Colonia, Yap, FM 96943, tel. 691-350-2300, fax 691-350-4567, e-mail: yapdivers@mantaray.com). It has the best equipment on the island. A half-day trip costs $35. **Yap Monarch Tours** at the Pathways Hotel also runs guided kayaking tours.

Shopping

The **YCA** (Yap Cooperative Association) store in the center of town is the best store for groceries on Yap. It also sells Yap T-shirts. **Family Chain Store** offers a wide selection of goods and keeps the longest hours in Colonia (7:30 a.m.-8 p.m. daily). The hardware department sells masks and snorkels.

You can buy a Yap State "Island of Stone Money" license plate at the police station for $5. Stamps and first day covers are available at the post office.

Services

The Bank of Hawaii (tel. 691-350-2129) has a branch in Colonia and is open Mon.-Thurs. 9:30 a.m.-3 p.m., Friday 9 a.m.-5 p.m. The Bank of FSM (tel. 691-350-2329) is in the YCA Complex.

You can place long distance telephone calls at the Telecommunications Corporation (open 24 hours). Rates are cheaper 6 p.m.-6 a.m. and on Sunday.

Address mail to Yap, FM 96943.

The FSM Immigration office (tel. 691-350-2126) is upstairs in the YCA complex.

There are free public toilets in the Marina Center and the YCA building.

You'll find a laundromat (open weekdays 8 a.m.-4:30 p.m., Sunday from noon) in an unmarked building next to Yap Divers. Another is located in the front of the ESA Bay View Hotel property.

Information

Marietta T. Fathal in the **Yap Visitors Bureau** (P.O. Box 988, Colonia, Yap, FM 96943, tel. (691) 350-2298, fax (691) 350-7015, e-mail: yvb@mail.fm, website: www.visityap.com) has information leaflets on Yap, can answer questions, and will even arrange accommodations in local homes.

The Yap Public Library (P.O. Box 550, Colonia, Yap, FM 96943, tel. 691-350-2793) on the marina pier is open Mon.-Fri. 1:30-4:30 p.m. There is a covered basketball court behind it.

GETTING THERE

Yap Airport (YAP) is 3.5 miles southwest of town. All hotel keepers meet the flights at the airport and provide transfers at about $5 pp each way.

Yap is a **Continental Airlines** stopover between Palau and Guam on Wednesday and Sunday, so the cheapest way to get there is to include Yap in a roundtrip Guam-Palau ticket. From Southeast Asia, you can purchase a Continental ticket from Manila to Guam to Koror to

Yap. Inquire whether there are any off-peak special fares.

Reconfirm your onward flight at the Continental Airlines office (tel. 691-350-2127) at the YCA building.

At the airport, take time to look at the monumental story board that tells the story of stone money on Yap.

Also at the airport is a café with outside tables and an air-conditioned bar. Five bucks gets you into the cool **Traders' Landing Club** (no admission charge for Continental's frequent flyers).

GETTING AROUND

The terrain of Yap can be a bit confusing and roads are seldom marked. While driving or walking, you come upon many dirt lanes too small to be placed on most maps. The easiest way to reach your destination is by consulting the large *Topographic Map of Yap,* produced by the United States Geological Service in 1983. The Land Resources office, above the office of the Telecommunications Corporation, sells it for $7.50. The map is extremely detailed and despite its age, it's still useful because most newer roads are merely upgrades of older roads or paths on the map. (Note: due to some linguistic convention, the map frequently places the letter "Q" before or after "A" in place names.) Most of Yap's roads are well maintained and in good weather can be driven in a conventional car.

Public buses connect the outlying villages to Colonia (50 cents) weekdays only, leaving the villages at the crack of dawn and departing from the park across the street from O'Keefe's Kanteen around 5 p.m. The buses are primarily for the use of students or people commuting to work.

Taxis cost 75 cents anywhere in town. They are surprisingly plentiful during the day and early evening, and you can usually catch one cruising by. If you need to call a cab, try **Target Taxi** at (691) 350-4403, **Midland Taxi Service** at (691) 350-2405, or **Island Mutual** at (691) 350-3401. It is sometimes cheaper to hire a cab for an afternoon of sightseeing than to rent a car for the day. Price must be negotiated in advance.

Car rentals run at $35-45 a day plus 10% tax, price determined by the age of the car and whether it has air conditioning, more than by whom you

local transport

rent from. Most rental agencies will also rent cars by the hour at about $10 per hour. None of the agencies have too many cars, though cars are usually available on the island. Try the **ESA Hotel** (tel. 691-350-2139, fax 691-350-2310); **Pacific Bus Company** (tel. 691-350-2266, fax 691-350-4116) in the hardware department behind Family Chain; **Target Car Rental** (tel. 691-350-3275); or **Island Rentals Company** (tel. 691-350-2566, fax 691-350-2555). Many car rental shops are not open on the weekend.

There is an excellent paved highway from the airport to Colonia, Tomil, Gagil, and Maap. When driving, observe the speed limit of 20 mph on roads, 15 mph in villages. Local chiefs often set "sand traps" (holes in the road filled with sand) in their villages to catch speeding cars.

To the Outer Islands by Air

Pacific Missionary Aviation (PMA; P.O. Box 460, Colonia, Yap, FM 96943, tel. 691-350-2360, fax 691-350-2539) flies Monday and Friday between Yap and Ulithi ($50 one way); Friday between Yap and Fais ($75 one way); every other Wednesday between Yap and Woleai ($150 one way); and on Friday roundtrip between Ulithi and Fais ($25 one way). Free baggage is limited to 30 pounds.

PMA was founded to support medical missionaries, but flights are available to visitors. This company carries out emergency medical evacuations and brings in medical supplies at no charge.

Field Trips
The **Yap State Transportation Field Trip Service** (P.O. Box 576, Colonia, Yap, FM 96943, tel. 691-350-2240, fax 691-350-4113) in the radio room of the government offices in Colonia runs the field trip ship MV *Micro Spirit* from Yap to Ulithi, Fais, Faraulep, Woleai, Ifalik, Eauripik, Sorol, and Ngulu about every five weeks. Actually there are two field trips: a short one from Yap to Ulithi and perhaps one other island, and a long one to the inhabited islands of eastern Yap. Try to get to Yap a week before departure to arrange required permits, extensions of stay, and trip bookings. On an outer island the radio operator will know the estimated time of arrival of the ship.

Seven simple double cabins are available on the first deck, but 95% of the passengers travel deck. Fares are roughly five cents a mile on deck or 20 cents a mile for cabin. Bookings have to be made a few days in advance, otherwise an additional fee may be charged. Meals in the officers' mess are $3 for breakfast, $4 for lunch, and $4.50 for dinner.

Take plenty of food with you from Yap (soups, coffee, tea, canned food) and be self-sufficient. Locals always have rice, taro, breadfruit, dried or smoked fish, and bunches of fresh coconuts, and they're always inviting you to meals. In return offer them canned food or meat, which they can't get without spending their very limited cash.

Take a few 10-quart plastic containers along to fill with fresh rainwater, or bring your own purification unit. The captain has a small shop to sell cigarettes, biscuits, and cold drinks, but these sometimes run out by the end of the trip.

On deck a straw mat and a thin sleeping bag will do for a bed and should be rolled out early upon boarding. The washing facilities are poor and only a half hour of water daily is allowed for military-style showers. Be quick so you don't end up with a soapy body and no water.

The Field Trip Officer (FTO) is the one responsible for the itinerary, payments, and cargo. He also has a cupboard with medications. A doctor is often aboard to check outer islanders at short stops. A field trip can seem very long if you're not making friends on deck and taking the supply boat ashore at stops. Always make sure to get back to the ship on time, as they could easily leave without you. Keep in mind that the field trips are meant to serve the outer islanders, not tourists.

THE OUTER ISLANDS

The Outer Islanders
The Western Caroline Islands east of Yap are among the most traditional in the Pacific. The men still pierce their ears and noses and tattoo their bodies. (They had continued to do this even when it was unfashionable in the West). They sing the chants of their ancestors and travel long distances by sailing canoe.

Women wear knee-length *lava lava* held in place by a string of shells or a girdle belt. Men wear a *thu* (loincloth) consisting of a long piece of cloth wrapped around the waist and between the legs. Neither men nor women wear any upper garment. Every outer island has a men's house or two. During menstruation women move to the *pal* (women's house).

Permissions
If you'd like to take the plane to Ulithi, Fais, or Woleai and stay a couple of days, you must first get clearance in Colonia. Apply at the Office of the Governor who may send you to meet with an outer island council in Madrich. The same procedure is required to spend time on an outer island between visits of the field trip ship.

You're supposed to apply one month prior to your scheduled arrival at the outer island. If you're really serious about going, call ahead at (691) 350-2108, fax (691) 350-4113, or write two months in advance to the Office of the Governor, State of Yap, Colonia, Yap, FM 96943, stating precisely which atoll you'd like to visit, when, and why. Upon arrival in Yap, check with the Outer Islands Affairs office at the governor's office. If you arrive in Yap not having applied for permission, with persistence, luck, and most of all a local contact, you may be able to obtain permission, sometimes with remarkable speed. You'll be expected to take enough food for the duration of your stay. Of course, take all medical supplies with you, and pay a courtesy call on the island chief upon arrival. An entry fee of $20 pp must be paid to the chief upon arrival at each island.

Advance permission is not required to visit the outer islands on a field trip ship as a through passenger, provided you only get off for a couple of hours to look around while the ship's there. Tourists are not allowed to disembark for longer stays without consent.

People on the outer islands are not used to tourists. Arriving foreigners usually have been missionaries, Peace Corps volunteers, anthropologists, fisheries researchers, etc. You will be treated like a guest. You will be offered food at many homes, and it is considered bad manners and suspicious behavior to decline. Don't eat too much at any one house as you may be called upon to eat at many. Coffee, tea, or betel nuts make welcome gifts to reciprocate the hospitality.

Ulithi

Ulithi (pop. 1,000), 106 miles northeast of Yap, has 49 small islets on its reef, which encloses a 183-square-mile lagoon. In 1731, a 13-member Jesuit missionary party under Father Juan Antonio Cantova landed on Ulithi. When the Spanish returned the next year, they found the islanders had wiped out the Jesuits.

The Japanese built an airstrip on Ulithi but evacuated to Yap when an American landing became imminent. On 20 September 1944, the United States Navy occupied Ulithi, unopposed. A thousand United States warships assembled in the Ulithi lagoon ("Flattop Row") prior to the landings on Iwo Jima and Okinawa in early 1945.

The presently inhabited islands of Ulithi are Asor, Falealop, Fatharai, and Mogmog. The airstrip, radio transmitter, administrative offices, post office, and Outer Islands High School are all on Falealop Island. The high school buildings were once part of a LORAN station, now closed. The school serves students from all the outer islands.

The field trip ship calls at Ulithi on both the outward and inward journeys. It delivers supplies to all the villages on the way out, but may stop only at Falealop on the way back.

Mogmog is the chiefly island, where men once went to have their bodies covered in tattoos. The chief of Mogmog is the high chief of the atoll. There is rivalry between the government representative in Falealop and the chief.

Western clothing and alcohol have been prohibited on Mogmog. As hurricanes destroy the old thatched houses, dwellings of tin and concrete appear. Much work is still done communally. The men catch fish and the women cook vegetables from the gardens. If a fishing boat hasn't returned by dusk, the village launches a rescue mission. If you are male, ask permission of the chief to stay in one of the two *fal* (men's houses). The stock in the couple of small stores often runs out, so bring food.

All this may be changing, however. There is a 14-room lodge under construction by Pacific Adventure Resorts. It is scheduled to open in 1999 and will have facilities for diving. When it opens, the rules will be changed so that Western tourists can wear Western clothing. What other customs of traditional life will also change because of the presence of tourists is not clear.

ULITHI

Fais

Fais (pop. 300) was once mined by the Japanese for its phosphate: the ruins of machinery and railroad can still be seen. Today the inhabitants live from fishing, vegetable gardening, and copra production, subsidized by assistance programs. This raised atoll has no lagoon.

Eauripik

Large ships cannot enter Eauripik's long, fish-filled lagoon. The 100 inhabitants crowded onto the tiny islet at the east end of the atoll don't make copra because they need the coconuts to eat. Instead they smoke fish to exchange at

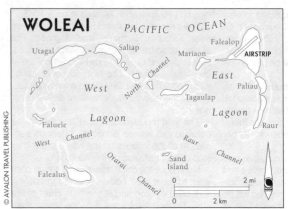

WOLEAI PACIFIC OCEAN

Utagal — Saliap — Falealop — Mariaon — **AIRSTRIP**

North Channel

West

Faluele

Lagoon

West Channel

Orarai Channel

Falealus

Channel

East

Tagaulap — Paliau

Lagoon

Raur

Raur Channel

Sand Island

Channel

0 ——— 2 mi
0 ——— 2 km

© AVALON TRAVEL PUBLISHING

Woleai, which they visit by sailing canoe. A passing freighter that lost a few big tropical logs recently was much appreciated by the skilled Eauripik canoe builders. They also make beautiful woodcarvings and other handicrafts of seashells. They build their houses on massive stone platforms to resist hurricanes, which flush waves over the islands.

Woleai

Woleai (pop. 850) is roughly in the center of the eastern outer islands. Five of the 22 islands around Woleai's two connected lagoons are inhabited. The others are used for copra and taro production. Woleai has the most breadfruit and the largest reef islands of any of the Yap atolls.

A junior high school and old Japanese airstrip remain on Falealop Island, where the high chief resides. Thousands of bypassed Japanese soldiers starved on Woleai in 1945. Wrecked planes, cannons, bunkers, and dumped heavy equipment still rot in the bush. Former railway tracks are used as curbs along the roads or as supports for cooking pots.

The FSM government hopes eventually to have internal flights from Chuuk to Yap that needn't pass through Guam. Woleai would make an ideal stop. Many islanders fear the changes this would bring.

The Japanese government donated a

traditional Yapese comb

modern ice plant to Woleai, but it's seldom in use due to maintenance problems and enormous fuel consumption. Aside from Western education, the school on Woleai teaches youngsters skills such as weaving, rope and canoe making, fish trap manufacturing, and traditional dancing. The graduation ceremony is the biggest event on Woleai, with dance practice beginning weeks before.

Satawal

Many Satawal islanders, from the easternmost inhabited atoll of Yap, have emigrated to work on Yap, leaving Satawal with a population of about 560. Some of the best traditional Pacific navigators live on Satawal, setting their course by the ocean swells and relative positions of the stars. In 1988 Lino Olopai of Satawal sailed his outrigger canoe to Saipan in this way. Mau Piailug, navigator of the famous Polynesian sailing canoe *Hokule'a,* is from Satawal lineage. The *Hokule'a* sailed with a native Hawaiian crew and no modern navigational devices from Hawaii to Tahiti.

Other Islands

Sorol atoll is no longer inhabited. Outboard motors are banned on highly traditional **Ifalik** atoll (pop. 650). Fish are mostly caught on an outer reef about 9.4 miles north of Ifalik, always by outrigger canoes. The Phallus of Maur stood in the meetinghouse (Tan Nap) on Ifalik until Catholic missionaries managed to engineer its removal.

Elato (pop. 120) and **Lamotrek** (pop. 400) are two of the most beautiful atolls of Yap, with a traditional way of life and sailing canoes. Lamotrek is well known for the traditional magic still practiced there. Together with Satawal these islands have been hard hit by both typhoons and drought in recent years, and there still could be a serious shortage of food and water, so check before heading that way.

GORDON OHLIGER

REPUBLIC OF PALAU
INTRODUCTION

Quite simply, above water, below water, Palau is pure beauty. The great cities of the world present visitors with surprises at every corner or hillcrest. Koror, capital of the Republic of Palau, does the same in a town of only 12,000 people. It's not the buildings or the neighborhoods, of course, but the breathtaking setting of the town, a fantastic crazy quilt of islands, bridges, and water that is like nothing else on earth. The otherworldly Rock Islands, looming like sculpted green mushrooms, dot the horizons. If you have one day to spend in Micronesia, spend it in Palau's Rock Islands.

With about 18,000 citizens, the Republic of Palau is the smallest of the four political units to emerge from the former Trust Territory of the Pacific Islands. Much to their credit, this small nation was the world's first to issue an Elvis stamp.

The correct Palauan pronunciation of the country is as if it were spelled "Belau," and many businesses use that spelling in their names. But the official name of the country is the Republic of *Palau,* the spelling we will use.

The Palau cluster consists of 343 islands strewn along a line that begins with Kayangel in the northeast and ends with Angaur, 125 miles southwest, most within one encircling barrier reef. This spectacular group, at the southwest corner of the Western Caroline Islands, offers great diversity, from tiny dots to 153-square-mile Babeldaob, the second-largest island in Micronesia (only Guam is bigger). In addition are the far-flung Southwest Islands, home to fewer than 100 people.

Only nine islands are inhabited. Two-thirds of Palau's population resides in Koror, the capital. This small island republic is equally distant from Guam and Indonesia, and only 550 miles east of the Philippines.

The Land
The east side of the giant lagoon created by the barrier reef, south of Koror, is riddled with hundreds of tiny umbrella-shaped islands, called the **Rock Islands** (*Chalbacheb* is the Palauan name).

These rounded, undercut mounds of limestone appear to float like emerald mushrooms on a turquoise lagoon. Formed from the weathering of ancient uplifted reefs, the islands have secluded beaches, tranquil channels, clear water, and unbelievably rich coral formations and marine life.

Babeldaob has a 700-foot-high volcanic center, fringed by mangrove forests. Add Babeldaob's freshwater Ngardok Lake (2,961 feet long) to Palau's perfect coral atoll (Kayangel) and two elevated limestone islands (Angaur and Peleliu), and you have one of the most varied, compact physical environments to be found in any ocean. Further, the Palau Visitors Authority promises, "At night the bright Southern Cross in clear sky will not fail to bring you a romantic mood."

Climate
Palau is alternately sunny and rainy, but always hot and humid. Due to its equatorial location, temperatures here tend to be slightly higher than elsewhere in Micronesia. Daily and seasonal variations in temperature are small. The heaviest rains occur early in the morning, with a second peak just after sunset.

Flora and Fauna
Palau's flora and fauna are the richest in Micronesia. The variety of habitats and proximity to the Indo-Malay faunal region explain the tremendous diversity of life in the lagoon. The enormous diversity of corals makes Palau one of the world's most favored dive sites. Scientists have found that as the distance from Southeast Asia increases, the number of species both above and below water decreases. Hawaii, for example, has only one-half to one-third as many varieties of fish and coral as Palau. Three nutrient-rich ocean currents merge here. In all, some 1,500 species of tropical fish and 700 different types of coral and anemones may be seen at Palau. Collecting coral and seashells is prohibited.

Palau's seagoing crocodiles, which inhabit the rivers and mangroves of Babeldaob, as well as other locations, probably arrived from New Guinea. They grow up to 16 feet long. Like all wild animals, they're shy and will flee from people if they can. Not a single crocodile incident

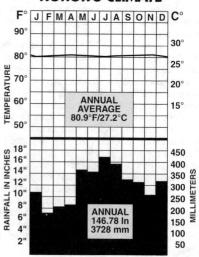

KOROR'S CLIMATE

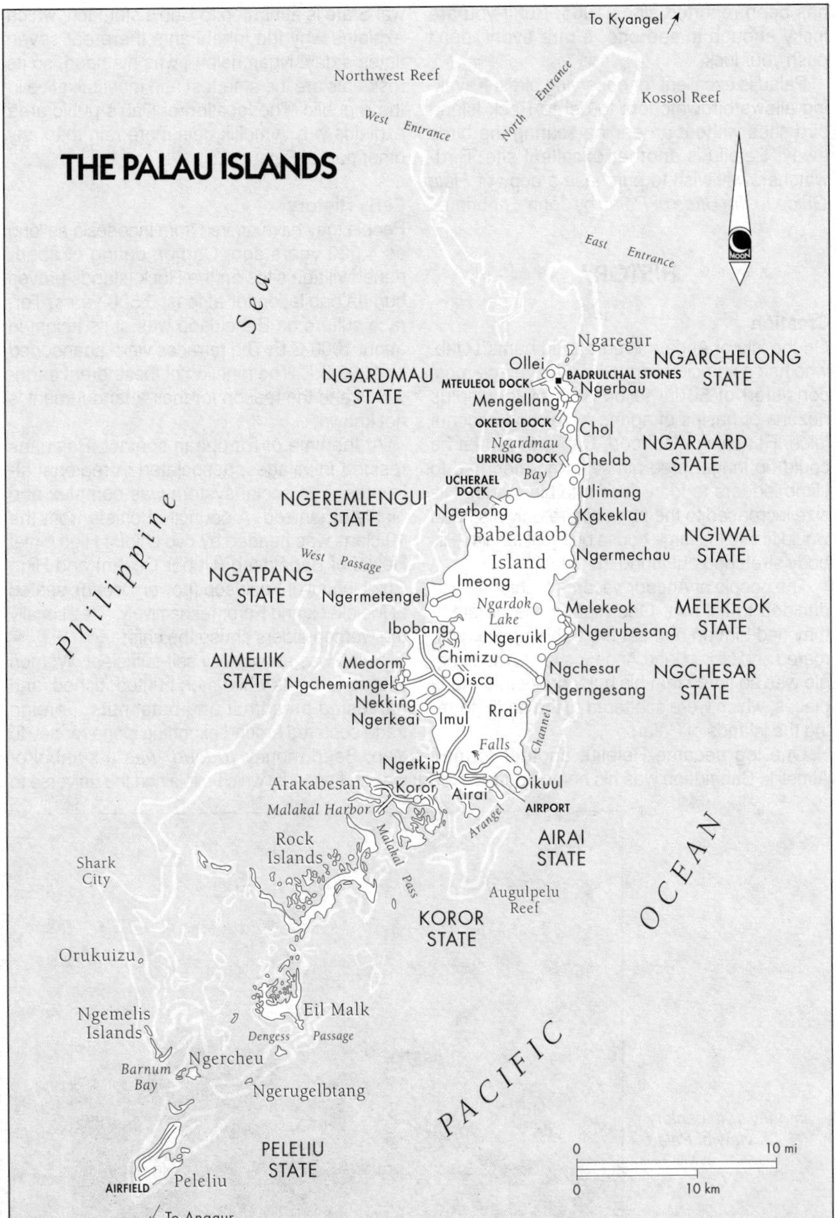

THE PALAU ISLANDS

To Kyangel ↗

Northwest Reef

Kossol Reef

West Entrance
North Entrance

East Entrance

Philippine

Sea

Ngaregur

Ollei • NGARCHELONG STATE
NGARDMAU STATE
MTEULEOL DOCK • BADRULCHAL STONES
Mengellang • Ngerbau
OKETOL DOCK • Chol
Ngardmau • Chelab • NGARAARD STATE
URRUNG DOCK *Bay*
UCHERAEL DOCK • Ulimang
NGEREMLENGUI STATE • Ngetbong • Kgkeklau
Babeldaob • Ngermechau • NGIWAL STATE
Island
West Passage
NGATPANG STATE • Imeong
Ngermetengel • *Ngardok Lake* • Melekeok
Ibobang • Ngeruikl • Ngerubesang • MELEKEOK STATE
AIMELIIK STATE • Chimizu
Medorm • Oisca • Ngchesar • NGCHESAR STATE
Ngchemiangel • Ngerngesang
Nekking • Rrai
Ngerkeai • Imul
Falls
Ngetkip • *Channel*
Arakabesan • Koror • Airai • Oikuul
Malakal Harbor • Airai • AIRPORT
Arangel
Rock • *Malakal Pass* • AIRAI STATE
Shark • Islands
City • Augulpelu Reef
KOROR STATE
Pacific
Orukuizu

Ngemelis Islands
Dengess Passage • Eil Malk
Barnum Bay • Ngercheu
Ngerugelbtang

OCEAN

PELELIU STATE
AIRFIELD • Peleliu

↙ To Angaur

| 0 | | 10 mi |
| 0 | | 10 km |

© AVALON TRAVEL PUBLISHING

has been reported since 1965. But if you are lucky enough to see one, a rare event, don't push your luck.

Palau is excellent for observing birds. Kayaking allows birdwatchers to get to Rock Island bird sites without an engine scaring the birds away. Peleliu is another excellent site. Birdwatchers will wish to purchase a copy of *Field Guide to the Birds of Palau* by John Engbring.

HISTORY

Creation

On the isle of Angaur lived a child named Uab, who had a voracious appetite. An average meal consisted of 50 large baskets of food, plus dozens of basins of spring water and coconut juice. Reaching manhood, Uab grew so fat he could no longer feed himself, and men had to climb ladders to force food into his mouth. His size increased to the point where only his head would fit into the large house built just for him. His body stretched out along the beach.

The people of Angaur became frightened and decided to kill him. One night while he slept, they tied him up and set fire to his house. Uab roared and kicked, and Angaur shook. The struggle was so fierce that his body broke into many pieces, which were scattered to the north, forming the islands of Palau.

One leg became Peleliu, another formed Aimeliik. Babeldaob was his body. Today's Ngi-wal State is attributed to Uab's stomach, which explains why the inhabitants there eat seven times a day. Ngarchelong was his head, so its residents are the smartest and most talkative in the republic. The location of Uab's pubic area explains why Aimeliik gets more rain than any other part of Palau.

Early History

People may have arrived from Indonesia as long as 4,500 years ago. Carbon dating of abandoned village sites on the Rock Islands proves human habitation for at least 3,500 years. Terrace culture on Babeldaob was at its height in about 1000 C.E. The terraces were abandoned by 1600 C.E. The function of these great earthworks and the reason for their abandonment is not known.

At the time of European contact, Palauans resided in villages, associated in regional alliances. The social system was complex and highly organized. A council of chiefs from the 10 clans was headed by two chiefs: High Chief Reklai of Babeldaob (Upper Ocean) and High Chief Ibedul of Youldaop (Lower Ocean), seated at Melekeok and Koror respectively. Traditionally the women elders chose the chief.

Palau was abundantly self-sufficient. Women tended taro pits while men hunted, fished, and harvested breadfruit and betel nuts. Foreign trade centered around exporting stone money to Yap. Bead money *(udoud)* was a symbol of wealth. Legends, which explained the universe to

an early 19th century view of Palau

M.G.L. DOMENY DE RIENZI

the people, appeared on men's meetinghouses *(bai)* and were painted in limestone caves.

European Impact

Although Spanish and Portuguese navigators visited as early as 1543, it was Capt. Henry Wilson of the East India Company's ship *Antelope,* wrecked in the Rock Islands in 1783, who first publicized Palau in Europe. A chief befriended Wilson and helped him build a schooner to return to Macau. This chief is known in the West as Abba Thulle, though it is probably not merely coincidence that the title for Koror's high chief is "Ibedul." His son, Prince Lebu (also spelled Lebuu or Lee Boo), sailed to London with Wilson, and the published account of the events made Palau briefly as famous in contemporary Europe as Captain Cook's Tahiti. Lebu died of smallpox after five months in England.

British traders introduced guns to the islands. During the century from 1783 to 1882, the population declined from upwards of 40,000 to only 4,000, primarily due to influenza and dysentery epidemics brought by Europeans. Early Spanish colonialists spread Catholicism. Germans, who succeeded them in 1899, concentrated on taking phosphates from Angaur and producing copra.

The Japanese Period

The Japanese, who seized Micronesia from the Germans in 1914, pursued economic development, largely for the benefit of the homeland, and sent large numbers of immigrants to Palau. They destroyed most of the tropical rainforest in order to plant sugar, rice, pineapples, and other crops. They paid Palauan laborers little to work in these fields or in the phosphate and bauxite mines. They taught Palauans to speak Japanese, took their lands, and replaced traditional chiefs with Japanese bureaucrats.

Koror became Japan's capital of Micronesia. Its population, more than twice the current population, was overwhelmingly Japanese. Before the war, a streetcar line ran through the city. In the late 1930s the Japanese built military bases, and after 1938 the area was closed to outsiders, a status that continued under the Americans until 1962.

In September 1944, a brutal battle exploded on Peleliu. Rather than meet the American landings on the beaches, as was the usual Japa-

nese strategy earlier in the war, the Japanese entrenched themselves in caves on a tangled limestone ridge. In two and a half brutal months, some 11,000 Japanese and nearly 2,000 Americans died. These deaths were particularly tragic since most military historians believe that the United States could have bombed and destroyed Japanese boats and planes, and bypassed the island, as it did with Koror and Babeldaob. There, 25,000 Japanese troops were left to sit it out. Prior to the Peleliu landings the Japanese had concentrated the Palauan population in central Babeldaob, where 526 (almost 10% of the indigenous population of the time) perished.

Recent History

In 1993, Palau voted to enter into a Compact of Free Association with the United States. In October 1994 the Republic of Palau became fully independent, after almost 50 years of trusteeship, and in December became the 185th member of the United Nations. Under the terms of the Compact, Palau will receive about $472 million over 15 years. But Palau's journey from trusteeship to independence was a rocky one.

In 1978 Palau voted to separate from the rest of Micronesia, and in 1979 the first Palau Constitutional Convention convened to write a constitution for a self-governing republic. The delegates incorporated provisions banning nuclear materials from Palau and preventing the government from using eminent domain powers for the benefit of any foreign entity. The United States, in its cold war mentality, would not agree to these provisions.

Over the next 15 years Palau was deeply divided on whether to accept a Compact of Free Association with the United States, which would

have negated these provisions. There were continual referenda over the issue. There was political violence, including the assassination of President Remeliik. There were charges of governmental corruption. No one could build a consensus on the terms on which to end the trusteeship.

Since Palau finally adopted a Compact that allows nuclear weapons to be stored on the islands as well as allowing access to the islands by the United States military, it can be said that the antinuclear forces, consistently a quarter to a third of the population, lost their fight. But with the cold war over, unless the world paradigm dramatically shifts once again, it's unlikely the United States military would now want to store nuclear weapons or build a military base in Palau. Thus, the antinuclear forces may have lost the battle but won the war.

During the 1970s, it was not only the United States that had designs for Palau's future. Nissho-Iwai and the Industrial Bank of Japan, backed by United States and Iranian interests, sought to create a $325 million central terminal station for oil storage on Palau's northern Kossol Reef. "Superport" was to have been used to transfer and store oil from jumbo tankers between the Middle East and Japan. Eventually the U.S. Environmental Protection Act managed to halt the project because of the havoc Superport could wreak on the wondrous seas around Palau.

GOVERNMENT

The three branches of government are executive, legislative, and judicial. The president and vice president are elected by the people for four years; the president chooses his cabinet. The Olbiil Era Kelulau is a bicameral legislature consisting of an elected house of delegates (one delegate from each of the 16 states) and a senate (14 senators elected from districts based on population). A presidential veto can be overridden by a two-thirds majority in both houses. There are two political parties. The chief justice of the Supreme Court is appointed by the president and confirmed by the senate.

For its population Palau is one of the most overgoverned places on earth. Aside from the national government and chiefs, each of the 16 states has a governor, chosen according to its state constitution, and a legislature. Some state governors are elected directly by the people, while others are the highest-ranking traditional leaders. One governor is picked from among members of the state legislature. In addition there's a traditional Council of Chiefs, with one chief from each state.

Palau has a federal system of government. But one of the 16 states, Koror, has about two-thirds of the country's population and asserts its muscle. It has enacted certain laws that some in the national government believe to be unconstitutional. For example, one statute (subsequently amended) had forbidden anyone except Palauan residents from using certain of the Rock Islands. Another Koror law forbids floating hotels and places a moratorium on additional live-aboard dive boats.

ECONOMY

Under the terms of the Compact, the United States made immediate payment of $172 million, with approximately $300 million to be paid over the next 15 years, in declining installments. These payments are a central feature of Palau's economy today, and as in the other Freely Associated States of Micronesia, it has been used to maintain a bloated bureaucracy.

There is relatively little commercial agriculture in Palau. There also is relatively little subsistence farming, though people may keep a garden or fruit trees. Consumer-oriented sales outlets are flourishing as much of the United States payments, directly and indirectly, goes into imported goods. Merchandising is dominated by the locally owned Western Caroline Trading Company (WCTC), Surangel and Sons, and Neco Group.

Tourism tripled from 1985 to 1995 to about 40,000 visitors per year. But the number of tourists from Korea, a significant percent of Palau's visitors, dropped dramatically after the Aug. 6, 1997, crash of Korean Air Flight 801 on Guam. Soon after came the economic downturn in Asia, which led to a significant decline in Japanese and Taiwanese tourism. Nonetheless, building continued. Approximately 200 new rooms were opened in 1998, including the 160 rooms of the new Outrigger Palasia Hotel Palau. By 1998, Palau had more than 800 hotel rooms, about one for every 20 of the country's citizens.

Palau appears to be betting its future on tourism. From a review of building permit applications, there are government estimates that by 2003, Palau may have 2,000 hotel rooms. There is even a plan to haul from Singapore to Palau a 200-room hotel built on a barge. Yet it is not clear whether tourism will rebound quickly enough to fill these new hotel rooms. Further, if the rooms do become filled, it is not clear whether Palau's limited infrastructure and fragile ecology will be able to bear it.

Palau has about 18,000 citizens. At least 5,000 workers from the Philippines and more than 1,000 citizens of other Asian nations work in Palau, usually remitting much of their income back to their home countries. About 500 Americans also live on Palau. As has happened in other Micronesian lands, increasingly the work in service industries, such as tourism, is being done by foreign labor rather than the local population. This leads to resentment by many citizens who feel alienated from the direction in which their leaders are taking the economy. Palau's total economy fared better in the 1990s than the other Freely Associated States: the Federated States of Micronesia and the Republic of the Marshall Islands. But it is not clear that the average Palauan has prospered. A quarter of all Palauans have opted to live abroad, many on Guam.

Foreigners may lease Palauan land but not purchase it; in a 1990 decision, the Palau Supreme Court ruled that 99-year leases by foreigners were the equivalent of ownership and therefore illegal. Subseqently, the legislature limited foreign-held leases to 50 years.

PEOPLE

Palauans *appear* to be the most Americanized of Micronesians; don't expect to see native dress. Beneath the surface, though, they are extremely tradition-oriented. While friendly, they'll often check you out by waiting for you to smile or say hello first.

Palauan culture was traditionally matriarchal, with women choosing which males would be the clan chiefs. Women owned and divided land.

Chiefly titles were, and still are, inherited through the mother.

The majority of Palauans are Roman Catholics, with a significant number in Protestant sects as well. However, a large percentage of Palauans still retain some of their traditional beliefs. This may in part be due to the United Sect, or Ngara Modekngei, founded by Temedad on Babeldaob in 1915. This belief system began as a nonviolent opposition to the Japanese occupation. It was a conscious return to beliefs that even at that time had been partially lost. It contains elements of ancestor worship and faith in protective spirits.

Both Palauan and English are official languages. Because of the 31-year Japanese occupation, the Palauan language still contains many words rooted in Japanese, particularly words describing 20th century technology.

In 1903, under the German administration, inhabitants from the Southwest Islands were relocated to Echang in Koror after a typhoon. In 1996, descendants of Palauans who claimed prior ownership in that land brought suit to recover title. In February 1998, the Palau Supreme Court ruled in favor of the Southwest Islanders. Those opposed to the decision then set up an ongoing "sleep-in" at the turnoff to the road leading to Echang. One sign left up by the protesters read, "NO MORE TYPHOON—GO HOME." Apparently to some whose families were from Koror before 1903, the fact that the families of the Echang residents had lived in Koror for four generations was outweighed by the fact that they had retained their own language as well as other traditions. After 95 years in Koror, they were still "outsiders."

ARTS AND CRAFTS

Palau has a rich artistic tradition and produces some of the most notable art work in Micronesia. Palauans' traditional communal meeting centers, *bai,* were built with excellent carpentry and powerful visual embellishment. Constructed under the direction of master craftsmen, a *bai* is made from interlocking pieces held together by a complex joiner system using removable pegs. The internal pillars and crossbeams of these buildings are carved and painted with Palauan stories, legends, and historical events, fashioned by master carvers.

an inlaid ceremonial vessel

In the 1930s the Japanese artist and folklorist Hisakatsu Hijikata worked with Palauan carvers to adapt traditional woodcarvings to a smaller format. The items, called story boards, were then exported to Japan. Story boards are not only carved on flat pieces of wood. They can be carved three-dimensionally to become various shapes, such as fish and crocodiles.

Replicas of traditional Palauan money *(udoud)* are made from pink and black coral and used as necklaces. The real money, still used in customary exchanges, was made from bits of glass or ceramic of unknown origin, quite possibly from Indonesia. Today, some island women wear a string of *udoud* as a necklace.

Tobi Island statues are another unique traditional item available for sale. These small squatting figures represent guardian spirits and ancestral deities. They were once placed in canoes with the deceased and set adrift for burial at sea. Other important Palauan art forms include distinctive carved wood containers and other objects, inlaid with beautiful shell designs.

Ancient Palauans made and used pottery. They also fashioned utensils from mother-of-pearl and tortoise shells.

HOLIDAYS AND EVENTS

Public holidays include New Year's Day (1 January), Youth Day (15 March), Senior Citizens' Day (5 May), President's Day (1 June), Nuclear-free Constitution Day (9 July), Labor Day (first Monday or Tuesday in September), Independence Day (1 October), United Nations Day (24 October), Thanksgiving (fourth Thursday in November), and Christmas (25 December).

Youth Day features open-air concerts and sporting events, while on Senior Citizens' Day there are dancing contests, handicraft exhibitions, and a parade with floats. Senior citizens are remembered on the fifth day of the fifth month because in Palau one attains official senior citizenship at age 55. The Palau Arts Festival on Constitution Day is also great for its traditional dancing, popular music performances, an arts and crafts show, and a culinary competition featuring local produce and cuisine.

During the *ngloik* dance, lines of Palauan women, their bodies glistening with coconut oil, chant legends to rhythmic movements. The Palauan men dance the *ruk* to celebrate a victory or inaugurate a new *bai*.

PRACTICALITIES

Accommodations

Most hotels are in or near Koror. Camping is not done in Koror. There's no problem, however, camping on Peleliu, Angaur, or Kayangel. On Babeldaob get permission before pitching a tent. Many of the states have offices in Koror that may be able to advise on village accommodations. The phone numbers for these offices are in the blue pages of the PNCC telephone directory.

Peleliu and Angaur have small guesthouses. It is now a local phone call to either island. Most guesthouses offer meals, but clarify prices in advance. You are permitted to cook at some guesthouses. Bring along all supplies as the stores have little to offer.

All hotel accommodations are subject to a 10% room tax, which is added to the bill. Hotels may also add a five or 10 percent service charge. Look for this on your bill when deciding on appropriate tips.

Visas

All travelers are required to carry a passport, even U.S. citizens. No visa is required for a stay of 30 days or less, although you may be asked to show an onward ticket. Permission for stay extensions costs $50 each, so on arrival ask for all the time you expect to need. Extensions are not automatic and will only be done twice, so three months is the longest you'll likely be allowed to stay as a tourist. For non-U.S. citizens, a visa may be required if you'll be transiting Guam.

Money and Measurements

United States currency is used. Restaurant tipping is usual. Since many restaurants add a 10% service charge, look at your bill before deciding on an appropriate tip. Credit cards are not universally accepted; many restaurants do not honor them.

Most government offices are closed 11:30 a.m.-12:30 p.m. When arriving in Palau from Guam or Yap remember that Palau is one hour earlier.

United States domestic postage rates apply, but Palau issues its own colorful stamps bearing its own name.

Services and Information

The **Palau Visitors Authority** (P.O. Box 256, Koror, PW 96940, tel. 680-488-2793, fax 680-488-1453, e-mail: pva@palaunet.com, website: www.visit-palau.com) is at the junction of the Malakal and Arakabesan roads. The office compiles very useful brochures on the country's hotels, dive shops, etc.

The air-conditioned public library opposite the old high school (P.O. Box 189, Koror, PW 96940) is open Mon.-Fri. 7:30-11:30 a.m. and 12:30-4:30 p.m. Before the war, the Japanese administration building stood on the site of the present library.

Palau Horizon is published every other week and the *Pacific Daily News* is flown in from Guam. CNN, CNBC and ESPN are available in real time. Other channels are prerecorded programming from San Francisco.

PALAU COUNTRY CODE: 680

Visitors, particularly divers, will wish to check out Nancy Barbour's richly illustrated description of Palau's natural and cultural history, *Palau* (Full Court Press, 511 Mississippi Street, San Francisco, CA 94107) and Tim Rock's *Diving and Snorkeling Guide to Palau*. Also of interest is *A Guide to the Palau Islands* (available to U.S. addresses for $20 postpaid from NECO Tours, P.O. Box 129, Koror, PW 96940) by Mandy Thyssen-Etpison, jammed full of color photos, line drawings, and useful information.

Tide charts can be found in the PNCC telephone book.

Getting There

Airai Airport (ROR) is on Babeldaob, 7.5 miles east of Koror by road. The taxi into town is around $15. Some hotels charge $10 for airport transfers; others are free. Car rental agencies are also located at the airport. The departure tax is $20 on international flights.

The Visitors Authority operates a desk at the airport, which opens for arrivals. The people working the desk are extremely helpful. If you arrive without reservations, they'll give you a complete hotel list with current rates. And they will offer advice if you have other difficulties.

Continental Airlines has daily flights to Koror from Guam and flights from Manila twice a week. A roundtrip from Honolulu to Koror with stops at Majuro, Kosrae, Pohnpei, Chuuk, Guam, and Yap costs about $1,200. From California the same ticket is about $300 more. Buying one ticket to Guam and another to Palau is much more expensive. Passengers to Koror must change planes on Guam and often must spend the night there. Yap is included as a stopover on the Koror to Guam flight on Wednesday and Sunday.

GETTING AROUND

Until 1998, **Paradise Air** (P.O. Box 488, Koror, PW 96940, tel./fax 680-488-2348) ran a commuter service to Peleliu and Angaur on six-passenger planes. In 1998, one of its planes had a tragic accident while attempting to land on Koror. Everyone on board died. As we went to press, no air service had resumed. However, a new outfit, **Belau Air Inc.** was in the process of trying to gain approval to provide inter-island service.

The best way to get information about a field trip ship to the Southwest Islands (Sonsoral, Pulu Anna, Merir, Helen Reef, and Tobi) is to call the Sonsoral State office in Koror at (680) 488-1237.

Local Boats

If you have a specific destination in mind, the best place to start gathering information is to call that state's office in Koror. Those phone numbers are listed in the blue pages of the PNCC telephone directory.

Boats to Peleliu and Angaur leave from the dock by the **Fisheries Co-op** on Malakal. The state boat to Peleliu leaves Tuesday and Friday ($3, two hours); it also sometimes makes extra trips. Due to varying tide conditions, it's best to check the precise departure times with the boat captain, either the night before or early on the morning of the day you wish to leave. Occasional fishing boats also head out from here to Ollei and Melekeok on Babeldaob.

Boats between Peleliu and Angaur are rare, although you might arrange for an Angaur boat to drop you off on Peleliu on its way back to Koror. Private boats to Peleliu leave from the anchorage beside the Peleliu Club.

Boats for Babeldaob and Kayangel leave from **T-Dock.** Although a few state boats to the north have regular schedules, the only sure way to get on is just to be there, ready to leave when they do. Friday afternoon and early Saturday morning are good times to look for speedboats to northern Babeldaob (up to $5 one way).

Surprisingly, Monday is a good day to head north, as the crowds are smaller and some boats that brought commuters may be returning empty. There's a concrete waiting pavilion by the dock.

Every other week a boat makes the four-hour trip to Kayangel ($6 pp). It usually leaves Koror on Saturday morning, returning Thursday afternoon a week and a half later. On its way back, the boat calls at Ollei, the northernmost village on Babeldaob, and sometimes another village halfway down—a good connection for those wanting to get off. Rides are scarce on the off weeks but are sometimes available from speedboats and fishing boats.

Tour boat companies will also take you to any place in Babeldaob they can safely anchor. The prices will vary depending on the distance, between $50-100 pp. As in much of Micronesia, tides will affect when a given trip can be made.

By Road

There's no bus service in Palau. Taxis work on standard fares: from the center of Koror to the Hotel Nikko Palau, $5; to the Palau Pacific Resort, $7; and to the airport, $15. Taxis are not shared, and the price is for the whole car, not per person. To call a radio-dispatched taxi, dial (680) 488-1519, (680) 488-2510, or (680) 488-2691.

Car rentals are $45-50 a day, with unlimited mileage. At the airport you can find: **1A Rent a Car** (P.O. Box 694, Koror, PW 96940, tel. 680-488-1113, fax 680-488-1115); **Toyota Rent-a-Car** (P.O. Box 280, Koror, PW 96940, tel. 680-587-3504); and, **Budget Car Rental,** tel. (680) 488-5611, fax (680) 488-5611. Hotels also often rent cars. Most car rental agencies will drop off and pick up at your hotel.

Most agencies want their cars driven only along Koror's paved roads and as far as the airport. If you want to explore Babeldaob by car, consider renting a pickup or jeep. They run between $60 and $85 a day. Take care with uneven driveways, which can scrape car bottoms. The speed limit in Koror is 25 mph, but most people drive more slowly.

It is also possible to hire a guide with a four-wheel drive or a pickup to drive you to sites in Babeldaob. The rate is negotiable, but probably will be about $20 per hour. The Palau Visitors Bureau can help you make arrangements.

KOROR

Koror is the most scenic town in Micronesia. You get excellent views of the fabulous Rock Islands stretching out to the south. From Airai Airport on southern Babeldaob, a well-paved road leads to Koror, the political and economic center of the republic. About two-thirds of the country's population now lives in Koror. The bustling prewar Japanese city was leveled by American bombing, although isolated relics remain.

Today Koror throbs again with a steady stream of traffic along the main road through town. There are traffic jams and even two traffic lights, though at rush hour, the lights are replaced by police. Bridges and causeways linking Koror Island to Babeldaob, Arakabesan, Malakal, and other islands make it a perfect base and an interesting place to explore.

SIGHTS

The **Palau National Museum** (tel. 680-488-2265; open weekdays 8-11 a.m. and 1-4 p.m., Saturday 10 a.m.-2 p.m., admission $2), the oldest, most extensive and most interesting museum in Micronesia, is a short walk up a hill from downtown Koror, located in the former Japanese Weather Bureau building. The displays, with their learned presentation, give a good look at Palau's rich artistic traditions.

In addition to paintings, exhibits include traditional shell-inlaid containers, native skirts, traditional mourning money paid to relatives who come to mourn, cooking utensils, spears (used for both warfare and fishing), hair combs, and traditional jewelry. The museum also has fragments and models of old *bai,* as well as photographs of old Palau and its people.

The museum has models of two traditional outriggers. One model is a war canoe, whose full size would be about 40 feet, holding 32 paddlers. The other is a sailing canoe in the style of the Southwest Islanders, the greatest sailors from the Republic of Palau.

The spectacular wooden carvings, some three-dimensional, some flat story boards, some recent, some old, are the highlight of the collection. One three-dimensional carving, crafted several years ago by artist Petrus Sikyang, tells the story of the giant Uab who was burned and then fell down, forming the islands of Palau. Petrus sculpts without sketches; he sees the sculpture on the uncarved wood. Another three-dimensional story board, by Isaac Klewei, carved on a curving wooden crocodile, tells the story of how taro growing came to Palau. Still another describes the division of work between men and women.

Upstairs is a room dedicated to the art of Hisakatsu Hijikata. Hisakatsu, a Japanese artist living on Palau in the 1930s, helped revitalize the Palauan story board tradition. This room shows how versatile the artist was in his own right, with drawings, watercolors, and carvings.

A varied botanical collection and a statue of the late President Haruo I. Remeliik (1933-85) spruce up the museum grounds. The traditional *bai* near the museum was erected in 1991 to replace an earlier one built in 1969 that burned down in 1979. A monument on the grounds states in English and Japanese:

May the souls of the people of Palau killed in the Pacific War rest in peace.

Scheduled to open during 1999, near the Outrigger Hotel, is the new, private **President Etpison Museum and Gallery.** The Etpison family owns what many consider to be the greatest collection of Palauan art. Some of the material that has been on exhibit in the Palau National Museum belongs to the family, and it is unclear whether that material will be transferred to the new museum. The museum will also contain rare shells from all parts of the Pacific. It is scheduled to have a coffee shop, a gift shop, and a local arts studio in the basement.

Malakal

Malakal Island, Koror's industrial suburb and commercial port, has a cold storage plant for tuna exported to Japan. The nearby **Fisheries Co-op** sells fresh fish daily.

At the end of the road on Malakal is the **Micronesian Mariculture Demonstration Center**

(MMDC), locally known as the "ice box" for a long-gone Japanese ice making plant. The MMDC, a major mariculture research center established in 1974, is the world's largest commercial giant clam farm. Through hatching and rearing, the MMDC hopes to save the giant clam (Tridacna gigas) from extinction. This species has been ravaged by Taiwanese poachers who take the clam's abductor muscle, supposedly an aphrodisiac. Millions of seed clams have been distributed throughout Palau as well as to foreign countries. In addition to four major clam species, hawksbill sea turtles are also reared in tanks here for release, and other marinelife such as commercial trochus and reef fish may be seen in outdoor tanks. Visitors are welcome weekdays 8-11 a.m. and 1-4 p.m.; $2 adult, $1 child.

Climb to the top of Malakal for a stunning view of the Rock Islands. Take the dirt road uphill from the sewage plant to the water tank, then make your way through the forest to the high metal tower at the summit (408 feet). On one side you can see across Babeldaob; on the other you look down on the great green arms enfolding the harbor. Very few places in the Pacific give you as much of an eyeful as this tower.

Arakabesan

The Japanese evicted all Palauans from Arakabesan Island and turned it into a military base. Great concrete football fields sloping down into the water remain from the **seaplane bases,** one beyond a school at Meyungs village not far from the causeway from Koror, two more on the west side of the island by the **Palau Pacific Resort.** If you are not staying at PPR, stop by to take a look and have a drink at their outdoor bar, set on a beautiful stretch of beach. Or, you can use its facilities, and snorkel from the beach or swim in their pool for $25 for the day.

On the south side of Arakabesan is the Southwest Islanders' village of Echang, discussed under **People** above. Turn to the left at the sign to the Sunrise Villa. Past the Sunrise, the road is unpaved but can easily be driven.

East of Town

Going east along the highway from central Koror, in about a mile you reach the section known as **Top Side.** Opposite the Dragon Tei Restaurant is a paved road to the right that goes 1.5 miles

down to the water. At the bottom is a basketball court and wonderful ruins of old Japanese brick buildings on a mangrove channel. The walk back up is a stiff uphill climb, through a lovely residential neighborhood.

Several hundred yards further, just beyond a couple of Japanese stone lanterns, go down a dirt track on the left beside the house marked QTR. NO. 03 to the evocative **Sakurakai Memorial.** The old Japanese cemetery and a cannon are just below.

Continuing east, past more stone lanterns, is a majestic stone stairway leading to a restored Japanese **Shinto shrine.** When opened in 1940 this was the largest of its kind outside Japan. Continuing along the road by the side of the shrine, you reach the Hotel Nikko Palau, which offers beautiful views of Iwayama Bay and the Rock Islands.

Ngermid village, beyond the turnoff to the Nikko Palau, is attractive and well worth strolling through. Halfway down to the dock at Ngermid are some old stone platforms and pathways, and beyond the houses, in a field to the left, the stone figure of a woman and child frozen on this spot when caught snooping on a gathering of men in a bai. Visible on the hillside is a Japanese cave containing a double-barreled AA gun.

Rock Islands

The Rock Islands, south of Koror, are wonders of the world. These wonders are made of soft limestone; the action of the ocean undercuts their base, making them appear to be emerald mushrooms floating in the lagoon. They are a wonderland of secret passages, and hidden tunnels and caves. Some islands have sandy beaches and virtually all are surrounded by astounding snorkeling sites. Because of the shade provided by the islands, one can see coral polyps out during the daytime. The islands are alive with birdlife.

On some islands you'll find inland lakes. The best known is **Jellyfish Lake** on Eil Malk. Cut off from direct contact with the lagoon, two species of jellyfish evolved here, with very little power to sting. Most jellyfish need stingers to kill their prey. But these two species became the ultimate vegetarians: within them is algae, which remains alive in their translucent bodies. The jellies float to the surface during daylight hours, the algae photosynthesize, and the jellyfish extract the energy produced. The jellies rotate around the lake to maximize their sunlight. You can swim with and hold these otherworldly creatures. Be careful. They are living beings. Also, some people develop a reaction to them through repeated touching.

Many dive companies, fishing outfits, and tour companies arrange day trips to the islands. Do not come to Palau and miss such an excursion. Perhaps the best way to get a feel for the Rock Islands is by kayaking.

The State of Koror imposes a $15 license for tourists to visit these islands. The license is good for one month.

ACCOMMODATIONS

Koror has a wide choice of hotels, from the luxurious Palau Pacific Resort to the best low-priced hotels in Micronesia.

Inexpensive

Locally owned **D.W. Motel** (P.O. Box 738, Koror, PW 96940, tel. 680-488-2641), at $35 s, 45 d, is perhaps the best buy in Koror. It is in a three-story building nicely set back from the main street, next to the Senior Citizens Center, one of the cultural centers of the island. The 17 clean, a/c rooms have private baths and hot showers. Airport transfers are free.

Tree D Motel and Apartments (P.O. Box 1703, Koror, PW 96940, tel. 680-488-3856, fax 680-488-4584) is another excellent low-cost choice at $45 s, $55 d. Its 22 units are very clean with a pleasant atmosphere. There is a laundromat next door. Located in Top Side, location is its only drawback, unless you have a car.

The **H.K. Motel,** formerly Ongdibel Bai (P.O. Box 61, Koror, PW 96940, tel. 680-488-2764, fax 680-488-1725), is located at a busy intersection opposite the Palau Visitors Authority. Rooms are plain and clean and rent for $25 s, $40 d. You can keep expenses down by using the on-premises kitchen.

The **Palau Hotel** (P.O. Box 457, Koror, PW 96940, tel. 680-488-1703, fax 680-488-1317) in central Koror is in a four-story building. The 38 rooms are air conditioned, but most do not have telephones, TVs or refrigerators. Rooms go for $50 s, $55 d, primarily to Asian businesspeople.

The bottom-end **New Koror Hotel** (P.O. Box 339, Koror, PW 96940, tel. 680-488-1159, fax 680-488-1582) in the heart of Koror town has little to recommend it. The rooms are plain and the main lobby has a very unpleasant smell. Do not stay here if you, or anyone staying with you, is six or more feet tall; the retrofitted air conditioners extend over the walkway, as the six stitches in my scalp can attest. Rooms begin at $33 s, $39 d.

Moderate

The three-story **Palau Marina Hotel** (P.O. Box 142, Koror, PW 96940, tel. 680-488-1786, fax 680-488-1070) is located at M-Dock, next to the Fish 'n Fins scuba shop. The 28 a/c rooms begin at $65 s, $80 d; all overlook the water. Alan's Restaurant at this hotel has a lovely bar with a great view across the water and a fairly lively dinner atmosphere. Some evenings there is live music.

The **V.I.P. Guest Hotel** (P.O. Box 18, Koror, PW 96940, tel. 680-488-1502, fax 680-488-1429) is located in the heart of central Koror, between the post office and the jail. The 10 a/c, balconied rooms in this pink three-story building are $65 s or $85 d. It's a bit overpriced, but a good location for commercial travelers.

Slightly more expensive, but better value, is the modern **Penthouse Hotel** (P.O. Box 6013, Koror, PW 96940, tel. 680-488-1941, fax 680-488-1442) is located in central Koror on a quiet back street. The rooms are small but clean and arranged well. The hotel has a nice warm feel to it. Rooms run $79 s, $85 d.

West Plaza Hotel, Inc. (a subsidiary of the Western Caroline Trading Company) operates five hotels in Koror. Each has a separate phone number, but reservations for all can be made by writing to Western Caroline Trading, P.O. Box 280, Koror, PW 96940 or faxing (680) 488-2136. All five hotels offer commercial discounts.

West Plaza Hotel by the Sea (tel. 680-488-2133, fax 680-488-2136) is located near T-Dock and is popular with divers. Rooms range $70-90. Many units have ocean views and kitchens. Closer still to the dock itself is the newer **West Plaza Coral Reef** (tel. 680-488-5333, fax 680-488-1783) which is overpriced at $120. **West Plaza Hotel Malakal,** (tel. 680-488-5290, fax 680-488-1783) another new West Hotel, with

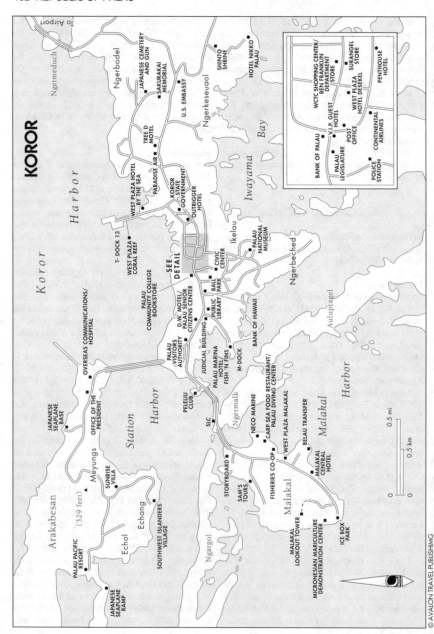

KOROR

To Airport

Ngetmeduch

Koror   Harbor

Ngerbodel

Ngerbodel

JAPANESE CEMETERY AND GUN

SAKURAKAI MEMORIAL

U.S. EMBASSY

Ngerkeseuaol

SHINTO SHRINE

HOTEL NIKKO PALAU

TREE D MOTEL

PARADISE AIR

WEST PLAZA HOTEL BY THE SEA

KOROR STATE GOVERNMENT

OUTRIGGER HOTEL

Iwayama   Bay

T-DOCK 13

WEST PLAZA CORAL REEF

SEE DETAIL

Ikelau

CIVIC CENTER

PALAU NATIONAL MUSEUM

PALAU COMMUNITY COLLEGE BOOKSTORE

D.W. MOTEL/ PALAU SENIOR CITIZENS CENTER

BALL PARK

PUBLIC LIBRARY

Ngerbeched

OVERSEAS COMMUNICATIONS/ HOSPITAL

PALAU VISITORS AUTHORITY

JUDICIAL BUILDING

PALAU MARINA HOTEL/ FISH 'N FINS

M-DOCK

BANK OF HAWAII

Auluptagel

JAPANESE SEAPLANE BASE

OFFICE OF THE PRESIDENT

PELELIU CLUB

SLC

NECO MARINE

CARP SEA FOOD RESTAURANT/ PALAU DIVING CENTER

WEST PLAZA MALAKAL

BELAU TRANSFER

Ngermalk

Malakal   Harbor

Arakabesan

Meyungs

SUNRISE VILLA

(329 feet)

Echol

SOUTHWEST ISLANDERS VILLAGE

Station   Harbor

PALAU PACIFIC RESORT

JAPANESE SEAPLANE RAMP

Ngargol

STORYBOARD

SAM'S TOURS

FISHERIES CO-OP

Malakal

MALAKAL CENTRAL HOTEL

MALAKAL LOOKOUT TOWER

ICE BOX PARK

MICRONESIAN MARICULTURE DEMONSTRATION CENTER

0   0.5 mi

0   0.5 km

Inset:

WCTC SHOPPING CENTER/ BEN FRANKLIN DEPARTMENT STORE

SURANGEL STORE

WEST PLAZA HOTEL DESEKEL

PENTHOUSE HOTEL

BANK OF PALAU

V.I.P. GUEST HOTEL

POST OFFICE

CONTINENTAL AIRLINES

PALAU LEGISLATURE

POLICE STATION

© AVALON TRAVEL PUBLISHING

most rooms overlooking Malakal Harbor, is a good buy at $70. **West Plaza Hotel Desekel** (tel. 680-488-2521, fax 680-488-2529) is centrally located and a good choice if you need to be in town for business. Rooms are $70 and up. **West Plaza Hotel Downtown** (tel. 680-488-1671) is old and rather dreary. Some rooms have no outdoor window. Room rates begin at $55.

Expensive

The four story **Malakal Central Hotel Annex** (P.O. Box 6016, Koror, PW 96940, tel. 680-488-1117, fax 680-488-1075) adjoins the commercial port. They've dropped prices to $100, which still is too high for this mediocre hotel.

Very Expensive

Sunrise Villa (NOTE—the reservation address is in Guam, not Palau: P.O. Box 12188, Tamuning, Guam 96931, tel. 680-488-4590, fax 680-488-4593) is located on a hillside on Arakabesan island. As you enter the hotel's front door, you look out at a sparkling view of town and water, the same view seen from each room. Service is good and the hotel is a fair value at $130. Suites, which easily sleep four, start at $210 and have kitchens. The hotel has a small swimming pool. Its indoor restaurant, Larry's, is quite respectable, and food is also served outdoors, at poolside, with one more terrific view.

The **Airai View Hotel** (P.O. Box 37, Koror, PW 96940, tel. 680-587-3485, fax 680-587-3533) is on southern Babeldaob, the closest hotel to the airport. Its rooms are $130, including tax and breakfast. The hotel caters mainly to Taiwanese tourists. The nicest feature is the fabulous large story board sculpture in the lobby, which is a nice spot for a drink.

The **Carolines Resort** (P.O. Box 399, Koror, PW 96940, tel. 680-488-3754, fax 680-488-3756) sits high on a forested hill on Arakabesan. The dirt road leading to it is bordered by many fortified tunnels built by the Japanese. Its seven rustic, individual cabins have air conditioning and TV. They go for $150, and most have great views. The rooms have balconies, but sometimes there is a mosquito problem. While the hotel has no regular restaurant, it does serve breakfast, wine, and coffee. There is a feeling of isolation, but the hotel's van will take you where you wish to go if you don't have a rented car. The hotel has

worked out a deal so that its guests can use, without charge, the oceanfront facilities of Palau Pacific Resort.

Luxury

The **Palau Pacific Resort** (P.O. Box 308, Koror, PW 96940, tel. 680-488-2600, fax 680-488-1606, e-mail: ppr@palaunet.com, website: www.panpac.com) on Arakabesan is the most luxurious hotel in Micronesia. Its 160 guest rooms are located on 64 landscaped, lagoonfront acres. The property looks out across a bay and no other buildings are visible. Single rooms start at $210 and go up from there. "Commercial rate" discounts of 10% may be available. If you can afford it, PPR, as it is locally known, is an incredible place to stay. The hotel has two restaurants, a beachfront bar, a swimming pool, tennis courts, its own hiking trails, and wonderful snorkeling from its white sand beach. Dive operators all pick up at the hotel's long concrete pier. **Splash** scuba program operates from the premises, as does an underwater photography center, **Photo Palau.**

For divers, PPR has a package rate, based on double occupancy of $414 for two, each person allowed a two-tank dive per day.

The newest luxury hotel in Palau is the 165-room **Outrigger Palasia Hotel Palau** (P.O. Box 1256, Koror, PW 96940, tel. 680-488-8888, fax 680-488-8880). From within the United States, reservations can also be made by calling (800) 688-7444. At this hotel located in downtown Koror, not on the water, rates begin at $220. It is the country's only high-rise building (six stories) and, unfortunately, intrudes on views from many points in Koror. Hopefully Palau will return to the unofficial zoning rule used through much of the Pacific: nothing higher than the coconut palms.

This said, the hotel is nicer on the inside than the outside. Built around two interior atriums, rooms are spacious and those above the third floor have excellent views. It offers many amenities—a lap pool, children's pool, gym, and three restaurants: one serving American food, another Chinese, and a sushi bar.

Until the Palau Pacific Resort went up in 1984, Palau's top hotel was the **Hotel Nikko Palau** (P.O. Box 310, Koror, PW 96940, tel. 680-488-2486, fax 680-488-2878), built by Continental Airlines in 1971. Now owned by Japan Air Lines, the Nikko Palau is spectacularly set on a hillside just east of Koror, with a breathtaking view of the Rock Islands. The hotel swimming pool is small and there's no beach, but dive boats can pick up and drop off passengers just below the hotel. Although the Nikko recently renovated some rooms, the hotel still feels down at the heels. Rates, starting at $150, are in the luxury range, but the facilities don't merit that term.

Island Base Camps

To avoid the long commute by speedboat from Koror to dive sites, some divers choose the **Carp Island Resort** (P.O. Box 5, Koror, PW 96940, tel. 680-488-2978, fax 680-488-3155) on Ngercheu Island near the fabulous Ngemelis Dropoff. The resort offers cottages with private baths, $65 s, $75 d (slightly higher in peak season). Bunk bed accommodations are available in a large "divehouse" of 10 four-bed dorms with shared bath ($30 pp). The island restaurant serves breakfast ($7.50), lunch ($7.50), and dinner ($20), but seafood specials ($30 pp) must be requested the day before. Bring food if you want to cook for yourself. **Palau Diving Center** handles the diving. Boat transfers from Koror are $30 pp, but free for divers. Day trips are also available.

You can also camp free on one of the Rock Islands, where shelters have been erected by the Koror government. Fish 'n Fins or Sam's Dive Tours will drop you off at the end of a snorkeling tour with a promise to take you back to Koror a day or two later at no additional charge. Be sure to take enough water and food, and do pack out all your garbage.

FOOD

Koror boasts quite a few good restaurants, with new ones appearing all the time. As in much of Micronesia, many of the best restaurants serve Japanese food. But Koror also now has variety. There are good Korean and Chinese restaurants, even a good Thai restaurant. If you do not like Asian cuisine, the choices are more limited, but there are also a number of acceptable American-style restaurants. Many restaurants do not take credit cards.

Locally caught fish, fresh produce, and inexpensive plate lunches are often available. At some point in your visit try *kankum,* a locally grown spinach. If you are a beer drinker, try the new, locally brewed **Red Rooster,** a nice dark beer full of gritty character. Buy local foods such as cold coconuts, hot tapioca, fried fish, and fresh fruit at **Yano's,** just north of WCTC Shopping Center. Fresh fish is sold daily at the fish market on the Fisheries Co-op dock at Malakal and at the Happy Landing gas station. Most of the local expats think **Surangel's** is the best grocery store in Palau, followed by **WCTC Shopping Center,** both located on the main street in downtown Koror. In the same building as the Rock Island Cafe (see below) is a deli selling cold cuts and other picnic items.

Restaurants

Yokohama Inn on Lebuu St. is a local favorite, serving inexpensive lunches, including fried fish and Japanese dishes from about $6. A good mid-priced choice is the **Furusato Restaurant** (tel. 680-488-2689) beside the Bank of Hawaii, with an extensive menu including Japanese, Filipino, and American dishes. It's a breakfast and lunch place for local politicos.

The **Carp Sea Food Restaurant** serves Japanese dishes such as tofu stew, sukiyaki, and tempura. Included is a plate of fruit for dessert. The portions are large and prices reasonable, with most dishes about $7. Full of colorful Gauguin-style art by owner Johnny Kishigawa, this rustic island restaurant is on the harbor but does not have air conditioning. It is located on a short dirt road, on the left as you drive out to Malakal. Signs will direct you.

Another Japanese restaurant, which is a local favorite, is the **Dragon Tei,** located in Top Side. Open every evening except Wednesday; dinner will cost about $20, more if you order crab or lobster. It has a very authentic style of Japanese food. Call for reservations at tel. (680) 488-2271.

Possibly the best meal on the island is the banquet at the **Fuji Restaurant** in the building south of West Plaza Hotel Downtown. The special dinner for $25 includes mangrove crab, lobster, sashimi, and steamed fish as well as a host of other dishes. Don't eat for a week before going if you hope to finish the meal. Call ahead for reservations at tel. (680) 488-2774, and specify if you wish the special seafood dinner.

Mingles, located on the main street downtown, is a reasonably priced restaurant that serves both Japanese and Palauan-style dishes. It's on the main street of downtown Koror, just west of Surangel's, on the second floor. Don't be surprised if the main dining room appears to be empty. In the evening, most people dine on the covered patio behind the main room.

Don't be put off by the surrealistic look of the **Thai Cafe.** Its food is good, its prices low (about $7 a dish), and its portions enormous.

Palau has many Chinese Restaurants. The **Crystal Palace Restaurant** above the Crystal Palace dance club in Malakal is a good Chinese restaurant with a Hong Kong chef. Another good choice is **Seahorse Restaurant,** newly opened in the West Plaza Hotel on T-Dock Road.

On the main road through Koror, opposite where the road to T-Dock cuts in, is the poetically named **Smoked Meat of Cake** Chinese Restaurant. Curiously, the smoked meat of cake is listed on the menu as "China Pizza" for $8. The dish, quite delicious, is fried flat Chinese pancakes in which the diner inserts hoisen sauce, scallions, and slices of meat—Hunan-smoked bacon one night, beef brisket the next. Also try Fender Fried Fish for $6.

Conveniently located downtown is the **Rock Island Cafe,** owned by Yutaka M. Gibbons, Ibedul, paramount chief of Koror. Next door to the law library, the café's location explains why so many local lawyers and government types hang out here. The great looking bar is one where you'll feel comfortable ordering a coffee, if that is your drug of choice. Pizza, Mexican dishes, and fried chicken are all good and will cost you about $7 pp. Rock Island Cafe T-shirts at $15 make great souvenirs. Best of all, it has a functioning espresso machine, perhaps the only one on Palau.

Larry's is the hotel restaurant of the Sunrise Villa, serving breakfast, lunch, and dinner. During the daytime, the restaurant has exquisite vistas over the city and water. The cuisine is varied, but primarily American in tone. Dinner without drinks will run you $12-15. Larry's will also serve at the hotel's outdoor terrace by the pool.

The following two waterfront restaurants offer hearty, basic food with a good selection of seafood dishes. The **Pirate's Cove Bar and Restaurant** is located on Malakal Island, at the port. It features a barbecue on Friday night. **Alan's** in the Palau Marina Hotel at M-Dock offers similar food. It often has music on the weekend.

The Palau Pacific Resort has two restaurants: the elegant and excellent **Meduu Ribtal** and the open-air **Coconut Terrace.** Meduu Ribtal can be very expensive, dinner for two with drinks can easily run $100. Seafood lovers will want to try their Taiwanese Steamboat special. The Coconut Terrace serves breakfast, lunch, and dinner. Each night of the week, it features an excellent dinner buffet for $24. The buffet changes nightly; for example, seafood one night and prime rib another. It's best to call for reservations at either restaurant, tel. (680) 488-2600.

Every other Thursday night at the Senior Center, the seniors prepare a dinner of local dishes. Traditional dancing as well as storytelling (in English) round out the evening. Admission and dinner is $25 pp. Make reservations with the Center by calling (680) 488-2165, or through your hotel.

OTHER PRACTICALITIES

Entertainment

The **Storyboard** in Malakal is the bar of choice among Palau's American and Australian expat community. The bar is made from a dozen or so story boards that purport to depict Palauan legends with an X rating. These scenes are not for the timid or the young. Drop in for a drink at 5 p.m. for happy hour prices.

Koror's nightlife kicks in after 9 p.m. by the Malakal causeway. The **Peleliu Club,** which also has a large sign proclaiming JOINUS CLUB, is on the right, on the Malakal Causeway, easily visible from the road. The **SLC** is right beyond it. Both are open air, with cha cha dancing on the weekend. SLC is more of a local scene.

Palau Pacific Resort features traditional dancing several nights a week at its 6 p.m. buffet. Call 680-488-2600 for information and reservations. Both **Pirate's Cove** and **Southern Cross** have live music many evenings.

If you go down the alley between WCTC and Yano's, you hit Lebuu Street. Turning toward the right, you come to a three-story building on your right, the first floor of which is **Q Ball,** a pool hall.

Sports and Recreation

Palau is one of the most sought after diving locales in the world. The diving season is year-round with visibility often 200 feet. There are a dozen blue holes along the southwest barrier reef, along with 60 identified dropoffs; Ngemelis Dropoff on Barnum Bay is considered the world's best. One minute you're in knee-deep water on the reef, the next you're plunging into 1,000-foot-deep ocean! This nearly vertical wall is covered with crimson and yellow sea fans, sponges, and soft corals. At Denges Dropoff is a plateau with giant tabletop corals. Blue Corner is noted for its fish life, including schools of barracuda.

Want to see fan coral, giant clams, or sharks? Just ask—the local divemasters know more than 50 great diving spots, including at least a dozen channel dives. Special trips can be arranged to the underwater cave system off Koror. Also ask about submerged Japanese ships and aircraft, including the well-preserved Zero sitting on a reef at Koror Road. Palau has almost as many wrecks to dive as Chuuk. See *WWII Wrecks of Palau,* by Don E. Bailey, North Valley Diver Publications, P.O. Box 991413, Redding, CA 96099.

Divers, of course, should carry their certifications. However, you can also speak to any of the following about introductory dives as well as scuba certification programs. Palau is a great place to learn to dive. The hospital has a recompression chamber.

Sam's Dive Tours (Sam Scott, P.O. Box 428, Koror, PW 96940, tel. 680-488-1062, fax 680-488-5003, e-mail: samstour@palaunet.com) prides itself on personalized, professional service. Remarkably, it has kept delivering this service despite having grown into perhaps the largest shop on Palau. A full two-tank dive day including lunch costs between $99 and $109, de-

pending on the destination. Snorkeling from a dive boat costs $55. Trips to northern Babeldaob are a specialty. Sam is noted for taking divers to a wide variety of locales. He'll even pick you up at your hotel. A PADI five- star dive center, it offers course instruction, from open-water certification through divemaster.

Catering to English speakers, the **NECO Marine** (Shallum and Mandy Etpison, P.O. Box 129, Koror, PW 96940, tel. 680-488-1775, fax 680-488-3014) on Malakal Island is another large dive shop. Its prices are similar to Sam's. Transfers from hotels are free. Full-day boat rentals to the Rock Islands are $350.

Fish 'n Fins Ltd. (P.O. Box 142, Koror, PW 96940, tel. 680-488-2637) beside the Palau Marina Hotel at M-Dock is a very experienced scuba operator. One-tank dives are $65; two-tank dives $90.

Splash (P.O. Box 308, Koror, PW, tel. 680-488-2600, fax 680-488-1601, website: www.divepalau.com) is located at the Palau Pacific Resort. It offers an excellent program and will also take divers who are not staying at the hotel. It is equipped to deal with English-speaking divers but is geared primarily for Japanese divers. It will make arrangements (including pick-up at PPR) with its sister company, NECO, which is better set up for those speaking English. Splash's prices are generally 20% higher than most other shops.

Palau Diving Center will also take divers from Koror at competitive prices.

Palau is a wonderful place to spend evenings on land. But for those who care about nothing except diving, there is the eight-cabin *Palau Aggressor.* Its trips are Sunday to Sunday for $2,295, meals included, based on double occupancy. For information and reservations, write Aggressor Fleet Limited, P.O. Box 1470, Morgan City, LA 70381, tel. (800) 348-2628 in the U.S., or internationally (504) 385-2628, fax (504) 384-0817, website: www.aggressor.com. Another live-aboard in Palau's waters is the *Sun Dancer,* with a seven-night trip for $2,200, less in summer. Contact Peter Hughes Diving, 1390 S. Dixie Hwy, Suite 1109, Coral Gables, FL 33146, tel. (800) 932-6237 or (305) 669-9391, fax (305) 669-9475, website: www.peterhughes.com.

Ocean kayaking is the fastest growing outdoor activity on Palau. In some cold water locales, kayaking is primarily for the young and rugged. In Palau, it is perhaps the best way to enjoy the sights and sounds of the unique ecosystem of the Rock Islands, without the intrusion of an internal combustion engine. It is no coincidence that Ron Leidich, who runs the largest kayaking operation on Palau (**Planet Blue**, P.O. Box 428, Koror, PW 96940, tel. 680-488-1062, fax 680-488-5003, e-mail: samstour@palaunet.com), has a master's degree in marine biology. Trips are designed to fit your ability and skill, and novices are quickly taught the fundamentals.

A typical outing might include a trip through mangroves and banyan trees. When the tide is right, there are places you can kayak or snorkel through tunnels to get to marine, saltwater lakes where you will see exotic fish, some that you are unlikely to see anyplace else, or fantastic soft corals out during the daytime. A day trip will include lunch, perhaps at a white sand beach, perhaps in a limestone cave.

A full-day tour at Planet Blue costs $85 pp. Two other kayaking companies that offer day outings at similar prices are **Splash Kayak Center** (P.O. Box 308, Koror, PW 96940, tel. 680-488-2600, fax 680-488-1601, e-mail: splash@palaunet.com) and **Palau Kayak Tours** (P.O. Box 1714-P105, Koror, PW 96940, tel. 680-488-5885, fax 680-488-1070, e-mail: kayakmary@palaunet.com).

Planet Blue is the only one of the three that uses "expedition caliber" gear. It also will arrange multiday trips that include camping on your own island.

Oceanic Society Expeditions (Fort Mason Center, Bldg. E, San Francisco, CA 94123, tel. 800-326-7491 or 415-441-1106, fax 415-474-3395, website: www.oceanic-society.org) is a nonprofit environmental travel organization. The Society organizes 10-day snorkeling and natural history tours to Palau in February and April. The tours are limited to 12 people. An expert naturalist leads the expedition, and costs $2,590 pp, including airfare from Honolulu, accommodations (at the Palau Marina Hotel), transfers, private boat excursions, picnic lunches, and guide.

The waters of Palau also offer plenty of good fishing. **International Anglers,** another component of Sam's Tours, tel. (680) 488-1062, will take you trolling for a half day for $125, a full day for $175, slightly more on a larger boat. **Palau Island Adventure Co.,** P.O. Box 1516,

Koror, PW 96940, tel. (680) 488-4511, e-mail: pia@palaunet.com, has similar prices. Both outfits have a minimum number of people going out for these prices, usually three or four depending on the size of the boat.

Shopping

With its rich artistic traditions, Palau is an excellent place to shop. Story boards are a unique Palauan art form. Other handicrafts are also available, as well as beautiful stamps and first day covers.

The **Palau National Museum** in Koror sells quality story boards, Tobi Island statues, other handicrafts, and books on Palau. First day covers, postcards, and prints designed by noted local artists Simeon and Samuel Adelbai are available. By making purchases here you help support this worthy institution.

The talented prisoners held in the **Correction and Rehabilitation Division Jail** (open 8-11:30 a.m., 12:30-3 p.m.) behind the downtown police station carve outstanding story boards. Purchases can be made on the spot or work can be done to order. This is a successful and innovative program, allowing prisoners to help support their families. Medium-size story boards cost $150 and up.

Ormuul Gift Shop at the Senior Citizens Center has a nice assortment of story boards and other handicrafts. The center is another key institution for keeping traditional cultural skills intact and is certainly worth a visit. You may see older men building a canoe or women weaving. It's located beside D.W. Motel.

Souvenirs at the **Hotel Nikko Palau** gift shop are expensive. It's also disappointing that the hotel still sells tortoiseshell items. They're illegal to import into the United States, Japan, and most European countries. **Duty Free Shoppers** at the Palau Pacific Resort sells story boards. The prices are high, but quality is good. It also sells first-day covers, T-shirts, and Palau videos ($30).

The post office offers Palau postage stamps and first day covers. They're only allowed to sell items less than one year old, however. Most souvenir shops on Koror sell older stamps and covers.

The **Ben Franklin Department Store** upstairs in the WCTC Shopping Center has a wide assortment of clothes and consumer goods, as well as souvenirs. There's a large supermarket downstairs at WCTC. **Surangel's** is across the street.

Services

The Bank of Hawaii (tel. 680-488-2602), Bank of Micronesia (tel. 680-488-1522), and Bank of Guam (tel. 680-488-2697) have branches in Koror. All are open Mon.-Thurs. 9:30 a.m.-2:30 p.m. and Friday 9:30 a.m.-5 p.m. To cash traveler's checks expressed in currencies other than US$ costs a hefty commission.

The post office in central Koror is open weekdays 8 a.m.-4 p.m. If you're considering mailing a story board, be aware it can't be more than 108 inches total length and breadth. To the United States, the maximum weight is 70 pounds, to Great Britain the maximum is 66 pounds. Address mail to Koror, PW 96940.

Most hotels allow long distance calls. They also can be made from the PNCC Overseas Communications office, on the hill just above the hospital on Arakabesan or at the downtown office. Charges are $9 for three minutes to Micronesia or the United States, and go up to $15 for a three-minute call to some other countries.

The Immigration office (tel. 680-488-2498) is upstairs in the Judicial Building. Enter from the back side.

The Palau Hospital is in a clean, modern building on Arakabesan, just across the causeway from Koror. The hospital has well-trained doctors. Its charges are always reasonable, and on a sliding scale based on the patient's ability to pay. It is one of the few hospitals in Micronesia into which you can safely go.

Tngeronger Laundromat is beside the National Development Bank of Palau on Lebuu Street below WCTC Shopping Center. There's also a small laundromat behind the reception area at D.W. Motel and another just past the hospital, on the opposite side of street.

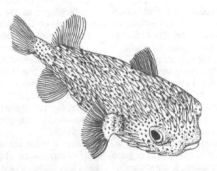

The dozens of sharp spines on the body of the porcupine fish (Diodon holacanthus) *make it almost inedible.*

DIANA LASICH HARPER

OTHER ISLANDS

BABELDAOB
(THE BIG ISLAND)

Palauans had been proud of the 775-foot long **K-B Bridge** completed in 1979, connecting Koror and Babeldaob. They would often tell visitors that it was the longest bridge of its kind in the world, though no one was ever too clear on what type of bridge it was (concrete box girder cantilever). But on September 26, 1996, the bridge collapsed. Miraculously, even though the collapse occurred at 5:35 p.m. on a weekday, only two people were killed.

The collapse also severed Koror's electricity and water, which came via the bridge from Babeldaob. Those services were quickly restored. By 1997 a temporary pontoon bridge was in place, and plans were underway to construct a new bridge of a different design.

Presently, southern Babeldaob is, in essence, a suburb of Koror. The airport is located here, and people commute to work. However, owing to the poor roads, the rest of Babeldaob remains an island of villages and open spaces.

All this may soon change, however. In 1999 work is expected to begin on a paved road around Babeldaob. The road is scheduled to be completed in three years. Everyone refers to it as the "Compact road" because the United States pledged in the Compact of Free Association with the Republic of Palau to fund this road, which is expected to cost $150 million.

The road will profoundly affect Babeldaob. At present, the roads to anywhere other than southernmost Babeldaob can only be negotiated in a pickup or a four-wheel drive and in wet weather may be impassible. Under the best of conditions now, a trip to the north end of Babeldaob takes at least three hours. After the road's completion, it may take as little as 45 minutes. The government is hoping that this may alleviate Koror's crowded living conditions by making it feasible for some who work in Koror but wish to live in Babeldaob, perhaps in their family's traditional village, to commute. However, conservation groups are concerned about the environmental effects of the road itself and the influx of population it may bring. Development of tourist facilities would further exacerbate the change.

Until the Compact road is completed, the trick to exploring any part of Babeldaob, other than the extreme south, is getting there. Many of Babeldaob's dirt roads dead-end, and few are named. You must either know the roads you wish to go on or have plenty of time on your hands to get lost. The roads along the west are better than those along the east side of the island. Thus, for example, if you wish to visit Melekeok on the east coast and are going by land, you first head up the west coast and then cut across. Your best bet for a land trip may be to make arrangements with a cab driver who has a sturdy vehicle. The Palau Visitors Authority can help you get in touch with someone.

If you have a specific destination in mind, it is frequently quickest to get there by boat. Most of the dive shops offer tours. Because of the coastal topography and the reefs, the east side of the island is also difficult to reach by boat. A tour operator may take you up the west coast and arrange for a local guide to drive you (or hike with you) to the site you wish to visit.

Southern Babeldaob

Like the mouths of its denizens, the **Palau Crocodile Farm** at the end of the causeway is open when it's open and closed when it's closed. At last count, it had 37 local crocs in captivity. Admission is $3 adults, $2 children. It additionally charges $5 to use a still camera and $10 to use a video, a bit excessive.

The paved highway passes the airport and extends almost as far as the concrete shell of the huge **Japanese Communications Center** at **Airai** (Irrai) village, split by American bombs in 1944. A Japanese tank and several anti-aircraft guns lie dumped beside the structure. Half a mile beyond is an authentic old *bai,* built in 1890, with painted facades, thatched roof, and finely carved beams. One is sometimes, though not always, asked to pay $5 to walk around it, $10 to take photos inside.

Near the *bai,* at the junction of four stone pathways leading in from the cardinal points, is the compass platform. The south path leads to the modern concrete **Bai ra Mlengl** (1983), painted with traditional scenes (notice the quarrying of Yapese stone money). Below this new *bai* is a dock from which you'll get a good view.

At the southern tip of Airai State, one can now easily visit *Metuker ra Bisech,* a quarry site for stone money. A recently completed stairway with handrail leads up a steep hill to the site.

Middle Babeldaob

A series of dirt roads lead north along western Babeldaob from near the temporary bridge to Aimeliik, Ngatpang, Ngchesar, and Ngardmau States. You will see a sign pointing to the left. It is an unpaved road that runs through beautiful green taro patches, cassava fields, and hilly countryside.

Six miles north of the bridge the road divides, with Aimeliik to the left and Ngchesar to the right. If you keep left toward Aimeliik, after a half mile you'll reach a turnoff to the left to Ngerkeai village. One and a half miles beyond this turnoff is the Chinese Agricultural Mission at **Nekkeng,** with the Oisca agricultural training school one half mile to the right.

North from Nekkeng another road climbs to a lookout above central Babeldaob with a view of a large bay which at first appears to be a lake. Visible on the east side of the bay is the Belau Modekngei High School at Ibobang, founded in 1974 with funding from the School of the Pacific Islands, Thousand Oaks, California. The school's emphasis is teaching self-sufficiency and preserving Palauan culture, history, and language. For more information call (680) 535-1038.

Four miles farther north on this road is the **Ngatpang** State Office and a half mile beyond it, over a hill to the right, a fisheries dock constructed with Japanese aid money in 1990.

The road to the left from Nekkeng runs three miles to **Ngchemiangel** village and terminates at the **IPSECO power plant** on the coast, about 16 miles from Koror by road. You get a good view of the ancient Aimeliik terraces from here. A short feeder road to the north runs to **Medorm** village, where old *bai* platforms may be seen: one on the ridge just before the village, another accessible from the dock. Visit nearby **Medorm Waterfalls.**

If back at the turnoff to Ngchesar you had turned right, after two and a half miles you would have reached a group of collapsed metal towers dating from Japanese times. Here the road divides again with **Ibobang** and the **Japanese war memorial** to the left and Ngchesar to the right.

The roads beyond the collapsed towers are in bad shape and four-wheel drive is essential. Be aware that all the dirt roads on volcanic Babeldaob can get very muddy and even become impassable after heavy rains.

Northern Babeldaob

Melekeok is the largest town on Babeldaob and well worth a visit. It is about an hour and a half drive from Koror. Melekeok was the traditional home of the High Chief Reklai, one of the two most powerful rulers of Palau. (The large church-like structure in town is the home of the current Reklai.) There is a proposal to make Melekeok the capital of Palau once the Compact road is completed

Begin by visiting the government house, the large yellow building, which has a large map of the area, including the best surf spots. Opposite the building is the old **Japanese pier,** which goes out to the base of the old lighthouse. From the end are magnificent views up and down the coastline.

Several hundred yards north, right beyond a church, are three large, ancient carved heads. To get permission to photograph them, ask at the house in whose yard they are located. Permission will cost $5, but you will also receive an explanation about them from the chief who lives there.

From a turnoff about 20 yards beyond the stone heads, one can go up the hill to reach a fascinating cultural area. Since there are a fair number of intersecting dirt roads, it may be best to ask at the government house whether a local child could accompany you to show you directions. (The child will be overjoyed with a tip of a couple of bucks.) Up the hill are the **Melekeok Bai** and the remains of a second *bai,* which was solely for the use of the local chiefs. There is also a paved ceremonial ground, from which ancient stone pathways spoke off.

On the way back down, look for the Japanese memorial stone on which is written:

All the souls of the fallen!
May they rest in peace!
In calm Melekeok

South of Melekeok is **Ngchesar,** a village that boasts a traditional war canoe. Inland from there is crocodile-inhabited **Ngardok Lake**(probably not a good place to swim), a two-hour walk from Ngchesar.

Visit the awesome five-ton basalt **stones of Badrulchau,** on a hilltop between Mengellang and Ollei, the northernmost villages. The story goes that spirits were working in the night to build a great *bai* at this spot. Then the sun came up, roosters crowed, and the spirits scattered, so the building was never finished. Today 37 monolithic blocks remain, six with carved faces on them. Like so many of the sites that ancient Micronesians chose for religious centers, the place itself is remarkable, with views of hills rolling down to the ocean and across to Ngaregur Island. **Sam's Tour Service** (P.O. Box 428, Koror, PW 96940, tel. 680-488-1062, fax 680-488-5003, e-mail: samstour@palaunet.com) can take you by boat to Ollei and arrange for you to be taken to the monuments and then to a white sand beach for a local-style lunch. If there are four people, the charge is $75 pp.

Ngardmau is noted for having the highest point in Palau (700 feet) and the tallest waterfalls. Also it contains the remains from the prewar Japanese bauxite mine. At **Taki Falls,** the Ngardmau River tumbles 80 feet into a lush jun-gle pool. The trail to the falls follows the one-and-a-half-mile route of an old Japanese mining railway through the rainforest.

Practicalities

The only place to stay on northern Babeldaob (other than with local families) is the **Ngaraard Traditional Resort** (P.O. Box 773, Koror, PW 96940, tel. 680-488-1788 evenings, fax 680 488-1725) in Ulimong. The establishment offers three thatched cottages at $45 s, $55 d, $75 t. The toilets and washing facilities are outside, and there is electricity from 6 p.m. to midnight. Ngaraard prides itself on its food, and meals must be arranged in advance. The cost for meals per person is $6.50 for breakfast, $8.50 for lunch, and $18.50 for dinner. Getting there from Koror by boat costs $50 pp roundtrip with a $100 minimum. It can be difficult to reach *Ngaraard* by phone, so start making arrangements as early as possible.

PELELIU

The little island of Peleliu (pop. 600), 31 miles southwest of Koror at the south end of the Palau lagoon, was a scene of intense combat from September through November 1944. Mercifully, the Japanese evacuated the Micronesian inhabitants to Babeldaob before the battle began. The defense of Peleliu marked a change in Japanese military tactics. Instead of defending the beaches, the 10,000 defenders holed up in entrenched po-

M.G.L. DOMENY DE RIENZI

an early 19th-century view of Peleliu

sitions in the island's tangled rocky interior. This strategy led to a drawn-out two-and-a-half-month struggle, with heavy U.S. casualties and devastating Japanese losses.

After the battle the United States made no attempt to capture Koror and Babeldaob, which remained in Japanese hands until peace came. Military historians now agree the whole campaign was ill-advised and the capture of Peleliu contributed nothing to the eventual defeat of Japan.

Today, Peleliu is a lovely, sleepy island once more. There are innumerable war sites to visit

on Peleliu. Remember it is illegal to remove war relics. One can visit the invasion sites and interior limestone caves and tunnels where the Japanese held out till the fatal end. (One determined group of 34 Japanese soldiers remained holed up until April 21, 1947). Peleliu also offers fantastic snorkeling from white sand beaches. Some of Palau's greatest dive sites are actually closer to Peleliu than they are to Koror.

If you will be staying on the island, pay a courtesy visit to the island's governor. He can direct you to homes in which you can stay or to places where you can camp. Peleliu's residents live in

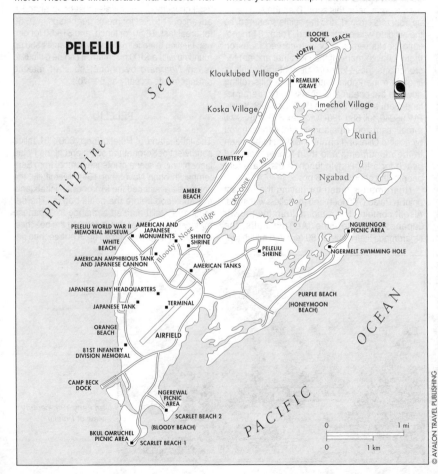

PELELIU

Philippine Sea

ELOCHEL DOCK
NORTH BEACH
Klouklubed Village
REMELIIK GRAVE
Koska Village
Imechol Village
Rurid
CEMETERY
CROCODILE RD.
Ngabad
AMBER BEACH
Bloody Nose Ridge
PELELIU WORLD WAR II MEMORIAL MUSEUM
AMERICAN AND JAPANESE MONUMENTS
SHINTO SHRINE
WHITE BEACH
AMERICAN AMPHIBIOUS TANK AND JAPANESE CANNON
AMERICAN TANKS
PELELIU SHRINE
NGURUNGOR PICNIC AREA
NGERMELT SWIMMING HOLE
JAPANESE ARMY HEADQUARTERS
PURPLE BEACH (HONEYMOON BEACH)
JAPANESE TANK
TERMINAL
ORANGE BEACH
AIRFIELD
OCEAN
81ST INFANTRY DIVISION MEMORIAL
CAMP BECK DOCK
NGEREWAL PICNIC AREA
SCARLET BEACH 2
(BLOODY BEACH)
BKUL OMRUCHEL PICNIC AREA
SCARLET BEACH 1
PACIFIC
PACIFIC OCEAN

0   1 mi
0   1 km

© AVALON TRAVEL PUBLISHING

three adjacent flower-filled villages at the north end of the island: Koska, Klouklubed, and Imechol. The people are friendly.

Sights

An excellent place to begin your visit is at the **Peleliu World War II Memorial Museum,** scheduled to open at its new location near **White Beach** in 1999. The museum has both American and Japanese artifacts from the war, patiently recovered in a two-year quest by Tangie Hesus, the museum's curator and a guide to the island.

The massive two-story reinforced concrete structure of the former **Japanese Communications Center** looms over the houses in Klouklubed village, just south of the school. Do not trespass to get to it. The large blue and white **grave** of Haruo I. Remeliik, president of Palau and a native of Peleliu, is on the corner opposite the baseball field in Klouklubed. Buried next to him is Mamoru Nakamura, Palau's first Supreme Court chief justice.

About a mile north of Klouklubed, a pleasant walk, is **Elochel Dock.** This is a nice spot to picnic. There is a fisherman's cooperative and public outhouses nearby. Several hundred yards south is a Japanese pillbox. Another hundred yards further south is the entrance to the **thousand man cave.** This massive burrow has 11 entrances and can take 20 minutes to explore. If you are not with a guide, be sure to have a flashlight and breadcrumbs so that you can find your way back out.

For touring the rest of the island, it is probably best to hire a guide: try Tangie Hesus, tel. (680) 345-1036. He will show you around the island from his minibus for $77 for up to four people (a bit more if you are traveling with more than four people). The underbrush of the island is such that you would not want to cut through it on your own. Even the road system can be confusing because there are remains of so many wartime roads.

A miniature Shinto shrine stands before the limestone cliffs of **Bloody Nose Ridge,** site of the fiercest fighting. Americans poured aviation fuel into caves sheltering diehard Japanese who would not surrender and ignited it. Three large **war memorials** stand on Bloody Nose Ridge. On the lowest terrace is the U.S. Marine Corps monument. From there a road winds up to the Japanese monument on a high terrace almost surrounded by jagged limestone peaks. This monument was erected in February 1989 on the site of the Japanese' last stand, where Colonel Nakagawa of the elite 2nd Infantry Regiment of the Imperial Japanese Army committed *seppuku* on 24 November 1944 after burning the regimental colors. At the very top of the ridge, accessible by a stairway, is the 323rd Infantry (U.S. Army) memorial and a flagpole on the uppermost peak. There's a superb view of the entire island from up there.

Several huge **Japanese buildings** stand half swallowed in the underbrush northwest of the airfield. **Orange Beach** is where the major American landing took place on 15 September 1944. At **Camp Beck Dock** is an assortment of abandoned U.S. ships and vehicles, plus wrecked planes bulldozed into mangled heaps of bent aluminum sculpture.

Most beaches on Peleliu have color names, though some also have other names. Heading counterclockwise from Klouklubed are: Amber Beach, White Beach, Orange Beach, Scarlet Beach (Bloody Beach) and Purple Beach (Honeymoon Beach). The color names are the code names used during the American invasion.

The **Bkul Omruchel Picnic area** on the island's southwest corner is a Japanese pilgrimage site. At high tide you can often see blowholes on this stretch of coast. At the cove between Scarlet Beach I and Scarlet Beach II (Bloody Beach) there is good snorkeling.

There is spectacular snorkeling from shore at Purple Beach (Honeymoon Beach) at the spot where the two roads intersect. If the surf is small, walk through the breakers and you come to a steep drop-off with huge fish swimming amidst fantastic coral gardens. Watch the current. If it's running, it's best not to snorkel.

Continuing on the road heading north from Honeymoon Beach is the **Ngermelt Swimming Hole,** a natural limestone sinkhole full of water that rises and falls with the tides—jump into the clear salt water and enjoy a refreshing swim.

Practicalities

Since the 1998 crash of a Paradise Air plane, there has been no air service to Peleliu. The only means to get there is by boat.

Peleliu has no restaurants, though most guesthouses will, for a fee, serve meals. There are a fair number of stores on the island, but they may be out of essentials. All things considered, if you are only spending a night or two on Peleliu, it may be best to bring in your own food and water. Beer and cold sodas are readily available.

Electricity is only on from 6 p.m. to 6 a.m. The island tends to be hot, sometimes extremely so in the afternoons. But there is, of course, no air conditioning until the electricity goes on.

Although Peleliu has no full-service hotel, it has a number of guesthouses from which to choose. In some you rent a room with a shared toilet, often an outhouse. A brief stay is an ideal way to observe contemporary outer island Micronesian life. You can usually just show up because the island's guesthouse rooms are seldom filled. Camping is an option also. Ask the governor for permission. Orange, White, Amber, and Purple Beaches are all good places to camp.

Mayumi's Inn (P.O. Box 482, State of Peleliu, PW 96940, tel. 680-345-1036) lies near the beach in Koska village. Mayumi and Keibo Rideb rent four air-conditioned rooms next to their store for $20 pp. You can also take meals: breakfast $7.50, lunch $9, and a special dinner with local lobster and crab at $16. You can also use the same phone number to make reservations at the **Peleliu Island Inn** in Klouklubed, which has six air-conditioned rooms with refrigerators and private baths at $50 d.

On the beach in Koska is the **Story Board Beach Resort** (P.O. Box 1561, State of Peleliu, PW 96940, tel. 680-345-1019), with A-frame cottages renting at $85 s or d. The rooms are clean and soft breezes come through the screened windows. This is a very pleasant place to stay.

In Klouklubed, **Reiko's Inn** rents air-conditioned rooms in a building behind the family's home. The stay is $20 pp, per night, with meals available for an additional $18 pp. Call (680) 345-1106. Nearby, also in Klouklubed, is the five-room **Wenty Inn,** tel. (680) 345-1080, at $16 pp, with no air conditioning.

ANGAUR

Angaur (pop. 206) is a quiet raised coral island, with few tourists and little traffic. This was also a major World War II battlefield, so you'll find the same sort of relics and caves as on the larger and more populated island of Peleliu, seven miles northeast. The 18 September 1944 American landings on Red Beach on the northeast side of Angaur were unopposed. The Japanese garrison had withdrawn to caves in the mined out central interior, which they held for more than a month. The Americans built the huge airstrip, which runs right across Angaur, in just 30 days, and B-24 Liberators became the main occupants.

Today the island is noted for the casual life in the one village, the attractive coastal scenery and beaches, and Micronesia's only monkeys, macaques that bred from two escaped German pets. With luck you may also see large monitor lizards, which were brought in by the Japanese. Palauans consider the monkeys pests because they eat crabs, so it's illegal to take them to other islands.

Central Angaur

Several half-submerged **American tanks** reinforce the breakwater of Angaur's harbor. The Japanese government spent $2.2 million on the harbor's new pier, but this reduced the available space, making it difficult for large fishing boats to maneuver, and the entrance is still treacherous. **Phosphate mining,** begun by the Germans in 1909 and continued through the Japanese period, finally ended under the Americans in 1954. The ruins of the bulk loading pier are just north of the harbor. Follow the remains of the fallen conveyor belt back through the bush to the skeleton of the phosphate crushing plant.

A ruined **Japanese lighthouse** rises high above the harbor, but it's not visible from the road, so it can be hard to find. Get there by taking the coastal road north from the phosphate plant less than a half mile, to a point where the route cuts between cliffs and begins to drop. Retrace your steps a little till you find your way into a small coconut grove on the southwest side of the road. Go in and look for a stone stairway leading past a square concrete water tank to the highest point. Your effort is rewarded with a good view of the island from the second-story roof. This place is perfect at sunset, and chances are you'll have a grandstand view of the antics of the local monkeys.

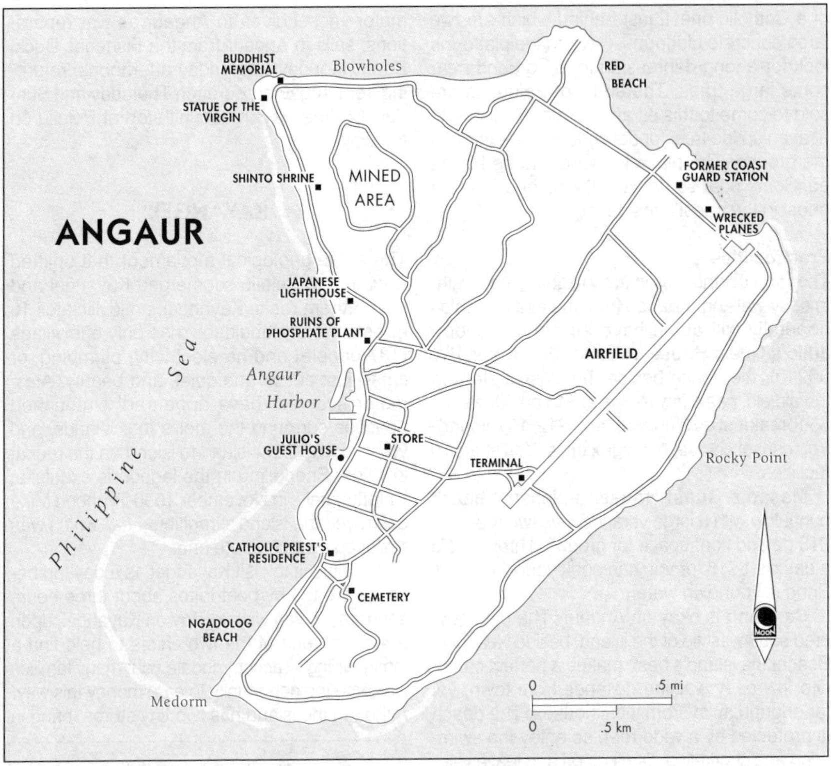

BUDDHIST MEMORIAL

Blowholes

RED BEACH

STATUE OF THE VIRGIN

SHINTO SHRINE

MINED AREA

FORMER COAST GUARD STATION

WRECKED PLANES

ANGAUR

JAPANESE LIGHTHOUSE

RUINS OF PHOSPHATE PLANT

AIRFIELD

Sea

Angaur Harbor

Philippine

JULIO'S GUEST HOUSE

STORE

TERMINAL

Rocky Point

CATHOLIC PRIEST'S RESIDENCE

CEMETERY

NGADOLOG BEACH

Medorm

0   .5 mi

0   .5 km

© AVALON TRAVEL PUBLISHING

Northern Angaur

A pleasantly shaded coral road runs right around Angaur, which you can cover on foot in a day, but carry plenty of water. The most attractive stretch skirts the stark limestone cliffs at the northwest corner of the island. This is where the Japanese army made its last stand during the American invasion; Shinto and Buddhist memorials mark the event. The miniature **Shinto shrine** is especially striking, with a good beach opposite. The snorkeling is good here when the water's calm, but beware of surf and riptides when it's not. Today this area is inhabited by large bands of monkeys, which dwell in the many huge banyan trees.

The ocean crashes relentlessly into the northwest cape of Angaur. A statue of the **Virgin Mary** was erected at this point in 1954 to protect the islanders from rough seas. Several spec-

tacular **blowholes** blow on the north coast, and the beat of the waves against the uplifted coral terraces can be hypnotic.

Between the abandoned buildings of the **former Coast Guard station** and the northeast end of the airstrip are **broken aircraft,** between the road and the coast. Included in this WW II aviation dump are fragments of a Corsair fighter and the wings of B-24 Liberators, half swallowed among the pandanus and ironwood trees.

Southern Angaur

Angaur is outside the protective Palau Reef. The impact of this can be appreciated at **Rocky Point** on the east side of the island: a blowhole and smashing surf. The far south end of the island has beautiful sandy beaches.

By the road at the north end of **Ngadolog Beach** is the former hospital, now the residence of a Catholic priest, just behind which are two large concrete platforms. Beyond the platforms look for a long depression in the ground near some large trees. The souls of Palauans are said to come to this pit after death to ascend to heaven up the trees or descend into hell through the ground. The place is thought to be haunted. Some hear screams in the night and see a ghost in the priest's residence.

Practicalities
The two guesthouses in the village are both within easy walking distance from the airstrip (which hopefully will again have air service soon). **Julio's Guest House** (P.O. Box 261, Koror, PW 96940), the house beside the closest store to the airfield, has a few rooms at $15 pp. Meals are $5 (breakfast), $8 (lunch), and $12-15 (dinner). You can, of course, bring groceries. You share all facilities.

Masao's Guest House, a pleasant beach bungalow with a large veranda, has two rooms at $15 pp and floor space for groups. Three meals a day cost $18, or you can cook your own food. Bring in your own water.

Camping is okay on Angaur. The pine-covered southwest tip of the island, beside Ngadolog Beach, the island's best, makes a perfect campsite. It's easy walking distance from town, yet far enough away from local houses. The beach is protected by a wide reef, so enjoy the swimming and snorkeling. Don't go off and leave valuables lying around, though.

Both camping and snorkeling depend on the direction of the wind: if it's out of the east, Ngadolog Beach will be calmer, but when it's out of the west Rocky Point or the promontory between Red Beach and the former Coast Guard station will be preferable. Much of the year Ngadolog Beach will be best, except during the southwest monsoon season from July through October, when this side of the island gets the most rain and wind.

The two small stores on Angaur are not always well stocked and are closed on Sunday.

Transportation
Since the 1998 crash of a Paradise Air plane, there has been no air service to Angaur. The only means to get there is by boat.

The *Yamato Maru,* a modern Japanese-made motor vessel given to Angaur as war reparations, sails to Angaur from the Fisheries Dock, Koror, Monday and Friday afternoons, returning from Angaur to Koror on Thursday and Sunday, $5 one way. It doesn't stop at Peleliu on the way.

KAYANGEL

The same geological movement that uplifted Angaur and Peleliu submerged Kayangel and the northern reefs. Kayangel, an idyllic atoll 16 miles north of Babeldaob, has only one village (137 people) and no electricity, plumbing, or cars—just peace and quiet, and beauty. Alas, motor scooters have appeared! Untouched beaches surround the atoll's four islands, and you can walk from island to island on the reef at low tide. Snorkeling in the lagoon is exquisite. Unfortunately, in November 1990 Typhoon Mike destroyed the island's traditional *bai,* which was replaced by a concrete one.

It is difficult to visit Kayangel as a day trip because the trip by boat takes about three hours each way. If you wish to stay on Kayangel, upon arrival ask one of the two chiefs to help find a family willing to accommodate you; many families welcome the opportunity to earn money this way. Although the island has two tiny stores, bring in

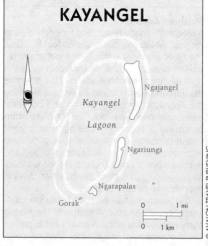

KAYANGEL

Ngajangel

Kayangel

Lagoon

Ngariungs

Ngarapalas

Gorak

0   1 mi

0   1 km

© AVALON TRAVEL PUBLISHING

your own food, water (or purification system), and insect repellent. Bread and coffee are appreciated as gifts, but beer is not allowed. Make your return plans before being dropped off.

THE SOUTHWEST ISLANDS

These five tiny islands between Koror and Indonesia are among the most remote in the Pacific. **Tobi Island** (Hatohobei), 372 miles southwest of Koror, is just 155 miles from the Indonesian island of Morotai. In 1990, Sonsorol State, which includes Tobi (148 acres) and Sonsorol (470 acres) Islands, had 61 inhabitants. About a dozen people may be on **Pulo Anna**

(198 acres) at any one time, while Merir (222 acres) and Helen (494 acres) are usually uninhabited. The main source of income is the sale of copra. **Sonsorol** consists of two islands, Fana and Sonsorol, about a half mile apart.

The people of the Southwest Islands speak the language of Woleai atoll, Yap State; Palauans cannot understand them. These islanders retain more of the traditional Pacific culture (leaf houses, canoe making, handicrafts, etc.) than any other group in Palau.

On remote **Helen Reef,** a sand spit east of Tobi, thousands of seabirds and turtles live in undisturbed bliss. Helen Reef has a 39-square-mile lagoon, but the other Southwest Islands are all low islands with only fringing reefs.

M.G.L. DOMENY DE RIENZI

TERRITORY OF GUAM
INTRODUCTION

Guam has wide streets and modern buildings. It does not have the exotic feel of the remote regions of Micronesia. But the sun is warm, the beaches beautiful; the streets are crowded, but clean; and the tap water is drinkable. United States military bases are physically and economically prominent. But increasingly, this is a land where brown-skinned islanders, Chamorros from Guam, Filipinos, and recent arrivals from the Federated States of Micronesia cater to Asian vacationers. People are busy spending or making money.

Guam is complex. It is a U.S. territory and military base. It is an Asian resort. But its southern half, still rugged from its volcanic origin, is a quiet place where modern Chamorro culture, a blend of indigenous Chamorro mixed with centuries of Spanish rule, thrives and rejuvenates itself.

It's not easy to pinpoint who visits Guam today. Even with the downturn in the Asian economies, numerically far and away the most prominent

are Japanese, and increasingly Taiwanese and Hong Kong vacationers seeking a fairly close, relaxing, short vacation. Some of these visitors are quite wealthy. Many others are young working people who can afford packaged tours. But Micronesians and expats living in Micronesia also come here for urban errands and pleasures. Still other visitors are family and friends of Americans stationed or working here.

Finally, there are American and European travelers, usually in transit to or from more exotic destinations. Too often they are in a rush to leave. This is unfortunate. Guam is a great spot to rest and relax after hard traveling in Micronesia or in Asia, or at the start of a vacation, to recover from jet lag.

The Land
The Pacific ends at Guam: on its western shores begins the Philippine Sea. This 209-

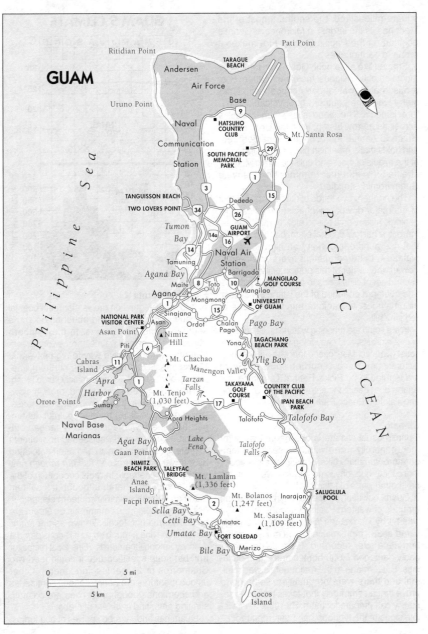

GUAM

Ritidian Point

Pati Point

TARAGUE BEACH

Andersen

Uruno Point

Air Force

Base

9

HATSUHO COUNTRY CLUB

Mt. Santa Rosa

Naval

Communication

SOUTH PACIFIC MEMORIAL PARK

29

Yigo

Station

3

1

Philippine Sea

TANGUISSON BEACH

TWO LOVERS POINT

Dededo

34

15

26

Tumon Bay

14a

GUAM AIRPORT

16

14

Naval Air Station

Tamuning

Barrigada

PACIFIC

Agana Bay

Maite

8 Toto

10

Mangilao

MANGILAO GOLF COURSE

Agana

1

Mongmong

Mangilao

UNIVERSITY OF GUAM

Sinajana

15

NATIONAL PARK VISITOR CENTER

Asan

Ordot

Chalan Pago

Pago Bay

Asan Point

Piti

Nimitz Hill

Yona

TAGACHANG BEACH PARK

OCEAN

Cabras Island

11

6

Mt. Chachao

4

Ylig Bay

Apra Harbor

1

Manengon Valley

Tarzan Falls

TAKAYAMA GOLF COURSE

COUNTRY CLUB OF THE PACIFIC

Orote Point

Sumay

Mt. Tenjo (1,030 feet)

17

IPAN BEACH PARK

Naval Base Marianas

Apra Heights

Talofofo

Talofofo Bay

Agat Bay

Gaan Point

Agat

Lake Fena

Talofofo Falls

NIMITZ BEACH PARK

TALEYFAC BRIDGE

Anae Island

Mt. Lamlam (1,336 feet)

4

Facpi Point

2

Mt. Bolanos (1,247 feet)

Inarajan

SALUGLULA POOL

Sella Bay

Cetti Bay

Umatac

Mt. Sasalaguan (1,109 feet)

Umatac Bay

FORT SOLEDAD

Bile Bay

Merizo

0   5 mi

0   5 km

Cocos Island

© AVALON TRAVEL PUBLISHING

square-mile island, the southernmost of the Marianas, is the largest in Micronesia. Guam's position on the Pacific Ring of Fire makes it prone to earthquakes.

Shaped like a footprint, Guam was formed by the union of two islands: the older northern one, a raised atoll, was already capped with limestone when the southern one, volcanic in nature, joined it. The island is less than five miles across its narrow instep, from the University of Guam to Agana, the commercial center. Legend holds that a great fish had been eating away at the middle of the island until the Virgin Mary restrained it with a hair from her head, saving Guam from destruction.

The northern two-thirds of Guam, where most of the major development is, shows clearly its geologic history as a raised atoll. In most places, there is a narrow coastal plain, backed by cliffs that rise hundreds of feet to a high limestone plateau with no permanent rivers or streams. Toward the center of this portion of the island, a second set of cliffs leads to a still higher plateau. The southern one-third of the island consists of mountainous, volcanic terrain with a ridge of red clay hills.

In the south are crashing waterfalls, seldom-visited rainforests, and easygoing villages along the coast (Umatac, Merizo, and Inarajan are the most picturesque). The best **surfing spots** on Guam are reputed to be Rick's Reef at Tamuning, the Agana Boat Basin, the entrance to Merizo harbor, and Talofofo Beach Park.

Climate

Guam's usual climate is one of endless summer, generally warm with little seasonal temperature variation. Like Hawaii, its air is liquid, though the humidity is not oppressive, as it can be in other parts of Micronesia.

Guam, however, is located within the breeding grounds of western Pacific typhoons. In 1997 it was hit by Hurricane Paka. Winds were measured at 237 mph, making it the most powerful hurricane ever recorded. Paka destroyed or badly damaged 8,000 homes and 2,000 buildings. But damage to the major hotels was minimal and there were no fatalities, seeming to prove that a community that takes typhoons seriously can prepare for them. By 1999, most visible signs of the typhoon had been repaired.

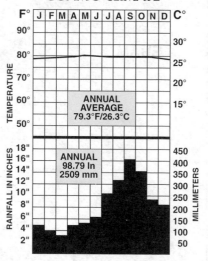

GUAM'S CLIMATE

ANNUAL AVERAGE
79.3°F/26.3°C

ANNUAL
98.79 In
2509 mm

Flora and Fauna

Salt-tolerant vegetation grows along the coastal strands, with swamps and marshes on some southern coasts and rivers. In the southern ravines are ferns and palms, then sword grass-filled valleys, which give way to high savanna. Dense forests once covered the northern limestone plateau, which today is mainly scrub brush.

The territorial tree is ironwood, or *ifil,* a slow-growing evergreen that throws out small cones, which makes walking barefoot painful. Its timber turns black with age. In 1947 *tangan tangan* brush *(Leucaena)* was seeded from aircraft to protect the island, which had been defoliated by the war, from erosion. *Tangan tangan* now grows in impenetrable thickets over much of the north end of the island, although it's seldom found on Guam's volcanic southern slopes.

The only indigenous mammals on Guam are bats. The fruit bat, locally known as the *fanihi,* has been having a rough go as it is considered a delicacy among Chamorros. (One local recipe for fruit bat soup specified that it could feed two Chamorros or 25 *haoles,* foreigners). Other unique creatures are nonpoisonous centipedes and scorpions (though their bites are painful), stinging ants, and a variety of crabs.

Guam has endangered species of sea turtles,

including the green and the hawksbill. Guam's sharks rarely attack humans. Guam's reefs harbor one of the most diverse fish populations in the world, with 110 families and 800 species of inshore fish identified. More than 300 species of coral are present, but in many places, the coral is stressed from the population of the island. The gathering of live coral is prohibited by law.

Guam may be one of the first places on earth to lose *all* its endemic birds, a disaster that could have serious ramifications on the pollination of native plants, dispersal of seeds, insect populations, and the whole ecological ladder. Introduced diseases, pesticides, hunting, and habitat loss have all been factors in the dramatic decline in birdlife over the past two decades. But in 1983 biologist Julie Savidge identified the main culprit as the brown tree-climbing snake *(Boiga irregularis),* introduced accidentally from the Solomon Islands from the hold of a navy ship or plane toward the end of World War II. The nocturnal snakes were first identified in the harbor area in the 1950s. Now some forested areas of the island have up to 12,000 snakes per square mile. The snakes can grow to more than six feet but are of little danger to people. They feed mainly on eggs and chicks, but can also be a danger to small domestic animals. Until the brown tree snake arrived, Guam's only serpent had been a blind, earthworm-like snake. Guam's native forest birds were helpless in the face of this new predator. There is now an experiment to see if even a small plot of undeveloped land can be cleared of this pest.

HISTORY

Early History

Guam's first people probably arrived from the Malay Peninsula around 5,000 years ago. They lived in small villages; the basic social unit was the extended, matrilineal family. After marriage, the man moved to the woman's house; land was inherited from the mother's brother. There were three social classes: nobles, commoners, and outcasts. Spirits of the ancestors were venerated.

The most intriguing remains left by the *taotaomona* (spirits of the before-time people) are *latte* stones, megalithic monuments up to 20 feet high. The *latte* were usually constructed in double rows of six to 14 stones, each composed of a *haligi* (pedestal) and a *tasa* (cap). The *tasa* are natural coral heads placed atop the *haligi* with the spherical side down, making the *latte* look like giant mushrooms with the tops inverted. Burial sites and artifacts are usually found in the vicinity of *latte. Latte* stones are found throughout the Marianas, the biggest on Tinian.

It is often written that the *latte* stones were used to support residences of the *matua* (upper class). I've never been convinced that this is a complete answer. Certainly the society that had the technology to transport and raise these stones could have devised a much simpler manner to raise houses, if that were its sole goal.

A Spanish Colony

Ferdinand Magellan, on the first known circumnavigation of the world, landed on Guam in 1521, his first stop after crossing the Pacific. Magellan landed three and a half months after rounding the tip of South America; his scurvy-ridden crew had been reduced to a diet of rats and leather after crossing the Pacific without sighting land. He saw Guam as a source of badly needed supplies. Magellan named Guam the Isle of Thieves when his skiff was stolen. He recovered the boat after personally leading a raid ashore, during which seven or eight islanders were killed and their village burned. Two months later, Magellan was killed in a similar fracas in the Philippines.

Miguel Lopez de Legaspi, colonizer of the Philippines, claimed Guam for Spain in 1565, but it was not until 1668 that Jesuit missionaries arrived at Guam to implant their faith. When persuasion failed, the Spanish resorted to force. From 1680 to 1695, troops under Capt. José de Quiroga waged a war against the native Chamorro people and, with the help of introduced diseases like smallpox and syphilis, reduced their numbers from 80,000 in 1668 to below 5,000 by 1741.

The survivors, mostly women and children, were relocated in controlled settlements where they intermarried with Spanish and Filipino troops and adopted much of those cultures, becoming the Chamorros of today. Clan-held lands were divided among individuals. In 1769 a power struggle between the king of Spain and the Jesuits led to the expulsion of the order from Guam (and all other Spanish colonies). The Chamorro population declined to 1,500 by 1783.

Today, a monument to the pro-Spanish collaborator Quipuha graces Agana's Marine Drive, while resistance leader Chief Matapang is not commemorated. Father Diego Luis de San Vitores, who used Spanish soldiers to carry out forced baptisms of Chamorros until they killed him in 1672, is now in the process of canonization.

Changing Hands

For 200 years, Guam was a source of food and water for Manila galleons plying between Mexico and the Philippines. It took three months to sail from Acapulco to Manila and six months to return. The Spanish traded silver from Mexico for gems and spices from Asia. The annual journeys ended in 1815 when Mexico became independent from Spain. After 1822, Yankee whalers became regular visitors.

Guam, Puerto Rico, and the Philippines became American possessions as a result of the Spanish-American War. On 20 June 1898 the USS *Charleston* entered Apra Harbor, firing as she came. Informed that their country was at war, the Spaniards promptly surrendered.

Military Rule

From 1898 to 1941 Guam was run as a United States naval station; U.S. Marines were the constabulary. To avoid provoking Japan, already a rising power, and in accord with a 1922 agreement between the two countries, the United States made no attempt to fortify the island. Just prior to World War II, Guam's defenses consisted of a few machine guns and several hundred rifles.

The Americans surrendered to a Japanese invasion force just two days after Pearl Harbor. The Japanese immediately forced the 2,000 Chamorro inhabitants of Sumay village on the Orote Peninsula to evacuate their homes. (They still live elsewhere on Guam; the area is a United States naval base today.) The Japanese renamed Guam *Omiyajima* (Great Shrine Island).

In March 1944, the Japanese deployed 18,500 troops to Guam to meet the expected American invasion. Guamanians were conscripted to work alongside Korean labor battalions. On 12 July, the Japanese beheaded Father Jesus Baza Duenas and three others accused of aiding a fugitive United States Navy radioman. A few days later all 21,000 local residents were herded into concentration camps such as the one at Manengon near Yona, a move that did separate the Chamorros from the crossfire of battle.

Some 55,000 Allied personnel landed at Agat and Asan on 21 July 1944. Organized resistance by the outnumbered and outgunned Japanese ended on 10 August, although some remained in the interior for years. The final cost to the United States came to 2,124 dead and 5,250 wounded, most of them marines. Only 1,250 Japanese were captured; the other 17,000 perished.

One diehard Japanese straggler, Sergeant Shoichi Yokoi, held out in the jungle near Talofofo until 24 January 1972, claiming he was unaware that the war had ended. Yokoi, who lived until 1997, became a controversial figure to Japanese. To the older generation, he represented the virtues of dedication, loyalty, and perseverance. But many in the postwar generation felt he carried those characteristics to a life-negating fault.

The United States turned Guam into a massive military base; by mid-1945 there were 200,000 servicemen on Guam. Large tracts of land appropriated at that time remain in the hands of the military today, and the private owners have not yet been fully compensated. In the late 1970s former landowners and their heirs launched a lawsuit against the United States demanding compensation. A $39.5-million out-of-court settlement was paid in 1986. But this settlement was not deemed fair by many landowners. Questions remain as to whether the landowners actually gave knowing consent to the settlement.

From 1945 to 1949, 144 Japanese defendants were tried by the United States in a Quonset hut on Nimitz Hill, Guam. Two Japanese lieutenant generals, two rear admirals, five vice admirals, and the commanding officers in the Marshalls, the Marianas, Tungaru, Bonin, Palau, and Wake were among the 136 convicted of war crimes. Fifteen of the 111 convicted of murder were executed. The rest served their sentences at Sugamo Prison, Tokyo.

In 1946 the United States granted independence to the Philippines but retained control of Guam. In 1950, the Department of the Interior took control of the island, at which time Guamanians became United States citizens. Until 1962, a military security clearance was required to visit Guam.

marines taking cover during the landings on Guam, 21 July 1944

Military Use

During the cold war, Guam's strategic importance to the U.S. came from its proximity to Russia, Japan, and China. Guam became one of the most heavily fortified bases. Andersen Air Force Base, the main Strategic Air Command (SAC) base in the Pacific, had the only B-52s based outside the continental United States.

The navy still controls a 1.5-mile runway at the Agana Naval Air Station beside the international airport. Guam is the communications center for naval forces in the western Pacific. But with the collapse of the cold war, the closing of United States bases in the Philippines, and a reduced U.S. presence in South Korea, the military situation in the western Pacific is changing. The number of military personnel on Guam has been drastically reduced. Guam's economic future seems tied more to Asian business than to the American military.

For more information on Guam's history, read Professor Robert Rogers's book, *Destiny's Landfall* (Honolulu: University of Hawaii Press, 1995)— an extraordinary discussion of the process of conquest and colonization, from the precontact era to the present-day struggle for autonomy.

GOVERNMENT

Guam is a permanent, unincorporated territory of the United States. In 1987 the Guam electorate approved a draft Guam Commonwealth Act, which was never approved by the United States Congress. The proposed Commonwealth Act would have given Guam control over immigration, veto power over certain federal laws, and a say in defense policy relating to the island. In many ways, this proposal gave Guam more attributes of sovereignty than given in Commonwealth bills to the Northern Marianas or Puerto Rico. Negotiations on the future status of Guam have occurred sporadically over the past decade.

At present, Guam has only one level of government: a 15-senator unicameral legislature (formerly 21-member) elected every two years. The people of Guam elected their own governor for the first time in 1970; both the governor and an elected lieutenant governor serve four-year terms. Since 1972 an elected, *nonvoting* member of Congress has represented Guam in Washington. Guamanians cannot vote in United States presidential elections, yet United States citizens living in Guam can vote in its elections. The government of Guam controls certain territorial departments and autonomous agencies such as the Commercial Port of Guam, Guam Airport Authority, Guam Power Authority, Guam Telephone Authority, and the University of Guam.

A "sovereignty" movement continues among Chamorros today. This concept has different meanings to different adherents, but for all, it means greater Chamorro autonomy. In the political realm, demands run the gamut from merely more local rule to complete independence. In the cultural realm, the movement includes relearning and using the Chamorro language and employing art forms that reflect traditional Chamorro expression.

ECONOMY

Tourism is Guam's biggest business. Guam receives more tourists than any Pacific island destination except Hawaii. In 1995, Guam passed the million visitors a year mark for the first time. More than 80% of Guam's tourists are Japanese. In 1996 Koreans were the second largest group of tourists, but the number of tourists from Korea dropped dramatically after the crash of Korean Air Flight 801 on Guam on 6 August 1997. Soon after came the economic downturn in Asia, which led to a significant decline in Japanese and Taiwanese tourism. Still, less than 10% of the tourists are American.

Military spending has been greatly reduced since the end of the cold war. It remains significant, though segments of the economy that were heavily dependent on the military had to endure hard times. As elsewhere, movement toward a peacetime economy causes economic dislocations.

Large military reservations account for 30% of the surface area of the island; more than half of this area is held for "contingency purposes" and is not currently being used. The Guam government holds another 25% of the land. The military recently released its hold on more than 15,000 acres of excess land, and the islanders are exerting enormous political pressure to release more. The Chamorro Land Trust Commission is charged with settling landless, indigenous Chamorros on returned land.

Guam is a free port, not part of the United States customs area. Import duties are charged only on tobacco, liquor, and liquid fuel. Manufactured goods with at least 30% value added by assembling or processing on Guam can be exported duty free to the United States. This was intended to spur industries that would assemble component parts produced inexpensively in Asia, but such industry has not yet developed to a significant degree.

THE PEOPLE

The pre-European people of the Marianas were culturally related to other Micronesians. Most Chamorros of today are of mixed Micronesian, Filipino, and Spanish ancestry. Ninety-eight percent are Roman Catholic.

Under a succession of colonial rulers the focus of Chamorro life shifted from the traditional men's house to the village church, the school, and finally the shopping mall and office. Chamorros underwent an assimilation crisis.

Today, Guam's total population is roughly 135,000, with less than half the population being Chamorro. Guam is home to many ethnic Filipinos, who make up more than 25% of the population. Statesiders are about 15% of the population. Chinese, Japanese, Koreans, and Micronesians from other islands form the other major groups on Guam.

The Filipino community on Guam is not homogeneous. The families of many Filipinos have lived on Guam for generations. But the 1990s saw a new wave of arrivals from the Philippines. They came in search of work, often to help support family members still in the Philippines. These new arrivals frequently wind up in the lowest paying jobs in the hotel and restaurant industries.

Many Chamorros share a very real fear that the growing influx of immigrants from east and west will make them a small minority on their own island. In 1940 they comprised 90% of the total population; today they're less than 45%. Some Chamorro leaders have demanded that a plebiscite on Guam's future be taken and that only those of Chamorro ancestry be allowed to participate in the vote. It is not clear whether the United States could constitutionally sanction such a vote.

The 5,000-plus Micronesians from the Freely Associated States (Republic of Palau, Federated States of Micronesia and Republic of the Marshall Islands) are resented by many of Guam's residents, including Chamorros. Guam has attempted to control immigration from the FAS and to limit Micronesian access to subsidized housing. It is unclear whether such limitations are legally permissible. Guam is a U.S. territory, and the Compacts of Free Association guarantee Micronesian access to the United States.

The *Pacific Daily News* has chronicled the usage and effect of "ice" on Guam (see *Pacific Daily News,* July 5, 1998, p. 3 for excellent reporting on this drug and its effects). "Ice" is a powerful form of methamphetamine used throughout the Asian Pacific. Its effect on a community can be as devastating as "crack" has been on the U.S. mainland.

Language

Chamorro went out of general use a generation ago, but today there is a revival of its use and it is again being taught in the schools. It is a rhythmic, melodic language. Spanish speakers generally have difficulty following a conversation, even though about 85% of the words in modern Chamorro derive from Spanish (*buenos dias*—good morning; *adios*—goodbye). Virtually all Chamorros speak English. One does, however, see many signs proclaiming *Hafa adai* which sounds like "half a day" but means something like "Hello, how are you?" More frequently than Chamorro, one hears the languages of foreign workers and tourists: Tagalog, Korean, Chinese, and Japanese.

ARTS AND CRAFTS

Guam has a lively arts scene. Artists trained in Western art, often in the United States, are creating a new school of painting that combines Western techniques with traditional values and themes. The **Guam Gallery of Art** in Chamorro village shows local artists.

In addition, Guam has two art museums. The **Guam Museum** is located at the government complex in Adelup. At the University of Guam, 15 Dean's Circle, you'll find the **Isla Center for the Arts,** which contains a collection of Pacific and Pacific Rim art, both indigenous and modern. Though currently closed, the old Guam Museum, located in Plaza de Espana, contains many artifacts relating to Shoichi Yokoi's 16 years of hiding on Guam.

HOLIDAYS AND EVENTS

Banks and government agencies remain closed on the following public holidays: New Year's Day (1 January), Martin Luther King's Birthday (third Monday in January), President's Day (third Monday in February), Guam Discovery Day (first Monday in March), Good Friday, Memorial Day (last Monday in May), Independence Day (4 July), Guam Liberation Day (21 July), Labor Day (first Monday after the first Tuesday in September), Columbus Day (second Monday in October), Veteran's Day (11 November), Thanksgiving Day (fourth Thursday in November), Feast of the Immaculate Conception (8 December), and Christmas Day (25 December).

Around 6 March a fiesta at Umatac village commemorates Magellan's landing. Many events take place in July to celebrate Guam's liberation in 1944, culminating in a large parade and fireworks on 21 July. Merizo's Water Festival is held in August. Feasts are commonly held to celebrate anniversaries, marriages, and births. The biggest procession of the year occurs on 8 December in Agana, to honor Our Lady of the Immaculate Conception, patron of the island. Fireworks at the Hilton mark New Year's Eve.

All 19 Chamorro villages on Guam celebrate their patron saints' day; since some villages have more than one saint there are 32 recognized fiestas a year. The best known fiestas are those of the Santo Niño Perdido, Asan (January); Nuestra Senora de la Paz y Buen Viaje, Chalan Pago (January); Our Lady of Lourdes, Yigo (February); St. Joseph, Inarajan (May); Assumption of Our Lady, Piti (August); San Roque, Barrigada (August); Santa Rosa, Agat (August); Dulce Nombre de Maria, Agana (September); San Miguel, Talofofo (September); St. Teresita, Mangilao (October); St. Jude, Sinajana (October); Our Lady of the Blessed Sacrament, Agana Heights (November); and Santa Barbara, Dededo (December).

The *Guam Phone Book, Yellow Pages Ink* provides a complete list of village fiestas with exact dates. Most of these feature a religious procession through the streets, followed by a feast. People are very hospitable on these occasions and you stand a good chance of being invited if you're in the right place at the right time. "Come and eat" is the usual greeting.

SIGHTS

AGANA

Looking at Agana from the sea, one realizes what a narrow band, above the ocean and below the cliffs, has been home to so much human drama. The town of Agana (a-GA-nya) is primarily low rise, tucked in a small coastal strip below the cliffs to the central plateau. The town is pleasant looking and clean, though the buildings themselves are not picturesque. What is missing is anything old. The 1920s wooden structures one finds in the towns of much of the tropical Pacific are missing. They have been destroyed by earthquakes, typhoons, and the United States retaking the island in 1944. Old in Agana means before 1977, the date of a severe typhoon.

Agana, particularly at night, is a sleepy town. Most of the action has moved up to Tumon Bay. However, some treats remain, tucked away.

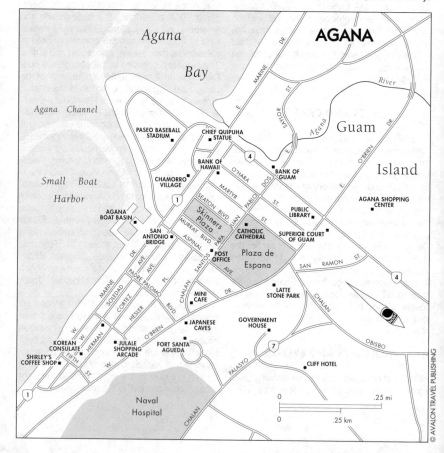

AGANA

Agana Bay

Agana Channel

Small Boat Harbor

Guam Island

River

Agana River

PASEO BASEBALL STADIUM

CHIEF QUIPUHA STATUE

BANK OF HAWAII

CHAMORRO VILLAGE

BANK OF GUAM

AGANA BOAT BASIN

AGANA SHOPPING CENTER

PUBLIC LIBRARY

Skinner's Plaza

SAN ANTONIO BRIDGE

CATHOLIC CATHEDRAL

SUPERIOR COURT OF GUAM

POST OFFICE

Plaza de Espana

SAN RAMON ST.

MINI CAFE

LATTE STONE PARK

JAPANESE CAVES

GOVERNMENT HOUSE

KOREAN CONSULATE

JULALE SHOPPING ARCADE

FORT SANTA AGUEDA

SHIRLEY'S COFFEE SHOP

CLIFF HOTEL

Naval Hospital

0   .25 mi

0   .25 km

© AVALON TRAVEL PUBLISHING

Many streets have not been named, and many buildings have no street address. Like residents on many small islands, nobody on Guam seems to know the street names that do exist, even if they know every building on the island.

The Spanish founded a town at Agana in 1668. A few physical reminders of the Spanish era remain. The **Plaza de Espana** in the heart of downtown Agana was the center of spiritual and temporal power during Spanish colonial times. Of the Casa de Gobierno (Governor's Palace), built in 1736 and enlarged in 1885, little survived the war. However, one can still see the *azotea* (terrace), the arches of the arsenal (1736), and the "Chocolate House," a summerhouse where Spanish ladies once gathered for late afternoon *meriendas* (teas). The former Spanish garden house, also in the plaza, has served as the **Guam Museum.** It was closed in 1995 and it's not clear when or if it will reopen. It housed a collection relating to the amazing story of Japanese sergeant Shoichi Yokoi.

To one side of the plaza is the **Catholic Cathedral,** first erected here in 1669 and rebuilt in 1955. The image above the main altar is Santa Maria Camalin. Legend says that this statue miraculously floated ashore on the beach at Merizo more than 200 years ago, guarded by two golden crabs bearing lighted candles in their claws. A revolving statue of Pope John Paul II (who said mass here in 1981) watches over Plaza de Espana.

Nearby, at the foot of Kasamata Hill, is **Latte Stone Park,** where eight ancient *latte* pillars, originally from the vicinity of Lake Fena in south central Guam, were re-erected in 1955. The stones are impressive, but not their setting, which is next to a busy street. Along the cliffs behind the park are **caves** where the Japanese ensconced themselves during the 1944 invasion by American forces.

Above Latte Stone Park at Agana Heights is **Government House** (est. 1952), residence of the governor. Inside you may visit the Governor's Museum, with its interesting displays on Guamanian history, and enjoy the view from the terrace. Just beyond this is the site of **Fort Santa Agueda** (1800). Although very little is left of the fort, you do get a splendid view of Agana from this hill. As with many attractions on Guam, you will enjoy the visit most if you can time it between tour bus arrivals.

Back near Marine Drive, northwest of the Plaza de Espana, is the **San Antonio Bridge** (1800). In 1676 the Presidio Agana, a small settlement surrounded by a stockade, was located between this bridge and the waterfront. The river itself was filled in after WW II.

The most interesting spot in town, particularly for the budget traveler, is **Chamorro Village.** It opened in 1994 and is located on fill from bulldozed World War II rubble, on a point opposite downtown, the former site of the public market. This great place to hang out is open during the day from 10 a.m.-5:30 p.m. It's also open till 9 p.m. most Wednesdays, except during the summer. During these evening the Village usually hosts live bands and dance groups.

The Village contains a series of small kiosks, made to resemble traditional housing. Only local produce and products can be sold here. The fish store sells reasonably priced sashimi to go. There are all types of gift shops, selling goods made by local artisans, using local products to the degree feasible. There are many food shops featuring the different ethnic cuisines of the people of Guam.

My favorite shop here is **Guam Chocolate and Pastry,** which sells fresh homemade chocolate. They do handicrafts in chocolate, such as chocolate baskets. A great, nonrenewable souvenir for $4.20 is a solid chocolate Great Seal of Guam. They will take orders at tel./fax (671) 472-1308. Another shop worth a look is **Marine Images** (P.O. Box 24666, GMF, Guam, GU 96921, tel./fax 671-472-9870), run by Larie Pangelinan, originally from Palau. The shop sells handicrafts from throughout Micronesia, such as story boards, carvings, and weavings. It also sells souvenir T-shirts and postcards with photos by Larie's photographer husband, Tim Rock.

Within the Chamorro Village, fronting on Marine Drive, is the Guam Gallery of Art, open during the day Monday through Saturday and in the evening by appointment (tel. 671-472-9659). Run by Fillamore Paloma, the gallery exhibits members of the Chamorro Artists Association. In the same room is a second gallery showing the work of the Castro family, perhaps Gaum's most renowned family of artists.

Right behind Chamorro Village is the **Paseo Baseball Stadium,** a charming, stadium that seats a couple of thousand, (340 left field line,

415 straight-away center, 325 right field line; $1.25 Spam burgers). It makes you remember why people play baseball for less than $3 million a year. If you see the lights on in the evening, go take a look.

The **Paseo de Susana Park,** behind the stadium, is a pleasant place to stroll or jog. Some tourists have their pictures taken in front of the **miniature Statue of Liberty** in the park. The mouth of Agana Boat Basin is a prime surfing spot.

AROUND THE ISLAND

Guam, though a large island for Micronesia, is only 30 by nine miles. Agana is located at the narrow waist of the island. One can travel the northern portion of the island in two to three hours, sightseeing included. A similar trip around the south takes four to five hours.

Guam recently took steps that greatly improve the quality of sightseeing there. First, the Department of Public Works identified and named 65 sites of interest. It issued **The Island of Guam Official Highway Map,** a beautiful piece of work that is not only a road map but also gives a succinct explanation about each site. The map is available at no charge from the Department of Public Works, 542 N. Marine Dr., Tamuning, GU 96911, or from the Guam Visitors Bureau, P.O. Box 3520, Agana, GU 96932, 401 Pale San Vitores Rd., Tumon, GU 96911, tel. (671) 646-5278, fax (671) 646-8861, e-mail: gvbgm@ite.net, website: www.visitguam.org. Most hotels also have copies for free distribution.

At the same time, solid, concrete gazebos were erected at most sites; these make lovely spots at which to picnic or merely sit down and enjoy the day.

North of Agana
Above Tumon Bay, on Route 1 between 14A and 34 (pretty much opposite and above the Sotetsu Tropicana), is a small park dedicated to **Confucius.** There is a nice view of the bay, and it's about as restful as anything could be in this busy location.

Beyond the north end of Tumon Bay is **Two Lovers Point,** a 350-foot basalt cliff where two young Chamorro lovers are said to have tied

their hair together and jumped to their deaths to avoid separation. A deep cave drops to the sea.

Gun Beach, beyond the Hotel Nikko on Tumon Bay, directly below the cliffs, is a favorite for swimming, snorkeling, scuba diving, and surfing. There is a parking structure just past the Nikko. It is fairly easy to get out past the reef here, but check for currents. Tumon Bay curves around between Two Lovers Point and the Hilton.

Heading north, Routes 3, 9, 1 and 15 create a loop around the island's northern plateau. The land here is flat, with dense scrub vegetation. The road is not near the ocean, because the coast is controlled by Andersen Air Force Base.

One of Guam's most beautiful beaches, **Tarague Beach,** is located on the base, east of Guam's northernmost spot, Ritidian Point. The road to the beach is not open to the public. However, if you make friends on the island who are in the military or even work for the federal government in another capacity, they can visit the beach and take you in as their guest. The beach is lovely and never crowded. Do not swim outside the reef here because of the powerful Rota channel. Military personnel and their guests can camp.

To the northwest and accessible from Tarague Beach is privately held land. With luck you will see some of the lovely fica butterflies that congregate here.

Toward the end of the battle for Guam in 1944, the Japanese withdrew northward. They made their last stand near Yigo; **South Pacific Memorial Park** marks the spot. Lieutenant General Hideyoshi Obata, commanding general of the Japanese 31st Army, had his headquarters in a network of tunnels below the park. On 11 August 1944 American soldiers tossed white phosphorous hand grenades into the tunnels and sealed the openings with blocks of explosives. When the tunnels were reopened four days later, 60 Japanese bodies were found inside, though Obata was never identified. Several of the tunnels can still be seen at the bottom of the hill behind the monument.

On Route 15, just past the junction with 29 (after the base) is the Mangilao Golf Club. From here you can see long stretches of the rocky coastline.

At Mangilao, north of Pago Bay and overlooking the ocean, is the **University of Guam,** founded in 1952 as a teacher's college. The university houses the Micronesian Area Research Center (MARC), the most important collection of material for serious Micronesia scholars. The university also has a big arena, called the Field House, that serves as a convention site for Guam. On the nearby new fine arts building is a large mural worth a look.

If you follow Route 32 past campus to the end, you come to a parking lot in front of WERI, University of Guam Water and Energy Research Institute. Behind the building is a path to the ocean. There is often surf here good for boogie boarders; the waves look a little too tight for board surfers and the bottom too rocky for body surfers. Even boogie boarders should be careful and ask locals for advice on the rock situation. Alternatively, you can work your way around the shore to the right for some beautiful high tide snorkeling.

The South
You can cross to the east coast of Guam either on Route 4 out of Agana or Route 8 and then Route 10 from Tumon Bay. The following discussion traces a trip along Route 4 (on Guam's east coast), heading to the south of the island then back north on the west coast, where the road's name is changed to Route 2. The sites discussed at the end of this section, particularly the **War in the Pacific National Historical Park Visitor Center,** can be reached much more easily by heading southwest out of Agana.

Once you get away from the Tumon Bay/Agana area, the island is no longer overwhelmed by tourists. No simple primitive, unspoiled Guam exists. But down south, you see mostly Chamorro faces. In the countryside, houses are spread out and there is not the apparent, grinding poverty one sees on some other islands of Micronesia.

There are a good number of public beach parks, most with toilets and showers. Along the east coast there are also a fair number of beaches with family names on them. They are *private* and should not be used without permission. If you meet a family member, permission to use the beach will usually be given.

You can get a good view of the cliffs lining Guam's windy east coast from the road leading to **Tagachang Beach Park** just below Yona. The beach sign is behind some ironwood trees and is a bit difficult to see. There is a paved road heading down to the beach. The park has a pleasant covered picnic area. It is not a good place to swim. Waves break on a hard reef and there are frequently rips. **Ipan Beach Park** is about five miles farther south. The setting is not as pretty as Tagachang, but it is better for snorkeling.

Right past Ipan Beach is **Ipan Beach Resort.** The water is too shallow to do anything with except near high tide. However, the resort has a swimming pool, restaurant, and bar. Admission for the day is $10 adult, $5 child. You can also pitch a tent and stay for the night. This costs an

M.G.L. DOMENY DE RIENZI

a view of Umatac in the early 19th century

additional $15 per adult and $13 per child.

Before reaching Ipan, however, Route 17 leads across to **Tarzan Falls,** near the center of the island. It takes 20 minutes to hike down a muddy track to the crest of the falls, and then there's a slippery climb down the side to a pool. Watch out for the sharp sword grass. The bottom of Tarzan Falls is idyllic. Route 17 leads back to the west side of the island.

At the junction of Routes 4 and 4A, drive a bit up 4A, where you will be rewarded with one of the best views of the southern, volcanic portion of Guam. You will be looking down into Talofofo Bay and the river which flows into it.

Talofofo Bay Beach Park is at the mouth of the river. This makes the water a bit muddy for snorkelers or divers, but prevents coral growth creating a reliable shore break for surfing. On storm surge, a long right comes off the point and can get pretty hairy. What is remarkable about this beach is that locals, military personnel, and tourists seem to coexist. Even more remarkable, the same can be said of body surfers, boogie boarders, and board surfers, all of whom use this wave. The shore break is soft mud, except for a couple of obvious rocks.

Talafofo Falls Park and Yokoi Cave is a great example of how to wreck a spot of natural beauty; at $7, it defines the term "tourist trap." Called the Guam Cultural Center, it is surrounded by an imitation European medieval wall. Management is planning to build a gondola so that you can go directly from the parking lot to the falls with almost no contact with anything natural. As to the cave where Yokoi supposedly lived from the end of the war until 1972, the attendant said, "It's just a big hole. No big deal."

Saluglula Pool, a popular saltwater swimming hole, is right beside the road at **Inarajan.** Founded by Governor Quiroga in 1680, this is the best preserved village on Guam, so take time to stroll around. Father Jesus Baza Duenas, the Chamorro priest beheaded by the Japanese in 1944, is buried beneath the parish church.

Merizo is the halfway point around the island—about 22 miles either way from Agana. Busloads of Japanese tourists are sent over from Merizo to **Cocos Island Resort,** (671) 828-8691, in a shuttle boat. There is good snorkeling off the island. The admission price, including the roundtrip boat ride, is $20 adult, $10 child. No food or drinks are allowed to be brought in so you must buy them on the island. At additional cost, the island offers such activities as parasailing and jet skiing, so don't expect to find peace and quiet on the island. The resort also offers diving lessons.

The **rectory** (El Convento) in front of the Merizo village church was occupied by the parish priest beginning in 1856; across the road is a **bell tower** (Kampanayun Malessu) built in 1910. The **Massacre Monument** in front of the church memorializes 46 Chamorros murdered by Japanese troops near here as the American invasion became imminent.

Umatac village was the docking site used by the Manila galleons; several forts built here in the early 19th century protected the area from English pirates. It remains brightly flowered and painted as many towns were in the past. Magellan has been said to have landed at Umatac on 6 March 1521; there's a monument to record the event. However, more recent scholarship doubts that this was the actual landfall.

Fort San Jose was on the north side of the bay, **Fort Soledad** on the south; not much is left of either, but Fort Soledad has a great view as well as a few canons of indeterminate age and the remains of a building.

The main road turns inland between Umatac and Nimitz. The road climbs through the rugged volcanic country of the slopes of **Mt. Lamlam** (1,336 feet), Guam's highest peak. A viewpoint above Sella Bay looks down on grassy red ridges trailing into the sea. A trail departing from the **Cetti Bay Overlook** leads up to the large cross atop Mount Lamlam (45 minutes each way), with a sweeping view of the entire island. On Good Friday a religious procession parades to this cross. It's possible to hike south along the ridge back to Merizo or Inarajan.

The West

Fish Eye Marine Park features a round circular room with many windows beneath the surface of Piti Bay. It gives those who don't snorkel or dive a chance to see undersea life. Admission with lunch included is $38 adult, $25 child. More expensive packages are available, including one with a Polynesian-style show.

Apra Harbor, between Asan and Agat, is one of the largest protected harbors in the world.

Guam's commercial port is here, though most of the south side of the harbor is taken up by a giant U.S. naval base. At **Gaan Point,** Agat, a couple of guns and tunnels recall the World War II fighting. Just south of Nimitz Beach Park is **Taleyfac Bridge** (1785), part of the old Spanish road from Agana to Umatac.

From Nimitz Hill high above Piti, an excellent hike follows a jeep track south from Mount Chachao to the summit of **Mt. Tenjo** (1,030 feet) with panoramic views along the way. As you drive up to Nimitz Hill from Piti, turn right onto Larson Road, the next street after Trans World Radio, and right again on Turner Road. Keep straight as far as Mount Chachao where the road swings left to the relay station atop Mount Alulom. The rough jeep track to Mount Tenjo, impossible for a car, is straight ahead, a two hour hike roundtrip.

Heavy fighting took place near Agana in July 1944. The main landings were at Asan and Agat; the Japanese commander directed the defense from the Fonte Plateau above Asan. **War in the Pacific National Historical Park Visitor Center** at Asan, one and a half miles southwest of Agana, offers a photo display and a 15-minute slide show about the war (tel. 671-477-9362; open weekdays 9 a.m.-4:30 p.m., weekends from 10 a.m.-noon and 1-4.30 p.m.). Even if you are coming from the south, rather than from Agana, go to this interesting center to get oriented, before you double back to the actual battlefields.

PRACTICALITIES

ACCOMMODATIONS

The geography of Guam controls its hotel scene. Most hotel rooms are along beautiful but developed Tumon Bay, or adjacent to it at the north end of Agana Bay. Hotels on the beach are at luxury prices. Many are Japanese-owned, however, and fail to provide luxury services for English-speaking guests. On the other hand, other luxury hotels, which also cater primarily to a Japanese clientele, work well for English speakers. It is not mere ownership, nor the language of the employees. Rather, at some "Japanese" hotels the staff's knowledge of dive shops, fishing boats, and other island activities may be limited to businesses where the proprietors speak only Japanese.

The hotels on the inland side of Pale San Vitores Road front a busy commercial street and generally are lower priced. Behind is a cliff, the remains of an ancient raised reef. Hotels on or above the cliff are close to the beach, though they may be several hundred feet above, a healthy climb in a wet bathing suit. Nonetheless, these are some of the best values on Guam and can provide an excellent choice for budget travelers. This area up the cliff is called Tamuning toward the south end of the bay and Upper Tumon toward the north.

Virtually all rooms in Guam have air conditioning, private bath, color TV, and room phones. The most crowded months are February, March, and October through December.

Many of Guam's hotels, including luxury hotels, will offer substantial discounts. These discounts fall into four categories: corporate, local, military, and government. Nobody is ever quite clear about the exact requirements for each. For example, do you qualify if you are in Guam to visit someone in the military? Discount qualifications are determined, in part, by how many vacant rooms the hotel has at the time. Be sure to inquire, particularly if you are calling from Micronesia to make the reservation.

Tumon Beach Enclave

Guam is a wonderful place to relax and enjoy yourself, in luxury if you wish. Tumon Bay is not a carbon copy of Waikiki. Yes, there are high-rise eyesores. But the hotels do not crowd each other the way they do on Oahu. The beach itself is never crowded and appears to be cleaned every evening. Pale San Vitores Road, behind the beach hotels, has restaurants and both elegant and schlock shopping. Like the rest of the world, it has a Hard Rock Cafe, a Planet Hollywood, and a Tony Roma's.

GUAM COUNTRY CODE: 671

Built in the late 1960s and recently refurbished, the Hilton International Guam is one of the largest hotels on the island.

ANTHONY CORN

The bay itself, backed by green cliffs, is stunning. The water is quite shallow and most enjoyable for snorkeling at high tide. When the water is calm, and if you are ocean-wise, it is relatively easy to work your way outside the reef, where ocean life is more varied. Watch out for occasional strong currents. As usual in shallow water, make sure your feet are covered to avoid injuries from the sharp coral.

The best luxury hotel for Westerners is the refurbished, 691-room **Hilton Guam** (luxury) (P.O. Box 11199, Tamuning, GU 96931, tel. 671-646-1835, fax 671-646-6038). Reservations can be made through its website: www.guamhilton.com). Rooms begin at $175. The hotel is located on 32 acres along Ypao Beach on Tumon Bay. Its beachfront seems even longer because it sits next to a large beach park. Like all of Tumon Bay's hotels, the clientele is mainly Japanese. But there are substantial numbers of other guests, and the Japanese guests here are a bit younger and more likely to be independent travelers. It is fun to sit in the lobby with a drink or a coffee and watch the scene.

The Hilton's location and service make it an excellent place for a business stay as well as for a vacation. It has a health club and all necessary business equipment.

The **Pacific Star Hotel** (luxury) (P.O. Box 6097, Tamuning, GU 96931, tel. 671-649-7827, fax 671-646-9335) is an architecturally interesting 19-story pyramid. The hotel has a quiet atmosphere, less festive than most of the other

hotels on this stretch. Rooms begin at $230. Special features of the hotel are six restaurants and a 24 hour coffee shop, three bars, a computerized business center, and a complete health club on the premises.

The 448-room **Hyatt Regency Guam** (luxury) (1155 Pale San Vitores Rd., Tamuning, GU 96911, tel. 800-233-1234 or 671-647-1234, fax 671-647-1235, website: hyatt.com) is a recently constructed luxury hotel. Despite the American name, this $150-million Hyatt belongs to EIE International of Japan. It appears able to provide good service to English speakers, however. Its grounds are lovely and worth a visit even if you are not staying there. The pricey rooms run from $290, with a deep discount given to locals. Also fun to visit at the hotel is T.J.'s Mexican restaurant (open for dinner or drinks at 6 p.m., live music at 9:30 p.m.) or La Mirenda for buffet ($20-26, depending on the night).

The **Pacific Islands Club** (luxury) (P.O. Box 9370, Tamuning, GU 96931, tel. 671-646-9171, fax 671-649-2434) is a 32-story eyesore on Tumon Bay. Not only is the hotel an eyesore, it is an ear sore, with messages continually blasted in English and Japanese with sufficient volume to disturb those relaxing on the beach. Forced "fun" runs rampant at this resort. Rooms without meals begin at $200. Apparently others appreciate this hotel more than I do. Business has been good enough, presumably, for it to build a second tower during 1999.

On 1 June 1999 Hawaii's Outrigger chain opened its 600-room, beachfront **Outrigger Guam Resort** (luxury) (1255 Pale San Vitores Rd., Tumon Bay, GU 96911, tel. 671-649-9000, fax 671-647-9048). Rooms begin at $240. The easiest way to reach the hotel is through the Outrigger reservation number at (800) 688-7444 or through its website at www.outrigger.com.

On the beach is the **Fujita Guam Tumon Beach Hotel** (luxury) (153 Fujita Rd., Tumon, GU 96911, tel. 671-646-1811, fax 671-646-1605), with its sprawling, low-rise 283 rooms at $170 s, $180 d. This was the first hotel along Tumon Bay. The outside of many of the buildings are decorated with fantastic tile mosaics, some 30 feet tall. The hotel has a 24-hour laundromat. It is primarily for Japanese clientele.

Holiday Plaza Hotel (luxury) (P.O. Box 12639, Tamuning, GU 96932, tel. 671-649-8001, fax 671-646-3400) is across the street on the inland side from the Fujita Guam Tumon Beach Hotel. It is mainly set up for Japanese tour groups. Its regular rate is $150, but its "local rate" is $120 and its corporate rate is a bargain at $85 if you can get it. Just down the road toward Tamuning lies **Dai-Ichi Hotel** (very expensive) (P.O. Box 3310, Agana, GU 96910, tel. 671-646-5881, fax 671-646-6729), with 333 rooms at $180 for ocean view, $140 hillside. Directly adjacent **Sotetsu Tropicana Hotel** (luxury) (P.O. Box 8139, Tamuning, GU 96911, tel. 671-646-5851, fax 671-649-9342) has 198 rooms at $160.

Overlooking Tumon Bay is the 18-story **Guam Reef Hotel** (luxury) (P.O. Box 8258, Tamuning, GU 96931, tel. 671-646-6881, fax 671-646-5200), owned by Japan Air Lines. You get excellent views from the balconies of the 458 rooms at the Reef. Rooms begin at $200.

The **Guam Hotel Okura** (luxury) (185 Gun Beach Rd., Tumon, GU 96911, tel. 671-646-6811, fax 671-646-1403) is quite elegant with a large crystal chandelier hanging in the lobby and a convention/banquet facility seating 450 guests. The 366 rooms at the Okura begin at $160 s, $250 d. It is primarily for Japanese travelers.

Although the **Hotel Nikko Guam** (luxury) (P.O. Box 12819, Tamuning, GU 96931, tel. 671-649-8815, fax 671-649-8817) is on a cliff, directly below it is the beach, at an excellent spot for low tide reef walking. It probably has the most luxurious grounds of any of Guam's hotels. The building is architecturally interesting with big open spaces. Not all staff speak English. The 500 rooms begin at $200.

Palace Hotel Guam (luxury) (P.O. Box 12879, Tamuning, GU 96931, tel. 671-646-2222, fax 671-649-5211), on Oka Point, offers some fabulous views, seen from within its vacuous architecture. It is overpriced at its regular rate of $210 s, $230 d, and even at its "corporate rate" of $150.

Though across the street from the beach, the new **Sherwood Guam Resort** (expensive) (P.O. Box 10479, Tamuning, GU 96931, tel. 671-647-1188, e-mail: sherwood@hafa.net.gu) is a good buy at $105 s, $119 d.

Closer to Agana and to be avoided is **Alupang Beach Tower.** This hotel is trapped behind a fortress-like parking lot. The hotel is set down on a narrow stretch of beach. It's a great place to go if your idea of fun is watching and listening to jet skis driven in incessant circles.

Near Tumon Bay

One of Guam's best bargains is the **Polynesian Hotel** (inexpensive) (P.O. Box 9014, Tamuning, GU 96931, tel./fax 671-646-8209), with its 13 rooms above a convenience store, all units with kitchenettes. The hotel is not far from the airport. It is on Ypao Road, above the cliff, but only about one mile from the Hilton and the adjacent public beach park. Studios are $50, and bedroom units are $65. You will wish to rent a car if staying here. The Polynesian will also rent weekly at $260, monthly at $780.

Another choice for a less expensive hotel near the beach is the **Guam Regency Hotel** (moderate) (1475 Pale San Vitores Rd., Tumon Beach, GU 96911, tel. 671-649-8000, fax 671-646-8738), on the road going up the cliff from the Reef Hotel. This Korean-run hotel is popular with expats traveling to Guam from other parts of Micronesia and strives to give good personal service to all its guests. Most rooms have spectacular views of Tumon Bay and are quite reasonably priced, beginning at $95.

Behind the Guam Regency is **Hotel Sunroute Oceanview** (very expensive) (1433 Pale San Vitores Rd., Tumon, GU 96911, tel. 671-649-9670, fax 671-649-0562). All units have kitchens. A one-bedroom unit is $128 and a two bedroom $160. The hotel offers substantial discounts to corporate customers.

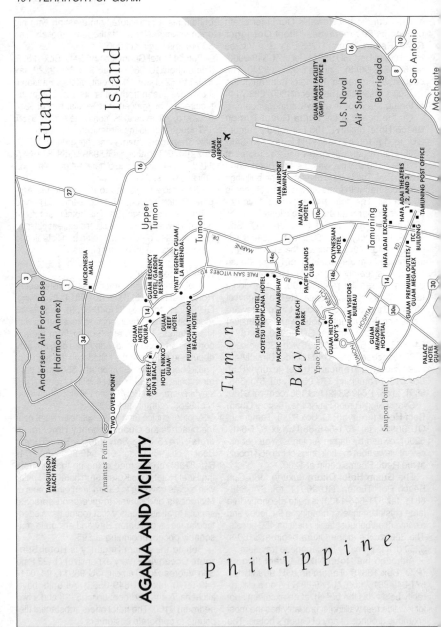

AGANA AND VICINITY

Guam Island

Philippine

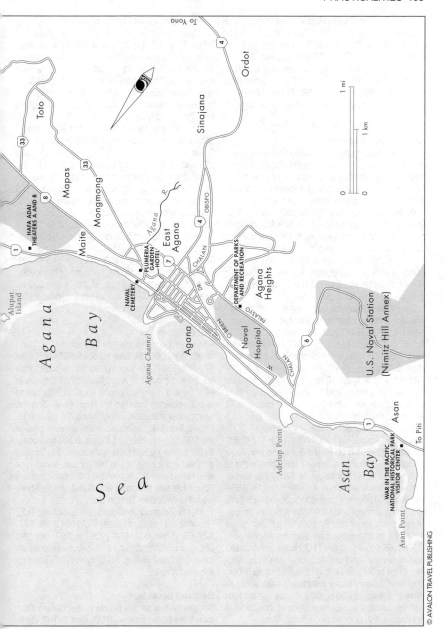

© AVALON TRAVEL PUBLISHING

The 520 room **Guam Plaza Hotel** (expensive) (P.O. Box 7755, Tamuning, GU 96911, tel. 671-646-7803, fax 671-646-3952) is up the hill from Pale San Vitores Road. Rooms begin at $110.

Farther up the hill is **Tumon Bay Capital Hotel** (moderate) (P.O. Box 10717, Tamuning, GU 96931, tel. 671-646-3903, fax 671-646-3902,. This small hotel is a very good buy at $75.

Other Agana Locales

Guam has a fair number of motels that Statesiders call "hot sheets motels" and the Japanese call "love hotels." Rooms can be rented by the hour. The difference in Guam is that these hotels usually have a number of rooms, perhaps a whole floor, dedicated to other use. Morality aside, most such hotels are not well kept, and the foot traffic is annoying. Hotels bearing a neon sign proclaiming "24 hours" usually fall into this category.

At any rate, there are a fair number of inexpensive hotels in and near Agana without the above drawbacks. Even if not luxurious, they may be suitable for a business visit.

On Route 8, about a quarter mile up from Marine Drive is the **Plumeria Garden Hotel** (inexpensive) (P.O. Box 7863, Tamuning, GU 96931, tel. 671-472-8831, fax 671-477-4914), under very pleasant new management. It is a motel-style establishment with lots of parking. It has 78 rooms at $50 s, $55 d, and offers discounts for stays of a week and longer. A laundromat is on the premises. This is a decent place, built around a swimming pool.

The **Maite Garden Hotel** (inexpensive) (P.O. Box 2925, Agana, GU 96910, tel. 671-477-0861, fax 671-477-0844) on Route 8, behind the Maite Shopping Town Plaza, has 47 units beginning at $55 s, $63 d. Suites begin at $75. Also sometimes available are units with kitchens for $650 per month. This may be a good choice for a family visiting someone in the military. Some people at reception know little English, which can make it difficult to arrange a stay over the phone.

The 45 rooms of the **ITC Hotel** are located on the seventh and eighth floor of an office building. (The hotel's desk is on the ninth floor.) This odd hotel is very funky but clean, safe, and relatively cheap at $55 s, $66 d. Ask for a room with an ocean view. Each room is air conditioned and has a TV, phone, and refrigerator.

The low-rise **Cliff Hotel** (moderate) (178 Francisco Javier Dr., Agana Heights, GU 96910, tel. 671-477-7276, fax 671-477-1044) is located near the old governor's mansion above central Agana. For $70 you'll get one of the 17 regular rooms; for $110, one of the larger units with cooking facilities. All rooms have individual balconies, most with spectacular views of Agana and Tumon Bay behind it.

The closest hotel to the airport is the **Hotel Mai'Ana** (moderate) (253 Chalan Pasaheru St., Tamuning, GU 96911, tel. 671-646-6961, fax 671-649-3230), good if you need a place for the night. It has free pick-up and drop-off at the airport. The U-shaped, three-story building (78 rooms) encloses a pleasant courtyard with pool. Studios with cooking facilities are $80, while spacious two-bedroom apartments go for $99. A second choice is the **Guam Airport Hotel** (expensive) (P. O. Box 10239, Tamuning, GU 96931, tel. 671-649-8402, fax 671-649-8401). We think it's less desirable because of its location on a noisy street. It charges slightly more, $92 for a studio and $102 for a one-bedroom, and also has free pick-up and drop-off.

Out of Town

Aston Inn on the Bay (expensive) (P.O. Box 8390, Agat, GU 96928, tel. 671-565-8521, fax 671-565-8527), a modern beachfront hotel to the south on the coast at Agat, has kitchen facilities in all rooms. It is the only hotel south of Agana and is conveniently located for families visiting the nearby naval station. Considering the kitchen facilities, it is quite reasonable: ocean-view studios are $96, one-bedrooms $110, and two-bedrooms $123. Military guests get a discount. It is located on the beach side of the main road. It has nice snorkeling and fishing out the front door, but is a 20-minute ride to Agana and about one half-hour from the airport or Tumon Bay.

Hotel Palmridge Guam (inexpensive) (122 Hasalao Street, Barrigada, GU 96913, tel. 671-477-6666, fax 671-472-7931) is $50, but also offers a military discount. It is conveniently located for those visiting the University of Guam on the east shore.

Bed and Breakfast

An alternative to the hotels is the **Guam Garden Villa** (inexpensive) (P.O. Box 10167, Sinajana, GU 96926, tel. 671-477-8166) at 193 Ramirez Dr., Ordot, off Route 4 southeast of Agana. This local homestay is run by Mrs. Herta K. Laguana, a German expat married to Romy, a local Chamorro. The charge for bed and breakfast is $40 s, $60 d with shared bath. Book well in advance—there are only three rooms and they're usually taken. Airport transfers are available at $10 each way, but you're better off renting a car upon arrival as the house, on spacious, flower-filled grounds, is isolated. It's also hard to find, so call Herta for detailed directions.

South of Agana in Piti, you can also call Ann Concepcion, who rents inexpensive rooms adjacent to her shop, the Treasure Chest (tel. 671-472-8380) in Piti. Ann and her husband are extremely helpful hosts.

Camping

Camping is allowed in all public parks administered by the **Department of Parks and Recreation,** and there are usually sites available. Call the office at (671) 475-6288 or fax (671) 477-2822. You need a camping permit, which costs $2 pp and can be picked up from 8 a.m. to 5 p.m. at Building 13-8, Tiyan, near the airport. Most sites have running water and a shower. Many also have shelters that can be rented for an additional $10 a day.

The accessible parks include Tanguisson Beach Park (near Two Lovers Point), Ypao Beach Park (Tumon Bay), Afflege Park (Agat), Nimitz Beach Park (Agat), Fort Soledad (Umatac), Saluglula Pool (Inarajan), Talofofo Beach Park (Talofofo), Ipan Beach Park (Talofofo), Tagachang Beach Park (Yona), and Francisco F. "Gonga" Perez Park (Pago Bay). At Fort Soledad pitch your tent inside the walls of the old Spanish fort. You may also camp anywhere in Guam Territorial Seashore Park (administered by Parks and Recreation), which includes much of the coast between Merizo and Nimitz Beach.

Remember that it's unwise to leave your tent unattended. Be prepared to be blasted by high volume music from cars parked nearby at night.

FOOD AND ENTERTAINMENT

Guam has a large number of excellent restaurants. Since most food, other than fresh fish, is imported, restaurants in all price categories will be more expensive than comparable dining Stateside. Some rules to lessen the burden:

- Food is more expensive in luxury hotels than in freestanding restaurants.
- Japanese food, particularly in hotels, is very expensive. Don't expect to have dinner for less than $50. (These prices still seem fairly cheap to tourists from Tokyo.)
- In hotels, a buffet is your best buy, particularly if it becomes your only serious meal of the day.
- Lunch buffets are cheaper than dinner buffets.
- Food is cheaper off Tumon Bay than on it.
- Beer is cheaper than wine.
- Stands are less expensive than sit-down restaurants.

Agana

In the **Chamorro Village,** by the Agana waterfront, are many food shops featuring the different ethnic cuisines of the people of Guam. They are located around a shaded center court with tables, a lovely spot to have an inexpensive lunch. Try **Terry's Chamorro Food Stand,** with such dishes as chicken, beef, or shrimp Kelaguen; fried fish; or Filipino-like Pancit. And yes, you can get a cappucino at **Cafe Latte.**

Shirley's Coffee Shop, located on West Marine Drive, is a local institution. Particularly at breakfast, it is a place where local businesspeople put together deals. Breakfasts are about $5. At lunch, sandwiches run $3-4. For lunch or dinner, Chinese dishes average about $7, a bit more for steak or salmon. Shirley's serves up good food at a reasonable price in a lively atmosphere.

The waterfront **Pacific Cafe,** located on Marine Drive offers outstanding Meditarranean style food for moderate prices.

Despite the unpretentious appearance, the **Mini Cafe** is very popular for its weekday Cantonese lunch combination specials.

Sizzler Steak House at the Agana Shopping Center has a good salad bar and fairly inexpensive steaks. In the center is also **Hava Java Cafe,** a comfortable coffee house.

In the Julale Shopping Arcade, the **Korea Palace** stylishly serves excellent and extremely authentic Korean food. Its crowd is mainly local. Lunches cost about $10. Complete dinners run $15-20. Call ahead at (671) 472-4000 if you wish to reserve a Korean-style "tearoom." For budget eats in the same arcade, try the counter at the **Doughnut Tree,** where a two-choice lunch, including fried chicken, fried noodles, or fried rice will cost $5.

House of Chin Fee on the west edge of town serves Filipino dishes as well as Chinese. The best deal is the special for $16.95 that includes big portions of three dishes as well as two bowls of rice. It is surrounded by tacky nightclubs and massage parlors in an unsavory part of town, but it does have an adjacent parking lot.

Tamuning/Upper Tumon
Guam is loaded with franchise eateries: **Taco Bell, Wendy's, Popeye's, Kentucky Fried Chicken, Shakey's, Pizza Hut.** They are inexpensive by Guam standards. Upscale chains also have arrived—**Tony Roma's, Lone Star Restaurant, Outback Steakhouse** and the ubiquitous **Hard Rock Cafe** and **Planet Hollywood.**

In the old Gibson's Guam Shopping Center were about a dozen shops around a central eating area where you could get inexpensive Chamorro, Vietnamese, Korean, and Chinese dishes. While Gibson's has been replaced by the mega **Guam Premium Outlets,** there is a plan for the old food court to be reopened. **King's Restaurant** (open 24 hours) survived the closure of Gibson's. It offers weekday breakfast specials. The portions are huge and it's very popular with locals.

Food served in the luxury hotels can be excellent but expensive. Perhaps the most inventive food is at elegant **Roy's** at the Hilton. Another choice favored by many locals is **Hy's Steakhouse** in the Parc Hotel, also very elegant and very expensive.

As we discussed above, most luxury hotels offer scrumptious buffets at least some of the days of the week. The meals will not be inexpensive, but often offer very good value. **La Mirenda** at the Hyatt has a buffet each night. Most nights the buffet is $20, but on Wednesday and Sunday when there is even more seafood than usual, the price is $26. The **Mabuhay,** located in the Pacific Star Hotel, has a Filipino buffet on Saturday nights for $22. The **Guam Regency Hotel** has a varied and filling Asian lunch buffet for $7. The **Parc Hotel** has a terrific lunch buffet in its main lobby for $9.50.

Many hotels have dinner shows including Polynesian-style music and dancing. Staged primarily for Japanese tourists, these shows are usually quite expensive and have nothing to do with Chamorro culture.

The rooftop **Garden Restaurant** at the Guam Regency Hotel serves up great Korean food in an outdoor setting, overlooking Tumon Bay. The prices are moderate if you stay away from the pre-arranged dinners served to Korean tour groups.

On West Marine Drive, past the ITC building as you head north, is the **Hafa Adai Exchange,** rebuilt on its prior site after being destroyed by

overlooking Tumon Bay

fire. At this market, many small clothing and sundries shops have small stalls. Spread throughout are a number of restaurants. Above it, immediately to the north, are two interesting restaurants. **Lieng's Restaurant** is a decent mid-priced Vietnamese restaurant. Next to it is the **Islands Fisherman Kamayan Restaurant,** a Filipino-style seafood restaurant that is large enough to be a stop for tour buses. Dinners are excellent but very expensive. One walks through a serving line, chooses one's dishes, and pays by the ounce. It is very easy to run up a $75 bill. Even the set dinners for parties of six run $45 pp. But the restaurant also has a lunch buffet from 11 a.m.-1:30 p.m. that offers salads, rice, chicken, beef, fish, and usually shrimp and crab. It is a great bargain at $11.50. Try to get to the restaurant before 12:30 p.m., when the tour buses begin to arrive.

Around Guam

Jeff's Pirates Cove (closed Monday), just north of Ipan Beach Park on the east coast, is a fun place to stop for lunch when driving around the island. Many tour buses stop here, so it's not cheap. The cold beer at the bar is fairly priced, and between bus arrivals, it is a pleasant place to sit and watch the scenery. The bar is open air, and there is a volleyball court you are welcome to use.

Entertainment

Karaoke (video sing-along) is still the rage at many bars and restaurants on Guam. Hostesses, working for tips, are often available to sing along with you. (In some places, they are available for more than that).

Tumon's most glitzy dinner theater and discotheque is the **Sand Castle,** tel. (671) 649-7469, next to the Hyatt Regency Hotel in Tumon. This $30-million entertainment center features a Las Vegas-style musical revue dinner show at 7 p.m. nightly except Wednesday. It's $90 pp, $50 for the show alone. The Sand Castle also contains the 750-person capacity **Onyx Disco.**

The luxury hotels have bars and usually discos.

Guam now receives first-run movies just days after they are released Stateside. Located in the same shopping center as the Guam Premium Outlets building is **Guam Megaplex,** with 10 or more movies showing. Right up the street is

Hafa Adai 1, 2 & 3. On Marine Drive is **Hafa Adai A & B.**

SPORTS AND RECREATION

Guam's greatest attraction is its surrounding sea, for snorkelers, surfers, kayakers, or just plain swimmers and beach loafers. It is an excellent dive site with much to see. Moreover, it is a good place for a "shakedown" dive if you are just arriving in Micronesia. If you have any difficulty with your equipment, it can often be repaired in Guam, which is not the case on more remote dive sites. If you need to replace equipment, it can be purchased duty free. And for the more casual diver, without equipment, it's safe to rent from the established dive shops.

Prices are competitive among the major dive shops. A two-tank dive will cost about $90. Most shops will offer "locals" a cheaper price, especially if the diver is experienced and needs little supervision.

Guam Tropical Dive Station (P.O. Box 1649, Agana, GU 96932, tel. 671-477-2774, fax 671-477-2775, e-mail: gtds@ite.net) is run by the knowledgeable John Bent, whose dive shop is on Marine Drive opposite Ace Hardware at the south end of Agana. This excellent and very professional shop offers one-tank night dives, as well as the more usual two-tank day dives, at $95 including gear.

The biggest dive operator on Guam is the **Micronesian Divers Association** (856 N. Marine Dr., Piti, GU 96925, tel. 671-472-6321, fax 671-477-6329, e-mail: mda@mdaguam.com, website: www.mdaguam.com) founded in 1975 by Pete Peterson. They frequent Blue Hole, Haps Reef, Crevice, and the twin shipwrecks in Apra Harbor. MDA is located in Piti but will pick up at hotels.

MDA also arranges kayaking trips. The cost is $25 for a half day, $40 for a full day. Kayaking can be done near the shop on Piti Bay. However, for those who wish to explore, MDA can coordinate a hike and a kayak trip.

A third dive shop, located in Agat, is **Professional Sports Divers of Guam** (P.O. Box 8630, Agat, GU 96928, tel. 671-565-3488, fax 671-565-3633, e-mail:psdivers@kuentos.guam.net).

Scuba Locales

Guam's proximity to the Marianas Trench means the offshore waters are constantly flushed, resulting in 200-foot visibility in the dry season, 100-foot plus in the wet. There are also 15 to 20 good walk-in locations.

Bile Bay on the southwest coast provides a gradual slope out, and some cave diving. Farther north a Japanese **Zero aircraft** rests in 60 feet of water off Umatac Point.

Blue Hole is just off the south side of Orote Point, right under the cliffs. Near Blue Hole is the Crevice, also an exciting experience.

A navigational buoy in **Apra Harbor** marks two wrecks next to each other at about 100 feet: the WW I German auxiliary cruiser SMS *Cormoran* and the WW II Japanese freighter *Tokai Maru*. This is one of the few places in the world where vessels from the two World Wars can be seen on a single dive. Visibility, however, is usually better at the wreck of a sunken U.S. tanker one and a half miles farther out. Apra Harbor also has several nice reef dives.

Guam's most colorful dive spot is **Double Reef** off Uruno Point near the northwest end of the island. Two parallel reefs about 1,000 feet apart have a channel 40 to 60 feet deep between them, with excellent visibility of the fine coral beneath.

To learn more about the dive sites of Guam, order the excellent *Dive! Snorkel! Kayak! Hike!* written by Virginia Jones and Pete Peterson of MDA. It can be ordered through MDA, listed above. It costs US$14.95 and an extra US$1 if it is to be mailed to outside the United States.

Hiking

Hiking in Guam? Better believe it. One can hike to waterfalls, along the beach, or to interior waterfalls. Forty hikes and their degrees of difficulty are set out in the excellent **The Best Tracks on Guam,** by David Lotz, former Guam Parks Administrator. The book is $15.50, which works out to 39 cents a hike. It's readily available in Guam bookstores or from Making Tracks, P.O. Box 20721, Barrigada, GU 96961.

Golf

Guam has many 18-hole public courses to accommodate golf enthusiasts. The most "local" and established of them is the **Country Club of the Pacific** (tel. 671-789-1362), which opened in 1971. It's in pleasant rolling countryside just north of Ipan Beach on Route 4 south of Yona. Greens fees are $85 weekdays, $110 weekends. If you want to do only nine holes it's cheaper. The clubhouse is impressive.

Similar, though slightly less impressive, is the **Takayama** or **Windward Hills Golf Club** (tel. 671-789-1612). It's located west of Talofofo in the center of the island, a bargain at $25 weekdays, $35 weekends. Prices can be considerably higher in busy tourist seasons.

A slick modern course popular with Japanese tourists is the **Hatsuho International Country Club** (tel. 671-632-0362) on Route 9 in northern Guam. A round of golf here will cost $110 weekdays and $150 weekends and holidays.

On Route 15, past the junction with 29, is the **Mangilao Golf Club** (tel. 671-734-1121) overlooking the ocean. With its rocky coastline and magnificent sights, it's not quite Pebble Beach, but close, which probably accounts for the high fees. Prices are $150 weekdays, $190 weekends. This is $10 a hole, or for most golfers, approximately $2 per shot. Off-island visitors must make reservations.

The **Leo Palace Resort** (tel. 671-888-0001) in Manengon Hills, Pulantat, Yona charges fees of $130 weekdays, $170 weekends.

You should call ahead to each course to check whether reservations are necessary. A dozen golf tournaments a year are held on Guam.

INFORMATION AND SERVICES

Shopping

Guam provides a good number of shopping malls and department stores if you need to restock and refit. Try the **Agana Shopping Center,** the **Ben Franklin Department Store, K-Mart** or the **Micronesia Mall** at the intersection of Routes 1 and 16 in Upper Tumon. This mall is Guam's biggest shopping center, anchored by a **Liberty House.** A shuttle bus connects Tumon Bay tourist hotels to the Micronesia Mall every 30 minutes.

In Tumon Bay you can find goods by Chanel, Lorenz, Hermes, Cartier, Gucci, Ferragamo—all the usual suspects of world hot spots. **Duty Free Shoppers** has more than 10 stores on Guam.

Visas

Entry requirements are similar to those for the rest of the United States: anyone not American needs a passport. People from most countries also need a visa. Visitors from certain countries now do not need a visa for stays of up to 15 days, and visitors from a few countries can stay without a visa for 90 days. Check with an American embassy or consulate in your home country.

American citizens need only show proper identification, such as a certified birth certificate or voter's registration card, if arriving directly from the States. Nonetheless, we urge any American traveling here to avoid possible confusion by carrying a passport. All passengers flying from Guam to Hawaii must pass U.S. Immigration controls at Honolulu.

Money, Measurements, and Services

Guam has many banks, the most ubiquitous one being the Bank of Guam. Banking hours at most Guam banks are Mon.-Thurs. 10 a.m.-3 p.m., Friday 10 a.m.-6 p.m., and Saturday 9 a.m.-1 p.m. Major credit cards are accepted at most business establishments. The American Express office is at 207 Martyr St., Agana, GU 96910, tel. 671-472-8884. You can receive mail at this office provided you have American Express traveler's checks or credit card; registered letters and parcels are not accepted.

United States domestic postal rates apply in Guam, making this a cheap, dependable place to mail things. General delivery mail is held at the inconveniently located Guam Main Facility (GMF) post office on Route 16 in Barrigada. The Tamuning post office behind the ITC Building is open weekdays and Saturday morning. For postal information call 671-734-3921. For Guam postal codes see the appendix at the back of the book.

Guam is finally on the U.S. phone "grid." This has drastically reduced phone rates from Stateside, with rates as low as 16 cents per minute. It also means you can now access toll-free numbers (800, 888, etc.) when in Guam. Remember, Guam's a day ahead of the rest of the United States, so if it's noon Monday in Merizo it's 7 p.m. Sunday in Seattle.

The electric current, as in the rest of the United States, is 110-120 volts AC, 60 cycles.

Information

The Guam Visitors Bureau (401 Pale San Vitores Rd., Tumon, GU 96911, tel. 671-646-5278, fax 671-646-8861, e-mail: gvbgm@ite.net, website: www.visitguam.org) is a great source of information. Ask for the excellent *The Island of Guam Official Highway Map, A Guide to the War in the Pacific Sites,* and William H. Stewart's *Pacific Explorer's Map of Guam,* all available free of charge. The Bureau's accommodations list is helpful, but it only includes information about members, not the cheapest places.

For an informative brochure on Guam's WW II history write: War in the Pacific National Historic Park, P.O. Box FA, Agana, GU 96910.

Weather information is available by dialing 117.

The **N.M. Flores Memorial Library** (254 Martyr St., Agana, GU 96910, tel. 671-472-6417) is open Monday, Wednesday, and Friday 9:30 a.m.-6 p.m.; Tuesday and Thursday 9:30 a.m.-8 p.m.; Saturday 10 a.m.-4 p.m.

Faith Book Store in the Agana Shopping Center specializes in books of Christian interest. It also has a first-rate section on Guam and Micronesia, including topographical maps. Located in the same center is the **Bookseller** store. In addition to its selection of books, the Sunday *New York Times* is available on the following Tuesday. For a list of academic publications write: Micronesian Area Research Center, University of Guam, UOG Station, Mangilao, GU 96923.

Guam has a good newspaper, the *Pacific Daily News* (P.O. Box DN, Agana, GU 96910), owned by the Gannett chain. It circulates throughout Micronesia. *Guam Business News* can fill you in on the local business and economic scene.

If you need to see a doctor, try the new **Guam Memorial Hospital,** located on Oka Point, near the Palace Hotel at 850 Governor Carlos Rd., Oka, Tamuning, GU 96911, tel. 671-647-2939.

GETTING THERE

Won Pat International Airport (GUM) at Tamuning is just a few miles from the Tumon Bay resorts. There's no bus service, and taxis to the hotels cost about $10-15. Gone is the sleepy airport of just a few years ago—it has been greatly expanded and updated. It now looks like any other modern airport, except, of course, for the views out over the ocean, wonderful permanent artwork, and ancient artifacts exhibited by the Guam Museum.

Continental Airlines (tel. 671-647-6453 or 800-231-0856, fax 671-646-9219) uses the new Guam airport as a transportation hub. **Air Nauru** (tel. 671-649-7107), **All Nippon Airways** (tel. 671-642-5555), **Japan Air Lines** (tel. 671-646-6245), and **Northwest Airlines** (tel. 800-225-2525) also provide service.

Travelers transiting Guam between Hawaii or the FSM and Yap, Koror, or Saipan have to change planes here, which often requires an overnight stay. The terminal is open 24 hours a day.

All **Continental Airlines** flights terminate on Guam. You can fly Los Angeles to Guam with a stop only in Honolulu for about $1,000. (Reduced fares are sometimes available). Continental's Island Hopper service between Honolulu and Guam stops en route at Majuro, Kwajalein, Kosrae, Pohnpei, and Chuuk. If you are coming from the U.S. mainland or Hawaii and going to Yap or Palau, it is cheapest to purchase a through ticket rather than separate tickets first to Guam and then to Palau. Points in Asia served by Continental directly from Guam include Denpasar (Bali), Hong Kong, Manila, and many Japanese cities.

All Nippon Airways, Continental Airlines, Japan Air Lines, and Northwest Airlines fly from Tokyo. Continental also serves Fukuoka, Nagoya, Okinawa, Osaka, Sapporo, and Sendai. Japan Air Lines has nonstop flights from Nagoya and Osaka. Northwest arrives from Fukuoka and Nagoya. JAL and Northwest offer direct connections to Guam from many North American cities like Tokyo (Narita), instead of the usual Los Angeles to Honolulu routing. Regular charters come from major Asian cities.

Both Continental Airlines and Freedom Air (tel. 671-647-8359, fax 671-649-2241) have regular service to Saipan.

GETTING AROUND

Unless you are planning not to leave your hotel and its grounds, you should consider renting a car. Cabs are quite expensive, and even two short round-trips a day will probably cost more than a car rental for the day.

When driving in Guam, be patient. It has the longest red light intervals on earth.

Many car rental agencies such as Avis (tel. 671-646-2847 or 800-331-1084), Budget (tel. 671-649-1243), Dollar (tel. 671-646-7000), Gordon's (tel. 671-565-5827), Hertz (tel. 671-642-3210 or 800-654-3131), Islander (tel. 671-632-6733), National (tel. 671-649-0110), and Toyota (tel. 671-646-1872) have offices on Guam. Their rates are fairly standard: beginning at about $40 a day with unlimited mileage, plus five percent tax. Always ask if they have any special discounted or business rates, or lower rates for older cars without air conditioning. Avis, Budget Hertz, Islander, and Toyota have locations at the airport.

Guam has an extensive **public bus system.** To use it, be prepared to spend a lot of time waiting. The system operates along nine routes, with important transfer stations at Micronesia Mall, Gibson's Guam Shopping Center, and the Agana Shopping Center. One of the most useful routes for visitors is the hourly Express Line from Micronesia Mall to the Tumon Bay tourist strip, then up to Tamuning, and down Marine Drive to the Agana Shopping Center. This service will stop anywhere along its route, so just flag down a bus.

Route PT-3 from Micronesia Mall to Guam Premium Outlet via Marine Drive runs only six times a day. Routes PT-4 and PT-5 from the Agana Shopping Center to the University of

Guam run once an hour. Routes PT-6 and PT-7 from the Agana Shopping Center do a circular loop around southern Guam seven times a day in opposite directions. This two-hour ride is Guam's best bargain island tour, and you can easily stop off at points along the way after confirming onward bus times with the driver.

Fares are $1 per ride or $3 for an all-day unlimited ride pass. Service ends around 7 p.m. and there are no buses on Sunday and holidays. For further information, call 671-475-7433 or pick up printed schedules at the Agana office of the Guam Mass Transit Authority, 236 East O'Brien Drive.

> *Raindrops hit water causing concentric circles before returning.*

GORDON OHLIGER

COMMONWEALTH OF THE NORTHERN MARIANAS
INTRODUCTION

The Commonwealth of the Northern Mariana Islands (CNMI) stretches north from Guam in a 426-mile-long chain. The 14 islands are weathered tips of a massive mountain range rising more than six miles from the depths of the Marianas Trench.

Saipan is the business, government, and tourism center, while Rota is a place even Saipan dwellers go for a nice quiet weekend. Tinian is attempting to redefine itself from a rural backwater to an international gambling destination. These islands (along with northern Guam) are all raised coral reefs, with level terraces and coral reefs.

Saipan is the largest and most populous island in the Commonwealth of the Northern Marianas. Because the United States won its war with Japan, CNMI now has roughly the same status and relationship with the United States as Puerto Rico. But more than 85% of its tourists (tourism is the major industry) are Japanese,

with less than five percent being American. More store signs are in Japanese than English; fewer still are in Chamorro, the native language.

The Land

Saipan, the second largest of the Mariana Islands, is a 14- by five-mile block with towering cliffs on the north, east, and south, and gentle hills rolling toward white sandy beaches on the west. A barrier reef protects the wide western lagoon, making this side of the island the favorite of swimmers, snorkelers, and windsurfers. Sunsets seen from these beaches are spectacular.

Except for a short stretch at Laulau, no reefs are off the east coast. Huge waves fanned by the northeast trades often crash into this shoreline during Saipan's winter (November to April), cutting deep scars. Small bays, tidal pools, blowholes, and craters dot the rocky, broken east coast. The highest cliffs are in the Marpi area of northeast Saipan, entwined with the tragic events of war in 1944.

Rota and Tinian, the other big islands of the Marianas, are geologically similar to Saipan, with Rota especially noted for its majestic coastline and upland plateaus. The towering northern islands, some still active volcanoes, are mostly uninhabited. There have been eruptions on Uracas, Asuncion, Pagan, and Guguan this century.

The Marianas Trench just east of the chain is the deepest of the world's trenches, a circular arc extending 1,865 miles from Japan to Ulithi atoll. The 47-mile-wide trench was discovered in 1899 when the Nero Deep was sounded at 31,702 feet. It's eight times longer, six times deeper, and two and a half times wider than the Grand Canyon, and as deep as Mount Everest is high. The islands of the Marianas are thus sitting on mountains taller than any on earth's surface.

Climate

The Marianas are the sunniest islands in Micronesia, though there is significant rain from July to September. From January to March conditions are best for swimmers and sailboarders. This is also the period when most tourists arrive to escape the Japanese winters. The northeast trades blow across the Marianas from November to March; easterly winds predominate from May to October. The Marianas get an average of one typhoon a year, usually between July and January.

Flora and Fauna

Saipan isn't as lush a tropical island as those farther south. To prevent erosion, the Americans sowed *tangan tangan* brush from aircraft over the defoliated landscape soon after the war. Saipan's soil was saved, but the *tangan tangan* has choked out indigenous plants. Still, there are lovely hikes to take. The flame or poinciana trees along Saipan's Beach Drive, as well as in the interior, bloom red and orange from May through August, a wonderful sight.

HISTORY

Early History

The earliest known archaeological remains are thought to date from about 2000 B.C.E. The

THE MARIANAS AT A GLANCE

	LAND AREA (SQ. MI.)	HIGHEST POINT (FEET)
Northern Marianas	184.51	3,175
Agrihan	18.30	3,175
Aguijan	2.78	553
Alamagan	4.36	2,448
Anatahan	12.47	2,593
Asuncion	2.82	2,931
Farallon de Medinilla	0.35	266
Guguan	1.62	990
Maug Islands	0.81	750
Pagan	18.65	1,882
Rota	32.90	1,615
Saipan	47.45	1,550
Sarigan	1.93	1,806
Tinian	39.30	612
Uracas	0.77	1,050
Guam	208.88	1,336

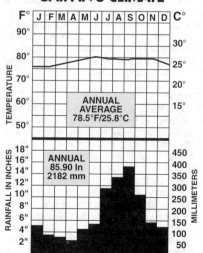

SAIPAN'S CLIMATE

ANNUAL AVERAGE 78.5°F/25.8°C

ANNUAL 85.90 In 2182 mm

people of Guam and the Northern Marianas were of one culture. They lived in small beach villages organized into matrilineal clans. Children belonged to the clan of the mother, and inheritance was through the female line. Colonialism altered this organization.

In 1668 Charles II of Spain dispatched Jesuit missionaries to Guam and named the island group for his mother, Queen Maria Ana of Austria. The Spanish defeated the Chamorros in 1689, after decades of heroic resistance, and relocated them to Guam where they could be more easily controlled. There they intermarried with the Spanish, adopting much Spanish culture.

In 1816, Chamorros began to return to the Northern Marianas, where they found communities of Carolinians from Lamotrek and Woleai had established themselves in their absence. The two cultures have lived peacefully through the generations, but to a considerable degree have maintained separate identities to this day.

Germany purchased the Northern Marianas in 1899 from Spain, which was afraid of losing the islands to the Americans. Governor Fritz built roads and required every family to plant food crops.

Japan seized the islands from Germany in 1914. It encouraged a migration of Japanese, Okinawans, and Koreans to develop large-scale sugarcane cultivation. The Nanyo Kohatsu Kaisha (South Seas Development Co., Ltd.) also built sugar mills fed by extensive rail networks. By 1938, and in clear violation of the League of Nations mandate, Asians outnumbered Micronesians almost 10 to one. Garapan on Saipan, the Japanese capital of the Marianas, had a Japanese population of 15,000.

The War

In 1941, the Japanese took a calculated gamble—they bet they could destroy the United States' ability to make war at sea in one decisive battle, allowing Japan to continue with her primary objective of domination of Indonesia and mainland Asia. The gamble failed. Over the next three years the United States simply out-produced Japan. By 1944 the outcome of the war was clear, as was the fact that the United States would accept nothing less than an unconditional Japanese surrender.

In June and July 1944 the United States took the Marianas from the Japanese. The landings at

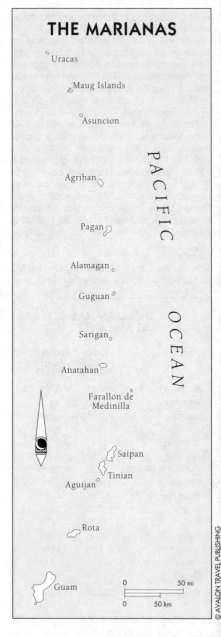

THE MARIANAS

Uracas

Maug Islands

Asuncion

PACIFIC

Agrihan

Pagan

Alamagan

Guguan

OCEAN

Sarigan

Anatahan

Farallon de Medinilla

MOON

Saipan

Tinian

Aguijan

Rota

0   50 mi

0   50 km

DAVID STANLEY

It is difficult to reconcile the beauty of Suicide Cliff with its deadly history.

Chalan Kanoa on the southwest side of Saipan led to a brutal three-week struggle for the island. After securing the south, the GIs began fighting their way up both sides of the island, hoping to meet on the Marpi plain below what was to become known as Suicide Cliff.

On 19 June the Japanese Navy sent three Zero-laden aircraft carriers to rescue their forces. The United States had no less than 16 carriers waiting west of the Marianas. During the Battle of the Philippine Sea, 402 Japanese planes and all three carriers were destroyed in a single day, against a loss of only 17 U.S. aircraft.

On 6 July the remaining Japanese troops, with little firepower left, launched a fanatical charge across the Tanapag plains, which continued until all 5,000 Japanese attackers had been killed. Of the 30,000-man Japanese garrison on Saipan, about 600 survived to be repatriated in 1945. Thousands of Japanese soldiers died making suicide attacks on the American forces. Hundreds of Japanese civilians tragically leapt to their death, jumping into the ocean from Banzai Cliff or onto land beneath Suicide Cliff, pushing their children ahead of them. More than 3,000 Americans were killed and another 11,000 wounded during the campaign. Some 419 Saipanese also died. Japanese memorials now stand at the base of Suicide and Banzai Cliffs. They praise loyalty, sacrifice, and courage, but no memorial attests to the stupidity of a world in which children are pushed off cliffs.

With Saipan in their hands, the United States landed on Guam on 21 July and Tinian on 24 July. Rota was bombed but not considered worth invading, so it remained in Japanese hands until the end of the war.

The islands became airbases from which American B-29s leveled the cities of Japan. At the height of the bombing campaign, North Field on Tinian was the busiest airfield in the world, with two B-29s taking off abreast every 45 seconds for the seven-hour ride to Japan. The nuclear age began here when the *Enola Gay* left Tinian for Hiroshima.

Americanization

The Marianas, except for Guam, became part of the Trust Territory of the Pacific Islands in 1947. Until 1962 the Northern Marianas were under U.S. naval administration and used as a training facility by the CIA.

Political status negotiations began in 1969. In February 1975 the Marianas Covenant was signed, slicing the Northern Marianas from the Trust Territory to become a part of the United States Commonwealth, akin to Puerto Rico. Of the approximately 5,000 voters, 79% approved the Covenant. On 24 March 1976 President Ford signed the Covenant. On 3 November 1986, the United States implemented the Covenant, and the residents of the Northern Marianas were declared American citizens. The Commonwealth elected a governor and legislature in 1977, and on 9 January 1978 the Commonwealth constitution came into effect.

The Covenant creates a political union between the United States and the Northern Marianas. The U.S. controls defense and foreign affairs, while the Commonwealth primarily is internally self-governing. The agreement can only be terminated by mutual consent.

GOVERNMENT

The autonomous Commonwealth of the Northern Marianas has a governor and lieutenant governor elected every four years. The bicameral legislature is made up of nine senators, three elected at large from each of the main islands every four years, and 15 representatives elected every two years, two each from six districts on Saipan and one each from Rota, Tinian, and the northern islands. A two-thirds vote in both houses is required to impeach a governor. Each of the four municipal jurisdictions is headed by a mayor. Commonwealth residents aren't represented in the United States Congress and can't vote in presidential elections. Both the Democratic and Republican political parties are active.

ECONOMY

The Commonwealth of the Northern Marianas' greatest resource is its location, near Japan, Guam, and the Philippines. The beaches, relaxed entry requirements, and easy access bring more than a half million tourists a year, the greatest bulk from Japan. However, locals have been given few opportunities to assume managerial positions in the tourist trade. A United States federal district court decision interpreted a Japanese-American friendship treaty as allowing Japanese-owned hotels and other businesses to ignore most of CNMI's local hiring preference laws. Despite widespread local underemployment, foreigners—mostly Filipinos, Chinese, and Koreans—compose almost 90% of the work force in Saipan's private sector.

Covenant payments and United States aid have equalled almost $3,000 per capita, much of it going to finance CNMI's government. The education system, however, is overwhelmed by a population explosion. Because of a lack of qualified local teachers, Statesiders and Filipinos make up a substantial percentage of the teachers. A Covenant provision prohibits the sale of land to persons of non-Marianas descent until 2011, but a substantial amount of prime beachfront property is under long-term lease.

Currently, the most controversial part of CNMI's economy is its garment industry. Garments assembled in CNMI can be shipped to the United States duty-free and with "Made in the U.S.A." labels. In 1997, Saipan shipped more than $800 million worth of garments to the United States. Saipan exacted $27 million in "user" fees from those companies. The garments are manufactured almost exclusively by foreign labor. Foreign workers are housed in compounds, often literally fenced in. Under CNMI law, these workers are paid only $2.90 per hour. President Clinton has urged the U.S. Congress to limit CNMI's open immigration policies and to make the ordinary U.S. minimum wage of $5.15 per hour applicable to the Saipan garment shops.

In 1999, a series of class-action lawsuits were filed against major U.S. retailers that purchase Saipan-made garments. The suits alleged basic human rights violations as to the work and living conditions of the "guest" workers. The allegations likened these workers to indentured servants because many cannot afford to leave CNMI until they earn enough money to pay back labor contractors who had arranged their transportation to Saipan.

WASTE DUMPING

In 1979 the Japanese government announced plans to dump 10,000 cement-solidified metal drums of dangerous nuclear wastes into the Marianas Trench halfway between Tokyo and the Northern Marianas. This was to be an "experimental" dump, followed by larger and continual dumping in the future. After widespread opposition erupted throughout the Pacific, Japan dropped its plan. A 1983 law created a 200-nautical-mile no-dumping zone around the Northern Marianas, but the proposed Japanese dump site is outside this area. An open-ended moratorium on nuclear waste dumping at sea, adopted by the London Dumping Convention in 1983, hopefully put an end to this ill-conceived idea.

THE TROPIC BIRD

Although graceful in the air, the white-tailed tropic bird *(Phaethon lepturus)* must crawl on its belly to move about on land. During courtship, male and female glide and circle one another high in the air, the upper bird sometimes touching the back of the lower with its two long, streaming tail feathers. Tropic birds often spend months at sea when not nesting, ranging hundreds of miles in search of food. Their bills have teethlike notches to help them hold their catch.

CNMI law exempts from the minimum wage maids, construction workers, fishermen, and farmers. These jobs are almost all held by foreign laborers, who often receive less than $200 a month. Filipinas are often brought in under false representations to work in Saipan's karaoke bars or to serve as housekeepers.

THE PEOPLE

Present-day Chamorros differ considerably from their ancestors, whose skeletal remains indicate a taller, larger-boned people. Modern Chamorros have a sense of ethnic identity, though most are descendants of not only the original Chamorros, but also of the Spanish, Filipinos, Chinese, Germans, Japanese, and Americans, with whom they intermarried through three centuries. Family names and social customs reveal a deep Hispanic legacy. Estimates indicate more than four-fifths of the words in the modern Chamorro language derive from Spanish roots.

One-fourth of the Micronesian population of the Northern Marianas is descended from Carolinians who arrived over a century ago by canoes. You can sometimes spot the Carolinians by the flower leis *(mwarmwars)* they wear in their hair. Since citizens of the FSM gained free entry to the United States and its Commonwealth in 1986, there has been a second wave of Carolinian immigration to Saipan.

About 63,000 citizens live in the Commonwealth, almost all on Saipan (56,000), Rota

(4,000), and Tinian (3,000). Additionally, there are about 35,000 registered alien residents, mainly contract laborers. Filipinos and Chinese are the two largest groups of contract laborers.

ARTS AND ENTERTAINMENT

The Commonwealth Council for the Arts sponsors exhibits throughout the year showcasing the arts, customs, and culture of all of Micronesia. No progress has been made on the plans to open a CNMI Museum of Culture at the old Japanese hospital building.

Fiestas

As on Guam, village fiestas take place every month of the year, except during Lent. These offer an excellent opportunity to try typical Chamorro food and to meet local people in an informal atmosphere. Since most of the population is Catholic, each fiesta begins with a procession and mass on the Saturday closest to the day of the village's patron saint, followed by feasting into the night. Sunday is the village open house when people open their homes. You can find the precise dates of fiestas from the Marianas Visitors Authority.

St. Joseph's Day (early May) is celebrated with great fervor at San Jose villages on both Saipan and Tinian. Other important fiestas include those dedicated to Our Lady of Lourdes (early February), San Vicente (early April), San Isidro (at Chalan Kanoa in mid-May), San Antonio (June), Our Lady of Mt. Carmel (at Chalan Kanoa in mid-July), San Roque (late August), San Francisco de Borja (on Rota in October), and Christ the King (at Garapan in mid-November). Other similar gatherings might commemorate a marriage, birth, or funeral. If you get invited to one, you'll long remember the hospitality of the local people.

Holidays

Public holidays include New Year's Day (1 January), Commonwealth Day (9 January), President's Day (third Monday in February), Covenant Day (24 March), Good Friday (March/April), Memorial Day (last Monday in May), Liberation Day (4 July), Labor Day (first Monday in September), Columbus Day (second Monday in October), Citizenship Day (4 November), Veteran's Day (11 November), Thanksgiving Day (fourth Thursday in November), Constitution Day (8 December), and Christmas Day (25 December).

Commonwealth Day (9 January) gives occasion to entertainment and feasts. Liberation Day (4 July) commemorates the day in 1946 when Chamorros were released from Camp Susupe, the U.S. internment camp at Chalan Kanoa, *not* the American Independence Day. The Flame Tree Festival occurs the week leading up to 4 July, with sporting events, handicraft shows, an agricultural exhibition, traditional food, and arts performances. On Liberation Day itself, expect a parade, firecrackers, carnival events, and feasting on Saipan. On All Souls' Day (1 November), cemeteries are visited and the graves are cleaned and adorned with candles and flowers.

PRACTICALITIES

Food

A Chamorro feast might consist of roast suckling pig cooked on a spit, red rice (white rice colored with achote seeds), a selection of fish, taro, crabs, pastries, and *tuba*—fermented coconut sap. Another favorite is chicken *kelaguen* (minced and prepared with lemon, onions, shredded coconut meat, and a touch of that super-hot *finadene* sauce that goes well on everything).

Also try *cadon guihan* (fish cooked in coconut milk), *lumpia* (pork, shrimp, and vegetables in a pastry wrapping), *pancit* (fried noodles), *poto* (rice cake), *bonelos aga* (fried bananas), and *bonelos dago* (deep-fried grated yam served with syrup). For dessert it's *kalamai* (sweet coconut milk pudding) or *ahn* (grated coconut boiled in sugary water). Those familiar with Filipino cooking will recognize similarities.

Visas

Since this is American territory, United States citizens are allowed to live and work in the Northern Marianas without restrictions. We do, however, advise Americans to come with a passport as this will speed entry.

Everyone but American citizens must have a passport to enter the Commonwealth. Passports must be valid 60 days beyond the date of entry. Visas are not required for tourist visits of up to 30 days.

Money and Measurements

United States currency, credit cards, and postage stamps are used. The electricity is 110 volts, 60 cycles. There's no sales tax in the Northern Marianas.

Information

Before arrival you can obtain a packet of colorful brochures and a "Travel Information Sheet" listing hotel prices by writing the **Marianas Visitors Authority,** (P.O. Box 861, Saipan, MP 96950, tel. 670-664-3200, fax 670-664-3237, e-mail: mva@saipan.com, website: www.visit!marianas.com). Ask for a copy of *Historic and Geographic Map of Saipan,* by William H. Stewart, which contains a wealth of information on the island's war record.

Saipan has two twice-weekly newspapers, the *Saipan Tribune* and the *Mariana Variety.*

Saipan has an air-conditioned library, on the left as you turn toward the Nauru building in Susupe. Faith Book Store opposite the Saipan Community Church on Beach Road has a large selection of books on Micronesia.

Address mail to Saipan, MP 96950; Rota, MP 96951; or Tinian, MP 96952.

Getting There

Saipan International Airport (SPN) is located eight miles south of Garapan. This is the former Aslito Airfield of World War II vintage, and there are still more than a dozen Japanese bunkers scattered around the airport. The terminal building is open 24 hours a day. There's no departure tax.

Some hotels offer free transfers from and to the airport, others charge up to $12 one way, so ask. A taxi to Garapan should cost about $20. Numerous car rental companies have offices in a kiosk in front of the airport terminal. Freedom Air flights leave from the commuter terminal next to the main terminal.

CNMI COUNTRY CODE: 670

Saipan is linked to Tokyo by **Continental Airlines, Northwest Airlines** and **Japan Air Lines.** Continental also arrives nonstop from Guam, Manila, Fukuoka, and Nagoya. Japan Air Lines also flies from Nagoya and Osaka. Northwest Airlines, which has an alliance with Continental, has direct connections in Tokyo to and from Atlanta, Cincinnati, Los Angeles, New York, Seattle, and other North American cities.

Continental passengers can connect in Guam with flights to and from Honolulu. To fly Continental between Saipan and Los Angeles involves changing planes in both Guam and Honolulu.

Getting Around

Continental Airlines flies between Guam and Saipan. **Freedom Air** (P.O. Box 239 CK, Saipan, MP 96950, tel. 670-288-5663, fax 670-288-5663) flies between Guam, Saipan, Tinian, and Rota. Different flights make different stops. It sometimes uses a seven-seat plane and other times a 30-seater. Inquire if this is an issue for you.

THE SNORKELER

Although he lived in an interactive universe turning toward pun, he resented being turned into a caterpillar as punishment for chasing a pair of butterfly fish.

SAIPAN

Saipan is a pleasant island where tourists, primarily from Asia, go to relax in the sun and in warm ocean waters. As you look toward the lagoon from the beach between the old sugar dock and the Saipan Grand Hotel, you'll see a partially submerged military tank several hundred feet from shore, its turret and gun out of the water even at high tide. I snorkeled to it, hoping the young Japanese tourists crisscrossing the lagoon on their jet skis would notice me in the water.

From looking at the tank I could not tell whether it was American or Japanese, but I knew it must be American because on 15 June 1944 it was the Americans who were attacking Saipan from the sea and the Japanese who were defending it from the land. The men in the tank most certainly died when their tank became stranded during the invasion.

Arriving at the tank, I rested, sitting on the main body, which was a foot or so beneath the water's surface. The tank was covered by algae and sea grass. Once rested, I snorkeled around the tank, which seemed larger in the sea than on land. Fish darted in and out through holes and ports.

Apparently other snorkelers had discovered this spot before me. The surrounding sand was covered with beer cans. Viscerally I hated this litter. But certainly it was more benign than the litter I had come to see: a weapon of war that had become a death trap.

Most of the island's tourist facilities run up the sunny west coast, from the commercial center of Chalan Kanoa to the entertainment district of Garapan. Some self-contained resorts are farther north. Near the north end of the island, in the rugged Marpi area, are Banzai and Suicide Cliffs, pilgrimage sites for many Japanese and a major attraction for all.

SIGHTS

Garapan

Little that is old remains in Garapan. This town, the Japanese capital of the Marianas, was destroyed during the war, but it has been rebuilt and is again the major town on the island. Garapan's center has a heavy concentration of restaurants, karaoke bars, souvenir shops, and such elite Western stores as Tiffany and Chanel. It is as if Rodeo Drive were deposited on the Jersey Shore and everybody started speaking Japanese. In the evening, the area is lively, with many tourists milling about. Bars have bar girls out in front, inviting customers to enter. Japanese tourists call this area Little Ginza. In 1998, CNMI passed legislation to make it easier to prosecute aggressive solicitation of prostitution. The stated need for the legislation was the fear that Garapan would lose its reputation as a place for Japanese family vacationers.

Nearby **American Marianas Memorial Park** and adjacent **Micro Beach Park** with its gentle lagoon are great places to catch the sunset or

the cold, forbidding walls of the old Japanese prison at Garapan

have a swim. In the memorial park is a small **WW II Museum.** The park also has a 2.5-mile jogging path.

Just south of the main tourist center you'll find **Sugar King Park,** complete with a 1934 statue of Haruji Matsue, head of the South Seas Development Company, which developed the sugar industry in the Marianas prior to the war. In the same park is a red **Japanese locomotive** used to haul cane to the old sugar mill at Chalan Kanoa. This park is now a botanical garden featuring a reconstructed Japanese shrine with examples of various tropical trees (open daily 8 a.m.-4 p.m., free). Across the road are the imposing ruins of the **old Japanese hospital,** and nearby on a back street to the south, the **old Japanese jail.**

On the street leading to the Sugar King Hotel is the **Saipan International House of Prayer** (not, to my knowledge, referred to as the IHOP). This hexagonal building, crafted in Japan, maintains a beautiful and peaceful elegance. In the center is a large bell, "the bell of peace, the bell of love." Coming here at sunset can make you believe striking the bell will bring peace to you and to the world at large. Do not miss this experience.

San Roque

The ever-growing **La Fiesta San Roque,** about five miles on the road north from Garapan, is a large tourist shopping center with many gift shops. It has a fair number of restaurants, mostly overpriced. Opposite the shopping center is **Pau** beach, a lovely safe beach to snorkel.

Nearby is the **Laderan Trail,** one of the nicest hikes on the island. It gives you a feel for the interior of this tropical island with its plant- and birdlife. As you head north from La Fiesta, the road to the trailhead is not marked, but it is the right turn immediately past the center. In a quarter mile, at a 1-million-gallon water tank, make another right and proceed three-quarters of a mile to a turnoff to the trailhead. There are few parking spots at the trailhead itself, so it may be best to park the car before this last turn.

Despite several exceptions, the trail is well marked by blue and orange plastic ribbon, usually on your left, though sometimes on the right. If you are hiking with someone, as you should, and cannot see the next marker, send one of the group ahead to find it before leaving the last one. There is a heavy canopy, and once off the trail it is easy to become disoriented.

The trail is on ancient raised coral so the bottom is rough. Wear good walking shoes. Though the trail is not technically difficult, the second half can be tiring because the ground becomes rougher and there are several long uphill stretches. The entire trail is about three miles.

There are 14 numbered markers but no explanation of what they are marking. (Make up your own—it's called interactive hiking.) Past marker 13 is a fork; one trail leads down to the right, the other slightly uphill to the left. To get back to the trailhead take the path to the left. After ascending a hill, you come to a small grass meadow. The grassed-over dirt road to the right leads back to the trailhead.

An alternative is merely to hike to marker 6 and return. This is the easiest part of the hike, and probably the most interesting as you won't have to watch your footing as much.

Managaha Island

Off the northwest coast lies Managaha Island, in the Tanapag lagoon—the most popular snorkeling site on Saipan. Captured from the Japanese only after the main island had fallen, a white sandy beach runs around Managaha. Three Japanese artillery pieces are still there, and an array of sunken barges, landing craft, ships, planes, and guns can be seen among the coral heads near the island, on a sandy bottom in only 20-40 feet of water. Look in particular for the Japanese Zero, the sub chaser, and the four-engine bomber.

Because of building and irrigation on this coast, and the runoff this created, the reef here is clearly distressed. It would be a tragic loss for Saipan if it does not take steps to reverse this process.

Numerous local tour operators run glass-bottomed boat trips over to Managaha Island, $43 pp with barbecue lunch. A good swimmer can make it out without too much difficulty. The greatest danger is from passing boats. One can also rent a kayak on the beach next to the Hyatt and paddle across.

Northern Saipan

The north end of Saipan was the scene of the last desperate Japanese resistance in mid-1944

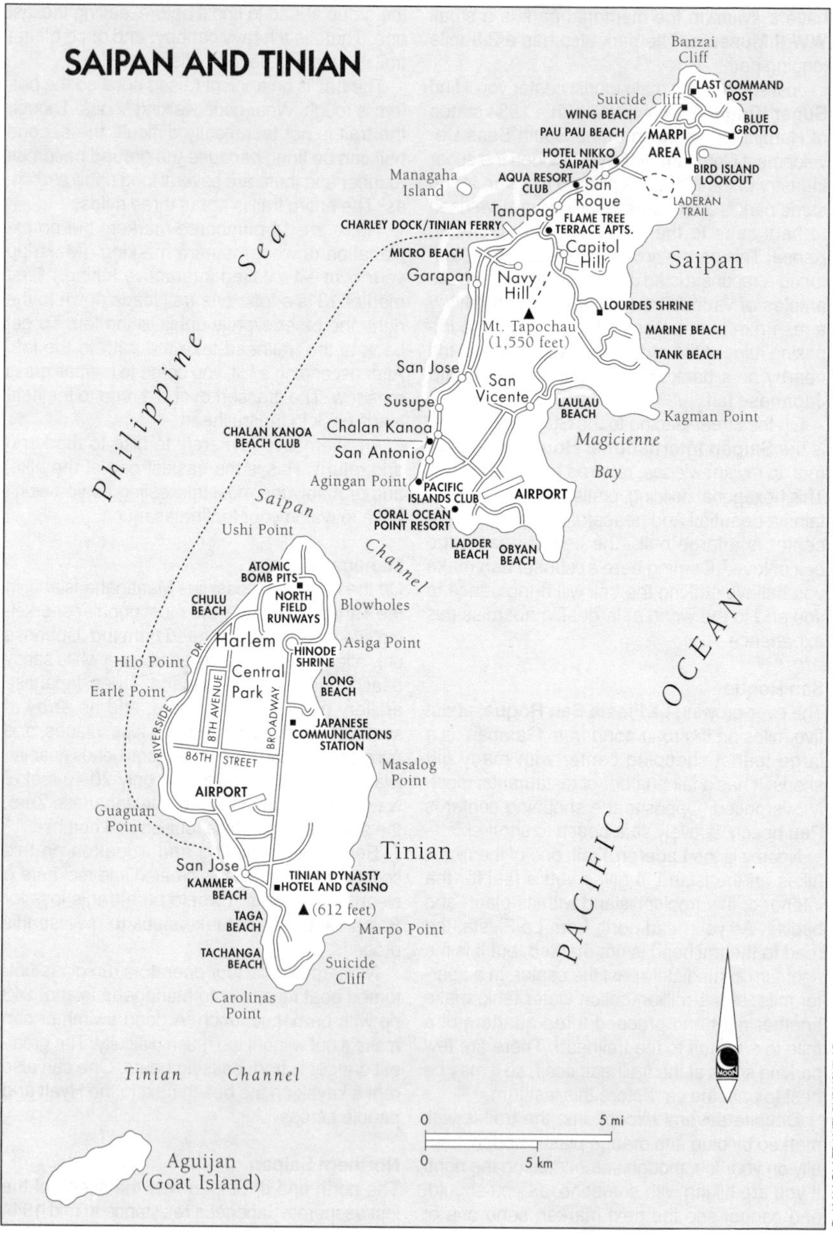

SAIPAN AND TINIAN

Banzai Cliff

LAST COMMAND POST

Suicide Cliff

WING BEACH

BLUE GROTTO

PAU PAU BEACH

MARPI AREA

HOTEL NIKKO SAIPAN

BIRD ISLAND LOOKOUT

Managaha Island

AQUA RESORT CLUB

San Roque

LADERAN TRAIL

CHARLEY DOCK/TINIAN FERRY

Tanapag

FLAME TREE TERRACE APTS.

Saipan

MICRO BEACH

Capitol Hill

Garapan

Navy Hill

LOURDES SHRINE

Mt. Tapochau (1,550 feet)

MARINE BEACH

TANK BEACH

San Jose

San Vicente

Susupe

LAULAU BEACH

Kagman Point

CHALAN KANOA BEACH CLUB

Chalan Kanoa

Magicienne Bay

San Antonio

Agingan Point

PACIFIC ISLANDS CLUB

AIRPORT

CORAL OCEAN POINT RESORT

LADDER BEACH

OBYAN BEACH

Ushi Point

Philippine Sea

Saipan Channel

ATOMIC BOMB PITS

CHULU BEACH

NORTH FIELD RUNWAYS

Blowholes

Harlem

Asiga Point

HINODE SHRINE

Hilo Point

Central Park

LONG BEACH

Earle Point

JAPANESE COMMUNICATIONS STATION

Masalog Point

86TH STREET

Guaguan Point

AIRPORT

San Jose

Tinian

KAMMER BEACH

TINIAN DYNASTY HOTEL AND CASINO

▲ (612 feet)

TAGA BEACH

Marpo Point

TACHANGA BEACH

Suicide Cliff

Carolinas Point

PACIFIC OCEAN

RIVERSIDE DR.

8TH AVENUE

BROADWAY

Tinian Channel

Aguijan (Goat Island)

0   5 mi

0   5 km

© MOON PUBLICATIONS, INC.

© AVALON TRAVEL PUBLISHING

DAVID STANLEY

TO THE CHILDREN
WHO DIED AT BANZAI CLIFF

How stupid is war.
Children pushed to early death.
Fish can swim away.

as well as mass suicides by Japanese soldiers and civilians to avoid capture. Later this area became a U.S. ammunition stockpile zone that was only cleared and reopened to the public in 1968. No stores are in this area so come prepared with drinks and snacks.

The **Last Japanese Command Post** is in a cave just below high cliffs next to the **Okinawa Peace Memorial.** Here, General Yoshitsugo Saito ordered his men to take seven lives each for the emperor. Not following his own advice, he then committed hara-kiri. From this post you can follow the Banadero Trail for an hour up to the top of **Suicide Cliff** where, high above the post, hundreds of Japanese soldiers jumped 820 feet to their deaths rather than surrender. You can drive the three miles to the top of Suicide Cliff by another road, which now has a "fitness path" with exercise stations alongside. Can bungee jumping from the cliff be far behind?

At **Banzai Cliff,** near the north end of the island, entire families lined up and jumped off, elders pushing the young. The Saipanese claim the white terns that ride the winds over these cliffs didn't exist before the war, that they bear the souls of the dead.

At times during the morning and afternoon, a great number of tour buses disgorge large numbers of Japanese tourists. If possible visit the cliff early in the morning or late in the afternoon. You will be profoundly moved, and perhaps be in the presence of Japanese mourning their lost loved ones.

Continuing around the point and heading south it is a three-mile trip from here to the **Bird Island lookout** from which you get a good view of the small cliff-girdled island the Japanese more poetically called Moon Viewing Island. On the way to the lookout, the road passes the turnoff to the **Blue Grotto,** a sunken pool connected to the ocean by twin underground passages. Steep concrete stairs lead down to this cobalt blue pool where a variety of fish reside—a favorite spot for divers. Because of odd tidal effects occurring in the grotto, do not swim here until you discuss it with locals.

Central and Southern Saipan
From 1951 to 1962 the CIA had a $28-million base on **Capitol Hill,** where Nationalist Chinese guerrillas were trained. Later Capitol Hill became the headquarters of the High Commissioner of the U.N. Trust Territory, and a ghetto for American expatriates. Today this is the location for most Commonwealth government offices.

From behind the Civil Defense Energy/MPLC office (the former Congress of Micronesia building) at Capitol Hill, follow a rough road two miles up to the top of **Mount Tapochau** (1,550 feet) for a good 360-degree view. A small statue of Christ was erected on the summit in 1987, and the Saipanese carry wooden crosses up every Easter. A sturdy car could navigate the road, but you may have to park and walk when it gets too difficult.

Southeast of Capitol Hill is **Our Lady of Lourdes Shrine,** marking an area where the Saipanese took refuge during the American invasion. It's a half mile off the main highway. Remote beaches on the east coast are accessible from the Cross Island Road. **Laulau Beach** near San Vicente has good coral and tends to be calm.

Some of the best conditions for walk-in diving and snorkeling are at Ladder and Obyan beaches in southern Saipan. Don't leave valuables unattended on the beach. An ancient Micronesian settlement at Obyan has been carbon dated to 1500 B.C.E. The remnants of *latte* stones can still be seen.

ACCOMMODATIONS

Most of Saipan's hotels are along the west coast sunbelt. Hotel rates in the Northern Marianas and on Guam are higher than elsewhere in Micronesia. As on Guam, at many Japanese luxury hotels the staff's knowledge of dive shops, fishing boats, and other island activities may be limited to businesses where the proprietors speak only Japanese.

Separately listed below with more details are hotels, some Japanese owned or managed, that do better with English-speaking guests. Many of the least expensive hotels are under Korean or Chinese management.

Many luxury hotels and car rental agencies on Saipan will have special "local" or "corporate" rates. These mean different things at different hotels. Discount application often reflects the vacancy rate of the hotel rather than the status of the guest. Sometimes, at some hotels, these discounts appear to be given to anyone with an American accent who asks. These rates are seldom given to Japanese. You stand a better chance of getting them by asking in person, rather than over the phone.

Saipan used to fill up during the summer and during the Japanese winter vacation periods. Perhaps that will occur again when the Asian economy turns around.

Budget

Contrary to popular belief, there are some nice budget hotels on Saipan. Perhaps the best, if you do not need to be by the beach, is the **Garden Motel** on Middle Rd. (Box 10000, Saipan, MP 96950, tel. 670-234-0320, fax 670-234-5446), with 17 rooms at $40 s, $50 d. It has a warm, old-time feel, as if you were in someone's home. The rooms all open to a lovely enclosed patio. The front desk is in the same room as the restaurant and TV.

Victoria Hotel (SVRB P.O. Box 7013, Saipan, MP 96950, tel. 670-233-2031, fax 670-233-2037) opened in June 1998. Located behind the Hyatt in Garapan, it has some rooms overlooking American Marianas Memorial Park. Rooms are $55 s, $65 d.

Capital Hotel (P.O. Box 3352 CK, Saipan, MP 96950, tel. 670-233-7820, fax 670-233-7822) is located on a quiet street behind Garapan. It is about a 10-minute walk to the beach and rooms are $42.

Micro Beach Hotel (P.O. Box 1328, Saipan, MP 96950, tel. 670-233-1368, fax 670-233-0301) is in the midst of Garapan. It is only one block from the beach, reached directly by walking down the alley south of the Hyatt. The rooms are small and a bit dreary, but clean for $45.

The **Remington Club** (P.O. Box 10001, Saipan, MP 96950, tel. 670-234-5449, fax 670-234-5619) is another good budget choice. The 14 regular rooms are on the second floor above its bar, and cost $55 s or $72 d; rooms with cooking facilities begin at $85. The hotel is near the beach and right in the heart of the action in the Garapan entertainment district.

The **Sun Palace Motel** (P.O. Box 920, Saipan, MP 96950, tel. 670-234-6639, fax 670-235-6062) is one of the least expensive places to stay on Saipan, located behind the ballpark beside Susupe's Marianas High School. The 18 a/c rooms here are $40 s, $50 d.

Moderate

The **Pacific Gardenia Hotel** (P.O. Box 144, Saipan, MP 96950, tel. 670-234-3455, fax 670-234-3411) at Chalan Kanoa calls itself "Saipan's Biggest Little Hotel." The 14 spacious rooms with cooking facilities and TV are $84 s or $95 d. There's a coin laundry. Usually on Friday evening, a local band plays on the sandy beach behind the hotel as guests wine, dine, and dance. Happy hour at the beach bar is Mon.-Sat. 4:30-6:30 p.m.

The 50-room **Gold Beach Hotel** (P.O. Box 2232, Saipan, MP 96950, tel. 670-235-5501, fax 670-235-5510), opposite the lagoon south of Garapan, has 46 rooms with rates between $45 and $80. The rooms have cooking facilities, but you may have to supply your own pots and pans.

Locally owned **Summer Holiday Hotel** (P.O. Box 908, Saipan, MP 96950, tel. 670-234-3182, fax 670-234-3077) is on Beach Road, Garapan. The 26 rooms in the attractive three-story building begin at an economical $50, cooking facilities included. A nice beach park is a two-minute walk from the hotel. A coin-operated laundromat is on the premises, and Martha's Store next to the hotel is open 24 hours.

The **Saipan Ocean View Hotel** (P.O. Box 799, Saipan, MP 96950, tel. 670-234-8900, fax 670-234-9428) is a three-story hotel on Beach Road, Garapan. The 20 rooms with fridge are $80. The hotel is located on a busy stretch of road, but faces a park.

Luxury

The **Hyatt Regency Saipan** (P.O. Box 87 CHRB, Saipan, MP 96950, tel. 670-234-1234, fax 670-234-7745), formerly owned by Continental Airlines, serves an international clientele in its plush seven-story hotel. The 325 rooms with balcony and fridge begin at $250, but they usually offer local and corporate discounts. It's nicely set on landscaped gardens facing Garapan's Micro Beach. Three wings of the hotel face a lush tropical garden with parrots in cages and colorful fish in the ponds. Most nights there's a show that includes dinner.

Pacific Islands Club Saipan (P.O. Box 2370, Saipan, MP 96950, tel. 670-234-7976, fax 670-234-6592) in San Antonio has 220 standard rooms beginning at $220. It also has plans including meals and a wide range of recreational activities. This hotel caters primarily to Japanese package tourists, but its staff is mainly American. Like its counterpart on Guam, its loudspeakers bark out "fun" activities, but at a much less frenetic pace. American expats working in the Far East often vacation here.

Saipan's smallest luxury hotel is the **Chalan Kanoa Beach Club** (P.O. Box 356, Saipan, MP 96950, tel. 670-234-7829, fax 670-234-6534) at the south end of Chalan Kanoa. The 28 deluxe units arranged in two-story buildings around the swimming pool are $180. There's a cocktail lounge and restaurant on the premises.

The elegant **Aqua Resort Club** (P.O. Box 9 CK, Saipan, MP 96950, tel. 670-322-1234, fax 670-234-1220), a low-rise complex, stands on the beach between Tanapag and San Roque in northern Saipan. The 91 rooms begin at $240.

Additional luxury-priced hotels, primarily for Japanese tour groups, include:

Hotel Nikko Saipan (P.O. Box 5152 CHRB, Saipan, MP 96950, tel. 670-322-3311, fax 670-322-3144) near San Roque, $230.

Saipan Grand Hotel (P.O. Box 369, Saipan, MP 96950, tel. 670-234-6601, fax 670-234-8007), Susupe Beach, rooms from $180.

Saipan Diamond Hotel (P.O. Box 66, Saipan, MP 96950, tel. 670-234-5900, fax 670-234-5909), Susupe Beach, $175.

Hafadai Beach Hotel (P.O. Box 338, Saipan, MP 96950, tel. 670-234-6495, fax 670-234-8912), south of Garapan, $170 and up.

Dai-ichi Saipan Beach Hotel (P.O. Box 1029, Saipan, MP 96950, tel. 670-234-6412, fax 670-234-7064), Garapan, $180.

Marianas Resort Hotel (P.O. Box 527, Saipan, MP 96950, tel. 670-322-0770, fax 670-322-0776), Marpi, near golf course, from $200.

Coral Ocean Point Resort Club (P.O. Box 1160, Saipan, MP 96950, tel. 670-234-7000, fax 670-234-7095), Marpi, near golf course, $160.

Apartments

Flame Tree Terrace Apartments (P.O. Box 86 CHRB, Saipan, MP 96950, tel. 670-322-3366, fax 670-322-3886) in Lower Capitol Hill rents nicely furnished condominiums on a monthly basis only. There are 35 units available, as well as a swimming pool. The condos cost $700 for a one-bedroom, $1,050 for a two-bedroom, and $2,000 for a three-bedroom. The apartments are often fully booked, so write or call as far in advance as possible to get on the waiting list. If there is a vacant apartment, it may be possible to rent by the day.

Camping

The parks along the west side of Saipan are for day use only, so if you want to pitch a tent consider the more remote east coast beaches, such as Laulau. On the south coast, Ladder Beach, less than two miles from the air terminal, has

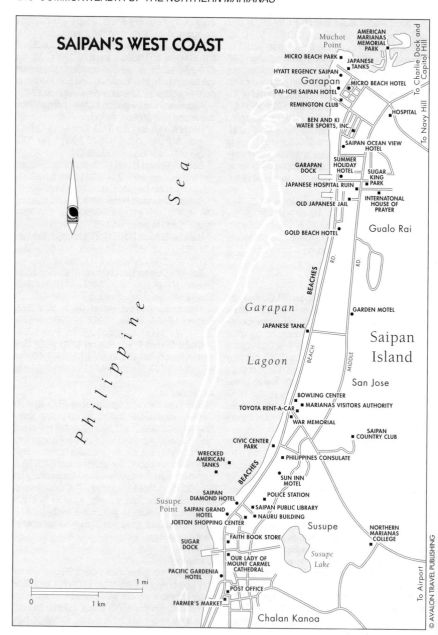

SAIPAN'S WEST COAST

AMERICAN MARIANAS MEMORIAL PARK

To Charlie Dock and Capitol Hill

Muchot Point

MICRO BEACH PARK
JAPANESE TANKS
HYATT REGENCY SAIPAN
MICRO BEACH HOTEL
DAI-ICHI SAIPAN HOTEL
REMINGTON CLUB

Garapan

To Navy Hill

HOSPITAL

BEN AND KI WATER SPORTS, INC.

SAIPAN OCEAN VIEW HOTEL

GARAPAN DOCK
SUMMER HOLIDAY HOTEL
SUGAR KING PARK
JAPANESE HOSPITAL RUIN
OLD JAPANESE JAIL
INTERNATIONAL HOUSE OF PRAYER

GOLD BEACH HOTEL

Gualo Rai

Philippine Sea

BEACHES RD.

RD.

Garapan

GARDEN MOTEL

JAPANESE TANK

Saipan Island

Lagoon

BEACH

MIDDLE

San Jose

BOWLING CENTER
MARIANAS VISITORS AUTHORITY
TOYOTA RENT-A-CAR
WAR MEMORIAL
SAIPAN COUNTRY CLUB

CIVIC CENTER PARK

WRECKED AMERICAN TANKS

PHILIPPINES CONSULATE

BEACHES

SUN INN MOTEL

SAIPAN DIAMOND HOTEL
POLICE STATION
SAIPAN GRAND HOTEL
SAIPAN PUBLIC LIBRARY
JOETON SHOPPING CENTER
NAURU BUILDING

Susupe Point

Susupe

NORTHERN MARIANAS COLLEGE

FAITH BOOK STORE

SUGAR DOCK

Susupe Lake

OUR LADY OF MOUNT CARMEL CATHEDRAL

PACIFIC GARDENIA HOTEL

POST OFFICE

To Airport

FARMER'S MARKET

Chalan Kanoa

0   1 mi
0   1 km

© AVALON TRAVEL PUBLISHING

caves with picnic tables. Otherwise camp by the Bomb Wing Memorial nearby. Obyan Beach is a better campsite, but it's two miles farther along.

No permit is required at these beaches and none of them have facilities. Don't go off and leave your gear unattended.

OTHER PRACTICALITIES

Food

Food in Saipan can be very expensive. Mediocre restaurants often charge very high prices. Prices are highest in the luxury hotels. But prices can also be very high at a restaurant along Beach Road, even if its front makes it look like a dive. Check prices before sitting down. Often restaurants will post a menu, visible from the outside. If the menu is in Japanese, as is frequently the case, walk in and ask to see an English menu. Saipan is one of the few places on earth where a perfectly fine but modest Chinese lunch can cost $30 pp, without drinks. Tips are expected, but there is no sales tax on meals.

One way to beat the high price of restaurant food on Saipan is to rely on its combination bakeries and takeaway places. Some even have tables to sit at if you so choose.

Try my favorite, **Marge's Kitchen,** a specialty bakeshop. You can buy fresh bagels or excellent local bread. Bento box lunches start at $2.50. The bakery is also a great place to cure a sweet tooth. Try the *lanpiyos,* a local dish of sponge cake smothered in a milky custard and flavored with cinnamon and coconut for $1.75. Forgive Marge's its hot dog-stuffed croissant. It is located on the side street immediately north of Our Lady of Mount Carmel Cathedral, north of Chalan Kanoa. It is open 6:30 a.m.-7 p.m.

Herman's Modern Bakery on the airport road serves breakfast and lunch specials (open 6 a.m.-3 p.m. Mon.-Sat.) and is popular among locals.

Right before Garapan as you drive from the airport, on the left, is **Hafa Adai Deli and Bakery.** Try the mango turnovers (85 cents). They have reasonably priced takeaway food that can also be eaten in the shop.

The large **supermarket** at Joeten Shopping Center is open until 7 p.m. on Sunday, 9 p.m. other days. **Aiko's Coffee Shop,** in the corner between this supermarket and Ace Hardware, serves a good breakfast, ramen soup ($2.45) and sandwiches anytime. Ask for the plate lunch (which may not be on menu), $4.25 for two scoops of rice, beef entree, and salad. It's open till 7:30 p.m. daily except Sunday, when it closes at 2 p.m.

J's Restaurant, at the Bowling Center in San Jose, is open 24 hours a day. It's good for breakfast and has cheap lunch specials.

Want to try some Chamorro cuisine? The **Chamorro Restaurant,** located in Garapan in the now-defunct Chamorro Hotel, is quite good. Try the tasty, spicy minced chicken *kelaguen.* Dinner will run about $15.

Poon's Restaurant, on Middle Road just north of Sugar King Park, serves Indonesian dishes.

The **Korea House Restaurant** serves full dinners, each with many side dishes, for $15-18.

The **Remington Bar** can be a fun place to hang out. Pleasant bar, nice company, and two pool tables. It serves up pretty good bar food, including $5 lunch specials.

Rudolpho's (tel. 670-322-3017), located at the intersection of Capitol Hill Road and Middle Road, bills itself as a Mexican and pizza restaurant. Although the food is mediocre, it's not too expensive. It is *the* place to meet young local *haoles* on the weekend; it has a good bar and an outside terrace. There is often live music on Saturday night.

For a delicious Sunday brunch, try the **Hyatt Regency Saipan.**

And of course, there are **Winchell's Donuts, McDonald's, Kentucky Fried Chicken,** and **Pizza Hut.** Garapan also has any number of ice cream and pizza stands.

Entertainment

Many of the large tourist hotels have happy hours at their bars with reduced drink prices, usually beginning around 5:30 p.m. Discos have stiff admission charges. There are also plenty of karaoke clubs, most with hostesses.

The Movie House (tel. 670-234-3456) beside the post office in Chalan Kanoa shows fairly current films. It opens at 7:30 p.m. daily.

You can also bowl at the old **Bowling Center** in San Jose and now the new **Capital Lanes,** behind Garapan.

Sports and Recreation

The following three dive shops are well suited for English speakers. Most of the many other scuba outfits on Saipan are geared mainly to Japanese tourists.

The largest dive shop for English speakers is **All American Divers** (PPP 245 P.O. Box 10000, Saipan, MP 96950, tel. 670-233-7056, fax 670-233-7055), located on Hotel Street in Garapan. Two-tank shore dives are $80 and two-tank boat dives are $110. The shop is PADI five-star and gives lessons for certification.

Saipan's oldest locally owned dive shop is **Ben and Ki Water Sports Inc.** (P.O. Box 5031 CHRB, Saipan, MP 96950, tel. 670-235-5063, fax 670-235-5068). They charge $100 for beach diving (two tanks) or $130 for boat diving (two tanks), lunch and gear included. Snorkelers can join the divers for $25 pp. A seven-hour diving expedition to Tinian and Goat islands is $120; a four-day certification course runs $500. Water-skiing is $30 for 20 minutes, and trolling costs $350 for four hours (up to six persons). The manager, Ben Concepcion, his son Lawrence, and son-in-law Duanne Pangelinan are very helpful. Visit their shop in Garapan or their kiosk facing the beach just south of the Hyatt. They pick up at hotels anywhere on Saipan.

You might also wish to try **Stingray Divers** (PPP 373 P.O. Box 10000, Saipan MP 96950, tel. 670-233-6100, fax 670-234-3709) which is a bit less expensive than the other two.

Because of environmental degradation, the diving at Saipan is not as good as at most other Micronesian sites. Decades of sugar production followed by decades of hotel building will do that. **Surfing** is poor on Saipan. One local surfer told me that when a swell hits, you reach the best surf by driving to the airport and taking the first plane to Guam. But **windsurfing** is good in the wide western lagoon. Boogie boarders can try Obyan Point or Coral Ocean Point.

Of Saipan's five golf courses, the nine-hole **Saipan Country Club** (Caller Box PPP 130, Saipan, MP 96950, tel. 670-234-7300) is the most "local." They have varying greens fees for varying clients: $20 for locals, $40 for Japanese tourists, $30 for other tourists. You can rent a full set of clubs for $15. On fairway four a ball passing to the left of a coconut tree is considered out of bounds, irrespective of where it comes to rest!

Saipan's top golf course is the **Coral Ocean Point Resort Club** (P.O. Box 1160, Saipan, MP 96950, tel. 670-234-7000, fax 670-234-7005) on the south coast at Koblerville. The resort's fantastic 18-hole golf course right on the coast is $70 a round if you're staying at the hotel, $120 otherwise. **Kingfisher Golf Links** (tel. 670-322-1100) is Saipan's newest, with ocean views from every green.

To the north **Mariana Country Club and Resort Hotel** (tel. 670-322-0770) at Marpi has another 18-hole golf course overlooking the sea. It's $100 a round for those not staying at the resort.

Midway between these two, **Laolao Bay Gulf Resort** offers the island's newest golf course, (tel. 670-256-8888).

Services

The Bank of Hawaii (tel. 670-235-5400; open weekdays 10 a.m.-3 p.m., Friday 10 a.m.-6 p.m.) is in the Nauru Building. There are also branches of the Bank of Guam (tel. 670-234-6467), Bank of Saipan (tel. 670-234-6260), and the Union Bank (tel. 670-234-6559) on Saipan.

The main post office is opposite the market in Chalan Kanoa and there's another, less crowded post office beside the CNMI Convention Center on Capitol Hill.

The Immigration and Naturalization Office (tel. 670-234-6178) is on the fourth floor of the Nauru Building.

The Japanese Consulate (tel. 670-234-7201) is on the fifth floor, Yarikuchi Building, opposite Garapan dock (open weekdays 9 a.m.-5 p.m.). The Philippines Consulate (tel. 670-234-1848) is in the CTC Building in Susupe (Mon.-Thurs. 8 a.m.-noon, 2-4:30 p.m.). You'll need a Philippines visa only if you want to stay longer than 21 days.

The main Continental Airlines reservations office (tel. 670-234-6491) is in the back of the Oleai Center in San Jose. There also is an office at the airport.

GETTING THERE

Saipan is linked to Tokyo by **Continental Airlines, Northwest Airlines** and **Japan Air Lines.** Continental also arrives nonstop from Guam, Manila, Fukuoka, and Nagoya. Japan Air Lines flies from Nagoya and Osaka. Northwest Airlines, which has an alliance with Continental, has direct connections in Tokyo to and from Atlanta, Cincinnati, Los Angeles, New York, Seattle, and other North American cities.

Continental Airlines flies between Guam and Saipan. **Freedom Air** (P.O. Box 239 CK, Saipan, MP 96950, tel. 670-288-5663, fax 670-288-5663) flies between Saipan, Guam, Tinian, and Rota. Different flights make different stops. It sometimes uses a seven-seat plane and on other flights a 30-seater. Inquire if this is an issue for you.

GETTING AROUND

By Boat
A large catamaran ferry now runs six times a day in each direction, taking passengers from Charley Dock on Saipan to San Jose on Tinian. Call (670) 328-2233 for the current schedule. The main purpose of the ferry is to take people to the **Tinian Dynasty Hotel & Casino** to gamble. The fare is normally $30, but look in the newspaper as the casino often runs special promotions of reduced fares. The ferry does not take reservations, but one can almost always get a seat by showing up 30 minutes before departure. One can easily go to Tinian, have lunch, gamble, and be back in Saipan before night.

By Road
Taxis now use meters in Saipan. A trip from the airport to Garapan usually runs about $20. The largest cab company is **Bo-Boy's Taxi,** tel. (670) 322-3822. You might also try **Prudy's Taxi Service,** tel. (670) 234-6502. You may, however, wish to rent a car upon arrival at Saipan. The main sights of the island can be seen in a day by rental car, and the car rental agencies at the airport (Hertz, Budget, Dollar, and Tropical) are competitive. The speed limit on Saipan is 35 mph unless otherwise posted. Your home driver's license is valid for 30 days after arrival.

OTHER ISLANDS

TINIAN

Only three miles south of Saipan, Tinian had been turned by the Japanese into a great sugarcane producer, supporting a population of 15,000 Japanese and Korean civilians. Today Tinian consists of a series of layered limestone plateaus covered by *tangan tangan.* Until 1998 one would describe it only as a "quiet backwater" of several thousand, an island for a peaceful vacation. In 1997 there were only 31 hotel rooms on the island. But then someone in Hong Kong must have seen *Field of Dreams* and thought "If I build it, they will come." Well over a hundred million dollars later, **Tinian Dynasty Hotel & Casino** was completed, adding more than 400 new rooms.

Tinian is betting its future on gambling. There are plans in the works to build more casinos and turn Tinian into *the* gambling center for Asia. But others say there is not yet any evidence that Tinian can support even one casino, that Tinian has as much chance to become an interna-

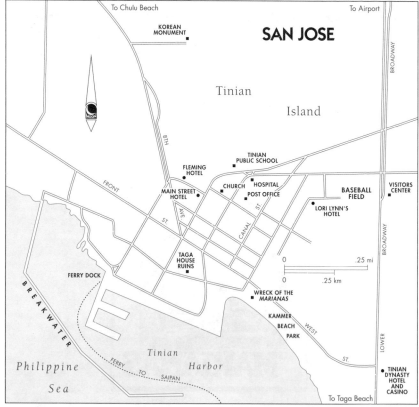

tional gambling destination as does Winnemucca, Nevada. Presently, one can fly from Tokyo, Taiwan, or Hong Kong to Las Vegas on charters for not much more than a trip to Tinian. But then again, people told Bugsy Segal to drop the crazy idea of Las Vegas.

San Jose

The island's only town is San Jose. It is a small town, with much open space. The town surrounds the harbor and goes up the hill behind it. Its main sight (other than the casino) is the **Taga House,** in a *latte* stone park not far from the harbor where the ferry lands. These stones are much larger than the *latte* stones of Guam. One still stands, and there are the remains of another 11. Next to the Taga House is a small Japanese war memorial. To the south are the remains of an ancient well.

Nearby lies the wreck of the freighter *Marianas,* thrown onto the beach by a typhoon in the late 1960s. From here you can look across to uninhabited Aguijan (Goat Island), five miles southwest. Another much larger shipwreck marks the entrance to Tinian harbor.

A paved bicycle and jogging path now runs south from **Kammer Beach** to **Taga Beach,** at the foot of Broadway to **Tachonga Beach.** On most Sunday afternoons, much of the island's adult population will be barbecuing and drinking Budweiser at Kammer Beach Park while their kids are swimming. At a point directly in front of the casino, you will sometimes see local kids jumping into a deep waterhole below. It's probably best not to try it, and certainly not before you check the tide and speak to some kids as to how and when it can be done.

Keep your eyes open while walking in town; you will see many remains of concrete Japanese buildings.

The **Korean Monument** off 8th Avenue just outside San Jose bears an evocative inscription dedicated to the 5,000 Koreans who:

suffered by chains of reckless imperial Japanese army, by whom they were deprived of their rights, and were taken to the islands here and there like innocent sheep, and then were fallen to this ground leaving behind them an eternal grudge.

South

At **Suicide Cliff** on the southeast side of the island, Japanese troops held out in caves for three months after the rest of Tinian fell. There are Japanese and Okinawan peace memorials here.

North

One can rent a car and see most of North Tinian's sights in a morning. Head up by driving on **Broadway,** which is a four-lane road until it reaches the airport. North of the airport, it now has only two lanes; the other two have been abandoned.

In 1944, even before the entire island had been secured, American Seabees began rebuilding a captured Japanese airstrip at the north end of the island in one of the largest engineering projects of World War II. Less than one year later **North Field** was the largest airfield in the world, with four 1.6-mile runways from which a total of 19,000 combat missions were made against Japan, under the direction of General Curtis LeMay, said to have been the prototype for Dr. Strangelove. To carry the huge quantities of bombs up from the port at San Jose, American soldiers built two divided highways across Tinian. As the island is shaped something like Manhattan, the GIs gave the roads names like Broadway, 42nd Street, and Riverside Drive. The monument to the Seabees is located at 86th Street and 8th Avenue.

About five miles north of the Airport turnoff is **Hinode Shrine.** This beautiful prewar Shinto shrine is now reduced to being a traffic circle on a road that has virtually no traffic. North of the circle, the road switches to one lane.

Right before the circle, on the left, are two *torii* gates (arches) leading to another Shinto shrine, built in 1941. Under Japanese rule, 80% of Tinian's land was under sugar cultivation by the NKK (Nan'yo Kohatsu Kaisha) company—the South Seas Development company. This shrine was built next to a spur of the cane railroad.

Heading north, after about a mile and a half, there are two small signs: one pointing to the right, leading to a **Blowhole,** and the other to the left, leading to the **Bomb Pits.** From the scenic ocean blowhole one sees much of Tinian's spectacular east coast. Though the walk to the blowhole is short, wear good walking shoes because of the coral outcroppings you must walk over.

an old engraving of the latte *stones of Tinian, all but one now toppled*

M.G.L. DOMENY DE RIENZI

To the left, if you follow the sign, you'll come to the massive World War II North Field. With so many old runways and roads, you can easily lose your direction. North of the runways, a large concrete platform is flanked by two Japanese air raid shelters on the west, and another concrete Japanese building and three American war memorials on the east. In the bush behind the middle memorial is the Japanese **air operations command post,** a massive, two-story reinforced concrete building complete with a Japanese bathtub.

However, if your main destination is the **atomic bomb loading pits,** don't turn off the road here. Instead, continue north on the main road. The road curves around toward the west, and in about a mile, you will see several small monuments to your left. At No. 1 Bomb Loading Pit an atomic bomb was loaded aboard an American B-29 dubbed *Enola Gay* on the afternoon of 5 August 1945, to be dropped on Hiroshima the next day. At nearby No. 2 Bomb Loading Pit a second atomic bomb was loaded on 9 August 1945 and dropped on Nagasaki. On 10 August 1945 Emperor Hirohito ended the Pacific war without his cabinet's consent.

West again is Chulu or **Invasion Beach,** where 15,000 U.S. soldiers landed on 24 July 1944. A concrete Japanese bunker stands watch.

Accommodations and Food

First, you must come to terms with **Tinian Dynasty Hotel and Casino** (inexpensive—if you don't lose too much money gambling) (P.O. Box 1133, Tinian, MP 96952, tel. 670-328-2233, fax 670-328-1133). Its sprawling seven stories contain more than 85% of the island's hotel rooms. From the outside it doesn't look like it cost more than $100 million to build. But inside, the hotel has recreated the type of public space where James Bond would have gambled. There is a giant marble-floored central lobby. Niches in the lobby contain replicas of Greek statutes, presumably to complement the mannerist murals in the casino. What all this has to do with creating a tropical gambling joint for well-heeled Asians is anybody's guess.

The Dynasty has a staff of 1,200. The fact that Tinian did not have the population to staff this hotel did not deter investors; they imported a staff from 27 nations. Much of the staff comes from the PRC, with many additional Filipinos, Nepalese, Thais, and a smattering of Australians and Europeans.

I went to Tinian expecting to see the same conditions for foreign workers as on Saipan. But things appear much better here. The workers live in buildings behind the hotel that look quite like my college dormitory. There are two workers per room, with each room having a bathroom. The staff receives not only English instruction, but cultural diversity training as well. The service these workers give is excellent, and for many of them, working at the Dynasty is an education. They will go back to their home countries after a couple of years with a good knowledge of the hotel industry.

Check prices and look for specials in the Saipan and Guam newspapers. The quoted price is often $100 per night, but the price for "locals," $50 a night, seems to be given to anyone with an American accent who calls up.

The rest of Tinian's hotels are small and not particularly luxurious or interesting. **Lori Lynn's Hotel** (inexpensive) (P.O. Box 478, Tinian, MP 96952, tel. 670-433-3256), a little east of San Jose city center, is probably the best choice. A comfortable, large a/c room with TV and fridge will be $40 s, $55 d. Reduced weekly and monthly rates are available. Lori Lynn's has a coffee shop with reasonably good Japanese food. You might also try the small, motel-style **Tinian Hotel** (inexpensive) at the first cross-street as you drive from the airport to San Jose. The Japanese-oriented **Fleming Hotel** (moderate) (P.O. Box 68, Tinian, MP 96952, tel. 670-433-3232, fax 670-433-3022) in central San Jose has 13 rooms at $60 s, $83 d. The Fleming complex also sports a restaurant, grocery store, laundromat, and bank.

Camping is possible at Chulu Beach at the north end of 8th Avenue or Long Beach halfway up the east coast. Bring all the food and water you might need.

The **Dynasty** has the best restaurants on the island. It has a Chinese restaurant, Japanese restaurant, and two separate buffets. The larger of the two costs $20 for a sumptuous meal. For simpler, less expensive meals, try **Mary's Bakery,** or the restaurants at the Fleming Hotel or Lori Lynn's Hotel.

Transportation
The best way to reach Tinian is to take the 300-person ferry from Saipan. The ferry covers the 23 nautical miles in 55 minutes.

West Field Airport (TIQ) is 2.5 miles north of San Jose village. Hotels will pick up, as they will at the ferry.

Freedom Air (P.O. Box 239 CK, Saipan, MP 96950, tel. 670-288-5663, fax 670-288-5663) flies between Saipan, Guam, Tinian, and Rota.

For car rentals, both **Budget** (tel. 670-433-3104) and **Avis** tel. (670-433-2847) have two offices, one located at the airport and the other about one-quarter mile before the turnoff to the Dynasty. Both will pick up and drop off at the Dynasty. Car rentals are $45 dollars a day and up. You can easily visit the sights on Tinian in half a day.

ROTA

Halfway between Tinian and Guam, Rota is an attractive, friendly island. People who live in Saipan or Guam come here to relax. As you walk or even drive around the island, people driving in the opposite direction will wave to you. They are not mistaking you for anyone; they wave to strangers as well as to friends.

The locals call their island Luta, the main town Songsong. A second village, Sinapalo, recently developed near the airport. The sea around Rota is very clear and the sunsets superb.

Sights
Shaped like a hand with a finger pointing at Guam, the flat mountain atop the finger is known as **Wedding Cake Mountain** because that's what it looks like. The village of **Songsong** is spread along a narrow neck of land between two harbors. It is on a low-lying strand of land that connects Mount Taipingot (Wedding Cake) to the rest of the island. Songsong's architecture may not be impressive, but there are views of water or mountains in almost any direction you look. Its location also allows the town to catch whatever wind is blowing.

The brick shell of an **old Japanese sugar mill** still stands beside Songsong's West Harbor, an old steam locomotive from the operation parked alongside.

At the end of the road west of Songsong is **Tweksberry Beach Park** below Wedding Cake Mountain. Tweksberry is an attractive place to sit and watch the day go by.

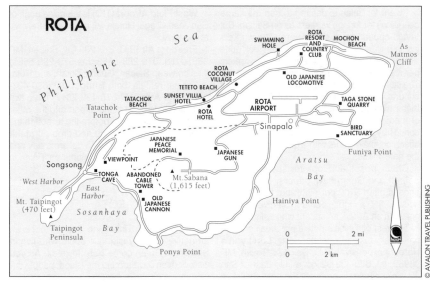

© AVALON TRAVEL PUBLISHING

Just above Songsong is **Tonga Cave,** with stalactites and stalagmites. The Japanese used it as a hospital during the war. Locals can still take shelter here during typhoons. There's a perfect short hike up the jeep track to the white cross directly above Tonga Cave. You'll get a great view of Songsong and Wedding Cake Mountain from this viewpoint, but it's too steep to drive a car up there.

The most complete collection of relics from Rota's history is at the **Rota Cave Museum,** a museum privately owned by Mattias Taisican, and located in Antigo Cave. Admission is $5 for adults, $3 for children. The museum is located about a mile from Songsong Village along the main road from the airport. Almost anywhere on Rota, one can find remains from the Japanese occupation.

Southeast

Heading southeast from Songsong, you'll soon be on a dirt road that sometimes hugs the rugged coastline. Some of the nicest homes in Rota are along the first mile of this road. See if you can spot the home built on one huge limestone outcropping. Then see if you can figure out how it was built.

A huge **Japanese cannon,** in a bunker beside the road three miles east of Songsong, overlooks Sosanhaya Bay, its camouflage paint still on. The abandoned **cable car towers** nearby once brought ore down from the phosphate mines in the interior.

Northeast

About three miles out of town, on the road to the airport, you'll pass the new campus of the **College of the Northern Marianas.** Immediately beyond is a well-maintained dirt road that leads up the mountain. First you'll pass on the left a small chapel dedicated to **Lourdes.** Another mile or so up, make a left at the sign pointing to **Taisacana's Botanical and Nature Trails.** A quarter mile down this lane, you'll reach the trailhead, opposite a beautiful overlook of the island, down perhaps a thousand feet to the ocean. On a clear day you can see Saipan, 70 miles away. The botanical trail is a level one-quarter mile. Rota is famous for its birdwatching, and this is one fine place to do it. Admission to the park is $5.

Returning to the northeast road, you'll soon reach **Teteto Beach Park,** probably the nicest beach on the island to snorkel. Like all of Saipan, a very uneven, craggy, sharp-fringing reef surrounds the beach. It is quite sharp; try not to swim or walk past it, even at high tide. However, an area within the reef can be snorkeled at high tide. There is interesting fish life, but no coral. Across the street from the beach are two snack shops, with fins and snorkels available for rent. There are bathrooms at the park.

Several miles beyond the Rota Hotel is a fork in the road. The paved road proceeds to the Rota Resort and Country Club and the airport. The dirt road continues along the coastline. Right at the fork, in very shallow water, are the remains of a **shipwreck.** Continuing on, you'll see a large, natural **swimming hole** in the reef and a perfect campsite. The stalactite-covered cliffs and blowholes (best at low tide) of **As Matmos Cliff** at Rota's northeast point are worth the drive.

If, instead, you take the paved road to the airport and continue about one and a half miles beyond the Rota Resort and Country Club, you'll reach a dirt road to the left that passes a Japanese cannon in two miles. In an additional three miles, you'll see a **Japanese Peace Memorial** on the Sabana Plateau near the highest point on Rota (1,615 feet).

If you return to the paved road and continue immediately beyond the airport, the pavement ends. If you continue straight ahead, on the dirt road, in about a mile and a half you'll reach the **Taga Stone Quarry.** The quarry is not well marked. Look for a small clearing on your left. In the quarry, nine megalithic *latte* stone pillars and seven still-unfinished capstones lie where they were being cut. Some caps are seven feet across, and some pillars at least 12 feet long. Is it possible that stones this large were never meant to be removed? Were they meant to befuddle future archaeologists? Their purpose is still unknown.

Where the pavement stops, beyond the airport, if instead of going straight you take the well-graded dirt road to the right, in about a mile and a half you reach a **bird sanctuary** and a view out over Aratsu Bay.

Accommodations
Penny's Meitetsu Hotel (budget) (P.O. Box 539, Rota, MP 96951, tel. 670-532-0468), also

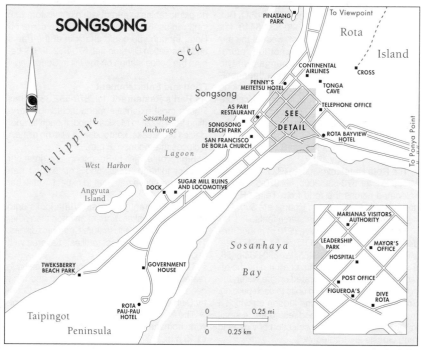

known as the Blue Peninsula Inn or "B.P. Hotel," in the middle of Songsong village, charges $30 s, $36 d for one of the 21 rooms with a/c and private bath. Penny's is pretty basic, with no phones in the room. It is not a hotel of choice, but will do if necessary.

The **Rota Bayview Hotel** (inexpensive) (P.O. Box 875, Rota, MP 96951, tel. 670-532-3414, fax 670-532-0393) in Songsong village has nine rooms, $45 s, $60 d, and is just a walk to the water's edge. It too is very basic, with no phones in the room.

Also in Songsong village and on the ocean is the **Coral Garden Hotel** (inexpensive) (P.O. Box 597, Rota, MP 96951, tel. 670-532-3201, fax 670-532-3204). Its 22 rooms are $44. The rooms have nice views, telephones, and TV, but are quite dreary.

Jotina Inn, (inexpensive) (P.O. Box 887, Rota, MP 96951, tel. 670-532-0500, fax 670-532-0703) the newest budget hotel in Songsong, has TV and phones in the room and is, at $40 per night, a cut above the other inexpensive hotels.

Rota Coconut Village (moderate) (P.O. Box 855, Rota, MP 96951, tel. 670-532-3448, fax 670-532-3449) is on the coast, west of the airport. An individual Japanese hot tub *(ofuro)* comes with each of the 18 bungalow-style rooms, which are $80 d. There's a three-foot-deep swimming pool on a terrace overlooking the sea, but no beach below, just a rocky shore graced by a shipwreck. The rooms are very charming and a good value for the price, but the staff speaks Japanese and has difficulty communicating in English. If that won't bother you, it's a lovely place to stay.

The **Rota Hotel** (expensive) (P.O. 878, Rota, MP 96951, tel. 670-532-2000, fax 670-532-3000) is located across the road from Teteto Beach and has a swimming pool. Rooms are $90. The hotel is new and still has a sterile feel to it.

Better and less expensive ($70 d) is the **Sunset Villia** (moderate) (P.O. Box 511751, Rota, MP 96951, tel. 670-532-8455, fax 670-532-8458, e-mail: sunsetv@gtepacifica.net) run by the affable Vianney Hocog. Located on the water, the hotel has 20 units, with two units to each building. Small porches overlook the lagoon on which it fronts. The hotel has a good restaurant, a small karaoke bar, and a large selection of videos to rent. Guests are treated well.

The two-story **Rota Pau Pau Hotel** (luxury) (P.O. Box 503, Rota, MP 96951, tel. 670-532-3561, fax 670-532-3562) stands on a terrace below Mount Taipingot at the south end of town, looking like a TraveLodge. All 50 rooms have a fridge and bathtub. Many rooms have good views over the East Harbor, but the hotel isn't near a beach. It does have a pool, but the hotel is isolated. Overpriced at $165 s, $194 d, it will offer a rate of about half that for "locals."

Rota Resort and Country Club (luxury) (P.O. Box 938, Rota, MP 96951, tel. 670-532-1155, fax 670-532-1156) is quite luxurious, located up on the plateau, overlooking the golf course and the ocean. It is the most sybaritic spot on Rota, and golfers love to stay here. It can be very expensive, but the resort frequently runs specials for those from Saipan or Guam.

Camping possibilities include the park in front of Tonga Cave, Tweksberry Beach Park, Teteto Beach Park, and Tatachok Beach. A lot of traffic passes Teteto and Tatachok, and Tonga Cave is probably better than Tweksberry as there are no picnic tables to attract late night visitors with loud radios. No permit is required to camp on Rota, though you could check in at the Parks and Recreation Division (tel. 670-532-4001), behind the police station on the hill in Songsong.

Food and Entertainment

As Pari's Restaurant (tel. 670-532-3356) has Rota's most extensive menu including everything from pizza to Mexican food, though its specialties are steaks, seafood, and Filipino dishes. It closes afternoons 1-6 p.m.

Figueroa's, also in Songsong, is a great bar in which to hang out. Its food is quite good, better than you have any right to expect from a bar in Rota.

The restaurant in **Sunset Villia** looks onto the lagoon. It makes more of an effort than other restaurants on Rota to feature Chamorro dishes. Try the *titiyas* (breakfast tortillas), flavored with coconut and fried.

The Pau-Pau Hotel and Coconut Village have restaurants that are fairly expensive and fairly good. The **Pacifica** at the Rota Resort and Country Club is an elegant and expensive restaurant.

The Mobil station at the entrance to Songsong from the airport sells groceries and is open till 10 p.m.

Sports and Recreation

Dive Rota (P.O. Box 941, Rota, MP 96951, tel. 670-532-3377, fax 670-532-3022, website: www.diverota.com) at East Harbor, Songsong, charges $50 for a one-tank morning or afternoon dive ($80 for two dives the same day). Americans Mark and Lynne Michael also offer night dives and trolling. They'll happily take snorkelers out in their boat for $25 pp. Even if you aren't a diver, visit their shop in Songsong for the wide selection of island T-shirts.

Most of the dive sites are near Songsong. The wreck of the WW II Japanese freighter *Shoun Maru* stands upright in about 100 feet of crystal-clear water in East Harbor. The wreck has been blown open to reveal trucks, bicycles, a deck crane, a bathtub, and two steam engines. Divers also can inspect the underwater debris near the phosphate loading cableway on the same bay and, of course, the usual marinelife on the reefs. It's possible to surface inside Senhanom Cave, among the moray eels, squirrel fish, and bronze sweepers.

In February 1999, the U.S. Coast Guard sank two boats in the harbor to create additional dive sites. The boats had been seized for smuggling immigrants.

Services

The **Bank of Guam** (tel. 670-532-0340) is below Penny's Meitetsu Hotel. International phone calls are more cheaply and easily placed on Saipan than on Rota and Tinian. There are several coin-operated laundromats in Songsong.

Transportation

Rota International Airport (ROP) is eight miles northeast of Songsong. The excellent highway along the north coast from the airport to Songsong. Hitching to the airport is easy, but little traffic runs along the other roads. Car campers should note that the toilets at the airport are open long hours. The Mayflower Restaurant upstairs in the terminal is nice for a cup of coffee.

There is no public transportation on Rota, though many of the hotels will shuttle you around. It is also an easy island to rent a car and explore on your own. Most of the car rental companies have counters at the airport, including **Budget** (tel. 670-532-3535, fax 670-532-0801) and **Islander** (tel. 670-532-0901 or 670-532-0902). Expect to pay $40 and up with unlimited mileage.

NORTHERN ISLANDS

Pagan, 201 miles north of Saipan, has a formidable volcano, hot springs, and winding beaches of glistening black sand. Bandeera village is on Apaan Bay, backed by the narrow isthmus that separates explosive Mount Pagan (1,875 feet) in the north from the two dormant volcanoes in the south. When the mountain exploded in May 1981, blowing a section off the summit, the 54 Chamorro inhabitants of Pagan escaped the flow of molten lava by huddling together in bat-infested caves until they were rescued by a Japanese freighter. A wrecked Japanese bomber and anti-aircraft gun remain beside Pagan's airstrip.

Only a handful of people live on **Agrihan** and **Alamagan.** The group on Agrihan are Carolinians, while Chamorros reside on Alamagan. The Chamorros made a last stand against the Spanish conquistadors on Agrihan in the 17th century. A hot spring is at the north end of Alamagan's west coast.

A wide caldera was created at the center of **Anatahan** when its volcano blew up. On the crater wall are two peaks, 2,349 and 2,593 feet high, on its northeast and west sides, respectively. In 1990 all 22 inhabitants evacuated the island due to continuing volcanic activity.

Asuncion's active volcanic cone rises to 2,931 feet. **Maug** comprises three steep islands, which remained when its volcano exploded and the sea flooded the caldera. The Japanese once used the submerged caldera as an anchorage and had a weather station here, but Maug is now abandoned. The Tropic of Cancer slices through Maug. **Uracas** (Farallon de Pajaros), northernmost of the Marianas, is a cinder-covered active volcano.

GORDON OHLIGER

REPUBLIC OF NAURU
INTRODUCTION

- *"What is Nauru?"*

- *"What is Nauru?" is the correct response to a $1,000 geography question on the TV show* Jeopardy. *It would also be the correct response to:*

- *This country's wealth was built on bird droppings.*

- *This country went from being the wealthiest per capita in the Pacific to economic chaos in about five years.*

- *This country's nearest neighbor is almost 400 miles away.*

- *This country is surrounded by ocean, but has almost no place to go in for a swim.*

Tiny, 21-square-km (eight-square-mile) Nauru built its economy on extracting large deposits of easily accessible, high-grade phosphates. For millions of years, billions of birds nested on

Nauru, and the excrement or guano (phosphoric acid and nitrogen) they left behind reacted through leaching with the coral (lime) of this upraised atoll to form a hard, odorless, colorless rock, averaging 85-88% pure phosphate of lime. This fertilizer kept the fields of New Zealand green and the farms of Australia productive. Ironically, the phosphate has no impact on the fertility of Nauru itself, as it must be treated with sulfuric acid before it can be used as fertilizer.

The Land
Oyster-shaped Nauru is one of the three great phosphate rock islands of the Pacific (the others are Banaba in Kiribati and Makatea in the Tuamotus). A fringing reef, bare at low tide, encloses glistening white sand beaches from which rugged limestone rock often protrude. A 100-300 meter wide (330-1,085 foot wide) coastal belt and a small area around the Buada Lagoon contain the island's only cultivable soil. Coral cliffs encircle an elevated interior plateau that

reaches 65 meters (214 feet) in altitude. Punctuated by white coral pinnacles left over when the phosphate was removed, much of the barren, moonscape interior is a scene of utter desolation, in striking contrast to the lush, tropical coastline. Even in the oldest fields, in which vegetation has begun to grow back, the land is now so jagged that it cannot be used.

Climate

Only 53 km (33 miles) south of the equator, there's no seasonal variation in Nauru's temperature. November through February are the wettest months; drier northeasterly tradewinds blow the rest of the year. Rainfall varies greatly from year to year with periods of prolonged droughts.

History

The exact origins of the Nauruans is not clear. Their language is neither like the Gilbert islanders, nor like the Polynesians'. Anthropologists find it difficult to classify the people of this island.

The first known European ship to arrive at Nauru was the British whaler *Hunter,* which arrived in 1798. Captain John Fearn named it Pleasant Island for the welcome he received. During the 1830s whalers began calling more often, a number of crew members deserting to remain on land. These men allied themselves with rival chiefs, and after 1878 there was continual fighting among Nauru's 12 tribes.

Germans from New Guinea landed in 1888 and suppressed the tribal warfare. Arms and ammunition were confiscated; liquor was banned.

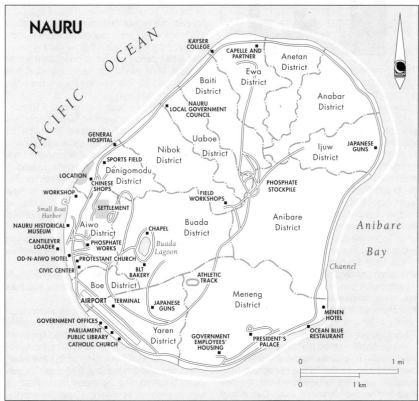

NAURU'S CLIMATE

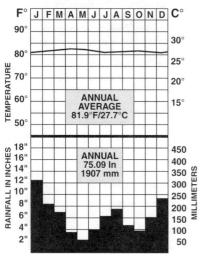

The Germans set about running their new colony as part of the Marshall Islands Protectorate, unaware of the wealth beneath their feet. The first missionaries showed up around 1899.

While visiting Nauru in 1896, trader Henry E. Denson picked up a stratified rock, assuming it was from a petrified tree. He took the rock back to Australia thinking perhaps it could be made into children's marbles. It kicked around the office of Denson's Pacific Islands Company for a couple of years and was being used as a doorstop when Albert Ellis, a young company employee in Sydney, noticed it. He had it analyzed and discovered that it contained 80% pure phosphate of lime. Today the original rock is in Auckland Museum in New Zealand.

The Germans had already claimed the island and set up a trading post and coconut plantation. As mineral rights negotiations proceeded on Nauru, an employee of the Sydney company found vast additional quantities of the same material on Banaba. Britain annexed Banaba on 28 September 1901.

It was finally agreed that the phosphates of Nauru would be exploited under joint British-German auspices, by the Pacific Phosphate Company. Profits were to be shared with the German firm on the Marshalls, Jaluit Gesellshaft.

The agreement made no provision for direct compensation to the Nauruans. Mining began in 1907, but the Germans lost their share when Australia took Nauru without a fight on 9 September 1914, at the beginning of World War I. A Japanese warship arrived soon after with the same intent, but turned back when it found the Australians already in control.

After the war, the League of Nations granted Australia the right to administer Nauru, on behalf of itself, New Zealand, and Britain. In 1920, the British Phosphate Commissioners (BPC), controlled by these three governments, bought out all rights to the deposits. Far from benefitting the Nauruans, the early days of phosphate mining witnessed a series of epidemics introduced by the foreign labor force: dysentery (1907), polio (1910), influenza (1919), and pneumonia (1920). Some 400 Nauruans died from these diseases, lowering the population to only 1,200 in 1920. In 1927, agreement was reached between the company and the island chiefs that a royalty of seven and a half pence per ton of phosphate would be paid. Mining land was to be leased at £40 an acre and 25 shillings paid for any food-producing tree cut down.

World War II came to the island on 6 December 1940, when the German raider *Orion* captured and sank the BPC vessel *Triona* bound for Nauru. The next day the *Orion* and its companion, the *Komet,* arrived at Nauru and sank four more phosphate freighters drifting offshore. On 27 December 1940 the *Komet* returned to Nauru and shelled the cantilever loader, putting it out of commission until 1948. Because of weather conditions, the Germans never attempted to land. On 9 December 1941 a Japanese plane bombed the radio station, making Nauru one of the few lands that was bombed by both the Germans and the Japanese. With the war situation deteriorating the British Phosphate Commissioners evacuated personnel and their families.

On 26 August 1942 a Japanese invasion force landed on Nauru and began to build the present airport. Of the 1,850 Nauruans present when the Japanese arrived some 1,200 were eventually deported to Chuuk to serve as slave labor. It was not until 31 January 1946 that 737 survivors returned. The Japanese solved Nauru's leprosy problem by loading 49 people with the disease into a boat and sinking it. The Allies bypassed Nauru; some 500 Japanese marines held it until the end of the war.

In 1947, Nauru became a United Nations Trust Territory administered by Australia. Phosphate shipments recommenced in July 1947, and payments to the Nauruans were increased. Despite the devastating and permanent effect of the mining on the land, until 1965 only a 2.5% royalty was paid to the Nauruans for the phosphate.

The first elected Local Government Council was formed in 1951. The Council began to press Australia for a greater share of the profits from the phosphate mining. Expenditures by the BPC administration for health, housing, and education increased nearly fivefold between 1951 and 1955. In 1953 public service employees launched a four-month strike led by Hammer DeRoburt, who was elected Head Chief in 1956.

In 1963 DeRoburt turned down an offer of Australian citizenship for his people and resettlement somewhere on Australian territory, such as Fraser or Curtis Islands off the coast of Queensland. In January 1966, with the establishment of legislative and executive councils, Nauruans became almost self-governing. The next year, it was agreed that Nauru could buy itself back from the British Phosphate Commissioners for A$21 million, payable over three years. On 31 January 1968, the 22nd anniversary of the return from Chuuk, Nauru became the world's smallest republic. DeRoburt was elected president in May 1968 and on 30 June 1970 the mines were formally transferred to the Nauru Phosphate Corporation.

Government

Two levels of government coexist. The Nauru Government, run by the elected president and his ministers, owns the Nauru Phosphate Corporation and Air Nauru, while the Nauru Local Government Council (NLGC), under an elected head chief and his councilors, controls trade, including the Nauru Insurance Corporation, the Civic Center complex, the Menen Hotel, and the Lands Committee. Nauru has an 18-member Parliament, which is elected every three years. It, in turn, elects the president from its ranks. During one period at the end of 1996, four presidents served in a three-month period. The five cabinet ministers are chosen by the president. The

Nauru Party, founded in 1975, was reformed as the Democratic Party in 1987. The Nauru Local Government Council consists of nine elected members under a head chief. There are 14 districts, each headed by a councillor (formerly the chief of the clan).

Economy

Since its independence in 1968 until 1990, Nauru exported 2 million tons of phosphate a year to Australia, New Zealand, Korea, and the Philippines, bringing in A$100 million. In 1990, shipments declined sharply, partly due to alternative agricultural techniques, but more fundamentally because the reserves of easily removable phosphate were being exhausted.

The Nauru Government takes half the revenue from phosphate sales; the rest is split between the Local Government Council, the Nauru Phosphate Royalties Trust, and landowners. The trust fund reached more than A$2 billion. It was designed to provide the inhabitants with a future income. Investments included flashy office buildings in Melbourne ("Birdshit Tower"), Honolulu, Manila, and Saipan, two Sheraton hotels in New Zealand, Fiji's Grand Pacific Hotel, and the highly successful Pacific Star Hotel on Guam.

Though financial reports are not published, other investments were disastrous, like the never completed Eastern Gateway Hotel on Majuro. Nauru is believed to have lost A$70 million on a fertilizer plant in the Philippines and millions more on a similar plant in India. Maintaining Air Nauru, necessary in order to connect Nauru to the rest of the world because no other airline goes there, has been a cash drain.

On the income from the phosphate, a nonrenewable resource, the Nauruans built an unsustainable economy. It became a consumption-oriented small island nation. A whole host of flim-flam outsiders descended on the island, with one project or another to separate Nauruans from their money. Today, Nauru realizes that the party is over. Economic self-sufficiency can only be achieved now by decreased personal consumption, greater efficiency in governmental operations, and most important, the removal of harder-to-reach remaining phosphate through "residual" mining techniques.

In 1989 Nauru filed suit before the International Court of Justice to get the governments of

Australia, Britain, and New Zealand to pay for damage to the land. In 1994, the suit was settled for A$107 million to be used to rehabilitate the island's interior. Work has not yet begun.

The People

Of the 10,000 people living on Nauru, about 70% are indigenous Nauruans. For many years, there also has been a large number of laborers from Kiribati. The rest of the population is made up of a mix of other Pacific Islanders, expat Australians, New Zealanders, and Chinese. The number of foreign contract laborers, who once made up almost 40% of the work force, is being reduced as Nauru's economy weakens. These foreign workers are housed in long, squalid tenements at **Location.** As the number of foreign workers decreases, Nauru has been tearing down some of these tenements to reduce overcrowding.

Nauruans have the world's highest incidence of diabetes—a shocking 30%. Medical journals cite Nauru's epidemic as a classic case of junk food-induced diabetes. High blood pressure, heart disease, alcoholism, and obesity are rampant, making a 50th birthday a big event.

Most Nauruans reside in single-story, tin-roofed family homes strung along the coastline and around the Buada lagoon. For now, the Nauruans' education, hospitalization, electricity, and housing are still provided free by the government, and there is no income tax, sales tax, or customs duties. School truancy has become an issue in Nauru. Some affluent Nauruans send their children to Australia or New Zealand in an attempt to obtain a better education than they perceive is available on Nauru.

Conduct

Be aware that Nauruans do not take kindly to argumentative foreigners. Many Nauruan men are large, strong, and not averse to being physical. A friendly, low-key approach is usually best. Although Nauruans are reputed to be the most loyal and caring of friends, they are not particularly friendly to newcomers, which is not surprising considering their treatment by foreigners. Be careful walking after dark as many Nauruans train their dogs to attack.

Holidays and Events

Public holidays include New Year's (1 January), Independence Day (31 Jan.-2 Feb.), Easter, Constitution Day (17 May), Angam Day (26 October), and Christmas (25 December). The Independence Day celebration includes fishing competitions, sports events, a parade by students, and a speech from the president. Angam Day commemorates the times (in 1932 and 1949) when the local population regenerated to 1,500, the minimum necessary, according to Nauruans, for the maintenance of a collective identity.

Island activity virtually stops on the afternoon of the first Tuesday in November when the Melbourne Cup horse race is run and shown live on Nauru television.

SIGHTS

Around the Island

Nauru has a well-maintained road that circles the island and is 19 km (12 miles) long. Driving is done in the left-hand lane. A cement sidewalk borders the road much of the way, and small stores and restaurants are well distributed, so you're never too far from a cold drink or snack. Thus, one can walk around Nauru, but remember, Nauru is just below the equator, making it very difficult to take this jaunt during midday. Reader John Connell writes: "Setting off at 6 one morning, I ran around the island without too much interference from dogs. I now claim to be one of the few people to have run around a country (even a republic) before breakfast!" Both the Menen Hotel and the Od-N-Aiwo offer guided tours, including trips to the phosphate diggings. Except for school buses, there is no public transportation on the island.

An alternative is taxis, which are not too expensive, once you've found them. The hotels serve as taxi stands. Taxis work on a meter, and the drivers will not set a flat hourly rate. A trip around the island, around Buada Lagoon, and through Top Side to see the phosphate fields costs about A$40, excluding waiting time. So make sure to negotiate ahead of time that the meter not run while the driver is waiting for you. The interesting parts of the island can be seen in about four hours, and you should set an outside limit of time to encourage the taxi driver to agree to turn off the meter when you leave the cab. If plane connections allow only a couple of hours on Nauru, hire a taxi to go up into the interior.

Cars can be rented for A$50, almost double that if you wish a new midsize car with air conditioning. Make arrangements through your hotel.

Bottom Side

The section of the Aiwa district on the around-the-island road serves as "downtown" for Nauru. The phosphate mined on the hot, dusty interior plateau (Top Side) is brought down by train to the works behind the **cantilever loaders** (Bottom Side). Here the material is crushed, screened,

Nauru phosphates are loaded onto ships for Australia and New Zealand from these giant cantilever loaders at Aiwo.

roasted, and stored. A **calcination plant** removes all carbon and most cadmium (a pollutant) from the phosphate.

The **buoys** off Aiwo are connected to the deepest water moorings in the world (518 meters, 1,704 feet). Two ships can be loaded from the cantilevers at a time. The **small boat harbor** nearby remains from the pre-1927 days when ships were loaded by lighter.

Just south of the cantilevers, on the inland side of the road, is the Civic Center Building. The main post office is there, open weekdays 8 a.m.- noon and 1:30-4:45 p.m. You can make overseas calls and fax from the post office. Nauru has some very pretty stamps that make wonderful, inexpensive souvenirs. The building also contains an **Air Nauru** office and a large market, with many bare shelves.

NPC Staff Club (Nauru Phosphate Corporation) is about three hundred yards north of the cantilever. This private club sells beer and has a snack bar. One of the "tropo" Aussies probably will offer to sign you in if you look respectable.

Running north from the NPC club is a little road that the locals call "The Boulevard." There are a number of thatched roof-covered tables overlooking the harbor and also a pizza stand. Bingo games run on Monday and Wednesday evenings.

Right before you reach the golf course, standing behind an old steam locomotive used by the Germans to bring down phosphate, is a small museum containing early 20th-century photographs, some weaponry and other materials left from the Japanese occupation, and a cabinet showing different forms of phosphate. The museum is seldom open, but if you call the director of works operation at (674) 555-6181, the office may send someone to open it for you. The Museum sells an interesting pamphlet, *Republic of Nauru, Historical Sites and World War II Relics*.

Location, the housing area for foreign workers, is just north of the boat harbor. In this hot, dusty, squalid area, large numbers of people have been packed into overcrowded two-story cinder block tenements. One can only wonder about the poverty on other islands that forced Pacific Islanders to choose to work in Nauru and live under such conditions.

Management housing sits on the hilltop above, at **Settlement,** and uses the nine-hole golf course abutting Location.

About 15 small Chinese-owned shops sit by the road in front of Location, selling clothing, household supplies, and foodstuffs. Each shop usually has three or four owners or family members sitting in its cramped space, though no store seems to have more than one or two customers at a time.

Waterfront

Leaving Aiwa and heading north around the island, you'll see the lushness of the coastal strip, with many plumeria trees breathing their fragrance into the air. Looking out to the ocean, at any time other than high tide, you can see an exposed, hard coastal reef. It is the presence of this reef that makes entry into the ocean so hazardous. On the reef are sharp coral pinnacles. The hard edge of the reef makes any return from the ocean hazardous, since waves make it very difficult to avoid being smashed into the reef. At two places, channels have been dug through the coral, one at the small boat harbor and the other on Anibare Bay. However, even trying to enter the ocean at the channels can be treacherous: water may be flowing into part of the channel while a vicious riptide can be flowing outward several feet away. Once in the riptide, you can be taken out of the channel and carried miles down the coast where you may have to try to get back to shore by going over the reef. To paraphrase the Ancient Mariner:

Water, water everywhere, but not a spot to surf.

Reef walking at low tide along the coast (especially at Anibare Bay, near the Menen Hotel) is fascinating. Corals, sea urchins, crabs, and small fish can be seen in abundance at the edge of the intertidal zone. Wear good strong reef walkers. Watch your footing, and unless you are a very experienced ocean-goer, do not get too close to the reef's edge. Along the bay are fantastic-looking limestone deposits, a photographer's paradise.

There is a memo of understanding with Japan to put in a small boat harbor at the Anibare channel. That channel originally had been dug to make it more likely that Queen Elizabeth could make it to shore from her royal yacht.

Frigate birds are often seen soaring above the shoreline. The keeping of these birds was a traditional pastime on Nauru. Young boys throw weighted nets to try to catch a bird. A bird that is caught will have its articulated wings taped back for a period of about a week. During that period, they are hand-fed fresh fish. After, the tape is removed and the birds are free to fly as they like. Needless to say, they always return to where they know a free meal is waiting. They are fed on a perch that stands in the water, but will rest on a roost placed on the shore.

In the 1980s this Nauruan custom almost died out. In 1994 President Dowiyogo announced plans to revitalize the tradition. The program has been enormously successful, and today you can see the roosts and their birds all around the island, tame enough to approach and photograph.

Buada Lagoon

A road goes uphill from the cantilevers to the interior. Shortly past the phosphate works it dead-ends into another road. If you take the turn to the left, the road circles the saltwater lagoon. The lagoon is used for raising milk fish and not for swimming, but it is picturesque. Circling the lake counterclockwise, you will reach the **BLT Bakery** in several hundred yards, a delightful place to have a cold drink and some fresh bread, or Chinese dishes for about A$3. The lagoon is nicely developed as all the homes are across the road, leaving open views of the water. Bananas, coconuts, and even some taro are grown. You'll also see large breadfruit and pandanus trees that provide shade as you walk. Wear bug repellent. You can walk up to the lagoon, stop at the BLT, walk around the lagoon and back to the Od-N-Aiwo in an hour and a half. Alternatively, a taxi can get you to the lagoon from the Od-N-Aiwo for about A$3, and you can walk around the lagoon and back down to town.

Top Side

A look at the mined-out **coral pinnacles** of the interior is an essential part of any tour of the island. You may visit the **phosphate fields** on foot. The walk is easy enough, but it is uphill. Don't try it in the heat of the day and bring plenty of water as there are no facilities along the way. It's about three miles to where mining is still going on. Cross-country hiking off the road through the pinnacles is very dangerous. If you fall into a pit, easy to do in the topsy-turvy topography of the fields themselves, you might never be found.

There are no restrictions on entry. Head inland from the Od-N-Aiwo Hotel. You come to a T intersection at the top of the hill. Take the road to the right to get to the current minefields (to the left, the road runs to the Buada Lagoon). While not paved, this road is well maintained and wide. It leads up to a flat plateau. At the next fork in the road, again go to the right. As you approach the active mining, you begin to see the "moonscape" scenery. There is an awesome ugliness to it all: limestone pinnacles protruding from land where phosphate has been removed. The pinnacles look like religious monoliths, and perhaps they are monuments to the religion of modernity, science, and exploitation.

In some of the older minefields, you will see vegetation fighting its way back, growing in the small amounts of topsoil left behind. But the topography remains. It is not clear whether the land ever can be meaningfully rehabilitated. One current idea is to bulldoze the pinnacles. This would help level out the fields. Residual phosphate could be recovered from beneath where the pinnacles now stand. Topsoil could then be brought in.

Great cranes load giant trucks at quite a slow pace due to the small size of the grab buckets on the crane. You'll often see lengths of steel cable protruding from the coral pinnacles with a grab bucket cut loose below. It was cheaper to abandon jammed buckets than to spend time trying to retrieve them. One of the few **railways** in the central Pacific operates here. The long phosphate trains traverse the narrow gauge tracks from the interior loader to Bottom Side below.

The interior of Nauru is in ecological chaos, but photographers will be intrigued, particularly early in the morning or late in the afternoon when the pinnacles cast shadows.

War Relics

Many wartime **Japanese pillboxes** dot the coastal fringe and more are slightly inland. Just a little north of Anibare Bay, on the inland side of the road adjacent to houses on the crest of a hill, are two large coastal defense guns. One is hard to find as a large workshop has been erected right next to it, but the other is in the open.

Many Japanese bunkers are around the Menen Hotel, including a well-hidden pillbox just off the steps to the tennis courts and a larger two-story observation post directly below the courts. An underground bunker is behind the volleyball court near the hotel entrance. A number of camouflaged bunkers are on the interior side of the airport runway.

A machine gun from an American Flying Fortress, shot down over Nauru during World War II, is mounted in the front yard of a private residence in Yaren, along the road from the airport terminal near the Meneng District boundary line.

PRACTICALITIES

Accommodations
There are two hotels on the island.

The government-owned **Menen Hotel** (P.O. Box 298, Republic of Nauru, Central Pacific, tel. 674-444-3300, fax 674-444-3595) was expanded and upgraded for the 24th South Pacific Forum, which was held in Nauru in 1993. Its modern facilities are spotlessly clean. It is the hotel of choice, particularly for business travelers. It has 119 well-designed rooms, with good air conditioning and TVs that bring in CNN and Australian MTV. The hotel is located on the water at the south end of picturesque Anibare Bay, four km (2.5 miles) east of the airport terminal. Prices for standard rooms are A$85 s, A$120 d. Prices are higher for ocean view rooms, but that can often be negotiated down. The hotel will work out a different pricing structure for those working in Nauru for an extended period.

Service is good at the hotel. It has a bar, restaurant, swimming pool, and all-weather tennis courts. The bar at the Menen is probably the best place to meet expat Aussies and Kiwis and business travelers to the island. The hotel's restaurant offers standard chicken, beef, and fish dishes, as well as popular outdoor barbecues (A$10) Wednesday and Friday nights. The restaurant has one of the best wine lists in Micronesia, left over from Nauru's glory days.

The island's other hotel, the family-operated **Od-N-Aiwo Hotel** (P.O. Box 299, Aiwo District, Republic of Nauru, Central Pacific, tel. 674-444-3283, fax 674-444-3720), located near the Civic Center and phosphate works downtown, is good if you want to observe local life. The 60 a/c rooms, many with ocean or port views, go for A$45 s,

A$60 d. The rooms are simply arranged with refrigerators but no TV. The hotel's biggest drawback is that, depending on the direction of the wind, it can become quite dusty from the cantilever or the phosphate-processing plant. The hotel's restaurant serves fixed-plate breakfast (A$5), lunch (A$10), and dinner (A$10). There is a different menu for each day of the week. On the hotel's first floor is also a Chinese take-away restaurant.

Food
Nauru has a fair number of restaurants in addition to those at the hotels. Several inexpensive Chinese restaurants are at the Chinese shops near the workers' housing area at Location. A good lunch of beef and rice goes for around A$3. The **Triton Restaurant** near the Od-N-Aiwo is good, and if you wish to spend a little more, the **Star Twinkles Restaurant** at Nibok is worth a try. The **Frangipani Cafe** at Boe is very reasonable. Small Chinese cafés dot the island. **Ocean Blue Chinese Restaurant,** about one km south of the Menen Hotel, serves small plates for about $6, a bit more for large. It serves breakfast, lunch, and dinner. Food is available at Capelle & Partners supermarket at Ewa, open late most evenings.

Sports and Recreation
Nauru's national sport is Australian Rules football. Games at the sports field by the road just north of the Chinese shops are played all day Saturday and some evenings. Admission is free. Fast-pitch softball is also popular on the island, and if there is only a pick-up game going on, you may well be invited to join in. The nine-hole golf course near Location is open to the public.

Local expatriate Ian Chapman got here working with Jacques Cousteau. He offers diving to certified divers only for A$45 pp and to snorkelers for A$20 pp, with a two-person minimum.

NAURU COUNTRY CODE: 674

Contact Ian through Pacific Blue Diving Company, Ewa, (tel. 674-555-4550, fax 674-444-3759). There are relatively few good sites to dive. Since Nauru has an exposed reef, there are no soft coral. But after a period of relatively little rain, there can be an enormous number of pelagic fish close to shore because the water gets very deep very quickly. One hundred meters from shore, the ocean is 100 meters deep. Ian warns that one can dive or snorkel only under certain weather conditions. These will occur about half the time. Ian checks the ocean each day to determine where, if anyplace, is safe.

Sean Oppenheimer runs the fishing side of the operation. Two modern vessels are available. The larger rents for A\$75 per hour and can accommodate five, while the other is A\$45 per hour and can accommodate three. Call ahead so that one of the boats will be ready for you. You have a shot at large game fish and are almost certain to bring in skipjack. Again, if weather or surf conditions are bad at Nauru's two channels, you may not be able to go out.

You can usually find Ian and Sean at their offices at Capelle & Partners.

Surf fishing can be done from the reef at low tide, but don't go out unless you are pretty experienced with surf and agile on your feet.

Shopping

Except for Toddy Soft Drinks and local fish, practically every consumable is imported. Because of shipping difficulties, store shelves are often bare. Look for expiration dates on any packaged food you buy because other nations are fond of dumping out-of-date products on Nauruan consumers. I saw a package of "Stainless Gillette Blue Blades" in the same cardboard package we used to get in the States 30 years ago. Thank goodness they were rustproof.

Nauru has a number of food shops. Far and away the best is **Capelle & Partners,** located on the inland side of the round-the-island road in the Ewa district. Usually available are frozen foods, ice cream, liquor, fruit juices, film, and the like. The small Chinese shops near Location are usually better stocked than the larger stores operated by the Local Government Council.

Most business needs can be tended to in the **Civic Center** at Aiwo, which includes the Air Nauru office, the bank, and the post office from which

This ancient coral hatchet was found behind Capelle's by Hailis Capelle.

you can make international calls and send faxes.

The **Central Pacific Bookshop** near the Od-N-Aiwo sells magazines and some good postcards of Nauru. The post office may also have postcards. Color print film is available at a small store opposite the Civic Center with 24-hour processing available.

Visas

All visitors must have a passport. A visa is not required if you'll be continuing to a third country on the first connecting flight and hold a confirmed seat reservation. In practice, this means that you do not need a visa for any reasonably short visit. Contrary to reports in prior editions of this book, the customs office is now polite and efficient. If you know a Nauruan family willing to sponsor you, a one-month visa may be possible, but application must be made at a Nauruan diplomatic office before your planned arrival.

For longer visits, apply for a visa. If the stay is for business, the nature of the business and any Nauruan contacts must be detailed. Write to Principal Immigration Officer, Nauru, Central Pacific. You can also apply for a visa in person or write: Consulate General of the Republic of Nauru, Level 50, 80 Collins Street, Melbourne, VIC 3000, Australia. Other consulate offices are:

Honorary Consul for Nauru, Level 5, 17 Castlereagh Street, Sydney, NSW 2000, Australia; Consulate General of Nauru, Sheraton Mall, 105 Symonds Street, Auckland, New Zealand; Embassy for Nauru, 7th Floor, Ratu Sukanu House, MacArthur Street, Suva, Fiji; Nauru Representative in London, Mairi Government Office, 3 Chelsham Street, London SW1-X8ND, U.K.; Consul General for Nauru, 7th Floor, Pacific Star Building, Makati Avenue, Makati Metro, Manila, Philippines.

Services

Nauru uses Australian currency. In recent years, the Australian dollar has been worth about two-thirds of an American dollar. Hotels change traveler's checks at a worse rate than the Bank of Nauru. Credit cards are now accepted at the two major hotels. International calls can be placed from your hotel or the main post office. Nauru uses the three-pin Australian plug and 240 volts, 50 cycles AC electricity.

Address mail to: Republic of Nauru, Central Pacific.

Free consultations are available weekdays at the general hospital at Denigmodu just up the road from the NPC staff hospital. Nauru doesn't have a tourist information office. The Australian High Commission in the Civic Center has a decent library where you can relax in comfort and learn about the wonders of Oz.

Information

The government publishes the *Bulletin,* in English, once a week. There are no tourist brochures available in the country.

Getting There

Nauru International Airport (INU), one km (two-thirds of a mile) southeast of the Civic Center at Aiwo, was extensively remodeled in 1993. Both hotels have courtesy buses meeting incoming flights. The Menen Hotel operates a café at the airport that serves a continental breakfast for departing and arriving morning flights. There also is a small bar. Next to the airport is Nancy's Chinese restaurant and a food market. Nancy's is quite expensive, with many dishes costing more than A$12. It has an indoor, air-conditioned room and outside eating as well.

Air Nauru, the only airline to land on the island, has flights to Australia: Brisbane ($328), Melbourne ($369), Sidney ($369). It also flies to Guam ($257); Manila, Philippines ($414); Nadi and Suva, Fiji ($214); Pohnpei, FSM ($219); and Tarawa, Kiribati ($109). All prices are in U.S. dollars for a one-way economy ticket. You can check dates and time of flights, as well as any price changes, at Air Nauru's website: www.airnauru.com.au.

Be sure to reconfirm your onward flight soon after you arrive. Call (674) 444-3758. Get to the airport early, as check-in is two hours before flight time and the counter closes 30 minutes before departure time. If your Air Nauru flight is delayed or canceled, politely ask the employee at the airport to give you a voucher for a paid room with meals at the Menen Hotel.

Visiting yachts must tie up to a ship's buoy, and someone must stay on the boat at all times. It's much too deep to anchor. Spending the night moored here is not allowed, however, and yachts must stand offshore overnight if they wish to stay a second day. Dinghies can land in the shallow small-boat harbor, though it does experience quite a tidal surge. Diesel fuel is usually available, but little water.

Nauruans have revived their tradition of keeping frigatebirds.

LOUISE FOOTE

GORDON OHLIGER

REPUBLIC OF KIRIBATI
INTRODUCTION

You've got to love a country that still uses five-digit phone numbers and doesn't yet have postal codes. If you're still not sold, let me quote from the introduction to the *Kiribati Visitor's Handbook* published by the Republic of Kiribati:

> *We hope you will appreciate the values we consider important: family, hospitality, peace and tranquility, time for conversation and sharing, time to relax.*
>
> *We put these values ahead of television (we have none), work, we do work, but we have not become slaves to it and the pressures of modern life.*

Kiribati is to the world as North Dakota is to the United States: even when there, you do not fully believe its existence. Is it any wonder that the co-directors of the Peace Corps in Kiribati claim a stateside address in North Dakota?

Mention to a friend that you've just returned from Kiribati (KIR-i-bas) and you will most likely hear, "What'd ya say?"

I have never been anyplace else in the world where you get as much mileage from one word: *Mauri* (hello). It is not pronounced with a hard American "R." Rather, there is a bit of a trill to the "R" or, when pronounced by people from certain home islands, a hint of a "D." *"Mauri"* will always get you a smile from whomever you say it to: children, adult men or women, even the type of teenager who almost anywhere else in the world would be unwilling to break from sullenness. And there are no smiles like those you see in Kiribati. Each smile seems to say, "How lucky, we share this moment."

> *Sudden connection.*
> *Why were we supposed to meet?*
> *Ah—the perfect smile.*

The islands the British called the Gilberts, as well as the Line Islands and the Phoenix Islands, now comprise the independent Republic of Kiribati. The name is an indigenous corruption of the name "Gilberts." To cause further confusion, the Kiribati name of the islands that form the Gilbert Islands group is Tungaru. The people of Kiribati, the Gilbertese, are known as I-Kiribati, and speak the language called Kiribati. I still have not heard a plausible explanation why after independence in 1979, the new republic chose to keep a corruption of the British colonial name.

Until recently, the International Date Line bisected Kiribati because most of the Line Islands, some 2,000 miles to the east, were east of the Date Line. But Kiribati declared that the Date Line within its territorial waters would be shifted to the east, supposedly so that the entire nation would share a common date. However, this move has not been recognized by all. Other nations near the Date Line view the move as a cynical ploy by Kiribati to cash in on the expected rush of tourists wishing to reach the new millennium as soon as possible. The king of Tonga was not pleased.

Kiribati more than any other Micronesian country has held onto traditional values and customs. The I-Kiribati are friendly, inquisitive, and terribly hospitable. They love fun and know how to party. As one Peace Corps volunteer, Kevin Campopiano, puts it, "What I love about these people is how they can always take a good thing and carry it to excess."

In Kiribati, visitors can participate in the daily activities of the village—mingling and observing customs, lifestyles, and behavior. It is very easy to fall in love with it. But Kiribati is not for everyone. Life is slow (very slow), and it is not near anywhere. Even Tarawa, the capital, isn't very modern. It is densely populated by 35,000 people, most living under thatched roofs. Pigs, chickens, and dogs run loose. A euphemism for relieving oneself is "nako tari," literally "going to the ocean." Yes, at times odors permeate the town.

The Land

The 33 low-lying atolls and coral islands of Kiribati total only 810 square km (313 square miles) in land area, but 3,550,000 square km (1,370,656 square miles) of sea are included within Kiribati's 200-nautical-mile Exclusive Economic Zone. No other political unit on earth is made up of such a large sea to land ratio. It is the largest atoll state in the world, straddling the equator for 3,235 km (2,010 miles) from Banaba to Christmas Island. Tarawa, the capital, is 2,815 km (1,750 miles) north of Fiji.

The islands are arrayed in three great groups: the 16 Gilbert Islands atolls (Tungaru), the eight Phoenix Islands, and the eight Line Islands, with little Banaba alone to the west between Tarawa and Nauru. Tungaru contains 280 square km

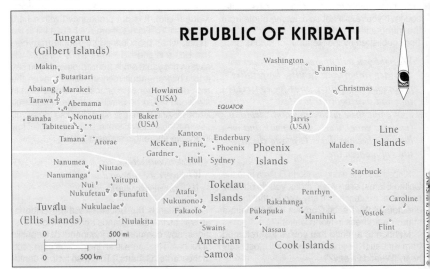

KIRIBATI AT A GLANCE

	POP. (1990)	LAND AREA (SQ. KM)
Tungaru		
(Gilbert Islands)	**71,418**	**279.23**
Abaiang	6,020	17.48
Abemama	3,442	27.37
Aranuka	1,015	11.61
Arorae	1,248	9.48
Beru	2,784	17.65
Butaritari	3,909	13.49
Kuria	971	15.48
Maiana	2,184	16.72
Makin	1,830	7.89
Marakei	2,724	14.13
Nonouti	3,042	19.85
Nikunau	2,009	19.08
Onotoa	9,198	15.62
Tabiteuea (North)	3,383	25.78
Tabiteuea (South)	1,404	11.85
Tamana	1,181	4.73
North Tarawa	4,004	15.26
South Tarawa	28,350	15.76
Banaba (Ocean Islands)	**339**	**6.29**
Phoenix Islands	**83**	**28.64**
Birnie	0	1.21
Kanton (Abariringa)	83	9.15
Enderbury	0	4.53
Gardner (Nikumaroro)	0	4.14
Hull (Orana)	0	3.91
McKean	0	1.21
Phoenix (Rawaki)	0	1.21
Sydney (Manra)	0	3.28
Line Islands	**5,818**	**496.52**
Caroline	0	2.27
Christmas (Kiritimati)	3,225	388.39
Fanning (Teraina)	978	33.73
Flint	0	2.43
Malden	0	43.30
Starbuck	0	16.19
Vostock	0	0.66
Washington (Tabuaeran)	1,615	9.55
TOTAL	**77,658**	**810.68**

(108 square miles) and most of the people of Kiribati. The flat, palm-studded Tungaru isles have a uniform environment of crushed coral surface, magnificent white beaches, lagoons, and reefs. Most of these atoll islands are no more than 200-300 meters (650-1,000 feet) wide, but the atoll lagoons are anywhere from 15 to 100 km (10 to 63 miles) long. Due to the action of the prevailing winds, the atolls' northeast coasts are generally higher than the west, but nowhere do they reach more than a few meters above sea level. The west sides are encumbered by shoals and reefs, making it a bit safer for ships to navigate the east coasts. All except Makin, Kuria, Nikunau, Tamana, and Arorae have central lagoons.

Banaba, 443 km (275 miles) southwest of Tarawa, is a raised limestone island. To the southeast of Tarawa are the uninhabited Phoenix Islands, and farther east, the Line Islands stretch between Hawaii and Tahiti. Christmas Island, largest atoll in land area in the world, accounts for nearly half the republic's dry land.

A United Nations report on the greenhouse effect (the heating of earth's atmosphere and resultant rise in sea level due to industrial pollution) lists Kiribati as one of the countries that could disappear completely beneath the sea in the 21st century unless drastic action is taken to prevent further global warming.

Climate

Robert Louis Stevenson wrote that the Gilberts enjoy "a superb ocean climate, days of blinding sun and bracing wind, nights of heavenly brightness." Remember that Kiribati is near the equator, with a brutal midday sun. At high noon, the sun is so directly overhead that your shadow is almost entirely beneath you, as if it too were hiding from the sun. In the shade, sea breezes often moderate the temperature. The best time to visit is March to November when the southeast trades blow; from November to March the westerlies bring more rainfall, in sharp irregular squalls. Droughts occur in southern and central Tungaru; considerably more rain falls on the northernmost atolls: Butaritari gets 3,114 mm (121 inches) of annual rainfall, compared to only 1,177 mm (46 inches) at Onotoa. The reduced rainfall in the south is caused by the upwelling of cold oceanic water, which reduces evaporation from the ocean surface. (Nutrients

TARAWA'S CLIMATE

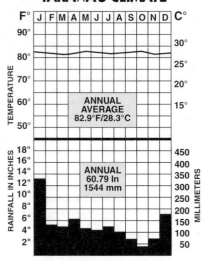

European Contact

Some of the islands may have been sighted by Spanish explorers in the 16th century. In 1765, Commodore John Byron of the HMS *Dolphin* chanced upon Nikunau. Tungaru received its European name from Capt. Thomas Gilbert of the British ship *Charlotte,* who passed in 1788. The first detailed observations and charts were made by Capt. Charles Wilkes of the U.S. Exploring Expedition (1840).

By 1840, whalers were active in the area. Although they had many skirmishes with the islanders, they also traded with them, and some even deserted to live there. Resident Europeans maintained continual contact with the outside after 1850, trading bêche-de-mer (edible sea cucumbers), turtle shells, and coconut oil. Between 1850 and 1875, slave traders, known as blackbirders, captured I-Kiribati laborers to work European plantations in other parts of the Pacific.

brought to the surface also make this a prime fishing area). Tarawa is usually less humid that the rest of Micronesia.

HISTORY

According to Kiribati legends, the god Nareau picked flowers from the ancestral tree and threw them north of Samoa to create the atolls of Tarawa, Beru, and Tabiteuea.

Perhaps 3,000 years ago, the ancestors of the Micronesians arrived in Tungaru from Southeast Asia, probably via the Caroline Islands. Several thousand years later Polynesian navigators came and intermarried with the original inhabitants. I-Kiribati legends tell how spirits left Samoa and journeyed to Tungaru, where they remained a long time before changing into humans.

Continual contact among the Tungaru atolls by outriggers led to a homogeneous culture. The inhabitants were fierce warriors, equipped with shark-tooth daggers and swords, body armor of thickly plaited coconut fiber, and porcupine-fish helmets. On the islands north of the equator district chiefs predominated; south of the equator, councils of elders *(unimane)* ruled.

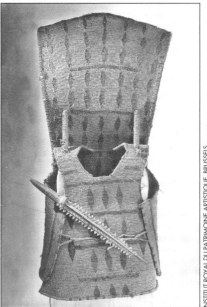

Gilbertese warriors wielding shark-tooth swords once donned heavy armor made from coconut fibers and human hair.

INSTITUT ROYAL DU PATRIMOINE ARTISTIQUE, BRUSSELS

preserved British eight-inch naval gun at the eastern end of Betio

American missionaries from Hawaii arrived in northern Tungaru in 1857; it was not until 1870 that the London Missionary Society sent representatives from Samoa to southern Tungaru. Catholic missionaries landed at Nonouti in 1888. When the Americans withdrew in 1917, the Catholics extended their influence in the north.

Colonialism
Britain established a protectorate over the Gilbert and Ellice Islands in 1892. When phosphate was discovered on Banaba (Ocean Island) in 1900, the British quickly annexed the island. From 1908 to 1941, the British governed the group from Banaba; the administration was not shifted back to Tarawa (where it had been before 1908) until after World War II. The protectorate became a colony in stages between 1915 and 1916. Britain annexed Christmas Island in 1919 and added the Phoenix Islands in 1937.

In the Guano Act of 1856, the United States claimed 14 islands in the Line and Phoenix groups, a subject of amicable dispute with the British until 1939, when they agreed to jointly control Kanton and Enderbury.

Under British colonial rule, factional and religious warfare decreased. The people, who had always lived in scattered family *(kaainga)* settlements, were concentrated into compact, easy-to-rule villages, connected by roads. Land ownership was registered.

The War
Most Europeans and Chinese laborers were evacuated from the Gilberts after the outbreak of World War II. The Japanese occupied Tarawa, Butaritari, Abemama, and Banaba in late 1941 and 1942. They did not fortify the islands or establish large garrisons until after an American raid on Butaritari on 17 August 1942. That day, 221 marines under Colonel Carlson landed on the south side of the atoll from two submarines, in a move to divert Japanese attention from the concurrent invasion of Guadalcanal in the Solomons. The marines dug in and easily beat back an attack by the 150 Japanese on the island. The U.S. force then withdrew before the Japanese could retaliate from their strongholds in the Marshalls. Nine unfortunate marines left behind in a mix-up were captured and beheaded. Two days after the raid, Japanese planes bombed a Gilbertese village in which they thought some Americans were hiding, killing 41 islanders.

As a response to the Carlson raid, Tarawa's Betio islet was heavily fortified by the Japanese, who built an airstrip down its middle. On 20 November 1943 a strong force of U.S. Marines landed at Betio and cleared the island in a brutal three-day struggle. During the Battle of Tarawa 4,690 Japanese soldiers and Korean laborers were killed (only 17 Japanese and 129 Koreans were captured); the number of United States troops killed, wounded, or missing reached 3,314. This was the Allies' first great amphibious landing against fortified positions and, though costly, provided valuable lessons for later operations, including the need to undertake massive bombardments from the sea and the air before landing. The Americans retook Butaritari at a cost of several hundred lives; the 22 Japanese on Abemama committed ritual suicide to avoid capture. The United States didn't consider it worthwhile to land on strongly defended Banaba and Nauru, which they bypassed but continued to bomb from the air.

Throughout the war Gilbertese civilians were used as slave labor by the Japanese. Later, the great quantities of supplies brought in by the Americans so impressed the Gilbertese that some developed a cargo cult and sent delegations to the military commanders requesting permanent American rule. This was denied, and several persistent petitioners were arrested. The British were not amused.

To Independence

The Gilbert and Ellice Islands Colony fell under the British colonial Western Pacific High Commission, headquartered in Fiji until 1953 and after in the Solomon Islands. In 1972 this administrative arrangement ended, and the British resident commissioner on Tarawa became a governor responsible directly to London.

The first formal steps toward self-government came in 1963 when the British appointed islanders to executive and advisory councils. In 1967 a House of Representatives with a majority of elected members replaced the Advisory Council. In 1971 the Legislative Council received greater powers. In 1974, the post of chief minister and a House of Assembly were created.

That same year the Polynesian Ellice Islanders voted in a plebiscite to be administered separately from the Micronesian Gilbertese and in 1975 independent Tuvalu was born. Banaba attempted, unsuccessfully, to secede from the soon-to-be country of Kiribati about the same time.

The British granted full internal self-government to the Gilbert Islands in 1977. Official independence followed on 12 July 1979, just as the phosphate deposits on Barnaba ran out. With no other easy resources to exploit, and a growing, impoverished population, the British were more than happy to leave. Probably no other former British colony got a worse deal at independence.

Also in 1979 the United States relinquished to the Republic of Kiribati all claims to the Phoenix and Line Islands in a Treaty of Friendship, which specified that none of the islands be used for military purposes by third parties without consultation. Kiribati didn't reach its present extent until 1982 when the country bought back Washington Island and Fanning Atoll from multinational Burns Philp.

GOVERNMENT

The Republic of Kiribati has a 41-member Maneaba ni Maungatabu (House of Assembly), elected every four years. The speaker is not a member, but rather an outsider chosen by the Maneaba. The Beretitenti (president) is elected by the people from among three or four candidates nominated by the Maneaba from its ranks. The Beretitenti chooses an eight-member cabinet from the Maneaba. Kiribati's first president, Ieremia Tabai, served from independence in 1979 until his statutory retirement in 1991.

The main political parties are partly divided along religious lines, with Protestants in the National Progressive Party and Catholics supporting the Christian Democratic Party. The Liberal Party and the New Movement Party complete the scene. Although government is centralized at Bairiki on Tarawa, small administrative subcenters are run by district officers on Abemama, Beru, Butaritari, Christmas, and Tabiteuea.

Kiribati was placed under a caretaker Commissioner in 1994 due to a vote of "no confidence" on the government of President Teatao Teannaki. Opposition leader Teburoro Tito was elected president in the ensuing election.

In 1998 a constitutional convention was held. Perhaps the most important issue was whether a president could be sued while in office. (Sound familiar?) Apparently the president had called the previous administration corrupt. The former president and other former high governmental officials brought suit for defamation. Since a president can stay in office for 12 years, immunity would have a long-time effect.

ECONOMY

Kiribati is the poorest country in Micronesia.

On the outer islands, most I-Kiribati live from

subsistence agriculture and by collecting seafood from lagoons and reefs. Pigs and fowl are common. Small amounts of copra are made from coconut meat, and seaweed is farmed to earn extra cash for essentials such as sugar, rice, flour, and kerosene. Farmland is often divided into scattered miniholdings. The most important subsistence foods are taro, pumpkin, breadfruit, coconut, breadfruit, and papaya.

Outside of South Tarawa, only the government compound at Beru and the main settlement on Christmas Island have electricity.

Many outer islanders have migrated to Tarawa in search of jobs that don't materialize. Crowded South Tarawa, with its polluted lagoon, is less amenable to subsistence living than the outer islands. Thus, many of these migrants wind up worse off than they started.

There is some industry in Kiribati, but not much. Coconut Products Ltd. (P.O. Box 280, Tarawa, Republic of Kiribati) uses copra to make coconut oil soap and cosmetics. In the Line Islands copra production is run by the government, while village cooperatives handle production in Tungaru. Government-run outfits export some fish.

In 1989 a small garment factory opened on Betio (Tarawa) with South Korean aid, and a year later British aid was used to establish a small industrial center on Betio, producing footwear, kamaimai (coconut molasses), and garments. Solar-evaporated salt is produced on Christmas Island. Seaweed farms export their harvest to be used as emulsifiers and pharmaceuticals.

Many I-Kiribati are still employed in the phosphate operation on Nauru, but those jobs will disappear as Nauru's mines are worked out. Remittances from I-Kiribati seamen serving on foreign ships are an important source of income for families.

Kiribati's greatest resource is its EEZ, encompassing 3.6 million square kilometers (1.4 million square miles) of rich fishing grounds. The royalties paid by foreign fishing vessels represent a significant portion of Kiribati' budget, though considerably less revenue than if Kiribati could exploit this resource by itself. The ecological havoc wreaked by modern fishing in a relatively short period of time may make it impossible for even outer islanders to remain self-sufficient.

Package tourism is insignificant and unlikely to develop due to competition from more accessible destinations and transportation difficulties within the Republic.

Kiribati could not survive at its current economic level without foreign aid. Australia, New Zealand, Japan, Canada, and Britain still offer support. The United States maintains 60 Peace Corps volunteers there, and the U.S. Coast Guard helps enforce Kiribati's EEZ. The newest player in town is the Republic of China, with the largest diplomatic station in the country. China recently built a satellite tracking station on South Tarawa. The United States was not pleased.

Aid, particularly direct services, often comes through private sources, such as churches. Australian Seventh-Day Adventists provide dental care to outer islanders.

THE PEOPLE

Customs

To understand the people of Kiribati, one must understand three institutions: the *maneaba,* the *botaki,* and *te Tuitit.*

Traditionally a *maneaba* was a thatched roof supported by pillars of coral and coconut palm trunks. The roof was overhanging so that unless rain was driving almost horizontally, the area underneath stayed dry. Under the roof, each family set its pandanus mats. The *maneaba* was large enough to seat the entire village.

Today, the *maneaba* may be constructed with a concrete floor and concrete pillars supporting a corrugated metal roof. But the *maneaba* remains the town meeting hall and then some. Here, marriages and funerals take place. And people sleep here during the heat of the day or on a particularly warm night.

There are manners to be observed in a *maneaba,* particularly during a meeting or celebration, though the village will be tolerant if you, an *I-Matong* (non-Islander), break a minor custom. If you want to indicate something, do not point with a finger; wiggle your lips in that direction or, at most, point with four fingers held low to the ground. While business is being discussed, everyone sits cross-legged; do not sit with legs outstretched, pointing toward anyone. After the official "business" is over, everyone relaxes and

the next generation of I-Kiribati

stretches out their legs, but it's rude to step over someone's legs.

The *maneaba* must be shown respect. When moving about in the *maneaba*, it's proper to stoop. Never stand upright, especially in front of seated people. Maintaining a low profile is a sign of respect to the *unimane* and others present. It's also polite to back out of the *maneaba* when exiting, rather than turning your back on the occupants. It's considered disrespectful to place your hands on the beams or roof. When driving past a *maneaba* in a car or motor scooter, slow down if something is happening inside, though this custom is in decline in crowded South Tarawa.

A *botaki* is an event that takes place in the *maneaba*. It might be a wedding, a wake, or a community, political or governmental meeting. If you attend a *botaki*, as a guest from afar, you will be seated in a position of honor, opposite the elders. You may have no idea what is occurring, but you'll be expected to make a short speech. Someone will translate. Tell them why you've come and how you're enjoying their island.

A *botaki* that takes place for a community meeting moves to a different logic than similar gatherings in industrialized nations. For example, in the United States, we would conduct business before eating for fear that if the food were served first, members of the group would simply eat and run. But in Kiribati events begin by sharing food. The act of eating bonds the group and welcomes everyone.

The I-Kiribati presentation of food at a *botaki* differs greatly from our potluck dinners. A serving dish may contain a multitude of foods. Placed on a bed of rice or ramen noodles may be cooked pumpkin, breadfruit, candied pandanus fruit, slices of fresh papaya, boiled meat of baby coconuts, some local wild greens or seaweed, and some small broiled or smoked local fish. After eating a great quantity of foods in the equatorial heat, some exercise must be done to work off the languor that the food produces.

Enter *te Tuitit* (the Twist). Exactly how the twist became Kiribati's universal dance seems lost in the history of some seedy bar on Tarawa. Yet today it forms an integral part of Kiribati culture. The dance they do may still be called the Twist, but it also includes elements of more recent club dancing styles and even line dancing. They consider the Macarena to be an American product—the best American export since the Twist. Most dancing is to fairly recent techno-music.

As an honored guest, you likely will be the first person asked to dance. A partner will approach you in the style of the islands, with lowered arms in a gesture that spells come hither in any language. While dancing, people will come up behind you, patting on talcum powder and spraying you with floral-scented water. At the end of the dance, lower your arms toward you partner and say, *"Ko raba"* (thank you).

In most personal situations, Gilbert Islanders are conservative. However, the dance floor is one place where they can compensate for the reserved demeanor required in other aspects of their lives. Their dancing is quite strenuous and sexually suggestive. There appears to be an unwritten rule (at least I assume no one wrote it down): the older the dancer, the raunchier the dance.

If you're invited to a *botaki*, you are expected to reciprocate with a gift. Cash has replaced products as a gift. The going rate seems to be about A$10 pp. The money should be placed in an envelope and given to whoever appears to be in charge. At a wedding, the gift should be given to the bridegroom; at a wake, to the head of the family.

Always have a supply of small gifts to repay anyone who invites you in for a drink of toddy or a meal. Matches, a package of tea leaves, and a tin of condensed milk could be presented to any family with whom you stay. If you stay more than one night with the same family, check out the village store and purchase something more substantial to give. Those staying more than a week should contribute a large bag of rice. Spend at least what you figure your meals were worth, then a little more. *Te ga'am* (chewing gum) is popular with children.

Don't verbally admire an islander's possession, or that person may feel obligated to give it to you. I-Kiribati are curious people who won't hesitate to ask your age, marital status, or occupation. Don't react as if they're invading your privacy.

Demography

More than a third of Kiribati's population lives in South Tarawa, primarily on Betio and the Bairiki-Bikenibeu strip. Most other Tungaru atolls have several thousand inhabitants each. The Phoenix and Line groups traditionally were uninhabited. To relieve the population pressure on South Tarawa, the Kiribati government has helped to resettle thousands of people to *Kiritmati* (Christmas) Island. But population growth remains high

on Tarawa, undercutting the benefits of the program. Forty percent of the population is 14 years of age or younger.

The northern atolls of Kiribati are predominantly Catholic, the southern mostly Protestant. The total population is 54% Catholic, 38% Kiribati Protestant Church. The remainder of the population consists of other Protestant groups, Seventh-Day Adventists, Mormons, and Bahai adherents. Most of the 142 resident Westerners and 688 Polynesians (primarily Tuvaluans) live in South Tarawa.

The ribbonlike I-Kiribati villages stretch out along the lagoon side of the Tungaru atolls. When you see a cluster of houses seemingly on top of each other, they usually house one extended family. Although thatched roofs still predominate, tin roofs are becoming popular because they require little maintenance and can be used to catch rain water. *Maneabas* continue to be village focal points.

Language

English is understood by many on South Tarawa, where it is an official language. On the outer islands, knowledge of it is less common, yet usually you will be able to find someone who understands it. Kiribati is in the Austronesian family of languages. It has elements of both Micronesian and Polynesian languages. It is related to Marshallese, though most residents of the two countries have great difficulty understanding each other.

ROD BUCHKO

the largest maneaba *in Kiribati, Nonouti atoll*

Pronunciation of the language is divided into northern and southern Tungaru dialects. The northern dialect is used on Abemama, Aranuka, Kuria, and all the islands northward, while the southern version applies on Nonouti, Beru, and the islands to the south. It's interesting to note that the northern dialect is also used on Mili atoll in the Marshalls and the southern dialect in the Line Islands and Nui in Tuvalu. On South Tarawa both dialects are used.

The 13-letter written alphabet developed by American missionaries has no letter "s" or "c," probably because these missionaries came from Hawaii. Hawaiian does not have an "s" sound. Rather than creating a new alphabet that would truly suit the Gilbertese language, the missionaries stayed with the alphabet they had developed for use by Hawaiians, using the letter combination "ti" for the "s" sound. This explains why someone who doesn't already know cannot guess how to pronounce "Kiribati" (KIR-i-bas).

HOLIDAYS AND EVENTS

Independence Day (12 July) features a parade at the Bairiki National Stadium (Tarawa), traditional dancing, and canoe races. Interschool sports and dance contests are held on Youth Day (first Monday in August). Public holidays include New Year's Days (1 and 3 January), Good Friday, Easter Monday, Independence Days (11 and 12 July), Youth Day (1 August), Human Rights Day (10 December), and Christmas Days (25, 26, and 27 December).

Music and Dance
The I-Kiribati, like many Pacific Islanders, exhibit extraordinary musical achievements. At the turn of the century, hymns had been brought to the Gilberts by transplanted Boston ministers, coming by way of Hawaii. These hymns now bear little relationship to the staid versions taught by those missionaries. The typical hymn today is performed in four-part harmony, with an infectious exuberance. The people of Kiribati learn these songs early in life, first by listening to singing at communal events. Singing is part of every gathering, whether an informal village *botaki* or a meeting of high government officials. As

children become older, they receive training in school and in their churches. It is as if singing were the national canon, and everyone knows the core songs and his or her part in each song. The effect is enchanting.

Try to visit the **Kiribati Protestant Church (KPC)** in Bikenibeu at 7 p.m. Sunday to hear some great religious singing. Be aware that at the end of the service you probably will be asked whether you wish to say a few words.

The I-Kiribati are also renowned dancers. In their traditional dances, the emphasis is on movement of the hands, head, and eyes, rather than the body or feet. A classical Kiribati dance is the *ruoia,* while the more vigorous *batere,* parts of which resemble a Samoan *siva,* was introduced from Tuvalu centuries ago. Children learn the technique early and practice all their lives. The *ruoia* was banned by the missionaries, but it has made a comeback in recent years. It's said that *ruoia* composers had special powers and could inflict curses and spells through their songs and chants. Talcum powder may be sprinkled on the backs of the necks of guests and performers at these gatherings. The **Otintaai Hotel** stages dances at its Thursday dinners.

PRACTICALITIES

Accommodations
The only hotels are on Tarawa and Christmas Island. All hotels have a 10% surcharge. Most outer atolls also have basic Island Council rest houses. (There are no rest houses on South Tarawa.) These houses were built to accommodate visiting officials from Tarawa. But when not serving that purpose, they are available to travelers. Most offer meal service, charging between A$15 and A$30 pp, including meals. A number have been upgraded for overseas visitors, but electricity and hot water are still an exception rather than the rule. Cooking materials are sometimes provided if the house does not serve meals. To be on the safe side, bring your own food, mosquito nets, insect repellent, and

KIRIBATI COUNTRY CODE: 686

CAPSULE KIRIBATI VOCABULARY

mauri — hello

tiabo — goodbye

ko uara? — how are you?

i marurung — I'm fine

kua — tired

taiaoka — please

ko raba — thank you

kom rabi — thank you (said to more than one person)

te raoi — you're welcome

antai aram? — what's your name?

kien ia? — where do you come from?

iraua am ririki? — how old are you?

i kan amwarake — I'm hungry

e kangkang te amwarake — the meal is delicious

teutana — a little

teutana riki — a little more

e a tau — that's enough

akea riki — no more

akea — none, nothing

eng — yes

tiaki — no

te ika — fish

kikao — octopus

te iriko — meat

te ben — coconut

te moimotu — drinking coconut

te tongo — fermented coconut milk

kabubu — pandanus drink

te babai — swamp taro

katei ni Kiribati — the Kiribati way

bula — platform with roof, but no walls

maneaba — meeting place

botaki — gathering

boti — place in a *maneaba*

uea — chief

unamane — group of elders

ka-ainga — group of extended families

utu — extended family

batua — eldest male in a *ka-ainga*

unaine — old woman

karimoa — the eldest son

I-Kiribati — Kiribati people

I-Matang — Europeans

riri — woman's coconut leaf skirt

tibuta — woman's short-sleeved blouse

baangota — spirit-worshipping place

te tuitit — the Twist

---

toilet paper. Most important, bottled water is usually not available on outer islands. Bring your own or a purification device. To book a rest house, contact the Visitor's Bureau (P.O. Box 50, Betio, Tarawa, Rep. of Kiribati, tel. 686-26-157, fax 686-26-233).

An alternative is just to head out and hope the facility is available and make arrangements on arrival. You could be out of luck as to the guest house, but someone will probably agree to put you up. Officials at the Island Council, or any Peace Corps volunteer you locate, can help facilitate arrangements. Keep in mind that this means adapting to the local way of doing things.

The first evening you spend in a private home, neighbors will come to visit. If the house is traditional, as a guest, you will eat first, having the choice of the best food. Once you have finished, the men will be served, before the women and children. Expect to sacrifice much of your privacy. Custom dictates that members of your host family accompany you everywhere, and you will be deemed rude if you resist. On Sunday, you will be expected to accompany the family to church.

Food

Te babai (swamp taro) is cultivated in large pits below the water table; it's eaten either boiled or made into several different puddings. Breadfruit is a staple which is boiled or fried in butter; fried as chips it makes a terrific snack. Boiled pumpkin, papaya, and plantain supplement the diet. Coconut and papaya are in abundance. The poor soil on the atolls, however, limits the variety of produce. On the southern islands *te roro,* a wafer-like food made from the boiled fruit of the pandanus tree, tastes like dates. It's often served with coconut cream spread on the surface. Formerly, *te roro* was eaten only in the *maneaba*. Ripe pandanus fruit is dark yellow or orange and sweet like pineapple, and is sometimes candied.

A fantastic variety of fish can be caught in the lagoons, reefs, and the open ocean. You'll usually eat fresh fish. Eels, crawfish, and various other shellfish are often available, including crawfish that resemble Australia's Morton Bay "Bugs."

Rice is consumed in phenomenal quantities, and when possible, canned corned beef. The latter usually is substandard—salty and fatty. The I-Kiribati go to great lengths to please foreigners (I-

Matang); for example, the frequent serving of cold, uncooked corned beef from the can! Chickens, eggs, and pork are not often served. Remember that food and all the basics may not be available on the outer islands due to erratic shipping. Take with you as much as you can.

Toddy

The drink of the islands is *te karewe* (sweet toddy), extracted from the coconut palm early in the morning and evening. The spathe of the tree is bound and cut, then the sap is collected in a coconut shell or bottle. One can drink it immediately—not sweet, but very refreshing. It's usually taken after meals and is even used to wean babies. Note: this liquid tastes very little like the "milk" one finds within a coconut itself.

Te kamaimai, molasses extracted from boiled *karewe,* is great in rice; diluted with water it makes a pleasing drink called *te katete. Te kamaimai* mixed with grated coconut and coconut cream makes a tasty sweet called *kati ni ben. Te karewe* fermented for three days becomes *te kaokioki* (sour toddy), a very smooth, potent drink. *Te kaokioki* can be readily obtained. The color varies from a milky white to light brown. A local sweetbread is made from *te kaokioki* yeast. *Kabubu* is a mixture of toddy, pandanus, and grated coconut, dried in the sun and pounded. It can be stored for long periods.

Toddy-cutting is a male profession passed from father to son, and the cutters are well respected in their village. In the 1990 census 1,638 I-Kiribati men listed their occupation as "tree workers," the highest number in any occupational category. As they work high up among the coconut palms they often sing Christian hymns or songs of praise for toddy, wives, girlfriends, lost loves, or even the adventures of the previous night. Said Robert Louis Stevenson, "They sing with a certain lustiness and Bacchic glee."

Visas

All visitors must have a passport and an onward ticket. Visa regulations are simple: nationals of countries that require a visa of I-Kiribati travelers must themselves possess a visa to visit Kiribati. Thus, Americans, Australians, Dutch, French, Germans, and Japanese should obtain a visa in advance. Most British subjects and nationals do not require visas.

The visa costs about A$20 and may be used anytime within three months of the date of issue. In the United States, contact Mr. William E. Paupe (850 Richards St., Suite 503, Honolulu, HI 96813, tel. 808-521-7703, fax 808-521-8304). In Australia, contact Mr. Bill Franken, Consulate General of the Republic of Kiribati (35 Dover Rd., Rose Bay, Sydney, NSW 2029, tel. 02-9371-7808, fax 02-9371-0248). In New Zealand, contact Mr. Raymond D. Mann (P.O. Box 40205, Glenfield, Auckland, tel. 09-419-0404, fax 09-419-1414). Japan: Mr. Tokugoro Kuribayashi, Consular Office of the Republic of Kiribati (Room 684, Marunouchi Building, 2-41 Marunouchi, Chiyoda-kr, Tokyo, tel. 03-3201-3487, fax 03-3214-1884). Germany: Frank Leonhardt, Leonhardt & Blumberg (Rodingsmart 16, 200 Hamburg 11, tel. 040-36-146-0, fax 040-36-146-123). Great Britain: Maurice Chandler CBE, Consulate of Kiribati (Faith House, Westminster SW1P 3QN, tel. 071-222-6952, fax 071-976-7180). South Korea: Mr. In Yung Chung, Consulate of Kiribati (Halla Building, 891-44, Daechi-Dong, Kang Num-ku, Seoul, South Korea, tel. 02-5591-114/837, fax 02-5591-699).

Curiously, by arrangement with Kiribati, some British consulate offices still seem to be issuing visas for Kiribati. It is best, however, to use a Kiribati consul if possible, or write: Principal Immigration Officer, P.O. Box 69, Bairiki, Tarawa, Rep. of Kiribati.

You run some risk of being immediately deported if you arrive without a visa. However, upon arrival without one, you'll usually be granted a stay until the date of your onward flights. You may even be allowed a stay for up to one month. Extensions can be obtained from the Office of Home Affairs, Bairiki, one month at a time for up to four months in any 12-month period. Bring along your onward ticket. If you are on an outer island, you must cable your request to this office in advance.

Ports of entry for cruising yachts are Banaba, Tarawa (Betio), Fanning, and Christmas. At Tarawa, yachts can obtain permission to cruise the outer islands of Tungaru but must return to Tarawa again to clear out of the country. Occasionally yachts en route to Majuro are allowed to stop at Butaritari without having to return to Tarawa.

Money and Measurements

Australian paper currency is used, although some Kiribati coins circulate. Most prices in this chapter are in Australian dollars (A$). It's usually impossible to change traveler's checks on the outer islands, so take enough Australian dollars in small denominations. It's also difficult to change A$50 and A$100 bills on the outer islands. It is still difficult to use a credit card in Kiribati. The few places that allow the use, such as the Otintaai Hotel, charge up to $15 to verify that your card can accept the charge. This may, however, be cheaper than paying in American dollar currency or traveler's checks at a poor discount rate. If you have not brought enough Australian dollars with you, your best bet is to convert American dollars at the Bank of Kiribati. Tipping is not usual, but of course is greatly appreciated.

Airmail between Kiribati and Australia takes about one week, and to Asia or America about two weeks, if you are lucky.

The electric voltage is 240 volts, 50 cycles, and the Australian three-pin plug is used. On Tarawa both the metric and imperial measurement systems are in use, although distances are usually stated in kilometers.

Health

Midday in Kiribati is not meant for walking. Why do you think lunch and the nap were invented? When walking about even in the morning or the late afternoon, be careful of the sun. Wear a hat and sunglasses. There's no malaria in Kiribati, but outbreaks of dengue fever sometimes occur. Anyone contemplating staying with locals should have a mosquito net. Do not drink untreated water. There are chronic medicine shortages on Kiribati. Take all medicines you may need with you, including those as common as aspirin.

Many homes do not have toilets, and thus it is common for locals (and travelers in distress) to relieve themselves on the beach or in the lagoon. This makes lagoons near population centers unsanitary. With a few exceptions, indicated in this book, do not swim in the lagoon at South Tarawa. In places, even the ocean is not clean enough to swim in without first inquiring locally. For example, raw sewage goes into the ocean from the local hospital.

Information

Tourist brochures on the country are available from the **Kiribati Visitors Bureau,** (P.O. Box 510, Betio, Tarawa, Rep. of Kiribati, tel. 686-26-157, fax 686-26-233). For information on Christmas Island, contact the Tourism Office (Ministry of Line and Phoenix Development, Christmas Island, Rep. of Kiribati) or call the Honolulu office of Air Kiribati, toll-free at (888) 800-8144

Topographical maps of Kiribati can be ordered from the **Lands and Surveys Division** P.O. Box 7, Bairiki, Tarawa, Rep. of Kiribati). A good selection of books on the country is available from the National Library (P.O. Box 6, Bairiki, Tarawa, Rep. of Kiribati).

Getting There

Tungaru's ties to the rest of the world are tenuous. Essentially one **Air Nauru** (tel. 674-444-3141, fax 674-444-3705) plane twice-weekly connects with Nauru, where you can catch flights to Australia, Fiji, FSM (Pohnpei), Guam, and the Philippines. For current information on the days and time of flight, check its website: www.airnauru.com.au. **Air Marshall Islands** has a plane that connects Tarawa to the Marshall Islands (Kwajalein and Majuro), where you can hook up to **Continental Airlines,** and to Fiji (Suva) and Tuvalu (Funafuti). Roundtrip excursion fares are cheaper, but they require a seven day advance purchase. A stopover at Tuvalu greatly increases the cost of a Fiji to Tarawa flight. AMI flights are often fully booked weeks ahead, so confirm your reservations. Baggage space may be limited. For current information on the days and time of flight, check its website: www.rmiembassyus.org/amisked.html, or call (692) 625-3733.

If either the Air Nauru or the Air Marshall Islands plane needs repair or even extensive service, you can get stuck in Tarawa for a number of days until a replacement plane makes it in. Do not go to Kiribati if a couple of days delay would be catastrophic for you.

To get from Tarawa to Christmas Island, also in the Republic of Kiribati but in the Line Islands, is more difficult. The only air transport at present to Christmas Island is a once-a-week flight from Honolulu. Thus, to get from Tarawa to Christmas Island would first require a flight on Air Marshall Islands to Majuro, then a flight on Con-

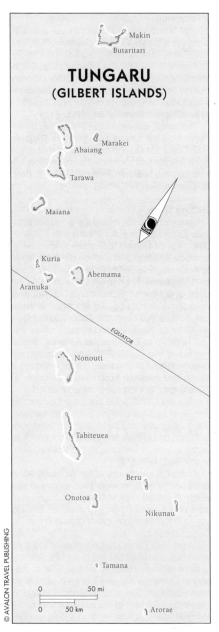

TUNGARU
(GILBERT ISLANDS)

Makin
Butaritari

Marakei
Abaiang

Tarawa

Maiana

Kuria

Abemama
Aranuka

EQUATOR

Nonouti

Tabiteuea

Beru
Onotoa
Nikunau

Tamana

0   50 mi
0   50 km   Arorae

© AVALON TRAVEL PUBLISHING

tinental Airlines from Majuro to Honolulu. From Honolulu there is a flight to Christmas Island each Tuesday. The flight is an Air Kiribati flight, but it uses an Aloha Airlines plane and crew. For reservations on this Air Kiribati flight, call (888) 800-8144 or (818) 839-6680, or fax (818) 839-6681.

Bonriki Airport (TRW) is five km (three miles) northeast of Bikenibeu on Tarawa. The airport bus to the Otintaai Hotel is free for guests with confirmed bookings, otherwise A$2 pp. Public buses (usually vans) also call on the terminal when Air Nauru or Air Marshall planes arrive. If you arrive on an interisland flight, unless you have made prior arrangements to be picked up, walk about 100 meters to the main road to catch a bus. The airport tax is A$10 on international flights.

Getting Around by Air
Air Kiribati (formerly Air Tungaru) operates a subsidized domestic air service to all the Tungaru atolls. Every atoll gets at least one flight a week, some several. It's best to book all your flights before you leave Tarawa. The Air Kiribati "office" on the outer islands usually operates out of the agent's attaché case when a flight is due at the airstrip. Reconfirm your onward reservation with the local agent immediately upon arrival at an outer island. If you want to change your reservation, simply go to the airstrip when the next flight is due and ask the agent to radio in your request. At other times the radio shack will probably be closed. You could also try forwarding written requests to Tarawa with the pilot. Plan your itinerary carefully, as it will be hard to make changes. Fares from Tarawa vary between A$29 (Abaiang) to A$116 (Beru). Children ages two to 11 fly for half fare and infants fly for 10% of adult fare. The baggage allowance is 15 kilos (33 pounds).

Be prepared for schedule irregularities and canceled flights. For example, if a fishing boat does not return in the evening, your plane may be diverted into search duties.

Getting Around by Sea
The Shipping Corporation of Kiribati, now known as the **Kiribati Shipping Services Limited** (KSSL) (P.O. Box 495, Betio, Tarawa, Rep. of Kiribati, tel. 686-26-195), is located at Betio har-

bor and operates five cargo/passenger ships. Fares range from A$13 deck to Abaiang; A$49 to Banaba; up to A$148 to Christmas Island. Every four to six weeks voyages are made to Majuro (A$76 deck), Funafuti (A$94 deck), and Suva (A$175). (From Suva, contact Williams & Gosling Ltd., Box 79, Suva, Fiji Islands, tel. 679-312-633, fax 679-300-367.) Often a diversion is made to Nauru (A$76 deck). Children under 12 pay half fare and cabin fares are usually double the quoted deck fare. Confirm all trips at the office. Don't trust local gossip.

MATS Shipping and Transport (P.O. Box 413, Betio, Tarawa, Rep. of Kiribati, tel. 26-355) in Betio runs its copra boat, the *MATS-1,* to the outer islands every couple of weeks with occasional voyages to Christmas Island, Fanning, Washington, Fiji, and Majuro. Fares are similar to those charged by KSSL. Another possibility is **Waysang Kum Kee** (tel. 21-036) above the Paradise Club on Betio.

Gilbertese *baurua* (large twin-sailed catamarans) travel between Tarawa and Abaiang (A$9 one way) three or four times a week; visitors can arrange to go along by asking at the harbor at Betio.

A final possibility is to try traveling as unpaid crew on a cruising yacht. Most private yachts sail north from Fiji and Tuvalu to Tarawa, then continue on to Majuro. From Tarawa to Hawaii is a long haul. As yachts usually are required to clear customs at Betio on both the inward and outward journeys, you may be lucky enough to be accepted for a cruise around the Tungaru atolls. Be prepared to do your share of work and to contribute a per diem amount toward costs. Yachts anchor in the lagoon just off Betio, and the only way to get on is to convince a captain you're a hand worth having aboard.

Getting Around by Road

On the outer islands, ask the Island Council clerk if he or she knows of anyone who might be willing to rent you a motorbike *(te reberebe).* If you can borrow a bicycle *(te batika),* you've got great and leisurely local transportation, and a barrier-free way of meeting people. A bicycle is good transportation on a flat atoll.

TARAWA

Tarawa atoll, just 130 km (81 miles) north of the equator, is the main center of the Tungaru group and capital of Kiribati. Most people live in South Tarawa, along the bottom side of this huge open triangle of long, low islands surrounding a lagoon. A single passage pierces the barrier reef along Tarawa's west flank, the route for contemporary shipping as it had been for the wartime American invasion force.

There is continual ribbon development along the 24-km (15-mile) lagoonside road from Bonriki to Betio. Most of the structures are still traditional, with palm frond roofs. The most important government offices are at Bairiki, though the health and education facilities are at Bikenibeu and communications at Betio. Densely populated Betio is the heart of Kiribati. It has stores, bars, war relics, and the port where the fishing and shipping industries are centered: commerce as well as squalor.

SIGHTS

South Tarawa
One does not go to South Tarawa to see the sights. It is the overcrowded, often dirty, capital of a poor country. Its population has increased more than 20-fold since the end of the war, and the infrastructure has not kept stride. Though it is surrounded by water, the lagoon is polluted. Even the ocean is polluted opposite such spots as the hospital. Further, as in much of Micronesia, there is a very long, hard shelf going out into the open ocean. Going in is only for people with good ocean swimming skills. Surfers—only go in within an hour and a half of high tide.

Yet if you can get past South Tarawa's difficulties, it is a very interesting place. The local people are extremely hospitable, which makes it easy to meet locals. The expat community (and other travelers) all seem to be sufficiently "off" to be amusing. Everyone has a story, and if you are there for awhile, you'll probably have one too. And there are almost enough sights so that you can pretend to have things to do.

The four-km (2.5-mile), A$10-million Nippon Causeway, built with Japanese aid, opened in 1987 connecting Betio to the rest of South Tarawa. The construction of causeways between the South Tarawa islands may be convenient for getting around, but a serious pollution problem has developed as wastes accumulate in the murky, trapped waters of the lagoon. Local fishermen complain that the causeways choke the lagoon and cause formerly clear passages to silt up. Large quantities of coral rock and sand are used to build the causeways, disrupting the ecology of reef and lagoon. Still, there's good swimming and snorkeling by the Betio causeway bridge when the tide's coming in. **Nauru Park,** on the lagoon on the Betio side of the causeway, is a nice place to picnic.

In 1943, more than 4,000 Japanese soldiers on Betio were sheltered underground in concrete blockhouses with walls 1.5 meters (five feet) thick, reinforced by palm trees and steel rails, roofed by a three-meter (10-foot) blanket of sand and coral. Facing the U.S. Marines, who landed on 20 November, was a solid wall of enemy gunfire coming from inside these pillboxes.

Today you can visit the four eight-inch **Japanese coastal defense guns** at the southeast and southwest ends of Betio. One of the guns has collapsed and is now half buried in the sand; another was restored in 1989. These guns bear British markings but were sold to Japan in 1904, *not* captured at Singapore as some assert.

You can find bunkers, dugouts, and trenches along the ocean side of the island, where the Japanese expected the landings, but the Americans came ashore on the northern and western beaches. About 20 rusting **landing vehicles** (LVT), visible at low tide, still lie stalled on the reef where they became stuck in 1943, due to a miscalculation of the tides. All that remains today is rusting engines and broken tracks.

On the south side of Betio, surrounded by smashed cement bunkers and fallen guns, is the local cemetery, with a simple **memorial** to the 22 British coast watchers beheaded here by the Japanese. Their epitaph reads, "Standing unarmed to their posts they matched brutality with gallantry, and met death with fortitude."

The **Marine Training Center** trains young islanders to work on vessels. This excellent program has given hundreds of I-Kiribati an opportunity to earn money, learn a trade, and see a bit of the world. Gilbertese are sought-after sailors. Some of the buildings of the school are World War II vintage American. But also note the Japanese bunker converted into a squash court.

The **Betio Catholic Church** has a tower. If it is a clear day and you can find a nun to let you in, you can see across to Abaiang atoll.

A very fine *maneaba* is located on the lagoon side of the main road in **Eita**. Out of respect, guests from other countries who are going to the Parliament for government business must first stop here.

The **Umwanibong Cultural Center and Museum** in Bikenibeu is worth visiting (admission A$2.50). The collection is rather sparse, but it does have two Gilbert Island coconut-thread suits of armor and traditional sharks-tooth spears. Two necklaces are on display—one made from porpoise teeth and the other from human teeth. If you ask, usually you will be allowed access to the nicely air-conditioned director's room, which has many other artifacts such as fishing hooks and adzes made from giant clam shells and coconut shell cups.

North Tarawa

You can see a more traditional lifestyle merely by leaving South Tarawa. As of 1998, causeways and electricity only went as far north as

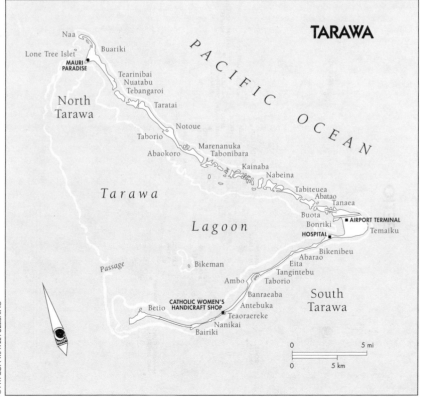

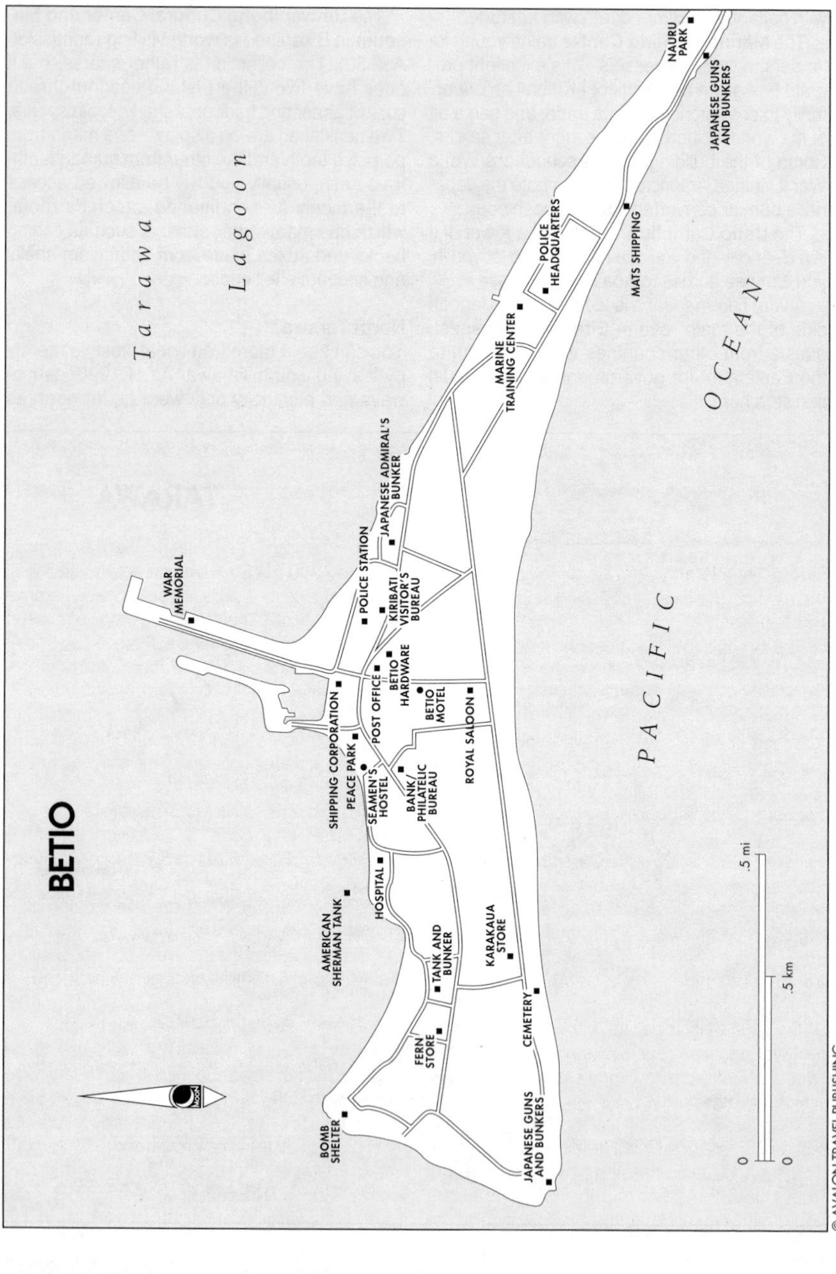

BETIO

Tarawa Lagoon

PACIFIC OCEAN

WAR MEMORIAL
AMERICAN SHERMAN TANK
HOSPITAL
SHIPPING CORPORATION
PEACE PARK
SEAMEN'S HOSTEL
POST OFFICE
POLICE STATION
KIRIBATI VISITOR'S BUREAU
JAPANESE ADMIRAL'S BUNKER
BETIO HARDWARE
BETIO MOTEL
BANK/PHILATELIC BUREAU
ROYAL SALOON
TANK AND BUNKER
KARAKAUA STORE
FERN STORE
CEMETERY
BOMB SHELTER
JAPANESE GUNS AND BUNKERS
MARINE TRAINING CENTER
POLICE HEADQUARTERS
MATS SHIPPING
NAURU PARK
JAPANESE GUNS AND BUNKERS

.5 mi
.5 km

© AVALON TRAVEL PUBLISHING

ANCIENT GILBERTESE WAR CHANT

Striking of my breath, here:
Breaking of light in the East.
For what do I approach?
I approach for anger.

For what do I approach?
I approach for readiness.
For I approach the thunder which
rattles at the side of Heaven in the East.

For I am not cowardly,
For I am not unwilling,
For I am not slow in war, but angry!
Anger! Readiness! Safety!

—from the Umwanibong
Cultural Center and Museum

Buota. All this may change by the year 2000; the electric grid is scheduled to reach north to Buota by then.

The South Tarawa bus service extends from Betio to the end of Buota, just beyond Tanaea. At slack tide, there is good swimming under the bridge linking Tanaea to Buota. From the bus terminus at Buota, you can wade northward to Tabiteuea at low tide. At high tide, if you whistle, a canoe may come to take you across. Be sure to make arrangements if you wish to be taken back across later that day.

If you wish an adventurous trip, at low tides you can wade through knee-deep water, across passages separating the string of reef islands as far as Tabonibara. With luck, you may be able to hitch a ride on a local canoe crossing the next passage. There, another continuous coral road begins, and you can walk right to Naa at the atoll's northern tip without getting your feet wet again. A few trucks ply irregularly between Abaokoro and Buariki. You can charter a minibus for about A$15.

This excellent walk allows a glimpse of Kiribati village life, especially in Nabeina and Kainaba. There's a Catholic mission at Taborio. Set out from Buota three hours prior to low tide. You could camp on uninhabited islands, stop at the rest house in Abaokoro, or sleep in a village *maneaba*. Bring in water, food, and any other necessary supplies. An unreliable launch runs back to South Tarawa approximately twice a week from Buariki and Tearinibai (A$4 pp), or just walk back the way you came. This trip is the perfect way to spend a couple of extra days on Tarawa and meet some friendly people.

Another way to visit North Tarawa is to stay at the **Mauri Paradise.**

PRACTICALITIES

South Tarawa Accommodations

The **Otintaai Hotel** (moderate) (P.O. Box 270, Bikenibeu, Tarawa, Rep. of Kiribati, tel. 686-28-084, fax 686-28-084) is the best hotel choice on Tarawa. It has 40 air-conditioned rooms with fridge and fan. Though the hotel usually has vacancies, make reservations; there is a great step down in quality to the next hotel, and occasionally, if there is a conference at the hotel, it will fill up. Prices begin at A$80 s, A$90 d. If you are on business, ask in advance for a 10% rate reduction. The hotel has a full-service bar and a dining room, discussed below. If you are going to be at the hotel on Friday or Saturday night, ask for a room other than 1-20, unless you would like to listen to the hotel's late-night disco. There is a barbecue every Saturday night from 7:30 to 9 p.m. that costs A$15 and often includes entertainment, with Gilbertese dancing or singing by the local choir.

The next best choice is **Betio Motel** (moderate) (P.O. Box 12, Betio, Tarawa, Rep. of Kiribati, tel. 686-26-361, fax 686-26-048) centrally located in Betio. Its 10 air-conditioned rooms rent for A$50 s, A$60 d. It has its own electric generator, for use when the town's system blacks out. The restaurant on the premises has a satellite dish so that sports junkies can catch ESPN.

Mary's Hotel (inexpensive) (Mary Teanako, P.O. Box 12, Bairiki, Tarawa, Rep. of Kiribati, tel. 21-164) is a neat, two-story, concrete block building near the landing at Bairiki. All five rooms have a/c, private bath, and fridge. Rates are A$50 s, A$60 d. Meals in the restaurant downstairs are A$5 and up. The walls are rather thin, so your comfort depends a lot on who your neighbors are.

The **Tarawa Motel** (inexpensive) (P.O. Box 59, Bairiki, Tarawa, Rep. of Kiribati, tel. 686-21-445) in

Ambo has four rooms with clean, shared bath and cooking facilities that go for A$25 s, A$35 d. Long-term rates are negotiable. It has a nice patio with a great view of an ocean bay, but the conditions are very basic and without air conditioning.

Sweet Coconut Hotel (budget) (Mr. Nani-matang Karoua, tel. 686-21-487) has two rooms on the ocean side of South Tarawa at Tebunia. Private cooking facilities are available, but the shower and toilet are shared. The rooms are basic but peaceful, costing A$15 s, A$30 d.

Seamen's Hostel (budget) (Mr. Teitia Binoka, P.O. Box 478, Betio, Tarawa, Rep. of Kiribati, tel. 686-26-133) has 10 rooms at A$15 pp, no double rooms available unless you sleep on the floor. It is in Betio, overlooking a junkyard. Try to avoid this hotel if possible.

For a longer stay, contact the Kiribati Visitors Bureau, P.O. Box 510, Betio, Tarawa, Rep. of Kiribati, tel. (686) 26-157, fax (686) 26-233. They may be able find a house that you can rent, or find a home that wishes to rent out a room.

North Tarawa Accommodations

The **Mauri Paradise** (moderate) (P.O. Box 26, Bairiki, Tarawa, tel./fax 686-21-646, e-mail: mp@tskl.net.ki) is a superb place to spend a day or two (or a week or two) away from crowd-ed South Tarawa. This unique eco-resort is lo-cated on Buariki, the rural, northernmost island on the Tarawa atoll. The hotel's 39-foot motor-ized outrigger will take you from Betio to Buari-ki in about an hour and a half. The resort is quite different from South Tarawa, having the feel of an outer atoll. It consists of three small, traditional Kiribati-style structures, open-sided platforms covered by a thatch roof. There is a shared, spotlessly maintained outhouse. The resort is quite small, sleeping about six or eight. Run by Kiyotaka Sosaki and Yasuhiro Sato, the mission of this resort is to introduce its guests to the native I-Kiribati culture. The re-sort is therefore well integrated into the local village, allowing you to observe and participate in village activities.

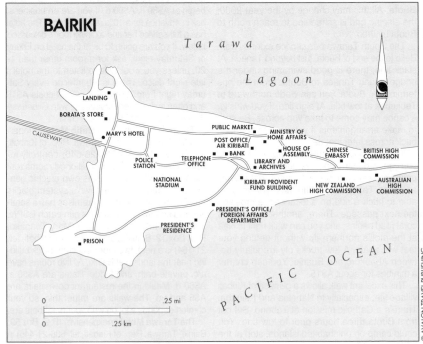

The lagoon on this end of the atoll is crystal clear. The hotel is equipped for diving and snorkeling, including introductory dives. It offers PADI certification courses. As for fishing, as I rode across the lagoon to the resort, three bonefish jumped into the boat. (Honest, I am not making this up or even exaggerating.) I've heard of good fishing, but this was ridiculous. Usually, the fishing, though good, requires placing a baited hook into the water in order to bring some fish home.

The resort costs A$80 pp. But this includes three wonderful meals a day, the best in Kiribati. Don't ask in the morning what you'll have for dinner, because it will be whatever is caught or gathered that day. Diving, (two-tank dive, A$88), snorkeling from a boat (A$28), and fishing (A$38 and up) is extra.

Food

The **Otintaai Restaurant** at the Otintaai Hotel is probably the best restaurant on South Tarawa. For breakfast, try pancakes with *te kamaimai* (molasses made from coconut sap).

Also quite good is **Matarena's,** located behind Mary's Hotel. As a starter, try the raw fish marinated in a coconut curry sauce. The fried fish makes an excellent main dish.

The restaurant in Mary's Hotel itself has a similar menu.

For lunch, you can buy locally prepared food from women with pushcarts at the Bairiki Market and around the high court offices in Betio. Make sure that your vendor appears to keep the product clean and sanitary.

In the mood for ice cream? Try **Molly's** on the road south of the Marine Training Center in Betio.

In the afternoons on Tarawa, women sit behind baskets of fish that their husbands caught earlier in the day, lazily fanning flies away from the fish. It may be boring, it may be low-paying (a three-pound skip-jack sells for between 50 cents and a dollar, depending on the day's catch), but it is not a high-stress job. I saw several women apparently able to sleep while continuing to fan. Fresh fish (and sometimes produce) is also available in the afternoon at the **Public Fish Market** in Bikenibeu, donated by the Canadian Government.

You can't always get what you want in Kiribati.

banana tree (Musa cavendishi)

For example, during 1998 when the country's one loading crane broke down, incoming freight had to be loaded onto smaller boats in Majuro, to then be trans-shipped to Tarawa. But if you have an insatiable urge for some utterly absurd Americana, such as Sarah Lee cheesecake, or some fresh greens, your best shot would be at the **One-Stop,** south of the Bikenibeu police station. The shop is expensive, but . . .

Entertainment

Young people in Tarawa like to dance at dance clubs. As Friday and Saturday night roll on, a good number of young men get drunk. Although there doesn't seem to be any pronounced anti-tourist feeling, fights do break out. It is probably best only to go to the clubs with local escorts, who will have better antennae about what might go down.

Probably the best club for visitors is **Sunrise Hall** on the grounds of the Otintaai Hotel. On Friday and Saturday nights it has live music 9 p.m.-midnight, and then a D.J. through most of the night. In Betio, the best bet is probably the **Royal Saloon,** which doesn't have live music. The **Betio Saloon** is similar. It's probably best to stay away from the **Kiosu,** the **Paradise Club** next to the Bank of Kiribati, and the **Seamen's Club,** all of which can get quite rough, particularly on Friday and Saturday nights.

On weekends you can watch model outrigger canoe races down the beaches at high tide. Look for these at Taborio, near the small causeway at Teaoraereke, or at Nanikai. You'll be amazed how fast they go when the breeze is right.

Divers should bring their own equipment. Only the small Mauri Paradise has all necessary equipment. Privately owned compressors exist on South Tarawa. A good place to inquire about both diving and sportfishing is **Betio Hardware** (tel. 686-26-130) in Betio. Also try to contact John Stripsky at tel. (686) 21-255; he's dive coordinator of the Kiribati Dive Club. For fishing, contact Louis Einkenhout at tel. (686) 26-130, fax (686) 26-332, or Norm Liven at tel. (686) 21-090, fax (686) 21-451. To charter a large trimaran with sails and an auxiliary motor, call (in advance) John Thurston, P.O. Box 228, Bikenibeu, Rep. of Kiribati, tel. (686) 28-661, fax (686) 21-451 or (686) 28-035.

Shopping

In Bairiki, opposite the post office, is a **market** that meets Monday through Saturday 7 a.m.-3 p.m. Mostly household goods are sold, but prepared food is also for sale.

Bikenibeu and Bairiki each have cooperative stores. Check out the small shopping plaza in the Kiribati Provident Fund Building next to the co-op in Bairiki for a variety of small shops. The best shopping is in Betio. Prices for the same items vary considerably. The **AMMS** stores at Antebuka, Bairiki, and Betio, and the **Fern Store** at Betio offer some of the best prices. Every village and housing agglomeration has a small store selling soft drinks, tobacco, matches, kerosene, corned beef, rice, flour, tinned butter, and a small number of other items.

The **Catholic Women's Handicraft Shop** in Teaoraereke is a good place to buy souvenirs. Pandanus purses cost A$6 and up. Also available are pandanus baskets, painted shells, cowrie shell barrettes, and small models of tra-

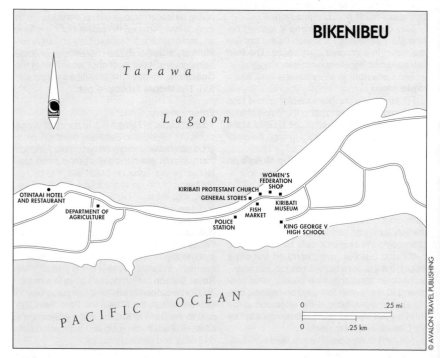

ditional Gilbertese boats. Several places in Bikenibeu also sell handicrafts: the gift shop at the Otintaai Hotel; and the **Women's Federation (AMAK)** shop, just a few hundred meters farther down the road. Hours are irregular, so just keep trying. Sleeping mats, sun hats, baskets, and fans are good buys. Check these shops regularly; new items are always coming in. Most Kiribati crafts are utilitarian, such as woven mats and thatch. There's no pottery or woodcarving, except for model canoes. On the outer islands, the co-op stores display items made by I-Kiribati families. Artifacts more than 30 years old and traditional tools cannot be taken out of the country.

The **Philatelic Bureau** (tel. 686-26-515) located in the same building as the post office in Betio sells Kiribati postage stamps—excellent gifts or souvenirs.

Services

The **Bank of Kiribati** branches at Bairiki and Betio open weekdays 9:30 a.m.-3 p.m., the Bikenibeu branch 9 a.m.-2 p.m.

Bikenibeu, Bairiki, and Betio have post offices. Address mail to: Rep. of Kiribati. Long-distance calls can be placed at the Telecom Services Kiribati Limited office next to the medical clinic in Bairiki, at the Ministry of Communications next to Betio post office, or at the Bikenibeu post office. If you are staying at the Otintaai Hotel, an overseas call can be placed from your room. Calls to Pacific countries are A$3/minute, to the rest of the world A$7.20/minute. (Yes, a fairly quick hello can run you $100.) You can direct dial from Tarawa to Christmas, Abaiang, Abaokoro (North Tarawa), Marakei, Abemama, Kuria, and Aranuka.

The Immigration office is located at the Ministry of Home Affairs and Rural Development (tel. 686-21-092 or 686-21-087) in Bairiki. Australia, China, South Korea, New Zealand, and the United Kingdom maintain diplomatic missions on South Tarawa.

The 120-bed **Tungaru Central Hospital** (tel. 686-28-081) is on the main road, between the airport and Bikenibeu. The branch hospital at Betio offers free medical service. Medical supplies are often limited. Due to chronic overcrowding patients may be transferred to the open-air *maneaba* next to the hospital, foreigners included. If a medical problem is serious, but

can wait a few days, leave Kiribati to seek medical attention.

Information

The **Kiribati Visitors Bureau** office (P.O. Box 510, Betio, Tarawa, Rep. of Kiribati, tel. 686-26-157, fax 686-26-233) is now located in Betio. The receptionists at the Otintaai Hotel are also very helpful.

The National Library and Archives at Bairiki stocks magazines and newspapers. The library also sells some interesting books on Kiribati. The Lands and Surveys office above the archives has excellent colored maps of most of islands.

The student bookshop in the forecourt area of the **Catholic Mission** at Teaoraereke has a comprehensive Kiribati dictionary (A$3.50). The University of the South Pacific Center is also at Teaoraereke. Visit the bookstore at King George V School, Bikenibeu, for books on the country and language of Kiribati.

GETTING THERE

Bonriki Airport (TRW) is five km (three miles) northeast of Bikenibeu on Tarawa. Buses serve the terminal. An **Air Kiribati** office (tel. 686-28-088) is located at the Bonriki Airport. For schedule and bookings, call (686) 21-550. If you are staying at the Otintaai, the receptionists can make arrangements.

It is not unusual for an international flight to be delayed a day or two. If you have to make plane connections, always allow at least a 24-hour layover to meet your connecting flight.

GETTING AROUND

By Road

South Tarawa has an efficient transportation system that revolves around vans acting as buses. You can flag down any van with a sign in the windshield that says "Bus" or "Hire." Despite the laws of physics, they always seem able to fit in one more passenger. When you want out, just shout *tei*. Buses run daily 5 a.m.-9 p.m., sometimes later on Friday and Saturday nights. The wait for a van is seldom more than 10 minutes. From the airport to Betio, the fare is $1.20. The minimum fare for trips within one village is 45 cents.

It is not unusual for no rental cars to be available. You may wish to make arrangements with a guide who has access to an automobile. We can recommend **Anita Awira,** who can be reached at tel. (686) 21-925.

If you are making advance hotel reservations, ask the hotel to reserve a car for you. You might also try **Avis** (tel. 686-21-090, fax 686-21-451), which rents modern Toyota cars. The **Otintaai Hotel** rents cars and motorbikes. The government **Plant and Vehicle Unit** (PVU) (tel. 686-21-174, fax 686-26-343) also rents vehicles to visitors from its compounds on Bairiki and Betio, as does the **Atoll Motor Marine Service** (AMMS) (tel. 686-21-113). Some local I-Kiribati also rent cars to visitors. Ask around. The Visitors Bureau keeps a list of car rental agencies and may offer to call around for you. A foreign driver's license is valid on Tarawa for two weeks, and driving is on the left. Beware of speed bumps.

Tuesday and Saturday you can catch a launch to North Tarawa (A$4). You can also rent a small launch from people at the wharf in Betio for about A$5 an hour with an operator. **Bikeman,** a small islet in the lagoon, is a nice destination for picnics.

OTHER ISLANDS OF TUNGARU

Abaiang

Abaiang, 51 km (32 miles) north of South Tarawa, is the most easily accessible outer island, with Air Kiribati flights three times a week (A$29 each way). The Island Council truck often meets flights.

In 1989 the Island Council built the **Nikuao Hotel** (Mr. Taata Tataua, Abaiang Island Council, Tabontebike, Abaiang, Rep. of Kiribati, tel. 686-27-102, fax 686-26-233) on one of the best and cleanest beaches in Kiribati. It consists of four traditional thatched bungalows and is located at Tabontebike village near the southern tip of the atoll. The bungalows, which cost A$30-40 pp including one meal, are quite comfortable. Mosquito nets are provided; toilet and washing facilities are shared. The council can arrange fishing and snorkeling off an outrigger canoe and trips to uninhabited Teirio Island. Traditional dancing is staged for groups and local meals are served. For reservations call the Abaiang Island Council clerk from South Tarawa or the Visitors Bureau at (686) 26-157.

There is an older rest house at Taburao, a few kilometers north of the airstrip. At Koinawa, further north, is an old Catholic church with a tower. Ask permission to climb up for the view. Heavily populated, villages are squashed together all the way up the thin strip of land along the lagoon's east side. Abaiang sour toddy has a distinct flavor. In 1991 Teatao Teannaki from Abaiang was elected president of Kiribati, but his government was suspended by a vote of "no confidence" in 1994.

Marakei

Marakei has an enclosed lagoon; two passages connect it to the sea at high tide, but at low tide it's entirely landlocked. It's customary for visitors to travel counterclockwise around Marakei (27 km, 17 miles). The airstrip is at the north end of the atoll, not far from Rawannawi village,

ABAIANG

Ribono

Takarano

Ubanteman

PACIFIC OCEAN

Nanikirata
Nuotaea

Tebunginako

Anariki

Borotiam

Aonobuaka

Koinawa

Morikao

Lagoon

Kuria

Taburao

Teirio

Tabwiroa

Tuarabu

AIRSTRIP

Bingham Channel

Tanimaiki

Tabontebike

Tebanga

0   5 mi
0   5 km

© AVALON TRAVEL PUBLISHING

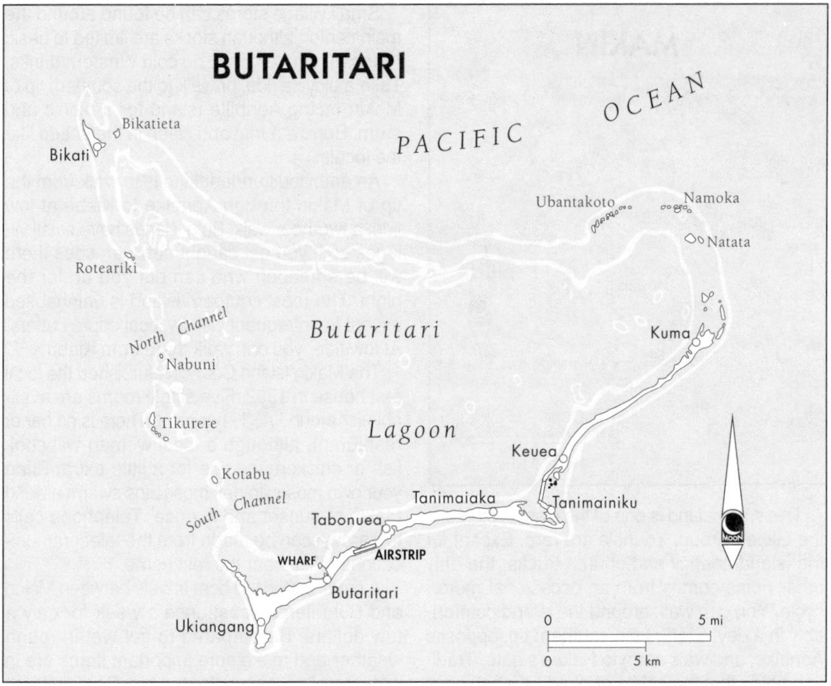

BUTARITARI

PACIFIC OCEAN

Bikatieta
Bikati
Ubantakoto
Namoka
Natata
Roteariki
North Channel
Butaritari
Kuma
Nabuni
Tikurere
Lagoon
Keuea
Kotabu
South Channel
Tanimaiaka
Tanimainiku
Tabonuea
WHARF
AIRSTRIP
Butaritari
Ukiangang

0   5 mi
0   5 km

which offers the rest house. Flights are three times a week and cost A$35 each way.

Butaritari

Due to regular rainfall, Butaritari is a very green atoll, with abundant vegetation and variety of food. Butaritari is known for its flavorful bananas, large quantities of which are shipped to South Tarawa. A causeway joins the two longest islands of the atoll, making it possible to walk the 30 km (19 miles) from Ukiangang to Kuma.

Butaritari has had long contact with Europeans; the first permanent European trading post in Tungaru was established here in 1846. At one time during the 19th century, 20 traders operated on the atoll. Many Western-style buildings remain today, intermingled with Chinese and local architectural styles. Americans and Japanese fought battles here during World War II, and rusted pillboxes still mar the island. The skeleton of a **Japanese seaplane** (minus wings and tail) lies beside the lagoon, opposite the small hospital in Butaritari village.

There's good anchorage for ships in the lagoon. Father Gratien Bermond, the Catholic priest in Butaritari village, also runs a small two-room **guesthouse** (A$15 pp including meals). There's a co-op and numerous privately owned shops on the island. Take care with the water, and always wear footwear, as the wetter climate encourages parasites such as hookworms. Air Kiribati flies to Butaritari three times a week (A$61). You can also check with the Kiribati Visitors Bureau to see if any boat is going over.

Makin

Butaritari's near neighbor, Makin, is the northernmost Tungaru island, 191 km (119 miles) north of Tarawa. (Formerly, Butaritari was known as Makin and the present Makin was "Little Makin.") The rest house is at Makin village, south of the airstrip. There are three flights a week (A$61).

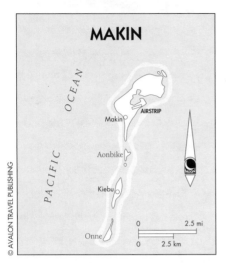

MAKIN

OCEAN

PACIFIC

AIRSTRIP

Makin

Aonbike

Kiebu

Onne

0   2.5 mi

0   2.5 km

© AVALON TRAVEL PUBLISHING

This small island is one of the least explored in the Gilbert group. Tourists are rare. Except for the island council and church trucks, the only other noise comes from an occasional motorcycle. You can walk around the island comfortably in a day. Start at the southern tip, opposite Aonbike, and walk north to Nakaa's gate. Tradition holds that the spirits of dead I-Kiribati pass this way on their journey to paradise or hell. Nakaa, the "Watcher at the Gate," waits at the northern end of Makin to catch the dead in his net. If you are adventurous and unafraid of ghosts, you can stay the night in one of the two *maneabas* nearby. The one near Nakaa's gate is said to be haunted, and you may find it difficult to get local I-Kiribati people willing to stay the night with you; the caretaker's house, in between the two *maneabas,* remains abandoned.

By walking at extreme low tide a short distance to the beach due west of the haunted *maneaba,* you will be able to see **Nakaa's tongue,** a rocky outcropping. Should you see flies on the rocks it's a sign that a spirit is passing through the judgement net. Tradition dictates that all who visit the tongue of Nakaa must cast offerings to the tongue from the beach.

For a panoramic view of Makin, ask permission to climb the stairs to the top of the Protestant church bell tower. Be careful of the slippery steps and lack of ladders on some levels.

Small village stores can be found around the main center, although stocks are limited to basic I-Kiribati requirements: no cold Western drinks. Take a bicycle ride, or walk to the southern tip of Makin facing Aonbike Island for a picnic and swim. Borrow a mat and sleep in the shade like the locals.

An ambitious undertaking is to walk from the tip of Makin through Aonbike to Kiebu at low tide, a two-hour walk. Both islands have small villages so if you get caught between tides there will be someone who can put you up for the night. The most southern island is uninhabited except for infrequent visit by local copra cutters. At low tide, you can walk there from Kiebu.

The Makin Island Council refurbished the local rest house in 1992. Five single rooms are available for around A$35 per night. There is no bar or restaurant, although a local woman will cook fish or chicken and rice for a little extra. Bring your own mosquito net; mosquitos swarm around Makin at sunset and sunrise. Telephone calls to Tarawa can be made from the telecommunications office near the rest home.

A small motorized boat travels between Makin and Butaritari at least once a week for only a few dollars. Be prepared to get wet in rough weather and make sure important items are in waterproof packaging for the trip. Confirm landing points to be made on Butaritari before leaving Makin to avoid ending up at the wrong island or village.

If you wish, you can join a fishing expedition outside the reef. However, proceed with caution; this is an arduous and potentially dangerous activity because the seas can become very rough. Canoes and their crews have been lost at sea.

Air Kiribati flies to Makin two to three times per week. Make sure to confirm your flight since these flights are often fully booked.

Kuria

Kuria, north of Tarawa, consists of a pair of triangular islands connected by a causeway; the airstrip and rest house (at Buariki) are on the southern one. Kuria has a fringing reef but no central lagoon. Near the north tip of the island are remnants of a former whaling station. Air Kiribati flies from Tarawa to Kuria twice a week (A$48 one way).

Banaba

Banaba (also known as Ocean Island) is a tiny, six-square-km (2.3-square-mile) raised atoll that claims the highest point in Kiribati—86 meters (283 feet). It lies 452 km (281 miles) southwest of Tarawa, closer to Nauru. Like the latter, it was once rich in phosphates, but from 1900-79 the deposits were exploited by British, Australian, and New Zealand interests in what is perhaps the best worst example of corporate, colonial exploitation of resources in the history of the Pacific islands.

After the Sydney-based Pacific Islands Company discovered phosphates on Nauru and Banaba in 1899, a company official, Albert Ellis, was sent to Banaba in May 1900 to obtain control of the resource. In due course "King" Temate and other chiefs signed an agreement granting Ellis's firm exclusive rights to exploit the phosphate deposits on Banaba for 999 years in exchange for £50 sterling a year. Of course, the local population had little idea what the whole transaction was about.

As Ellis rushed to put mining equipment and moorings in place, a British naval vessel arrived on 28 September 1901 to raise the British flag, joining Banaba to the Gilbert and Ellice Islands Protectorate. The British government reduced the term of the agreement to 99 years, more than enough years for the Pacific Phosphate Company, formed in 1902, to strip out the resource.

Things ran smoothly for the British until 1909, when the islanders refused to lease the company any additional land after 15% of Banaba had been stripped of both phosphates and food trees. The British government granted a somewhat better deal in 1913, but in 1916 changed the protectorate to a colony to prevent the Banabans from withholding their land again. After World War I the company was renamed the British Phosphate Commission (BPC), and in

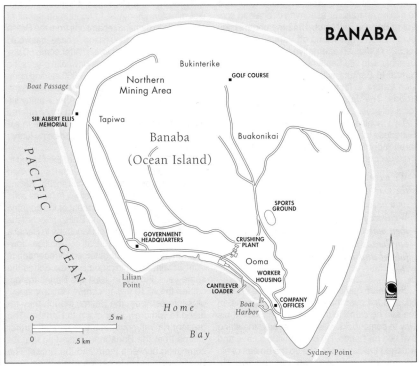

1928 the resident commissioner, Sir Arthur Grimble, signed an order expropriating the rest of the land, against the Banabans' wishes. The islanders continued to receive a tiny royalty until World War II.

On 10 December 1941, with a Japanese invasion deemed imminent, the order was given to blow up the mining infrastructure on Banaba, and on 28 February 1942 a French destroyer evacuated company employees from the island. In August some 500 Japanese troops and 50 laborers landed on Banaba and began erecting fortifications. The six Europeans they captured eventually perished as a result of mistreatment. All but 150 of the 2,413 local mine laborers and their families were deported to Tarawa, Nauru, and Kosrae. As a warning, the Japanese beheaded three of the locals and used another three to test an electrified anti-invasion fence.

Meanwhile the BPC decided to take advantage of this situation to rid itself of the island's original inhabitants to avoid any future hindrance to mining operations, assuming it regained control of Banaba. In March 1942 the commission purchased Rambi Island off Vanua Levu in Fiji for £25,000 as an alternative homeland for the Banabans. In late September 1945 the British returned to Banaba with Albert Ellis the first to step ashore, to find only surrendering Japanese troops. The Japanese had destroyed all the local villages.

Two months later an emaciated and wild-eyed Gilbertese man named Kabunare emerged from three months in hiding and told his story to a military court:

We were assembled together and told that the war was over and the Japanese would soon be leaving. Our rifles were taken away. We were put in groups, our names taken, then marched to the edge of the cliffs where our hands were tied and we were blindfolded and told to squat. Then we were shot.

Kabunare had either lost his balance or fainted, and fell over the cliff before he was hit. In the sea he came to the surface and kicked his way to some rocks where he severed the string that tied his hands. He crawled into a cave and watched the Japanese pile up the bodies of his companions and toss them into the sea. He stayed in the cave two nights then made his way inland where he survived on coconuts until he was sure the Japanese had left. Kabunare said he thought the Japanese had executed the others to destroy evidence of their cruelties and atrocities on Banaba.

As peace returned the British implemented their plan to resettle all 2,000 surviving Banabans on Rambi. The first group arrived on Rambi on 14 December 1945 and in time adapted to their mountainous new home and traded much of their original Micronesian culture for that of the Fijians. They and their descendants live there today.

During the 1960s the Banabans saw the much better deal Nauru was getting from the BPC, mainly through the efforts of Hammer DeRoburt and the "Geelong Boys," who were trapped in Australia during the war and thus received an excellent education and understanding of colonialism.

In 1966 Mr. Tebuke Rotan, a Banaban Methodist minister, journeyed to London on behalf of his people to demand reparations from the British for laying waste to their island, a case that would drag on for many bitter years. After some 50 visits to the Foreign and Commonwealth offices, he was offered (and rejected) £80,000 sterling compensation. In 1971 the Banabans sued for damages in the British High Court. After lengthy litigation, the British government in 1977 offered the Banabans a payment of A$10 million in exchange for a pledge that there would be no further legal action.

In 1975 the Banabans asked for their island to be separated from the rest of Kiribati and joined to Fiji, their present country of citizenship. Kiribati politicians, anxious to protect their fisheries zone and wary of the dismemberment of the country, lobbied against this, and the British rejected the proposal. The free entry of Banabans to Banaba was guaranteed in the Kiribati constitution, however. In 1979, Kiribati obtained independence from Britain, and mining on Banaba ended the same year. Finally, in 1981 the Banabans accepted the A$10 million compensation money, plus interest, from the British, though they refused to withdraw their claim to Banaba. The present Kiribati government rejects all further claims from the Banabans, asserting that it's something between them and the British. The British are trying to forget the whole thing.

Some 284 people now practice a subsistence lifestyle on Banaba. There's no airstrip so the only way to get there is on the quarterly supply ship from Tarawa (A$25 deck one-way). Anyone wishing to spend three months on Banaba must obtain advance permission from the Home Affairs Office in Bairiki (Tarawa). No permit is required to visit the island for a few hours while the ship is in port.

Abemama

Abemama ("Island of Moonlight"), just north of the equator 153 km (95 miles) southeast of Tarawa, is a crescent-shaped atoll with a lagoon on its west side. Two passages give access to an excellent anchorage. There's good snorkeling here. A visit to Abemama is a trip to an earlier period in the Pacific: beautiful, clean beaches and beautiful, warm, and friendly people.

Transportation on Abemama consists of several church trucks, a few owned by the Island Council and a few more privately owned. One or more of these trucks will meet your incoming plane, and you will have no trouble getting a lift. There also are a fair number of motor scooters on the atoll.

Kariatebike is the government center, with a small hospital, administrative building, police station, and co-op. The store usually is not well stocked. so bring in any food and drink you may need. Causeways have been built linking Kariatebike to the islets south, making it possible to drive all the way to Kabangaki.

Near Tabontebike, north of the Catholic *maneaba,* is the tomb of the tyrant chief Tem Binoka. Robert Louis Stevenson, who lived just north of Kariatebike for several months in 1889, made Tem Binoka famous (read *In The South Seas*). War relics on Abemama include the airstrip at the north end of the atoll and a wrecked Corsair fighter aircraft set up in front of the hotel.

Formerly, the island had several small hotels, but all have closed. However, there is an inexpensive Island Council guest house on the oceanfront in Kariatebike. The rooms are small, simple, and clean. You may also be able to sleep in the *bula* (a traditional Gilbertese sleeping platform covered by a thatched roof but without walls). It is truly a wonderful experience to wake up during the night, feel the cool nighttime breezes, and watch the stars). Meals are provided. The extremely gracious Tekakia Unkenio runs the house and serves up some of the best meals in Kiribati.

Air Kiribati flies to Abemama three times a week (A$45), but the flights are often full. After heavy rains the journey from Kariatebike to the airport can be slow due to potholes and water on the road, so allow extra time when leaving.

Nonouti

The **government rest house** at Matang, four km (2.5 miles) south of the airstrip, faces the ocean and is cooled by prevailing winds. The manager can provide food, if you need it. Nearby are a post office, a couple of small shops, and a local hospital with a nurse. The cooperative store is located at the government wharf at Aubeangai, just south of Matang. One bus, even if running, provides an erratic, unscheduled service the length of the road—two trips each way daily. Most people travel by motor scooter.

Visit Kiribati's largest *maneaba* at Umantewenei village. The Makauro *maneaba* is the oldest on Nonouti; visitors traditionally spent their first night on the island here, though this custom need not be followed today. A monument in the form of a ship at Taboiaki village recalls the arrival of the first Catholic missionaries to Tungaru in 1888. At the north end of the atoll are several small islets, accessible by boat, where large numbers of seabirds nest. Inquire at the council offices for a visit. Kiribati's first president, Ieremia Tabai, hailed from Temotu village on Nonouti.

Air Kiribati flies to Nonouti twice a week (A$76 one way).

Tabiteuea

This 72-km-long (45 miles) island, 296 km (184 miles) southeast of Tarawa, is the longest in Tungaru. The name Tabiteuea ("Forbidden to Kings") was chosen for this island, since it traditionally had no kings. Fences erected around houses delineated private property. Anyone entering without first seeking the owner's permission could be attacked. You can still sees vestiges of this way of life in the well-maintained flower gardens surrounding houses, and in the more evident retention of fences.

In 1881 the population of Tabiteuea South was almost wiped out by an army from Tabiteuea North, organized by a pair of Protestant missionaries from Hawaii wishing to spread their faith by force. Most of the inhabitants of the atoll are now Catholic. Rest houses are at Utiroa, near the airstrip on Tabiteuea North, and at Buariki, near the airstrip on Tabiteuea South. Tabiteuea is known for its dancers.

TABITEUEA

Tabiteuea North

Tekabwibwi
Tekaman
Tanaeang
Buota Terikiai
Eita
Utiroa **AIRSTRIP**
Tauma
Kabuna
Tenatorua Bangai
Aiwa
Tabiteuea South
South Lagoon
Tewai Taungaeaka
AIRSTRIP
West Passage Buariki
Katabanga Nikutoro
Taku

PACIFIC OCEAN

0   10 mi
0   10 km

© AVALON TRAVEL PUBLISHING

Air Kiribati flies to Tabiteuea North and Tabiteuea South twice a week; one way to either is A$94.

Onotoa

Onotoa Island is named for six giants who created it by throwing stones into the sea. Its houses and *maneaba* are still built on coral slabs. Much land has been reclaimed from the lagoon by building coral walls around an area, and then filling in with broken shells and coconut husks. There's no causeway to the southernmost islands of the atoll, so you must wade at low tide or borrow a canoe. The postman delivers mail to the southern villages once a week and might give you a lift. The rest house is at Buraitan, seven km (4.5 miles) southeast of the airstrip. Flights are twice a week at A$116, one way. Transportation is sometimes available in the Catholic mission's truck.

Beru

The bones of Kourabi, a famous 18th-century Beru warrior, hang in a basket in the Buota Maneaba Atianikarawa, with a huge turtle shell suspended above. Once every eight years the bones are washed in the ocean, and the villagers celebrate a great feast. The London Missionary Society ran its Tungaru mission from this island for many years. Beru is the only place in Tungaru outside South Tarawa that has electricity. A well-furnished rest house is at Tabukiniberu, a few kilometers northwest of the airstrip. Ships cannot enter the lagoon.

Southern Tungaru

The three small islands at the southeast end of the Tungaru group, Nikunau, Tamana, and Arorae, are all without central lagoons. To stay at the rest house in Rungata village on **Nikunau,** see the manager of the co-op. The rest house on **Tamana,** smallest atoll of the Tungaru group, is cooled by sea breezes. The deep *babai* pits, about a 15-minute walk northeast of the government center, are impressive. **Arorae,** 624 km (388 miles) from Tarawa, has a basic rest house opposite the co-op at Taribo, three km (two miles) south of the airstrip. At the northwest tip of Arorae are the Atibu ni Borau, large coral "navigation stones." The ruins of an old village and a cemetery are nearby.

THE PHOENIX ISLANDS

Archaeological remains indicate that some of the Phoenix and Line Islands were once inhabited, probably by Polynesians. By the time the first Europeans arrived, however, these people had died or left. Guano was collected on these islands during the mid-19th century, but the deposits were soon exhausted. Britain annexed the group in 1889, although the United States had a vague claim dating from the guano-collecting era.

In 1937 Phoenix was joined to the Gilbert and Ellice Islands colony, and a year later, to reinforce their claim, the British resettled about a thousand people from overcrowded southern Tungaru on Gardner, Hull, and Sydney. Americans visited Kanton and Enderbury in 1938; in 1939, as their value as stopovers on the trans-Pacific aviation route between Fiji and Honolulu became apparent, the two islands were placed under joint British-American administration for 50 years.

By 1952 the strategic value of the islands had declined, and the colonists were undergoing serious difficulties due to saline well water and droughts. They also suffered from isolation and unrealistic expectations. Some returned to Tungaru, but most were taken to the British Solomon Islands Protectorate, where large numbers live today. By 1964 all the Phoenix Islanders had left.

Kanton

Kanton (Canton) is the largest and most northerly of the Phoenix group. The 14-km-long (nine miles) lagoon is surrounded by a narrow triangular strip of land, broken only on the west side. Despite strong currents, large ships can enter the lagoon. The island was named for the New Bedford whaling boat *Kanton,* wrecked here in 1854. The 32 survivors sailed from Kanton to Guam in an open boat, a distance of 2,900 nautical miles. (Captain Bligh's epic open-boat journey from Tonga to Timor totaled 3,618 nautical miles.)

Wildlife on Kanton consists mostly of birds, fish, and rats. Large colonies of white fairy terns and red-footed boobies nest on the atoll. Giant hermit crabs are plentiful all over Kanton and, together with the frigate birds, are useful scavengers. Tiny insect-eating lizards dart through the ruins of the base. A kaleidoscope of tropical fish fills the lagoon: triggerfish, damselfish, puffer, parrot fish, sharks, and moray eels.

Pan American Airways used Kanton's lagoon as a stopover for its trans-Pacific seaplanes in the 1930s. In 1938 it built an airstrip on the atoll and cleared the coral heads from a seaplane runway in the lagoon. During World War II, the United States Air Force built a new airstrip at the island's northwest end. This was maintained as an emergency landing field until the 1960s when it was abandoned.

A NASA satellite tracking station established in 1965 closed in 1967, when the island passed to the U.S. Air Force. The unused facilities stand intact on Kanton, taken care of by an I-Kiribati family. An American-built wharf on Kanton is capable of handling large freighters. The United States has turned these abandoned facilities over to the Kiribati government.

In 1990 the government installed firefighting equipment and refueling capacity beside Kanton's airstrip to provide emergency landing facilities for flights between Tarawa and Christmas Island. Presently, there are no scheduled flights, but Shipping Corporation of Kiribati ships sometimes call on their way to Christmas Island

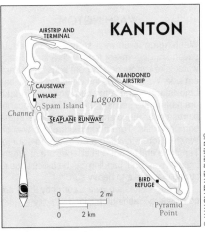

© AVALON TRAVEL PUBLISHING

every three months. On the return voyage the ship will bypass Kanton unless there's enough cargo or passengers to be picked up. Ask about this before disembarking or be prepared to pay a substantial "diversion fee" if the ship is forced to return only to evacuate you.

THE LINE ISLANDS

The five central and southern Line Islands, worked for guano more than a century ago, are now uninhabited. None of the five (Malden, Starbuck, Caroline, Vostok, and Flint) has a safe anchorage, although landings have been blasted through the reefs at Starbuck and Flint, and an airstrip was built on Malden in 1958 as part of a nuclear testing program.

Plantation workers live on Fanning and Washington. In 1983 the Kiribati government purchased the coconut plantations on Fanning and Washington from the Australian trading company Burns Philp, and leased them to the former employees, who produce copra for their cooperative.

In an attempt to reduce the overcrowding on Tarawa, Kiribati has encouraged resettlement on Christmas Island. But the extremely isolated nature of these islands has created serious transportation and administrative problems for the government. The deep seabed around the Line Islands contains some of the richest known deposits of cobalt, nickel, platinum, and manganese in the world.

WASHINGTON

Washington is an oval-shaped island about seven km (four miles) long, with a large freshwater lake surrounded by peat bogs on its eastern side. Washington is the wettest of the Kiribati Line Islands, and after heavy rains the lake drains into the sea through a sluice. Coconut palms cover the island, with pandanus in the damper areas. Taro and breadfruit do well on Washington, providing a steady food source. Tangkore and Nanounou villages are at Washington's west end. Landing can be difficult due to strong currents and heavy surf.

Although it has a runway, currently there are no flights to Washington Island

FANNING

Fanning is also known as Tabuaeran, a corruption of a Polynesian name meaning "sacred footprint." It is an 18 by 11 km (11 by 7 mile) atoll, 286 km (178 miles) northwest of Christmas Island and 141 km (88 miles) southeast of Washington. Three channels lead into the wide lagoon. In 1798 Capt. Edmund Fanning reached the island, 3,020 km (1,875 miles) east of Tarawa. It was once the mid-ocean station of the undersea cable running from Fiji to Vancouver, which is now closed. Most of the land area is planted with coconuts. The number of seabirds nesting here is limited due to the activities of feral cats. The main village, English Harbor, is on the southwest side of the island.

Visiting yachts are charged A$3 a day to anchor at English Harbor in the Fanning lagoon. The Shipping Corporation of Kiribati runs a supply boat to Fanning three times a year. One-way deck fares are A$17 from Christmas, A$116 from Tarawa, double fare for a B class cabin, triple for A class.

Although it has a runway, currently there are no flights to Fanning Island

CHRISTMAS ISLAND (KIRITIMATI)

This large island, 2,110 km (1,310 miles) southeast of Honolulu, 2,715 km (1,690 miles) north of Tahiti, and 3,220 km (2,000 miles) east of Tarawa, accounts for nearly half the land area of Kiribati. Deserted beaches surround the 160-km (100-mile) perimeter, with many small lakes in the interior. The huge tidal lagoon on the island's west side covers 160 square km (62 square miles). Christmas's southeast "panhandle" has no palm trees, only bushes, and many seabirds.

Captain Cook reached the island on Christmas Day 1777; the British annexed it in 1888. (Another Christmas Island, a dependency of Australia, is in the Indian Ocean.) To the locals, it's known as **Kiritimati,** the Kiribati spelling of Christmas.

During World War II the United States built the airport on Christmas to refuel planes flying southwest toward Australia. From 1956 to 1962 the United States and Britain tested nuclear weapons in the atmosphere at Christmas and Malden Islands. The British tested their first hydrogen bomb at Malden on 15 May 1957; over the following 15 months they exploded six more, plus two atomic bombs.

Because of the Tarawa relocation program whereby I-Kiribati are encouraged to settle on Christmas Island, there are now almost 4,000 people living on the island. It has been trying to establish itself as a tourist destination—offering some of the world's best bonefishing and excellent birdwatching.

Sights

Large colonies of 18 species of rare migratory seabirds, all quite tame, nest on Cook Island and Motu Tabu. Christmas Island has the world's largest colony of sooty terns; eight million birds nest here in June and December. Other tame birds nesting on the ground at camera level include noddies, fairy terns, boobies, tropic birds, frigate birds, wedgetailed shearwaters, and petrels. The seabirds have breeding seasons spread throughout the year, though the best months to visit are March-July and October-December. It's illegal to hunt them, and possession of birds, nests, eggs, and even feathers is prohibited.

The island swarms with scavenging land crabs and the reefs teem with fish. Christmas Island is famous for sportfishing, particularly for the **Pacific bonefish** found on the coral flats of the shallow interior lagoon. Anglers wade out watching for a bonefish, then cast their fly toward it and experience the fight of their lives. Gray sharks are numerous along the drop-off. Beyond the reef papio, ulua, waho, marlin, and stingrays are abundant.

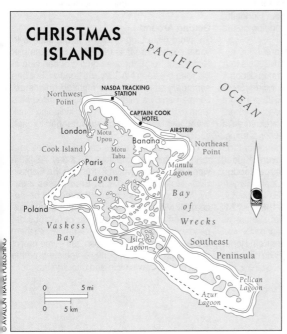

The lee shore between Northwest Point and London is the safest diving or snorkeling area, but it can be dangerous to fight your way through the surf. The coral surge channels through the reef teem with fish. You can combine a little snorkeling with your visit to the bird sanctuary on Cook Island.

At the north end of the island, the National Space Development Agency of Japan (NASDA) has a downrange **satellite tracking station,** which controls satellites launched from Tanegashima, Japan, during the early stages of orbit.

Practicalities

Opened in 1994, the **Mini Hotel Kiritimati** (moderate) (tel. 686-81-225, fax 686-31-316) offers a small number of rooms, which can be rented with or without meals. Motor vehicle hire can be arranged for about A$100. For further information about the hotel, contact Mark Somers, **Christmas Island Outfitters,** P.O. Box 669, Crozet, VA 22932, tel. (800) 694-4162, fax (800) 550-1906. Outfitters specializes in fishing trips, offering, for example, a one-week excursion for roughly US$2,000 pp, including airfare from Honolulu, based on double occupancy, depending on the season.

The 36-room **Captain Cook Hotel** (very expensive) (Boitabu Smith, tel. 686-81-230) is four km (2.5 miles) northwest of the airstrip. Rooms have twin beds and private bath. Standard rooms are A$165 s or A$264 d, about A$20 per night extra for air conditioning. Fairly expensive American-style food and local fresh fish are served in the dining room. The bar is open every evening, and Monday is Island Night, with typical food cooked in an *umu* (underground oven). Kiribati dance shows are arranged if a large enough group is present. JoAnn Poffel or Susie Fitzgerald at **Fish and Game Frontiers** (P.O. Box 959, Wexford, PA 15090, tel. 800-245-1950 or 724-935-1577, fax 724-935-5388), website: www. frontierstrvl.com) can make reservations for you. They also sell packages with airfare from Honolulu, including fishing and diving. Prices based on double occupancy range from US$1,720 to US$2,535 a week, depending on the activities you wish included.

Camping on the island is prohibited.

There are plantation stores in all the villages, plus a hospital in London. A large map of the island is available from the Land Development Officer.

Getting There

As of 1999, there was no regular airline service from Christmas to Tungaru. **Air Kiribati,** using an Aloha Airlines plane and crew, flies from Honolulu to Christmas each Tuesday. The return flight is the same day (Wednesday: Kiribati time). For reservations on this flight, call (888) 800-8144 or (818) 839-6680, or fax (818) 839-6681. You may wish to have either Christmas Island Outfitters or Fish and Game Frontiers, discussed above, make flight arrangements for you.

Kiribati's newest interisland container ship, the *Nei Matangare,* operated by Kiribati Shipping Services, serves Christmas from Tarawa at least once every two months to pick up copra. Cabins are often booked in advance.

Getting Around

To avoid disturbing breeding birds, access to some seabird areas is restricted. For example, Northwest Point, the area on the ocean side of the road between NASDA and London, is a bird sanctuary, and entry is prohibited unless accompanied by a wildlife warden. Escorted boat tours to the accessible reserves, including Cook Island and Motu Tabu, can be arranged through your hotel.

Other breeding areas can be reached in a rental Isuzu pickup truck (A$75 a day, A$450 a week, plus gas), available through the Captain Cook Hotel or from **J.M.B. Enterprises** nearby. Your overseas driver's license will be accepted. Motor scooters are sometimes available. Some of the vehicles are of dubious dependability, and traveling any distance with them is risky. However, J.M.B. also has some newer pickups for hire. Don't drive a vehicle onto the coral flats. It may sink in and damage the reef.

GORDON OHLIGER

AMERICAN POSSESSIONS

The United States government holds as possessions a number of scattered islands and atolls on Micronesia's northeast fringe. They have historical and geographical links to the rest of the region. Midway atoll is geologically part of the Hawaiian chain. Johnston and Wake atolls are stepping stones to the Marshalls. Kingman Reef, Palmyra Atoll, and Jarvis Island are part of the Line Islands (the rest of which are included in the Republic of Kiribati). Howland and Baker are just northwest of Kiribati' Phoenix Islands. Until the last several years, none of these islands could be visited by tourists. But since 1997, Midway atoll has accepted a limited number of tourists, no more than 100 at any given time.

Originally uninhabited, these islands came under United States sovereignty during the 19th and early 20th centuries. They were not considered important until 1935, when they began to be used as aviation stopovers and military bases. Today, Howland, Baker, and Jarvis as well as Johnston form the **Pacific Islands National Wildlife Refuge** (P.O. Box 50167, Honolulu, HI 96850, tel. 808-541-1201). Entry to these islands is restricted to scientists and educators,

who must obtain a permit from the Refuge Manager prior to landing.

There have been periodic attempts to incorporate Baker, Howland, Jarvis, Kingman, Midway, and Palmyra into the State of Hawaii and annex Wake to Guam. To date, nothing has come of these proposals.

MIDWAY

Near the northwest end of the Hawaiian chain, 1,469 miles from Oahu, Midway measures two square miles. The 15-mile-long barrier reef around this circular atoll encloses two small islands, Sand and Eastern. The atoll is midway between California and Japan, hence the name. Captain N.C. Brooks of the Hawaiian ship *Gambia* arrived in 1859, and the United States annexed the atoll in 1867. In 1903 it became a station on a submarine cable that is no longer used. Until 1997, it was controlled by the U.S. Navy, under the command of Barbers Point Naval Air Station, Hawaii.

Pan Am China Clippers began refueling here in 1935. Soil was shipped in from Guam, and

Norfolk pines were planted on the island. In 1941, the United States completed an important submarine base. The Battle of Midway took place early in June 1942, marking a turning point in World War II. In a massive sea battle, the United States halted Japan's eastward expansion. During the Vietnam War, Midway again became an important naval air station with several thousand residents. After 1978 the population fell sharply.

Since 1997, Midway has been opened to a limited number of tourists. No more than 100 can be on Midway at any given time. Control of the island was turned over to the Interior Department's Fish and Wildlife Service. FWS then contracted with the **Midway Phoenix Corporation** to run visitor services.

Midway's main attraction is its wildlife, particularly its bird populations. It is home to 71% of the world's Laysan albatross, nicknamed gooney birds by sailors during WW II. Each November, about 400,000 pairs of these birds come to Midway to nest (very few make advance reserva-

tions). Chicks are born in January and fly off in June or July—until they return to Midway to mate. More than 75,000 pairs of sooty terns *(Ewa Ewa)* return to Midway each year. The chicks born to these birds will fly off and not touch land for seven years—until they return to Midway to mate.

Midway is also gaining a reputation as a fishing, snorkeling, and diving destination. It is home to spinner dolphins, rare turtles, and the endangered Hawaiian monk seal. Because there has been so little tourism to Midway, birds and sea life are often much more approachable than those found in more populated areas.

The accompanying table, compiled by the San Francisco-based nonprofit Oceanic Society Expeditions, tells you the best months to see specific wildlife. The Society also keeps a hotline at (415) 440-2473 to let you know of any unusual wildlife patterns. Please also note on the accompanying chart that because of Midway's relatively northern location, winter weather is considerably colder than that in the summer.

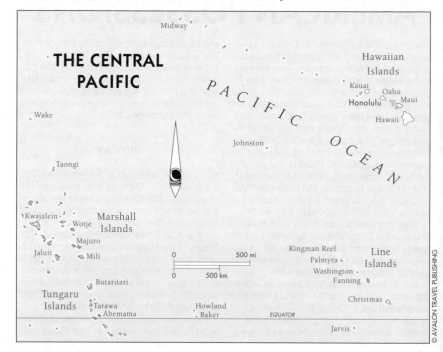

MIDWAY WILDLIFE CALENDAR

KEY ● = ABUNDANT ◗ = LESS ABUNDANT | = FEW PRESENT

FISH & WILDLIFE	JAN	FEB	MAR	APR	MAY	JUN	JUL	AUG	SEP	OCT	NOV	DEC
Laysan Albatross	●	●	●	●	●	●	●				●	●
Black-footed Albatross	●	●	●	●	●	●	●			◗	●	●
Short-tailed Albatross	|	|	|	|						|	|	|
White Tern	●	●	●	●	●	●	●	●	●	●	●	●
Sooty Tern		●	●	●	●	●	●	●	◗			
Gray-backed Tern			●	●	●	●	●	●				
Black Noddy	●	◗	●	●	●	●	●	●	●	●	●	●
Brown Noddy				●	●	●	●	●	●	●	●	
Wedge-tailed Shearwater			●	●	●	●	●	●	●	●	●	
Christmas Shearwater			●	●	●	●	◗	●	●	◗		
Bonin Petrel	●	●	●	●	●	●		●	●	●	●	●
Red-tailed Tropicbird	●	●	●	●	●	●	●	●	●	●	◗	◗
White-tailed Tropicbird	|	|	|	|	|	|	|	|	|	|	|	|
Great Frigatebird		●	●	●	●	●	●	●	●	●		
Red-footed Booby	●	●	●	●	●	●	●	●	●			
Masked Booby	|	|	|	|		|	|		|	|		
Pacific Golden Plover	●	●	●	●				●	●	●	●	●
Ruddy Turnstone	●	●	●	●				●	●	●	●	●
Bristle-thighed Curlew	●	●	●	●				●	●	●	●	●
Wandering Tattler	●	●	●	●				●	●	●	●	●
Sanderling	●	●	●	●				●	●	●	●	●
Hawaiian Monk Seal	●	●	●	●	●	●	●	●	●	●	●	●
Hawaiian Green Sea Turtle	●	●	●	●	●	●	●	●	●	●	●	●
Hawaiian Spinner Dolphin	●	●	●	●	●	●	●	●	●	●	●	●
Lagoon Fish (200+ species)	●	●	●	●	●	●	●	●	●	●	●	●

COURTESY OF OCEANIC SOCIETY EXPEDITIONS

MIDWAY

Islet

Center

Lagoon

Seaward Roads

LANDING

Wells Harbor AIRSTRIPS

Eastern Island

Sand Island

Brooks Channel

PACIFIC OCEAN

0   3 mi

0   3 km

© AVALON TRAVEL PUBLISHING

You can visit Midway a number of different ways: as an independent traveler, on an organized tour, or on a work project.

Flights to Midway depart from Honolulu. (There is no longer a flight from Lihue, Kauai, Hawaii). The flights are chartered by Phoenix Air. On Wednesday, it uses its own 19-passenger Gulfstream twin turboprop airplane, which takes five hours to get to Midway. On Saturday, it charters an 85-seat Aloha Airlines 737, which takes two and a half hours flying time. Independent travelers can make reservations either through **Oceanic Society Expeditions,** Fort Mason Center, Building E, San Francisco, CA 94123, tel. (800) 326-7491 or (415) 441-1106, or

Midway Sport Fishing and Diving, P.O. Box 217, Newnan, GA 30264, tel. (888) 244-8582 or (770) 254-8326. Airfare for the roundtrip from Honolulu is $750, sometimes less.

Either company can book you at Midway's only hotel, which is in Midway's old Bachelor Officers Quarters. The accommodations are clean and comfortable, though not luxurious. Rooms with shared baths begin at $120, with a private bath $150. Suites are also available. All accommodations are air conditioned. Food is available at the old Navy cafeteria and the new, more upscale Clipper House. There is also a pub.

Even if you don't ordinarily travel on organized tours, you might wish to do so on Midway. This is not a location where, for example, your independence would bring you a wide choice of restaurants to sample. Oceanic Society Expeditions has both a five-day tour (cost including airfare from Honolulu, $1,654) and a nine-day tour ($2,289). This nonprofit, membership organization is dedicated to worldwide conservation projects. Its guided tour programs are crammed with opportunities for you to learn about the fascinating wildlife that probably brings you to this destination.

While Midway Sport Fishing and Diving doesn't offer an educational program, it can arrange all your diving, snorkeling, and fishing needs.

Feel like making a contribution with your vacation? Oceanic Society Expeditions organizes nine-day research expeditions. At Midway, it has had ongoing research projects on: seabird mon-

smoke rising from an American installation on Midway, hit by Japanese aircraft in early June 1942

NATIONAL ARCHIVES, WASHINGTON, D.C.

A Pan American Airways Martin M-130 at Wake in 1936, the year Pan Am started trans-Pacific passenger service. The first airmail flight from San Francisco to Manila passed through a year earlier.

itoring; native plant restoration; spinner dolphins; and historical preservation. These projects cost about $2,000, including accommodations, meals, and roundtrip airfare from Honolulu to Midway.

The United States Fish and Wildlife Service also has a program for volunteers. You will need to make a three-month commitment and will be expected to put in an honest week's work. You will get free transportation, a food allowance, and a free room. For further information, write U.S. Fish and Wildlife Service, Midway Atoll National Wildlife Refuge, Box 29460, Honolulu, HI 96820-1860, tel./fax (808) 599-3914.

To answer most of your questions about Midway, visit its website: www.midway-atoll.com.

WAKE

Wake (Enen Kio) is located between Guam and Midway, 750 miles north of Kwajalein. The three islands of this 2.5-square-mile atoll—Wilkes, Wake, and Peale—enclose a horseshoe-shaped lagoon, sealed on the northwest by a barrier reef. The channel between Wilkes and Wake islands, now blocked by a solid causeway, once gave entry to the lagoon. A small-boat harbor presently occupies this channel, but ships over 22 yards must moor to offshore buoys.

Although Enen Kio traditionally probably had no permanent population, Marshallese navigators visited to hunt sea turtles and birds. Sighted by the Spaniard Mendana in 1568, Wake is named for the British sea captain William Wake, who arrived in 1796. In 1840 the atoll was charted by Capt. Charles Wilkes of the United States Exploring Expedition; Peale Island was named for the expedition's naturalist. The Republic of the Marshall Islands claims the atoll, though the United States is unlikely to give it up.

The United States annexed Wake in 1898 for use as a cable station. A Pan American Airways refueling base and 48-room transit hotel opened on Peale in 1935.

At the outbreak of World War II, 1,200 civilian workers were on Wake, completing a major air and submarine base. On 11 December 1941

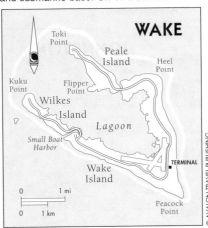

WAKE

Toki Point

Peale Island

Heel Point

Kuku Point

Flipper Point

Wilkes Island

Lagoon

Small Boat Harbor

TERMINAL

Wake Island

Peacock Point

0   1 mi

0   1 km

the construction workers and 523 marines re-pelled a Japanese invasion, but on 23 December, Japanese troops from Kwajalein landed in force. The Japanese forces took the surviving Americans to POW camps in China and Japan. The Japanese held Wake until the end of the war for use as a submarine base.

Today, civil aircraft are allowed to land and refuel, but prior permission is required; write Detachment 4, 15th Air Base Wing, APO San Francisco, CA 96501-5000, or call (256) 955-5932.

JOHNSTON

Johnston atoll, about 800 miles southwest of Honolulu, is 12 miles around. Its four islets, Johnston, Sand, Akau (North), and Hikina (East), now total 1.1 square miles, increased from its natural state by dredging during the 1960s. The military believed in straight lines, so today, from the air Johnston Island looks like a large aircraft carrier.

Crew members of the brig *Sally* of Boston sighted this island in 1796. Charles James Johnston, captain of HMS *Cornwallis*, landed in 1807. In 1856 Johnston Island was claimed by both the United States and the Kingdom of Hawaii (which called it Kalama Island). That year, an American company began to extract guano. In 1934 the United States Navy assumed jurisdiction of the atoll. Jurisdiction was transferred to the U.S. Air Force in 1948.

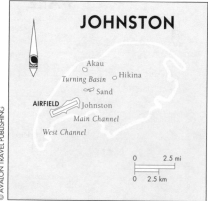

After the end of WW II, the United States military used Johnston for nuclear testing. It then turned it into a large incinerator complex for the destruction of chemical warfare weapons, under the auspices of the Johnston Atoll Chemical Agency Disposal System (JACADS). American chemical agents were brought to Johnston from storage in Okinawa and Germany. Destruction of the weapons began in 1990 and is expected to be completed in the year 2000. The United States had considered using Johnston to destroy chemical weapons for other nations with less advanced destruction plants. The U.S., however, dropped those plans, yielding to pressure from other Pacific Island countries that feared the possibility of a mid-Pacific disaster.

It is not yet clear whether the United States will simply close down the facility in 2000. Till then, the population consists of about 300 enlisted and 1,000 civilian employees, overwhelmingly male. All personnel are required to have gas masks ready. All temporary guests are also issued masks and instructed in their use. Military personnel on Johnston are given fairly extensive leaves in Hawaii because of the combination of stress and boredom for those working here.

Although some Continental Airlines flights between Honolulu and Majuro touch down on Johnston, it is virtually impossible for anyone without business there to get permission to visit. Very few would want to, even though, despite the nearby toxicity, Johnston is a national wildlife preserve with more than 300 species of fish, 20 species of birds, 32 coral species, green sea turtles, dolphins, humpback whales, and the endangered Hawaiian monk seals.

KINGMAN

Kingman Reef, between Hawaii and Samoa, is a triangular-shaped atoll, the apex of which points northward. On the east side is a barren speck of sand about 130 feet long and only three feet above the high tide mark. This low profile makes the atoll a navigational hazard. An American, Capt. Edmund Fanning, found Kingman Reef in 1798, but it is named for Capt. Kingman, who visited in 1853. The United States annexed the reef in 1922, and in 1934 turned it over to the U.S. Navy, which retains jurisdiction. Pan Am

PALMYRA

Strawn
AIRSTRIP
Aviation
Quail
PIER
Center Lagoon
East Lagoon
West Lagoon
Portsmouth Point
Eastern
Barren
Entrance Channel
Sand
Marine
Home
Paradise
Kaula
Engineer
Pelican
Penguin Spit
Holei
Bird

0   1 mi
0   1 km

© AVALON TRAVEL PUBLISHING

China Clippers bound for New Zealand touched down in the lagoon from 1937 to 1938. Today the Kingman lagoon is abandoned.

Just 156 miles northwest of Kingman, within the United States Exclusive Economic Zone, is an extinct undersea volcano covered by a three-quarter-inch-thick manganese crust containing 2.5% cobalt, the richest deposit of its kind ever found. Other rich nickel and platinum deposits lie on the seabed near the Line Islands at depths up to 6,500 feet.

PALMYRA

Palmyra atoll, 33 miles southeast of Kingman Reef, is at the north end of the Line Islands, 1,056 miles south of Honolulu. Dredging has been used to increase the acreage of the atoll's 50 tiny reef islets from 500 to 3,000 acres. The barrier reef encloses three distinct lagoons known as West, Center, and East. West Lagoon provides large anchorage areas and can be entered through a narrow dredged channel on the southwest side of the atoll, adjacent to Sand Island. A dredged seaplane landing area connects the West and Center lagoons.

Fish caught at Palmyra are often poisonous. Several years ago scientists in Tahiti determined that the cause of ciguatera (fish poisoning) is a microalgae called a dinoflagellate. Normally these algae are found only in the ocean depths,

but when a reef is disturbed, as happened at Palmyra during World War II, the algae can multiply dramatically and enter the food chain.

Captain Sawle of the American ship *Palmyra* reached the atoll in 1802. It's rumored that Spanish pirates from Peru left buried treasure in 1816. Since the Kingdom of Hawaii claimed the atoll in 1862, the United States annexed it by annexing Hawaii. In 1911 Judge Cooper of Honolulu acquired title to Palmyra, which he used as a coconut plantation. Before his death in 1929 the judge sold all but Home Island to the Fullard-Leo family of Honolulu. During World War II Palmyra had a 6,000-man naval air station and was an important link in the aerial supply route to Kanton and Bora Bora in the South Pacific. The navy transformed the atoll, dredging the lagoon for a harbor and seaplane landing area while building a 6,000-foot coral airstrip on Cooper Island and connecting most of the islets by causeway. The sea has now severed the connecting causeways in several places.

In July 1990 Honolulu realtor Peter Savio (Suite 202, 931 University Ave., Honolulu, HI 96826, tel. 808-942-7701) leased Palmyra from the Fullard-Leo family. Plans to build "an away from it all resort" seem to have stalled. Cruising yachts on their way from Hawaii to the South Pacific have long called here, though Mr. Savio now requires yachties to obtain advance permission. The island's huge wartime rainwater catch basin is usually full.

HOWLAND

Howland Island, 719 miles east of Tarawa, is only 385 acres in area. Pigweed and a few scrawny *kou* trees survive on this dry, flat island, 1.5 miles long, 2,928 feet wide, and nowhere over 15 feet high. There's no anchorage, but in emergencies small boats can land on the west side beach.

In 1937 three dirt airstrips were constructed so that Howland could be used as a refueling stop for Amelia Earhart and Fred Noonan on their around the world flight. They left Lae, New Guinea, on 2 July 1937, never to be seen again. A lighthouse (actually a day beacon painted with red and white stripes) called **Earhart Light** in memory of the aviator was constructed a year after the loss, some 500 feet inland on the western side of the island.

Just after Pearl Harbor, two colonists were killed during attacks on undefended Howland by Japanese submarines and Kawanishi flying boats from the Marshalls. Although the Japanese didn't land, the remaining colonists were evacuated and the island abandoned for the duration of the war. In 1974 Howland, Baker, and Jarvis were placed under the supervision of U.S. Fish and Wildlife Service. The only inhabitants today are reptiles, crustaceans, green and hawksbill turtles, and millions of birds.

BAKER

Baker Island, just north of the equator, 36 miles southeast of Howland, is a flat, oval 320-acre island. Scattered herbs, grass, and low shrubs grace this hot, dry island. A 2,000-foot-long sandy beach runs along the southwest side, but Baker has no lagoon or anchorage. Feral cats were eradicated on Baker in 1964, and nesting brown noddies are now undisturbed.

In 1839 Capt. Michael Baker of the New Bedford whaler *Gideon Howland* discovered guano on the island while burying one of his crew and claimed the island for himself and the United States. The American Guano Company later bought his rights and worked the deposits from 1859 to 1878; from 1886 to 1891 a British firm carried on the work. In 1935 American colonists landed and founded Meyerton to reassert the United States claim, but Japanese air raids following Pearl Harbor prompted their removal in early 1942.

JARVIS

Jarvis Island is located just below the equator, 250 miles southwest of Christmas Island. This saucer-shaped island of coral and sand is only

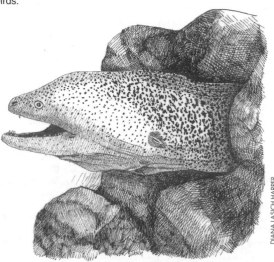

Active mostly at night, the fierce-looking leopard moray eel (Lycodontis javanicus) attacks only when threatened. Since the moray hides in holes and crevices in rock or coral, a careless diver can inadvertently have a bad encounter with one. The flesh of this species is often poisonous to eat.

DIANA LASICH HARPER

1.7 square miles in size and has no lagoon. The beaches slope steeply to a 20-foot-high ridge, which entirely surrounds the flat interior. Due to little rainfall, only sparse bunchgrass, prostrate vines, and low shrubs grow. Boat channels cut through the reef on the west and southwest sides of the island lead to landings, but there's no anchorage.

Captain Brown of the English ship *Eliza Francis* spotted Jarvis in 1821. The island has had many names: Brock, Brook, Bunker, Jarvis, and Volunteer. The American Guano Company dug guano from 1858 to 1879. Britain annexed Jarvis in 1889 and leased the island to a London and Melbourne guano company in 1906. Little was extracted, and low-grade deposits remain on the island today. In 1935 the United States landed colonists on Jarvis, who founded Millerville and erected a monument to make a point of the change in ownership. The British did not respond and the island remains in American hands today, uninhabited.

> *Rain falls from grey clouds*
> *over the steely lagoon.*
> *A tuna jumping.*

BOOKLIST

DESCRIPTION AND TRAVEL

Ashby, Gene. *Pohnpei: An Island Argosy.* Pohnpei: Rainy Day Press, 1993 (P.O. Box 574, Kolonia, Pohnpei, FM 96941). A comprehensive summary of the history, flora and fauna, culture, and attractions of Pohnpei with numerous maps, illustrations, and a complete subject index. About as good as a travel book gets.

Barbour, Nancy. *Palau.* San Francisco: Full Court Press, 1995. A wonderful, richly illustrated description of Palau's natural and cultural history.

Christian, F.W. *The Caroline Islands.* London: Frank Cass & Co., 1967. Christian's detailed account of his journey through Micronesia in 1896, when Spanish colonial rule was still in place.

Grimble, Sir Arthur. *A Pattern of Islands.* London: John Murray, 1952. Grimble served as British resident commissioner in the Gilberts 1926-32 and left behind this classic narrative of Kiribati life as he observed it during his first six years there (1914-20). In the U.S. the same book was published as *We Chose the Islands.* A sequel, *Return to the Islands,* dating from his second tour of duty, appeared in 1957.

Hinz, Earl R. *Landfalls of Paradise: The Guide to Pacific Islands.* Ventura, CA: Western Marine Enterprises, 1980. The only genuine cruising guide to all 32 island groups of Oceania.

Kluge, P.F. *The Edge of Paradise: America in Micronesia.* New York: Random House, 1991. Kluge's long association with the region began with the Peace Corps and continued as speech writer for Lazarus Salii, Palau's second president. This sweeping survey, bursting with vignettes of island players and politicians, is a full-length feature portrait of the place.

Lewis, David. *We, the Navigators.* Honolulu: University of Hawaii Press, 1972. A definitive work on the ancient art of landfinding as practiced by Micronesians.

Lotz, Dave. *The Best Tracks on Guam.* Guam: Making Tracks 1997. Forty hikes to take on Guam, rated for degree of difficulty. Well-written book by former Parks Administrator for Guam.

Price, Willard. *Pacific Adventure.* New York: John Day, 1936. A rare English language eyewitness account of Micronesia during the Japanese period. An updated abridgement of the same book appeared in 1944 under the title *Japan's Islands of Mystery,* then again in 1966 as *America's Paradise Lost: The Strange Story of the Secret Atolls.*

Rock, Tim. *Diving and Snorkeling Guide.* Houston: Pisces Books, 1994. Beautiful guides for Palau, Guam, and Yap, and Chuuk lagoon. Must-have book for divers.

Segal, Harvey Gordon. *Kosrae: The Sleeping Lady Awakens.* Kosrae: Kosrae Tourist Division, 1989. A 382-page compilation of all kinds of hard-to-obtain background information about the island.

Stanley, David. *South Pacific Handbook.* Chico, CA: Moon Publications, 2000. Covers the South Pacific in the same manner as the book you're reading. *Fiji Handbook, Tahiti Handbook,* and *Tonga-Samoa Handbook* are also by the same author.

GEOGRAPHY

Couper, Alastair, ed. *The Times Atlas of the Oceans.* New York: Van Nostrand Reinhold, 1983. A superb study of the oceans of the world in their contemporary context.

Karolle, Bruce G. *Atlas of Micronesia, Second Edition.* Honolulu: Bess Press, 1993. A basic reference emphasizing the natural, manmade, and human resources of the Marianas, Carolines, and Marshall Islands.

Oliver, Douglas L. *The Pacific Islands.* Honolulu: University of Hawaii Press, 1989. Updated edition of the important 1951 study of the history and economies of the entire Pacific.

Ridgell, Reilly. *Pacific Nations and Territories.* Honolulu: Bess Press, 1995. One of the few high school geography texts to the region. Bess Press also publishes Bruce G. Karolle's *Atlas of Micronesia.*

Wruble, F. Boomer *My Years Underseas.* Kalamazoo, MI: Lobo Press. Discusses some of the author's not-so-secret trips.

SCIENCES

Amesbury, Steven S., and Robert F. Myers. *Guide to the Coastal Resources of Guam: The Fishes.* Guam: University of Guam Press, 1982. A comprehensive, profusely illustrated handbook, useful to laypeople and specialists. Unfortunately, a matching volume, *The Corals,* is less comprehensible, as only scientific terminology is used.

DeLuca, Charles J., and Diana MacIntyre DeLuca. *Pacific Marine Life: A Survey of Pacific Ocean Invertebrates.* Rutland, VT: Charles E. Tuttle Co., 1976. An informative 82-page pamphlet.

Engbring, John. *Field Guide to the Birds of Palau.* Illustrated by Takesi Suzuki. Koror: Conservation Office, 1988.

Engbring, John, and Peter Pyle. *Checklist of the Birds of Micronesia.* Honolulu: Hawaii Audubon Society. This excellent six-page publication lists both the scientific and common names of 244 species. A detailed bibliography and precise sighting information are provided. Hawaii Audubon also sells a *Checklist of the Birds of the Mariana Islands.*

Hinton, A.G. *Shells of New Guinea and the Central Indo-Pacific.* Australia: Jacaranda Press, 1972. A photo guide to shell identification.

Jaffe, Mark. *And No Birds Sing: The Story of an Ecological Disaster in a Tropical Paradise.* New York: Barricade Books, 1997. Chronicles the work of Julie Savidge in discovering the tragic effects of the brown tree snake on Guam's ecology.

Martini, Frederic. *Exploring Tropical Isles and Seas.* Englewood Cliffs, NJ: Prentice-Hall, 1984. A fine introduction to the natural environment of the islands.

Mayr, Ernst. *Birds of the Southwest Pacific.* Rutland, VT: Charles E. Tuttle Co., 1978. A reprint of the 1945 edition.

Merrill, Elmer D. *Plant Life of the Pacific World.* Rutland, VT: Charles E. Tuttle Co., 1981. First published in 1945, this handy volume is a useful first reference.

Myers, Robert F. *Micronesian Reef Fishes.* Coral Graphics, P.O. Box 21153, GMF, Guam 96921. Three hundred pages of beautiful photos and thorough information on identification of coral reef fishes. A must for snorkelers and divers.

Nelson, Bryan. *Seabirds: Their Biology and Ecology.* New York: A & W Publishers, 1979. A fully illustrated manual.

Pratt, Douglas. *A Field Guide to the Birds of Hawaii and the Tropical Pacific.* Princeton, NJ: Princeton University Press, 1986. The best of its kind; essential reading for birders.

Sacks, Oliver W. *The Island of the Colorblind.* New York: Knopf 1997. Fascinating account of the author's investigation of the totally colorblind on Pingelap and those with a rare neurological disease on Guam.

Tinker, Spencer Wilkie. *Fishes of Hawaii: A Handbook of the Marine Fishes of Hawaii and the Central Pacific Ocean.* Honolulu, HI: Hawaiian Service, Inc. A comprehensive, indexed reference work.

Wilson, Roberta, and James Q. Wilson. *Watching Fishes: Understanding Coral Reef Fish Behavior.* Houston, TX: Pisces Books, 1992. A wonderful description of the behavior of the not-so-simple creatures that live in the seas.

HISTORY

Brower, Kenneth. *A Song for Satawal.* New York: Penguin Books, 1984. Discussion of three islanders, one each from Yap, Satawal, and Palau, and their efforts to preserve their cultures.

Carano, Paul, and Pedro C. Sanchez. *A Complete History of Guam.* Rutland, VT: Charles E. Tuttle, 1964. A comprehensive history, with a particularly important discussion of Spanish colonial rule in Guam.

Denfeld, D. Colt. *Hold the Marianas.* Shippensburg, PA: White Mane Pub. Co., 1997. Describes the Japanese defense of the Marianas in 1944.

Hanlon, David L. *Remaking Micronesia.* Honolulu: University of Hawaii Press, 1998. A study of United States policies in Micronesia from 1944-1982.

Hezel, Rev. Francis X. *The First Taint of Civilization.* Honolulu: University of Hawaii Press, 1983. A History of the Caroline and Marshall Islands in precolonial days, 1521-1885.

Hezel, Rev. Francis X., and M.L. Berg, eds. *Micronesia: Winds of Change.* Saipan: Omnibus Social Studies Program of the Trust Territory, 1980. A huge book of readings on Micronesian history intended as a textbook for social studies and cultural heritage courses.

Labby, David. *The Demystification of Yap: Dialects of Culture on a Micronesian Island.* Chicago: University of Chicago Press, 1976. Comprehensive work on the symbolic cultural significance of land.

Lavesque, Rodrigue. *History of Micronesia.* Honolulu: University of Hawaii Press, 1993. Two-volume historical resource book.

Lessa, William A. *Drake's Island of Thieves: Ethnological Sleuthing.* Honolulu: University of Hawaii Press, 1975. A fascinating examination of Drake's 1579 visit to Micronesia aboard the *Golden Hinde.*

Liebowitz, Arnold H. *Embattled Island: Palau's Struggle for Independence.* New York: Praeger Pub., 1996. A former representative for Palau before the federal government tells all.

Meller, Norman. *Constitutionalism in Micronesia.* Honolulu: University of Hawaii Press, 1986. An account of the factors that led to the fragmentation of the Trust Territory of the Pacific Islands.

Nufer, Harold. *Micronesia Under American Rule: An Evaluation of the Strategic Trusteeship (1947-1977).* Hicksville, NY: Exposition Press, 1978. Includes interviews with Micronesians about WW II.

Oliver, Douglas L. *The Pacific Islands.* Honolulu: University of Hawaii Press, 1989. A new edition of the classic 1951 study of the history and economies of the entire Pacific.

Oliver, Douglas L. *Native Cultures of the Pacific Islands.* Honolulu: University of Hawaii Press, 1988. A text for college-level courses on the precontact societies of Oceania.

Parmentier, Richard J. *The Sacred Remains.* Chicago: University of Chicago Press, 1987. Myth, history, and society in Palau.

Peacock, Daniel J. *Lee Boo of Belau.* Honolulu: University of Hawaii Press, 1987. The story of a 20-year-old island prince taken to London by an English sea captain in 1784.

Peattie, Mark R. *Nan'yo: The Rise and Fall of the Japanese in Micronesia, 1885-1945.* Honolulu: University of Hawaii Press, 1988. Micronesia, not from the viewpoint of the Micronesians, but from the imperialist Japanese perspective.

Prange, Gordon W., with Donald M. Goldstein, Katherine V. Dillon. *Miracle at Midway.* New

York: McGraw-Hill, 1982. Account of the decisive battle of Midway during World War II.

Rogers, Robert F. *Destiny's Landfall*. Honolulu: University of Hawaii Press, 1995. Although dealing only with Guam, also an extraordinary discussion of the process of conquest and colonization.

Sanchez, Pedro C. *Guahan: The History of Our Island*. Guam: Sanchez Publishing, 1989. "Doc" Sanchez's *Complete History of Guam*, a primary source for more than two decades, was updated in this well-illustrated new volume.

Smurthwaite, David. *The Pacific War Atlas 1941-1945*. New York: Facts on File, 1995.

Stevenson, Robert Louis. *In the South Seas*. The writer's cultural observations during his travels through the Marquesas, Tuamotus, and Gilbert Islands between 1888-90.

Stewart, William H. *Ghost Fleet of the Truk Lagoon*. Contains 60 photos and maps of the February 1944 bombings, plus considerable general information on Chuuk. Missoula MT: Pictorial Histories Publishing Co., 1985.

White, Geoffry M., and Lamont Lindstrom, eds. *The Pacific Theater: Island Representations of World War II*. Pacific Islands Monograph Series, No. 8. Honolulu: University of Hawaii Press, 1989. An outstanding portrayal of what the war meant to the indigenous peoples of the Pacific.

PACIFIC ISSUES

Bradley, David, with a foreword by Jerome B. Wiesner. *No Place to Hide 1946/1984*. Hanover, NH: University Press of New England, 1983. A key book in the development of the antinuclear movement, written by a physician assigned to the Bikini atoll bomb tests.

Firth, Stewart. *Nuclear Playground*. Honolulu: University of Hawaii Press, 1987. The story of the nuclear age in the Pacific.

Johnson, Giff. *Collision Course at Kwajalein: Marshall Islanders in the Shadow of the Bomb*. Honolulu: Pacific Concerns Resource Center, 1984. Though dated, this referenced study continues to provide useful background information on the effects of U.S. nuclear and missile testing in the Marshall Islands.

Marshall, Mac, and Leslie B. Marshall. *Silent Voices Speak: Women and Prohibition in Truk*. Belmont, CA: Wadsworth Publishing Company, 1990. Fascinating reading for anyone interested in the role of women in Micronesian society and the influence that grassroots community groups can exert on the political process.

Report of the Global Conference on the Sustainable Development of Small Island Developing States, Bridgetown, Barbados, 26 April-6 May 1994. New York: United Nations Publications, 1994. A thorough discussion of ecological issues facing small island nations, such as those of Micronesia.

Smith, Roy H. *The Nuclear Free and Independent Pacific Movement: After Mururoa*. New York: Tauris Academic Studies, 1997.

White, Geoffrey M., and Lamont Lindstrom. *Chiefs Today: Traditional Pacific Leadership and the Postcolonial State*. Palo Alto, CA: Stanford University Press, 1998. Describes the conflict and accommodations between the traditional chief system and modern democracy in the Pacific Islands.

SOCIAL SCIENCE

Alkire, William H. *An Introduction to the Peoples and Cultures of Micronesia*. Menlo Park, CA: Cummings Publishing Co., 1977. An anthropological survey.

Howell, William. *The Pacific Islanders*. New York: Scribner's, 1973. An anthropological study of the origins of Pacific peoples.

Damas, David. *Bountiful Island: A Study of Land Tenure on a Micronesian Atoll*. Waterloo, Ontario, Can.: Wilfred Laurier University Press,

1994. A scholarly account of land tenure on Pingelap atoll, FSM.

Kiribati: A Changing Atoll Culture. Fiji: Institute of Pacific Studies, 1984. A team of 14 I-Kiribati writers examines island life.

Kirch, Patrick. *The Lapita Peoples: Ancestors of the Oceanic World.* Cambridge, England: Blackwell, 1997. Excellent scholarly archeological work.

Kiste, Robert C., ed. *American Anthropology in Micronesia: An Assessment.* Honolulu: University of Hawaii Press, 1998. Includes extensive bibliography.

Koch, Gerd. *Material Culture of Kiribati.* Fiji: Institute of Pacific Studies, 1987. The English translation of a classic work; dozens of line drawings of everyday objects.

Moore, Albert. *Arts in the Religions of the Pacific: Symbols of Life.* London and Washington, Cassell Academic, 1997. Significant work on the importance of the arts in Pacific Island religions.

Oliver, Douglas L. *Oceania: The Native Cultures of Australia and the Pacific Islands.* Honolulu: University of Hawaii Press, 1989. A massive two-volume anthropological survey.

Tamanaha, Brian Z. *Understanding Law in Micronesia.* New York: E.J. Brill, 1993. Discusses the collision of traditional Pacific legal systems with modern Western systems.

Thomas, Nicolas. *In Oceania: Vision, Artifacts, Histories. Durham, NC: Duke University Press, 1997. Collection of scholarly essays.*

Ward, Martha C. Nest in the Wind: Adventures in Anthropology on a Tropical Island. Prospect Hills, IL: Waveland Press, 1989. Ward spent several years managing a scientific research project on Pohnpei in the early 1970s. This is her very personal account of how she adapted to Pohnpeian ways.

ART

D'Alleva, Anne. *Arts of the Pacific Islands.* New York: Harry N. Abrams, 1998. Excellent survey of visual arts of the Pacific Islands, with a chapter on Micronesia. Many color plates.

Browning, Mary S. *Micronesian Heritage.* Dance Perspectives, no. 43. New York: Dance Perspective Foundation, 1970. A historical overview of Micronesian dance.

Feldman, Jerome. *The Art of Micronesia.* Honolulu: University of Hawaii Art Gallery, 1986. This exhibition catalog includes three scholarly articles that discuss form, style, and ritual use in Micronesian art. The catalog also includes photographs and drawings of art objects.

Handicrafts of the Marshall Islands. Majuro: Republic of the Marshall Islands, 1993. This government brochure consists of color photographs of various handicrafts and brief historical commentary.

Kaeppler, Adrienne, et al. *Oceanic Art.* New York: Harry N. Abrams, 1997. Major new, beautiful book on oceanic art with more than 900 illustrations.

Morgan, William N. *Prehistoric Architecture in Micronesia.* Austin, TX: University of Texas Press, 1988. Beautifully illustrated large-format book. Excellent text as well.

Mulford, Judy. *Decorative Marshallese Baskets.* Los Angeles, CA: Wonder Publications, 1991 (2098 Mandeville Cyn Rd., Los Angeles, CA 90049). A good book authored by a contemporary basketmaker on the process of Marshallese basket construction, including how to prepare plants and weaving techniques. Photos and drawings included.

Owen, Hera Ware, ed. *Palau Museum Guide.* Koror, Palau: Palau Museum Publications, 1978. Reviews the important art collection of the Palau Museum.

Wells, Marjorie D. *Micronesian Handicraft Book of the Trust Territory of the Pacific Islands.* New York: Carlton Press, Inc., 1982.

LITERATURE

Ashby, Gene, ed. *Micronesian Customs and Beliefs.* Pohnpei: Rainy Day Press, 1983 (P.O. Box 574, Kolonia, Pohnpei, FM 96941). A treasure trove of Micronesian legends and traditions, as related by the students of the Community College of Micronesia. This and the following entry are among the only cultural writings by Micronesians presently in print.

Ashby, Gene, ed. *Never and Always: Micronesian Legends, Fables and Folklore.* Pohnpei: Rainy Day Press, 1983. Another 86 traditional stories by CCM students.

Flood, Nancy. *From the Mouth of the Monster Eel.* Golden, CO: Fulcrum Pub., 1996. Five illustrated Micronesian legends, suitable for young children.

Kellerman, Jonathan. *The Web.* New York: Bantam Books, 1996. Another suspense novel in the Dr. Alex Delaware series, this one set on an unspecified Micronesian island.

Knight, Gerald. *Man This Reef.* Majuro, Marshall Islands: Micronitor Press, 1982. This translated autobiography of a Marshallese storyteller takes more concentration to read than others of its kind because Knight went out of his way to retain the language patterns and structure of the original. This gives the book its depth and indirectly conveys the Marshallese concept of life.

Tator, Elizabeth, ed. *Call of the Morning Bird.* Honolulu: Bishop Museum, 1985. This unique cassette bears the chants and songs of Palau, Yap, and Pohnpei collected by Iwakichi Muranushi in 1936. It's a basic document for the study of Micronesian music.

Te Katake. Fiji: Institute of Pacific Studies. Traditional Kiribati songs.

REFERENCE BOOKS

Pacific Islands Yearbook. The bible of facts and figures for the Pacific, published since 1932. Usually a new edition comes out about every three years, most recently in 1998. Copies may be ordered through *Pacific Islands Monthly,* G.P.O. Box 1167, Suva, Fiji Islands, or through the *Fiji Times, Suva.*

Dennon, Donald, et al. *The Cambridge History of the Pacific Islanders.* New York: Cambridge University Press, 1997. Authoritative history of the Pacific Islands.

Far East and Australasia. London: Europa Publications. An annual survey and directory of Asia and the Pacific. Provides abundant and factual political, social, and economic data; an excellent reference source.

Fry, Gerald W., and Rufino Mauricio. *Pacific Basin and Oceania.* Oxford: ABC-CLIO Press, 1987. A selective, indexed Pacific bibliography that describes the contents of the books instead of merely listing them.

Goetzfridt, Nicholas J., and William L. Wuerch. *Micronesia 1975-1987: A Social Science Bibliography.* Westport, CT: Greenwood Press, 1989.

Haynes, Douglas, and William L. Wuerch. *Micronesian Religion and Lore: A Guide to Sources, 1526-1990.* Westport, CT: Greenwood Press, 1995. Excellent comprehensive bibliography to all aspects of traditional Micronesian religion.

Jackson, Miles M., ed. *Pacific Island Studies: A Survey of the Literature.* Westport, CT: Greenwood Press, 1986. Comprehensive listings, as well as extensive essays that put the most important works in perspective.

Layton, Suzanne. *The Contemporary Pacific Islands Press.* St. Lucia, Queensland, Australia: Department of Journalism, University of Queensland, 1992. Updated listing of print and broadcast media organizations, news services, and professional associations.

Marshall, Mac, and James D. Nason. *Micronesia 1944-1974: A Bibliography of Anthropological and Related Source Materials*. New Haven: Hraf Press, 1975.

Stewart, William H. *Business Reference Guide to the Commonwealth of the Northern Marianas Islands*. Saipan, MP: James H. Grizzard. An economic atlas including 90 maps and 50 charts.

Oceania: A Regional Study. Washington, DC: U.S. Government Printing Office, 1985. Extensive bibliography and index. This 572-page volume forms part of the area handbook series sponsored by the U.S. Army, intended to educate American officials. A comprehensive source of background information.

Wuerch, William L., and Dirk Anthony Ballendorf. *Historical Dictionary of Guam and Micronesia*. Metuchen, NJ: The Scarecrow Press, 1994. An excellent compilation of historical terms and people of Micronesia.

MAP PUBLISHERS

American Pacific Islands Index. U.S. Geological Survey, NCIC, M/S 532, 345 Middlefield Rd., Menlo Park, CA 94025. A complete list of recent topographical maps of Micronesia.

Charts and Publications, United States Pacific Coast Including Hawaii, Guam and the Samoa Islands. National Ocean Service, Distribution Branch (N/CG33), Riverdale, MD 20737-1199. Nautical charts put out by the National Oceanic and Atmospheric Administration (NOAA).

Defense Mapping Agency Catalog of Maps, Charts, and Related Products: Part 2: Hydrographic Products, Volume VIII, Oceania. Defense Mapping Agency Combat Support Center, Attn: DDCP, Washington, DC 20315-0010.

Index to Topographic Maps of Hawaii, American Samoa, and Guam. Distribution Branch, U.S. Geological Survey, P.O. Box 25286, Denver Federal Center, Denver, CO 80225.

Pacific Historical Maps. Economic Service Counsel, Inc., P.O. Box 201 CHRB, Saipan, MP 96950. These fascinating tourist maps by William H. Stewart are packed with information. Copies often are available from local tourist offices.

PERIODICALS

Atoll Research Bulletin. Washington, DC: National Museum of Natural History: Smithsonian Institution. A specialized journal and inexhaustible source of fascinating information (and maps) on the most remote islands of the Pacific. Consult back issues at major libraries.

Commodores' Bulletin. Seven Seas Cruising Assn., 1525 S. Andrews Ave., Suite 217, Fort Lauderdale, FL 33316. This monthly bulletin is loaded with useful information for anyone wishing to tour the Pacific by sailing boat.

The Contemporary Pacific. University of Hawaii Press, 2840 Kolowalu St., Honolulu, HI 96822. Publishes a good mix of articles of interest to both scholars and general readers; the country-by-country "Political Review" in each issue is a concise summary of events during the preceding year. Those interested in current topics in Pacific Island affairs should check recent volumes for background information.

Guam Business News. P.O. Box 3191, Agana, GU 96910. An informative newsmagazine published monthly on Guam.

Isla, A Journal of Micronesian Studies. University of Guam Press, UOG Station, Mangilao, GU 96923.

Journal of Pacific History. Carfax Pub Ltd. P.O. Box 25, Abingdon, Oxon, OX 14 3UE, England. Since 1966 this publication has provided reliable scholarly information on the Pacific.

Micronesia. The Marine Laboratory, University of Guam Press, UOG Station, Mangilao, GU 96923. A journal devoted to the natural sciences in Micronesia.

Pacific Affairs. University of British Columbia, 1855 West Mall, Suite 164, Vancouver, BC V6T 1Z2, Canada (quarterly).

Pacific Islands Monthly. Fiji Times Ltd., P.O. Box 1167, Suva, Fiji Islands. Founded in Sydney, Australia, by R.W. Robson in 1930, *PIM* is the granddaddy of regional magazines.

Pacific Magazine. P.O. Box 25488, Honolulu, HI 96825 (every other month). This excellent business-oriented magazine, published in Hawaii since 1976, will keep you up-to-date on what's happening around the Pacific and, in particular, Micronesia.

Skin Diver. Petersen Publishing Co., Circulation Division, 6420 Wilshire Blvd., Los Angeles, CA 90048. This monthly magazine carries frequent articles on Micronesian dive sites and facilities.

Tok Blong Pacific. South Pacific Peoples Foundation of Canada, 415-620 View St., Victoria, BC V8W 1J6, Canada. This quarterly of news and views focuses on regional environmental, development, human rights, and disarmament issues.

REFERENCE WEBSITES

The following websites are useful for general reference, containing many links to more specialized sites. For websites of Visitors Bureaus, airlines, and the like, see the section of this book titled *APPENDIX: Travel Information and Diplomatic offices.*

Bank of Hawaii Economic Research Center: www.boh.com/econ/index.asp
In-depth studies of the economics of various Micronesian nations.

The CocoNet Wireless-Pacific Islands News and Information:
www.uq.oz.au/jrn/coco/index.htm
Compiled at the University of Queensland.

Pacific Islands Internet Resources:
www2.hawaii.edu/~ogden/piir/index.html
Probably the best website about Micronesia; it is maintained at the University of Hawaii.

The South Pacific Information Network:
sunsite.anu.edu.au/region/spin/

APPENDIX

TRAVEL INFORMATION AND DIPLOMATIC OFFICES

REGIONAL

Pacific Asia Travel Association, Administrative Headquarters, One Montgomery St., Telesis Tower, Suite 1000, San Francisco, CA 94104, tel. (415) 986-4646, fax (415) 986-3458 website: www.patamicronesia.com.

Pacific Asia Travel Association, Pacific Division, P.O. Box 645, Kings Cross, 80 William St., Level 2, Suite 203A, Woalloomooloo, NSW 2011, Australia, tel. 61-2-9332-3599, fax 61-2-9331-6592

Pacific Asia Travel Association, Europe Division, Les Eucalyptus (Block 1), 11 Avenues des Guelfes, Zone E Fontvieille, MC 98000, Monaco, tel. (377) 92-05-61-32, fax (377) 92-05-61-33

Pacific Asia Travel Association, Micronesia Chapter, 970 South Marine Dr., Suite 10-PATA, Tamuning, GU 96911

Office of Territorial and International Affairs, Room 4312, United States Dept. of the Interior, Washington, DC 20240

Office of Freely Associated States, Dept. of State EAP/FAS, Room 5317, Washington, DC 20520-6310

MARSHALL ISLANDS

Marshall Islands Visitors Authority, P.O. Box 5, Majuro, MH 96960, tel. (692) 625-6482, fax (692) 625-6771, e-mail: tourism@ntamar.com

Embassy of the Marshall Islands, 2433 Massachusetts Ave. NW, Washington, DC 20008, tel. (202) 234-5414, fax (202) 232-3236 website: rmiembassyus.org/

RMI Permanent Mission to the United Nations, 220 E. 42nd St., Suite 3105, New York, NY, 10017, tel. (212) 983-3040, fax (212) 983-3202

Embassy of the Marshall Islands, 41 Borron Rd., Suva, Fiji Islands, tel. (242) 387-899, fax (242) 387-115

Embassy of the Marshall Islands, Meiji Park Heights, Room 101, 9-9, Minamimoto-Machi, Shinjuku, Tokyo, Japan, tel. 81 (3) 5379-1701, fax 81 (3) 5379-1810

FEDERATED STATES OF MICRONESIA

FSM Visitors Board, Palikir, Pohnpei, FM 96941, website: www.visit-fsm.org/

National Government of the FSM, P.S. 12, Palikir, Pohnpei, FM 96941 website: www.fsmgov.org/

Division of Tourism, Kosrae State Government, P.O. Box 600, Kosrae, FM 96944, tel. (691) 370-2228, fax (691) 370-2187 e-mail: kosrae@mail.fm

Pohnpei Tourist Commission, P.O. Box 66, Kolonia, Pohnpei, FM 96941

Chuuk Visitors Bureau, P.O. Box 1142, Weno, Chuuk, FM 96942, tel. (691) 330-4133, fax (691) 330-4194 website: www.fsmgov.org/info/chuuk

Yap Visitors Bureau, P.O. Box 988, Colonia, Yap, FM 96943, tel. (691) 350-2298, fax (691) 350-7015, e-mail: yvb@mail.fm, website: www.visityap.com

FSM Information Office, P.O. Box 490, Kolonia, Pohnpei, FM 96941

Embassy of the Federated States of Micronesia, 1725 N St. NW, Washington, DC 20036, website: www.fsmembassy.org/

Permanent Representative of the FSM to the United Nations, 820 Second Ave., New York, NY 10017, website: www.fsmgov.org/fsmun/

Federated States of Micronesia Consulate, 3049 Ualena St., Suite 408, Honolulu, HI 96819, tel. (808) 836-4775

Federated States of Micronesia Consulate, P.O. Box 10630, Tamuning, GU 96911, tel. (671) 649-4000, fax (671) 649-6320

Embassy of the Federated States of Micronesia, 2nd Floor, Reinanzaka Bldg., 14-2 Akasaka, 1-Chome, Minatu-Ku, Tokyo 107, Japan

Embassy of the Federated States of Micronesia, P.O. Box 15493, Suva, Fiji Islands

PALAU

Palau Visitors Authority, P.O. Box 256, Koror, PW 96940, tel. (680) 488-2793, fax (680) 488-1453.

Palau/Washington Liaison Officer, 2000 L St., NW Washington, DC 20001, tel. (202) 452-6814

Palau/Guam Liaison Officer, P.O. Box 9457, Agana, GU 96911

GUAM

Guam Visitors Bureau, 401 Pale San Vitores Road, Tumon, GU 96911, tel. (671) 646-5278, fax (671) 646-8861, e-mail: gvbgm@ite.net, website: www.visitguam.org

Guam Visitors Bureau, Kokusai Building, 3-1-1 Marunouchi, Chiyoda-ku, Tokyo 100, Japan

NORTHERN MARIANAS

Marianas Visitors Authority, P.O. Box 861, Saipan, MP 96950, tel. (670) 664-3200, fax (670) 664-3237, e-mail: mva@saipan.com, website: www.visit-marianas.com

Resident Representative, Commonwealth of the Northern Mariana Islands, 2121 R St. NW, Washington, DC 20008

CNMI Liaison Office, 1221 Kapiolani Blvd., Suite 348, Honolulu, HI 96814

CNMI Liaison Office, P.O. Box 8366, Tamuning, GU 96911

KIRIBATI

Kiribati Visitors Bureau, Ministry of Natural Resource Development, P.O. Box 251, Bikenibeu, Tarawa, Rep. of Kiribati, tel. (686) 28-287

Tourism Office, Ministry of Line and Phoenix Development, Christmas Island, Republic of Kiribati

ALTERNATIVE PLACE-NAMES

Abariringa—Canton
Abariringa—Kanton
Babeldaob—Babelthuap
Babelthuap—Babeldaob
Banaba—Ocean Island
Belau—Palau
Bokaak—Taongi
Canton—Kanton
Canton—Abariringa
Chrlstmas—Kiritimati
Chuuk—Truk
Dublon—Tonoas
Ellice Islands—Tuvalu
Emwar—Losap
Enen Kio—Wake
Enewetak—Eniwetok
Eniwetok—Enewetak
Fanning—Teraina
Gardner—Nikumaroro
Gilbert Islands—Tungaru
Gilberts—Kiribati

Houk—Pulusuk
Hull—Orana
Jabat—Jabwot
Jabwot—Jabat
Kanton—Abariringa
Kanton—Canton
Kiribati—Gilberts
Kiritimati—Christmas
Kosrae—Kusaie
Kusaie—Kosrae
Losap—Emwar
Manra—Sydney
Moen—Weno
Mokil—Mwoakilloa
Mwoakilloa—Mokil
Ngatik—Sapwuahfik
Nikumaroro—Gardner
Ocean—Banaba
Onoun—Ulul
Orana—Hull
Palau—Belau

Phoenix—Rawaki
Pis—Pisemwar
Pisemwar—Pis
Pohnpei—Ponape
Ponape—Pohnpei
Pulusuk—Houk
Rawaki—Phoenix
Sapwuahfik—Ngatik
Tabuaeran—Washington
Taongi—Bokaak
Teraina—Fanning
Tonoas—Dublon
Truk—Chuuk
Tungaru—Gilbert Islands
Tuvalu—Ellice Islands
Ulul—Onoun
Wa'ab—Yap
Wake—Enenkio
Washington—Tabuaeran
Weno—Moen
Yap—Wa'ab

GLOSSARY

archipelago—a group of islands

atoll—a low-lying, ring-shaped coral reef enclosing a lagoon

bai—a traditional Palauan men's meetinghouse

barrier reef—a coral reef separated from the adjacent shore by a lagoon

bêche-de-mer—sea cucumber; trepang; an edible sea slug

benjo—an overwater toilet

betel nut—the fruit of the areca palm, chewed together with pepper leaves and a little lime

botaki—communal gatherings in Kiribati

blackbirders—European Pacific Ocean slave traders during the 19th century

breadfruit—a large, round fruit with starchy flesh, grown on a breadfruit tree *(Artocarpus altilis)*

cassava—manioc; a starchy edible root from which tapioca is made

Chamorro—the indigenous inhabitants of the Mariana Islands

ciguatera—a form of fish poisoning caused by microscopic algae

CNMI—commonly used abbreviation of the Commonwealth of the Northern Marianas

coast watchers—Australian intelligence agents who operated behind Japanese lines during WW II, spotting approaching planes and ships

copra—dried coconut meat used in the manufacture of coconut oil, cosmetics, soap, and margarine

coral—usually a hard, calcareous substance of various shapes, comprising the skeletons of tiny marine animals called polyps. There are also soft corals.

coral bank—a coral formation more than 500 feet long

coral head—a coral formation a few feet across

coral patch—a coral formation up to 500 feet long

cyclone—also known as a hurricane (in the U.S.) or typhoon (in the Pacific). A tropical storm rotates around a center of low atmospheric pressure; it becomes a cyclone when its winds reach 64 knots. In the Northern Hemisphere cyclones spin counterclockwise, while south of the equator they move clockwise. The winds of cyclonic storms are deflected toward a low-pressure area at the center, although the "eye" of the cyclone may be calm.

direct flight—a through flight with one or more stops but no change of aircraft, as opposed to a nonstop flight

ecotourism—a form of tourism that emphasizes limited impact participation in the natural environment

EEZ—Exclusive Economic Zone; a 200-nautical-mile offshore belt where a state controls mineral exploitation and fishing rights

endemic—something native to a particular area and existing there only

faluw—a Yapese young men's house

fringing reef—a reef along the shore of an island

FSM—common abbreviation of the Federated States of Micronesia

guano—manure of seabirds or bats, which after being treated can be used as fertilizer

lagoon—an expanse of water bounded by a reef

latte stones—large limestone pillars left by pre-contact Chamorros

lava lava—a wraparound skirt

leeward—downwind; the shore (or side) sheltered from the wind; as opposed to windward

LORAN—Long-Range Aids to Navigation

maneaba—a Kiribati community meetinghouse

mangrove—a tropical shrub, capable of living in saltwater, with branches that send down roots forming dense thickets along tidal shores

manioc—*see* cassava

matrilineal—a system of tracing descent through the mother's familial line

Melanesia—the high island groups of the western Pacific (Fiji, New Caledonia, Vanuatu, Solomon Islands, and Papua New Guinea)

Pacific Rim—the continental landmasses and large countries around the fringe of the Pacific

PADI—Professional Association of Dive Instructors

pandanus—screw pine with slender stem and prop roots. Fiber from the sword-shaped leaves is used for weaving.

parasailing—being carried aloft by a parachute pulled behind a speedboat

pass—a channel through a barrier reef

passage—an inside passage between an island and a barrier reef

patrilineal—a system of tracing descent through the father's familial line

pebai—a traditional Yapese community meetinghouse

pelagic—relating to the open sea, away from land

Polynesia—divided into Western Polynesia (Tonga and Samoa) and Eastern Polynesia (Tahiti-Polynesia, Cook Islands, Hawaii, Easter Island, and New Zealand)

purse seiner—a tuna fishing boat that encircles fish by using a net that is drawn up like a purse

Quonset hut—a prefabricated, semicircular metal shelter popular during WW II

rai—Yapese stone money

reef—a coral ridge near the ocean surface

sakau—found on Pohnpei, this anesthetizing and mildly narcotic drink is made from the root of the pepper plant; called *kava* in Polynesia

sashimi—edible raw fish

scuba—self-contained underwater breathing apparatus

shoal—a shallow sandbar or mud bank

shoulder season—a travel period between high/peak and low/off-peak

SPARTECA—South Pacific Regional Trade and Economic Cooperation Agreement; an agreement that allows certain manufactured goods from Pacific island countries duty-free entry to Australia and New Zealand

subduction—the action of one tectonic plate wedging under another

subsidence—geological sinking or settling

tangan tangan—a thick brush found in the Mariana Islands

taro—a starchy, elephant-eared tuber *(Colocasia esculenta),* a staple food of many Pacific islanders

thu—a Yapese male loincloth

toddy—The spathe of a coconut tree is bent to a horizontal position and tightly bound before it begins to flower. The end of the spathe is then split and the sap drips down a twig or leaf into a bottle. Fresh or fermented, toddy *(tuba)* makes an excellent drink.

tradewind—a steady wind blowing toward the equator from either the northeast or southeast, depending on the season

trench—an ocean depth marking the point where one tectonic plate wedges under another

tridacna clam—eaten everywhere in the Pacific, its size varies between four and 40 inches

tropical storm—a cyclonic storm with winds of 35 to 64 knots

tsunami—a fast-moving wave caused by an undersea earthquake, sometimes called a tidal wave

TTPI—Trust Territory of the Pacific Islands

udoud—Palauan traditional money

windward—the point or side on which the wind blows, as opposed to leeward

wunbey—a Yapese stone platform

yam—the starchy, tuberous root of a climbing plant

zoris—a Japanese term still used in Micronesia for rubber shower sandals, thongs, or flip-flops

ACCOMMODATIONS INDEX

INDEX

LEGENDS AND MYTHS

SNORKELING

ABOUT THE AUTHOR

In the early 1970s, Neil M. Levy and his bride Jane bought a Land Cruiser, drove from California to the Panama Canal, sold the car, and headed to South America.

They landed back in the San Francisco Bay Area several years later, Neil confident he had conquered his accursed wanderlust. For the next two decades he seemed to be right—he became a law professor, the father of three, and a homeowner.

Professor Levy is an expert on the legal rights of native people. He has spent summers in Hawaii, first researching, then writing about the rights of Native Hawaiians. He later applied his knowledge by working for Native Hawaiian community groups. Some say had there been better surf in South Dakota, he might have become an expert on the law of the Sioux tribes.

Neil has traveled extensively in the South Pacific and Micronesia during the past six years. With their children off at college, Neil and Jane now travel guilt-free to Micronesia. Jane contributes to the diving and arts and crafts sections of this book. When not traveling, they reside in the Bay Area.

LOSE YOURSELF IN THE EXPERIENCE, NOT THE CROWD

For more than 25 years, Moon Travel Handbooks have been the guidebooks of choice for adventurous travelers. Our award-winning Handbook series provides focused, comprehensive coverage of distinct destinations all over the world. Each Handbook is like an entire bookcase of cultural insight and introductory information in one portable volume. Our goal at Moon is to give travelers all the background and practical information they'll need for an extraordinary travel experience.

The following pages include a complete list of Handbooks, covering North America and Hawaii, Mexico, Latin America and the Caribbean, and Asia and the Pacific. To purchase Moon Travel Handbooks, check your local bookstore or check our Web site at **www.moon.com** for current prices and editions.

"An in-depth dunk into the land, the people and their history, arts, and politics."
—*Student Travels*

"I consider these books to be superior to Lonely Planet. When Moon produces a book it is more humorous, incisive, and off-beat."
—*Toronto Sun*

"Outdoor enthusiasts gravitate to the well-written Moon Travel Handbooks. In addition to politically correct historic and cultural features, the series focuses on flora, fauna and outdoor recreation. Maps and meticulous directions also are a trademark of Moon guides."
—*Houston Chronicle*

"Moon [Travel Handbooks] . . . bring a healthy respect to the places they investigate. Best of all, they provide a host of odd nuggets that give a place texture and prod the wary traveler from the beaten path. The finest are written with such care and insight they deserve listing as literature."
—*American Geographical Society*

"Moon Travel Handbooks offer in-depth historical essays and useful maps, enhanced by a sense of humor and a neat, compact format."
—*Swing*

"Perfect for the more adventurous, these are long on history, sightseeing and nitty-gritty information and very price-specific."
—*Columbus Dispatch*

"Moon guides manage to be comprehensive and countercultural at the same time . . . Handbooks are packed with maps, photographs, drawings, and sidebars that constitute a college-level introduction to each country's history, culture, people, and crafts."
—*National Geographic Traveler*

"Few travel guides do a better job helping travelers create their own itineraries than the Moon Travel Handbook series. The authors have a knack for homing in on the essentials."
—*Colorado Springs Gazette Telegraph*

MEXICO

"These books will delight the armchair traveler, aid the undecided person in selecting a destination, and guide the seasoned road warrior looking for lesser-known hideaways."
—*Mexican Meanderings* Newsletter

"From tourist traps to off-the-beaten track hideaways, these guides offer consistent, accurate details without pretension."
—*Foreign Service Journal*

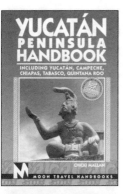

Archaeological Mexico	**$19.95**
Andrew Coe	420 pages, 27 maps
Baja Handbook	**$16.95**
Joe Cummings	540 pages, 46 maps
Cabo Handbook	**$14.95**
Joe Cummings	270 pages, 17 maps
Cancún Handbook	**$14.95**
Chicki Mallan	240 pages, 25 maps
Colonial Mexico	**$18.95**
Chicki Mallan	400 pages, 38 maps
Mexico Handbook	**$21.95**
Joe Cummings and Chicki Mallan	1,200 pages, 201 maps
Northern Mexico Handbook	**$17.95**
Joe Cummings	610 pages, 69 maps
Pacific Mexico Handbook	**$17.95**
Bruce Whipperman	580 pages, 68 maps
Puerto Vallarta Handbook	**$14.95**
Bruce Whipperman	330 pages, 36 maps
Yucatán Handbook	**$16.95**
Chicki Mallan	400 pages, 52 maps

"Beyond question, the most comprehensive Mexican resources available for those who prefer deep travel to shallow tourism. But don't worry, the fiesta-fun stuff's all here too."
—*New York Daily News*

LATIN AMERICA
AND THE CARIBBEAN

"Solidly packed with practical information and full of significant
cultural asides that will enlighten you on the whys and
wherefores of things you might easily see but not easily grasp."

—Boston Globe

Belize Handbook	**$15.95**
Chicki Mallan and Patti Lange	390 pages, 45 maps
Caribbean Vacations	**$18.95**
Karl Luntta	910 pages, 64 maps
Costa Rica Handbook	**$19.95**
Christopher P. Baker	780 pages, 73 maps
Cuba Handbook	**$19.95**
Christopher P. Baker	740 pages, 70 maps
Dominican Republic Handbook	**$15.95**
Gaylord Dold	420 pages, 24 maps
Ecuador Handbook	**$16.95**
Julian Smith	450 pages, 43 maps
Honduras Handbook	**$15.95**
Chris Humphrey	330 pages, 40 maps
Jamaica Handbook	**$15.95**
Karl Luntta	330 pages, 17 maps
Virgin Islands Handbook	**$13.95**
Karl Luntta	220 pages, 19 maps

NORTH AMERICA AND HAWAII

"These domestic guides convey the same sense of exoticism
that their foreign counterparts do, making home-country
travel seem like far-flung adventure."

—Sierra Magazine

Alaska-Yukon Handbook	**$17.95**
Deke Castleman and Don Pitcher	530 pages, 92 maps
Alberta and the Northwest Territories Handbook	**$18.95**
Andrew Hempstead	520 pages, 79 maps
Arizona Handbook	**$18.95**
Bill Weir	600 pages, 36 maps
Atlantic Canada Handbook	**$18.95**
Mark Morris	490 pages, 60 maps
Big Island of Hawaii Handbook	**$15.95**
J.D. Bisignani	390 pages, 25 maps
Boston Handbook	**$13.95**
Jeff Perk	200 pages, 20 maps
British Columbia Handbook	**$16.95**
Jane King and Andrew Hempstead	430 pages, 69 maps

Canadian Rockies Handbook	**$14.95**
Andrew Hempstead	220 pages, 22 maps
Colorado Handbook	**$17.95**
Stephen Metzger	480 pages, 46 maps
Georgia Handbook	**$17.95**
Kap Stann	380 pages, 44 maps
Grand Canyon Handbook	**$14.95**
Bill Weir	220 pages, 10 maps
Hawaii Handbook	**$19.95**
J.D. Bisignani	1,030 pages, 88 maps
Honolulu-Waikiki Handbook	**$14.95**
J.D. Bisignani	360 pages, 20 maps
Idaho Handbook	**$18.95**
Don Root	610 pages, 42 maps
Kauai Handbook	**$15.95**
J.D. Bisignani	320 pages, 23 maps
Los Angeles Handbook	**$16.95**
Kim Weir	370 pages, 15 maps
Maine Handbook	**$18.95**
Kathleen M. Brandes	660 pages, 27 maps
Massachusetts Handbook	**$18.95**
Jeff Perk	600 pages, 23 maps
Maui Handbook	**$15.95**
J.D. Bisignani	450 pages, 37 maps
Michigan Handbook	**$15.95**
Tina Lassen	360 pages, 32 maps
Montana Handbook	**$17.95**
Judy Jewell and W.C. McRae	490 pages, 52 maps
Nevada Handbook	**$18.95**
Deke Castleman	530 pages, 40 maps
New Hampshire Handbook	**$18.95**
Steve Lantos	500 pages, 18 maps
New Mexico Handbook	**$15.95**
Stephen Metzger	360 pages, 47 maps
New York Handbook	**$19.95**
Christiane Bird	780 pages, 95 maps
New York City Handbook	**$13.95**
Christiane Bird	300 pages, 20 maps
North Carolina Handbook	**$14.95**
Rob Hirtz and Jenny Daughtry Hirtz	320 pages, 27 maps
Northern California Handbook	**$19.95**
Kim Weir	800 pages, 50 maps
Ohio Handbook	**$15.95**
David K. Wright	340 pages, 18 maps
Oregon Handbook	**$17.95**
Stuart Warren and Ted Long Ishikawa	590 pages, 34 maps

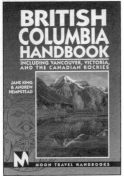

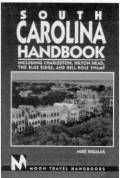

Pennsylvania Handbook	**$18.95**
Joanne Miller	448 pages, 40 maps
Road Trip USA	**$24.00**
Jamie Jensen	940 pages, 175 maps
Road Trip USA Getaways: Chicago	**$9.95**
	60 pages, 1 map
Road Trip USA Getaways: Seattle	**$9.95**
	60 pages, 1 map
Santa Fe-Taos Handbook	**$13.95**
Stephen Metzger	160 pages, 13 maps
South Carolina Handbook	**$16.95**
Mike Sigalas	400 pages, 20 maps
Southern California Handbook	**$19.95**
Kim Weir	720 pages, 26 maps
Tennessee Handbook	**$17.95**
Jeff Bradley	530 pages, 42 maps
Texas Handbook	**$18.95**
Joe Cummings	690 pages, 70 maps
Utah Handbook	**$17.95**
Bill Weir and W.C. McRae	490 pages, 40 maps
Virginia Handbook	**$15.95**
Julian Smith	410 pages, 37 maps
Washington Handbook	**$19.95**
Don Pitcher	840 pages, 111 maps
Wisconsin Handbook	**$18.95**
Thomas Huhti	590 pages, 69 maps
Wyoming Handbook	**$17.95**
Don Pitcher	610 pages, 80 maps

ASIA AND THE PACIFIC

"Scores of maps, detailed practical info down to business hours of small-town libraries. You can't beat the Asian titles for sheer heft. (The) series is sort of an American Lonely Planet, with better writing but fewer titles. (The) individual voice of researchers comes through."

—Travel & Leisure

Australia Handbook	**$21.95**
Marael Johnson, Andrew Hempstead,	
and Nadina Purdon	940 pages, 141 maps
Bali Handbook	**$19.95**
Bill Dalton	750 pages, 54 maps
Fiji Islands Handbook	**$14.95**
David Stanley	350 pages, 42 maps
Hong Kong Handbook	**$16.95**
Kerry Moran	378 pages, 49 maps

| Indonesia Handbook | **$25.00** |
| Bill Dalton | 1,380 pages, 249 maps |

| Micronesia Handbook | **$16.95** |
| Neil M. Levy | 340 pages, 70 maps |

| Nepal Handbook | **$18.95** |
| Kerry Moran | 490 pages, 51 maps |

| New Zealand Handbook | **$19.95** |
| Jane King | 620 pages, 81 maps |

| Outback Australia Handbook | **$18.95** |
| Marael Johnson | 450 pages, 57 maps |

| Philippines Handbook | **$17.95** |
| Peter Harper and Laurie Fullerton | 670 pages, 116 maps |

| Singapore Handbook | **$15.95** |
| Carl Parkes | 350 pages, 29 maps |

| South Korea Handbook | **$19.95** |
| Robert Nilsen | 820 pages, 141 maps |

| South Pacific Handbook | **$24.00** |
| David Stanley | 920 pages, 147 maps |

| Southeast Asia Handbook | **$21.95** |
| Carl Parkes | 1,080 pages, 204 maps |

| Tahiti Handbook | **$15.95** |
| David Stanley | 450 pages, 51 maps |

| Thailand Handbook | **$19.95** |
| Carl Parkes | 860 pages, 142 maps |

| Vietnam, Cambodia & Laos Handbook | **$18.95** |
| Michael Buckley | 760 pages, 116 maps |

OTHER GREAT TITLES FROM MOON

"For hardy wanderers, few guides come more highly recommended than the Handbooks. They include good maps, steer clear of fluff and flackery, and offer plenty of money-saving tips. They also give you the kind of information that visitors to strange lands—on any budget—need to survive."

—US News & World Report

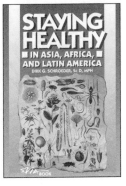

| Moon Handbook | **$10.00** |
| Carl Koppeschaar | 150 pages, 8 maps |

| The Practical Nomad: How to Travel Around the World | **$17.95** |
| Edward Hasbrouck | 580 pages |

| Staying Healthy in Asia, Africa, and Latin America | **$11.95** |
| Dirk Schroeder | 230 pages, 4 maps |

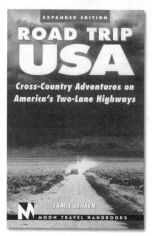

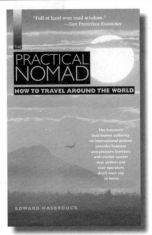

U.S.~METRIC CONVERSION

1 inch = 2.54 centimeters (cm)
1 foot = .3048 meters (m)
1 yard = 0.914 meters
1 mile = 1.6093 kilometers (km)
1 km = .6214 miles
1 fathom = 1.8288 m
1 chain = 20.1168 m
1 furlong = 201.168 m
1 acre = .4047 hectares
1 sq km = 100 hectares
1 sq mile = 2.59 square km
1 ounce = 28.35 grams
1 pound = .4536 kilograms
1 short ton = .90718 metric ton
1 short ton = 2000 pounds
1 long ton = 1.016 metric tons
1 long ton = 2240 pounds
1 metric ton = 1000 kilograms
1 quart = .94635 liters
1 US gallon = 3.7854 liters
1 Imperial gallon = 4.5459 liters
1 nautical mile = 1.852 km

To compute celsius temperatures, subtract 32 from Fahrenheit and divide by 1.8. To go the other way, multiply celsius by 1.8 and add 32.

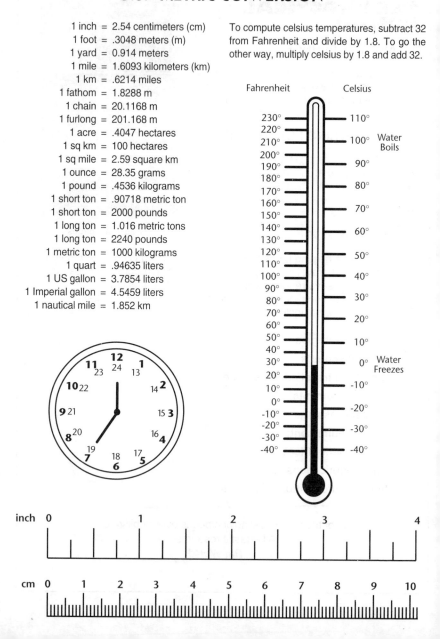